D0205512

The Armenian Genocide

The Armenian Genocide

Cultural and Ethical Legacies

Edited by

Richard Hovannisian

Transaction Publishers
New Brunswick (U.S.A.) and London (U.K.)

Second printing 2008

This book is printed on acid-free paper that meets the American National Standard for Permanence of Paper for Printed Library Materials.

Library of Congress Catalog Number: 2007011673
ISBN: 978-0-7658-0367-2 (cloth); 978-1-4128-0619-0 (paper)
Printed in the United States of America

Library of Congress Cataloging-in-Publication Data

The Armenian genocide : cultural and ethical legacies / Richard G. Hovannisian, editor
p. cm.
1. Armenian massacres, 1915-1923. 2. Armenian massacres, 1915-1923—Historiography. 3. Armenians—Turkey—History. 4. Collective memory. 5. Genocide. I. Hovannisian, Richard G.

DS195.5.A736 20007
956.6'20154—dc22 2007011673

Dedicated to the Great Faith and Commitment

of

ARCHBISHOP MESROB ASHJIAN

Scholar—Servant—Steward

Contents

Preface

The Legacy

This volume is the outgrowth of a UCLA conference in April 2005 titled "After Nine Decades: The Enduring Legacy of the Armenian Genocide." The conference and this publication have been supported by the Souren and Verkin Papazian Fund at UCLA. It is the fifth volume that I have edited and contributed to relating to the Armenian Genocide. Two of the preceding four books have also been published by Transaction Publishers. The fact that these have enjoyed multiple printings indicates that scholarly and general interest in the subject has grown during recent decades. What once was referred to as the "Forgotten Genocide" is clearly no longer forgotten, as the Armenian case finds a place in most comparative studies of genocide and in many works pertaining to collective human rights. At the same time, however, there remains significant resistance among scholars specializing in Middle Eastern studies to deal with the issue. Some try to ignore it altogether, while others seek to contextualize the violence in such a way as to rationalize and relativize the extreme measures taken by the Young Turk government during World War I. There may even be a conscious or unconscious desire to justify the present geopolitical structure of the Middle East by giving reasonable explanations to the circumstances that brought about its division into four unequal but clearly identifiable parts: Arab, Iranian, Turkish, and Israeli. The existence and aspirations of other groups within that framework may be regarded as potentially destabilizing and delegitimatizing and is therefore troubling to some scholars dedicated to the study of a particular people or state. For a long time, the Kurdish question, for example, was certainly viewed as such, and just as certainly, at least for the Turkish government and some associated scholars, the Armenian Genocide was and remains a significant irritant.

It is among this group of Middle Eastern scholars that one of the last bastions of academic denial is centered. At the other end of the spectrum, however, there is a small but growing number of Turkish academic and literary figures who are raising their pens and their voices to challenge the state's narrative of events and to expose the errors and transgressions of propagators of that narrative among the scholarly community. This strong ethical position requires both commitment and courage and is not without personal and professional risks.

Yet the positive effects of this development are already becoming obvious as Armenian, Turkish, and other interested scholars willing to confront this difficult issue are involved in ongoing exchanges and dialogue, and the Turkish scholars in particular are helpful in filling in the many gaps in understanding the decision-making processes and procedures relating to the Armenian Genocide. Such exchanges heighten the prospect of eventual Armenian-Turkish conciliation and raise the related question of "What after recognition?" The last two chapters of this volume by Elazar Barkan and Simon Payaslian begin to address that highly sensitive topic and the role of bodies such as truth commissions or commissions for transitional justice.

The opening chapter by Richard Hovannisian is related to those chapters in the sense that it explores the differing interpretations of the Armenian Genocide as either a continuum from the 1890s through the 1920s or a swift radicalization of measures by the Young Turk perpetrators under the immediate impetus of World War I, a situation that in turn is linked to the issues of premeditation and intent.

With advances in the study of the long-term and immediate antecedents, the implementation, and the consequences of the Armenian Genocide, the legacy of that momentous event has found an important place in literature and is beginning to be reflected in philosophy and theology, in art, music, drama, and film, and in education and curriculum development. Most of the contributors to this volume focus on these themes. Using the paradigm of Christian ethical approaches to the Holocaust, Michael Papazian wonders about the absence of a Muslim mood of responsibility or introspection concerning the Armenian Genocide. Henry Theriault challenges the view that dehumanization of victims is an essential precondition of genocide and argues that it was in fact the very humanity of the Armenians that exacerbated the violence against them. Marc Nichanian considers the value and place of survivor accounts and addresses the complex question of when and how, if ever, does "testimony" become "monument."

The volume includes three different literary themes. Barlow Der Mugrdechian explores reflections of the genocide in the literary and semi-autobiographical accounts of Armenian-American writers Michael Arlen, Michael Krekorian, and David Kherdian. Marc Mamigonian tries to make sense out of the puzzling tangle of Armenian-related words and names in James Joyce's *Finnegans Wake*, and Rubina Peroomian develops a relatively new area for scholarly research—the genocide and historical memory in the literature of Soviet and post-Soviet Armenia.

In the realm of art, Jean Murachanian argues that the legacy of the Armenian Genocide is clearly evident in the self-portraits and abstractions of French-Armenian painter Léon Tutundjian. Ramela Grigorian Abbamontian examines the very different forms, sometimes startling, that contemporary Armenian artists in California use to depict the impact of the genocide. Literature, art, and film are combined by Hrag Varjabedian as he looks at the process of historicization in the writings of Peter Najarian and Micheline Aharonian Marcom and the films of Atom Egoyan and Tina Bastajian. Jack Der Sarkissian surveys the musical legacy from the elegiac pop-styled "Ils Sont Tombés" of Charles Aznavour and the mystical chords of Alan Hovhaness, neither of whom use the word "genocide," to the free-form jazz style of Gregg Bendian's "After Chomaklou Was a Desert" and the angry cries for "Recognition, Restoration, Reparation" of the hard-metal group "System of a Down."

The Armenian Genocide is slowly finding a place, albeit often very small, in middle school, high school, and college textbooks and even more in comparative studies of genocide. An entire resource book prepared by Facing History and Ourselves, Inc. has now been released and the pedagogical philosophy behind it is discussed by Adam Strom. But the dissemination of genocide education through mandated state or district curriculum guidelines must compete for precious time in a crowded school day in a period of "high-stakes testing," as explained by Nicole Vartanian. An important component in education and research relating to genocide has become the Worldwide Web, as tracked by Hagop Gulludjian, who makes a comparative analysis of the exposure "in cyberspace" of the Armenian Genocide vis-à-vis the Holocaust and other twentieth-century genocides.

Several other chapters also have comparative components. Anahit Khosroeva draws attention to the little-known case of the Assyrian Christian population, which in many parts of the Ottoman Empire was equally victimized with the larger Armenian element. Speros Vryonis, Jr. presents a single literary-historical work by the Greek prose writer Elias Venezis to portray the tribulations of the Greek men and youth who were conscripted into brutal labor battalions in the wake of the Turkish Nationalist triumph over the Greek army in Asia Minor in 1922. Tigran Matosyan returns to one of the earliest themes in comparative genocide studies—linkages between the Armenian Genocide and the Holocaust. Nora Arissian examines for the first time the coverage of the Armenian Genocide in the contemporary Syrian press, both within and beyond the Ottoman Empire. Suzanne Moranian surveys the U.S. official response to the Armenian Genocide, in what she terms "a legacy of paradox." Philippe Videlier traces the migration and memories of the French Armenian community as it spread from Marseilles northward into the industrial towns of the Rhone River Valley and the working-class suburbs of Paris in the 1920s.

The final section of the volume, aside from the chapters on the preconditions for reconciliation, includes two chapters on Turkish historiography. Fatma Müge Göçek assesses the direction and changes in writing about what she terms "the unbearable weight of 1915." Bedross Der Matossian, as if in response, describes and evaluates the approaches taken by liberal Turkish scholars such as Göçek who are boldly "venturing into the minefield."

The twenty-four chapters of *The Armenian Genocide: Cultural and Ethical Legacies* draw together what may seem to be rather far-ranging and somewhat disparate subjects. Yet all are linked by a striving, although not yet achieved, to cope with and move beyond the great calamity that claimed the ancient homeland of the Armenian people and reshaped for all time the course of Armenian history.

Richard G. Hovannisian

Part 1

History and Philosophy

1

The Armenian Genocide: Wartime Radicalization or Premeditated Continuum?

Richard G. Hovannisian

World War I was a watershed, a defining moment, in Armenian history. Its effects were unprecedented in that it resulted in what no other war, invasion, or occupation had achieved in more than 3,000 years of identifiable Armenian existence. This calamity was the physical elimination of the Armenian people and most of the evidence of their ever having lived on the great highland called the Armenian Plateau, to which the perpetrator side soon assigned the new name of Eastern Anatolia. Bearers of an impressive martial and cultural history, the Armenians had also known repeated trials and tribulations, waves of massacre, captivity, and exile, but even in the darkest of times there had always been enough of them remaining to revive, rebuild, and go forward.

The Total War Ethic

The technology and totality of twentieth-century warfare changed all of this and no longer facilitated just oppressive rule but also the virtual annihilation of the targeted group. Total war and genocide are often associated with modernism and industrialization, but even in the backward Ottoman Empire in 1915 possession of the telegraph alone was a major asset in the hands of the perpetrators, ensuring coordination and surveillance of the genocidal operations, allowing Talaat Pasha in the Ministry of Interior to cajole and intimidate recalcitrant officials and to be kept informed by Dr. Behaeddin Shakir and other Young Turk central committee members in charge of overseeing the cleansing process.

The combination of a xenophobic nationalist mindset and a total war ethic produced a lethal atmosphere from which the Armenians could not escape. In recent years, renewed interest has been shown in the concept of total war, a strategy that views all of the enemy's resources as being valid, justified targets in order to break and demoralize the opponent's armed forces and civilian population in order to attain a swift victory. Terms such as "collateral damage" or "shock treatment" are now used as euphemisms for civilian casualties in time of war, usually with the intent to display such an awesome show of power as to bring about the collapse of the perceived enemy. Of course, one need not look simply at military operations in Panama, Serbia, or Iraq to discover such examples, for like examples can be found in whole or in part much earlier in the German Blitzkrieg, the saturation bombings at Dresden and Leipzig, and the mushroom clouds at Hiroshima and Nagasaki.

Some scholars have linked these tactics to those of the Prussian military school and perhaps specifically to Helmuth von Moltke and his strategy of an overpowering show of force as demonstrated in the Prussian offensives in Denmark, Austria-Hungary, and France in the process of German unification.[1] Von Moltke previously served as a military adviser in the Ottoman Empire, assisting the sultan to reorganize his outmoded and inefficient armed forces, introducing Prussian models and the structure of a regular army supported by reserves and a home guard or gendarmerie. The Prussian model approached the concept of total war, which was adopted in the Ottoman Empire even before World War I. It has been suggested that the principle of total war is applicable both in a "small war" and in a "great war" situation. The chronic crises in the Balkans during the nineteenth century might be regarded as "small war" situations involving insurgent districts and guerrilla fighters that the Ottoman sultan dealt with through tactics of total war on a local scale. Some regular army detachments joined larger irregular forces to attack all elements of the restive group, whether or not they were involved in the fighting. Hence, the massacre of entire villages of Greeks, Serbs, and Bulgars as a means to quell uprisings and preserve the status quo became a recognizable model. In such cases, the participation of the regular armed forces might be only ancillary to the *bashibozouk* and irregular mounted units that generally were employed.[2]

The pattern of a small total war also held true on a larger scale for the widespread massacres of Armenians in the Asiatic provinces of the Ottoman Empire during the 1890s. In that decade, tens of thousands of Armenians lost their lives, and nearly all Armenian communities suffered enormous individual and collective material losses. The armed forces often stood on the periphery while frenzied mobs, Kurdish irregulars, and Muslim refugees (*muhajir*s) from the Caucasus and the Balkans vented their rage on Armenian businesses, city quarters, and villages and on any hapless Armenian who was unable to hide or flee. The mayhem lasted from a day to a week, but eventually the regular army interceded to reestablish order. Sultan Abdul Hamid II had given a frightful lesson to the Armenians, whose leaders had solicited outside pressure on the sultan to bring about reforms to safeguard Armenian life and property in a time of heightened insecurity and arbitrariness.[3]

Whether or not one wishes to view the Hamidian massacres of the 1890s as an adaptation of total war tactics applied to a "small war" (which was also used to force semi-autonomous Muslim chieftains into submission), there can be no doubt that World War I was in fact a "great war" in which the total war ethic with all its implications prevailed. It was no longer primarily irregulars and mobs that engaged in the operations, although they were always present, but rather the regular armed forces and the shady Special Organization that functioned under the Young Turk central committee and especially the Ministry of War (Enver Pasha) and Ministry of the Interior (Talaat Pasha). Now, the impact of total war struck with full force. Nearly all Armenians without regard to age, sex, economic status, or religious denomination were targeted for elimination while they were also dispossessed of everything they owned personally and communally. The result was genocide.[4]

Incremental Cleansing or Premeditated Genocide?

To a large extent, the escalation of the massacres of the 1890s into the genocide of 1915 is accepted by almost all serious scholars. What still is open to differing views and interpretations is whether the genocide was premeditated before the outbreak of World War I in 1914 or whether the "total war" policies simply got rolling after Turkey entered the conflict and things then progressed from bad to worse, with the various repressive measures and the decision to deport most of the Armenian population deteriorating or radicalizing into the most extreme form of persecution and a point of no return—genocide.

By and large, Western scholars such as Jay Winter, Norman Naimark, Ronald Suny, and Donald Bloxham adhere to the latter position. Explaining that when mixed with other ingredients the conditions of total war led to the Armenian Genocide, they do not necessarily negate a preexisting Turkish desire to be rid of the Armenians, just as the Nazis wanted to be rid of the Jews. They maintain, however, that without the Great War there would not have been or could not have been a genocide. Most scholars in Armenia, on the other hand, and a number of their American and European colleagues such as Yves Ternon, Vahakn Dadrian, and Tessa Hoffman believe that the genocide was premeditated and that figuratively the death warrant for the Armenian people had already been issued in secret meetings of the Young Turk dictators before the Ottoman Empire entered the war as an ally of Germany. Various plans to deal with the Armenians, they assert, had been devised previously in the inner circles of the Ittihad ve Terakki (Committee of Union and Progress—CUP) ranks. All concur, however, that the war created the conditions in which the genocide could be implemented, whether its blueprint had been drafted earlier or evolved as the war progressed.

The attempt of Minister of War Enver Pasha in December 1914 to encircle the Russian army at Sarikamish as a way of achieving a swift victory in the Caucasus and advancing as far as Baku and even beyond reflects the strategy of taking risks in an all-out offensive to catch the enemy by surprise, break military and civilian morale, and emerge auspiciously triumphant. Yet Enver disregarded the advice of his general staff in throwing an army of 90,000 men into an impossible campaign in blizzard conditions. What had served the Prussians well decades earlier spelled defeat and humiliation for Generalissimo Enver by the first week of January 1915, when he returned to Constantinople/Istanbul feigning success but smoldering with humiliation and rage.[5] His praise of the valor of the Armenian troops notwithstanding, it was the Armenians who were to be made the scapegoats for his defeat. Among the first tangible steps in the Turkish final solution to the Armenian Question were the directives to dismiss Armenians in the local militias and gendarmeries and most civil servants, to segregate the Ottoman Armenian soldiers into unarmed labor battalions (where most would die or be killed), and the decision in March 1915 to deport the proud and defiant Armenians of the mountainous stronghold Zeitun (Zeytun) in the region of Cilicia.[6]

I can make no claim to having the answer to many questions relating to the Armenian Genocide. Here, there will be only an attempt to offer an overview of the arguments and evidence relating to the issues of intent, premeditation, and timing. Unless and until the records of the Ottoman government, Young Turk central committee, and the Special Organization (*Teshlikat-i Mahsusa*)—if such exist—are made available and examined thoroughly, a final determination of the question of premeditation cannot be made with absolute certainty. At present, one must rely on memoirs, testimonies of Turkish, Armenian, and other officials, reports of foreign diplomatic, missionary, and relief personnel, incomplete and often sanitized compilations of documents, and unconfirmed and contested yet probably largely truthful diaries and accounts, and circumstantial evidence.

In courses on modern Armenian history, I present the arguments for and against a continuum of genocidal intent and contend that these are not mutually exclusive. The genocide of 1915, I believe, was different quantitatively and qualitatively from the Hamidian massacres of the 1890s.The Hamidian regime used plunder and massacre in a desperate, futile effort to preserve the status quo, that is, to keep afloat the sinking ship of state. Forces loyal to Sultan Abdul Hamid intended to punish the Armenians for seeking European intervention, to set them back economically, and to alter the demographic balance and advance the process of Islamization. Yet it is unlikely that the sultan thought he could simply eradicate all Armenians.

The extreme wing of the CUP, on the other hand, did not want to maintain the status quo but rather to alter it drastically by creating a new society based on a single ethno-religious, linguistic, and cultural identity. In espousing the concept of Turkism, the Talaat-Enver-Shakir-Nazim clique rejected the old system of plural society and the confessional-based *millet* system. Rather, they sought means to accelerate the new order in which the Armenians, along with

Assyrians, Greeks, and other non-Turks and non-Muslims, had either to be assimilated fully or else eliminated in one way or another. Hence, there were essential differences between the 1890s and what transpired under the cover of World War I.

That important difference notwithstanding, the entire period from the 1890s (perhaps even from the 1870s) to the 1920s also constituted a continuum of ethnic cleansing, forced religious conversion, and de-Armenianization of the Ottoman Empire and the Republic of Turkey. Throughout this period, Armenians were being dispossessed of their lands, entire villages were being coerced into conversion under threats of death and destruction, and growing numbers of people fled or immigrated to other lands. The murderous raids after the Russo-Turkish war of 1877-78 and Russian withdrawal from Erzerum, Bayazid, and Alashkerd were followed in 1894 by the indiscriminate massacre in Sasun, which drew the European powers limply back to the Armenian Question. Then came the 1895-96 general massacres, which affected virtually every Armenian-inhabited city, town, and village in the six Ottoman Armenian provinces and adjacent regions. Many thousands of people were killed or maimed as the Armenian quarters and villages were looted and burned. This deadly violence gave way in 1909 to the Cilician inferno in which an estimated twenty to thirty thousand more Armenians were killed and the entire Christian population of the Adana *vilayet* and the northern counties of Aleppo (Aintab and Marash) were terrorized.[7] It was only five years after that round of bloodletting that the wholesale destruction of the Armenians of the Ottoman Empire began during the first year of the Great War. It may be concluded, therefore, that a valid case can be made for both interpretations—a clear and sharp distinction between the massacres of the nineteenth century and the genocide of the twentieth century, yet also a continuum with the incremental use of unbridled violence that reached a crescendo in 1915-16.

The Degeneration of War

Was the Armenian Genocide premeditated outside the context of the totality of World War I and as a fundamental policy that linked the nineteenth and twentieth centuries and the seemingly incongruous regimes of Sultans, Ittihadists, and Kemalists? A number of scholars do not think so. They maintain that without the war there would not have been, indeed could not have been, genocide. In his development of the "total war" thesis, American historian Jay Winter describes the Armenian Genocide as incremental. He doubts that there was a single decision or order to annihilate the Armenian population. Enver's failure at Sarikamish was followed by the daring British plan to knock Turkey out of the war by striking at the Ottoman capital through the Gallipoli peninsula in the spring of 1915. These factors only added to the Young Turk junta's sense of fear and danger and triggered the decision to deport the Armenians. Winter says:

> What turned a war crime into a genocidal act was the context of total war, a context that transformed deportation swiftly into the mass slaughter, abuse, and starvation of an entire ethnic group potentially troublesome to an authoritarian regime at war. . . . Total war entailed the obliteration of the distinction between military and civilian targets and the ruthless use of terror in the suppression of domestic groups suspected of offering the enemy tacit or active support.[8]

Though the assessment seems logical, there remains the question of why even a sense of endangerment would turn the full fury of the state against entirely helpless Armenians in western Anatolian districts where they constituted no more than 2 or 3 percent of the total population.

Like Winter and in an approach somewhat analogous to the "intentionalist" and "functionalist" interpretations used in the study of the Holocaust, Norman Naimark concludes: "The genocide was planned within this dangerous vortex of Ittihadist nationalism, resentment against the Armenians, and mobilization for war. No single order, or single meeting, or single action initiated the events. Much as in the case of the Holocaust, orders from the top are hard to find and substantiate; precise dates for the beginning of the genocide and unambiguous initiatives that prompted it are difficult to document."[9] This echo of the "functionalist" interpretation may certainly be challenged, but until such time as there is unobstructed access to the Turkish records such objections must rest largely on circumstantial evidence and the reports and declarations of third parties, whether defenders or opponents of the Young Turk regime.

Ronald Suny argues that the Young Turks viewed themselves as leaders of an embattled empire more than of a Turkish nation whose heartland was the Armenian Plateau. They strove not only to preserve the empire through a radical transformation of its composition and character but to enfold within it the Caucasus and possibly even Central Asia. The Armenian Genocide, he says, was "a major strategic decision by elites in power" as a "final, desperate effort to revive and expand the empire."[10] Suny does not view the genocide as a natural, inevitable extension of Turkish racial or religious hatred for the Armenians. He concludes:

> Rather than a long-planned and carefully orchestrated program of extermination, the Armenian Genocide was more a vengeful and determined act of suppression that turned into an opportunistic policy to rid Anatolia of Armenians once and for all, eliminating the wedge that they provided for foreign intervention in the region, and open the way for the fantastic dream of a Turanian empire.[11]

British historian Donald Bloxham, too, sees the deadly atmosphere created by Turkish military setbacks and anxieties as the trigger for genocide. The defeat at Sarikamish and the difficulties on all other fronts created an "existential crisis" for the Ottoman Empire. "Given these awkward circumstances, we might suggest that the wartime anti-Armenian measures had their genesis in the immediate-term of the war, or that if they were planned beforehand that this was in the form of a contingency plan."[12] He notes:

> [G]enocide involves mass, sustained, and indiscriminate killing, and often a period of the expansion of murder from individuals, even in large numbers, to whole groups. Pinpointing the precise time within the period of radicalization at which a state framework that is demonstrably permissive of murder and atrocity becomes explicitly genocidal is extremely difficult and unlikely ever to be achieved definitely.[13]

Nonetheless, by the spring of 1915, the Allied threat had become so grave and the parallel anti-Armenian measures so intense that a genocidal program began to crystallize. "At one and the same time the CUP leaders were put in the position of having nothing left to lose since their criminal culpability had already been invoked on the international stage [by the public proclamations of the Allied Powers in May 1915], and they were—in their own perception—given an incentive by external 'provocation' finally to solve the problem of the 'inner enemy' in its entirety." Bloxham concludes: "The very nature of the deportations is sufficient evidence of genocidal intent if such needs to be sought."[14]

The Armenian Genocide as a Continuum

Most scholars in Armenia have maintained that the destruction of the Armenian population in the Ottoman Empire began long before World War I and that the specific blueprint for the 1915 genocide was drawn up prior to the outbreak of hostilities. Mkrtich Nersisyan, Ruben Sahakyan, Jon Kirakosyan, and Ervand Sargsyan, who were among the first Soviet Armenian historians to write on what had been a taboo subject in the Soviet Union, point to a continuum since the 1870s and, using various Western sources and documents, argue that the specific groundwork for the genocide during World War I had been laid as early as 1910.[15] Sargsyan states that "in principle, the Young Turkish clique had decided to annihilate the entire Armenian population of Turkey before World War I." He cites what is said to be one of Talaat's communiqués to the provincial authorities in April 1915, declaring: "Although the elimination of the Armenian element in Turkey was decided upon earlier, circumstances did not allow us to accomplish this sacred duty."[16]

Such assertions are not limited to Soviet Armenian authors: British historian David Marshall Lang draws similar conclusions:

> At secret meetings of the Committee of Union and Progress, the fate of the Armenians had been discussed in principle months, if not years, before the outbreak of war. . . . Right in the middle of the projected pan-Turkic empire lay a monstrous blot on the horizon—the Armenian tableland, inhabited by well over two million Christian non-Turks. They were in the way—and were duly scheduled for elimination.
>
> The fact that the Armenian genocide was planned by the Young Turk junta well before the outbreak of the First World War is shown by the skillfully laid plans for the scheme and its lightning execution when the signal was given in the late spring of 1915. From 1913 onwards, in all towns and villages inhabited by Armenians, governors and police chiefs had been appointed who were known for their devotion to the aims and dictates of the Young Turk regime.[17]

Lang adds: "The Turkish Committee of Union and Progress had already realized that war could provide them with ideal conditions in which to carry out the extermination of the Armenians which they had long meditated."[18]

Manoug Somakian emphasizes the anti-Armenian measures that were implemented much before Turkey's entry into the war, including the wholesale confiscation of goods and properties in many provinces.[19] The Armenian bazaar in Diarbekir, for example, was plundered and set on fire in August 1914 while the authorities looked on. An Armenian notable reported: "Our people have not seen such a systematic pillage since massacres even under the last Sultan [Abdul Hamid]. Government mercilessly confiscates everything in Armenian houses."[20] From Erzerum, there were reports of attacks on Armenian villages in the eastern districts, of an Ittihadist member of Parliament from Bayazid openly proclaiming "death to the Armenians," and of arms being distributed among the Muslim population for an "impending massacre of the Armenians."[21] The prelate of the Mush district of Bitlis province wrote to the Armenian Patriarch of Constantinople in November 1914: "The times are pregnant with danger. The people are prepared to suffer any kind of privation in exchange for security of life. But the government, which is the source of all the turmoil and evil, is inciting the dark forces and arming them against the Armenians."[22] Somakian and other researchers see the genocide of 1915 as the logical culmination of the steadily intensifying Armenophobia manifested in the Ottoman Empire.

This situation, according to many authors, did not change with the Young Turk revolution in 1908. French author Yves Ternon writes: "And it was following the massacres in Cilicia [in 1909] that Dr. Nazim declared: 'The Ottoman Empire must be exclusively Turkish. The presence of foreign elements is a pretext for European intervention. They must be forcibly Turkified'."[23] Then after Turkey's entry into the Great War in 1914, the government used the pretext of unrest at Zeitun to have the army besiege the city and deport its inhabitants. Ternon explains: "The fact that at the beginning of April 1915, long before the Van rebellion, the government sent the deported peoples to two different places, one of which (Konya) proved to be undesirable and the other a good choice for later, suggests that Zeytun was a trial run for the deportation program."[24] He then lists a series of anti-Armenian measures by the government, which, taken together, can be interpreted as preliminaries to the genocide. The Young Turk regime simply used the excuse of an Armenian uprising at Van (late April 1915) to begin the genocidal operations in earnest. The fact that so many Armenian leaders were arrested in one day, on April 24, shows that the government "had to have been ready to act at the drop of a hat and had to have prepared a list of names in advance."[25] Armenian sources, too, list scores of incidents in the latter part of 1914 and early 1915 that, taken together, may be termed state-sanctioned actions aimed at debilitating the Armenian population in preparation for the full-scale genocidal operations. One may add that when the deportations and massacres became nationwide in May 1915 the swiftness of their implementation starting from the border and coastal areas and working inland, as well as the rapid resettlement of Muslim refugees in the Armenian city quarters and villages, lends support to the existence of at least preexisting contingency plans.[26]

Vahakn Dadrian, a widely published author, has written on the historical, social, and religious, and legal components of the Armenian Genocide, the legal ramifications and postwar trials of the Young Turk perpetrators, the role of Germany, and comparative analyses with other instances of ethnic cleansing and mass killing. He maintains that the massacres of the 1890s and the events of 1915 did not differ in intent. "Sultan Abdul Hamit's restraint in the matter of selecting the target population and the duration of the organized mass murder appear as signs of exigency and expediency rather than of moderation and mercifulness." The Hamidian massacres were not just an episodic occurrence but had consequences far beyond the event, paving the way to 1915 by providing the Young Turks with "a predictable impunity." The absence of adverse consequences for the sultan in the 1890s encouraged the Young Turks to proceed without fear. "One is dealing here with the reality of a historical continuum in which the lethal character of a perpetrator-victim relationship is not only sustained but its level is escalated and its dimensions are amplified to the point of the termination of the existence of the victim, i.e., the vast Armenian population of the Ottoman Empire."[27]

The fact that the anti-Armenian measures took place under separate consecutive Turkish regimes shows the constancy of the wish to obliterate the targeted population. Even after the Young Turks had been defeated and dispersed in 1918, the Turkish Nationalist forces of Mustafa Kemal took over from their predecessors and completed the process of cleansing all of the Asiatic provinces of the Armenian remnants. The overriding operative factors superseded the differences in the structure and circumstances of the successive perpetrators. Yet the perpetrators had to be concerned about the viability of their plans and about internal and external variables. Sultan Abdul Hamid could not be certain that the European powers would not intervene, and he therefore had to limit the extent and form of the atrocities. As it happened, Europe remained inactive, a lesson quickly learned and remembered by the Young Turks in their decision-making processes. Dadrian states: "It may be argued that the Abdul Hamit-era massacres were a testing ground, an opportunity, to probe the limits, if any, of the scope and methods of destruction one may dare launch against a targeted population." Hence, it became a prelude and part of the continuum leading to the genocide during World War I.[28] Further in support of the judgment of continuum are the Cilician massacres of April 1909, occurring less than a year after the Young Turk revolution in July 1908.

A number of authors maintain that by early 1910 certain Young Turk leaders were insisting that it was imperative to "Ottomanize," that is, "Turkify," all elements of the empire. Talaat is reported to have expressed contempt for the infidels, rejecting their right to equality. They could expect equal treatment only when they abandoned their ethnicity or nationality to become Ottomans.[29] Jon Kirakosyan is among the authors who accepts accounts that during an Ittihadist meeting in October-November 1910 the slogan of "Turkey for the Turks" was adopted, with the decision that if this could not be achieved by persuasion then it would be realized by force. Moreover, in 1911, Ittihadist central committee member Dr. Nazim went so far as to call for the expulsion of the Armenians if they did not accept Islam as proof of their being "Ottomans."[30]

Conditions became worse after the Balkan wars of 1912-13. A Russian diplomat reported from Erzerum in December 1913: "Secret meetings are being held here, and people are talking about the forthcoming Armenian massacres. Everything is ready to start the carnage; they are only waiting for orders from the capital."[31] Turkish scholar Taner Akçam has also noted that by the end of the Balkan wars, decisions had been taken to diminish the Armenian concentration in the Asiatic provinces by limiting the number of Armenians in any given district to 5 or 10 percent.[32] Still, it may be argued that such goals may have been a part of a "wish list," but that neither the precise means nor time for fulfillment of the objective was foreseen. It took the Great War to present the welcome opportunity and to transform desires for ethnic cleansing to actions for ethnic annihilation. Akçam believes that the decision for physical elimination was taken during deliberations of the Ittihadist leadership in Constantinople at the end of March 1915 when it was stipulated that Dr. Behaeddin Shakir should henceforth turn his concentration away from assisting the war effort beyond the borders to operations solely against "internal enemies."[33] Akçam adds: "It is possible to conclude that the decision for deportation directly aimed at liquidation, when one looks at the dismissals and even killings of officials who thought that the 'deportation' should be mere resettlement."[34]

All positions are not without some inconsistencies. In the evidence presented in support of the theme of a single-minded and consistent process of eradication, for example, Dadrian and others acknowledge that the early atrocities against Armenians in the war zones in 1914-15 were primarily acts of vengeance prompted by Turkish military failures and frustrations, especially as several Armenian detachments were fighting alongside the Russian army. There is also the episode in which a Young Turk delegation led by Behaeddin Shakir arrived at Erzerum in the summer of 1914 to urge the international congress of the Armenian Revolutionary Federation (Dashnaktsutiun) to foment an anti-Russian rebellion among the Russian Armenians in exchange for a degree of autonomy. The evasive reply of the Armenian leaders and their appeal for Ottoman neutrality in the erupting European war deepened the Young Turks' distrust of all Armenians, but the question remains, why would the ruling clique have solicited Armenian subversion against Russia if their plan for obliteration had already been adopted. There are, of course, grounds to argue that Shakir was not sincere and that his mission to Erzerum was part and parcel of a clever scheme of deception and that, in any case, his main objective in the region was to direct anti-Russian subversive activities across the border. In fact, he is reported to have ordered the (unsuccessful) ambush and murder of Armenian delegates en route back to their homes.[35]

In what they do not regard as a contradiction at all, those who believe that there was premeditated intent to eliminate the Armenians incorporate the "opportunity" thesis. They have gathered evidence from statements ascribed to Young Turk leaders and from reports of German, Austrian, and other military officers and civil officials to show that the Ittihadists had consciously planned the genocide and merely awaited the right moment to implement it. The decision to commit genocide was not spontaneous or incremental; it was not "a crime of passion." Rather the war afforded the perfect historic moment to execute a long-held secret plot. The Young Turks, Dadrian suggests, might actually have joined the war as Germany's ally to create just such an opportunity. He quotes from the indictment against the primary Young Turk culprits by the Ottoman Military Tribunal following the defeat of Turkey and its wartime allies: "The massacre and destruction of the Armenians were the result of the decision-making by the Central Committee of Ittihad ve Terakki . . . . This question has been determined upon following extensive and profound deliberations."[36] And there is much more incriminating testimony gathered by the Turkish courts-martial that ultimately condemned to death (in absentia) Enver, Talaat, Behaeddin Shakir, and others guilty of war crimes.

There are also the reports of German and Austrian officials and even of Turkish notables regarding the planned annihilation of the Armenians. In August 1915, a German officer who was in command of a unit of the Special Organization reported from Erzerum to the German military mission in Constantinople that the massacre of the Armenians was part of "a plan conceived a long time ago."[37] And after the cleansing process was nearly completed at the end of 1916, the German vice consul at Erzerum, Max von Scheubner-Richter, informed his government: "A large part of the Young Turk Committee maintains the viewpoint that the Turkish empire should be developed on a purely Muslim, Pan-Turkic basis. The non-Muslim, non-Turkic inhabitants must be forcibly Islamicized and Turkified and, whenever this should prove impossible, destroyed. The liquidation of the Armenians was at the top of their program."[38] At the end of the war in 1918, the heir apparent to the Ottoman throne stated that upon hearing of the intended extreme anti-Armenian measures planned by Talaat and Enver, he had confronted Enver, who had replied simply: "It is decided. It is the programme."[39]

Conclusion

This substantial evidence of premeditation and continuum does not directly contradict the views of scholars who connect the genocide with total war and the escalation and degeneration of conflict into mass killing. Winter, Suny, and others agree that once the decision for eradication had been made it was carried out ruthlessly and mercilessly. This follows the conclusion of the U.S. Ambassador to Turkey, Henry Morgenthau (1913-16), who wrote:

> When the Turkish authorities gave the orders for these deportations, they were merely giving the death warrant to a whole race; they understood this well, and in their conversations with me, they made no particular attempt to conceal the fact.[40]

American-educated Turkish journalist and public figure Ahmed Emin [Yalman] rationalized the removal of the Armenians from the war zones in the context of wartime exigencies, admitting, however, that most of the deportees were women and children (implying that the males had already been killed) who suffered terribly and that the Special Organization actually provoked attacks on the unarmed caravans. He adds: "The deportations taken as a whole were meant to be only a temporary military measure. But for certain influential Turkish politicians they meant the extermination of the Armenian minority in Turkey with the idea of bringing about racial homogeneity in Asia Minor." Those responsible for "the policy of general extermination" knew that they would be universally condemned and believed that their personal sacrifice for the national cause would be recognized "only in a very distant future."[41] Ironically, their prediction has come to pass, as the remains of Talaat and Enver have been repatriated and given places of honor in the Republic of Turkey, and there has been a general rehabilitation of persons widely regarded as prime organizers of the Armenian Genocide.

Emin's explanations can be used to support both the theses of degeneration of war into genocide and of actual premeditation among the most influential and powerful decision makers of the empire. The deportations, he contends, were justified, but the circumstances surrounding them led to undue suffering and death. War deteriorated into the massive loss of life of innocent civilians. But Emin also indicates that the war presented the opportunity for Enver, Talaat, and other Young Turk leaders to implement a preexisting plan of elimination for the sake of creating a homogeneous realm.

One may conclude based on the available information that the Armenian Genocide was indeed premeditated but not necessarily inevitable. Developments in World War I provided the cover under which to intensify and accelerate the cleansing process and to turn the possibility of a final solution into an accomplished fact. It is probable that more precise and compelling evidence, perhaps even the proverbial "smoking gun," exists among the extensive archival materials and private collections in Turkey. A few Turkish colleagues have begun to explore the subject. Hopefully, like German historians who have studied and written about the Holocaust, its causes, implementation, and effects, a new generation of Turkish scholars will be able to find the missing links that will remove any existing tentativeness regarding the genocide that took place under the canopy of the Great War and that sadly became the prototype of subsequent twentieth-century mass killings.

Notes

1. See, for example, James J. Reid, "Total War, the Annihilation Ethic, and the Armenian Genocide, 1870-1918," in *The Armenian Genocide: History, Politics, Ethics*, ed. Richard G. Hovannisian (New York: St. Martin's Press, 1992), pp. 29-30.
2. Ibid., pp. 31-37.
3. Of the extensive materials on the 1894-96 massacres, see the following collections of documents: Great Britain, Parliament, *Sessional Papers*, 1895, vol. 109, c. 7894, Turkey no. 1, pt.1, 7894, and pt. 2, 7894-1; 1896, vol. 95, c. 7927, Turkey, no. 2; vol. 96, c. 8108, Turkey no. 8; 1897 vol. 101, c. 8305, Turkey no. 3; France, Ministère des Affaires Etrangères, *Documents diplomatiques: Affairs arméniennes, 1893-1897,* and *Supplément, 1895-1896* (Paris: Imp. Nationale, 1897); Germany, Auswärtiges Amt, *Die Grosse Politik der europäischen Kabinette, 1871-1914*, 40 vols. (Berlin: Deutsche Verlagsgesllschaft für Politik und Geschicte, 1922-1927), vols. 10 and 12 *passim*. For a useful bibliography, see George N. Shirinian, "The Armenian Massacres of 1894-1897: A Bibliography," *Armenian Review* 47, 1-2 (2001): 113-164.
4. The literature on the Armenian Genocide is voluminous. For selected bibliographies, including denial literature, see the following sources: Richard G. Hovannisian, *The Armenian Holocaust: A Bibliography Relating to the Deportations, Massacres, and Dispersion of the Armenian People* (Cambridge, MA: Armenian Heritage Press, 1980); idem, "The Armenian Genocide: A Critical Bibliographic Review," in *Genocide: A Critical Bibliographic Review,* vol. 1, ed. Israel Charny (London, Mansell, and New York: Facts on File, 1988), pp. 89-115, and, from vol. 2 (1991), the following chapters: Roger Smith, "Denial of the Armenian Genocide," pp. 38-85; Vahakn N. Dadrian, "Documentation of the Armenian Genocide in Turkish Sources," pp. 86-138.
5. On Enver's failed campaign, see W. E. D. Allen and Paul Muratoff, *Caucasian Battlefields* (Cambridge: Cambridge University Press, 1953), pp. 240-283; Richard G. Hovannisian, *Armenia on the Road to Independence, 1918* (Berkeley and Los Angeles: University of California Press, 1967), pp. 45-46.
6. See, for example, Christopher J. Walker, *Armenia: The Survival of a Nation* (London: Croom Helm, 1980), pp. 203-205.
7. See Hakob Papikian [Hagop Babigian], *Adanayi egherne* [The Adana Calamity] (Constantinople: Kilikia, 1919); Duckett Z. Ferriman, *The Young Turks and the Truth about the Holocaust at Adana in Asia Minor during April, 1909* (London: n.p., 1913); M. Seropian, *Les Vêpres ciliciennes* (Alexandria: Della Roca, 1909); Walker, *Armenia,* pp. 182-189; Vahakn N. Dadrian, *History of the Armenian Genocide: Ethnic Conflict from the Balkans to Anatolia to the Caucasus* (Providence, RI: Berghahn Books, 1995), pp. 179-184.
8. Jay Winter, "Under Cover of War," Robert Gellately and Ben Kiernan, *The Specter of Genocide* (New York: Cambridge University Press, 2003), p. 208.
9. Norman M. Naimark, *Fires of Hatred: Ethnic Cleansing in Twentieth-Century Europe* (Cambridge, MA: Harvard University Press, 2001), p. 28.
10. Ronald Grigor Suny, "Empire and Nation: Armenians, Turks, and the End of the Ottoman Empire," *Armenian Forum* 1, 2 (1998): 17.
11. Suny, "Empire and Nation," p. 46.
12. Donald Bloxham, "The Beginning of the Armenian Catastrophe: Comparative and Contextual Considerations," in *Der Völkermord an den Armeniern und die Shoah/*

The Armenian Genocide and The Shoah, ed. Hans-Lukas Kieser and Dominik J. Schaller (Zurich: Chronos, 2002), p. 104.

13. Donald Bloxham, *The Great Game of Genocide: Imperialism, Nationalism, and the Destruction of the Ottoman Armenians* (Oxford: Oxford University Press, 2005), p. 95.
14. Ibid., p. 86.
15. See, for example, Mkrtich Nersisyan and Ruben Sahakyan, *Hayeri tseghaspanutyune Osmanyan Kaysrutyunum: Pastatghteri ev nyuteri zhoghovatsu* [The Armenian Genocide in the Ottoman Empire: Collection of Documents and Materials] (Erevan: Hayastan, 1964); John S. Kirakossian [Jon Kirakosyan], *The Armenian Genocide: The Young Turks before the Judgment of History* (Madison, CT: Sphinx Press, 1992); Ervand Gh. Sargsyan, *Turkian ev nra nvajoghakan kaghakananutiune Andrkovkasum* [Turkey and Its Policy of Conquest in Transcaucasia] (Erevan: Hayastan, 1964).
16. Sargsyan, *Turkian*, p. 231.
17. David Marshall Lang, *The Armenians: A People in Exile* (London and Boston: Allen & Unwin, 1981), p. 19.
18. Ibid., p. 23.
19. Manoug Joseph Somakian, *Empires in Conflict: Armenia and the Great Powers, 1895-1920* (London and New York: Tauris, 1995), p. 77.
20. Ibid.
21. Ibid.
22. Quoted in Vahakn N. Dadrian, *German Responsibility in the Armenian Genocide* (Watertown, MA: Blue Crane Books, 1996), p. 27.
23. Yves Ternon, *The Armenians: History of a Genocide* (Delmar, NY: Caravan Books, 1981), p. 168.
24. Ibid., p. 211.
25. Ibid., p. 217.
26. For an outline of the deportations and massacres, province-by-province, see Walker, *Armenia*, pp. 209-230; Ternon, *Armenia*, pp. 221-247.
27. Dadrian, *History of the Armenian Genocide*, p. 172.
28. Ibid., p. 174.
29. Ibid., pp. 99-100 (citing British documents).
30. Kirakossian, *Armenian Genocide*, pp. 86-87. See also Dadrian, *History of the Armenian Genocide*, pp. 179-180.
31. Aramayis N. Mnatsakanyan, "Hai zhoghovrdi mets egherne ev azgayin veradznunde" [The Great Calamity of the Armenian People and the National Revival] in *Hushamatian mets egherni, 1915-1965* [Memorial Volume of the Great Calamity, 1915-1965], ed. Gersam Aharonian (Beirut: Zartonk, 1965), p. 30. See also Antranig Chalabian, *General Andranik and the Armenian Revolutionary Movement* (Southfield, MI: Antranig Chalabian, 1988), pp. 223-225.
32. Taner Akçam, "Rethinking the Ottoman Archival Material: Debunking Existing Myths," in *Der Völkermord an den Armeniern und die Shoah/The Armenian Genocide and The Shoah*, ed. Hans-Lukas Kieser and Dominik J. Schaller (Zurich: Chronos, 2002), p. 104.
33. Taner Akçam, *Dialogue Across an International Divide: Essays Towards a Turkish-Armenian Dialogue* (Toronto: Zoryan Institute, 2001), pp. 53-54.
34. Ibid., p. 55.
35. Vahakn N. Dadrian, *The Role of the Special Organisation in the Armenian Genocide during the First World War* (Oxford: Berg Publishers), pp. 16-17. See also Akçam, *Dialogue Across an International Divide,* p. 45.

36. Vahakn N. Dadrian, “A Textual Analysis of the Key Indictment of the Turkish Military Tribunal Investigating the Armenian Genocide,” *Armenian Review* 44, 1 (1991), p. 21.
37. Vahakn N. Dadrian, *Documentation of the Armenian Genocide in German and Austrian Sources* (New Brunswick, NJ: Transaction Publishers, 1994), pp. 110-111.
38. Vahakn N. Dadrian, *Ottoman Archives and the Denial of the Armenian Genocide* (1992), p. 19.
39. *The Morning Post*, December 7, 1918, p. 5, as cited in Vahakn N. Dadrian, *Documentation of the Armenian Genocide in Turkish Sources* (Jerusalem: Institute on the Holocaust and Genocide, 1991), p. 111.
40. Henry Morgenthau, *Ambassador Morgenthau's Story* (Garden City, NY: Doubleday Page, 1918), p. 309.
41. Ahmed Emin [Yalman], *Turkey in the World War* (New Haven, CT: Yale University Press, 1930), pp. 219-221.

2

Philosophy and the Age of Genocide: Reflections on the Armenian Genocide

Michael Papazian

Ninety years after the Armenian Genocide, there has not yet emerged an extensive discussion by philosophers about the significance of this event. This is in stark contrast to the Holocaust, about which there is a very rich and provocative philosophical literature.

This contrast is not surprising. The Holocaust was a German event, carried out by Germans in the heart of Europe, in the land of Kant, Hegel, and Nietzsche. Many of its victims and survivors were people educated in German universities and familiar with the strong philosophical traditions of Germany and Europe. Indeed, one of the aspects of the Holocaust that makes it philosophically interesting is that it was perpetrated by the most philosophically vibrant nation in Europe, nurturing and producing some of the foremost influential philosophers in twentieth-century thought in the years prior to the Nazi ascendancy. In this sense one can speak of the Holocaust as a challenge to philosophy itself that begs to be addressed by philosophers.

This has not been the case with the Armenian Genocide. The image of Turkey in the European imagination, certainly, was one of barbarism and savagery. Thus, a genocide perpetrated by Turks in the Ottoman Empire does not, at least for Europeans, pose the kind of issues that a genocide carried out by "cultured" and "learned" Germans and other Europeans in the aftermath of the Enlightenment and the Age of Reason does.[1] In addition, the Genocide was directed against Armenians living in the Ottoman Empire, that is, a people who for the most part did not directly live or think within the context of modern European thought. Therefore Armenian philosophical responses to the Genocide would have to wait longer to emerge than did Jewish philosophical responses to the Holocaust.

Given the close similarities and parallels between the Armenian Genocide and the Holocaust, it is sensible to look at the treatment of the Holocaust within contemporary Jewish philosophy as a model for Armenian philosophers wishing to come to terms with the *Aghet* (Catastrophe). The similarities are striking even to philosophers like Emil Fackenheim, who strongly asserts that the Holocaust is unique but nevertheless recognizes that the "Jewish genocide resembles most closely the World War I Armenian genocide":

> Both were (i) attempts to murder a whole people; (ii) carried out under cover of war; (iii) with maximum secrecy; (iv) after the deportation of the victims, with deliberate cruelty, to remote places; (v) all this provoking few countermeasures or even verbal protests on the part of the civilized world. Doubtless the Nazis both learned from and were encouraged by the Armenian precedent.[2]

This discourse focuses on a number of responses to the Holocaust in Jewish philosophy and explores the ways in which these responses can be appropriated in the development of an Armenian philosophical response to the Genocide. Given the similarities between the two genocides and the fact that discussion of the Holocaust is so much more extensive, it seems that much can be learned by studying the response in Jewish philosophy, not only for the positive insights but also to avoid some of the errors and less promising avenues of thought we may find there. Hopefully this discussion will contribute further to the development of the philosophy of genocide more generally and will encourage further comparative study of genocides among philosophers.

Three questions or areas of discussion among philosophers of the Holocaust and what those studying the Armenian Genocide may learn from their discussion are as follows:

1. What is an appropriate philosophical response to genocide?
2. Does the Holocaust constitute a new and different kind of evil unlike the pogroms and persecution of the Jews in the past, and, if it is different, in what respects is it different?
3. What consequences does the Holocaust have for Christianity?

These are questions that may also be asked of the Armenian Genocide, making the necessary changes. Thus, for the Genocide, question 3 would be: "What consequences does the Genocide have for Islam?" I briefly discuss some responses to these questions found in the philosophical literature on the Holocaust and the relevance of these responses to the Genocide.

First, what is an appropriate philosophical response? Almost unanimously, philosophers who have written on the Holocaust dismiss all attempts to make sense of the Holocaust either by pointing to a greater good that has emerged from the evil or by asserting that the Holocaust was God's punishment, a view that is supported by some ultra-orthodox Jews. There is a consensus that theodicy, or the traditional attempt to explain the presence of evil in the world, fails in the face of the Holocaust.[3] It is futile for philosophers to try to *explain* the Holocaust; at best, they can only seek *responses*. The proper philosophical question to ask is not *why* there is evil, but *how* we should act in the aftermath of the evil.

Fackenheim is the most prominent exponent of this approach to the Holocaust. He argues that the Holocaust has created a new commandment for Jews. Fackenheim writes, "nothing less will do than to say that a commanding Voice speaks from Auschwitz, and that there are Jews who hear it and Jews who stop their ears."[4] The Voice commands Jews that they not grant "*posthumous victories to Hitler*."[5] In particular, an "authentic response to the Holocaust … is a commitment to the autonomy and security of the state of Israel."[6]

Fackenheim's ideas will resonate among Armenians who already have responded to the Genocide by their determination to make sure that the Young Turks not be granted a posthumous victory and to ensure the survival of the Armenian nation by supporting their fledgling and beleaguered state, fighting the present Turkish campaign of denial, and perpetuating Armenian life and culture in the Diaspora. While not necessarily articulated in the profoundly theological language that Fackenheim uses, Armenians still hear a commanding voice from the desert of Deir el-Zor.

Before accepting Fackenhem's response, though, one needs to be aware of criticism that his view has provoked from other Jewish thinkers. Perhaps the most compelling critique is that of Michael Wyschogrod, who wonders why he is required to "preserve Judaism because Hitler wished to destroy it."[7] He recognizes the command to destroy Hitler but fails to see why he, as a secular Jew, bears any "Hitler-derived burdens" to remain a Jew. At most he is commanded to "struggle against evil and injustice wherever perpetrated." The danger of Fackenheim's approach, Wyschogrod argues, is that it makes the Holocaust the "dominant voice that Israel hears," eclipsing the acts of redemption and joyful events in Jewish history. Wyschogrod warns against Jewish fixation on the Holocaust, a fixation that makes destruction and death the central event of Jewish history.

Wyschogrod's cautionary note is one that applies to Armenians as well. The Genocide is becoming, if it is not already, the central event in Armenian history. In many ways, this is unavoidable. The continued Turkish denial of the Genocide as well as the fact that the Genocide, unlike the Holocaust, occurred on the traditional homeland of its victims rather than in the Diaspora have forced Armenians to fixate on the *Aghet*. This means that the danger of fixation is even greater for Armenians since the Genocide is the source of current grievances and is relevant to Armenian political demands in a way that the Holocaust is not for Jews today. Therefore, Armenians need even more so to be mindful of what the centrality of the Genocide is doing to their sense of national identity, and also what it has done to Armenian theology. Wyschogrod suggests that Fackenheim's response to the Holocaust has distorted the Jewish faith by turning it away from a religion of redemption and salvation and toward one of suffering and death. Correspondingly, Armenian fixation on the Genocide may very well have distorted their traditional Christian theology, making death and destruction central to it rather than life and resurrection. This is something that the Armenian Church and theologians must recognize.[8] Any genuine Armenian response to the Genocide must come to terms with the effects of its centrality in Armenian history. On this point, Armenians can learn from Jewish philosophers like Wyschogrod who discuss the problems that people face when a destructive event like genocide becomes a focus of their history and identity.

Fixation on the Holocaust takes us to the second question, for the reason that Jewish thought focuses on the Holocaust is due to the sense that the Holocaust is a different kind of evil than the pre-Holocaust persecution of the Jews. As Wyschogrod points out, the claim of uniqueness or difference is a consequence of the desire to justify fixation on it.[9] The reason why the Holocaust is deserving of attention is because it is radically different from all previous forms of persecution due to some "existential feature or objective quality" that sets it apart. Although Wyschogrod may be correct that the uniqueness or difference claim (and here I am focusing on uniqueness within Jewish history rather than world history) is used as justification, that claim of uniqueness may still be true. Likewise, I would argue that the Genocide is a unique event in Armenian history. Throughout their history Armenians have been victims of massacres and war, but the Genocide constitutes a break, a different kind of violence.

But in what ways is the Genocide different? Here again, Jewish thought on the difference of the Holocaust may be helpful. There are different reasons given for the special character of the Holocaust. Some point to its totalitarian nature—this is the first time that a regime attempted to destroy every Jew. Fackenheim notes that the Holocaust was not like pogroms carried out by Cossacks: "The Holocaust was not a gigantic pogrom from which one could hide until the visitation of the drunken Cossacks had passed. This enemy was coldly sober, systematic rather than haphazard; except for the lucky few, there was no hiding."[10] The same can be said about the Genocide. It was more total and systematic than previous massacres. It effectively erased Armenian presence from Western Armenia just as the Holocaust in effect erased Jewish presence in Europe. As Richard Hovannisian has noted:

> The major difference between Abdul-Hamid and his Young Turk successors was that [the former] unleashed massacres in an effort to maintain a state structure in which the Armenians would be kept in their place without the right to resist corrupt and oppressive government, whereas the Young Turks were to employ the same tactic in 1915 on a grander scale to bring about fundamental and far-reaching changes in the status quo and to create an entirely new frame of reference that did not include the Armenians at all.[11]

The important question is why these more total and systematic forms of violence emerged in the twentieth century. Such questions cannot have easy answers but it is difficult not to conclude that various elements of modernism have made both the Genocide and Holocaust different from all previous persecutions. By "elements of modernism," I mean the fruits of the various ideological movements associated with the modern age beginning with the rise of modern science and the rejection of traditional authority as embodied in religion and the state rather than the popular or individual will. The elements of modernism include the technology resulting from science that produced more effective ways of slaughtering masses of people but also ideologies such as secularism, nationalism, and pseudo-scientific racism that made the idea of the wholesale murder of ethnic groups more imaginable.[12] Some of these ideologies have their roots in Enlightenment philosophy with its rejection of traditional authority and its embrace of secularism and individualism, but especially pernicious are the anti-Enlightenment movements of nationalism and racism that developed in nineteenth-century France and Germany.

Consider the consequences of secularism with respect to the Holocaust. Arthur Cohen has noted: "the church never undertook to kill the Jews. Certainly the church had the opportunity; it did not have the intent."[13] The massacres of the Middle Ages were driven by popular hostility and were often contained and suppressed by the church. Christian ideology, though it does lead to anti-Judaism, cannot justify but only contribute to genocidal intent. It is only with the rise of secularism as well as the nationalism and racism current in post-Enlightenment European, and most notably nineteenth-century German thought, that the Holocaust becomes a reality.

It seems that one can say much the same about the Armenian Genocide. The concept of *dhimmi* (or the People of the Book as a protected class) has had a similar effect within Islam as the acknowledgement of its Jewish roots has had for Christianity. One may also add the implicit anti-racism and anti-nationalism of both of these world religions. The Young Turk regime, like the Nazis, owed more to secular and nationalistic ideas blowing from the West. The Pan-Turkic ideology[14] found in the writings of Tekin Alp (1883-1961) and Ziya Gökalp (1876-1924) clearly owe much to Western ideas of nationalism and secularism.[15] Thus, Shaw and Shaw write:

> Much of the rationale [for Pan-Turkism] came from European philosophers and Orientalists. The Frenchman de Gobineau [1816-1882] had developed the idea of blood and race as the most important influences on human development and history, with some races naturally superior to others.[16]

So while Islamic hostility toward Christians had a contributing effect on the Genocide, Islam probably would not by itself have produced it. Indeed in many cases Islam tempered and resisted it just as, to some limited extent, the Church in Europe resisted Nazism.

Much more would have to be said and argued to establish the case, but at this point I will simply suggest the possibility that it is modernism, not only modern technology, but perhaps more importantly it is ideology that made the difference between the Genocide and Holocaust, on the one hand, and all previous persecutions directed against Armenians and Jews, on the other. If so, a proper response to genocide should be a realistic skepticism about modernity and its connection to progress. In particular, as more of the world falls under the spell of modernization, new cases of genocide might be expected.[17]

This leads to my final question—what consequences does the Holocaust have for Christianity? One of the striking features of the philosophical discussion of the Holocaust is the number of Christian writers attempting to come to terms with the Holocaust and what it means for Christianity. There is a very rich and fruitful Christian discussion of the Holocaust. But so far there has not been to my knowledge a corresponding debate on the part of Islam concerning the Genocide. I have already noted that Islam is not directly responsible for the Genocide, but it cannot be exonerated either. Centuries of Islamic hostility toward Christianity, like centuries of Christian hostility toward Judaism, were a contributing factor. Indeed, some Islamic philosophers treat the evils of genocide as well as totalitarianism and nihilism as uniquely Western phenomena. One example of such thinking is found in the works of the Swiss Islamic philosopher Tariq Ramadan.[18] The danger here is that Islamic societies may consider isolation from Western influences to be a desirable response, thereby cutting themselves off from the positive ideals of the West and blinding themselves to the possibility that the "pristine" form of Islam espoused by Islamicists is itself tarnished by elements of modern Western ideology.[19]

One argument that should be made in the pursuit for further recognition of the Genocide is that Islamic failure to come to terms with the Genocide is bad for Islam and for Islamic societies. Belief that one is exempt from the genocidal and totalitarian impulse will make Islamic societies more prone to injustice because such societies will not be as insistent in codifying safeguards and minority rights into their laws and institutions. Furthermore, they will not fully recognize the dangers that modernization poses for their societies, if I am right to suggest that the distinguishing feature of genocide is due to the elements of modernity. Denial of genocide is dangerous. It is not simply that it erases the memory of a people and rejects truth; it also results in a distortion of our understanding of human nature and politics.

This brief discussion should be viewed at best as a prolegomenon to future philosophical reflection on the Armenian Genocide and on genocide in general. In particular, the thesis concerning the relation of modernity to genocide needs to be expanded to encompass other examples of genocide in order to determine if modern ideology is a decisive factor in transforming "ordinary" political violence into genocide. It would be helpful to see if something similar can be said about the more recent cases of genocide in Cambodia and Rwanda. It is my hope that an awareness and understanding of the common ideologies underpinning genocidal movements may contribute to prevention of any further instances of the modern political pathology of genocide.[20]

Notes

1. A point brought out by Emil Fackenheim, "The Holocaust and Philosophy," *Journal of Philosophy* 82,10 (1985): 511: "Since Socrates, philosophers have known of evil as ignorance; but the Auschwitz operators included Ph.D.s."
2. Ibid., p. 509.
3. Fackenheim, p. 506, refers to the Holocaust as a "*novum* in the history of evil."
4. Fackenheim, "Jewish Faith and the Holocaust," in *A Holocaust Reader: Responses to the Nazi Extermination,* ed. Michael L. Morgan (Oxford: Oxford University Press, 2001), p. 119.
5. Ibid., p. 120.
6. Emil Fackenheim, "The Holocaust and the State of Israel" in Morgan, *A Holocaust Reader*, p. 135.
7. Michael Wyschogrod, "Faith and the Holocaust," *Judaism* 20 (1971): 289.
8. A critique of a dominant response to the Genocide on the part of the Armenian Church is given by Vigen Guroian in "Armenian Genocide and Christian Existence," *Cross Currents* 41, 3 (1991): 322-343. Guroian believes that the Church has to a large extent adopted a "rhetoric of national or collective resurrection." The survival and prosperity of Armenians after the Genocide is often characterized as the resurrection after the Golgotha of 1915. Guroian sees this rhetoric as dangerous and a distortion of Christianity. Thus Guroian recognizes a danger in the Armenian theological context analogous to the danger that Wyschogrod points to in the Jewish one.
9. Wyschogrod, "Faith and the Holocaust," pp. 291-292.
10. Emil Fackenheim, "Holocaust" in *Jewish Philosophers and Jewish Philosophy*, (Bloomington: Indiana University Press, 1996), pp. 126-127.
11. Richard G. Hovannisian, *The Armenian Genocide in Perspective* (New Brunswick, NJ: Transaction Publishers, 1986), pp. 25-26.
12. Military historians have also noted that these ideological factors have changed the nature of modern warfare. Martin Van Creveld, *The Transformation of War* (New York: The Free Press, 1991), p. 64, writes that "in the nineteenth century swelling national feeling, deliberately spurred and abetted by the state, was turned into chauvinism. Earlier restraints, whether imposed by religion or natural law, were discarded as irrelevant." In these circumstances each nation "employed every available means and went to the utmost lengths to defeat its rivals, it brazenly proclaimed its right, and even its duty, to do so."
13. Arthur Cohen, *The Tremendum: A Theological Interpretation of the Holocaust* (New York: Crossroad, 1988), p. 12.
14. For a treatment of Pan-Turkism, see Jacob Landau, *Pan-Turkism in Turkey: A Study of Irrendentism* (Hamden, CT: Archon Books, 1981), pp. 33ff.
15. Christopher Walker, *Armenia: The Survival of a Nation* (New York: St. Martin's Press, 1990), p. 189, notes that Ziya Gökalp is "curiously…hailed today by experts on Turkish history…as a 'progressive intellectual'." If it is true that genocide is a product of "modern progress," there is nothing curious or necessarily false about this.
16. Stanford J. Shaw and Ezel K. Shaw, *History of the Ottoman Empire and Modern Turkey*, vol. 2 (Cambridge: Cambridge University Press, 1977), p. 260. James W. Ceasar, *Reconstructing America* (New Haven, CT: Yale University Press, 1997), p. 89, notes that some distinguish between Gobineau's "aristocratic" racism and the

"crude, lower-class, populist racism of Hitler," but he points out correctly that "if Nazism is not the inevitable or only result of [Gobineau's] thought, it is certainly a logical conclusion. Prescient thinkers at the time, among them Alexis de Tocqueville, easily foresaw the dangerous effects of Gobineau's ideas, although no one could begin to imagine the horrors that these ideas would be used to sanction." Thus, just as the philosophical racism of Gobineau in the West was adopted by populist movements such as Nazism in Germany and by supporters of slavery in the United States, his ideas influenced the thought of Gökalp, which in turn became a part of the Young Turk ideology and an impetus for genocide.

17. I have not said anything about the trend in Jewish thought that asserts the uniqueness of the Holocaust as a world-historical event (rather than as a unique event in Jewish history). I will note here only that I find Wyschogrod comments on this question illuminating:

It is true that the Holocaust is *our* catastrophe and one is entitled to mourn more intensely for the death of a relative than for that of another. But this consideration cannot have ultimate significance. On the psychological plane such partiality is understandable; on the final, moral plane, all men enjoy the same dignity as my relatives and it therefore follows that crimes against them cannot be qualitatively different from those against others. (Wyschogrod, "Faith and the Holocaust," pp. 169-170)

The tendency to move from the psychological to the moral plane is one to which perhaps all victims of genocide are prone. There is such a thing as a narcissism of the oppressed that leads people to make claims of the uniqueness of their own suffering. While such claims may have historical validity, nations that have suffered genocide need to be aware of the detrimental effects of such thinking.

18. Ramadan sees the idea of rebellion against God, embodied in the myth of Prometheus, as specifically Western. See Tariq Ramadan, *Islam, the West and the Challenges of Modernity* (Leicester: The Islamic Foundation, 2001), p. 215. The idea, he argues, is not found in Islamic traditions. In contrast to Western rationalism, which posed "the greatest peril" to clerical authority in the West, reasoning in Islam has as its goal "to come closer to God...one cannot find the expression of Promethean temptation at any moment in the evolution of Islamic civilization." (p. 217). As a result, "the level of 'security' of Muslim societies is particularly impressive. With such misery, poverty and destitution, one is astonished to notice so little delinquency, acts of vandalism or other 'kinds of social violence'" (p. 249). For Ramadan, the evils ("loss of values, nihilism, the idea of suicide, and blind violence") that threaten Islamic societies are all due to external (i.e., Western) causes (p. 250).

One would be more impressed by the level of security of Muslim societies if those societies were not virtually all governed by authoritarian regimes. It is doubtful that Ramadan would attribute the low level of "social violence" in the old Communist states to the ideological purity of Marxism. Of course, Ramadan entirely ignores the violence visited upon minority communities in the Islamic world. I recognize the aggravating effect that modernity has had on the problems of Islamic societies, but unlike Ramadan, do not see it as their primary cause. Nor do I think that the tendency toward totalitarianism and nihilism is uniquely Western.

An interesting discussion and critique of Ramadan is in Paul Berman, *Terror and Liberalism* (New York: W. W. Norton, 2003), pp. 24ff.

19. A compelling case for the latter is made by Paul Berman and also by Ian Buruma and Avishai Margalit, *Occidentalism: The West in the Eyes of Its Enemies* (New York: The Penguin Press, 2004).

20. I am grateful to Berry College students Zachary Greene and Marisa Hinchcliff for their assistance in the preparation of this chapter.

3

Rethinking Dehumanization in Genocide

Henry C. Theriault

It has become an article of faith that a condition necessary for genocide is the dehumanization of the victims in the minds of perpetrators. In conjunction with greed for land or an ideology of hatred, viewing the target group as less than human allows perpetrators to conceive of genocide. For on-the-ground direct killers and enabling bystanders, the dehumanized status of victims is necessary for overcoming ethical compunctions against killing. This view has become so prevalent that it functions as an axiom in case studies and general discussion. So certain an axiom is it that it is rarely even pointed out—it is woven into the very conceptual framework through which the data of a genocide are typically perceived. It is never challenged.

There is good reason for attention to dehumanization, as it typically is a major factor in genocide. There is ample evidence of this in both the stated ideologies of the major perpetrators and in the motives, mind-sets, and acts of direct killers. The propaganda images and concepts of Jew as vermin and subhuman creature, Armenian as disease and infidel, or Native American as nit and soulless heathen are all too vivid. Philosopher André Mineau takes this a step further, arguing that under Nazism Jews became mere things.[1]

While the concept of dehumanization is a valuable tool for understanding genocide, a problem arises when it is misconceived as the exclusive psychological component making genocide possible. Regarding the Armenian Genocide, the case examined in this discussion, choosing to view the historical data through the prism of dehumanization alone can prevent perception of other just as important factors and render central features ancillary aspects. In order to support a better and more comprehensive view of genocide in general and the Armenian Genocide specifically, the framework of analysis must be expanded. This does not mean displacing the concept of dehumanization but rather adding to it a complementary and inverse feature that is just as significant.

From Ethical Question to Practical Cruelty

In response to Mineau's approach, philosopher Daniel Shartin poses a profound question: Is it morally worse to kill a being one has dehumanized or a being one considers a full person?[2] Of course, from the perspective of the victim and with regard to objectively measured human suffering and injustice, they are equally bad. But Shartin means this as a question about the motives of the perpetrator and the level of hatred and violence from the perpetrator's viewpoint. Does a perpetrator think that murdering those considered fully human is doing something more than is done by killing subhuman beings or destroying non-human things? From a perpetrator's perspective, is genocide the equivalent of spraying pesticide on a bunch of ants in one's yard, or is it something more momentous?

While except for extreme deontologists no one would base ethical evaluation of an act of genocide solely on the perpetrators' intentions, considering the reasons perpetrators act is crucial to understanding why a genocide has occurred and, perhaps, even more importantly, why future genocides could occur. The evidence of the Armenian Genocide indicates that, while dehumanization was certainly part of the process, it is clear that the perpetrators at every level not only recognized the humanity of their victims but, in fact, killed Armenians precisely because of their fully human, not subhuman, status.

A key to seeing this is in the actual methods used to annihilate the Armenian population. It is common to posit the instrumental rationality of the methods used to execute a genocide and to argue that the killers sought to be as efficient as possible. The argument goes, for instance, that under conditions of war scarcity, Turkish gendarmes employed alternative forms of killing that saved on the cost of bullets. They stabbed people with bayonets and walked them to death in deserts. They even tied two people together, threw them in a river, and shot only one to let the other be pulled under and drown, all to kill two Armenians with only one bullet. Yet, the efficiency argument with respect to at least some murder techniques seems a stretch. If the goal was to save bullets and effort, why take the time and effort to tie people together and throw them in water while still using one bullet for every two? Surely a quicker and more efficient method could have been found. Why have contests to see who could throw Armenian babies up and catch them on bayonets, instead of stabbing the victims right away? During the desperate military conditions of World War I, why devote considerable numbers of military age and trained men to lead and guard deportation caravans for weeks and months, to kill slowly Armenians who could have been killed quite easily immediately?

Given the unconcern about killing some Armenians on the caravan paths and leaving their bodies to rot, which resulted in various epidemics in the Turkish population, it could not have been to remove Armenians from places where their corpses might spread disease. If, as has been argued,[3] it had been to separate

Armenians more cleanly from their immovable and movable property, why not march them just outside the town or village before killing them, as was typically done to military-age males, rather than extending the moves and the resource drain by a factor of 100 to 1,000 through the prolonged death marches?[4]

While of course it might be defended, even at this point one can see that the efficiency argument is at best only one possible explanation and not particularly convincing. Attention to other aspects of the killing leads to a compelling alternative. On the ground, Armenians were often killed in festivals of cruelty that involved rape and other forms of torture. Village-level participants—direct killers and bystanders—enjoyed these spectacles precisely for their inefficiency. The treatment of deportation caravans maximized cruelty for direct victims of given acts as well as for other Armenians present (who would, themselves, become direct victims sooner or later), for instance as gendarmes or villagers raped and/or killed individuals in front of other family members, causing intense emotional anguish, and in front of all caravan members, heightening fear and traumatizing them through the witnessing of such brutal suffering and death. In full view of government agents leading the caravans and directly because of conditions imposed by the deportation process, mothers were tortured in the deepest ways because of their love for their children. Mothers (few if any fathers remained to make the death marches) lost adolescent daughters who jumped off cliffs to avoid being gang-raped to death in bloody violence. Mothers walked on as their beloved infants died in their arms of heat exhaustion, starvation, or disease in their arms. Women giving birth en route to nowhere had stillborn babies only because the caravans were ordered to keep moving forward—for no reason other than to keep sadistic pressure on Armenians.[5]

Even in the central government, cruel treatment of Armenians for its own sake, not to increase efficiency of killing, was a matter of policy. In his memoir, United States Ambassador Henry Morgenthau relates a discussion with a government official charged with torturing Armenians. He joined his colleagues at the headquarters of the Committee of Union and Progress in enthusiastic nightly high-level discussions of the details of their torturing of Armenians. The pleasure of this and other officials is clear from the passage in question. In these discussions,

> Each new method of inflicting pain was hailed as a splendid discovery, and the regular attendants were constantly ransacking their brains in the effort to devise some new torment.[The official] told me that they even delved into the records of the Spanish Inquisition and other historic institutions of torture and adopted all of the suggestions found there. He did not tell me who carried off the prize in this gruesome competition, but common reputation throughout Armenia gave a preeminent infamy to Djevdet Bey, the Vali of Van. . . .[6]

From this passage, it appears that pushing the anguish of Armenians to the highest possible level was its own reward. Of course, even beyond this kind of torture, for the main directors of the genocide—Talaat, Enver, Jemal, and others—there could have been no doubt about the misery they were inflicting on Armenians through the deportation program, the Special Organizations, and encouragement of Kurdish raiders and Turkish villagers—it was understood and the unmistakable product of explicit policies.

As these examples suggest, at every level perpetrators maximized the agony of Armenians, not the mere efficiency of the killing. It was not just the deaths of Armenians they sought, but "death-through-torment." And, death-through-torment is possible precisely because of the human status of the victims. To understand cruelty on the ground and as an intended feature of the overarching plan of the Armenian Genocide, it is essential to recognize the pleasure perpetrators derived from the ordeals of the victims. Philosopher Friedrich Nietzsche was the first to draw attention to the pleasure people experience in witnessing the suffering of others, not as an aberration but as a philosophically significant common feature of human psychology.[7] His moral assessment is clearly problematic: he holds that the prevalence of this gratification makes it normal and thus ethically legitimate, while its suppression is perverse and mentally unhealthy. Yet, his recognition of this phenomenon is nonetheless vital for those who oppose such cruelty.

This phenomenon has two relevant dimensions. The first, identified by Nietzsche, is that the pleasure at witnessed suffering derives from the sense of superiority it gives to those who are not suffering, precisely because they are in a better situation. This is increased when those who relish it cause the suffering—where it is an expression of the perpetrators' power over the victims. In this regard, it is noteworthy that eyewitness accounts of the Armenian Genocide indicate that rape was more or less universal. This pleasure-producing feature of inflicted torment meshes with accounts of rape, both in general and as a method of genocide.[8] Though some treatments tend to assume dehumanization as part of the process of rape without clarifying whether it is beginning or terminus, they also stress rape as a form of violent domination of its direct victim, people who care about her and her community more broadly. The pleasure of rape is not sexual, but rather is experienced as sexual because the perpetrator gets sexual pleasure from violent domination. Sexual enslavement of Armenian women and girls, including through coerced or forced marriages, allowed perpetrators a related avenue of dominion that could be extended out in time.

Second, the suffering of victims is a function of their humanity and, thus, the pleasure derived from their suffering is directly proportional to the level of humanity perpetrators ascribe to the objects of their violence. Elements of Nietzsche's account perhaps hint at this, but he does not develop the idea. The reason for the first point should be obvious. Suffering is a function not simply of direct physical pain but of the psychological registry of that pain—including recognition of its duration through a sense of the passage of time, trauma based on memory of the past and anticipatory anxiety over the future, and feelings of degradation and humiliation. It is also a function of more developed human capacities, such as love for others, a sense of duty to others, and empathy. Indeed, these features of Armenians had to be assumed by perpetrators in order for many forms of cruelty, such as raping of women and girls in front of husbands, siblings, or their children, to be considered meaningful. Perpetrators could have elicited a mother's distress at the effects of deportation on her children only if the mother had the capacity for deep human love for her children, which would have been confirmed immediately and continually by the anguish of mothers in the caravans. Had Armenians been considered akin to animals, the pleasure would have diminished considerably;[9] had they been conceptually dehumanized to the point of "thingness," the pleasure would have evaporated entirely, as for instance kicking a rock in anger gives no pleasure insofar as the pain of the rock is considered.[10]

This is not meant to suggest that the process of deportation did not in objective terms strip victims of their human status and features. Violence and degradation as well as physical deterioration through starvation and disease certainly combined to render deportees less and less human at the functional and psychological levels.[11] As Morgan Blum points out, the goal of the three genocidal processes she treats was to reduce human beings to sub-humanity, that is, to make their dehumanization an objective fact. From my perspective, it is not the endpoint that should be the focus, but the process itself, through which genocide perpetrators consume the humanity of their targets by converting it into their own pleasure, in what might be termed a "genocidal exchange economy of suffering." If victims were left at the end of the process without humanity conceptually and literally—they usually died or were murdered at this point—their recognized humanity was at the core of a process the goal of which was to destroy it.

Imperial Dominion and Anti-Democracy

Asserting dominance over other human beings either achieves or issues from the perpetrators' sense of superiority over members of the victim group. Thus, rather than victims beginning with low status or having their status lowered, through domination the perpetrators' status increases. And, the increase depends in part on the "worthiness"—that is, the humanity—of the victims. One might call the genocidal extreme of such supremacy "hyper-domination," to differentiate it from other, more stable forms of domination. In genocide, the subjugation of the target group is not fixed but rather accelerates toward their total destruction. Genocide maximizes the differential status between god-like superior and human inferior whose existence itself is erased.

It is possible at this point to reintroduce dehumanization into the emergent model of the Armenian Genocide. Certainly some aspects included dehumanization, and it would be just as bad to ignore them as to ignore the element of hyper-domination. In maximizing the differential status of perpetrator and victim, both "superiorization" and dehumanization occurred in different combinations depending on the aspect of the genocide. Rather than posing the two concepts in an exclusive opposition, one should view them as linked inversions of each other and even in a complementary or mutually supportive relationship that maximized the differential in perpetrator and victim status.

At the same time, the superiority of the perpetrators and not the dehumanization of victims was the ultimate key to the genocide. In the previous section, I argued that recognition of the humanity of the victims, and not their dehumanization, explains the ways in which Armenians were exterminated. In this section, I will go further to make the case that imperial arrogance coupled with the humanity of the victims drove the Armenian Genocide itself.

Hyper-dominance comes in different forms. It can be an exceptionalness that grants the perpetrators special moral status that allows them the right to destroy others, perhaps as a vaguely conceived means of "protecting" the world as the benefactor of humankind. It can be paranoia that authorizes every extreme in supposed defense against some "menace." It can be a self-justifying self-interest that deems the ambitions of its own society of special importance that justifies and authorizes any mistreatment of other groups. In the Ottoman case, it was imperial dominance that assumed the right of rule over and mistreatment of Armenians and other conquered peoples. Through centuries of the confessional-based *millet* system that institutionalized the hierarchy produced by earlier aggressive conquest, most Turks had come to see themselves as inherently superior to their subject peoples.[12]

This dominance had become normalized, such that the superiority of Turks was taken as a natural condition. When, as a response to severe repression by the Ottoman government, Kurds, and others, Armenians in the second half of the nineteenth century began asking for basic human rights, many Turks experienced this as an aggressive attack on the legitimate status quo, a dangerous disruption by Armenians. When Armenians pushed for an end to the attitude that it was morally acceptable to steal from, rape, and murder Armenians, they were in effect challenging the right of conquest at the foundation of Ottoman imperial identity.

Responsible employment of Nietzsche's analysis in reference to the Armenian Genocide requires two caveats. First, as my frequent use of the term "perpetrator" rather than "Turk" conveys, by no means were all Turkish individuals in the Ottoman Empire perpetrators of the Armenian Genocide. Many Turks at each level of Ottoman society refused to participate as direct killers or supportive bystanders, while some even actively resisted the genocide. Second, while attention to social and political factors specific to the Ottoman Empire and the emergent Turkish nationalist identity is crucial to understanding the genocide, the attitude of superiority and pleasure at suffering inflicted on others is not unique to Turkish culture; as Nietzsche maintains and world history confirms all too clearly, they are potentials in any social and cultural context. The subject at hand is why, in the particular context of the Ottoman Empire, the potentials became actualized in the form of the Armenian Genocide. Beyond the scope of this paper but potentially quite fruitful is a comparative application of this paper's model to a range of genocides and other instances of systematic mass violence.

The rationale of the Turkish reaction is reflected in the denialist argument claiming that Armenian rebelliousness and aggression provoked a response by the Ottoman government that, if possibly excessive and not well organized, was nevertheless justified. The main perpetrators themselves made this argument to cover up their act, and later deniers have developed it further. Renowned Ottoman specialist and long-time Armenian Genocide denier Bernard Lewis' version is perhaps the most prominent.[13] A more extreme iteration of this argument that focuses on the last quarter of the nineteenth century is that of the late Middle East Studies scholar Elie Kedourie, whose 1960s theory of nationalism is still considered pioneering by some.[14] Both accounts place blame on Armenian nationalist insurrection aimed at independence. For Lewis, the biggest problem was the intermixture of Armenians and Turks together. Unlike "conquered" territories, say in the Balkans, the Armenian areas were fully integrated and in the heart of "Turkey-in-Asia." The separatist movement he attributes to Armenians required not merely revolt against the government, but expulsion of Turks from a central homeland area. The result of Armenian separatism was a struggle in the heartland between Armenians and Turks that resulted in great death on both sides. Kedourie asserts that violent Armenian nationalist separatists attacked the Ottoman government and social order, thereby triggering an understandable reaction. After each governmental response, Armenians irrationally kept increasing the level of violence, to the point where the government had to take decisive steps, by which Kedourie appears to mean the 1894-96 massacres. He conveniently avoids discussing the 1915 period.

Beyond criticisms of the historical inaccuracies pervasive in these provocation claims, there have been a number of important theoretical replies. Vahakn Dadrian has opposed the view that, in the pre-genocide period, Armenians were driving the conflict with or causing the reaction by Turks.[15] He argues convincingly that Armenian political attitudes and acts were themselves predictable responses to the oppression Armenians experienced within the Ottoman system. Dadrian demonstrates that, from the mid- to late-nineteenth century on, oppression produced legitimate responses by Armenians that in turn were met with increased oppression in an escalating ethnic conflict that the Young Turks ultimately decided to end through the radical solution of exterminating the other party. Dadrian is clear about the one-sided nature of this tension, both in terms of the great military and political advantages of the Ottoman government and Turks generally relative to Armenians and the fact that the oppressiveness of the Ottoman government and society caused the conflict with Armenians.

Robert Melson takes a different approach.[16] From his standpoint, it is not simply the imbalance of power and Turkish aggression that exonerates Armenians but their own quiescence. While there were some separatist elements within the Ottoman Armenian community, their overall presence and effects were negligible. The Armenian Genocide was a function of the Young Turk ideology, which required strict ethnic purity for the new Turkish state, not of the actual dynamics of Turkish-Armenian political relations.

Both approaches contain elements that add appreciably to an understanding of the Armenian Genocide. But each also misses a key element. Dadrian does not question the "conflict" model but merely shows that Turks were at fault, in effect inverting Kedourie's account. Dadrian fails to theorize the qualitative differences between Turkish nationalism and Armenian nationalism. He relies on a reductive ethnic essentialism that misses the complexities of identity in each group. In effect, his model accepts the genocide perpetrators' faulty conceptualization of their world as constituted by two homogenous ethnic entities each vying for its own advantage. The difference was only in the means they used to pursue that advantage and the nature of the advantage (dominance versus emancipation).

Melson rightly points out that nothing the Armenians could have done justified genocide, but at the same time explicitly downplays various aspects of Armenian political agency. For instance, he emphasizes that prior to the genocide the Armenian Revolutionary Federation, the largest Armenian political force in the Ottoman Empire, had not adopted a separatist position and highlights Enver's praise for Armenian soldiers during the first months of the war, in order to show that any purported provocation by Armenian separatist nationalism was false.[17] He fails, however, to explore the significance of the ARF's actual political program and role in the 1908 Young Turk revolution, or that of Armenian soldiers' loyalty in the Ottoman military. More broadly, though he is quite sympathetic to Armenian political concerns, he does not give an account of the diversity of Armenian political attitudes and agency. In this way, his approach refutes the provocation thesis without transcending the conceptual limits imposed by it.

What was the nature of Armenian political agency, which both Dadrian and Melson miss? Following the above clue and looking at the Armenian Revolution Federation's political activities, as analyzed incisively by Dikran Kaligian, one finds not a separatist force but a political party committed to working with the Young Turk movement to improve the situation of Ottoman Armenians.[18] This was true in the lead-up to the 1908 revolution that overthrew the sultan and restored a liberal constitution that granted full citizenship rights to non-Muslims. It was true as well from 1908 right up to the genocide itself. If there was a shift among some Armenian activists after the 1912 Turkish losses in the Balkans, when they pushed successfully for renewed European intervention to protect minorities, Armenians not only declared their loyalty but acted on it when World War I broke out in 1914. Had Armenians been intent on separation, they would have seized the opportunities the Ottoman Empire's difficult wartime situation and military failures provided to revolt—as propaganda from the Young Turks to justify the deportations later claimed but against which the historical evidence is clear. They did just the opposite, with a multitude of Armenian men fighting loyally in the Ottoman military until they were killed as part of the genocide.

The great majority of politically active Armenians had committed themselves to the Ottoman Empire through an integrationist politics advanced by an "advocative" nationalism, a nationalism that focused on advocacy for the basic civil rights of Armenians. While it is easy to see Armenians as just another minority in the line of Greeks, Serbs, and others who had split from the Ottoman Empire, one must examine the former community in its own light. The new citizenship rights offered something that groups that separated before the 1908 revolution did not see, the possibility of retaining their group identity, including non-Muslim religion, while at least in theory still participating as equals in the new Ottoman society and state. Thus, 1908 was a decisive break from the sultanate past, in which Armenian identity meant oppressed second-class status.[19] Armenians could remain Armenians and still become full citizens of the new Ottoman state. This promise of the 1908 revolution was highly attractive, especially because it offered a way for Armenians to overcome deep oppression without entering into a dangerous separatist movement. Hence, even from a realpolitik perspective, integration made sense: substantive participation in a new multinational state that Armenians could have a role in forming and that would be at the least a secure regional power was a markedly better alternative to a smaller and weaker Armenian state in the midst of the complicated political terrain of early twentieth century Western Asia and in the face of powerful Russian imperialism.[20]

This path is not surprising, given the basic features of Armenian political history stretching back to ancient times. While there had been periods in which an independent Armenian political entity existed, pre-national Armenian identity was forged within the boundaries of large empires. The Byzantine Empire, for instance, allowed great Armenian participation. The focus on Armenian separatism, whether to exaggerate or downplay it, echoes the error of Benedict Anderson as critiqued by Partha Chatterjee,[21] of assuming all national identities and nationalisms in non-European areas to be modular imports derivative of European forms. As the success of the flexible diasporan Armenian identity after the genocide suggests, Armenian national identity was not tied to Armenian statehood in the unforgiving way of many European cases. While separatism was one type of Armenian nationalism in the pre-genocide era, the integrationist form also emerged as a variation mixing Armenian political history with received European concepts of the nation.[22]

The question now is why did the Armenian bid for integration fail so completely as to give way to genocide? From 1894 to 1896, Sultan Abdul Hamid

II ordered a set of massacres against the Ottoman Armenian population. His intent was not total extermination, but elimination of Armenian communities that were sites of active resistance to repression from the central government as well as local Turks and Kurds and the unleashing of a generally murderous terror on the broader Armenian population to intimidate them into remaining in their lowly position within the millet system. That place was a secondary rank through a form of institutionalized discrimination that, in addition to eroding the viability of the community politically and culturally, left Armenians physically and legally defenseless against depredations committed against them. While he might not have acknowledged that his own repression was why Armenians were beginning to challenge his authority over them, the sultan did recognize that they were becoming a serious problem and effected the mass killing of as many as 200,000, on the order of 10 percent of their population.

In 1894, the sultan had the option of trying to put Armenians back in their subservient position in the Ottoman Empire. By 1915, however, two important developments had occurred. First, through the revolution of 1908 and their subsequent integrationism, Armenians had humanized themselves within Ottoman society. This does not mean they had full equality, but they had become much fuller participants in the political and social life of the empire. At the very least, more and more Armenians tried to take their place as equals and began to see participation in the life of the empire as a normal thing.

Second, the Young Turk movement came to be dominated by an ultra-nationalist ideology that, as Melson says, called for a homogeneously Turkish society to replace its multinational Ottoman predecessor. In emphasizing the conversion and assimilation of non-Turks into Turkish identity as the basis of a new Turkish Ottoman Empire, Young Turk ideologues developed an extremist nationalism that melded the nineteenth-century German romantic form[23] and their own imperial mindset. German romantic nationalism began with the notion that national identity was egalitarian in the sense that members of a given nation were all supposed to share a core identity and the leaders of the nation ruled legitimately when they represented that core national essence. In reality, of course, the elites denoted as this true national essence their own views of what the nation should be, typically in line with the personal interests and dispositions. As for the homegrown imperial element, the Ottoman Empire had been built through conquest and assimilation of some members of the conquered societies. This method was now joined to the imported concept of nationalism. The goal was a homogeneous national state, through assimilation and consolidation of Young Turk authoritarian rule over this national state.

Hence, there was no longer a place in the new society for those who could not be assimilated. Their transformation had left Armenians too human to be forced back into an inferior status-position. And they had entered the new society without sacrificing their Armenian identity, which rendered them effectively incapable or unworthy of assimilation. The Young Turks themselves had come to see the Armenians as "essentially other," that is, as an alien presence that would continue without assimilation to Turkish identity. This kind of integration of Armenians would have undermined the utility of ethno-nationalism for legitimizing the Turkish state without democracy. Inclusion of Armenians as Armenians would have forced or marked some level of truly democratic popular participation reflecting the actual residents of the state and not an idealized exclusive ethno-nation, while calling the whole basis of the Young Turk ethno-nationalist dream into question. The ideological impossibility of democratic integration and the de facto pluralism accomplished by the large unassimilated Armenian population led the Young Turks to a different solution, the elimination of the Armenians. It was not the fact that Armenians rejected participation in the new Ottoman Empire; on the contrary, it was their eager willingness to become part of a liberal Ottoman state constructed around religious and cultural tolerance that was unacceptable to the Young Turks.

One could argue that, because of their agency as a progressive political force as well as their perceived association with the European powers, Armenians came to be perceived as a corporate personification of democratic, liberalizing change in the Ottoman Empire.[24] Eliminating Armenians came to mean eliminating the democratic, liberalizing forces threatening the old Ottoman hierarchy still embraced by reactionary elements as well as threatening to derail the new ethno-nationalist fantasy of a romantic rather than democratic Turkey.

In a sense, the 1915 genocide made good on Abdul Hamid II's threat, that if Armenians continued advocating for their rights, they would be punished by general massacre. Put another way, the Young Turks exterminated the Armenians because the Armenians were human beings and had come to act like it in the public sphere. The genocide was not due to Armenian provocation, except insofar as their acting like human beings triggered an imperialist reassertion of Turkish superiority. Through genocide alone, participating Turks could re-impose their dominance over Armenians and the Young Turks could ensure dominance over the newly nationalized Ottoman Empire.

Concluding Implications

Aside from offering a new perspective on the Armenian Genocide that might help advance understanding of it, my account could have two other benefits. First, I have already used it to reframe the usual understanding of the post-genocide relationship between Armenians and Turks.[25] Proper comprehension of the impact of the genocide on contemporary relations is especially vital in this time of dialogue and growing concerns about reparations. On the dehumanization model, genocide results from a conceptual error in which human beings are not recognized as such. Not only does this suggest that the Armenian Genocide was a historical aberration but also that its impact on contemporary Turkey and Turkish individuals can be negated simply through recognition of the humanity of Armenians. The conception of the Armenian Genocide as a function of a Turkish imperial mindset and dominance over Armenians, however, implies that the success of the genocide consolidated a new level of Turkish imperial dominance. This dominance has persisted to the present and has pervaded all aspects of the Armenian-Turkish relationship. Rectifying the legacy of the genocide for the Armenian-Turkish relationship requires much more than a simple shift in attitudes about Armenians; it requires a much more difficult process of cultural and psychological transformation away from imperialism—indeed, a rethinking of Turkish identity itself, even in its progressive forms.

Second, my account offers a new framework through which to examine contemporary events that could become or already are genocidal, in the hope of prevention or at least effective intervention. One of the key problems since the United Nations Genocide Convention was adopted has been getting official recognition that what is occurring is or is on the path to becoming genocide. Instead, member governments, UN officials, journalists, and academics frequently misconstrue cases of genocide as intractable mutual ethnic conflicts. This misrepresentation dominated accounts of the genocides in Rwanda and Bosnia throughout the periods when prevention or effective intervention might still have been possible. In these two cases together, perhaps 1 million people were killed because of the failure to intervene. Of course, one could add cases such as Bangladesh, East Timor, and many others to this list. The model advanced in this chapter focuses on the qualitative differences between the motives, political agendas, and even nationalisms of the perpetrator and victim groups, so that the distinction is no longer blurred. What is more, it is based on recognition of the dominance relation of imperial superior over subjugated inferior, not on a conflict model in which dehumanization might occur on both sides and confirm a relativistic appraisal. I have been especially intent on challenging the tendency to view victims' human rights activism against pre-genocidal oppression and genocide as qualitatively and quantitatively similar to perpetrator superiority and aggression. It is crucial that those looking at potential and actual genocides think more complexly about the political agency of victims, so that basic self-defense against genocide as well as victims' desperate efforts at positive political change to avert mass violence will no longer be used to justify a refusal to intervene. At present, it is only after the victim group has proven its utter passivity and vulnerability by sustaining a large number of losses that intervention becomes a geopolitical possibility.[26]

Notes

1. André Mineau, "Reification as a Precondition of Genocide," Society for the Philosophic Study of Genocide and the Holocaust panel, American Philosophical Association Central Division Meeting, Chicago, April 23, 2004.
2. Daniel Shartin, panel of the Society for the Philosophic Study of Genocide and the Holocaust at the American Philosophical Association Central Division Meeting, Chicago, April 23, 2004.
3. Hilmar Kaiser, "After All, Who Remembers the Genocide of the Armenians?" Lecture, Clark University, February 13, 2001.

4. Armenian Genocide deniers might take this as an opening to argue that, since deportations were not an efficient way of killing Armenians, it must be that killing Armenians was not the goal of the deportations, and any deaths were an unfortunate byproduct. But, just because perpetrators did not kill Armenians as efficiently as they might have does not entail that they did not mean to kill them. What is more, examination of the deportations and related facts demonstrates clearly that the goal and effect of the deportations was the destruction of deportees, as has been extremely well argued in the literature. The mere fact that men in villages were killed immediately supports this, as do the conditions of starvation and extreme violence from all quarters, including governmental Special Organizations and other sanctioned groups, imposed on deported Armenians. The fact that the Committee of Union and Progress chose to deport Armenians into a desert in the first place perhaps says all that needs to be said on this point.
5. For especially telling survivor testimony and insightful analysis of these kinds of violence, see Donald E. Miller and Lorna Touryan Miller, *Survivors: An Oral History of the Armenian Genocide* (Berkeley, Los Angeles, London: University of California Press, 1993), esp. chap. 5, "The Experiences of Women and Children," pp. 94-117. Eyewitness testimonies further supporting my characterization of violence against Armenians can be found, for instance, in *United States Official Records on the Armenian Genocide, 1915-1917*, comp. and intro. Ara Sarafian (Princeton, NJ: Gomidas, 2004).
6. Henry Morgenthau, *Ambassador Morgenthau's Story* (Garden City, NY: Doubleday, Page., 1918), p. 307.
7. Friedrich Nietzsche, Essay II, *On the Genealogy of Morals and Ecce Homo*, trans. Walter Kaufmann and R. J. Hollingdale (New York: Vintage/Random House, 1989), pp. 57-96.
8. See especially the following chapters in *Mass Rape: The War against Women in Bosnia-Herzegovina*, ed. Alexandra Stiglmayer, trans. Marion Faber (Lincoln: University of Nebraska Press, 1994): Ruth Seifert, "War and Rape," pp. 54-72; Alexandra Stiglmayer, "The Rapes in Bosnia Herzegovina," pp. 82-169; Vera Folnegovic-Smalc, "Psychiatric Aspects of the Rapes in War against the Republics of Croatia and Bosnia-Herzegovina," pp. 174-79; Catharine A. MacKinnon, "Rape, Genocide, and Women's Human Rights," pp. 183-96; and Rhonda Copelon, "Surfacing Gender: Reconceptualizing Crimes against Women in Time of War," pp. 197-218.
9. This is not to deny that in some cases people derive pleasure from abusing animals. For instance, it is often pointed out that adult men who commit domestic violence sometimes abused animals while growing up. But, the pleasure derived from abuse of animals would seem to result from the personification of those animals, that is, the ascription to them of a human capacity for suffering—driven presumably by the desire to cause human suffering. It is telling that such animal abusers often turn to abuse of people later in life, apparently to boost their sense of power and pleasure at the abuse.
10. If, in frustration, some individuals do vent their anger on inanimate objects, they do so to make an owner suffer the object's destruction, personify the object by blaming it, or soon realize the pointlessness of their behavior (perhaps leading to even greater frustration).
11. For an excellent comparative analysis of this type of dehumanizing process in the Holocaust, the Armenian Genocide, and indigenous American genocides, see Morgan Blum, "Dehumanization as a Process of Genocide," Undergraduate Honors Thesis, Clark University, 2002.

12. The millet system was the organizing hierarchy of the Ottoman Empire. In it, Muslims had full legal and social rights, while non-Muslim "people of the book," that is, Jews and Christians, had a second-class subject status that entailed, among other things, higher taxes, exclusion from the military and political spheres, and strict limitations on legal rights. The second-class subjects were further divided according to their particular religious institutions. Thus, the Armenians, on the basis of their branch of Christianity, formed their own millet. Each millet's internal affairs were largely administered by its religious leadership structure.
13. Bernard Lewis, *The Emergence of Modern Turkey*, 2d ed. (New York: Oxford University Press, 1968), p. 356.
14. Elie Kedourie, *The Chatham House Version and Other Middle-Eastern Studies* (New York: Praeger, 1970), pp. 287-300. See also Elie Kedourie, *Nationalism*, 3rd ed. (London: Hutchinson UL, 1966).
15. Vahakn Dadrian, *The History of the Armenian Genocide: Ethnic Conflict from the Balkans to Anatolia to the Caucasus* (Providence, RI: Berghahn Books, 1995).
16. Robert Melson, *Revolution and Genocide: On the Origins of the Armenian Genocide and the Holocaust* (Chicago: University of Chicago Press, 1992), pp. 41-69, 137-170, 245-286.
17. Melson, *Revolution and Genocide*, pp. 157-159.
18. Dikran Kaligian, "The Armenian Revolutionary Federation under Ottoman Constitutional Rule from 1908 to 1914," Ph.D. Diss., Boston College, 2004.
19. Taking this hope seriously requires suspending knowledge of its ultimate futility and the need for an independent state to ensure the human rights of Armenians against Turkish violation.
20. Earlier *Tanzimat* reforms (1839-76) promised something similar, but remained mere promises, with no transformation of the empire. It took an overthrow of the government to effect real change in the situation of Armenians.
21. Partha Chatterjee, *Nationalist Thought and the Colonial World: A Derivative Discourse?* (Minneapolis: University of Minnesota Press, 1986).
22. This could represent a genuinely Armenian contribution to the evolution of "nation" and "nationalism" in the nineteenth and twentieth centuries—though a contribution no doubt shared with certain other minority groups in other contexts.
23. My understanding of nineteenth-century German romantic nationalism comes from Martin Thom's masterful *Republics, Nations and Tribes* (London: Verso-New Left Books, 1995).
24. See British Ambassador Sir Philip Currie's 1894 letter to Sultan Abdul-Hamid II, quoted in Melson, *Revolution and Genocide,* pp. 59-60, for evidence of this perception of Armenians.
25. Henry C. Theriault, "Toward a New Conceptual Framework for Resolution: The Necessity of Recognizing the Perpetrator-Victim Dominance Relation in the Aftermath of Genocide," 7th Biennial Conference of the International Association of Genocide Scholars, Boca Raton, Florida, June 7, 2005.
26. I wish to thank Daniel Shartin for the brilliant ideas he imparted in thoughtful conversations that provided the starting point for this essay and to Adam Strom for his insightful remarks in discussions regarding the key points that I have developed.

4

Testimony: From Document to Monument

Marc Nichanian

In memory of Grigor Hakobyan

Historicity and Representation

Nearly twenty-five years have passed since I wrote the essay "Le style de la violence," based on Hagop Oshagan's reflections about the possibility or impossibility of representing the Catastrophe. The essay was subsequently translated into English and was published in the *Armenian Review* in 1985. Meanwhile, there have been numerous developments in the field. Historians of the Holocaust, alongside philosophers on both shores of the Atlantic, have repeatedly asked the same questions: on the one hand, about the implementation of the genocidal will, the modernity of such a will, the perverted role of historiography, and, on the other hand, about the "limits of representation" when confronted with the reality of concentration camps, programs of extermination, and genocidal violence. In fact, there are three levels of concern that rise in this field and need to be distinguished carefully, because of the discontinuity of their historical occurrences and especially because no interrogation can be conducted about each of them in relation to the others if the distinction has not been made in the first place. Of these three ranges, the first one is concerned with the historicity of genocidal events; the second, with the possibility and decency of any artistic approach to extreme mass violence, to physical destruction, and to cultural annihilation; and the third, simply put, with the phenomenon of testimony. Recent decades have witnessed an astonishing phenomenon in the discursive field that relates historiography as a discipline, testimony as a genre, and what in general is called fact. The stable (and immemorial) coexistence between historiography, testimony, and the factuality of facts has been suddenly put into question through a number of debates among historians, partly provoked by the change of nature of "testimony" and the philosophical reflection brought about by this phenomenon. Of course, it had already been shaken by the very nature of the genocidal will, but without being accounted for until the recent testimonial revolution.

This slow change in the meaning of the word "testimony," this emergence of a crisis in the very field of historiography due to the necessity of rethinking the status of testimony, put an abrupt end to two or three decades of unhampered work by historians and literary critics. Both sectors had shared the pending work on the Catastrophe, and apparently both had a clear idea about the difference between testimony as a document and testimony as a piece of writing that could be discussed in terms of artistic value (and sometimes, of course, pure authenticity passed as artistic value). One particular expression of this heated debate came with the 1991 conference organized by Saul Friedlander at UCLA and subsequently published under the title of *Probing the Limits of Representation.*[1] The obsession of the 1991 conference about the question of "truth in history" was the consequence of an internal crisis within the discipline itself. In the United States, this crisis absurdly crystallized around the intellectual configuration named "post-modernism" and the figure of Hayden White. It is true that American "post-modernism" wanted to be "relativist" about historical truth. But it is ironic to see that the 1991 historians created a representation of their own crisis in a colloquium on the historiography of the Extermination by refiguring their own dissension under the features of revisionism and by assigning a scapegoat—Hayden White himself. At stake in that debate was the significance of testimony. It was around an indestructible and unshakable idea of testimony that Carlo Ginzburg constructed his devastating critique of White's position.

Ginzburg's contention was that the modern implementation of genocidal will does not radically change our ways of writing history and our views on the task and the nature of historiography. This argument drew upon J. F. Lyotard's *The Differend*, from which historian Ginzburg quoted the following passage:

> But, with Auschwitz, something new has happened in history (which can only be a sign and not a fact), which is that the facts, the testimonies which bore the traces of here's and now's, the documents which indicated the sense or senses of the facts, and the names, finally the possibility of various phrases whose conjunction makes reality, all this has been destroyed as much as possible. Is it up to the historian to take into account not only the damages, but also the wrong? Not only the reality, but also the meta-reality that is the destruction of reality? Not only the testimony, but also what is left of the testimony when it is destroyed?[2]

With this selection from Lyotard, Ginzburg showed that he was perfectly aware of the stakes involved in the debate, which is all the more remarkable that the French original of these lines was written in 1983 in direct reference to

Hayden White's 1982 article, "The Politics of Interpretation." The problem was that Ginzburg did not quote Lyotard's answer to his own question, although (or because) this answer addresses the responsibility of historians. Here is Lyotard's complete answer:

> Yes, of course, if it is true that there would be no history without a *differend*. . . . But then, the historian must break with the monopoly over history granted to the cognitive regimen of phrases, and he or she must venture forth by lending his or her ear to what is not presentable under the rules of knowledge.

Yes, it is up to the historian to take into account not only the damage—that which can be formulated in a tribunal by speaking an audible and controvertible language in exchange for retribution—but the wrong, for which no audible language exists which could engage the endless game of historical and judicial refutations; not reality, but this meta-reality which is, as Lyotard superbly states, the destruction of reality; not testimony, but what is left of testimony when it has been destroyed in its validity if not in its concrete presence within archives. Yes, it is up to the historian. This is part of his metaphysical responsibility. And yet, if he could do that, if only one of them could do that, he would already have departed from the historians' history. This is why Ginzburg skips the passage, which he probably considers as being purely rhetorical, and rather quotes: "[Auschwitz's] name marks the confines wherein historical knowledge sees its competence impugned."

And it is here, after this quotation, that Ginzburg finally comes forth to declare: "Is this last remark true? I am not fully convinced. Memory and the destruction of memory are recurrent elements in history." The destruction of memory is nothing new. It is a constitutive part of history, no less than memory itself. Conquerors have always destroyed the archives of conquered nations. Colonizers have always been sufficiently astute for ensuring that archives reflect their own point of view on history and not that of the colonized. There always have been forced conversions, massacres, extermination, annihilation, where the very memory of conversion and annihilation have been annihilated, monuments have been demolished, tombs, funeral steles, places of worship, traces of life and death have been erased. Not only have conquerors suppressed lives but, everywhere in the world, they also saw to it that these lives were never lived. Thus, so many times in history, archives have been destroyed that would have made possible the validation of facts and the memory of their own destruction. The result is that there is nothing at all new with Auschwitz and the genocides of the twentieth century. As a consequence, there is also nothing new in the status of the survivor and the witness after Auschwitz. Already for the Romans, one of the words for "witness" was *superstes*, which also meant "survivor." The rules of the testimonial narrative are the same today as they were yesterday, the strategies for the validation of these narratives are the same, the historians' doubts when confronted with these narratives are the same (Just one witness? Is the totality of testimonies tantamount to acceptable evidence for establishing the reality of the facts?).

This whole argumentation concerns the interrogation on the "historicity" of facts and on the question as to how the facts, taken together, constitute what is generally accepted as history. But similarly, the whole debate with Hayden White was also bringing up different kinds of elements and arguments, this time related to the realm of representation, to the limits of a representative language in its confrontation with the Catastrophe, to the ways of adequately representing events, to the rhetoricity of language, and, with this last feature, to the whole question of the impossibility of distinguishing between fact and fiction. The Nietzschean argument about "politics of interpretation" and the so-called relativist argument about the fictitiousness of historiography overlapped completely. Finally, testimony intervened within the argument, both in Lyotard's treatment of White's assessment and in Ginzburg's gentle skepticism. The three ranges formerly introduced (historicity, representation, and testimony) were interwoven to the point of being indistinguishable. The problems that the resistance to admit historiography's crisis in the face of the inhuman nature of genocidal events was redoubled by a similar resistance to admit that testimony as a concept (if not as a practice) went through a profound change of status and significance in the last two decades. It is in this change of status that, albeit belatedly, the particular nature of the genocidal will can be recognized. This will is not (or not only) a will to eliminate lives or to destroy the social texture of a living community but a will to eliminate facts or rather the *factuality of facts* as the basis of everything that is known under the name of humanity.

Therefore, the change in testimony's status needs to be taken into consideration. For lack of a better characterization and on a provisory basis, it will be admitted that it is a change from testimonies serving as *documents* to testimonies becoming *monuments*. The term is borrowed from Michel Foucault, who introduced the distinction document/monument in a different context and never explicitly harkened back to it:

> I shall call an *archive* . . . the series of rules which determine in a culture the appearance and disappearance of statements, their retention and their destruction, their paradoxical existence as *events* and *things*. To analyze the facts of discourse in the general element of the archive is to consider them, not at all as *documents* (of a concealed significance or a rule of construction) but as *monuments*.[3]

The paradox is that what Foucault calls "archive" is almost contrary to what is ordinarily understood with the archive as being a depository of texts and traces left by a civilization. By using the term archive, Foucault uses *the same word* both to describe the "general element" in which monuments appear and to refer to the collection of documents. This equivocation has its profound reasons and, obviously, its dangers. Some of them have since been made explicit by

Giorgio Agamben in his reworking of the concept of testimony in *Remnants of Auschwitz* (from which I received the impetus for rethinking the historical meaning of "testimony" between document and monument), and more precisely at the beginning of the chapter titled "The Archive and Testimony."[4]

As long as testimonies were documents and only documents, they were read (if they were read at all) as if they were either quiet remnants that could help reconstruct the facts or traces of a tragic experience left behind by survivors for future generations. In both cases, they could supposedly be made available for reclaiming the truth of the facts, of the experience. They were dependent on a reality perpetually hidden behind them, awaiting its rediscovery, its deployment before the eyes of the civilized world, for all eternity. Once they have become monuments, the same testimonies can finally be considered for what they are, independently of any reconstructing gaze and any will to make them function as evidence. A document is always already instrumentalized, it is always for something else: for a possible biography, for revealing thrashed and maimed existences, for restoring a context, for describing a larger set that would encompass the particular events documented in the document. A monument is only for itself. It is on this basis that I offer an abridged account of the production of Armenian testimonies in the twentieth century, read as monuments and not as documents.

Armenian Testimony between Art and Document

The Armenian discussion on the question of testimony was manifest during the last century. The discussion is somewhat difficult to follow, not only because of its multiple ramifications, but because it is often inexplicit and has to be worked out of the narratives. The authors of the first generation of literate survivors who wrote down their experience in the form of reports, memoirs, accounts, stories, often also wrote residual remarks on the necessity of bearing witness, of keeping a live memory of the events, of recounting their gruesome experiences and their miraculous escapes. These remarks do not say much about the nature of testimony and the way they conceived their task. We will read here some of these reflections. Sometimes, as is the case for Zabel Esayan, they pronounced the demise of literature in a few sentences and opened an abyss of questions about the capacities of art when confronted with collective atrocity. But sometimes on the contrary, as is the case for Aram Andonian, they considered that only literature could answer their own interrogations about the necessity of coping with the entire scope of the atrocities. Almost immediately, however, there is a series of testimonies that do not belong to these categories and are not concerned with this dilemma of art/testimony. Their authors would never have thought of writing if they had not been obsessed by the memories of the deportation. In this new category are a few intellectuals who came back from exile in Changere or Ayash and also persons who were not intellectuals at all but who decided that what they went through was worth recounting and being transmitted to their contemporaries. All these authors were doing a personal work and offering an account of their own experience. Others devoted themselves, sometimes for years and decades, to the work of gathering a multitude of testimonies of all sorts and became the "documentarians" of the testimonial narrative. This work of gathering had begun very early, in one case (the British *Blue Book* prepared by Arnold Toynbee and Lord Bryce) under the impulse of external motives. Already in 1916 Vahan Totovents was at work in Erzinga/Erzinjan (introduced by Esayan to a project initiated and commissioned by Levon Shant) gathering testimonies from survivors of the first wave of extermination. In 1917, Esayan was working as a documentarian in the Caucasus. Later, in 1918, Aram Andonian devoted his energy to the same enterprise, this time in Aleppo.

Perhaps these two endeavors, the personal recounting and the gathering of testimonies have to be distinguished and do not obey the same imperative. The fact is that this incredible fever and fervor around the work of bearing witness lasted until 1922.[5] After that date (the end of Armenian cultural and literary life in Constantinople, when most of the writers who had survived the deportation escaped the city along with their students), writing on the years of deportation became more of an individual project. Other categories have to be recalled at the outset of this inquiry: (1) the individual testimonies of many semi-literate survivors who nevertheless wrote their memories in Armenian or Turkish;[6] (2) the contributions of people who were literate and even intellectuals but did not belong to the circle of Constantinopolitan writers (several Evangelical ministers and priests from the region of Kharpert (Harput), for example, wrote interesting survivor memories);[7] (3) those who were very young in 1915, had learned Armenian in their village or in orphanages in the Middle East, and wrote their memories much later.[8] Of course, with the exception of the testimonies written in Turkish (of which, as far as I know, none was published in its original form), everything listed above was written in Armenian and constitutes the bulk of the Armenian testimony in the course of the twentieth century. But there are also testimonies in other languages. Two of the first testimonies in English were Elizabeth Caraman's *Daughter of the Euphrates* (1939) and Zaven Surmelian's *I Ask You, Ladies and Gentlemen* (1946).[9] In more recent years, there has been a resurgence of this infinite will to bear witness (or simply to show one's wounds) with a last wave of published testimonies, either translated by the sons and daughters of the survivors, or written directly in English. The latest and probably final wave in this succession of endeavors stirred by the paradoxes of memory is the spectacular gathering of oral testimonies and creation of various collections throughout the United States and Canada.

This long list suggests that a large part of the Armenian energy during the last century was devoted to the production of testimonies, yet none of them has ever been studied as such. There are only two books in English that concern themselves with testimonies at large, one by Lorne Shirinian, which gives a general idea of the survivors' memoirs available in English,[10] and the other one by Donald and Lorna Miller, which uses a limited number of oral narratives by survivors and the common historical knowledge about the events for recreating both the world of the Armenian village, with the beauties and the harshness of its everyday life, and the ways this world has been systematically destroyed.[11] Clearly, testimony is used here for the purpose of the historical restoration of a vanished reality and an excruciating experience of loss. Although the endeavor is perfectly legitimate according to the criteria of oral history, it is also apparent that testimony itself vanishes behind reality and experience. It is conceived and read as a document, never as a monument. The same holds true for Shirinian's definition of a survivor's memoir: "A memoir is a prose story that a real person has written about his or her own life; the individual acts as a witness, and what is emphasized is the individual point of view. However a memoir has a broader dimension than just the individual life."[12] This is a strange definition on all accounts, first because a non-real person would have some difficulty writing about his or her own life, unless we are already in a novel (and this remark is far for being trivial: at stake is the whole status of literary testimony), and second because there is a certain awkwardness in the use of the word "witness." An individual can do many things. He can witness the death of others and bear witness to it, but there is one thing that is impossible: he cannot bear witness to his own death and his own incapacity of bearing witness. Yes, this is a paradox, and the paradox is still more acute than just explained, because it is also true that in order to be able to remember and to describe, to recount and to record, what happened to them, survivors needed to describe everything as though it were slightly external, as though they had been only witnessing—witnessing the sufferings and the thousand deaths of others. If they had done more than only witnessing, with the very thin but also very immoral distance between witnessing and bearing witness, they would not have survived. Did I say immoral? Again, yes. In the thousands of pages of survivor testimonies that are at the disposal of everyone in Armenian and now sometimes in English, the word "shame" is never encountered. Isn't it shameful to show one's wounds? I read recently the words written or pronounced by an anonymous Armenian survivor, printed in the *New Republic* on June 29, 1921: "We cry in anguish and pain. We show our wounds. We call for help. The crowd on the shore throw out handfuls of pennies which fall leaden into the waters. Our cry has not been understood." I do not know who this Armenian survivor was, I do not know if he or she was literate and in which language, if the words quoted above were pronounced in Armenian or directly in English. But all the same, these short sentences have in themselves the germ of a work of art. They speak metaphorically. They imagine a crowd on the shore, they imagine the reception of testimony. But they also imagine a showing of the wounds. How does one show one's wounds? What is imagined in these lines, these unbearable lines, is a space of visibility. The wounds have to be shown and they need a public, a crowd, that sees them. They have to be visible, or at least they have to be made visible. But already decades ago, these few lines were also saying that "our cry has not been understood," and obviously for eighty-five years the survivors and their descendants have kept repeating, "Our cry has not been understood." In order to make the cry understood, the survivors have asked for more visibility, more images, more paintings, more representation, more films. It is the fate of testimony, it is part of its essence or its structure. Testimony calls for more visibility. There is never enough visibility. Our cry has never been understood enough. Testimony calls for the gaze of the civilized world. With the call for visibility shame comes up, which lies at the core of the testimonial narrative because of the very thin, almost indiscernible distance between witnessing and bearing witness, which is also the indiscernible distance between document and monument, and because, at the very beginning, before any documentary use of testimony or definitions of survivor memoirs, it was the convention of the genre.

An Ethics of Representation

Only witnessing. This is what Ervant Odian says on the last page of his own narrative, his voluminous survivor's memoir, *Anitsial tariner* (Accursed Years), serialized as early as 1919 and only recently published as a book in Erevan. The following is my translation from Armenian:

> Here is the story of my three and a half years of deportation. Of course the readers have noticed that I wrote that story in the simplest way possible and even with an uncultivated literary style. Before everything else I wanted to be truthful [*chshmar-tapatum*] and to say things exactly as they happened, without distorting any fact, without exaggerating any event.
>
> And yet the reality was so horrible that many readers thought I was exaggerating. Those who went through the sufferings of deportation and were able to survive, those will testify that I did not alter the truth.
>
> Let me say also that, in spite of all the evils that I had to endure, I have been one of the most fortunate among the deportees. The other ones, men or women, suffered and grieved much more than what I had to suffer and grieve for.
>
> They were entire families, who lived through the extremities of bitterness and misery: the death of their children or parents on deserted roads, the abduction or rape of their daughters in front of them, under the tents, looting by bandits, theft by the gendarmes, illness, starvation, thirst, all the ways of torturing.
>
> I myself was alone, I had only myself to care for. I had no belongings, no money, that I could fear of being stolen or becoming the aim of the greed of policemen. On the contrary, always and everywhere, there was an acquaintance or someone entirely unknown but sympathetic to me, who as soon as he heard my name, immediately came to my help and brought as much benevolence as he could.
>
> My three years of deportation replaced my thirty years of literary activity.[13]

He will be as sober, as restrained, as possible. He will only recount what he has seen, as though he was merely an observer, which he was not of course. But again this is the indispensable convention of survivor testimonies. If they had done more than only witnessing, they would have died or become mad in the very moment when they were speaking/writing. As is known from the flurry of philosophical reflections on that matter, the witness is never the one who is really "there." He is not (in the moment of his witnessing/bearing witness) at the very core of the event or the experience, he is not the one who died or became mad. Primo Levi would say: he is not the "integral witness," he is not the one who passed the inhuman limit of humanity and never came back. And consequently the usage of the word witness by Shirinian is quite understandable but for me nonetheless shocking. It bears repeating: the survivors who spoke and wrote are those who bore witness. To be a witness and to bear witness are not exactly the same. Primo Levi and other Jewish survivors of the Holocaust are today called "witnesses" because they bore witness, not because they were the witnesses of atrocities. But what Odian says on the last line of his memoir, "My three years of deportation replaced my thirty years of literary activity," is more difficult to grasp. Here, suddenly, he is beyond the convention. Does he want to say that he learned more during his deportation than in his thirty years of being a writer or that he survived because he was well known? Or, more to the point, that he had *to abandon literature* in order to be faithful to his experience as a deportee? To tell the truth and only the truth would thus require to put aside any preoccupation of style. What Odian is formulating here is an ethics of representation. This ethics of representation, formulated nearly nine decades ago, was buried in the pages of the journal *Zhamanak* (*Jamanag*) of Constantinople, and it came to the attention of the general reader only in 2005, thanks to the publication of those pages by Grigor Hakobyan, to whose memory this essay is dedicated.[14]

Grigor Hakobyan died in Erevan on April 2, 2005, at the age of forty-six.[15] He was a member of the Institute of Literature, the youngest ever Doctor of Letters in Armenia when he received the title in 1997, the best and probably only specialist of Western Armenian and Diaspora literature in a country where the literary tradition of the Diaspora has never been taken seriously. He was a theoretician of the literary phenomenon, well versed in modern and modernist approaches. Among many other publications, he had prepared a new, scientific edition of Hagop Oshagan's novel *Haji Abdullah.* He also had a book on the novels of Ervant Odian, and most recently, after great effort, he was the one who published Odian's *Accursed Years*, which describes his deportation and his return to Constantinople after three years through the hell of his torment and the death of his people. As noted, these memories had been written and published by Odian in serialized form in 1919 in the journal *Zhamanak.* They had never before seen the light of day as a single volume. The book was released at the beginning of 2005 as Grigor Hakobyan's last philological achievement. Although Hakobyan's life tragically ended shortly thereafter, the volume is a sign that something has changed in the Armenian reception of the Catastrophe and in the concept of testimony. So long as in everyone's mind testimonies were equated to "documents," so long as the move from document to monument had not taken place, these testimonies belonged to the archives and did not deserve any other treatment but being shelved in libraries and lost from the collective memory of Armenians. Today, finally, testimonies have begun to acquire a value in and for themselves, and they can be studied as such, in their structure, their temporality, their narrative devices, their claims, their historicity, their representational function. And this is also the way we gradually, almost naturally, came to use in Armenian a word which now is the equivalent of testimony as monument (as opposed to testimony as document). The term is *vkayagrutiun*. Grigor Hakobyan used the word spontaneously when in his preface he spoke of Odian's *Accursed Years*, with no special emphasis on the fact that it is a new word in Armenian. Before, they said *hushagrutiun* (memoir; memory writing), *hush* (memory), *hushapatum* (narrative), or simply *vkayutiun* (testimony in the sense of an eye-witness account). And this is why now a reflection on testimony is needed, a history of Armenian testimony, and a better understanding of the ways testimony functions as representation of the Catastrophe. With his work on Odian's memoirs and the precious preface that he wrote for the volume, Grigor Hakobyan was one of those who have contributed to this ongoing reflection.

But there is more about Ervant Odian. He was the most prolific of all Armenian novelists. He wrote regularly two novels a year, very often two novels at the same time, and they were always serialized in the Armenian newspapers of Constantinople. He was arrested in August 1915 and did not return until after the end of World War I in November 1918. He then immediately resumed his activity and began to write the detailed account of his years in deportation. At the same time, he started to write a novel, *Tiv 17 Khafien* (Spy Number 17), which is set precisely in 1914-18, with the usual elements of his other novels: adventures, complicated plots and powerful intrigues, young Armenian revolutionaries, spies and traitors—the Armenian word, full of idiosyncratic meaning, is *matnich*, denouncer—but also (and this is the most amazing) with real figures, real characters, real names (Armenian intellectuals, directors of newspapers, political activists, deputies in the Ottoman Parliament, well-known writers, and, of course, also informers).[16] This last feature transforms the 1,200 page novel into a strange mixture of fact and reality, fantasy and history, all the more strange when one knows that most of these intellectuals, writers, and political activists whose names and figures appear on these pages were killed in the summer and fall of 1915, barely four years before the time of Odian's writing. And the reader asks himself: how did he dare do that? How did he dare transform the dead into characters in a novel, a novel written with the sole purpose of entertaining the masses or, more precisely, what remained of the masses. Was this not for him a kind of desecration, a sacrilege? These are legitimate questions. But it seems that Odian did not have these kinds of qualms. As stated, at the same time he was also writing a detailed account of his deportation, in a sober manner, without any literary ingredients—or at least that was his contention. This duality is interesting in itself. It prefigures the question that would obsess a number of novelists and eventually would constitute the core of the discussion concerning testimony among Armenian writers in the Diaspora: is it possible to transform the Deportation and the utter destruction of the Armenians into literature?

In the short foreword that precedes the novel and presents its subject matter, Odian explains that he has personally known one of those who collaborated with the Turkish police as a *matnich* and was responsible for the death of thousands of Armenians, adding: "I want to recount all these facts in a novelistic way [*vipakan dzevov*] to the readers of *Verjin Lur*, being sure that they will read with interest these events related to our recent past, in which many well known and loved personalities took part, and a number of them, alas, after tasting the bitterness of the Deportation, also endured the sufferings of martyrdom."[17] The truth is that Odian's posterity was particularly harsh with this novel. In spite of its several editions in the Diaspora, it has been entirely forgotten and apparently will remain deprived of a careful reexamination before Odian scholars in Armenia exhume it from oblivion and offer it to the public as the novel of the Catastrophe par excellence.[18] One of the justifications of the newly sprawling interest in Odian's *Tiv 17 Khafien* lies in the fact that in a way Odian was the only Armenian established novelist who as a survivor endeavored to mold the Catastrophe into something resembling the genre of the *historical novel*. The others ones (Andonian, Esayan, Oshagan) adopted different attitudes, and in the final analysis they escaped before the task or they refused to fictionalize the events. Only Oshagan toyed with the idea until the end of his life but abandoned it. The real problem was not art's alleged lack of power for the rendering of genocidal events (as Oshagan's formulations could be interpreted). It was not an undue respect for the unprecedented scope of the victims' sufferings (as Esayan wants it to be). The problem was the status and the fate of testimony when we are still unable to see it as a monument.

Against Fiction: A Moral Imperative

In 1943, when Levon Shant was writing his history of Armenian literature, *Endhanur aknark me hay banahiusutian vra* (General Overview of Armenian Literature), he came to the names of Siamanto first and then of Suren Bartevian (Partevian) and Aram Andonian. Each time, he felt the need to express his disapproval with the type of literature they cultivated, and this for a very specific reason linked with the literary treatment of what, according to him, should have remained in the exclusive domain of the already numerous collections of testimonies and survivors' accounts. In the chapter on Siamanto, Shant writes:

> Art strives to move and to awaken emotions, but it does so aesthetically, that is, it awakens not real pain and suffering, rather only the distant resemblances of pains and suffering in a milder and non-poisonous form. When, in order to stir one's emotions, such events from reality are depicted, that cause fear, suffering, pain and deep sorrow not aesthetically but rather really, they then cease belonging to art. Such writings can

> be used to elicit vengeance, so as to keep the fire of hatred burning, but not in order to awaken aesthetic emotions.
>
> The descriptions of the bestial and savage treatment the Armenian people were subjected to cannot benefit anyone, nor are such descriptions in need of the benefits that art might bestow upon them. The reality is already atrocious and powerful. It is best that [these descriptions] remain in the white, blue, yellow—or whatever color they may have—collections of governmental documents gathered from the lips of the witnesses.[19]

I will not open here a new round of reflections on the difficult questions of the artistic representation of the bestial, the inhuman, the atrocious. Is it possible to represent it? Shant does not say anything about its being possible or not. Does it have to be represented? This is where Shant has something to say. He formulates a sort of moral imperative against the artistic representation of atrocities. The description of everything that is really atrocious does not belong to art. As seen in the case of Ervant Odian, there is here an ethics of representation but not exactly in the same terms. Odian strove for faithfulness to the reality of his experience as a survivor. His was a testimonial ethics, which did not prevent him from using the same material for a work of art or, say, a work of literature and fiction, with no claim of exclusiveness on the one side or the other. In Levon Shant's approach, atrocities are the domain of the testimonial narrative, not the domain of art. But, of course, Shant also had a particular view on what is now called "testimony." The word *vkayagrutiun* was not available to him and in the present context he does not use any other word that could have an equivalent meaning. For him, "testimony" is nothing that is worth reflecting on or for that matter that should be kept in the written annals of the nation. It is something purely political, or a pure document which as such does not deserve to enter the realm of art. No philosophical privilege needs to be attached to it. The "white, blue, or yellow" collections of documents that he mentions are among others (and rather contemptuously) referring to the British *Blue Books* and the French *Yellow Books*. Both series devoted hundred and thousand of pages to the first wave of partial extermination in 1895-1896 and to the all-encompassing genocidal thrust of 1915. The witnesses and the victims can recount their experience and their testimonies can appear in these diplomatic publications as documents. That is where their place is and, more precisely, that is what their function should be limited to. Shant was perfectly aware of the existence of all sorts of testimonies. But for him, the category of "testimony" had to be confined to the domain of documents and not transgress into the domain of art. He repeated the same idea a few pages later, this time in his comments on the Western Armenian novelists and authors of short stories: "Suren Bartevian, Aram Andonian, and one or two others authors have tried to depict [*patkerel*] aesthetically the national grief of our massacres and deportation in short stories. A very superfluous and very difficult endeavor."[20]

Why is this depiction superfluous and difficult? Again for two reasons: on the one side, art will suffer from it, for real sorrow has nothing to do with art; on the other hand, political strivings will also suffer because art is the realm of imagination and therefore the impression left by the sense of reality (on the civilized world!) will be weakened. The goal is to impress the civilized world with our open wounds, isn't it? But what is more interesting is Shant's insistence on the fact that testimony should be confined to the domain of politics. This is what the author says still more explicitly in the following lines:

> What is the aim of those writings? The creation of an aesthetic work? As stated, aesthetics will gain nothing, and the reader will feel more pain and real sorrow than aesthetic pleasure and enjoyment. And if the purpose be exactly the production of such pain and sorrow, if it be to elicit vengefulness in the readers' souls in order to shake them from their indifference, in that case, putting what we have to narrate in an aesthetic form amounts to a great impediment and it disturbs, because we are used to looking at an aesthetic piece of writing as if it were the fruit of the imagination, as an adapted thing, which weakens the effect conveyed by true reality.
>
> These stories of suffering, grief, and torture relative to our cruel reality have to be recounted carefully in details, in perfect nudity, without any embellishment, without fictitious complements, without any exaggeration [as they were gathered], from the lips of witnesses and the official documents, always avoiding the allure of an aesthetic writing. In this state only can these raw descriptions attain their highest level, as the exact representation of a bestial reality.[21]

Is it possible to disagree? It is true that any "embellishment" would deprive a testimony of its value as the report of a lived experience. This was already what Odian was saying in his own context, which is the context of testimony as monument. But in reality what Shant is saying here is truly appalling. In his mind, the survivor's memories and narratives have a value only as documents, never as monuments. They only have an instrumental value; their goal is to elicit vengeance or pity; they have to be a pure exhibit of atrocity. There is no middle way. Testimony has to be either artistic or political. Shant is the impassioned advocate of the "political" usage of testimony. The opposite choice, the "artistic" reception of testimony, has been represented in the twentieth century by the powerful figure of Hagop Oshagan. It should be clear that the two choices, albeit antithetic, are purely symmetrical. Testimony as document excludes any sort of art, as though this exclusion was an ethical imperative, and thus instrumentalizes the utterances of the survivor. Conversely, the upholder of a literary rendering of the genocidal experience must accept the documentary conception of testimony (he has no other conception at his disposal), which nevertheless prevents him from any artistic use.

Two Illustrations of the Deadlock: Esayan, Andonian

This typical deadlock is well illustrated by the positions and activities of Zabel Esayan and Aram Andonian after 1915.

Zabel Esayan

Esayan was the most distinguished woman writer from Armenian Constantinople. In 1911, she wrote a remarkable book titled *Amidst the Ruins*, a book of suffering and mourning, following the massacres of Cilicia in 1909.[22] At that stage, mourning was still possible. It was possible for a modern Antigone to rise up against the interdiction on mourning and to raise a monument in the form of a testimony. Was it a work of literature or a reportage? No one has been able to decide which genre this great book belongs to. No one could conceive testimony as monument. But it seems that the reversal of testimony into the archive had not yet occurred. This was just before the Catastrophe. After 1915, Esayan, who had miraculously escaped from the round-ups of intellectuals and taken refuge first in Bulgaria, then in the Caucasus, wrote, at least once, the story of how she had fled and gone into hiding; but she was perfectly incapable of writing a new monument of mourning like the one she had written in 1911. Instead, she devoted almost three years of her life to collecting testimonies, transcribing them, translating them into French, in order to present them to civilized humanity, to show the Armenian wounds to the crowd assembled on the shore. Thanks to Esayan's contribution and translations, the French journalist Henry Barby published *Au pays de l'épouvante* in 1917.[23]

The very first testimony published was thus the testimony of a survivor, Haig Toroyan, which Esayan personally transcribed and rewrote in its entirety. That was in February 1917. Toroyan had come down the Euphrates from October to December 1915 in the company of a German officer for whom he worked as an interpreter. He had therefore seen, one by one, all the concentration camps in Mesopotamia. He and the German officer had taken photos and notes. When they arrived in Iran, where they were supposed to hand over their arms, the German soldier became delirious and killed himself. Toroyan was able to continue on to the Caucasus where he recounted his story to Esayan, who published it under her own signature, with a two-page preface. The substance of the preface was that literature is not capable of rendering the Catastrophe; literature is superfluous. This did not mean that she would stop writing. She wrote a great deal after 1918 but not a single line directly related to the genocidal atrocities. Here is what she wrote on the impotence or the demise of literature:

> Painfully impregnated with the task that had fallen to me as my lot, I considered it a sacrilege to transform into literature the suffering in which an entire people agonized, the unutterable story of the profaned girls, and the wrecks of a civilized nation that has been reduced to the level of bestiality by pain and misery. . . . Consequently I approached this work with utmost simplicity and respect.[24]

Esayan, the greatest woman writer of her time, thus became a substitute witness, a pen at the service of the true witness; she became *the secretary of the archive*. She was haunted by the survivor. She took dictation; she transcribed.

She submitted herself to the reign of the archive, to the immediate transformation of testimony into the archive. She became, in her very life and body, an archiving machine. She exposed herself to the original moment of shame. She became a willing instrument in the ongoing and pervasive process of the archivization of testimony, which for nine decades now has short-circuited the victim's memory and its impossible mourning.

Aram Andonian

Aram Andonian was deported to Changere. He was part of one of the macabre convoys that once upon a time, from July to September 1915, transported the deportees of Changere to the place of their death. The extraordinary fortune of Andonian was that on that morning he fell from the oxcart and broke his leg. Brought to a hospital, he eventually healed, was convicted by a tribunal in Ankara and deported again, this time all the way to the deserts of Syria—Ras-ul-Ain and Meskene. He survived. In 1919, immediately upon his return to Constantinople, Andonian began to set down his recollections in the form of a testimony written in the first person. He never completed this personal recounting. The portion that is available was published in 1919-20 in the Parisian journal *Veratsnund*. Instead, he completed and published two books, which are the best illustration of the deadlock brought about by the antithetical but symmetrical consideration of testimony as document against the use of testimony for aesthetic purposes. In 1919, he published *Ayn sev orerun* (In Those Dark Days), and, in 1921, *Mets vochire* (The Great Crime).[25] The first is a volume of literature. Instead of having testimony in the first person, suddenly there is a collection of short stories, all of them horrifying, as though it were possible to exhaust the recording of atrocities with short stories. In these stories written in the heat of the moment, Andonian apparently wanted to speak of the victim's abject state through a series of unbearable descriptions. It is bad literature quite simply because it is literature. From the beginning, Andonian knew, with a knowledge that imposed itself on him beyond all reflection, that it was necessary for him to write literature in order to escape the becoming-archive of testimony. Thus, driven by the logic of the inescapable symmetry between the political choice and the artistic choice, he had no other solution but to write *Ayn sev orerun*.

Now, it was Andonian himself, the same Andonian, who led the first systematic campaign to collect testimonies. This took place in 1918, in Aleppo, the hub of the 1915-16 deportation. It is in Aleppo that he began to collect testimonies from everyone who was more or less willing or able to speak. Here is what he says about this enterprise in the first pages of his 1921 book:

> When the British entered Aleppo, I used the opportunity in order to save the history [of events] and I began to interrogate those among the survivors who were still able to remember the unspeakable awe and the atrocities of the past five years. Thousands

> of women, girls, men, came to me, they spoke and wrote. Each of them had his/her own story to tell, and not a single one of the tortures that they endured was similar to the other. Very often I thought that for each one of them a whole volume would be necessary in order to render these sufferings at least in their broad features. And they were more than a hundred thousand who had a whole volume of things to be told. And even if this were done, we wouldn't have the story of those who had fallen, bringing away with them the loss of more than a million volumes.[26]

Andonian put together a book partly based on these testimonies, written in Armenian, but immediately translated into French (it was practically a commissioned work). The version in French appeared in 1920 (before the version in Armenian). The testimony, in its archival dimension, was addressed to civilized humanity. And there is not, there never was, any testimony outside the dimension of the archive; this is the stunning, vertiginous paradox of testimony. Instead of writing a testimony in the first person, instead of working out testimony as monument, Andonian devoted the rest of his life to the collecting of testimonies and their transformation into archival material for a possible history of the Extermination. Andonian, who lived until 1952 and was the librarian of the Armenian Nubarian Library in Paris, not only collected this material, elicited more and more recollections from survivors, classified them according to their region of origin, but also wrote monographs about the process of deportation and extermination for each and every region concerned. All this material (tens of thousands of pages) is gathered in Paris and has remained unpublished, awaiting a researcher for so many years after the facts. Raymond Kevorkian is working on this material as a historian. One of my ambitions is to publish some of these testimonies and Andonian's monographs in their original language and hence to save the work of testimony from its archivization, its transformation into documents and evidence, in order to let it be as a monument. But not only have testimonies never been studied as such but the historians themselves have not done their work, perhaps for the same reasons, and today, ninety years later, there is no informed, comprehensive history of the Armenian Extermination.

To Approach the Catastrophe

A singular law of distribution led Levon Shant to distinguish between the "historical-political" and an "artistic" usage of testimony and to decide in favor of the political usage, expressing an impassioned (and embarrassing) disagreement with any past or future attempt to receive testimony within the field of art or aesthetics (*gegharvest*). Hagop Oshagan, the predominant figure in twentieth-century Armenian literature, embraced the opposite position. In 1931, ten years after Andonian's *The Great Crime*, Oshagan was in the midst of writing *Mnatsortats* (The Remnants). In this novel, after two parts on the pre-Catastrophe world, he wanted to write a third part in which he would "approach the Catastrophe." This third part was never written. It was to be called "Hell." In 1934, after writing the 2,000 pages of the first two parts, Oshagan stopped. He stopped on the threshold of "Hell" and never went back to the novel. Much later, in 1944, he said that it would have meant "marching straight toward death," his own death, of course, which was also the extermination of his people. In volume 9 of his *Panorama of Western Armenian Literature*, written between 1937 and 1944, there is a monograph on Andonian in which Oshagan reflects once again on the Catastrophe, on the apparently impossible writing of the Catastrophe, and in particular on Andonian's two books published in 1919 and 1921.Concerning *Mets vochire* he writes: "I wonder what he had in mind by putting forward these few telegrams, when deep in his conscience . . . he knew perfectly well who the authors of this drama were and what goal they were pursuing. It was the extermination of his people."[27] The work of memory should therefore guard against the trap of having a proof to administer and against the documentary use of testimony. Oshagan indeed makes the objection that would occur to anyone: "Civilized humanity?" he asks, and answers this himself: "History can prove nothing, because it is a tissue of disavowals and denials."[28] It is clear that, with this formulation, Oshagan situated himself at the first level of questioning, among the three that were mentioned at the very beginning of this essay, that is, the level of historicity. Contrary to Levon Shant's reactions, Oshagan maintains that testimony does not belong to this sphere.

But then to what sphere does it belong? To the sphere of literature, of art and aesthetics? Several times between 1931 and 1947, Oshagan reflected lengthily on the testimonial phenomenon and the conflicting relationship between testimony and literature. A first occurrence of an implicit discussion on testimony appears as early as the summer of 1931, in the long interview conducted by Beniamin Tashian and eventually published in two installments under the title of *Mayrineru shukin tak* (In the Shadow of the Cedars).[29] Oshagan was in Cyprus at the time, and his novel had begun to appear in the Cairo journal *Houssaper*. At a certain juncture in the interview, when asked about the third part of his novel, he declares: "It will require at least a topographical study, a reading of thousands of stories and hundreds of volumes and many memoirs, before being able to begin to write the last volume."[30] These lines remind the reader of Andonian's declaration: "And they were more than a hundred thousands who had a whole volume of things to be told." Clearly, what Oshagan wanted to have at hand was an "archive." He wanted in reality or metaphorically the testimonies collected by Andonian and, of course, they were not available to him. This is why he was *condemned* to literature: "I must be content with what I have. Hence, the necessity of the novelistic form." He needed the "raw" materials, the thousands of testimonies, the survivor stories, but for what purpose, if literature was only the second choice? (These testimonies are perhaps to be found today on the shelves of American universities. No one reads them, no one listens to them). So the formulation is, at the very least, quite strange. Should these formulations be interpreted as a sign that Oshagan himself was caught in the deadlock of the symmetrical and reciprocally exclusive usages of testimony? Or was it possible that Oshagan was already announcing testimony's change of value and meaning, which was still to come, its move from document to monument, from the documentary archive to a monumental archive, without being able to accomplish it himself? Of course, both are possible. The fact is that he was never able to "approach the Catastrophe." His explicit project was literary.

In the seventh volume of his *Panorama*, Oshagan devotes a whole monograph to Ervant Odian, and it is here that for the first time he takes into consideration the testimonies left by intellectuals or literary figures: Krikoris Balakian, Hovhannes Kapigian, Doctor Salpi, Payladzou Captanian, and, before them, Odian, Mikayel Shamdanjian, and Andonian. Obviously, these were not part of the "thousands of testimonies" that Oshagan was looking for as a pure fantasy or a simple metaphor in 1931. Why not? Probably because in his eyes they had already done the work of "aestheticization" on the raw materials and this work was not satisfying. He writes:

> They did not elevate themselves to the level of literature and henceforth they are out of our sphere of interest. In the daily and monthly *Hairenik* and in the journals of the Diaspora, the stories that have been published for the last twenty years were not fortunate enough for being signed by an authentic writer. And the terrible event remained unconquered [*ev ahavor depke mnats annvach*].[31]

As to Odian's *Accursed Years*, Oshagan's dislike of the work was so powerful that, after devoting a hundred pages or so to the analysis of the novelist's other works, he wrote dismissively about it: "I have no place and no time to analyze the book."[32] He considered Odian's testimony a pure failure. The only reason he advances for this failure or his own distaste is that "Odian could not conceive of the breadth of the Catastrophe."[33] If this is true, then what exactly were Oshagan's expectations? Was he waiting for a text that would be written by an "authentic writer" (these are Oshagan's words), like Esayan's *Amidst the Ruins* thirty years before? What was there to expect from Odian's testimony, from a testimony which declared that it was written without embellishment and without exaggeration, which according to Odian meant: devoid of literature? Oshagan was expecting a text as huge, as terrible, as unprecedented as the event itself. That, in fact, was what he expected from himself. But, even by himself, the terrible event remained unconquered.

Later, in the monograph devoted to Andonian, after quoting the same names like a litany, and after each one, again and again, expressing his dissatisfaction, Oshagan adds the following: "If ever writing is a power (*uzh*), to prove this power we have no better material than the Deportation of Western Armenians."[34] In the same note, literature is defined as "the awesome witness of the most solid, profound, ineradicable experiences of a nation."[35] Yes, but again he himself was unable to implement this power of writing in relation to the Catastrophe, at least with respect to testimony and on the basis of a realist account. Like Shant in the same period, like Andonian before him, Oshagan was caught in a deadlock: on the one hand, the document, the unembellished authenticity of the document, which accounts for the survivor's pure experience and offers the material for the historian's endeavor; on the other hand, art; in between, no place for testimony as monument. But, to express again the same hesitation as above, maybe it was not a deadlock after all. The pages on Andonian, written by Oshagan in 1943, are the only place where an Armenian author has ever reflected on the nature, the essence of testimony and has advocated for a testimonial literature liberated from the archive. This could have been done only in Armenian—not because the task of thinking about these questions is impossible in other languages. Rather it is because we will not cope with the question of testimony, we will not be able to accompany testimony on the path that transforms it from a document to a monument, by keeping it in the sphere of the "raw" experience eternally deposited in the archive and occasionally shown to the "Other" as an open wound, our dearest wound. This is why Daniel Varoujan (Varuzhan), the writer closest to Oshagan's heart, in his 1909 poem "Kilikian mokhirnerun" (To the Ashes of Cilicia) addressed the Other as the "foreigner," to whom he had shown and recounted the ashes of Cilicia, of this field of ruins and devastation, in the following way:

> Foreigner, go now. You see that I too go down
> From these heights, and wrapped in my sad cassock
> I go to wander again in the city of the sacrifices.
> I must bury the dead, I must anoint the holocaust.
> The head of a wounded man moans on the altar stone. . .
> Next to the fountain, oh, a sister agonizes with no one there to watch over her. . .
> Tonight I must dig countless graves,
> I must weave shrouds of light until morning comes
> I must build mausoleums, I must erect monuments,
> And into marble I must carve my songs as an epitaph.[36]

These are the last lines of the poem. I will not comment on them. Krikor Beledian has devoted beautiful pages to these lines in his book on the poet. I wish simply to note along with Varoujan that Art as mourning (the activity of erecting monuments of mourning, building mausoleums, carving epitaphs into marble) only begins when we give up discourse as exhibit and testimony as document. Oshagan and Varoujan, the two Dioscuri of Armenian literature, fully agreed on this point. But what happens then to testimony? Where is testimony as monument? Sixty more years were needed after Oshagan's reflections, ninety more years after Varoujan's poem, to see how testimony could appear as a monument. Oshagan and Varoujan had opened the way. They were the Moses of this promised land. Like Moses, they were forbidden to enter.

Notes

1. Saul Friedlander, ed., *Probing the Limits of Representation, Nazism and the "Final Solution"* (Cambridge, MA: Harvard University Press, 1992).

2. Jean-François Lyotard, *The Differend: Phrases in Dispute*, trans. George Van den Abbeele (Minneapolis: University of Minnesota Press, 1988), p. 57.
3. See *Essential Works of Foucault*, Paul Rabinow, ed., vol. 2 (New York: The New Press, 1998), p. 310 and p. 333 note.
4. Giorgio Agamben, *Remnants of Auschwitz* (New York: Zone Books, 1999), pp. 137-146. Significantly, the subtitle of the book is *The Witness and the Archive*.
5. Among the most famous testimonial works produced by the Constantinopolitan intellectuals and writers who came back after years of deportation are the following: Grigoris Palakian [Krikoris Balakian], *Hay Goghgota: Trvagner hay martirosagrutenen* [The Armenian Calvary: Episodes of the Armenian Martyrology], vol. I (Vienna: Mekhitarist Press, 1922); Mikayel Shamdanjian, *Hay mtki harke Eghernin* [The Tribute of the Armenian Mind to the Catastrophe] (Constantinople: Vosdan, 1919); Aram Antonian [Andonian], *Ayn sev orerun* [In These Dark Days] (Boston: Hairenik, 1919), and his *Mets Vochirë* [The Great Crime] (Boston: Pahak, 1921); Teodik, *Hushardzan Abril 11-i* [Memorial to April 11 (April 24)] (Constantinople: Arzuman, 1919), and his *Banti ev aksori tariner* [Years of Prison and Deportation] (Constantinople: Arzuman, 1919). Other works of testimony published in the same period include those of Payladzou Captanian, Dr. Salpi, Dr. Avedis Nakashian, and Hovhannes Kapigian.
6. Among those testimonies, one written in Turkish by Vahram Altounian and translated into French by Krikor Beledian was published by his daughter in Janine Altounian, *Ouvrez-moi seulement les chemins d'Arménie* (Paris: Belles-Lettres, 1990). Altounian wrote a beautiful commentary on her father's memoir, "De quoi témoignent les mains des survivants?" in Jean-François Chiantaretto, ed., *Témoignage et Trauma* (Paris: Dunod, 2004), of which a new version will be published in English translation in my *Art and Testimony*.
7. In this category, see Abraham Hartunian, *Neither to Laugh, Nor to Weep,* trans. from the Armenian manuscript by Vartan Hartunian (Boston: Beacon Press, 1968).
8. In this category, see Armen Anush, *Arian chanaparhov* [On the Way of Blood], published posthumously in Beirut (1959); English trans. Ishkhan Jinbashian as *Passage Through Hell* (Studio City, CA: H. & K. Manjikian, 2005).
9. Elizabeth Caraman, in collaboration with William Lytton Payne, *Daughters of the Euphrates* (New York and London: Harper, 1939). Caraman came from a well-educated Protestant family in the region of Kharpert. Zaven Surmelian, *I Ask You, Ladies and Gentlemen* (New York, E. P. Dutton., 1945). This book was received extremely well. Surmelian had been a student of Hagop Oshagan and Vahan Tekeyan in Constantinople between 1920 and 1922, before immigrating to the United States, and had, with Tekeyan's blessing, published a book of poetry, *Loys Zvart* (1924), which immediately placed him in the pantheon of precocious Armenian writers. Oshagan devoted a long, laudatory article to Surmelian's *I Ask You* in the newspaper series "Kiankin het" [With Life], *Haratch* (Paris), April 6-19, 1947.
10. Lorne Shirinian, *Survivor Memoirs of the Armenian Genocide* (Reading: Taderon, 1999).
11. Donald Miller and Lorna Touryan-Miller, *Survivors: An Oral History of the Armenian Genocide* (Berkeley, Los Angeles, London: University of California Press, 1993).
12. Shirinian, *Survivor Memoirs*, p. 19.
13. Ervant Odian [Ervand Otian], *Anitsial tariner, 1914-1919 (andznakan hishatakner)* [Accursed Years, 1914-1919 (Personal Memories)], ed. and pref. Grigor Hakopyan (Erevan: Nairi, 2004), pp. 531-532.
14. The only available collection of *Zhamanak* today is in Vienna in the library of the Mekhitarist Congregation. Unfortunately, the series of 1919 was not complete and Odian's memoir has been published with one installment missing.

15. Grigor Hakopyan's obituary appeared in the literary journal, *Grakanagitakan handes* (Erevan), 1 (2005).
16. One of my uncles, Onnik Nichanian, appears in the novel, with his real name and his real activity in Konia during the war. *Tiv 17 Khafien* was first published in Constantinople, in the journal *Verjin Lur* [Latest News], from November 1, 1919, to October 2, 1920. It was republished for the first time in 1938 in Cairo in four volumes (by the printing house Cineveb), and serialized again by the journal *Zartonk* of Beirut in 1957. A new edition in three volumes was published in Erevan in 2000 by the Museum of Literature and Art, marking "the 85th anniversary of the Armenian Catastrophe." In the preface, Samvel Muradyan states that he considers the novel as the first great artistic work aimed at the novelistic representation of the events in the years from 1913 to1918. This is an exaggeration. In a letter to Arshag Chobanian on January 23, 1919, Odian wrote: "I am alive, after an incredible, terrible odyssey that lasted three years and a half. I was pushed until Der Zor and still farther, to the desert of Mesopotamia, El Bousera, between the Euphrates and the Kopar, where Ezekiel had his visions. I do not know if I will be able to recount faithfully what I saw, but I will try. This will be a large work, maybe a few volumes." See Ervand Otian *Namakner* [Letters] (Erevan: Museum of Art and Literature, 1999), p. 244. According to Muradyan, this refers to *Spy Number 17*, which of course is wrong. Grigor Hakobyan had already noted the mistake. Odian's hint obviously refers to his forthcoming *Accursed Years*. His phrase "faithfully recount what I saw" foreshadows what he says a few months later on the last page of his memoir.
17. *Tiv 17 Khafien*, vol. 1, p. 25.
18. The novel was forbidden in Armenia in the Soviet period, although the name of Odian was not. The voluminous "Complete Works" of Odian have been published in Erevan, but this novel was condemned to remain in the secret dungeons of the regime. Why? Partly because the very mention of the Armenian Genocide was forbidden and partly because everything that more or less challenged the Soviet interpretation of the genocidal events had to be kept under lock and key.
19. *Levon Shanti erkere* [The Works of Levon Shant], vol. 9: *Endhanur aknark me hay banahiusutian vra* [General Overview of Armenian Literature] (Beirut: Hamazkayin, 1950), p. 371. These lines and the next citation were used in a different context by Krikor Beledian, *Krake shrjanake: D. Varuzhani shurj* [Circle of Fire: Around D(aniel) Varoujan] (Antelias: Catholicosate of Cilicia, 1986).
20. Levon Shant, *Endhanur aknark*, p. 377.
21. Ibid.
22. *Averaknerun mej* (Constantinople: H.H.E., 1911).
23. Henry Barby, *Au pays de l'épouvante: L'Arménie martyre*, pref. Paul Deschanel (Paris: A. Michel, 1917).
24. The points discussed in this paragraph are developed in my study of Zabel Esayan, appearing in *Writers of Disaster*, vol. 1 (London: Gomidas, 2002), pp. 187-242. An English translation of her preface to Haig Toroyan's testimony is printed in its entirety on pp. 221-222.
25. Aram Andonian, *Ayn sev orerun* (Boston: Hairenik, 1919), was written in part in the camp of Meskene in 1917. *Mets vochire* (Boston: Bahag, 1921; repr., Erevan: Arevik, 1990) was first published in its French version in 1920. An English translation was also published shortly thereafter: *The Memoirs of Naim Bey: Turkish Official Documents Relating to the Deportations and Massacres of Armenians* (London: Hodder and Stoughton, 1920; repr., Newton Square, PA: Armenian Historical Research Association, 1964).

26. *Mets vochire*, p. 2. In his monograph on Andonian, Hagop Oshagan paraphrases this passage almost word for word. See *Hamapatker arevmtahay grakanutian* [Panorama of Western Armenian Literature], vol. 9 (Antelias: Catholicosate of Cilicia, 1980), p. 271.
27. Oshagan, *Hamapatker arevmtahay grakanutian*, vol. 9, p. 272. This multivolume work is an immense history of the literature of the Ottoman Armenians from 1850 to 1915. The tenth and final volume, *Vkayutiun* [Testimony], written in 1944, is devoted to Oshagan himself, in the third person, as the endpoint and fulfillment of this literature in the "after-effect" of the Diaspora.
28. Ibid., p. 278.
29. The interview appeared in the monthly *Hairenik*, in March and May 1932. It has been reprinted as a book prepared by Boghos Snabian in the Centenary series (Antelias: Catholicosate of Cilicia, 1983), with several other pieces that Tashian published along the years and that derived more or less from the days when he traveled to Cyprus to visit Oshagan to urge him to speak on *Mnatsortats* and Armenian literature in general.
30. Beniamin Tashian, *Mayrineru shukin tak* (Beirut: Altapres, 1983), p. 16. The word that I translated here as "memoir" is *hushagir*, which could as well be rendered as "testimony" if we ignored the fact that in the movement from document to monument, a "testimony" is not exactly a "memoir."
31. Oshagan, *Hamapatker arevmtahay grakanutian*, vol. 7, p. 429.
32. Ibid.
33. Ibid., p. 430.
34. Ibid., vol. 9, p. 244.
35. Ibid., p. 245.
36. The poem was the last piece Varoujan wrote for his book *Tseghin sirte* [The Heart of the Race], published the same year, 1909, in Constantinople. For the quoted lines, see Daniel Varuzhan, *Erkeri liakatar zhoghovatsu* [Complete Collection of Works], vol. 1 (Erevan: Armenian Academy of Sciences, 1986), p. 151.

Part 2

Literature, Art, Film, and Music

5

Across the Chasm: From Catastrophe to Creativity

Barlow Der Mugrdechian

During the nine decades since the Armenian Genocide of 1915 a vast corpus of Armenian-American literature has developed, some of which deals with the varied responses to the Catastrophe. In particular, during the past thirty years, a generation of writers has begun to explore the consequences and impact of the Genocide on Armenians living in America. The works of three representative authors is the subject of this preliminary study: Michael Arlen's *Passage to Ararat*,[1] Michael Krekorian's "Avedis,"[2] and David Kherdian's *Asking the River*.[3] Each author presents a different perspective on the impact of the Genocide on his person and on the community in general and each has his own distinctive approach. This assessment is based on the premise that the Genocide remains a powerful force in Armenian literature and that the act of writing and creating has been a means to bridge the gap from catastrophe to creativity.

There are many themes in these stories, but they ultimately return to the *Aghed* (Catastrophe) itself and revolve around the key issue of how the children and grandchildren of genocide survivors have assimilated the trauma of their forebears in a creative manner. Thus, the writers have bridged the chasm from catastrophe to creativity by unleashing their creative literary efforts and by the *act of writing*. The Catastrophe of the Genocide has been marked in Armenian literature by the absence of the ability to articulate the experience of the Genocide in a way that was productive.

The term Catastrophe and its relation to literature is discussed by Marc Nichanian in *Writers of Disaster*.[4] The Catastrophe looms over Armenian literature. Nichanian describes the "Event" as "the total extermination of the Western Armenians, those who lived in the Ottoman Empire." He continues: "This bears a name in Armenian, a name among others, a name that did not really prevail in popular consciousness and henceforth in everyday language, a name which is still waiting for its full understanding. This name is *Aghed*, which means Catastrophe, like Shoah in Hebrew. *Aghed* is the proper name of the event."[5] Nichanian later points to something else when he writes: "Why is the Catastrophe catastrophic? Because it coincides, collectively, with the impossibility of mourning."[6] Thus, it is through writing that the authors presented in this study have been able at least partially to overcome the chasm between catastrophe and creativity.

Lorne Shirinian has discussed the Genocide as a symbol in Armenian literature, and one of his main premises is that "the collective symbol of the Armenian genocide is the basis for understanding the body of texts I wish to call Armenian-North American literature."[7] This in Armenian history has become a powerful symbol that has penetrated into literature and every facet of Armenian cultural life.

All of the works discussed in this survey were originally written in English. They fall, however, in the general realm of Armenian literature because of their content. They share a consistency in the way the main characters function in the context of the societies in which they live, in particular the impact of life in America. They express a resilience and vibrancy that demonstrates the ability of the Armenian-American to move forward in a positive and creative way.

Michael Arlen, Jr.

Michael Arlen's *Passage to Ararat* is a semi-autobiographical work that became an American bestseller in 1975. It has received much attention because of its reception among a non-Armenian audience. *Passage to Ararat* represents a very different style of literature than Michael Krekorian's "Avedis," although at their core they share a common theme, that of the Genocide. The style of *Passage to Ararat* is relaxed and descriptive, with more time to develop themes. The author himself is more introspective, concerned with finding the motivation behind his own father's distance from his son.

Passage to Ararat is told through the voice of Michael Arlen, Jr., a second generation Armenian, who at the beginning of the narrative clearly states his purpose: "At a particular time in my life, I set out on a voyage to discover for myself what it is to be an Armenian."[8] What at first seems a straightforward proposition actually becomes the complex and multi-tiered revelation of a man's inner voyage toward self-discovery. Arlen's voyage takes him through an awareness of his own relationship with an emotionally distant father, one whom he really never understood, as well as to an awareness of Armenian history, and ultimately his own place in the context of that history.

Early in the work the reader is made aware that the Genocide is a main focus, although it is only obliquely referred to. When Arlen's father is asked to speak with an Armenian professor, he responds coldly: "Tell him I'm out. . . . He'll only want to talk about Armenian problems."[9] The "Armenian problems" which Arlen Sr. was so reticent to discuss with his son is a clear, but again understated, reference to the Armenian Genocide of 1915. The connection of an Armenian (any Armenian) to a terrible past is what causes both an emotional and psychological dislocation for Arlen Jr. This is his personal *catastrophe* that he must bridge in order to attain his own creativity. Arlen is initially unaware of the event that had such a widespread and profound impact on the Armenians. His father's attitude remained with him as he expressed his own feeling of being "marked" by the association of Armenians to the Genocide:

> For the most part I was content to leave things as they were. I was only slightly curious about my Armenian background—or so I thought, although, if I had understood how to acknowledge such matters, I might have known that I was haunted by it. Mostly I was afraid of it. . . . What was I afraid of? It's difficult to remember now. Probably of being exposed in some way, or pulled downby the connection: that association of "difference," one's own "difference," with something deeply pejorative, with sin.[10]

Arlen begins his journey at the age of forty after the death of both his father and mother. His inability to understand his father fully is directly related to the impact of the Genocide on his family. Arlen must reconcile with his father to unleash his own creative energy. His first association with Armenians takes place in an Armenian church at the beginning of his own journey. Later, visiting the home of two elderly cousins he is reminded of the centrality of the Genocide by their mournful recollections of death and catastrophe. The brutalization of the cousins jolts Arlen because he is still unable to connect with his father. He is still unwilling or unable to connect emotionally and remains "repelled by the tale of misery."[11]

The Genocide or the "Armenian problems" dislocate Arlen in time and space. He is removed in time by some sixty years from the Genocide but is still, willingly or unwillingly, tied to it. Shirinian discusses this concept of temporal dislocation brought on by the Diaspora and how the literary texts that are produced in Diaspora can be part of the desire for cultural preservation: "The problem is that in the residue of history, these cultural objects are divorced from their content. Diaspora and home cultures are not synchronous . . . . The Armenian genocide has rewritten the discourse of the Armenian nation, and Armenian-North American literature is a response to this tragedy, which forced the diaspora of the previous generation from the Armenian homeland."[12]

Arlen is also dislocated from a sense of belonging or identification with the Armenian people. His father's absence, in both a real and metaphorical sense, has left him no way to connect with the past. He is far removed from the locale of the Genocide since he is an American who lives so far from historic Armenia where the event occurred. The absence of the father is a recurring theme in the works of many Armenian-American writers, notably in those of William Saroyan, reflecting the loss of cultural continuity and transmission because of the absence of the father.[13]

Arlen must come to grips with the Genocide in order to resolve his own internal paradoxes. He must travel to Fresno, to New Jersey, and to Erevan to make his journey a meaningful one—so that he can make sense of his own life in America and ultimately to bridge the gap from catastrophe to creativity. It is the Genocide that he must understand both on a rational and an emotional level.

Arlen journeys to Armenia where he meets unexpectedly with a man named Sarkis, who becomes his self-appointed guide.[14] Sarkis' first action is to take Arlen to the Armenian Martyrs Monument and in doing so to make the inevitable connection that binds the Armenians of the present with those in the past.

In Armenia, the Genocide again becomes a locus for Arlen as he buries himself in books, especially learning the history of the Armenians. Sarkis recounts episodes from the Genocide to try and awaken a sense of belonging in Arlen, a sense of his past. Initially, Arlen is intellectually unable to comprehend the gap from catastrophe to life. He has not yet come to terms with the Genocide nor has he been able to resolve its hold on him. The Genocide hovers over the story but Arlen does not come into contact directly with it until later in his journey. He wrestles with the idea of the Genocide as a defining aspect of the Armenian experience of the twentieth century: "Sarkis has been trying to define me as an Armenian—but a certain kind of Armenian. Those damned massacres, I thought. That chauvinism, such a chauvinism of misfortune!" [15]

Arlen must also discover the "other" of Armenian literature—the Turk. He learns about the Turks in order to disarm them of their power over him. "Maybe you won't understand this, I said, but I want to know everything about the Armenians, and that seems to include knowing something about the Turks."[16] His relationship to his own father is another facet of the search for self and is also intimately linked with the Genocide. Michael Arlen, Sr. ended up in a European society that rejected the Armenians as equals, stamped by the mark of the ghastly Genocide. Yet, Arlen Sr. adapted himself to the very society that rejected him. But at what cost? In order to fit, he had to "become" less Armenian, less different than his compatriots appeared.

Arlen Jr. utilizes the literary technique of interspersing his own activities with a recounting of important points of Armenian history. Thus, the book becomes a means for those who are unaware of Armenian history to come into contact with it. The emotional weight of Armenian history is constantly being brought to Arlen's attention. Sarkis says: "To be an Armenian is to have this intolerable weight of sadness on one's soul. This is what one of our Armenian poets said. Is it not true?" And later: "Armenians can never forget what happened to them. Armenians must never forget. It was a genocide."[17] Sarkis represents the idea of the "Armenian" who cannot and does not want to let go of the Genocide, the Catastrophe that has had such an indelible impact on the Armenian people.

Arlen must come to terms with his past before he can begin to understand his current position. It is finally an expression of anger that triggers his first self-realization. Stereotypes of the Armenians as rug merchants by Western

European sources make Arlen angry and in fact remind him of things in his own life that had led him to hate his Armenian background. Thus it is through the catharsis of self-realization that healing can take place.[18] Arlen "hated" being an Armenian because he had been given the values of others (through his father) over his own history.

It is to the twentieth century and to the Armenian Genocide to which Arlen is inevitably led in his search, because to understand the Armenian soul of the twentieth century one has to understand the Armenian Genocide. For Arlen, he must understand the Genocide on a rational level, but it is on the emotional level that he will actually make contact with his Armenian self. By the latter part of the book, the Genocide has become so important to Arlen that it becomes the focal point of the remainder of the book. Trying to understand the Genocide becomes the impetus for the story itself.

As he prepares to leave Armenia, his final act is to pay a return visit to the Armenian Martyrs Monument. There he is touched by the memory of his father. He even cries—the first time that he expresses any real emotion. Although at the end of the book Arlen returns to America with little more than a *feeling* of an emotional tie with Armenia, clearly the central axis of the book is the Genocide. In the end Arlen was able to reconcile himself to his place and time, to come to grips with the past, and in his own experience to move on creatively to the literary career that he had chosen.

Michael Krekorian

Michael Krekorian's *Corridor* is a collection of short stories, and constitutes the work of a third-generation Armenian born in Los Angeles in 1949. Krekorian is a frequent contributor to *Ararat* magazine and has had his works published in many periodicals and magazines. In "Avedis," from the collection of short stories in *Corridor*, Krekorian has in fifteen pages crafted a fully developed story that unfolds on various levels of creative reality. In his alinear style of writing, time is not an important element. There is no beginning or end to the story, which revolves around three complementary narratives, two of which are based purely on direct and terse delivery of information and the third which is based on a contemplation and development of more complex actions and emotions involving the protagonist, Avedis Der Zakarian, and later his oldest son George.

The first two narratives are in a direct action/reaction relationship. One narrative is the Turkish government position on the Armenian Genocide, as it develops over time. In a succinct few lines the Turkish government's position is related at different points in time; for example: "The Turkish government claims that the Armenian Genocide is an eighty-year-old myth. The Treaty of Lausanne is signed between Turkey and the superpowers with no mention of the Armenians. What does Wilson say now? What will Hitler say 16 years later?"[19] This narrative thread is continued throughout the story and is central to the work, because the other narratives are interrelated to this one and react to it.

In response to the Turkish government's position, the second narrative line tells of the actions taken by certain Armenians:

> January 28, 1982, Los Angeles. The Turkish Consel drives his late model sedan through the rush hour traffic. He comes to a stop at the corner of Wilshire and Comstock. The red light seems unusually long. The Consul General is alone. Before the signal changes, two men step out from behind a hedge and empty the contents of their pistols into the driver's side of the car. The Consul General is shot in the face, head, and chest. He slumps in the seat, his foot slips off the brake pedal. The vehicle rolls forward striking two cars, then comes to rest against a silver-dollar eucalyptus across the street.[20]

The consul general is assassinated—the political violence expressed in "Avedis" is a reaction, juxtaposed with the Turkish position of denial of the Genocide. In the narrative, acts of political violence are discussed from Gourgen Yanikian in 1973 through the 1980s.

The third narrative, which surrounds and encompasses the other two and which could stand alone, is structurally interspersed with the other two narratives and revolves around the life of Avedis Der Zakarian and his awakening self-realization of the effects of the Genocide. In its basic structure then, this short story is shaped around the Genocide (the Catastrophe), although it nominally takes place some fifty-three years after 1915. Real time for the book is 1968 but linear time is no barrier to the development of the major theme.

The story recounts the life of Avedis Der Zakarian, a survivor of the Armenian Genocide. A common thread ties the story together—a litany of Armenian names is being read by Der Zakarian from a small notebook—the names flowing on and on, periodically in the story, take on a life of their own, resembling a mantra: Aaronian, Abadjian, Abassian, and ending with Zahabian, Zaharian, and Zakarian. The family names are a reminder of those who died in the Genocide, but they are also a living reminder that there were survivors and that they are being remembered. This affirmation of memory and life is in direct opposition to the Turkish government's position of erasing memory. Abcarian, Abdalian, Abdosian, Abdulian, Abedian, Abelian, Abgarian—the names are a totem that informs the reader of the importance of the Genocide. It is Avedis' own connection with his past, with the Genocide. From death and catastrophe arises life.

"A branch snaps from a poplar in a high wind. An old Armenian man awakens to the events of May 1968."[21] After fifty years, the story of the Genocide is revisited as an old man awakens and becomes aware of his surroundings, that he is alive and that he has a purpose. This awakening occurs through the narrator's voice. The scene is Paris in the midst of a crowd of Maoists, Troskyites, and anarchists who are demonstrating in the streets. They are against something, which is not clearly stated, but it is against the status quo. Disorder, chaos, the beginning, the Genocide.

April 1915—Upper Khokh (Kharpert-Historic Armenia). Avedis Der Zakarian. Finally, the name of the old man is revealed and through the naming we are drawn into his story and his life. The massacres take place in his village and while Avedis is spared, his family is destroyed, and his people exiled and dispersed: "Genocide victims fade from the memory like the details in an overexposed photograph. Survivors scatter across the globe like the smear of constellations across a crisp winter sky."[22]

The third generation, in this case through Michael Krekorian's riveting short story, attempts to recreate what happened in the Genocide through the only means it has at hand—namely through an exploration of the memory of the survivors. It is only through the survivors that the memory can be recovered and through memory that the third generation is able to recreate their life in foreign countries—in the Diaspora. This is how they can bridge the chasm from catastrophe to creativity. Only through the freedom of creative literature can this take place, far from a Turkish government that seeks to eliminate the very presence or memory of the Armenians.

"Survivors scatter across the globe like the smear of constellations across a crisp winter sky." The line is repeated again and again and is a metaphor for the Armenian experience—forced exile as a result of the Armenian Genocide and the subsequent Diaspora. While others who arrive at Ellis Island changed their names and became part of the new society, Avedis Der Zakarian refused to do so. He did not submit to the changing of his identity.

The Genocide is explicitly described in a few short paragraphs. The steps taken by the Turkish government to execute the catastrophe are tersely related. Krekorian does not overstate events but using words sparingly he paints a more effective picture that comes alive. Avedis Der Zakarian finds himself in a new environment in America, the very symbol of life with its flow of immigrants that contribute to its wealth. Der Zakarian is only seventeen years old when he arrives in New York. He tries to forget but he cannot. The family names that are interspersed with the text are a constant reminder of the Genocide and speak to the suffering that he endured. Der Zakarian has a son George with whom he shares his fear of the coming of the Turks.[23] George is told to gather the gold that Avedis has buried in the basement and to flee with his mother and sisters: "Talaat Bey, Turkish Minister of the Interior, in 1916 claims that he has accomplished more toward solving the Armenian question in three months, than Abdul-Hamid has accomplished in thirty years."[24]

George leaves his father to move to Los Angeles. Avedis says nothing when his son leaves, as the psychological distance between father and son is again manifested. Avedis is not quite free of the bonds of memory, while George has grown up in America and is both temporally and psychologically far from the Catastrophe.

Statement, response, reaction. Krekorian's "Avedis" is a densely constructed and interwoven series of narratives which explores the effects of the Genocide and its continued denial by the Turkish government. George feels an undefined pain that is at the same time sharp and diffuse. He in his own way is coming to terms with the Catastrophe from which his father is still suffering:

> The Turkish government claims that the Armenian Genocide is a twenty-four-year-old myth. Armenians gather quietly around a simple cylindrical stone monument erected in Beirut, Lebanon, honoring the Armenian victims of a genocide erased from the world's memory. Exactly three months later, on August 22, 1939, Hitler orders the mass extermination of the Polish people with these words "Who remembers today the extermination of the Armenians."[25]

The old Armenian reads day after day. Avedis Der Zakarian remembers his own family. Time is in abeyance, as he sees his loved ones even though they are dead. Krekorian ties George to the story of Gourgen Yanikian, as George is a recipient of a letter sent by Yanikian to the Santa Barbara community.

Gourgen Yanikian—the memory of the Genocide haunts him. The Turkish government never acknowledges the Genocide. "I am not Gourgen M. Yanikian but unacknowledged history coming back for the 1,500,000 Armenians whose bones desecrate my invisible existence."[26]

On January 28, 1973. Yanikian shot and killed two Turkish consular officers in Santa Barbara, California.

Tonian, Tokalian, Tokatelian. . . .

George Der Zakarian, Avedis' son, wishes that he had written down his father's story. Avedis has moved to France and now that he is no longer in the United States, it is only through the reaffirmation of life that George Der Zakarian can continue with his own life. He reflects: "Yanikian will spend the rest of his days in prison." George wants to remember his father's words and wishes that he had written it all down:[27]

> The Turkish government declares the Armenian genocide is a sixty-five-year-old myth perpetrated by liberation armies, international communists, red brigades, American racists, Armenian extremists, news media, Armenian revisionists, the scourge, assassins, accomplices of international conspiracy.[28]
>
> January 1984. Los Angeles. Hampig Sassounian is ordered to stand while the verdict is read. The court finds Hampig M. Sassounian guilty of the assassination of a Turkish Consul General. He is found guilty of first degree murder with "special circumstances." The special circumstances are that the Turkish Consul General was killed because of his *nationality*.[29]

It is ironic that the Catastrophe which was so devastating to the Armenian people and was based to a large extent on nationality has now become the reason for special circumstances.

Zakarian, Zadekian. . . . As Avedis drifts deeper into his memories, the story comes to an end. Although the names finally end, the story of Avedis Der Zakarian does not end and cannot so long as there is a Turkish government that refuses to acknowledge and accept responsibility for the Genocide. Yet through his short story, Krekorian, too, has been freed of the paralysis of the Catastrophe and moved on to creativity.

David Kherdian

David Kherdian's *Asking the River* is a novelette by one of the most prolific of Armenian authors writing in English in America. Kherdian, who was born in Racine, Wisconsin, in 1931, has authored more than sixty books and booklets of poetry and prose. His later works have captured the Armenian experience in America and the difficult adjustments required to come to terms with life in America. The earlier *Finding Home* is an account of family and friends based in Kherdian's hometown of Racine, Wisconsin.[30] Along with other volumes, it explores a world of experiences that have become extremely important for Armenian-American writers. Margaret Bedrosian has written: "Like Diana Der Hovanessian, David Kherdian turns to his past to 'gain the future'."[31] She continues:

> One of the major problems in dealing with contemporary Armenian experience lies in the Armenians' general inability to articulate what the massacres have meant to them as a people, not as an event , but as a stepping-stone in the Armenian myth. For if the Armenians were frozen with frustration before the massacres, they were frozen with pain afterwards. This account of meaning cannot be given by political history or documentation or even through massacre narratives, of which there are many. . . . At the most profound level, only a resumption of the myth by a gifted bard can free and heal the collective psyche.[32]

Thus, writers such as David Kherdian and those previously discussed have begun the process of healing.

In the semi-autobiographical *Asking the River*, young Stepan Bakaian is the protagonist who is searching for his identity while at the same time experiencing all of the emotional turmoil of adolescence. *Asking the River* follows Stepan through several years of his life and his transition from grammar school to middle school. Again, the Genocide looms as the ever-present backdrop to the story, although more subtly expressed than in *Passage to Ararat* and "Avedis." The Genocide is not explicitly discussed except in several brief passages, however the Genocide, as an experience that has had a broad impact, is central to the development of the entire story.

From the earliest part of the book, one senses the deep uneasiness that young Stepan (Steven) feels, when he is daydreaming in his classroom:

> Now we were cooped up in our classroom, which for me was a prison. It was a prison for all of us who felt unwanted. Not just the other Armenian kids like me, but anyone whose parents were foreign, or any of those who thought of themselves as something other than American.[33]

Thus, Stepan is seen through his own prism of perception as the "other" and as such he feels out of place in the school and in society at large. His being Armenian is always brought to his attention. The differences are felt in his small classroom and even his name is a cause for concern, as the Armenian Stepan is soon replaced by the American Steven. He says:

> All the Americans ever said about us was that we were the starving Armenians, which in their mind was anything but fascinating. They talked about us as if we didn't exist—like we were so far away in their minds that we were nowhere at all. Well those starving Armenians happened to be my relatives. . . . This was during World War I, when the Turks tried to get rid of all the Armenians living in the country.[34]

The Genocide is referred to here, again not explicitly but clearly present in the reference to "getting rid of all the Armenians." Stepan feels marginalized in America, as if he didn't exist, and this is part of the inner conflict raging in this sensitive boy, whose thoughts and ideas often touch on greater issues of identity. Self-identity is a critical element in the story. Who is Stepan Bakaian? Is he Armenian? Or is he American? In a conversation with his mother, he expresses this dilemma, which he has yet to resolve:

> "You see, you are not so different from your father."
>
> "I'm an American."
>
> "You are also an Armenian."
>
> "Yes," I admitted, "an Armenian American. That's what everyone tells me."
>
> "You're grumbling again. Now what is it?"
>
> "I'm one thing inside-myself—but on the outside I'm these two things, and I don't know what either one is supposed to be."[35]

Stepan cannot yet make sense of his purpose in life—what is it that he should be or do? His inability to resolve this inner division is what bothers him throughout most of the book. The Genocide of 1915 became the major cause for Armenian emigration and for large numbers of Armenians to settle in America. While Kherdian's narrative provides no clear answer to the questions that plague Stepan, it does suggest that the definition of identity is a process, one that constantly changes over time, and that understanding and awareness of identity are achieved through that process.

If Stepan is still trying to make sense of his identity, for his mother it is very clear, as she says: "Listen to me. I want you to be a proud Armenian. We are a great people with a great history. We were the first nation to adopt Christianity."[36] Stepan, in reference to his mother, says: "She was a foreigner. But I *was* an American, or rather an Armenian-American. Did being both make me neither? I wondered. Was that my nationality—neither? Is that why I was always uncomfortable with myself, with my parents, and also with the Americans?"[37]

Whether at home or at school Stepan felt uncomfortable and in school especially he is made to feel an outcast. He is faced with a teacher who tries to make him an American—the Americanization of his name to Steven is only one example. He has failed the second grade once and the fifth grade twice, and it is in school that Stepan feels most ill at ease, the most unwanted, the loneliest. The new principal of his high school is somewhat different than his teachers who show no understanding. This principal is the first American with whom Stepan feels comfortable. He invites Stepan to play baseball with him, without judging him in any other respect:

> All kinds of thoughts were flying around in my head. I was sure I had learned something big, I couldn't say that I knew what it was. Mr. Huber had made me feel important, and that was enough in itself, because I realized that I had never felt that way in all the years I had been at Garfield (high school).[38]

Stepan ponders the non-existence of Armenia because Armenia is never mentioned in the history books that he must read. Where did the Armenians go? The Genocide, the calamity of deportation and destruction, has left its mark on Stepan. The Catastrophe had as its intention the nullification of identity, the destruction of the spiritual as well as physical existence of the Armenian people. But Stepan is not willing to give up what is Armenian just to fit into American society: "We envied the Americans—as everyone else excepting the blacks was called—and would have liked to be American ourselves, but not if it meant giving up whatever else we were."[39]

This is the paradox of the Armenian in the Diaspora—forever cast out of land and home by the Genocide, with no immediate hope of return, yet facing the daunting task of preserving his heritage. Stepan envies the Americans, but is not willing to give up everything that he is in order to become American.

If Stepan is unhappy at school, then home is only slightly better. At home, Stepan communicates with his father very little or not at all. The absence of the father, as mentioned earlier, is also a theme that is common in Armenian-North American literature of the post-Genocide period. Either directly absent through death, or indirectly through the inability of father and son to communicate, the absence of the father is a recurring and central theme to this book. Stepan's father is an interesting character—born to be a cook, but forced by circumstances to work in a factory. He works a lot in the garden, and interacts with his son, but even what seems to be a mundane chore, like painting a fence, also sparks an inner struggle. Stepan's mother says: "The garden reminds him of Armenia, the dirt reminds him of his village, the vegetables he grows remind him of his home in Kharpert. That's why he is so angry. He's tormented by remembering, and he feels tormented when he forgets. Let him have his way."[40] Memory then is so central to Stepan's conception of self and the world that he inhabits. It permeates the relationship between father and son, and Stepan can never escape the memories, some of which he cannot understand.

Stepan's mother is the central familial figure. The problem is again that Stepan has no clear conception of his identity. "I'm one thing inside myself—but on the outside I'm these two things, and I don't know what either one is supposed to be."[41] The two things on the outside—an Armenian and an American—are the central axes in the book. The tension created by resolving the inherent conflict between the two identities gives the book its dynamic quality.

Stepan encounters numerous friends in short vignettes on his life in America. Time is spent with family or friends, but always with a sense of uneasiness. Nicky Tekeyan, Willy Springer, Joe Perch, and Kirk Ohanian are among the friends of his own age that he visits and shares time with. He perhaps is most at ease with friends, those who share his own ambivalent attitudes on identity and fitting in.

The Genocide continues to be a locus for conversation within the home as Stepan and his mother constantly argue about the past and the present:

> I seemed to surprise her when I asked, "Are the Turks like us?"
>
> "Of course not. What a question. They murdered our tiny nation."
>
> "But do they look like us? You know what I mean."
>
> "They are Moslems. We are Christians."
>
> "But are they dark like us, or are they maybe even darker?"
>
> "About the same—some darker, some lighter. They are a mixed up race, not like us—pure!" My mother was darker than my father, and I took after her.
>
> "So that wasn't it then—they weren't prejudiced against us because we were different looking?"
>
> "I told you—we were Christians."
>
> "That was the prejudice?"
>
> "Hatred! Discrimination!" [42]

Attending an Armenian school a few hours a week was no better and no easier for Stepan. He couldn't stand going to Armenian school, where his mother was the teacher, perhaps because he was embarrassed:

"If I don't know what's bothering you, I can't possibly understand, can I?"

"I don't want to be a sad Armenian. I don't like being looked down on. I feel backward and unwanted, and it's worse when I'm with the Armenians."

"They embarrass you."

"Yes."[43]

Later, Stepan explores the depths of his mother's feelings:

My mother looked at me for a long minute. "I am part of two worlds, one lost and shattered, the other a compromise. Now you tell me it is the same with you."

"It's not your fault," I said. "It's just the way it is."[44]

In Book II, Kherdian's character begins a process of self-reflection, using the river alongside which he grew up as the metaphor for life. As he sits next to the river, Stepan contemplates life:

I began to wonder, as I had so often, why it seems that everything was more possible at such moments. I looked down at the river and dreamed its meanings. It seemed so different from ours. Whenever I dreamed the river I dreamed myself, not as I was, with all my problems, but as someone free, yet still connected to everything. . . . It didn't seem to me that life should be as difficult as it was. And I couldn't understand why my thoughts and feelings should remain as they were, confused and without direction. [45]

In speaking to his friend Nicky's sister Lily, he begins to understand what life may mean for him. Stepan wants to find out what life is for. This is the key question that arises out of the discussion of the two young people. For him to understand this question will allow him to begin his life and to become a creative contributor in life. He will be able to come to grips with the past, with the Catastrophe, to cross the chasm to creativity, and to move on with his life.

Stepan's Uncle Mihran is also an important figure in the story, because he seems to understand Stepan. In an argument among the family members as to the internal divisions of the Armenians, especially in America, Uncle Mihran says:

We cannot fight the Turk, so we fight one another. The Turk hates us, and we have come to hate ourselves, and only because their hatred worked, it was effective. What they couldn't kill off they expelled, and now we are like an angry cloud blown across the face of the land. Strangers take us in, but among ourselves we argue and fight. [46]

For Uncle Mihran, the Genocide is also the center and still the cause for much of the unhappiness for the Armenians. This interpretation by Uncle Mihran of self-hatred parallels that of Michael Arlen in *Passage to Ararat*.[47] The Genocide is a great burden for the Armenians, because the perpetrator side has refused to acknowledge the crime.

The story of the black stockings told by Stepan's mother also deals with the effects of the Genocide, this time in a real physical sense with physical scars.[48] By talking with his mother as time passes, Stepan begins to understand more:

> And the river was always there, waiting, in movement, promising change, promising that life could be different because it didn't always have to be the same:[49]

> How to achieve freedom. And then it came to me. I was holding the broken part of a twig in my two hands. *It has to be accomplished.* Freedom has to be accomplished. It has to be achieved, realized. Yes, that's it: freedom cannot be given; it can only be earned by my own efforts. Did that make it inner freedom? I wondered. Well, it didn't matter how you defined it.[50]

It is the future that Stepan is trying to uncover—this is the creativity which must come after the Catastrophe. Uncle Mihran reiterates the truth of life when he talks to Stepan in his garden, as they are looking at his fruit trees:

> Your parents love you. Maybe not the way you like, but it's their love, given in their way. You see, our paths have been shattered but now we have the young ones. You are our future. . . . Then be your own future—*make* your own future. It is the same. It is nothing to be angry about.[51]

As the book ends, Stepan is turning fourteen and setting out for a new future in junior high school. Stepan is as curious as ever as he ponders his future. "I feel like life is a gift, but that it has to be earned. And I want to *earn* it. Maybe then I will understand what life is for. Do you know what I mean?"[52] Stepan ends his journey by understanding that it is through action that he will achieve the meaning of life that he is seeking. So Stepan has bridged the chasm of catastrophe to creativity by understanding that creativity is the action of doing and, in his specific case, the act of writing.

* * * *

The three works that have been considered share a common set of conditions. All have the Armenian Genocide (the Catastrophe) as a locus for the background of the story. Although it sometimes recedes, the Catastrophe is always there, unexplained and the unexplainable. In order to bridge the chasm from catastrophe to creativity, each story involves an awakening sense of change and expectation. The protagonist evolves toward an understanding of self—based on a realization of the power of the Genocide. In each story, he is able to move on. It is through literature that he is able to resolve inner tensions and is freed to become what he wants to be. This freedom is the creativity that arises from within the individual.

Armenian-American literature has thus developed into a mature form of expression, able to distinguish subtly between genres and to break free of the bonds of the past, even as the authors have used the past to free themselves. They have jumped across the chasm from catastrophe to creativity.

Notes

1. Michael J. Arlen, *Passage to Ararat* (New York: Farrar, Straus & Giroux, 1975).
2. Michael Krekorian, *Corridor* (New York: Ashod Press, 1989). "Avedis" is one of eleven short stories that comprise *Corridor*.
3. David Kherdian, *Asking the River* (New York: Orchard Books, 1993).
4. Marc Nichanian, *Writers of Disaster: Armenian Literature in the Twentieth Century*, vol. 1: *The National Revolution* (Princeton, NJ, and London: Gomidas Institute, 2002). Nichanian provides a fundamental framework for an understanding of the role of the Genocide, which for the purposes of his work, is characterized as the *Aghed*—the Catastrophe. His introduction, "The Horizon of the Catastrophe" offers a theoretical discussion of the issue.
5. Nichanian, *Writers of Disaster*, pp. 10-11. He goes on to discuss his own attempt to liberate the event from the historical and political meanings attached to it.
6. Ibid., p. 167.
7. Lorne Shirinian, *Armenian-North American Literature: A Critical Introduction: Genocide, Diaspora, and Symbols* (Lewiston, Ontario: Edwin Mellen Press, 1990), pp. 90-115.
8. Arlen, *Passage to Ararat*, p. 3.
9. Ibid., p. 11.
10. Ibid., p. 11.
11. Ibid., p. 24.
12. Shirinian, *Armenian-North American Literature*, pp. 55-58.
13. Lorne Shirinian, *The Republic of Armenia and the Rethinking of the North-American Diaspora in Literature* (Lewiston, Ontario: Edwin Mellen Press, 1992). Shirinian provides a thorough discussion of the "absence of the father" in modern Armenian literature in the chapter "Lost Fathers and Abandoned Sons: The Silence of Generations in Armenian Diaspora Literature." This is "an essential feature of Armenian Diaspora literature." Examples from various authors and texts are given to illustrate the point.
14. Arlen, *Passage to Ararat*, p. 64.
15. Ibid., p. 79.
16. Ibid., p. 135.
17. Ibid., p. 70.
18. Ibid., p. 101.
19. Krekorian, "Avedis," p. 60.
20. Ibid., p. 56.
21. Ibid., p. 55.
22. Ibid., p. 59.
23. Ibid., p. 60
24. Ibid., p. 59.
25. Ibid., pp. 62-63.
26. Ibid., p. 65.
27. Ibid., p. 68.
28. Ibid.
29. Ibid.

30. David Kherdian, *Finding Home* (New York: Greenwillow Books, 1981).
31. Margaret Bedrosian, *The Magical Pine Ring: Culture and Imagination in Armenian-American Literature* (Detroit, MI: Wayne State University Press, 1991), p. 168. Bedrosian examines the work of major Armenian-American writers and provides a framework for understanding modern Armenian literature.
32. Ibid., p. 133.
33. Kherdian, *Asking the River*, p. 3.
34. Ibid., p. 4.
35. Ibid., p. 9.
36. Ibid., p. 10.
37. Ibid., p. 35.
38. Ibid., p. 75.
39. Ibid., p. 3.
40. Ibid., p. 54.
41. Ibid., p. 9.
42. Ibid., p. 34.
43. Ibid., p. 60.
44. Ibid., p. 62.
45. Ibid., pp. 80-81.
46. Ibid., p. 88.
47. See Arlen, *Passage to Ararat,* pp. 248-249. Arlen's conclusions about this self-hatred and the reasons for it are an important moment of self-realization for the author.
48. Kherdian, *Asking the River*, pp. 90-92.
49. Ibid., p. 93.
50. Ibid., p. 94.
51. Ibid., p. 98.
52. Ibid., p. 101.

6

The Armenian Genocide in James Joyce's *Finnegans Wake*

Marc Aram Mamigonian

James Joyce wrote his final book, *Finnegans Wake*, between 1923 and 1939, in the years following the destruction of the Armenians of Asia Minor. Joyce, one of the high-priests of literary modernism, whose earlier novels *A Portrait of the Artist as a Young Man* (1916) and *Ulysses* (1922) were in many ways the ultimate expression of that movement, in *Finnegans Wake* demolished the very notion of a unified work of art, of literary structure, and of the English language itself. "I have finished with English," Joyce said while writing the book. Unquestionably, Joyce's revolution of the word was in part a reaction to the chaos of World War I, and finding a place in his decentered universe are the Armenians and the Armenian Genocide, references to which dot the book.

Joyce, ever-alert to historical-mythical parallels, saw the Armenians as like the Irish (as, in a more explicit way, he had paralleled the Irish and the Jews in *Ulysses*), both nations of "people living in the same place . . . or also living in different places," as the character Leopold Bloom defines the term nation in *Ulysses*; dispersed, oppressed, persistent in their refusal to be destroyed. Both are ancient nations that embraced and preserved Christianity at an early date; both suffered conquest, colonization, and exploitation at the hands of a more powerful imperial neighbor; both suffered massacres and dispersals and existed to a great extent as a nation of exiles. Joyce, who created a persona for himself as the ultimate Irish exile, was always sympathetic to other outcasts; and his inclusion of the Armenians in *Finnegans Wake* is a gesture of solidarity and an acknowledgment of fellowship.

This analysis builds on work that has already been done on the subject of Armenian in *Finnegans Wake* by Vrej Nersessian, Danis Rose, and Ian MacArthur;[1] by Petr Skrabanek[2] —an important and pioneering work that entailed identifying in the *Wake* text the words and phrases from Armenian that Joyce had listed in his notebooks; by Nathan Halper, who began the work of placing the Armenian in some meaningful context[3]; and my own "All Abunk for Tararat!: Armenian in *Finnegans Wake.*"[4] Here the focus is on the ways in which Joyce used the Armenians and the Armenian Genocide to support *Finnegans Wake's* major themes of death and rebirth, the Fall from Grace, and the cyclical nature of history.

Since *Finnegans Wake* is structured so that it has neither beginning nor end, and thus, by its very nature, it has no center, the comparatively small light that the Armenian references cast into the novel's vast obscurity is not merely peripheral. On a personal note, having struggled with *Finnegans Wake* for years now, focusing on the Armenian references and taking the part for the whole has been enormously helpful to my better understanding of the book.

It has been powerfully argued that the book of Genesis, especially the third chapter, "reinterpreted and repeated hundreds of times, is the narrative base of *Finnegans Wake*. There is no action that does not contain [it]."[5] Similarly, the story of the "second creation"—the landing of Noah's Ark at "the mountains of Ararat" and the story of Noah and his sons (Gen. 6-9)—bulks very large in *Finnegans Wake*. As Armenians are always fond of recalling, these biblical events unfolded in Armenia's backyard; and while they are among the formative myths of Western civilization, they are also particularly cherished by Armenians. The fact that the people of Ararat survived down to the twentieth century and had a major role in the latest of mankind's calamities, World War I, was too rich a source of material for Joyce to ignore, as it so strongly buttressed his idea of history constantly repeating itself with a difference.

On the one hand, it is not surprising to find Armenian in *Finnegans Wake*, albeit as a miniscule part of the whole, because everything else is there; but, on the other hand, it is somewhat startling because Armenia and Armenians do not enter into Joyce's pre-*Wake* work at all. And indeed, why should they? Although Joyce, who was born near Dublin in 1882, left Ireland in 1904 more or less for good, he basically wrote about Dublin and only Dublin in his stories, novels, and play. Dublin was his world. *Finnegans Wake*, in its way, is a book of Dublin and its environs, even if it takes the microcosm of Dublin as the macrocosm of all human existence everywhere. As far as I can tell, there were no Armenians in Dublin in Joyce's time (that is, there are no references to any Armenians nor are there Armenian names in the Thom's Official Directories of the United Kingdom of Great Britain and Ireland for that era that were consulted). But the Hamidian massacres of the 1890s would have been in Dublin newspapers, and Joyce, after all, spent his post-Dublin life in the cosmopolitan worlds of Trieste, Zurich, and Paris, where Armenians were present, even abundant; and Armenians were much in the public consciousness during the World War I and postwar era. By the early 1920s, when Joyce moved to Paris, France was home to tens of thousands of Armenians, mostly in Paris and Marseilles. The fact is, however, that one will search in vain for references to Armenians in Joyce's pre-*Wake* writings, both published and unpublished.

There are, then, at base, two fundamental reasons for the one hundred or so explicit references to Armenia or Armenian words. These are Armenia's relationship to major antediluvian and immediately post-diluvian events related in the Book of Genesis and the then-recent Armenian Genocide. I have focused on the former elsewhere[6] and will only touch on it here in an effort to focus on the latter, but the two go hand in hand and cannot be separated.

Joyce wanted *Finnegans Wake* to go beyond *Ulysses* in being all-encompassing in its scope and its connection to many of the great myths and epics of (especially Western) world civilization. Joyce wrote *Ulysses* mainly during World War I but the events of that time could find no place in that work, which was conceived before the war and, at any rate, takes place on a single day in Dublin in 1904. *Ulysses*, a work of enormous complexity and imagination, which is encyclopedic in its range of references and allusions, is tethered to a particular time and place in a way that *Finnegans Wake* decidedly is not.

Joyce seems to have considered *Finnegans Wake* to be truly universal and thus equally accessible to all. And so, in a certain sense, it is: it is very nearly as obscure to the English reader as to the rest of the world. The literary scholar Hugh Kenner has described reading *Finnegans Wake* as being "like going to a Berlitz school to learn a language that is useful nowhere on earth."[7] As an enticement, a reward, perhaps, Joyce included something for everybody; one might say, then, that the Armenian content serves, for those who encounter it and recognize it in the text, as a little prize and an encouragement to soldier on through the book. Clive Hart writes that Joyce "needed constant reassurance of [*Finnegans Wake*'s] relevance to the outside world. This relevance he tried to ensure by making its scope as wide as possible so that it might include not only all given experience but every possible permutation of experience as well."[8]

It is not possible here to attempt any kind of substantial account of what *Finnegans Wake* is about. But since many people have not read the book, a brief sketch of the bare-bones elements of the book may be useful. *Finnegans Wake* concerns primarily five characters who flow in and out of the book in countless guises but in their most basic forms are a father who is called by the initials HCE, his wife who is known by the initials ALP, or Anna Livia Plurabella, their two sons Shem and Shaun, and their daughter Issy. HCE is involved in some scandalous fall from grace; his wife strives to defend him; his sons alternately clash with each other and their father and come together to fuse with each other and with him; the daughter is an innocent child and a temptress. Their conflicts are repeated or refracted through hundreds of parallel or analogous conflicts that are enacted throughout the book.

The book, in all its complexity, is based on a short list of basic principles derived from the eighteenth-century *New Science* of Giambattista Vico and the sixteenth-century writings of Giordano Bruno: (1) History is cyclical and consists of four stages, within which the same basic situations are perpetually repeated with minor variations; (2) Each age echoes the others in its events and personages; (3) The rise of man foreshadows his fall, and his fall foreshadows his rise; (4) Etymology recapitulates history; (5) Conflicts between people are at their base conflicts over language and interpretation; (6) God manifests himself on earth in the principle of *coincidentia oppositorum*, the unity of opposites, wherein opposing halves form a unified and coherent whole; (7) each element of the universe contains, in microcosm, the entire universe; and (8) the actual and the possible are the same in eternity.[9]

Of the intimidating and impenetrable prose style he formulated for *Finnegans Wake*, Joyce wrote: "One great part of human existence is passed in a state which cannot be rendered sensible by the use of wideawake language, cutandry grammar and goahead plot."[10] Joyce drew on dozens of languages in creating the "night language" of *Finnegans Wake*; among them languages he knew fluently or nearly fluently such as English, Italian, French, Danish, and German; languages of which he had a substantial knowledge or interest, such as Latin, Irish Gaelic and other Celtic languages, Hebrew, Gypsy (Romany), and Russian; and the many, many other languages of the world of which he had little or no actual knowledge. Within this last category falls Armenian. The Joyce scholar Matthew Hodgart rather condescendingly states that Joyce "included many thousands of words from Hebrew, Arabic and Chinese (admittedly great cultural languages) and *even* from Armenian and Albanian."[11] Setting Hodgart's assessment of cultural greatness aside, the Armenian, like all of the languages used by Joyce, is put in the service of the book's larger goals.

Inevitably, for one who understands Armenian, these linguistic nuggets and references set off chains of association that do not exist for readers who do not know Armenian—and this included Joyce himself. (The same is true, of course, of all of the other languages the book draws upon.) Joyce could no more control where these associations would lead than any other artist. But unlike works of art that the artist wishes to keep as a closed system, one in which all meanings are, in principle, at least, circumscribed by the creator, *Finnegans Wake* deliberately is an endlessly open system: it has no beginning, no end, seemingly little of the formal structures that one looks for in books, and the potential for infinite interpretation and reinterpretation. Some critics will have it that this is true of all literary texts, and it may well be so. *Finnegans Wake* is, then, an extension of this open-ended principle to a logically absurd extreme.

There are just under one hundred Armenian-language words and phrases or else phrases with Armenian references in *Finnegans Wake*'s 628 pages. (That is to say, that is how many have been identified as such. There may be more.) They are not evenly distributed: the vast majority appears within the first two books (i.e., the first 399 pages), and they usually appear in clusters within these books. The Armenian tends to be associated with HCE. Book I deals mainly with HCE, Book II mostly with his sons; but the Armenian recurs when HCE comes to the fore. Nathan Halper perceptively writes:

> Notice that, in a number of allusions, being an Armenian is a metaphor for [HCE] himself or for one of his personae. . . . He is the victim, the old, impotent, defeated, the Mark who is a cuckold, the General who is about to be shot by Buckley. But, as we saw, the killing engenders "abnihilization." The same anew. The end of a cycle: beginning of a new one. The Armenian motif is involved with Creation! The finding—in the old dump—of a new letter.[12]

Thus, at 72.11, in the "long list (now feared in part lost) to be kept on file of all abusive names [HCE] was called" we find "Armenian Atrocity." Because HCE is both victim and victimizer, it is impossible to know exactly how to interpret this epithet. Is HCE an "Armenian Atrocity" in the sense of being a victim or is he an "Armenian Atrocity" in the sense of being a personification of those who committed them? No definitive answer can be given. Just nine lines above he is called "Sublime Porter"—part of a network of references to HCE as a "tarrable Turk," as he is called at 520.02. ("Sublime Porte" was, of course, the name for the seat of the Ottoman government.). Armenian-ness, then, carries with it the same dualities as everything else in the book.

HCE's sons Shem and Shaun form a pair of opposites who intermittently coalesce to form an opposition to HCE, with whom they also intermittently unify. Shem, who is the character in the book most closely identifiable with Joyce himself, is said by his brother Shaun to be "as popular as an armenial with the faithful" (190.25), that is, with the Muslim Turks. Similarly, several pages earlier, Shaun insults Shem, saying "no-one, hound or scrublady, not even the Turk, ungreekable in purscent of the armenable, dared whiff the polecat at close range" (181.22), which plays on Oscar Wilde's famous witticism on fox hunting ("the unspeakable in pursuit of the uneatable") as well as Thomas Carlyle's phrase "the unspeakable Turk." Shem is the artist figure in *Finnegans Wake*, something of an heir to Joyce's earlier fictional alter ego Stephen Dedalus, whereas Shaun is generally meant to be seen as a self-righteous poseur. The play on the Wilde quip reconnects Shem to his father—the Armenian association is one that bridges the generation gap. Wilde, who fell from grace because of a so-called sin, is alluded to throughout the book as a kind of exemplar of man's fall, and his name is evoked many times throughout the book, including on page 241 as "osghirs," from the Armenian word for gold.

This same network of allusions comes together once again later in the book. Shem, now appearing under the name of Glugg, is described: "He, through wolkenic connection, relation belong this remarklable moliman, Anaks Andrum, parley-glutton pure blood Jebusite, centy procent Erserum spoking" (240.26). "Anax andron" is Greek for Lord of Men; but Anak was the father of Grigor Lusavorich (who is himself invoked at *Finnegans Wake* 69.12; see below). "Erserum spoking" combines the Erse language—that is what the Irish call the

Irish Gaelic language—with Erzerum, the Armenian city and, of course, one of the major centers of massacre during the Genocide. The same combination recurs on page 344 in slightly different form: Eirzerum. A similar effect using different elements is achieved in the exclamation "All abunk for Tarararat!" (p. 267), which deftly fuses the Hill of Tara, the legendary seat of Ireland's high kings, with Mt. Ararat, a nice conjoining of two national symbols.

The great majority of Armenian references, or more specifically, Armenian words, do not explicitly refer to the Genocide. Nonetheless, the Genocide and Joyce's sympathy for the Armenians and their plight, as well as perception of the crucial elements of death and rebirth in the Armenians' story, are the principal reasons for the Armenians to be in the book in any substantial manner. This is not to say that Joyce was turning the Armenians or the Armenian Genocide into a metaphor, because making a metaphor out of the Genocide would be grotesque. Rather, Joyce looked at Armenia and saw a land where, biblically speaking, the first crime against humanity occurred in the Garden of Eden, and also where a recent crime against humanity had occurred.

The story of Noah and his sons, Shem, Ham, and Japheth, and Noah's drunken exposure of himself (and the resulting curse on his son Ham for, shall we say, his lack of enthusiasm for the job of concealing his father's nakedness and his subsequent announcing of the event to his brothers) is tied in *Finnegans Wake* to the protagonist HCE's obscure crime, which may or may not have been exposing himself in the Phoenix Park to three soldiers or two girls. It may be worth noting here, in passing, that one of Joyce's most-favored Church Fathers, St. Augustine, finds in the story of Noah's drunkenness an allegory of redemption and renewal: Noah's nakedness prefigures the Passion of Christ, Ham's behavior represents those who outwardly "glory in the Christian name, and at the same time lead abandoned lives," while Shem and Japheth represent the Jews and Greeks who receive the Gospel. Augustine's interpretation, which I find somewhat puzzling, is found in *The City of God*, Book XVI, Chapter 2 ("What Was Prophetically Prefigured in the Sons of Noah").

Armenians fashion themselves as the descendents of Hayk, the great-great grandson of Japheth (and thus the great-great-great grandson of Noah). According to the "Father of Armenian History," Movses Khorenatsi, writing in the fifth century (or later, depending on whom you ask), Shem, too, is closely connected with Armenian origins. (Note Joyce's confusing formulation "all the sems of Aram" [p. 228], that is, sons of Aram, the Armenians—but Aram is descended from Japheth, not Shem.) Khorenatsi writes of Shem that after the ark landed Shem dwelled for a time in a plain near a mountain and the mountain is called Sim after him to this day.[13] This is Mt. Sim, where the Armenian district of Sasun is located. Joyce mentions Sasun at 344.01 in the portmanteau word "unglück**sarsoon**" (emphasis added). "Ungluck" is German for misfortune. "Sarsoon," besides evoking Sasun, is also Armenian for shiver. The word as a whole also suggests "Anglo-Saxon" and Siegfried Sassoon, the doomed World

War I poet. This is a good example of how Joyce packed multiple meanings into a single term.

It is possible that Joyce had heard of Sasun because it was one of the hotbeds of conflict during the massacres of the 1890s and during the Genocide of 1915. However, of course, the region looms large in Armenian culture as the setting of the Armenian national epic *David of Sasun* or *Daredevils of Sasun*. It is not possible to establish that Joyce knew of the epic, which, while of great antiquity, was only written down in the late nineteenth century. Partial translations of it in English had appeared before the writing of *Finnegans Wake*, though. Joyce was deeply interested in national epics, however, so it is plausible that he would at least have been aware of the epic, whether or not he had read any of it.

The structural similarities of the epic to *Finnegans Wake* are intriguing, I think, and deserve greater investigation than can be undertaken here. The Sasun epic, which like *Finnegans Wake* has four parts or branches, concerns four generations of a family and their exploits. (The epic, that is, in its final form, has four parts: but other versions or recitations of the epic did not adhere to this structure.) It begins with the birth of warring twins, Sanasar and Baghdasar, born of a woman named Dzovinar, whose name connects her with water (*dzov* = sea). The similarities between Shem and Shaun and their watery mother Anna Livia, who is Dublin's River Liffey personified, are clear, if not necessarily conscious. The epic ends with Pokr Mher, the last of the four generations of heroes (that is, Little Mher, the name Mher being derived from Mithra), imprisoned in a mountain above Lake Van in Armenia, from which he will only return when the sinful world has been destroyed and remade again—shades of Giambattista Vico's cycles of history.[14]

The point of this digression on the Armenian epic is not to assert that Joyce was steeped in Armenian history and mythology. He may or may not have even been aware of them to any significant degree. But he was very skillful at choosing materials that dovetailed with archetypes that appear in many different ancient mythologies. The echoes of Armenian epic and myth in *Finnegans Wake* stand as a tribute, then, probably not to Joyce's vast learning so much as his ability to tap into Indo-European archetypes.

"Unglucksarsoon" as well as another dozen Armenian references appear on pages 344-50, the core of the "How Buckley Shot the Russian General" episode, which takes place during the Crimean War (1853-56), and in which the Russian general is an extension of HCE and Buckley a fusion of his sons. (The war was fought for dominance in the Near East, and the Crimea was known as Maritime Armenia in medieval times.) The general is shot after defecating and wiping himself with a piece of sod; thus connecting him to Noah's exposure and his son's informing on him rather than discreetly covering him, as well as, of course, HCE's self-exposure in the park.

Adaline Glasheen writes of this section: "it seems plain that the Russian general is every tyrant and father, slain by every son."[15] The story is related as a kind of televised comedy routine between two characters named Butt and Taff, who are representations of Shem and Shaun. At one point, Buckley explains why at first he was unable to act and shoot the Russian general:

> But, meac Coolp, **Arram of Eirzerum,** as I love our **Deer Dirouchy**, I confesses withould pridejealice when I looked upon the **Saur** of all the **Haurousians** with the weight of his arge fullin upon him . . . there was fear on me the sons of Nuad for him it was heavy for me then the way I immingled my **Irmenial hairmaierians** ammongled his Gospolis fomiliours till . . . I adn't the art to. [344-45; Armenian and related words in boldface]

In this passage, Buckley sounds as if he is Armenian (is he speaking to someone named Aram from Erzerum?), with his "Irmenial hairmaierians" (does this mean he is praying in Armenian?) contrasting with the Russian's "Gospolis fomiliours" (Old Church Slavonic: Gospodi pomilui, Lord have mercy). Or is the General himself Armenian, the "Saur (combining Armenian *sur*, sword, and Greek *souros*, lizard) of all the Harousians" (combining "Russians" with Armenian *Harutiun*, resurrection), weighed down by "arge" (age, of course, but also Armenian *arch*, bear, the symbol of Russia). Once again, the Armenian references tend to unify the opposing forces and blur distinctions, which makes sense in this context since, if as Glasheen suggests, in slaying the General Buckley is slaying the material universe, then he is slaying himself as well.

Most of the Armenian words, which come from both Classical Armenian (*grabar*) and modern Western Armenian, were very late additions to *Finnegans Wake*. Danis Rose and others have established conclusively that Joyce compiled the Armenian lists (in workbook VI.B.30, VI.B.45, VI.B.46, and VI.B.47) and incorporated the material into *Finnegans Wake* in late 1938—very late, indeed, in the composition of a book that was published on February 2, 1939.

Joyce had intended at least one Armenian element in *Finnegans Wake*, however, as early as 1928 when he included the Armenian word for peace (*khaghaghutiun*, which comes out as "Ghugugoothoyou!" [471.02]) in a passage that incorporates numerous other international words for "peace." Why Armenian? One can only assume it was a gesture of sympathy on Joyce's part to a people who had so recently suffered such devastation. So the concept of using Armenian elements was not necessarily one that came late in the process of writing the book; but unquestionably the bulk of its execution was. It is not yet known, however, how Joyce came by the list of Armenian words.[16]

It is possible that Joyce became especially aware of the Armenian language and things Armenian through his early and intense interest in Lord Byron, who studied Armenian in Venice with the Mekhitarist monks at San Lazzaro in 1816-17, did translations from the Armenian, and collaborated on an Armenian grammar and the first Armenian-English dictionary. Byron's Armenian episode has been well documented,[17] and Joyce must have been aware of it from biographies of Byron and his published letters. Byron seems to have visited the island for lessons and exercises daily for nearly two months. His teacher, the great Armenian scholar Father Paschal (Poghos) Avgerian, wrote: "He learned to read the Armenian language very well, and also to understand it a little." Byron himself was more modest about his achievement.[18]

Joyce may also have come to awareness of Armenians through a now little read but deeply influential work by another Romantic giant, Johann Christoph Friedrich von Schiller's *Der Geisterseher* ("The Ghost Seer," 1789). The first English translation, *The Armenian, or the Ghost-Seer, A History Founded on Fact*, was published in 1800, and was known by Byron and influenced Samuel Taylor Coleridge. In the novel, the narrator is stalked on the Piazza San Marco in Venice during Carnival by a masked Armenian who reappears in various guises later in the novel and turns out to be the Wandering Jew himself.[19] Given Joyce's extensive use of the Wandering Jew legend in *Ulysses*, it is probable he had read Schiller's novel or at least was aware of it.

Although he refers not to Armenian but to another "exotic" language that comes into *Finnegans Wake*, Clive Hart's words are relevant here:

> People only casually versed in Joycean studies are often highly sceptical of the suggestion that such things as Swahili words *really* are in *Finnegans Wake*. One glance at the MSS will dispel any doubts that these words really are to be interpreted as Swahili—*at least in the initial stage of their addition to the text*. Whether they are to be so interpreted in the final version of the book is a more sophisticated question.[20]

This "sophisticated question" must be asked of the Armenian in *Finnegans Wake* as well. In other words, while it is inarguable that Joyce compiled a list of Armenian words which were added to *Finnegans Wake*, by the time the reader encounters them in the text are they still to be regarded as (primarily? exclusively?) Armenian words or as something else altogether—that is, as components of the language of the *Wake* that may or may not bear the trace of their original meaning.

In Joyce's sigla, that is, the shorthand visual representations he devised for each of the characters in *Finnegans Wake* as he was composing it, and by which he referred to them in his letters and notes from very early on in the book's composition, HCE is represented through various rotations of the capital letter **E**: one of HCE's manifestations is as the E recumbent—Joyce said this is HCE interred in the landscape (his head at Howth and his feet at the Phoenix Park), where he lies dead only to rise again.[21] This is made explicit on page 6 of *Finnegans Wake*. While it has long been noted that this is the Chinese pictograph for mountain, I am not aware that anyone has pointed out that it is also the Armenian ա (*ayp*), the first letter of the alphabet. Joyce wrote in a letter that "A Chinese student sent me some letterwords I had asked for. The last one is ա. It means 'mountain' and is called 'Chin,' the common people's way of pronouncing Hin or Fin."[22] This may well bc true. (As far as I can determine, the Chinese word for mountain is "shan," which would have been just as good for Joyce's purposes, with its echoes of both Shem and Shaun). Did Joyce also know that *hin* is Armenian for old, a very apt term for HCE in his dying state, or is this another happy coincidence?

Since so much of the evocation of Armenia is tied to Mt. Ararat (all mountains in the book tend to be versions of Ararat), the association of HCE=mountain=Armenian gains strength. Furthermore, that the fall of HCE should have its visual equivalent in the beginning letter of the Armenian alphabet and be linked to the rebirth of mankind at Ararat has a particularly Joycean/Viconian logic: in the end is the beginning, in the beginning is the end.

One cannot say for certain if Joyce knew that one of the manifestations of his hero was the first letter of the Armenian alphabet, since he has left no evidence in his notes; nonetheless it is so. Thus, not only is HCE, as the prototypical progenitor (thus his nickname Haveth Childers Everywhere) connected with Hayk, eponym of the Armenian nation, who is mentioned at 367.05 and possibly elsewhere; but he is also linked with the Armenian alphabet itself, one of the most potent symbols of the Armenian people, created by Mesrob Mashtots and traditionally said to have been directly received from God. Mashtots, then, was the creator and deliverer of the Letter—linking him to HCE's son Shaun the Post in *Finnegans Wake*. (Mashtots is not directly alluded to in *Finnegans Wake* in any recognizable manner.) Shem, too, known as Shem the Penman, the forger, is linked to the alphabet through his many associations with the Egyptian god Thoth. (Thoth is the scribe-god who invented letters, among other things.)

The opening page of the book announces almost all of the themes of the book: "riverrun, past Eve and Adam's, from swerve of shore to bend of bay, brings us by a commodius vicus of recirculation back to Howth Castle and Environs" (1.1). Howth Head functions as a kind of Mt. Ararat for Joyce in *Finnegans Wake*. The Phoenix Park, mentioned a few lines below, serves as the Garden of Eden, its very name a convenient emblem of rebirth, no matter that its etymology does not tie it to the mythic bird but rather to the Irish Gaelic *fionn uisce*, "clear water." The rivalry of brothers—a major theme of *Finnegans Wake* that draws on the story of Noah's sons Shem, Ham, and Japheth (among many others)—is touched on: "Rot a peck of pa's malt had Jhem or Shen brewed" (1.12); as is Noah's rainbow: "and rory end to the regginbrow was to be seen ringsome on the aquaface."

The first significant cluster of Armenian words in the book falls on pages 69-75. The page 69 cluster is, unsurprisingly, tied to HCE's crime and fall from grace.

> Now by memory inspired, turn wheel again to the whole of the wall. Where Gyant Blyant fronts Peannlueamoore There was once upon a wall and a hooghoog wall a was and such a wall-hole did exist. Ere **ore or** ire in Aarlund. Or you **Dair's Hair** or you **Diggin Mosses** or your horde of **orts and oriorts** to garble a garthen of Odin and the lost paladays when all the eddams ended with aves. **Armen**? The **doun** is theirs and still to see for **menags** if he strikes a **lousaforitch** and we'll come to those baregazed

> **shoeshines** if you just **shoodov** a second. And let oggs be good old gaggles and Isther Estarr play Yesther Asterr. In the drema of Sorestost Areas, Diseased.
>
> [*ore or*: day by day; *Der Hayr*: Reverend Father; *vorti*: son; *oriort*: maiden; *dun*: house; *minag*: alone; *lusavorich*: enlightener; *shushan*: lily; *shudov*: hurry]

"The whole of the wall" was a location at Dublin's Phoenix Park, which serves in *Finnegans Wake* as the Garden of Eden. "Once upon a wall" suggests Humpty Dumpty's fall, which is repeatedly associated with HCE in this book. "Aaarlund" conflates Ireland and Armenia with the Danish "aar," year—HCE is of Scandinavian stock. Joyce may have been aware of the proto-Indo-European root **ar*- [to join together], from which such words as army, aristocrat, art, order, as well as, less obviously, reason, rational, read, and real derive. John Bishop seems to think so; thus the etymological chart for **ar*-, which he ties to Joyce's knowledge of Vico's etymological principle that all words carry a subliminal record of the past.[23] How pleasing, then, that here **ar*- joins together Ireland and Armenia! Joyce yokes the nations of Ireland, Denmark, and Armenia together once again on page 387: "But now, talking of **hayastdanars** and wolkingology and how our seaborn isle came into exestuance" (or *Hayastan*: Armenia).

"Dair's Hair" alludes to a possibly ribald music hall song, perhaps to HCE's exposure of himself, and certainly to Armenian priests. "Orts and oriorts" seem to refer to HCE's children, who tend to blur with the three soldiers or the two girls in the park, that is, the "lost paladays." The "baregazed shoeshines" are undoubtedly the two girls in the park, elsewhere embodied by Jonathan Swift's Stella and Vanessa (who were both named Esther—thus "Isther Estarr play Yesther Asterr"). "Shoeshines"—from *shushan*, lily—evokes the name of the wife of Magrath, the Cad with the Pipe, who needs a match (thus "lousaforitch"), and who helps bring about HCE's downfall. She is also tied to Lilith, the demoness who is dubbed the "patroness of abortions" in *Ulysses*.

The next cluster is on page 75 and begins the fourth part of Book I:

> As the lion in our teargarten remembers the nenuphars of his Nile (shall **Ariuz** forget **Arioun** or **Boghas** the **baregams** of the **Marmarazalles** from **Marmeniere**?) it may be, tots wearsense full a naggin in twentyg have sigilposted what in our brievingbust, the besieged bedreamt him stil and solely of those lililiths un-deveiled which had undone him, gone for age, and knew not the watchful treachers at his wake, and theirs to stay.

Once again, we are dealing with HCE—the lion, *ariuz*—and the two girls in the park (**baregams** of the **Marmarazalles** from **Marmeniere**, liliths, etc.) Ariuz links HCE with the Armenian epic of Sasun, where the hero of the second branch of the epic is called Ariudz Mher—Lion Mher. It is impossible to insist on the connection but it is there if one's ears are so attuned.

There is another outbreak of Armenian on pages 107-108 in the midst of the discussion of ALP's letter, the so-called "mamafesta," written to clear the name of her husband. One would not necessarily expect the Armenian to be here. But on page 107 it crops up when the question of the authorship of the letter is in doubt. It is suggested that HCE is himself the author of the letter, "in which the eternal chimerahunter Oriolopos . . . persequestellates his vanessas from flore to flore." The "vanessas" are the two girls in the Phoenix Park once again, whom HCE pursues ("persequestellates"). Thus, we are back at the Garden of Eden again and a flurry of Armenian results:

> Somehows this sounds like the purest **kidooleyoon** wherein our **madernacerution** of **lour** lore is rich. All's so **herou** from us him in a **kitchernott** darkness, by **hasard** and worn rolls arered, we must grope on till **Zerogh** hour like **pou** owl **giaours** as we are would we salve aught of moments for our **aysore** today. **Amousin** though not but.
>
> [*kidutiun*: knowledge; *madenakrutiun*: bibliography; *lur*: news; *heru*: distant; *kisher*: night; *kisheranots*: pajama; *hazar*: thousand; *tsereg*: daytime; *pu*: owl; *giaours*: (Turkish) infidels; *aysor*: today; *amusin*: husband]

HCE's authorship is dismissed, though, and the discussion meanders on, provoking the outburst: "Say, **baroun lousadoor**, who in **hallhagal** wrote the durn thing anyhow?" [*baron*: mister; *lousavor*: bright; *khaghal*: play] On page 113, we read:

> "**Grabar** gooden grandy for **old almeanium** adamologists like Dariaumaurius and **Zov**otri**maserovmeravmerouvian**; (dmzn!)" [*grabar*: Classical Armenian language; *dzov*: sea; *maserov* (*mazerov*): with hair; *merav*: died],

where the Adam/Armenian conjunction is hardly unexpected.

The final Armenian cluster is a group of twenty words that lies between pages 387 and 397, within a section that is obscure even by the standards of this book. One of the earliest sections to be drafted, it deals with the story of King Mark of Cornwall, his nephew Tristan, and Isolde. The tale is one of the major structural pillars of *Finnegans Wake*. Drawing on Roland McHugh's description, the chapter under discussion, which concludes Book II, "concerns the climactic point in the relationship of Tristan and Isolde, as they return to Cornwall from Ireland, having drunk the love potion. But [and] it is presented entirely as a fantasy" of The Four, who are variously the four evangelists, the four kingdoms of Ireland, the four points of the compass, and virtually any other quaternity one can think of.[24] The Four are, in this section, almost completely merged with HCE, of whom they almost seem to be a fourfold emanation. This, presumably, accounts for the Armenian, much of which is even more twisted out of recognition than elsewhere. This is merely speculation on a passage with which this reader, at least, has not yet come to terms.

* * * *

Noah, his sons, the Garden of Eden, the Ararat region: these are critical pieces to the great puzzle that is *Finnegans Wake* and they are connected directly to Armenian legendary history and geography. The Armenian references and allusions reinforce, bolster, and add depth of meaning to the book. The Armenian acts as a signpost for major themes of *Finnegans Wake*: the Fall from Grace, Rebirth, and the creation of the Letter.

Joyce was probably aware that before Indo-European had been theorized Armenian was thought by some to be the ur-language or *Stammsprache*, an important idea in *Finnegans Wake* because Joyce's new language created for the book can be taken as either the pure, pre-Tower of Babel, intelligible-to-all language; or, more ominously (and more convincingly to the average reader), the post-Tower confounded tongues. He may also have known (or at least would have been delighted to know) that in one of the earliest treatises in English on Indo-European language origins, James Parsons' *The Remains of Japhet, being historical enquiries into the affinity and origins of the European languages* (1767), the "Japhetic" languages were derived not from Armenian but from Irish. He might also have been pleased to know that there is a growing body of research on the connections between Armenia and Ireland, especially in early Christian times. The similarities between Irish high crosses and Armenian *khachkars* (stone crosses) have been noted often enough to be something of a cliché. What is undeniable is that both nations have undergone death and rebirth enough times that geographical distance is easily breached and the Armenian and the Irishman can nod knowingly to one another across the obscure pages of *Finnegans Wake*.

It is my opinion, and my hope, that Joyce, in his own strange way, points the way towards a better understanding of the Armenian Genocide. Joyce's countryman William Butler Yeats, who also believed in the cyclical nature of history, in his great poem "Easter 1916" viewed the failed Irish uprising of that fateful day as leaving the country "changed utterly:/ A terrible beauty is born." For Yeats, those who sacrificed their lives that day did so to transform Ireland from England's plaything, the place "where motley is worn" into something greater. I do not believe it is possible to see a "terrible beauty" being born from the Armenian Genocide, but there is no question that all was, indeed, "changed utterly."

For Joyce, the Armenian calamity was part of the story of humanity and worthy of inclusion in the book to which he devoted most of the last two decades of his life. Joyce's sense of inclusivity and fair play, perhaps made more acute by being part of an oppressed group, should lead Armenians to seek connections with other victimized groups, to see our story in theirs and theirs in ours. Armenians feel, quite rightly, too often pushed to the margins of history. Yet Armenians find themselves in the pages of one of the masterpieces of twentieth-century literature, and the role of the Armenians in this wonderful and insane book has barely begun to be explored. Professor Richard Hovannisian has spoken of the need to "integrate the Armenian experience into the collective human experience." In his own way, this is precisely what Joyce accomplished in *Finnegans Wake*.

Notes

1. "Armenian in *Finnegans Wake*," *A Wake Newslitter* 18:3 (June 1976), 48-51; "Armenian in II.4," *A Wake Newslitter* 17, 2 (April 1980), 26-27; "Armenian Notes," *A Wake Newslitter* 17, 2 (April 1980), 27.
2. "Notes on Armenian in *Finnegans Wake*," *Finnegans Wake Circular* 1, 3 (Spring 1986), 45-58.
3. Nathan Halper, "Armenian," *A Wake Newslitter* 16:2 (April 1979), 19-24.
4. Marc Aram Mamigonian, "All Abunk for Tararat!: Armenian in *Finnegans Wake*." Paper delivered at the International James Joyce Foundation's "Bloomsday 100" conference, Dublin, June 2004.
5. Harry Burrell, *Narrative Design in Finnegans Wake: The Wake Lock Picked* (Gainesville: University Press of Florida, 1996), p. 7.
6. Mamigonian, "All Abunk for Tarararat!"
7. Quoted in John Bishop, *Joyce's Book of the Dark: Finnegans Wake* (Madison: University of Wisconsin Press, 1986), p. 326.
8. Clive Hart, *Structure and Motif in Finnegans Wake* (Chicago: Northwestern University Press, 1962), p. 27.
9. This list is derived from Cyrus R. K. Patell, *Joyce's Use of History in Finnegans Wake* (Cambridge, MA: Harvard University Press, 1984), pp. 15-16. On Joyce's use of Vico, the most comprehensive study is Donald P. Verene, *Knowledge of Things Human and Divine: Vico's New Science and Finnegans Wake* (New Haven, CT: Yale University Press, 2003). On Bruno, see Frances Motz Boldereff, *Hermes to His Son Thoth: Being Joyce's Use of Giordano Bruno in Finnegans Wake* (Woodward, PA: Classic Non-Fiction Library, 1968).
10. James Joyce, *Selected Letters* (New York: Viking, 1975), p. 318.
11. Matthew J. C. Hodgart, *James Joyce: A Student's Guide* (London: Routledge & Kegan Paul, 1978), p. 136; emphasis added.
12. Halper, "Armenian," p. 23.
13. See Moses Khorenatsi, *History of the Armenians*, Robert W. Thomson, trans. and comm. (Cambridge, MA: Harvard University Press, 1978), p. 80.
14. On the eschatology of the epic, see numerous articles in James R. Russell, *Armenian and Iranian Studies* (Cambridge, MA: Harvard University Press and Armenian Heritage Press, 2004).
15. Adaline Glasheen, *Third Census of Finnegans Wake* (Berkeley and Los Angeles: University of California Press, 1977), p. 42.
16. It is possible that Joyce "commissioned" a list of specific words, but this is unlikely. The Armenian list is a strange one, and in many ways not the list of words one would expect to encounter in that many of them have no particular relevance to *Finnegans Wake*. It is not clear to me at this point whether Joyce wanted *this* Armenian list, per se, or merely *an* Armenian list. Vrej Nersessian is of the opinion that Joyce "must have been transliterating the spoken word, rather than reading from a dictionary." See "Armenian Notes," *A Wake Newslitter*, 13, 3 (June 1976): 27.
17. See, for instance, Noubar Maxoudian, "Lord Byron and the Armenians," *Armenian Review* 8, 4 (Winter 1955-56): 47-48; Ladis B. Kristof, "Lord Byron and the Monks of St. Lazarus," *Armenian Review* 9, 1 (Spring 1956): 65-76.

18. Kristof, "Lord Byron," p. 66.
19. See James R. Russell, "A Scholium on Coleridge and an Armenian Demon," *Journal of the Society for Armenian Studies* 10 (1998-99, 2000): 63-71; also a lecture given by Russell at the National Association for Armenian Studies and Research on "The Near East in the Mind of America" in 2001, online text available at www.commercemarketplace.com/home/naasr/Near_East_in_the_Mind_of_America_3-_Russell.htm
20. Clive Hart, "An Elephant in the Belly: Exegesis of *Finnegans Wake,*" *A Wake Digest* (Sydney: Sydney University Press, 1968), p. 6; the emphases are Hart's own.
21. The sigla are treated exhaustively in Roland McHugh, *The Sigla of Finnegans Wake* (Austin: University of Texas Press, 1976).
22. James Joyce, *Letters of James Joyce*, vol. 1, ed. Stuart Gilbert (London: Faber and Faber, 1957), p. 250.
23. Bishop, *Joyce's Book of the Dark*, pp. 204-205.
24. See McHugh, *The Sigla of Finnegans Wake*, p. 104.

7

Historical Memory: Threading the Contemporary Literature of Armenia

Rubina Peroomian

"'History is an unending dialogue between the past and the present.' History is a constant process of rethinking, rewriting and reinterpretation."[1] Every generation of every community or people tends to judge, reevaluate, and reconstruct the events of pivotal importance of the past in the light of knowledge of hindsight as well as the present exigencies and objectives. A people's past, and especially significant events of the past, are indelible landmarks in that people's collective memory. And that memory, that historical memory, finds different representations and different meanings in the process of its passage from generation to generation and under the dictates of the time. Literature is the locus of these representations. It is the place where the relationship between the self and the social and the constantly changing factors that influence these relationships are registered and represented. Literature purports revelations as the synthesis of the relationship or the dialogue of the self with the collective past in the context of the present.

The memory of the Genocide, as the most important event in the recent history of the Armenian people, the unresolved injustice, the indomitable pain and mourning over the colossal loss, persisted in the Diaspora and served as the common thread stringing together the diasporan literature. The memory of the Genocide reverberated in literature as a source of identity, a leitmotiv or a hidden theme. Successive generations of diasporan writers tried to confront the Catastrophe (*Aghet*), comprehend it, and deal with it. diasporan Armenian literature in one way or another relates to the Genocide.[2]

This was not the case in Soviet Armenia. Historical memory, the memory of the Armenian past and especially that of the Genocide of 1915, was abruptly switched off with the Sovietization of Armenia in December 1920. At least, that was what the official line mandated. The future of the Armenian nation under Soviet rule was not to converge with the past. Razmik Davoyan, a contemporary poet in Armenia, challenges this policy, stressing the importance, for the present and the future, of the path a nation's ancestors crossed, that is, the bearing of the past on the present and the future:

And if you reach your forefathers,
Then, you are close to your future;
Before you, long before you,
They set off thousands of years ago
And they are the ones closest
To all futures old and new.

And if, on your way,
You don't meet your forefathers,
You are on the wrong path
And no miracle can save you now.[3]

A nation without a past was much easier to rule and assimilate or Russify—to use the term befitting the goal. However, even if the officially accepted norms of proletarian literature did not allow the Armenian writers of the 1920s to write about the very recent memory of painful displacement, suffering, and death, the stories of this human ordeal were being told by the survivors within the confines of their family. Davit Muradyan, a contemporary writer, pictures his protagonist in "Hrazhesht" (Farewell) reminiscing the cozy nights when the elders spoke of the Old Country, and their stories permeated pain and yearning: "No! You cannot evoke these nights by simply depicting them. There are things that cannot be put in words. You have to be seated on your father's lap, devour these stories, and catch the gleam and the sadness in the eyes of these men."[4]

The collective memory was being transmitted orally but always challenged by the tenets of the new regime. How long would this unmediated transmission endure in that hostile atmosphere? Arsen, the protagonist of "Hrazhesht," hopes that this memory would accompany his son as he grows up, and as "he in turn tries to find and not lose the thread, the invisible silver thread that grows thinner with time but, curiously, never breaks, that is if you hold it between your fingers and walk in its path."[5]

The mediated transmission, the ever-thinning silver thread of collective memory, unfolded either through orally preserved stories of the survivors, who are mostly long gone now, or through literary representations of the Event. The latter, despite its shortcomings, was in full force in the Diaspora as a vehicle of transmittance, as a feeder for new creations. But in Soviet Armenia, the political atmosphere certainly did not accommodate the flow of literary responses to the recent traumatic experience, what would only be a natural way of dealing with it. Soviet Armenian literature was deprived of the immediate responses. The tradition of the poetics of genocide was not in place for a natural, vertical that is, temporal development of Genocide literature.

Soviet Armenian Literature in the Changing Political Atmosphere

With the Sovietization of Armenia, a drastic change was introduced not only in the political atmosphere, but also in the understanding of cultural and moral values, lifestyle, outlook, even norms and concepts pertaining to art and literature. A change in themes, ideas, and form was imposed. Literature had to follow the Soviet model: "national in form, socialist in content." It was to grow with no ties to its roots. Recourse to the past, even to deal with its psychological impact (let alone its political effect) on the present, had no place. The new path prescribed by the regime led to "socialist realism" in art and literature. Nationalistic themes were renounced and nationalism as an ingredient of Soviet identity was ruled out. The Congress of Soviet Writers in 1934 reiterated the goal to reach socialist realism, reinforcing again literature that was national in form and socialist in content. Andrei Zhdanov, secretary of the Central Committee of the Communist Party, declared, "Such a method in belles-lettres and literary criticism is what we call the method of socialist realism." This kind of literature, he explained, was intended to convey ultimate meaning through the most transparent literary forms and, thus, help to "remold and educate the working people in the spirit of socialism." Zhdanov admitted, "Our Soviet literature is tendentious, and we are proud of its tendentiousness. Stalin defined it correctly when he called the [Soviet] writers 'engineers of human souls.'"[6]

To deviate from the official line was impossible. The government controlled virtually all publications. But what was worse, in order to protect their careers and sometimes even their lives, writers would exert upon themselves an unyielding self-censorship before submitting a manuscript, to the extent of distorting the truth, to comply with the prevailing ideology.

Looking back onto the literature of that period, one can read between the lines to discover the untold truth about life in those difficult years. But more important, one tends to weigh what is told and to measure the suppressed or alluded truth against the inevitable distortion and misrepresentation in the process of multilevel censorship, which the truth often underwent. From the distance of seven decades, one even tends to question if it would not be wiser to keep silent rather than bend to the rules, disguise the truth, or even misrepresent it. Wouldn't it be wiser to remain faithful to one's own art and the history of one's people, produce art in all honesty and keep it in "the drawers" with no hope of its seeing the light of day? Isn't that what some Russian dissident writers did? Decades later, just before and after the collapse of the Soviet Union, when the restrictions were lifted, a renewed interest for the Armenian past found its way into literature. But this recourse to the past is somewhat problematic, because the source of information and inspiration, and the raw material from which to draw historical knowledge is mostly the early Soviet Armenian literature. David

Roskies notes, "Artistic expression draws in equal measure from earlier art as from observable reality."[7]

Suren Sahakyan's *Herosapatum* (Tales of Heroes, 1990), for example, is no doubt a genuine attempt to eternalize the life and deeds of *fedayis* (freedom fighters) and to describe the suffering of the Armenian people at the hands of the Turks. In fact, it is one of the first ventures after the blackout of the Soviet era. Yet, the book suffers from historical discrepancies and a tendency (implanted by Soviet indoctrination) to trivialize the role of the national political parties in organizing and training the troops of fedayis, procuring arms, and planning the strategy of self-defense. On the contrary, in scarce references to their existence, political parties are shown to be involved in petty skirmishes among themselves and therefore a hindrance in the Armenian national struggle for freedom.[8] Given the systematic and continuous indoctrination of generations, this distortion was not intentional. Obviously, the literature these writers produced reflected what they were led to believe. They read about the Armenian armed struggle only in the works that were published after extensive changes and cuts to make them acceptable to the regime. Generations were educated with less emphasis on Armenian history, literature, and culture, and obviously, no emphasis on the traumatic experience of their forefathers. "These were the times of fear and shackles," Suren Sahakyan reminisces:

> We were afraid to talk to Mshetsi Smbat, or any other former soldier of Andranik. Our parents were alien to us. We could get so many stories, true stories from them. We did not, and we lost a great deal. They came and passed away "sighing." They took with them many real life stories, episodes of the past that will never be told. Yet, we were being fed false history. Thus, came the years of brainwashing, making us forget the call of our blood, years of drought that only produced and eulogized men with no will and no homeland.[9]

Sparks of a Rekindled Fire of Past Memories and the Years of Terror

The Bolshevik regime was successful in enforcing the prescribed literature. But as it were, memories of the past, raw and unattended, lived buried in the depths of the minds of even the most dedicated proletarian authors.

Eghishe Charents, the strongest proponent of the new wave of internationalism, was the first to backtrack. His inner conflict made him struggle to find the synthesis of nationalism (through the traditions of prose and poetry) and the revolutionary or rather the revolutionized reality. He chose "to look at the world with the eyes of an Armenian," that is to sustain the national characteristics of the new lyric hero and still remain in the domain of socialist realism and internationalism. Aksel Bakunts, Stepan Zoryan, and others also followed that path, and their endeavors marked the rebirth of national—but of course, not nationalistic—themes and content in Soviet Armenian literature. Historical themes from the Armenian past permeated the autobiographical novels.

The increased manifestations of nationalism in the works of Charents, Bakunts, Gurgen Mahari, Mkrtich Armen, and a few others turned other, more orthodox "internationalist" proletarian writers such as Azat Vshtuni and Nairi Zaryan against the "nationalists" and critics like Gurgen Vanandetsi, Norair Dabaghyan, Hayk Giulikevkhyan, and Tsolak Khanzadyan who supported them. The censorship escalated and the purging of "dissident" intelligentsia began in 1936, dealing a deadly blow to Soviet Armenian literature. Even the most dedicated Communists were not spared. Both the "nationalists" and the "internationalists" came under suspicion. They were branded as traitors and anti-revolutionaries and were persecuted. The year 1937 symbolized the bloodiest time in the history of the Soviet Union. The rule of terror also prevailed in Armenia. Under coercion and from fear for their own lives, people informed on their neighbors and even on family members. Writers betrayed their closest colleagues, accusing them of subversive activities. Family members disowned the arrested one, vowed to forget him or her, and never maintained a relationship or correspondence with that "enemy of the people." Sons and daughters were forced to denounce their parents publicly and expose their "wrongdoings and repulsive deeds."

The full extent of Stalinist persecutions did not come to light until long after Stalin's death and the following period of political and social de-Stalinization. Until then, state censorship continued to prevail in the Soviet Union and was especially strong in Armenia. Memoirs of the victims of Stalin's terror were denied publication. Two of the most significant forbidden topics were the prison experience during Stalin's persecutions and any reference to the Armenian Genocide. It was only when the wave of Perestroika reached Armenia that the rejected memoirs, stories, and articles began to appear in the Armenian press and inspired new creations on the topic of Stalin's rule of terror.

The year 1937, the symbol, the wound, lives in the heart of every Soviet Armenian, since very few families escaped its effects. Ruben Zaryan writes: "If someone who managed to survive 1937 without an incident tells you that he has forgotten what happened and that it was a nightmare that came and is gone now, don't believe him. Look in his heart and you will see the smoldering wounds."[10] For Davit Muradyan, the story of the Gisakyan family is an Armenian story, "whichever door you knock on, you will hear a story like this or even sadder."[11] Armenians believe that they suffered more than any others in the Soviet Union. The Armenian secret police truly outdid itself. It was not enough to arrest and liquidate the Armenian writers and poets of significance. The police would raid their houses and the archives of the Writers' Union and destroy the manuscripts of the arrested literati. In some late-Soviet literary works, the terrors of the Stalin era are paralleled with the Genocide, two catastrophes twenty-five years apart. The memory of the Genocide of 1915 has resurfaced to serve as a parallel and a precedent.

In an interview in 1988, Sero Khanzadyan spoke of the years of Stalinist terror and the impact on Soviet Armenian literature: "For fifty years, they made our literature bend over and be subservient. It was forbidden to mention the names 'Western Armenia,' 'Armenian Karabagh,' 'Armenian Nakhijevan.' They shut our mouths to the word '*Eghern*' [Event, meaning genocide]. They crossed out and threw away anything in our writings which alluded to the concepts of exile, prison, Siberia. . . . [The memoirs of ex-prisoners show us today] that not only our literature but also the entire country was in a state of incarceration and exile."[12]

National Sentiments Aroused

Throughout the years of Soviet domination, the expression of nationalism in Armenia has fluctuated according to the political climate in Moscow. Proletarian, internationalist literature gave way to patriotism if there was a need to arouse the people's sentiments against foreign invaders—as it happened during World War II—or if the central government, entangled with internal sociopolitical problems, was unable to press hard and reinforce full censorship. An escalation of Armenian nationalism began with the outbreak of World War II, as Stalin's wartime policy called for Soviet patriotism to encourage the defense of the "motherland." In Armenian, the war was labeled as Patriotic War (Հայրենական պատերազմ). Patriotism, however, was diverted toward love for Armenia and, even more dangerously, toward the Armenian past and into a nostalgic recourse into the glories of historic Armenia.

The lenient central policy also resulted in the reevaluation and publication of the forbidden literature of the past. After all, Khachatur Abovian (1805-1848) was not a "backward bourgeois-liberal worshiper of the Russian capital but a true son of the Armenian people, a selfless, sacrificing symbol of love for the people."[13] (Notice that the carefully chosen word is people not nation—ժողովրդասիրութիւն not ազգասիրութիւն). Mikael Nalbandian's (1829-1866) yearning for freedom, Ghevond Alishan's (1820-1907) eulogy of Armenia, Mkrtich Peshiktashlian's (1828-1868) call for armed struggle to free the homeland, (Abovian's and Raffi's 1837-1888) dramatization of Armenian heroes in their struggle against foreign oppressors were published and widely read. Soon, original creations with nationalistic themes followed. The Great Patriotic War provided the subject; Armenian patriotism embellished the theme. The return to Armenian history to find parallels was another unique wartime phenomenon. For the first time in Soviet Armenian history, the subject of Armenian statehood and independence, albeit in the distant past, and the nation's struggle to keep that independence was undertaken in literature. Stepan Zoryan's *Pap Tagavor* (1943), Derenik Demirchyan's *Vardanank* (1943), and Nairi Zaryan's *Ara /ev Shamiram* (1944) are examples.[14] Soviet Armenian critics confirm that the concept of homeland in the wartime literature gradually evolved to encompass centuries-old history, the traditions, the past, the present, and the dreams of the future. These visions certainly did not belong to the "Great Homeland" (Մեծ Հայրենիք)—the Soviet Union.

Recourse to the distant past was tolerated, but writing openly about the Catastrophe of 1915 (Aghet) and the lands lost to Turkey was a political stance still off limits, unacceptable to the regime. Hovhannes Shiraz's "Hayots Danteakan" (The Armenian Dante-esque) was one such daring expression that crossed the line. This young and sensitive soul was deeply impressed by the stories he had heard from survivor-refugees with whom he liked so much to associate. He adopted their grief, made it his own tragedy and expressed it repeatedly in his literature. "Hayots Danteakan" was his masterpiece.

The first version of this long poem was written in 1941 (titled "Danteakan epopea"). Shiraz had gathered authentic photographs and documents from the Genocide and intended to publish them together with the poem in a separate volume. Publication was denied. Censors labeled the work as too nationalistic and suggested to delete some passages and to leave the photos and documents out completely. Shiraz was not ready to compromise. Short passages from the poem were published during the poet's life. Some chapters were published in Beirut and Tehran, significantly, before they appeared in the Soviet Armenian press. The entire work, over 8,000 lines in twenty-four chapters, with the photo-documents was published posthumously in 1990.[15] "Hayots Danteakan" reveals the author's perception of the Armenian Genocide, his philosophy of life, his humanistic views, and his urge to erect a spiritual monument in the memory of the victims of the Genocide. He speaks to the nations of the world reassuring that if anything like the Armenian Catastrophe were inflicted on any one of them, his heart of an Armenian poet would not remain silent as did theirs. He would scream in horror and sound the alarm with the bell of his conscience and the agony of his father. He would roar with the wail of a doleful nation and cry out for their deaths.

After World War II, nationalism was no longer needed. It had already served its purpose and had to be abolished. Indeed, nationalistic sentiments reverberating in wartime Soviet Armenian art and literature had gone too far. The poetry of Hovhannes Shiraz did not even have the camouflage of the trite themes such as the union of nations or the great homeland of the Soviet Union. It was physically woven around Armenia with all its spiritual, geographical, and historical attributes, with the freedom-loving Armenian nation at the core.

The task of suppressing nationalistic outbursts was accomplished with a strong wave of censorship on cultural expressions. A reevaluation of published works of past Armenian nationalist writers was made, and Raffi was condemned once again. To halt the tremendous impact of his novels, his books were banned and the Association of Soviet Armenian Writers published a declaration (1951) in which the "shortcomings" of Raffi's novels, especially *Kaitser* (Sparks) were pointed out. The declaration concluded that the publication of *Kaitser* was a "political mistake."[16] The persecution and purge of living writers followed. Gurgen Mahari, Vagharshak Norents, Vahram Alazan, and others were labeled as too nationalistic and were imprisoned or exiled, some for the second time.

Ironically, 1951 was the year when Shiraz, perhaps ignorant of the new policy, or rather in spite of it, wrote the poem "Ani," dedicated to the splendorous Armenian medieval capital city now under Turkish occupation, calling her home, pledging to do anything to bring her home. Despite his nationalistic aspirations, Shiraz was still a product of the system. He, too, sang the praise of the "Leader," Stalin, the "Father" of all nations. But even in these poems, he did not forget to appeal for the good of the nation, the return of Turkish-occupied historic Armenian lands. He called on Stalin, grateful for bestowing him a homeland—"You gave me my homeland. You won't let Ararat remain in exile."

This was not the approach of Shiraz's former wife, Sylva Kaputikyan, to Armenian history. Like many other young writers of her time, she was a true Communist, a believer in Stalin's ideal. Late in her life, she recalls a speech she delivered in 1952 in an Armenian writers' contest to win the Stalin medal. After forty years, she reads again the text of her zealous praise of Stalin and communism and asks herself: "Were these words sincere?" And she confesses in all honesty, "Yes, much to my chagrin and shame, they were sincere."[17]

Wounds of the Past and Irredentism

Artistic ideology was shaken after Stalin's death in 1953 and during the relative respite during the Khrushchev Thaw of the late 1950s and early 1960s, resulting in the revival of nationalistic literature in Armenia. This began with Anastas Mikoyan's statement in Erevan (1954), in which he reinstated the value of the works of Raffi and Rafayel Patkanian, despite what he termed their excessively nationalistic character. The purged Armenian writers and poets also were reinstated posthumously, and Mikoyan, who played a decisive role in Charents's imprisonment and murder, was the one praising his art.[18]

This was to be a period of uncertainty with contradicting vibes. It took much courage for Verjiné Svazlyan, a young researcher repatriated from Egypt, to travel around the country in 1955 and record tales and folksongs that the survivors of the Armenian Genocide had brought with them from the *Erkir* (Homeland)—Western Armenia—long ago and had kept them hidden in deep layers of their memory, safe from scornful and hostile surroundings. In the relatively more favorable conditions of the 1960s she initiated the collection of the survivor testimonies and eyewitness accounts of the Genocide. Despite the threatening atmosphere of Soviet censorship, the historical memory of the people persisted. Svazlyan collected this valuable material but without the hope of publishing it someday. In fact, it was only in the year 2000 that her monumental work was published.[19]

The strong censorship was yielding in the 1960s. European contemporary literature was filtering into the country, and the younger generation was avidly absorbing it. In that context, Karen Simonyan's publication of a series, in 1965, titled *Hamashkharhayin poezia* (International Poetry), was a welcomed initiative. Six issues were published before the project was condemned and halted. But this fresh air from Europe had already made a phenomenal impact.

Again in this same context, the publication of Hrand Hrahan's *Im kyanki vepe* (The Novel of My Life) in 1956 by the state publishing house Haypethrat was interesting. This "novel" is actually an autobiography, childhood memories of pain and suffering on the deportation routes during the 1915 Genocide. The annotation on the back of the title page clearly notes the topic to be "the mass extermination of the Western Armenian segment at the hands of Talaat, Enver and their colleagues, the leaders of sultanic Turkey (Սուլթանական Թուրքիա)." The narrative evolves around episodes of Turkish atrocities and provides historical information about the arrest and tragic fate of Komitas (1869-1935), Grigor Zohrab (1861-1915), and Ruben Sevak (1885-1915). After roaming the world as refugees, the surviving remnants of Hrahan's family repatriate to Soviet Armenia. "In Lieu of Epilogue" is a laudation of Soviet Armenia, "the revived and flourishing homeland of Armenians," and how happy Hrahan's family is in that paradise. Perhaps, this Epilogue was the price that Hrahan had to pay to publish the book.

Khachik Dashtents's *Khodedan* (the name of the protagonist) was published the same year and *Ranchparneri kanche* (The Call of the Tillers) a few years later. They are fictionalized realities to leave for posterity the homeland and the people that no longer exist. They were autobiographical novels of the Armenian collective experience under the Ottoman yoke. *Ranchparneri kanche* depicts the armed defense of Sasun against Turkish assaults. Here, in these two novels, the villages of Sasun, swept clean today of their indigenous Armenian population, come alive again. Dashtents takes your hand and leads you through the mountain passes and idyllic villages perched on the mountain skirts. The majestic landscape of Sasun is painted with vivid colors intermingled with village life from the author's childhood memories. He takes you inside the shacks where the *tonirs* are smoking, bread is baking, and children are playing. Life is going on, and then the Catastrophe, the massacres in Mush and Sasun.

Dashtents lived with the hope to see his birthplace, Sasun, free again. He dreamed of the day he could return to it. He spoke of the yearning that nested in many survivors' hearts in Armenia:

> My years, my years are passing.
> One is, you think, the repetition of the other.
> My eyes are always on the same light,
>   The same hope,
> To go and get to,
> To go and get to
> The mountains of Taurus.

Dashtents audaciously describes in his novels life as he sees it, hopeless monotony, eyes fixed on an uncertain unfeasible future. And this is in contradiction with the rosy image of life in the Soviet Union that the prescribed literature was to portray. Moreover, Dashtents dated *Khodedan*'s foreword 1956, May 28. One wonders if this is a coincidence or a deliberate mention of a significant date, May 28, the date of the birth of the first independent Republic of Armenia in 1918.

Curiously, government censorship had become more lenient toward literature that took its inspiration from the pre-Soviet Armenian past. Mourning the tragic loss of life and ancestral lands in 1915, demanding justice, pledging solemnly to bring home the Holy Mountain of Ararat and the occupied lands of historic Armenia were tolerated if these stayed within limits. That may have been in line with and served Soviet foreign policy of the time.

In this precarious period of fluctuating censorship, Paruyr Sevak's daring venture into capturing in poetry of epic grandeur the horrors of the Armenian Genocide for the first time in Soviet Armenia was another courageous deed. *Anlreli Zangakatun* (Ever-Tolling Bell Tower), a poem of more than 7,000 lines in forty-six chapters, was ready for publication in 1958. But the obstacles were many. Permission to publish was granted only on condition of heavy censorship. Thanks to Hamo Sahyan's intervention, the poem avoided the process and was published a year later with Sahyan as the editor. Stepan Alajajyan attests that heeding Stepan Zoryan's recommendation, Sevak added "Herosakan ghoghanch" (Heroic Peal), a chapter portraying the Armenian armed resistance against Turkish atrocities. This addition was made in the second edition of the poem. Alajajyan also remembers how Sevak bitterly asserted that Nairi Zaryan did not like the manuscript; Sergey Sarinyan reviewed it and liked only half of it, and Mkrtich Mkryan rejected it completely to earn membership to the Soviet Armenian Academy of Sciences.[20]

Anlreli Zangakatun embodies the life and work and the tragic fate of the great Armenian cleric composer Komitas Vardapet, ultimately a victim of the Genocide. But in reality, it is the story of Turkish atrocities and European politics. It is the songs, the labor, the customs, the joy and the tears, and the tradition of the Armenian people. It is the history of the Armenian national movement and armed struggle. Sevak was aware of the power of poetry and its "greater ability than prose to generate the most exact correlatives for feelings and states of consciousness,"[21] as Frieda Aaron puts it, and this, in response to an immense cataclysm like the Genocide. The impact was immense, and the work is still one of the most powerful literary responses to the Armenian Genocide.

Sero Khanzadyan's historical novel *Mkhitar Sparapet* (Commander Mkhitar, 1961) and Vahagn Davtyan's historical dramatic poem *Tondraketsiner* (The Tondrakians, 1960) are also brave explorations of the past, deliberations on the fate of the nation, and eulogies to the struggle for freedom. They, too, contributed to paving the way for a renewed Armenian national character and identity.

The popularity of *Tondraketsiner* was amazing. The authorities found in it all the tenets of Marxism-Leninism applied to the ninth-century "heretics" of Tondrak. There was the people's struggle against the exploiting clergy and the despotic rulers. There were victims and victimizers. But there was also a subtle undercurrent of alluding to the disillusion and disappointment caused by the unfulfilled promises of the Soviet regime. Vahagn Davtyan's reputation and popularity kept him away from the malice of the authorities. Collections of his poems were being published indiscriminately, without the omission of the ones where he sang the love of his birthplace in the province of Kharpert (Kharberd), his homeland lost.

In this proliferation of unconventional materials in the early 1960s, also noteworthy is Stepan Alajajyan's novelette *Piunik* (Phoenix, 1962). The novelette was published in the foray of many obstacles and was rejected a few times. It was an autobiography, the story of a repatriated family and the hardship it faced and the discontent and disenchantment it experienced in Soviet Armenia. To be sure, the author came under suspicion. He was ranked among the dissident writers of the 1960s and was called by the KGB for explanations.[22]

The rise of nationalism in the early 1960s in Armenia was significantly coupled with irredentism. The relatively relaxed atmosphere preceding 1965 had paved the way for a semi-secret national movement, which was also largely responsible for the turn of events on April 24, 1965, during the commemoration of the Armenian Genocide, a first in Armenia. The commemoration began with an innocent rally, soon to turn into a turbulent demonstration. People took to the streets demanding the return of Armenian lands under Turkish occupation. Historical memory had shattered its fetters and, bursting into the open, was gradually impregnating the ignorant masses, those who hardly knew about the scope of the colossal catastrophe that had befallen the nation fifty years ago.

In an article titled "Ayspes kochvats nasionalizmi masin" (About So-Called Nationalism), written in 1977 and published only posthumously in 1988, Mushegh Galshoyan chastised Soviet Armenian leaders for having denied the Armenian people the knowledge and awareness of the greatest tragedy in their history. By doing that, Galshoyan maintained, they had also denied the world the knowledge about this fateful event in the history of mankind. The first genocide of our century was turned into an Armenian *Eghern* [a strictly Armenian issue] and kept under locks, he writes. And then, they hesitantly and fearfully pulled this fragment of Armenian past out from under the locks and organized a formal commemoration of the *Mets Eghern* (The Great Event/Genocide) for the first time on April 24, 1965. Galshoyan attests that the masses on the street were confused, not knowing what the demonstrators were demanding. Many heard the word "*Eghern*" for the first time in their lives. They repeated the word, first without knowing the exact meaning of it, even distorting it to sound like *eghevni* (pine tree). But as Galshoyan puts it, the ignorant crowd grew larger and larger. The word passed on mouth to mouth and with it the imprisoned history was gradually being emancipated.[23]

"We have not forgotten the Մեծ Եղեռն (The Great Calamity). . . . Մեր Մեր հողերը . . . Մեր հողերը . . . (Our lands . . . Our lands)," the demonstrators shouted. The memory had been transmitted, no doubt. As Silva Kaputikyan writes, "it turns out that yes, they had not forgotten. The memory, the nation's historical memory, interwoven in the sighs of our grandparents, the constant grief in their eyes and their voices trembling with tears and yearning had really done the job."

You, unending anguish of the last tragedy,
When did you wake in my veins?
Did you come to spread into my eyes
From the yearning eyes of my Vanetsi grandmother?
Or spreading out of our orphan lands
You came as bushy thorns to wrap around me?
Or it was Komitas the embalmed grief
Who brought it to us when he returned home?
Or poor Tekeyan the exhausted singer of death
Shared with me his burden of sorrow?
Or maybe the fever of the wavering Diaspora
Shattered the peace of my soul . . .[24]

The poem manifests the influence of the Diaspora in veering Soviet Armenian political thought from the official line toward that which was dictated by national interests. The Armenian diasporan thoughts, ideologies, and especially patriotism, together with the liberalism of the West, had found their way into Armenia. Thus, once again nationalistic sentiments were let loose and patriotism as a theme began to reverberate in literature as an indication of the identity of Soviet Armenia leaning toward Armenianness. The works of purged writers like Charents and Bakunts were published and studied. The tragedy of 1915 took center stage.

Vahagn Davtyan, as a trusted established writer, was granted permission to make a pilgrimage to Deir el-Zor in 1977. His encounter with the open graves of the victims of the Genocide was phenomenal, and the outcome: his masterpiece, his most famous poem, "Rekviem" (Requiem). Later, in 1981, in a poem titled "Hogh im kisvats" (My Divided Land), he speaks of a remorse piercing his heart, an ever-burning wound: why was he born so late not to be able to shed his blood in the battle for the freedom of his homeland like a wounded fedayi in the mountains of Erzerum. He yearned for his blood to mix with the tears of Aratsani, the river running through his native land, and become a part of the mystery of his people's perpetuation.

Meanwhile, Vardkes Petrosyan's *Haykakan eskizner* (Armenian Sketches, 1969) had come as a natural evolution in this ongoing process. It was a search for a modern nationalism, a necessary ingredient for nation and state building. It elevated patriotism to a new level of consciousness, drawing its meaning and implications closer to that which prevailed in the Diaspora. Irredentism was the new dimension of this concept.

The Stalin Purges as a Second *Eghern* in Armenia

Significantly, while the political atmosphere in Soviet Armenia had become more permissive toward the Armenian past, it was still risky to talk about the years of Stalin's reign of terror. Of the thousands of exiled literati not many had returned, and those who returned after Stalin's death did not dare speak out about their ordeal, their torturous life in the gulags. Encouraged by the government's more tolerant approach to the freedom of art and literature and by the reassurance, or rather by wishful thought that the days of Stalinist censorship were over, the former victims began to put their memoirs in writing. Not one of them received permission to publish. This, of course, does not mean that these memoirs remained unknown and unread. The manuscripts were circulated. People knew about their existence and the overall content. That was the Armenian underground *Samizdat*.

Gurgen Mahari's memories of his exile, *Haykakan brigad* (Armenian Brigade) was ready in 1964. Publication was denied until the years of Perestroika in 1989. Nairi Zaryan's *Hartagoghi chamban* (The Milky Way), another eyewitness account of life in Stalin's prisons, was denied publication in 1963. That was also published in 1989.

Suren Ghazaryan, a former Chekist, and a victim of Stalin's persecutions, titled his memoirs written in the Russian language "That Should Not Be Repeated" and sent it to *Novyi Mir* monthly in 1967. In response, the editor, Russian poet Aleksandr Tvardovski praised Ghazaryan's courage, his determination to endure the tortures to stay alive and tell the world about his ordeal. He complimented the author's style, clarity of diction, and the vivid imagery but added that the publication of this work was out of the question. Tvardovski was nonetheless hopeful: "Some day, this and many other memoirs like this will be published and will render service to communism." Ghazaryan's memoirs were translated into Armenian as *Da chpetke krknvi* and published in 1987.[25] It was one of the earliest of such publications in Armenia, before others found their way out of the locked drawers into the light of day. The possible reason is that Ghazaryan's memoirs were published in Russian first. Thus, it was all right to translate and publish it in Armenia.

Gurgen Mahari's novelette, *Tsaghkats pshalarer* (Blooming Barbed Wires), a testimony of torture and death in Stalin's prison camps, was published in 1988. But as Davit Gasparyan attests, the work was already known to the public after it was first published in installments in *Nayiri* in Beirut, between 1971 and 1972. Throughout the narrative, together with scenes of torture and agonizing life in the prison camps and dark solitary cells, echoes Mahari's unquenched yearning for his birthplace of Van. Nostalgic reminiscences reveal themselves in the most unexpected places in *Tsaghkats pshalarer*. "I quenched my longing for the rivers of my birthplace from Hrazdan, my longing for Van from Erevan. And they thought it was too much. They deprived me of that; they made me a criminal in one night and locked me in a dark prison cell."[26] Mahari was a wretched, broken man when he returned. His youthful vigor, he confessed, his love for life and his stamina to create had fallen victim to the suffocating atmosphere of Stalin's prisons, as his happy childhood remained buried under the thick walls of the citadel of his beloved Van.[27]

The era of relative freedom had been coming to a gradual end with Brezhnev's rise to power and his efforts to close the hatches of the post-Stalin relative leniency. The mysterious deaths of Paruyr Sevak in 1971, Minas Avetisyan, the distinguished painter, in 1975, Mushegh Galshoyan in 1980, and still others were seen as evidence of renewed covert persecutions. Even the concept of *dissidentia* had acquired a fluid meaning to rationalize persecutions.

Was Arshak (Sergey Arshakyan) a dissident? He was an amateur writer, a metallurgist by profession, in the 1960s writing about the love of freedom, the love of homeland, and childhood reminiscences of the persecutions of the Stalin era. That was not permissible. The KGB called him in for some "explanations." *Gnchuhin* (The Gypsy Woman), the novel he wrote in 1977, was denied publication. Arshak had gone too far. Hrach Simonyan, the protagonist in this novel is a young man of dreams and imagination. He is the leader of a group of Russian miners, but he feels inferior, because he has lost a homeland (Western Armenia). The rivers Tigris and Euphrates have turned their backs to him. And yet, these elements are the main ingredients of his identity. He is ashamed in front of his Russian co-workers, because he does not have seas and rivers. He dreams of them but does not have the power and the will to get them back.[28] He is in love. He is under the spell of a gypsy woman not only because of her extraordinary beauty but also because of her people's spirit of freedom and the universal love that she embodies.[29] In her wisdom he sees the secret of "the evil that threatened to annihilate my people, that put the sword on the throat of my city as a boundary line."[30] Simonyan's childhood memories are shrouded by the repressions of the Stalin era. He has made all the decisions of his life not by his own will but by following orders "in the nightmare of those dark years." As a young boy he accompanied his mother to the party meetings every night, "as a shield and a protector." Because "if she didn't go to these meetings, it would prove that she was an accomplice to my executed father and shared his enmity against the Leader [Stalin]. And they would take her too. . . . She took me along, so that they would not take her temporarily—because she was very pretty—or for good, because she was my father's wife."[31] This novel along with other provocative works by this author was published beginning from 1995.

The Nationalistic Movement and the Karabagh Conflict

According to a survey on Soviet dissident artists, "the nonconformist movement began [in Russia] in the late 1950s and ended in Perestroika in 1987 when artists who had not adhered to the acceptable styles and ideology of socialist realism came out, as it were, from underground."[32] But state censorship before

Perestroika had been harsher in Armenia than in Russia itself, as evidenced by the fate and relatively small quantity of the nonconformist writings in Armenia. It also took longer for the Armenian KGB to loosen its grip—if it ever did—on Armenian life. And then, there was the even harsher self-inflicted censorship, "Would they publish this? No, this is not publishable. They will once again reject it." The wave of Perestroika, thus, was late in reaching Armenia. Publications of rejected material proliferated in the years between 1988 and 1991. These were mostly reminiscences of the devastating years of Stalin's rule of terror. The works of older generation poets were also being pulled out of their coffins, the boxes locked in the archives, and published.

It was time for the public to know about what remained under locks for decades. Among these were Avetik Isahakyan's "Hayduki erger" (Fedayi Songs) and two poems by Hovhannes Tumanyan, "Hin krive" (The Old Fight) and "Verjin ore" (The Last Day). Isahakyan's "Hayduki erger" obviously praised the Armenian freedom movement of the late nineteenth century, scorned and neglected by the Soviet historiography. These poems also manifested that the author's political orientation was not congruent with the Communist ideology. Tumanyan's "Hin krive" was written in the late 1890s and, as Hovhannes Ghanalanyan attests, was confiscated and destroyed by the tsarist authorities because it laid bare the Russian stance against the Armenian Cause and the tsarist real politic. Russians came to rescue Armenians in the name of Christ, Tumanyan wrote, and they thanked God to see the carnage and the Armenian lands devoid of Armenians. Soviet censorship continued the trend and the poem was left out of the publication of his *Erkeri zhoghovatsu* (Collection of Works). "Verjin ore," on the other hand, was an ode to the military operations of the Armenian volunteer army in 1915.[33] That, too, was censored.

The Iron Curtain separating the Soviet Union from the Western world had been lifted even long before Perestroika. European trends and ideas kept penetrating. The Armenian youth growing up in the 1970s and the 1980s zealously read the Soviet dissident literature, especially that of Solzhenitsyn. They inhaled the nationalistic air of the Armenian Diaspora, and followed the road set forth by the more daring, rebellious souls. Henrik Edoyan, Armen Martirosyan, Davit Hovhannes, Hrach Sarukhan, Hovhannes Grigoryan, Alvart Petrosyan, and others were able to forge modern Soviet Armenian literature, which was not necessarily nationalistic but certainly national. They were not the propagandists of the Soviet official line but modern nationalists who were able to absorb the new, the Western, the diasporan Armenian, and to create the spiritual atmosphere for a national revival. In a way, the dissident generation of 1965 had with its writings prepared the ground for the movement of 1988, which reached its apex in the massive demonstrations demanding the liberation of Mountainous Karabagh (Artsakh) from repressive Azerbaijani rule.[34] The leaders of this movement were none other than the writers and poets of yesterday, now turned political activists.

Between the years 1988, the beginning of the Karabagh movement, and 1991, the birth of the independent Republic, Armenians suffered two major cataclysms. One was a natural disaster, the terrible earthquake that left entire cities, towns, and villages in ruins—more than 50,000 dead and a population of survivors maimed physically and emotionally. The other was a manmade disaster, an echo of the 1915 Genocide, now against the Armenians of Azerbaijan—massacres and flight in Sumgait, Baku, and Ganja. Characteristically, the memory of the Genocide of 1915 was resurrected in the literary responses to both catastrophes.

Just a few weeks after the earthquake, Davit Hovhannes composed a free verse, an emotional response to this disaster. "Haverzhakan haye" (The Eternal Armenian) embodied the determination of the Armenian people to persevere and perpetuate against all odds, be it the *Eghern* or the earthquake. In this poem the eternal Armenian, a collective persona, is God, a Son of God, a mother gone mad, an unburied father, a son under the wreckage. It encapsulates at the same time the images of a wretched victim and a triumphant and omnipotent God as a symbol of eternity.

The memory of the earthquake and its physical impact persisted for more than a decade. Arevshat Avagyan's poem "Mite pordzadasht e Hayastane" (Is Armenia a Testing Ground?) is a protest against the universe, which brought about that horrendous disaster, just as it is against the perpetrators of the Genocide. "Is Armenia a testing ground where *Eghern* and earthquake and the blockade are tested?" The Armenian patience is strong, but it, too, has its limits. "Maybe, indeed, Armenia is a testing ground to reach the eternity of spirit."[35] Avagyan strikes a familiar note, a traditional explanation for extreme suffering which lasted for centuries and helped the disaster-stricken survivor reach a healing catharsis. God is always testing the love of his most devoted people. Martyrdom in the name of God is rewarded with eternal life.

Many poets sang the courage of the new fedayis in the battle against the Azeri oppressors. Fallen victim once again to the Azeri-Turkish atrocities, it was impossible not to remember the genocide committed by the forefathers of today's perpetrators. It was not possible to mourn the loss of the districts of Shahumyan and Getashen and not to remember Mush and Van. Robert Karayan's poetry is recourse to this past. It evokes the memory of the massacres of 1915 and the acts of self-defense against the Turkish army. "Shushva krvi vordik kajazun" (The Brave Sons of the Battle of Shushi), "Hnik erger" (Little Old Songs), "Enkats kajordinerin" (To the Fallen Brave), "Te es enknem" (If I Fall) manifest the parallel imagery between two tragedies that befell the Armenian nation seventy-two years apart.[36]

The massacres in Sumgait, Baku, and Ganja reawakened the memory of the Genocide in Maksim Hovhannisyan and are reflected in his collection of stories and essays, *Artsakh im, tsav im* (My Artsakh, My Pain). The memory of the past tragedies reverberates in the contemporary carnage. The struggle in Artsakh, the life and the joys and pains of its people—the Artsakhtsis—come alive in these stories. Here, Heydar Aliev, the Azeri president is described as "the new leader of genocide, a new shoot from Talaat's generation."[37]

In a satirical rendering of an Azerbaijani professor's presentation at a conference at Columbia University, Hovhannisyan quotes the professor bragging about the historical truth he had revealed in that conference and how he declared that Armenians were newcomers who settled late in Transcaucasia. They were mostly refugees from Iran and Turkey, he had explained. And to update his audience, he added, "As you know, Armenians lived in Eastern Anatolia before, not now."[38]

Ruzanna Asatryan's *Shushi* (2003) is a narrative poem of more than 450 lines, an ode to the liberation of Shushi, the jewel city of the old Armenian culture. The city was Turkified after Stalin granted the control of Mountainous Karabagh to Azerbaijan. The poem depicts the heroic battle the new fedayis waged to accomplish that amazing feat. And the massacres of 1915 are in the background, appearing as parallel situations, as metaphor, as sources of historic interpretation. The memory of the old fedayis of Western Armenia adorns the images of new bravery.[39]

The Literary Milieu of Independent Armenia

In the atmosphere of independent Armenia, one can suggest that all the basic components of a modern national literature are now in place. The atmosphere is ripe for the rebirth of national literature: the language, the soil, the presence of a common history and common destiny for almost three million people living in their homeland, sharing the same ethnic identity. The interruption of historical memory is mended. The Turkish-Armenian restrained relationship is a part of everyday life in Armenia. The memorial complex of Tsitsernakaberd and the majestic duo of Sis and Masis (the two peaks of Mount Ararat) that hover above the Erevan landscape are constant reminders of the historical injustice. Metakse, the renowned poetess of Armenia, who sings of a woman's most intimate sentiments, the beauty, the pain, and the pleasures of love, who sings the glory of God and exalts nature's splendor, could not remain indifferent toward that monument that embodies so much meaning, the suffering of the past and the aspirations of the future. In the poem "Tsitsernakaberdum" (At Tsitsernakaberd), she pictures the poetic grandeur of the sky above the monument, the gathering of the clouds and nature's preparation to mourn over the victims of the Armenian Genocide. And the sky is shedding tears; the clouds bow in reverence to lament the spilling of Armenian innocent blood.[40]

After more than a decade of independence, however, the Soviet experience still weighs heavily in the minds of the masses. Mushegh Galshoyan's thoughts back in 1977 negating this mentality have not yet taken root. "While weeping and wailing are useless," he wrote, "writing about twisted fates and shattered spirits as the effects of the Catastrophe is a very contemporary issue."[41] There are still those who believe that the Genocide concerns the Diaspora alone. It is the Diaspora's source of pain, political aspirations, and literary inspiration. There are still those who follow the line of thought imposed by Soviet-Turkish politics that writing or speaking about or even remembering the Genocide is masochism. Soviet citizens, the official line propagated, should always look forward to the future. What is the use of digging into the past? It was with the dissemination of this mentality, together with calculated policies vis-à-vis the Armenian Diaspora that the Soviet regime succeeded in creating a chasm between the two segments of the Armenian nation, a chasm that still refuses to bind.

The rediscovery of the past and the confrontation with the Catastrophe have not gone very far among Armenian writers. Instead of finding their way into the world of fetter-free, non-tendentious literature, instead of impregnating the soil for the rebirth of a national literature, many writers are engaged in a reactionary exercise against the Soviet era. This reaction is not about returning to the forbidden roots of the tradition of the nineteenth-century Armenian literature. The nationalistic themes permeating the literature of that era do not speak to the souls of today's Armenians in Armenia. The reactionary exercise is the experimentation in other forbidden grounds: the realistic description of life and morality or rather immorality as it is, the reality that existed and was carefully covered up in the Soviet era and not that which was prescribed to be recorded by the Soviet authorities. Graphic accounts of sexual encounters, perverted love affairs, and street life are abundant in some post-Soviet works of writers such as Gurgen Khanjyan, Norair Adalyan, and Violet Grigoryan.

These observations lead one to think, however, that the literature of Armenia of the 1990s represented a reactionary phase or, more optimistically, a transitional one. And that is a normal phase after an era of prescribed content in socialist realism. I can see the seeds of a healthy national literature sprouting its delicate shoots. The Armenian literati still bears the flag of nationalism, which brought about its crucifixion in the Soviet era and is leading people today toward national aspirations. Robert Yesayan, Ludvik Duryan, Ruben Vardanyan, Gurgen Gabrielyan, voices, young and new, echo the sufferings of the past and demand justice and retribution.[42]

The old yearning becomes a source of inspiration and finds a new outlet in the free atmosphere of independent Armenia:

> I saw a dream. It was Van and Aigestan,
>
> . . . .
>
> Three girls of the same age are murmuring in secret.
> Young and slim three girls like three sisters,
> I realize suddenly it's grandma, mother, and I.
>
> . . . .
>
> It is war in Van, fires, the loud fanfare is calling.
> Tired and miserable the three women carry bread to the battlefield,
> Three women are walking with difficulty on the deportation route,

It seems they stop near the walls of Erevan.
Do not ask. That's us again, grandma, mother, and me.[43]

The memory of the catastrophic events in her grandmother's birthplace is so vivid that Silva Kaputikyan sees herself caught within that tragedy. She is a player in that tragedy as a young girl living in Van, then as a new bride participating in the self-defense of Van, and finally, as a wretched refugee behind the walls of Erevan. Is it possible to live in a catastrophic event in the past just like the present without having been there? Elie Wiesel says: "Yes, one can live a thousand miles away from the Temple and see it burn. One can die in Auschwitz after Auschwitz."[44]

The discovery of the past and gradual awareness of the transmitted memory is best exemplified in Arevshat Avagyan's poetry. This accomplished poet and painter published several volumes of poetry, the first in 1963. But historical memory began to creep into his poetry only after 1974, reflecting more intensely in his last collection in 2003. He is the son of a refugee from Mokats Ashkharh (Moks). He is a continuation of his father's hopes and dreams, and the seeds of historical memory are cultivated in his soul through the reminiscences of his childhood—a father's yearnings and a mother's anathema. He knows how to fly through time, through centuries of Armenian history for the sake of the future renewal. In the poem "Patgam" (Bidding), he admonishes the new generation to love the light of knowledge, fellow human beings, and,

Before everything else
And after everything else
Love your homeland which is red in your veins
Its sky that shines deep in your eyes
And love the road to eternity
That continues through your feelings and your days.[45]

Avagyan's poetry is a struggle for the perpetuation of universality and the continuity of Armenian life and spirit, the continuation of historical memory. His art is a bridge between the past and the future, lest the future is severed from its roots in the past as was done once in the author's lifetime. Characteristically, his art becomes more and more deeply embedded in history and in the memory of his forefathers, the battles they fought, the identity they carved in his soul.

Rafayel Ghazanchyan initiates the publication of the memoirs of his father, a Genocide survivor. In the introduction of the volume he writes: "How is it possible not to see the enchanting images of lost horizons in the gazes of these eyewitnesses of the Catastrophe, not to feel their hope and aspiration to return to their homes? The silly preaching of some not to 'dig up' the past sounds totally absurd."[46]

The contemporary writer looks to the past for an answer to the historical injustice, and the echoes of present Turkish-Armenian relations come across in various voices. Aghasi Aivazyan's "Antun turke" (The Homeless Turk) and Henrik Edoyan's call "Hey, Turkish Poets" in "Turk banasteghtsnerin"(To Turkish Poets) are significant achievements.[47]

Davit Muradyan depicts life in Armenia in the 1950s in "Hrazhesht," but the thread of memory extends far back, the odyssey of the Gisakyan family of Kharpert, the hardship and loss of loved ones in the deportation route and exile, and the continuing predicament under Stalin's rule of terror in Soviet Armenia. Muradyan has a unique delineation of how memory is transmitted or "how the memories of others suddenly become yours."

> Not suddenly though, but slowly growing in your life. Like a stone tied to your foot, or like the rope connecting mountaineers together, something you have no right to let go. Complete strangers appear before your eyes. You even hear their voices. Things that you have never touched seem to have been seen a thousand times. Episodes that you have not been a part of, you live them through as an eyewitness. Those who pass away leave their life to us. This is the silver thread.[48]

The horrors of the Stalin era continue to appear at least as a secondary theme in literature, as they are certainly a part of the childhood memory of today's older Armenian writers. Interwoven with that life is yet the silver thread coming from farther back. Ruben Hovsepyan's *Levon Pap* (Grandpa Levon) has gone through many a hardship during the deportations and then in Soviet Armenia during the difficult years of Stalin's reign. His family history is an evidence of the lifestyle prescribed by the regime. In it the ties with the old and the traditional are disrupted. Levon Pap is a sad witness to that. He tries to salvage something from the past by adopting an orphan from Mush, a boy who faced death, as did many others like him. He endured hardship, famine and cold on the road of deportation. "The snow in the valley of Mush is red now."[49] There are such deep and rich implications in this brief but mysterious statement. The link with the past, the historical memory, manifests itself in Levon Pap's hopeless struggle to salvage and revive the discarded and despised culture of Cochineal; for him that red worm has become the symbol of national values trampled upon.

Aghasi Aivazyan writes about contemporary life in Erevan but the silver thread of memory expanded back in history. "On New Year's day in 1892 we were 27 of us," Kirakos remembers, even though he was generations away from being born, and by saying "we" Kirakos means his family, his forefathers. "On New Year day in 1916 we were three. He [Kirakos's father] celebrated the New Year alone in 1920 in our home in Erevan. He was almost dead when they became two again. . . . The second was my mother, another starving refugee, who stood on the threshold of my refugee father's home and said, "Happy New Year."[50]

****

There is renewed interest in Armenia to rediscover the past and deal with it. This interest stretches among the entire scope of intelligentsia in various domains and among the literati for that matter. The impetus is certainly the closer relationship with the Diaspora and thus acquaintance with and understanding of the diasporan Armenian psyche, goals, and aspirations. Then, there is the Turkish-Armenian, and in that context also the Azerbaijani-Armenian relationship with most recent tragedies, and on top of it all the continuing denial of the truth of the Armenian Genocide that challenges the minds and the sanity of sensitive souls and demands response, literary response as a catharsis, as a protest, and as a sanctuary of historical memory. This is the thread, the silver thread that grows thinner with time but never breaks, that is if those in the Diaspora and in Armenia hold it between their fingers and walk in its path.

Notes

1. Israel Gershoni, "Imagining and Reimagining the Past," in *History and Memory* 4, 2 (1992): 5, quotation from E. H. Carr, *What is History?* (London, 1964), p. 30.
2. See Rubina Peroomian, *Literary Responses to Catastrophe: A Comparison of the Armenian and the Jewish Experience* (Atlanta: Scholars Press, 1993), in which the literary responses to historical catastrophes culminating in the Genocide of 1915 are analyzed; idem, "New Directions in Literary Responses to the Armenian Genocide," in *Looking Backward, Moving Forward: Confronting the Armenian Genocide*, ed. Richard G. Hovannisian (New Brunswick, NJ, and London: Transaction Publishers, 2003), pp.157-180, in which responses of the second- and third-generation writers are examined.
3. From the poem, "Champortutiun 1" [Journey 1] in *Selected Poems*, a bilingual edition, trans. Armine Tamrazian (Macmillan Education, printed in Malaysia, 2002), p. 110.
4. Davit Muradyan, "Hrazhesht" [Farewell], a novella in *Gnatskner ev Kayaranner* [Trains and Stations] (Erevan: "Van Aryan," 2001), pp. 115-184, quotation, p. 123.
5. Ibid., p. 124.
6. "Socialist Realism and the Holocaust: Jewish Life and Death in Anatoly Rybakov's *Henry Sand*," in *Publication of the Modern Language Association of America (PMLA)* (March 1996): 240-255, quotations, endnote N-2 and p. 241.
7. David Roskies, "Foreword" to Frieda W. Aaron's *Bearing the Unbearable* (New York: State University of New York Press, 1990), p. ix.
8. Suren Sahakyan, *Herosapatum* [Tales of Heroes] (Erevan: Arevik Press, 1990). The passage on p. 118 is an example. The political atmosphere of the time and especially the ongoing conflict with the Azerbaijanis made it necessary to resurrect hitherto forgotten individual fedayis of the Armenian armed struggle and glorify them as national heroes and inspiring role models, deliberately leaving out the details of planning and organizing the movement. The Communist regime had set the trend and the Armenian National Movement, the party at the center stage and ruling the newly independent Republic, reinforced it.
9. Ibid., p. 5.
10. Ruben Zaryan, "Erku khosk" [Two Words], *Bagin* [*Pakine*], no. 7-9 (1995): 125.
11. Muradyan, "Hrazhesht," p. 148.
12. See Sero Khanzadyan's interview in *Grakan Tert* (1988), no. 49, quoted in *Bagin*, no. 9-10 (1991): 26.
13. Zvart Ghukasyan, *Sovetahay grakanagitutyune* [Soviet Armenian Literary Criticism] (Erevan: Armenian Academy of Sciences, 1981), p. 234.

14. *Pap Tagavor* is about the deeds of Pap, a fourth-century Armenian king, known for his strong stand for Armenian statehood and for the structural reforms he imposed on the Armenian Church. *Vardanank* is the story of the historic battle that the Armenians waged in A.D. 451 against the Persian king to defend their political independence and freedom to practice their Christian religion. *Ara ev Shamiram* is based on a legend depicting the Armenian struggle against the legendary Assyrian queen Semiramis's assaults and encroachments.
15. See *Bagin*, no. 9-10 (1991): 44-47, for an interview with Sipan Shiraz, the author's son, on the occasion of the publication of *Hayots Danteakan* [The Armenian Danteesque] and a segment from the poem. The interview had been originally published in *Grkeri Ashkharh*, no. 6 (1990).
16. See Levon Ghazaryan's article on the impact of Raffi's *Kaitser*, in *Hay grakanutyune patma-gortsarakan lusabanutiamb* [The Armenian Literature by Historio-Practical Explanation] (Erevan: Armenian Academy of Sciences, 1989), p. 324.
17. Silva Kaputikyan, *Echer pak gzrotsnerits* [Pages from Closed Drawers] (Erevan: Apolon, 1997), p. 14. This interesting collection of unpublished essays, texts of various speeches, letters, and poetry is divided into three parts: "Before 1988," "1988," and "After 1988." This categorization demonstrates Kaputikyan's perception of 1988 (the year the Karabagh movement was unleashed) not only as a turning point in the history of Armenia but also as a turning point in her own political activism. Many pieces included in this book speak of the author's nationalistic sentiments and her covert sense of belonging to the spiritual homeland she came to know through her grandmother's stories of pain, hope, and yearning.
18. In a poem dedicated to Charents, long before the exoneration of the poet, Khachik Dashtents expressed confidence that there will come a day when Charents will rise again from the dead and his art will find its deserved appreciation. And on that day, Dashtents asserts, those who condemned him most zealously will be the ones who will rush to the podiums to anoint their cursed past with the light of his memory. His prediction came true. See *Bagin*, no. 7-9 (1995): 88.
19. Verjiné Svazlyan audio-recorded or videotaped and authenticated testimonies and songs of historical significance of the survivors over the last fifty years both in Armenia and abroad. *Hayots Tseghaspanutyun, akanates veraproghneri vkayutyunner* [The Armenian Genocide, Testimonies of Eyewitness Survivors], published in 2000, contains 600 testimonies. In *Hayots Tseghaspanutyune ev patmakan hishoghutyune* [The Armenian Genocide and the Historical Memory, 2003], Svazlyan describes how in these difficult years of Soviet rule, in dire conditions and circumstances beginning in 1955, she initiated the collection of folk songs and tales of the Old Country and expanded her search in the 1960s to collect survivor testimonies of the Turkish atrocities of 1915.
20. For more details, see Stepan Alajajyan, *Champezri vra* [Alongside the Road] (Los Angeles: Nor Kyank, 1998), p. 53. *Champezri vra* is a compilation of his memoirs, notes, and reminiscences about contemporaries and overall life in the trying years of the 1960s in Soviet Armenia.
21. Aaron, *Bearing the Unbearable,* p. 1.
22. Alajajyan speaks of his bitter experience when his novelette, "Piunik," was being scrutinized in *Champezri vra.*
23. Galshoyan's article was eventually published in *Garun,* no. 8 (1988), quoted in *Bagin*, no. 9-10 (1991): 110-123, quotation p. 111.
24. Silva Kaputikyan, *Tsave nuynpes tsnum e neruzh* [Pain Can Also Give Birth to Inner Strength] in *Hayatsk Erevanits*, no. 4 (25) (April 2000): 5. The last two lines are, most likely, a reference to her visit to the diasporan Armenian communities in 1962. From this journey she returned transformed, full of awe and praise for the spirit,

the Armenianness, and the struggle against assimilation she had witnessed. She even had the audacity to suggest that the KGB follow the example of the Diaspora to commemorate April 24 every year (See *Echer pak gzrotsnerits*, p. 58).

25. For information about this memoir and a segment from it, see *Bagin*, no. 9-10 (1991): 3-21, and for the letter, 3-4.
26. Gurgen Mahari, *Tsaghkats pshalarer* [Blooming Barbed Wires] (Erevan: Sovetakan Grogh, 1988), p. 21.
27. Ibid., p. 48.
28. Arshak, *Gnchuhin* [The Gypsy-Woman] (Erevan: "Vark", 1995), p. 13.
29. Ibid., p. 59.
30. Ibid., p. 45.
31. Ibid., p. 20.
32. Renee Baigell and Matthew Baigell, *Soviet Dissident Artists* (New Brunswick, NJ: Rutgers University Press, 1995), preface, p. xi.
33. Hovhannes Ghanalanyan's article "Erku khosk" [Two Words] was published in *Hayastani Hanrapetutyun*, April 2, 1991, and quoted in *Bagin*, no. 9-10 (1991): 66-70.
34. Dissidence or dissident literature does not have the same connotation in Armenia as in the rest of the Soviet Union. While the Moscow dissidents were in disagreement with the Communist regime, the Armenian dissident literature was national in spirit, rooted in history, connected to the past, stemming from the impact of the Armenian Genocide, the loss of life and homeland.
35. Arevshat Avagyan, *Hangrvanner* [Phases] (Erevan: "Nor Dar," 2003), p. 353.
36. Robert Karayan, *Lusabatsnerin endharaj* [Welcoming the Dawns] (Los Angeles: Hayasa, 1999).
37. Maksim Hovhannisyan "Terunakan aghotk" [Lord's Prayer], in *Artsakh im, tsav im* [My Artsakh, My Pain] (Erevan: Nayiri, 1998), quotation, p. 151.
38. Ibid., from an essay, *Mister Sviatikhovskin haytnagortsum e* [Mr. Sviatikhovski is Making a Discovery], pp. 237-238.
39. Ruzanna Asatryan, *Shushi* (Erevan: "Amaras," 2003).
40. Metakse, *Erb es galu Ter?* [When Are You Coming, Lord?] (Erevan: Nayiri, 2003), p. 93.
41. See note 23, quotation on p. 114.
42. For more works of contemporary artists in response to the Genocide of 1915, see Peroomian, "New Directions in Literary Responses," pp. 174-178.
43. Silva Kaputikyan, "Hin karot" [Old Yearning] from *Echer pak gzrotsnerits*, p. 658.
44. Alan L. Berger and Naomi Berger, eds., *Second Generation Voices: Reflections by Children of Holocaust Survivors and Perpetrators* (Syracuse, NY: Syracuse University Press, 2001), p.1.
45. Avagyan, *Hangrvanner*, p. 107.
46. Rafayel Ghazanchyan, *Hayrakan tseragir* [Father's Manuscript] (Erevan: Graber, 2003), p. 3.
47. For a discussion of these two works, see Peroomian, "New Directions in Literary Responses."
48. Muradyan, "Hrazhesht," p. 143.
49. Ruben Hovsepyan, *Es tser hishoghutyunn em* [I Am Your Memory], collection of short stories and novellas (Erevan: Armenian Writers' Union, 2003), quotation from *Vordan Karmir* [Cochineal Red] novella, p. 30.
50. Aghasi Aivazyan, *Entir erker* [Selected Works] (Erevan: Nairi, 2001), from the story *Kirakos*. p. 9.

8

Léon Tutundjian—TRAuma in ART

Jean Murachanian

The following analysis considers the artistic legacy of an Armenian artist, Léon Tutundjian, who survived the Armenian Genocide of 1915 as a young boy. He later immigrated to Paris where he eventually established himself as an artist. In 1915, the Armenian people suffered a near annihilation and were driven from their historic homeland in the Ottoman Empire. The Turkish government insisted the catastrophe was an unfortunate side effect of World War I, but the survivors knew that was not the case. As one of many survivors who made their way to France, Tutundjian's artistic legacy provides a pictorial account of how this first generation dealt with its painful memories in the aftermath.[1]

Tutundjian was a prolific and talented artist. His extensive body of work includes a repetition of faces in various media and styles which I have interpreted as self-portraits. Utilizing trauma theory, I argue that the portraits reveal the repercussions of his genocide experience and its effect on his sense of self.

Like many survivors, Tutundjian never talked about his genocide experience. In the aftermath most avoided discussing their distressing past and repressed the associated memories.[2] Tutundjian was a man of few words and instead expressed himself visually through his art, though he even avoided elucidating and titling his images.[3] Hence, trauma theory provides a new avenue with which to access Tutundjian's art.[4] In an effort to further my understanding of this artist, I also met with his only child, Léa Vinet in Paris.

Looking at Tutundjian's artistic legacy through the lens of trauma theory, one can discern the repercussions of his genocide experience and the resulting fracturing of his psyche. Tutundjian had a seeming fascination with his self-portraits, which communicate his trauma through their repeated return to the scene of the shock during his youth. The self-portraits reveal a split sense of self as evidenced by a doubling within the portraiture, and a disconnection from himself and the world around him due to the fragmented nature of his representation and the lack of background settings. Subtle changes in his portraits over time suggest a gradual working through of his trauma as he began to reconnect and integrate his painful past through the process of narration—the telling of his story through art.

Biography

Léon (Levon) Tutundjian was born in Amasia, in Sivas (Sebastia) province in the Ottoman Empire in 1905. According to his daughter, Léa Vinet, Tutundjian came from a relatively wealthy and educated family—his father and his grandfather were teachers. He went to good schools, learned to speak French, and dreamed of moving to Paris.[5] Unfortunately, the family moved often so his father could procure teaching jobs. Tutundjian's life changed dramatically when his father died from a cerebral hemorrhage around 1915.[6] Without a primary provider, the family was soon destitute and Tutundjian's mother was forced to sell the family's possessions to care for her children.[7] However, the family did settle down for a time and Tutundjian was able to study at the Berberian and Getronagan schools in Constantinople since his father had taught there.

In 1921-22, Tutundjian's mother placed her son on a boat with other Armenian orphans headed to Greece from Constantinople.[8] He was sixteen or seventeen years of age at the time, older than most of the orphans, but the separation from his mother was still difficult for him. According to Vinet, because of the sad memories associated with this parting, Tutundjian always hated to travel, particularly on boats. In 1923, he stayed briefly at the Armenian monastery of the Mekhitarist Brotherhood in Venice, Italy, where he studied science and Armenian illuminated manuscripts.

In 1924, at the age of nineteen, Tutundjian arrived in Paris and studied art at the École des Beaux-Arts. His mother remained behind and stayed in touch with her son through letters, though Tutundjian was often remiss about corresponding.[9] Nevertheless, he waited until his mother's death to marry his French bride in 1933. The couple had one child, Léa, in 1935. According to Vinet, her father was loving but tended to keep to himself. He did have some close friends, such as the Armenian artist Ervand Kochar, and would occasionally visit the cafés of Montparnasse in the evenings. Vinet described her father as being completely consumed by his work and "always in his head," constantly working through ideas for his visual expression.[10]

Tutundjian showed early artistic promise. Within two years of his arrival in Paris, he exhibited at the opening of the Galerie Surréaliste, and three years later he was the featured artist in a group show at the Galerie des Editions Bonaparte. Over the years he exhibited widely, though at times sporadically, and generated various reactions from the critics. He was a prolific and driven artist, creating more than a thousand images in several media and styles. He never concerned himself with becoming famous. Fortunately, he supplemented his income by working as a ceramicist, a skill he learned while in Greece.[11]

Tutundjian came of age artistically in the early twentieth century when international struggles, reeling under the impact of modernity, nationalism, and technological warfare, resulted in the explosion of numerous artistic styles and movements in response to a rapidly changing world. Early in his career he experimented with several abstract or non-figural styles. In 1930, he co-founded the abstract *Art Concret Group* with well-known artists, Théo van Doesburg, Jean Hélion, and Otto Carlsung, heady company for a young Armenian immigrant. In 1933, he changed styles abruptly with the figural language of surrealism, which occupied him until 1960, though this long period was interrupted by the events of World War II; first by his brief military service and then by the difficult years under Vichy rule and the war's aftermath. In 1960 he returned to abstraction until his death in 1968.

Tutundjian changed styles frequently early in his career, suggesting that he was searching for a mode of expression that could adequately express his internal misery. Surrealism, therefore, might have been especially attractive to him because its associations with dreams and the unconscious could have provided him with the means to work through the genocidal horrors his conscious mind could not address directly. When he arrived in Paris at the age of nineteen he had not only experienced the Genocide, but the shuffling through several countries, the loss of his father, and the separation from his mother. Most likely it was difficult for him to sort through his traumatic past, particularly as he adjusted to life in a foreign land.

Trauma Theory

Advances in trauma theory from developments in the field of psychoanalysis, identification of post-traumatic stress syndrome, and scientific study of the brain provide new approaches for understanding the past. Only recently, however, has the theory been applied to the reading of visual imagery. In 1988, noted psychoanalyst Alice Miller postulated that whenever creative adults have been traumatized as children, evidence of their ordeal will be apparent in their artwork.[12] She first considered the visual imagery of artists she suspected were traumatized as children based on various elements in their work. She then researched their childhood histories and indeed found evidence of trauma.[13] Miller states that "the works of writers, poets, and painters tell the encoded story of childhood traumas no longer consciously remembered in adulthood."[14]

Building on Miller's findings and informed by Freudian theories of trauma, I suggest that evidence of shock is apparent in Tutundjian's pattern of images, most significantly those I have interpreted as self-portraits. According to Freud's repetition theory, people who have experienced trauma are often compelled to perform recurring actions as a mean of maintaining control over their lives because the habitual actions enable them to predict the outcome and retroactively prepare the unconscious for the event that caused their neurosis.[15] In other words, they repeatedly return to the scene of the trauma to master their reaction to it after the fact.

Throughout Tutundjian's varied oeuvre a pattern of images emerges, the most prominent being his own portrait. The recurrence of these portraits, particularly those of himself as a young boy, correlate with a working through the trauma of his youth. Substantiating my identification of Tutundjian's self-portraits is confirmation by Vinet that figural depictions of a detached and sorrowful young boy are, in fact, images of her father in his youth.[16] French scholar Gladys Fabre noted Tutundjian's repetition of faces in a 1994 monograph, but did not address their possible identity or the reason for their recurrence.[17]

As observed by Judith Herman, clinical professor of psychiatry at Harvard Medical School, traumatic events invariably cause damage to the self because there is a breach of basic human trust.[18] Thus, the self that is formed in relation to others is shattered. The victims are dissociated from themselves and others. The severity of the damage will depend on the psychological strength of the individual and his or her age at the time of the event. Children are believed to suffer greater damage because they do not have the life experiences to draw upon to mentally prepare for such an event. Based on Herman's findings, Tutundjian would have been vulnerable to psychological damage because he was only ten years old at the time of the Genocide and would not have had the emotional maturity with which to brace himself for such a catastrophic event.

Applying Herman's conclusions, I suggest that the manner in which Tutundjian repeatedly portrays himself reveals a psyche that is fractured and disconnected from himself and the world around him. First, a majority of his likenesses reveal a dual image—profile and anterior view simultaneously—implying that his sense of self is split. Second, Tutundjian always depicts only a portion of himself—the head—never showing his entire image as a cohesive whole. Third, the face is consistently displayed against either a nonexistent or otherworldly background, suggesting separation from the real world. Substantiating my theory of detachment from others is the description by his daughter that Tutundjian usually kept to himself and was "always in his head."[19]

Further, the mere multiplicity of Tutundjian's self-portraits points to a splintering of identity elements. As noted by literature professor Jenijoy LaBelle in reference to the repetition of one's likeness, "the multiplication of images is tantamount to a fragmentation of identity. There is no single, continuous conception of ego but a breakdown of that unity . . . . To exist in multiplicity is, in a sense, not to exist at all, because self-conception requires some conviction in the singularity of one's being."[20] Additional evidence of a shattered self is found in Tutundjian's use of multiple signatures throughout his life, signifying that he had difficulty unifying or settling on a single identity.

The Images

Face-Plate

From the beginning of Tutundjian's body of work the viewer becomes acquainted with the face of a young boy with a crooked nose and a small rosebud mouth. In a ceramic plate (Fig. 8.1) from his earliest period, dated circa 1920, Tutundjian's childlike vulnerability seems particularly accentuated as he peers out with a wide-eyed look, a thin neck, and a slightly exposed tiny bare shoulder.[21] He stares straight ahead and up slightly, as evidenced by the greater expanse of the whites of his eyes below the irises, as a little boy would be when looking up at an authority figure. He gazes out not to engage the viewer, but instead looks as if he has been caught off guard and is gripped by fear. He is young, motionless, and alone. In keeping with Freudian theory, he appears to return to the scene of the crime, so to speak, to the time when he experienced the traumatic event as a ten-year-old.

In all of Tutundjian's self-portraits one eye is larger than the other, alerting the viewer that something is amiss. Along with this variation are other facial elements that are either out of proportion or are depicted from diverse angles. As will become more evident, the resulting effect of these peculiarities is the formation of a double portrait—profile and anterior views concurrently. His left eyebrow is bushier than the right and his chin terminates on dissimilar planes. His hair is cropped short in an odd shape that exposes only his left ear and outlines the top of his head with a slight concave dip. The nose is long and narrow and appears to be depicted in profile while the remainder of the face is seen from the front.

I suggest that this duality signifies a fragmentation or splitting of Tutundjian's psyche. As Herman explains, the shattering of the self is caused by the feeling of terror and disempowerment during the traumatic event, which compromises the person's sense of safety in the world. It is the feeling of security, acquired at the very beginning of life in the "relationship with the first caretaker," which forms the basis of all subsequent relationships and shapes the foundation of human life.[22] In other words, when the victim's sense of safety is tarnished it damages his or her relationships with others.

Another commonality found in Tutundjian's self-portraits is the isolation of the head against a nonexistent or otherworldly background. In Figure 8.1 the face is detached from the body and suspended within blotchy colors of variegated density. There is no sense of space or setting. The resulting desolation references Tutundjian's disconnection from himself and the world. Conceivably, he would have felt removed from the boy of his youth who had experienced the Genocide and would have had difficulty integrating that experience into his new life in Paris. The lack of setting implies that he may have felt disengaged from his surroundings, an assumption supported by his tendency to keep to himself.

Figure 8.1
Léon Tutundjian, Untitled (Self-Portrait), ceramic plate, c. 1920s

As Herman notes, traumatic events "shatter the sense of connection between individual and community, creating a crisis of faith."[23]

The self that emerges from Tutundjian's self-portraits is not whole or connected, but split, distorted, and distanced from its nonexistent background.[24] According to Jacques Lacan's theory of the mirror stage, an infant's encounter with his reflection results in the child's sense of himself since it is at this point that he sees himself as an object available to the gaze of others.[25] The self-portrait, like the mirror, serves as a reflection, informing the self of its identity and its existence.

Samuel Bak

This early image of Tutundjian as a young boy bears a striking resemblance to *Self-Portrait at the Age of Thirteen* by Holocaust survivor and child artist Samuel Bak (Fig. 8.2), in terms of compositional layout and gaze of the sitter. Bak painted this self-portrait in 1946 before he fled Europe.[26] Like Tutundjian, Bak depicts only his head suspended in midair against a nondescript background of encircling colors. He also stares straight out without engaging the viewer. Bak does not depict the horrors he witnessed, but instead presents a picture

Figure 8.2
Samuel Bak, Self-Portrait at the Age of Thirteen, 1946 (artist's collection)

of himself seemingly reliving the catastrophe within his mind. Art historian Amishai-Maisels says of Bak's self-portrait that "the boy-artist gazes wide-eyed in horror . . . , still seeing before him the hell he had witnessed."[27] One might interpret Tutundjian's self-portraits in much the same way.

Gouache Face

In a 1925 image of colored ink, gouache and watercolor the face on Tutundjian's ceramic plate reappears, only here it is barely legible from its surrounding multicolored acid-like background (Fig. 8.3). Like the plate, it has no foundation in space or setting, suggesting a lack of grounding and disconnection.

Similarly, the eyes are distorted, only this time they are reversed—his right eye is now larger than the left. I should stress that while Tutundjian repeats the ocular defect in all his self-portraits, he constantly shifts the distortion, from

Figure 8.3
Léon Tutundjian, *Untitled (Self-Portrait)*, gouache, 1925

one eye to the other. The movement of this imperfection suggests that on an unconscious level Tutundjian was emphasizing the psychological nature of the flaw.[28] In other words, the malformation could not have changed locations on his face if it was solely physical.

As mentioned, the combination of the optical distortion and the positioning of the nose effectively render the image a double portrait—profile and anterior view simultaneously–only here the dual image is more readily discernible. This doubling within his self-portraits more explicitly reflects a split self-image.

The gouache is also compelling because it appears to be simultaneously emerging and submerging from its background of engulfing colors. It is the India ink that gives the head its shape, while the plethora of surrounding colors overlap it, making the face quite difficult to discern. Such vagueness of intent gives the impression that the likeness is at once overcome by obliteration and emerging from a murky past. Given Tutundjian's recent history, both scenarios are plausible. His actual existence would have been threatened during the Genocide and he has yet to surmount the associated trauma.

Grimmaced Face

A similar portrait (Fig. 8.4) provides different clues with which to access Tutundjian's psyche. It is the same face with distorted eyes, a long nose, and a small mouth, though here the image is seen from a slight angle. Like the others, it is a double portrait, but the eyes do not vary quite so daringly and the eyebrows are more uniform.

Like the gouache, the background is comprised of various colors, but they have a smoother, watery look and do not intrude upon the face as directly. The image seems less overcome since it is more readily discernable, suggesting that the artist is beginning to feel less trapped by his dark past. At first glance nothing seems radically different, until one notices subtle changes. The figure sports longer hair extended in mid-air, its jagged lines adding an aura of agitation. The mouth no longer forms its usual rosebud shape. Instead, the lips are separated

Figure 8.4
Léon Tutundjian, *Untitled (Self-Portrait)*, gouache and India ink, c. 1920s

slightly, bearing two rows of small teeth, the effect of which is a disturbing grimace. Could this portrait be a representation of Tutundjian's reaction to the horrors he experienced? Indeed, he may be purging, or reliving the event as evidenced by his physical reaction.

As posited by Freud, victims of trauma will repeat scenes from their past, but will not understand the compulsion or recognize the relation to their neurosis.[29] It is only through remembering and narrating the past that victims of trauma can resolve their troubled past. In Tutundjian's self-portraits as a young boy, he repeatedly returns to the scene of the trauma. Perhaps he did not initially understand why he painted these portraits. However, as a man of few words, who was obsessed with expressing himself visually, it seems he eventually found his way to narration through art. As reflected in this image, he appears to be visually narrating his past and identifying the horrors he experienced.

However, as evidenced by the two abstract self-portraits that follow, it seems that Tutundjian did not make steady progress in working through his trauma. In fact, he may have retreated further. As Amishai-Maisels has noted, the use of abstraction by traumatized artists is a distancing device, although it is usually applied in two fundamentally different ways: (1) to provide a safe distance from which to face the horrors of trauma, or (2) to distance oneself as quickly and as far as possible from the horrors.[30] Based on the visual strategies used in the following abstract images, I suggest that Tutundjian was separating himself from his disturbing memories. In other words, he began to retreat from his past because his encounter with it had become too overwhelming.

Abstract Face

In Tutundjian's abstract phase, I propose that the self-portrait materializes in a 1927 watercolor with India ink (Fig. 8.5). Here the face is stripped down to its bare identifying markers—the distorted eyes that are floating in an undefined space, suspended on different horizontal planes, staring straight out without engaging the viewer. Isolating the eyes in this manner, Tutundjian signifies their importance and calls even greater attention to their deformity. He moves the distortion again—this time the right eye is larger. I emphasize that Tutundjian's constant flipping of this disfigurement signifies a mental rather than a physical malady. As windows to the soul, the ocular irregularity implies a psychological disruption.

Floating Watercolor

Tutundjian created a similar abstract (Fig. 8.6), although it is different enough to perhaps confirm the preceding self-portrait (Fig. 8.5). The optical distortion repeats, but this time one eyeball is missing completely, its intended place reserved by an empty eye socket. Once again the irregularity has changed sides.

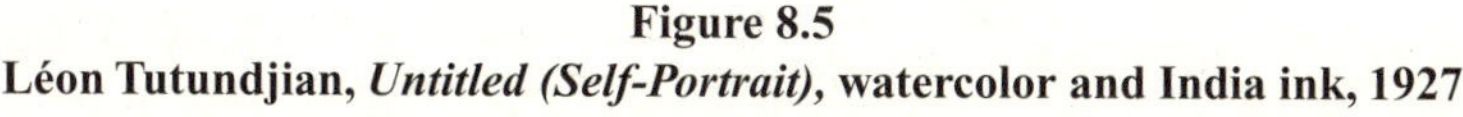

Figure 8.5
Léon Tutundjian, *Untitled (Self-Portrait),* watercolor and India ink, 1927

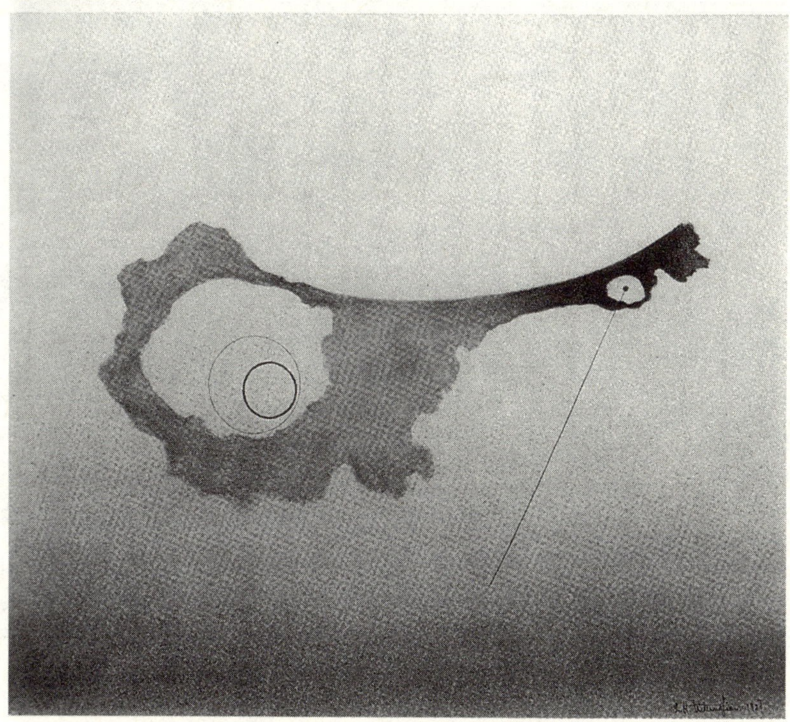

As will become more apparent in Tutundjian's later works, he seems to offer clues to identify the eyes by drawing thin lines around them.

Like the other faces, Figure 8.6 appears to be a double portrait. The eye peers out, toward the viewer, while the remainder of the image, an eerie mass with an almost cloud-like quality, forms a profile along the upper horizontal axis of the composition, in the area previously reserved for the crown of the head. All the facial elements are referenced in this horizontal profile; the forehead, eye, nose, mouth, and chin. Cleverly, the space for the lone large eye depicted from the front also forms the eye in profile.

The faces in Figures 8.5 and 8.6 have ethereal qualities, implying that their mere existence, like Tutundjian's, is tenuous. Associated with this reading is Tutundjian's tendency to avoid snapshots of himself, as if he were shunning documented proof of his existence.[31] Given his seemingly fractured identity and lack of grounding, his avoidance of concrete representations of himself is not surprising.[32] Like all of Tutundjian's faces, the images are detached, suspended in an undefined space, and completely removed from any realistic setting. No indication of time or space is provided. They float in what appears to be mid-

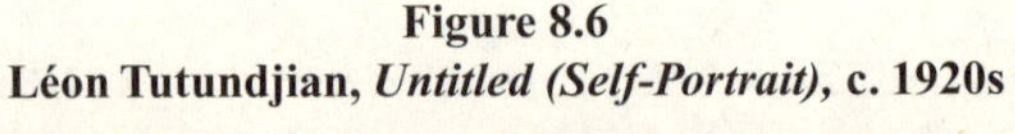

Figure 8.6
Léon Tutundjian, *Untitled (Self-Portrait)*, c. 1920s

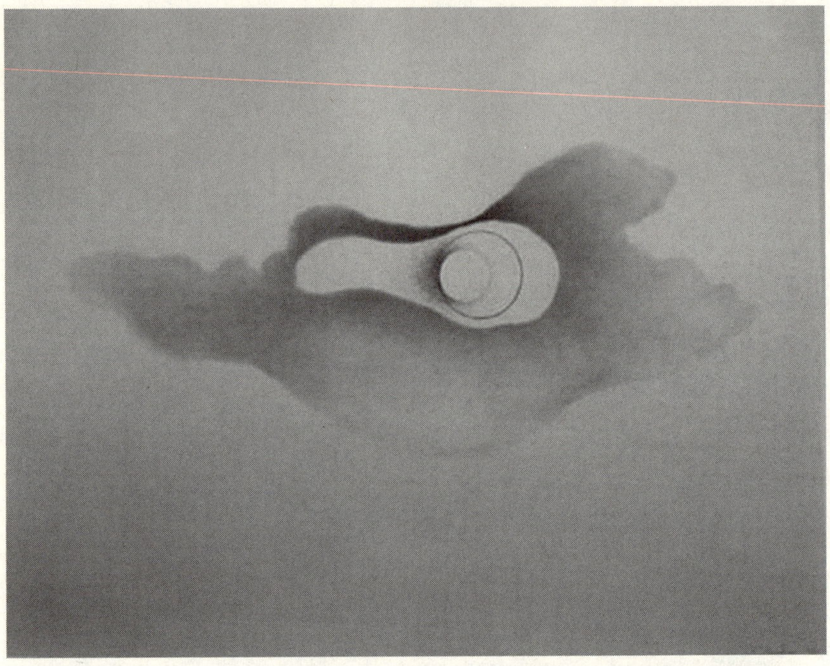

air, the graininess of the background referencing the molecular structure of air particles, implying perhaps that it is difficult to breathe, to take in the surrounding air. Is the air heavy with haunting memories?

Four Quarters—Young Boy in Fictive Landscape

I have also identified several self-portraits Tutundjian painted during his surrealist period. As mentioned, he worked in this mode for the majority of his career—from 1933 until 1960—making his attraction to this style significant in and of itself. As noted, he may have been instinctively drawn to surrealism because its association with dreams and the unconscious may have provided him with a suitable outlet to work through his trauma.

At the beginning of Tutundjian's surrealist phase his personal life changed when he married in 1933. This development suggests that he may have begun to heal since he was able to establish a close intimate relationship. Herman states that the most fundamental step in recovery is the reestablishment of personal connections.[33] It is the sense of safety provided by meaningful interactions that enables a person to reconnect and solidify his or her identity. As seen earlier, Freud discovered that a critical step in the therapeutic process is the need to

Léon Tutundjian, *Untitled (Self-Portrait)*, gouache, 1925 (Chapter 8)

Léon Tutundjian, *Untitled (Self-Portrait)*, gouache and India ink, c. 1925 (Chapter 8)

Léon Tutundjian, ***Untitled (Four Quarters with Self-Portrait)*****, oil on canvas, c. 1940s-1950s (Chapter 8)**

Léon Tutundjian, ***Untitled (Self-Portrait/Red Mask)*****, oil on canvas, c. 1940s-1950s (Chapter 8)**

Alina Mnatsakanian, closeup of *Box/Cross/Dismemberment/Genocide*, 1997 (Chapter 10)

Sophia Gasparian, *What Have You Done to Assist the Armenians?*, 2001 (Chapter 10)

Raffi, in *Ararat*, showing his video diary of Ani to the customs officer (Chapter 9)

***Jagadakeer . . . between the near & east*, a short film by Tina Bastajian (Chapter 9)**

Gregg Bendian Project, *Counterparts*, 1996 CIMP (Chapter 11)

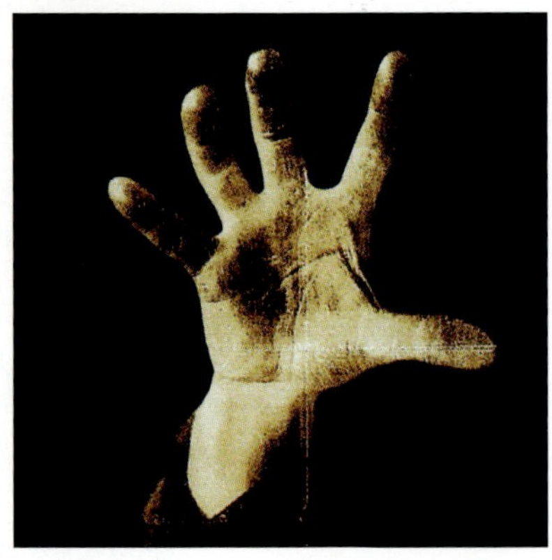

***System of a Down*, 1998, American Recording (Chapter 11)**

narrate, to tell the story of the event, which in Tutundjian's case occurs visually rather than verbally.[34] While his art may have facilitated his healing, he does not appear to have made steady progress, as evidenced by the last three images (Figs. 8.4, 8.5, and 8.6). His surrealist images reveal a continuation with the same markers of detachment and fracturing, however there is also a sprinkling of subtle positive signs.

In his surrealist period, Tutundjian created a series of paintings divided into four quarters, which author Gladys Fabre labeled the *Four Elements* because she considered each segment representative of different stages of the artist's life and work.[35] It is indeed interesting to note that Tutundjian repeats imagery from his earlier periods in this series.[36] In Figure 8.7 he includes the face of the young boy from Figure 8.1. However, in Figure 8.7 the boy is depicted as a painting within a painting, set in a barren, desolate landscape. He is trapped, boxed-in within the fictive picture, unable to move and engage with his surroundings. Following Fabre's lead and interpreting this composition as a reference to different stages in Tutundjian's life, the self-portrait, or self, might be seen as disconnected from the artist's own life. With the division of the canvas into quarters, it seems that Tutundjian is representing his life, his identity, as divided

Figure 8.7
Léon Tutundjian, *Untitled (Four Quarters with Self-Portrait)*, oil on canvas, c. 1940s-1950s

rather than whole. In addition, the overall feeling conveyed by this painting, as well as most of Tutundjian's images, is isolation. He depicts desolate, vacuous spaces suggestive of a deep-rooted void.

Based on what is known about Tutundjian, these portraits might reveal his lack of feeling connected to others. The Armenian community in Paris, particularly the artistic groups, could have provided Tutundjian with a sense of belonging and comfort in the familiar, but Tutundjian chose to keep his distance from his compatriots.[37] He may have avoided such contact to evade his past and to be seen as a more professional artist.[38] Factors also suggest that he was never fully embraced by his European contemporaries, as evidenced by the fact that he was unable to make a name for himself and by comments made by some of his peers, which reveal that they saw him as a foreigner, an other, an outsider.[39]

Once again there is the dual portrait—or conflation of identities—except that here it is slightly different since the right side of the face bears what looks like a five o'clock shadow, suggestive of a man rather than a young boy. At the time Tutundjian painted this image he was thirty-five to fifty-five years old, which may explain why part of the image looks older.[40] His tiny bare shoulder is not revealed as it was in Figure 8.1, rendering the image less childlike and less vulnerable. Nonetheless, Tutundjian continues to depict himself in very much the same manner as the boy from his youth, indicating that he most likely still had difficulty moving beyond his boyhood experience.

Masks

Tutundjian also painted two single-image surrealist self-portraits, which bear disturbing monstrous qualities (Figs. 8.8 and 8.9). Once again there is the large isolated face with distorted eyes, set in a desolate setting. Both face and backdrop look otherworldly, suggesting a complete disconnection from reality. Each face is now a mass of solid color, one red, the other yellow, with moon-like surfaces with perforations for the eyes and the mouth. Their facial texture is reduced to the craggy features of a rocky surface. The giant morphed faces gaze out and like all of Tutundjian's portraits do not engage the viewer. The eyes are delineated by the thin oval-shaped line around the larger eye, as seen in Tutundjian's more abstract portraits. Gone is the youthful rosebud mouth. In its place is a grimace, harkening back to the agitated mouth seen in Figure 8.4, only now it reveals sparsely spaced rotting teeth. The innocent face of the detached and sorrowful young boy is nowhere to be found. Instead there is a craggy, surreal face with decaying teeth, suggestive of an older person, perhaps one shaded by the cruel realities of the world.

Like the prior surrealist image, these massive faces are set in desolate landscapes with scattered rocks. The faces are elevated from the ground, signifying that they are detached, ungrounded, and homeless. Does the land beneath them refer to

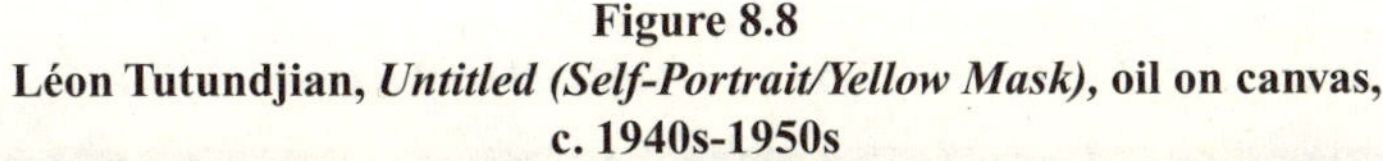

Figure 8.8
Léon Tutundjian, *Untitled (Self-Portrait/Yellow Mask)*, oil on canvas, c. 1940s-1950s

Tutundjian's homeland in Turkey, which no longer exists in its original form and to which Tutundjian cannot return? Or does the land represent his new home in Paris where he is not firmly rooted within the French or Armenian communities?

In each canvas there is a rock or clump of dirt in the foreground. (A similar mass also appeared in the prior surrealist painting). But what are these clumps? In the yellow image the rock seems to have broken into pieces that litter the ground. Might these pieces represent symbolic fragments of Tutundjian's homeland or his rocky past, which are always with him, but can never be integrated into his sense of self? The clumps look useless to him, as evidenced by their placement within the canvases—they are just there, as props on a stage. But again, what is he to do with these piles of dirt and rock, these bits of possible homeland? Tutundjian seemed to be proud of his ethnicity as revealed by his refusal to Europeanize his name as did famous Armenian artists Jean Carzou (Karnig Zouloumian) and Jean Jansem (Hovhannes Semerdjian).[41] As noted earlier, however, his ethnicity may have hampered his ability to assimilate fully into French society since it seems that his European contemporaries saw him as a foreigner.

The yellow image is propped up by a dead tree, thereby conceivably preventing the face/Tutundjian from taking root, from establishing a self that is connected to the earth or the rest of his body. He is left in mid-air, unable to

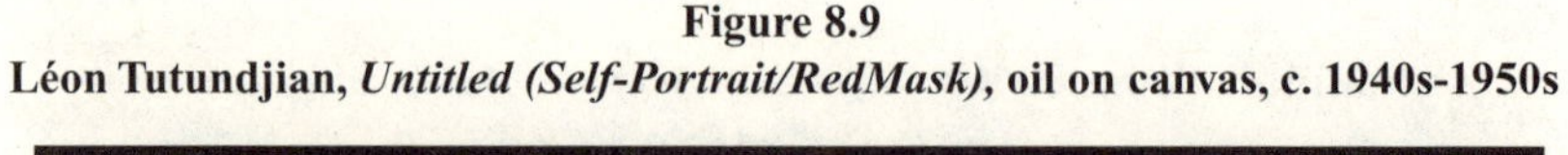

Figure 8.9
Léon Tutundjian, *Untitled (Self-Portrait/RedMask)*, oil on canvas, c. 1940s-1950s

ground himself physically or mentally. His detachment is laid bare for all to see. There are no signs of life, only desolate landscape as far as the eye can see. Yellow typically denotes jealousy. Perhaps Tutundjian is depicting his envy of those around him who have bonded and found their place in the world.

The red face is held up by what appear to be poles and sticks of varying sizes. Upon closer inspection it becomes apparent that many resemble needles, poking holes into the surface of the face, creating painful wounds, or memories. Red is suggestive of injury and anger. Is this image a manifestation of Tutundjian's painful past? The wounds cannot heal because they continue to be prodded by that which prevents the self from connecting to the ground below. Is he angered by the obstacles of his past, which keep him from making contact with others? A single ladder seems to provide passage to the world below. Or is it escape from his torment? The only signs of actual life are at the top of the red face in the miniature green trees sprouting from the crown of the head directly below the area of the ladder's placement. Might the correlation of the ladder with the live trees suggest that if Tutundjian had access to the ground, if he were connected in some way, his life would become more lush and real? Or does their placement refer to the small connection and sense of safety he was most likely enjoying as a result of his nuclear family?

Like the others, the red face includes a double portrait, but here it is seen in the mask-like shadow cast by the face to its right. Its silhouette is barely legible, but it is delineated by the gaps for the eyes and mouth. Hence, the face (Tutundjian) is able to touch the ground, but only as a shadow of himself and only for a fleeting moment. Again, the contact might refer to his sense of connection provided by his new family, while the faintness of the image might reflect the fragility of these new bonds. And perhaps the mask-like quality of the shadow implies that only by hiding behind a mask, by taking on a false identity, can he see himself making contact with the world around him.

Four Quarters—Sculpture

In another surrealist painting in four segments (Fig. 8.10), the face of the young boy is repeated, only now it is in the form of a marble bust rather than a fictive painting. The solidity of the material provides it with stability, a significant improvement from the ethereal qualities seen in Tutundjian's earlier works. The bust is angled to the viewer's right and the eyes gaze out in the same direction, lending the image a pensive and mature appearance. The firm and thoughtful qualities of the face, as well as the broader and more pronounced nose, give the face a slightly older look. Might these changes correlate with Tutundjian's own aging and solidification of his own identity?

Figure 8.10
Léon Tutundjian, *Untitled (Four Quarters with Self-Portrait)*, oil on canvas, c. 1940s-1950s

As might be expected, there is no indication of the precise setting. The landscape is bare and flat, except for the suggestion of mountains in the far distance and the inclusion of two pieces of giant fruit in the foreground, in front of the bust. Like the clumps of dirt in the previous surrealist images, the fruits seem to provide no useful purpose, other than their decorative contribution. However, I suggest that their inclusion is a positive sign since they denote nourishment and regeneration. Even their placement is more advantageous. The clump of dirt in the previous images was placed to the side and/or below the face, but here the fruit is directly in front of the face and its mouth, acting almost as a barrier insisting on its consumption before allowing passage.

A surprising change from the other portraits is that the face now has direct contact with the landscape. The neck rests directly on the ground, which no longer looks quite so desolate due to the golden glow emanating from the orange sky above. The changes taking place in this image—the solidity of the face, the existence of life-giving fruit, the direct contact with land, and the glow of the sky—point to positive changes in Tutundjian's life. He seems to be forming a more solid sense of himself and is able to connect with the ground beneath him. No longer is he depicted as an ethereal mass being threatened by a murky background or left to flounder in vacuous space. He now has direct contact with solid ground ablaze from the rays of the sun. The inclusion of the fruit is significant, as denoted by its enormous size. Fruit trees flourish with nourishment from contact with the ground and provide sustenance to those who partake of their creation. Thus, the symbolic elements reflected in this final surrealist image suggest positive changes of solidity, connection, and life. The sense of safety provided by Tutundjian's marriage probably enabled him to reconnect with his sense of self and the world around him, albeit over time.

A final image, an abstract drawing in India ink and charcoal on paper dated 1965 (Fig. 8.11) from Tutundjian's last period of artistic activity points to a reconciled and contented self.[42] There are two familiar circular shapes of different sizes—one larger than the other. The circular shapes are shaded over by two rectangular patches which leave a long narrow opening between them along the longer side. Below is a fine slightly curved line, which starts from the two circular shapes and dips to an area below the shaded patches. The image appears to depict two eyes, a nose and, alas, a smile. The distortion of the eyes is still there, perhaps suggesting that the pain of Tutundjian's past will always be a part of him, though he seems to have integrated the memories as evidenced by the satisfaction revealed through the smile.

As an artist, Tutundjian may have had an advantage over most survivors because he possessed an innate propensity for expressing his inner side through visual expression, and this may have enabled him to find his way, eventually, to the other side. As theorized by Freud, the need to narrate is a crucial step to recovery from trauma because it is through the telling of that story that an

Figure 8.11
Léon Tutundjian, *Untitled (Self-Portrait)*, India ink and charcoal, 1965

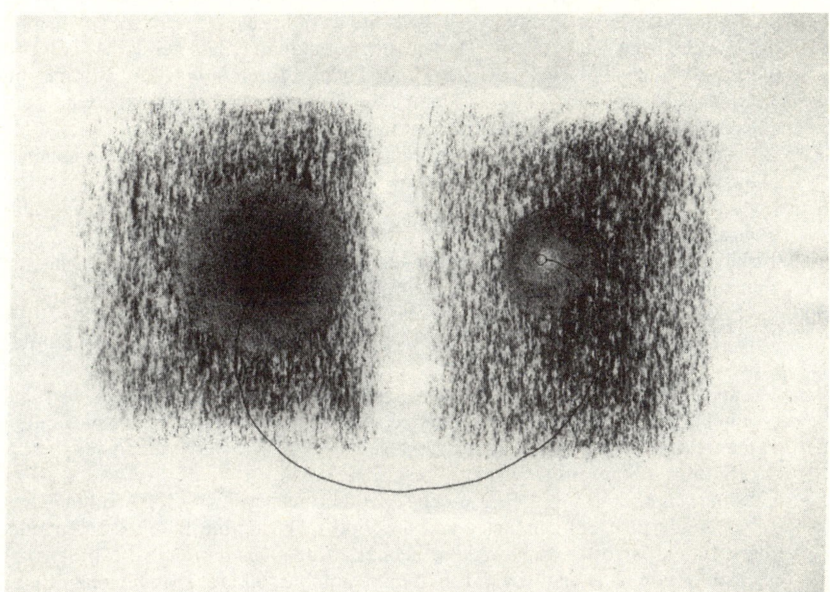

individual comes to understand what happened, to integrate his memories into his conscious mind. For Tutundjian that narration would have occurred visually rather than verbally.

Judith Herman has noted that reestablishing meaningful relationships is another key element for healing because it provides a sense of safety, enabling a person to reconnect with himself and others. Tutundjian's marriage in 1933 may have provided him with that nucleus of safety. Following this period there are subtle signs in his work suggesting that he began to form a more solid sense of himself and connect with the world around him.

The analysis of Tutundjian's self-portraits utilizing trauma theory reveals that his early experience of the Armenian Genocide resulted in a trauma to his sense of self. Hence, he arrived in Paris as a young man shattered by this ordeal. The repetition of his self-portraits, particularly as a young boy, suggests a repeated return to the scene of the trauma. The manner in which he consistently depicted himself intimates a fractured psyche—doubling within the portraiture, fragmentation of representation, and detachment from background settings. Like many survivors, Tutundjian's road to recovery was not an easy one. His portraits periodically reveal the inner horrors he faced as he grappled with his past. By forging ahead, however, he seemed gradually to find reconciliation. Tutundjian's pictorial tour de force lays bare the psychic repercussions of his genocide trauma.

Notes

1. Since Tutundjian's death, interest in his work has increased because the bulk of his output reached the art market when the contents of his atelier were sold at auction in the years from 1969 to 1987. As a result, Tutundjian only recently has come to the attention of scholars. Please see: Gladys Fabre, *Tutundjian* (Paris: Editions du Regard, 1994). Fabre notes Tutundjian's ethnicity and his genocide experience, but does not take these factors into account in her analysis.
2. Donald E. Miller and Lorna Touryan Miller, "Survivor Responses to the Genocide," in *Survivors: An Oral History of the Armenian Genocide* (Berkeley, Los Angeles, London: University of California Press, 1993; repr., 1999), pp. 155-181 (page citations are to the reprint edition). Basic information about Tutundjian's childhood in Turkey is available, but details of what he may or may not have endured during the Genocide are not known.
3. Interviews with Léa Vinet, Paris, France, December 12, 2003, January 4, 2004. Tutundjian also felt his work was not properly understood by his contemporaries.
4. The application of trauma theory has been utilized extensively in literary theory and is only beginning to be directed toward art history. For the most recent contribution to the field, see Jill Bennett, *Empathic Vision: Affect, Trauma, and Contemporary Art* (Stanford: Stanford University Press, 2005).
5. Interviews with Léa Vinet, December 12, 2003, January 7, 14, 2004. Tutundjian's father taught physical chemistry and the violin. During the family's prosperous years, Tutundjian often eschewed the niceties afforded his station in life, preferring instead the company and way of life of more humble folk. He spent a great deal of time at the house of a friend whose family had limited means. Often, he refused the delicate pastries his father would bring home from an expensive bakery because he thought such finery was unnecessary. However, when the family's situation changed, he regretted that he had not indulged himself when he had the opportunity. As an adult in Paris, he would, like his father, occasionally bring home to his small family delicacies from an expensive bakery.
6. Fabre, *Tutundjian*, p. 13. Interviews with Léa Vinet, December 12, 2003, January 4, 2004. Fabre and Vinet indicate that it was a result of bombings related to the Genocide.
7. Interviews with Léa Vinet, December 12, 2003, January 7, 14, 2004. According to Vinet, her father had one older sister who married at the time of the Genocide and left the country with her husband. Vinet remains in contact with her aunt's only son, but he was unable to provide any further details about the family's early years in Turkey.
8. Fabre, *Tutundjian*, p. 13. Interviews with Léa Vinet, December 12, 2003, January 7, 14, 2004. At the orphanage Tutundjian took the initiative to start a small orchestra and choral group. He had learned to play the violin from his father.
9. It is unclear exactly where his mother stayed—most likely she remained in Constantinople. Interviews with Léa Vinet, December 12, 2003, January 7, 14, 2004.
10. Interview with Léa Vinet, January 7, 2004.
11. He always had two workshops—one for his fine art and another for his ceramics, a necessity because of the dust created by the ceramics. Interviews with Léa Vinet, December 12, 2003, and January 7, 14, 2004.
12. Alice Miller, *The Untouched Key: Tracing Childhood Trauma in Creativity and Destructiveness*, trans. Hildegarde and Hunter Hannum (New York: Doubleday, 1990; repr., New York: Anchor Books, 1991). Originally published as *Der gemiedene Schlüssel* (1988).

13. For example, she looked at the works of Pablo Picasso and Käthe Kollwitz and determined that Picasso had been traumatized as a child by an earthquake in Málaga and Kollwitz suffered from psyche death, or depression, because she was brought up in a repressive household by a mother who had never recovered from the death of three of her children, particularly her first- and last-born in infancy.
14. Miller, *Untouched Key*, p. 73.
15. Sigmund Freud, *Beyond the Pleasure Principle (1920) Standard Edition*, trans. and ed. James Strachey (New York: W. W. Norton and Company, 1961). As the father of psychoanalysis, Freud was one of the first to unravel the human response to traumatic events. Although his theories have been criticized over the years for some of his more outrageous claims, such as penis envy, Freud laid the ground work for much of what we know today about the human psyche. As argued by clinical psychologist Drew Westen, current research in psychology is consistent with Freudian thought. See Richard J. McNally, *Remembering Trauma* (Cambridge, MA: Harvard University Press, 2003), p. 170.
16. Interviews with Léa Vinet, December 12, 2003, and January 7, 14, 2004.
17. Fabre, *Tutundjian* passim.
18. Judith Herman., *Trauma and Recovery: The Aftermath of Violence—from Domestic Abuse to Political Terror* (New York: Basic Books, 1992; repr., 1997), pp. 51-73 (page citations are to the reprint edition).
19. Interview with Léa Vinet, January 7, 2004.
20. Jenijoy LaBelle as quoted in Gannit Ankori, *Imaging Her Selves: Frida Kahlo's Poetics of Identity and Framentation* (Westport, CT: Greenwood Press, 2002), p. 250.
21. This is the only instance in which Tutundjian shows more than just his head and neck.
22. Herman, *Trauma and Recovery*, pp. 55-73.
23. Ibid., p. 55.
24. Other artists, such as Vincent van Gogh and Frida Kahlo, have shown a preoccupation with self-portraits which have also been seen as indicative of inner turmoil or trauma. See James Risser, "Self-Portrait as Self-Image" in *Van Gogh 100,* ed. Joseph D. Masheck, (Westport, CT: Greenwood Press, 1996), pp. 151-158; David Lomas, "Body Languages: Kahlo and Medical Imagery" in *The Body Imaged: The Human Form and Visual Culture Since the Renaissance*, ed. Kathleen Adler and Marcia Pointon (Cambridge: Cambridge University Press, 1993), pp. 1-19; Ankori, *Imaging Her Selves*.
25. Jacques Lacan, "The Mirror Stage as Formative of the Function of the I as Revealed in Psychoanalytic Experience," in *Ecrits: A Selection* (New York: W. W. Norton, 1977), pp. 1-7.
26. Ziva Amishai-Maisels, *Depiction and Interpretation: The Influence of the Holocaust on the Visual Arts* (Oxford and New York: Pergamon Press, 1993), pp. 5, 46-47, and Colorplate 1.
27. Ibid., p. 5.
28. Initially, I thought the variation was possibly a misprint in the reproductions with which I was working, but then realized this was not the case when I viewed the originals in Paris.
29. Sigmund Freud, "Remembering, Repeating and Working-Through," in *The Standard Edition of the Complete Psychological Works of Sigmund Freud*, trans. James Strachey et al., vol. 12: *1911-1913* (London: Hogarth Press and Institute of Psycho-Analysis, 1958), pp. 147-156.
30. Amishai-Maisels, *Depiction and Interpretation*, p. 272.
31. He would volunteer to be the picture-taker to avoid being in photographs. Interview with Léa Vinet, January 7, 2004.

32. Herman, *Trauma and Recovery*, pp. 53-54.
33. Ibid., pp. 51-73.
34. Freud, *Remembering, Repeating and Working Through*. On the other hand, Herman indicates that there must be a "sharing of the traumatic experience with others" for healing to occur. She also indicates that "the response of the community has a powerful influence on the ultimate resolution of the trauma." Herman, *Trauma and Recovery*, pp 61-73 (quotation, p. 70).
35. Fabre, *Tutundjian*, p. 140.
36. Because of the scope of this chapter, the other quarters in this and another work from the series will not be analyzed.
37. Interviews with Léa Vinet, December 12, 2003, and January 7, 2004. This was also confirmed by the managing editor of *Haratch*, Arpik Missakian (daughter of the founding editor, Chavarch Missakian).
38. Nubar Tildian, "French Armenian Painters," *Ararat* 9, 1 (Winter 1968): 36-44. According to Tildian, the more successful artists sought the prestige of solo exhibitions and representation by official art dealers, rather than exhibiting with Armenian art groups such as *Ani* or the *Union of Free Armenian Artists*. He indicated that they felt the "ethnic association might tend to restrict serious consideration of their work."
39. Critic and author, François Pluchart, wrote in 1966: "The constructive rigor of Tutundjian was always moderated by a certain Orientalism." François Pluchart as quoted in Fabre, *Tutundjian*, p. 157 (my translation).

    Tutundjian's long-time friend and co-founder of the *Art Concret* movement, noted modern artist Jean Hélion, stated in an interview published in *La Connaissance* in 1975: "Tutundjian came from the East. He was an imperious and noble man, as one may be noble with a certain level of misery." Jean Hélion as quoted in Fabre, *Tutundjian*, p. 94 (my translation).

    Finally, the following quotation by art critic Gérard Bertrand, writing in the Drouot catalogue of 1970, with its references to Indian and Persian miniatures, suggests that Tutundjian's peers were either not sure of his exact place of origin or simply saw in his imagery the centuries of cultural influences to which Armenia has been exposed: "Tutundjian expresses himself through symbols. A tree, a severed hand, a rope, a pomegranate sliced open, these are all there to represent invisible truths. . . . Perhaps in this lies some distant similarity with the mysterious symbols of Indian and Persian miniatures, which gives his work a rare charm." (Bertrand as quoted in Shahen Khachaturyan, *Armenian Artists: XIXth & XXth Centuries* (Erevan: National Gallery of Armenia, 2001).
40. Fabre does not give a precise date for this image, but includes it in her chapter covering the years from 1940 to 1959, pp. 135-152.
41. Interviews with Léa Vinet, December 12, 2003, January 7, 2004. According to Vinet, her father never considered changing his name and was upset with Armenians who did change their names to become successful in French society.
42. Although I have just presented Tutundjian's faces from his surrealist period in a particular order, we do not as yet know in what order he painted these images. Consequently, it is difficult to accurately map a trajectory of his surrealist period to assess whether he successfully reconciled his past and unified his sense of self. However, I suggest that by looking briefly at his last period of artistic activity, his second abstract period from 1960 until his death in 1968, clues may be discernible.

9

Historicization of the Armenian Catastrophe: From the Concrete to the Mythical

Hrag Varjabedian

There has been a surge in the number of artistic works produced by a generation of Armenian-Americans relating to the rupture created by the Event (*Eghern*) of the Armenian Catastrophe (*Aghed*),[1] which began to appear in the mid-1980s and continued to build during the following two decades. Even though these non-Armenian speaking authors and artists live and create on the continent most distant and removed both in time and space from the homeland of their ancestors where the actual historical rupture took place, nevertheless its legacy and its unresolved issues are very much alive within their creative work. Viewed collectively, their work becomes part of a unique historicization project—the process of integrating the rupture created by the Event of the Catastrophe into the continuity of Armenian history and personal identities—within the history of diasporic Armenians.[2] The events of 1915 have created a rupture not only within the historiography of diasporic Armenians who are the descendants of Ottoman-Armenians, but also within Turkish historiography and society.[3] There has been a silence on both sides regarding the events of 1915, selective amnesia and denial on the part of official Turkish historiography regarding the decimation of Ottoman-Armenians, and a lack of self-reflexivity on the part of the descendants of Armenian survivors regarding the Catastrophe and its effects. It is within this context that a break in this wall of silence is suddenly manifested.[4] Therefore, not only those culturally constructed texts that make specific histories must be studied, but also the historicity of the events that creates a framework within which those histories become meaningful. This implies the investigation of cultural representations and attitudes that give meaning to a specific past, something that gets constantly reinterpreted, reinvented.

The production of these specific artistic texts, related to representations of collective and historic memories of Armenians of this specific time and locale, coincides with an era where there has been a sudden proliferation in scholarship related to *memory*, particularly to historical and collective memory.

Historical Memory and Collective Memory

Generally, scholars of history tend to separate history and memory depending on their functions and operatives. The differentiation between history and memory started in the early nineteenth century, with the development of historicism within European historiography, where a whole culture of collection and preservation took hold. The role of preserving the past was sanctioned to professional historians who became the official guardians of the past, both of objects and of memory. But in addition to the development of history, there was another vehicle through which the transmission of identity and memory was taking place. This vehicle was namely "collective memory," functioning parallel to history.[5]

The concept of "collective memory" emerged as a topic of scholarly research in the early part of the twentieth century, at the same time as the crisis of historicism was developing. The French sociologist Maurice Halbwachs was the first to systematically develop and theorize the concept of "collective memory." In his work of 1925, *The Social Framework of Memory*, and later in *The Collective Memory*, a collection of essays published posthumously in 1950, Halbwachs distinguished personal memory from social or collective memory, and collective memory from historical memory. He used the concept of "collective memory" to show that memory is particularly a social phenomenon, and only in the social setting in which it has been constructed can individual memory be recalled.[6] Without a shared social context, an individual is not able to remember the totality of the experience. Individuals belong to multiple social and communal groups, and within each of these social settings there is an intrinsic collective memory.[7] Furthermore, Halbwachs clearly distinguished the differences between collective and historical memory. For him, collective memory exists and is propagated within a distinct social group, delimited in space and time, within which individuals can remember and articulate their own personal memories. As for historical memory, it is formed when memory is detached from its social setting and is embedded within the structure of historical records and details. In this context, the past is remembered through autobiography and memories of individual constituents of a social group where lived experiences and collective memory "interpenetrate" one another.[8]

According to Halbwachs, one of the main differences between collective memory and historical memory, or general history, is that collective memory is continuous and retains from the past whatever is still alive within the consciousness of the group, keeping memory alive, whereas historical memory deals with the description of a past that is lost; a past that is no longer part of the collective memory. Therefore, within collective memory, there is no rupture between the consciousness of the past and its existence in the present, thus nothing is lost and nothing can be lost in this continuum. There is a continuum in the interpenetration between lived individual history (personal experiences) and collective memory. On the other hand, historical memory begins when all living experiences are lost with the past. What are left are only fragments that have become commemorative relics. Therefore, collective memory represents lived experiences, whereas historical memory functions to preserve lived experiences.[9] And the historian tries to create a totality of all the various stories and information that he has collected, in the hope of presenting wholeness to the lived reality and the past.[10]

Memory as a Historical Agent

Another French sociologist and ethnologist, Roger Bastide, took Halbwachs's model of memory and worked out the nuances. Through his ethnography on African cultures in America, he was able to develop further the concepts of collective and individual memory.[11] He enhanced and developed Halbwachs's analysis in three main directions. First, he agreed with Halbwachs that recollection can occur in social settings, but the role of the body and its performative aspects were as important in realizing recollections of the social group.[12] Second, he elaborated on the relationship between the individual and the social group. The social group was made up of individuals who engage with each other based on networks that complement each other. Even though collective memory is that of a social group, the group is seen as an organization, a "system of relationships between individuals." And in Bastide's case, it was this structured organization that slavery and dislocation had destroyed within the Africans who were brought to America. And if there is a de-structuring of the social group, then there will also be a de-structuring of the collective memory, too, which accounts for the selective memory of the group and its lapses of memory. Because of this de-structuring, there will literally be *gaps* in the collective memory of the group. Hence, the social group will look elsewhere for images to fill in the gaps that have been created, thus bringing in new meanings to the structure of their collective memory. These meanings will be based on the way the new elements are organized within the structure and not simply on their individual meanings. The work of Bastide becomes important in understanding the development of the Armenian collective memory of the Diaspora, following the destruction of its structured social organization as a result of the massacres and dislocations from its indigenous homeland.

Postmemory and Narrative Practices

This group of Armenian-American artists and authors is composed of the children and grandchildren of survivors. The fragments of postmemories that they have inherited are experienced once or twice removed from the actual traumatic events. Multiple layers and crosscurrents of both visible and invisible histories and historicities are encountered in their work. Here the identities of the artists, both on a personal and national level, are constructed through historicization of inherited fragmented narratives, as well as the noticeable gaps between those fragments. If histories are socially constructed texts of past events, then historicities provide the frameworks within which those histories become meaningful as they enter the consciousness of individuals within the social group. This implies that investigation of cultural representations and attitudes that give meaning to a specific past gets constantly reinterpreted and reinvented by individuals who give meaning to this specific past. Those reinterpretations and reinventions manifest themselves through various modes of representations, be they artistic or otherwise.

A few Holocaust scholars have used the term "postmemory" in trying to understand the way in which effects of the traumatic events of the Holocaust are negotiated by a generation that is the descendants of survivors, in constructing its own identity and their familial identity. Postmemory becomes the continuance of inherited memory and its renewal in different modes of representation.[13] In trying to negotiate between history and memory, these scholars arrive at the conclusion that traditional means of understanding history are not satisfactory and strive for nontraditional means of understanding the effects of history. Through visual arts, autobiography, memoirs, family pictures, and literature, they attempt to come to an understanding of the traumatic events of the Holocaust and its effects on the descendants of the survivors.

This study examines one aspect in the work of four Armenian-American artists, two novelists, and two filmmakers.[14] It follows the process of embarking on the venture of historicizing the rupture created by the Catastrophe within their historical consciousness, through the process of unearthing layers of histories, historicities, and inherited fragments of memories that are part of their constructed collective memories. The historicization process becomes essential, since within those remembrances there will always be chronological gaps, fusions of incongruities, and a constant transformation of past events. This discussion will specifically look at Atom Egoyan's feature film, *Ararat* (2003), Peter Najarian's novel, *Daughters of Memory* (1986), Tina Bastajian's short film, *Jagadakeer . . . between the near & east* (2001), and Micheline Aharonian Marcom's novel, *Three Apples Fell from Heaven* (2001). Their combined work takes us within the historicization process from the concrete to the imaginary to the mythical. En route, they illuminate a range of fragmentary pieces of revealed memories and historicities, as well as what lies beyond memory and language. These creative works have been produced after decades of official Turkish denial. Ever since the collapse of the Young Turk regime that carried out the decimation of the Armenian population subsequent governments of the Republic of Turkey have denied that there was a genocide. For the Armenians, this denial has not been merely rhetoric. Rather it has been preventing the historicization of the rupture.

The Story of Raffi

In the film *Ararat*, Raffi is at the customs station at the Toronto International Airport. He is just back from Turkey, bringing with him film footage, supposedly to be incorporated into the making of *Ararat*, the film within the film.[15] Raffi is trying to explain to David, the customs officer, the reasons behind his mission to Turkey. The customs officer is doubtful of Raffi's story and is suspicious that he is smuggling drugs in the film canisters. In order to convince David, Raffi gradually ends up telling the officer the whole history behind the conflict between Armenians and Turks, and in the process unravels his own personal issues and personal involvements with the project. In the course of telling his story, Raffi starts to amend it, revealing the true reasons for his trip. He shows his video diary of the ancient city of Ani,[16] now in ruins, to the officer.

Raffi, in Ararat, showing his video diary of Ani to the customs officer.

> I am here mom, Ani. In a dream world, the three of us will be together: dad, you and me. I remember all the stories I used to hear about this place; the glorious capital of our kingdom, ancient history, like the story of dad being a freedom fighter, trying for the return of this, I guess. And then he died too. What am I supposed to feel when I look at the ruins? Do I believe that they are damaged by time, or do I believe they are willfully destroyed? Is this proof of what happened? . . . Why was he prepared to give up himself for that, mom? What is the *legacy* that he was supposed to have given me? Why can't I take comfort in his death? When I see these places, *I realize how much we have lost. Not just the land and the lives, the loss of any way to remember it. There is nothing here to prove that anything has happened.* [emphases mine]

In his video diary to his mother, Raffi acknowledges the breakdown of both his familial and national history. His father has died fighting for the Armenian cause, and Raffi is trying to deal with the consequences of both disasters.[17] In composing his video diary to his mother Ani (named after this ancient site) Raffi is trying to repair the breakdown of history and to undo the effects of the rupture caused by both familial and national calamities. He is deeply engaged in the process of integrating his own personal ruptured history into a continuum that would fit the linearity of histories the way he envisions them. For him to succeed in his project, he needs concrete evidence of events that have transpired in the homeland, now in ruins. And like Raffi, Atom Egoyan himself, is involved in the historicization project of the Armenian Catastrophe, but, of course, on a much grander scale.[18] After all, his film is a project of integrating, on a national level, ruptured Armenian history back into History itself. Egoyan very clearly states the historicization theme in the first sentence of his commentary on the film:

> I am going to take a particular route through this commentary which is talking about the importance of symbols and objects that people make and the notion of cultural transposition and how ideas are communicated from one generation to the other, because I think that is at the core of this film, and the object and things that people make are essential to the understanding of the history . . . the way that things are mutated, or changed, as they are being interpreted, as they are given from one person to another. Those are very important themes.

Egoyan believes in the importance of continuity, the passing down of things (items, ideas) from one person to another, from one generation to another and the transformations that take place in the process. For Egoyan himself, there has to be cultural and historical continuity in this national process; never a breakdown even though a rupture in the personal stories of some of his characters is seen, such as Raffi, and the disruption of practically all the stories of his characters. For the filmmaker, there is no rupture within Armenian patrimony and historical consciousness—history and memory. It is a continuum. There is a scene in the movie in which this comes across very explicitly. Raffi, in educating the customs officer on Armenian history, is narrating the story of Van's self-defense by the Armenians:

> Raffi: They were heroes. What happened in Van in April of 1915 was an amazing act of self-defense . . . like the Jews in the Warsaw ghetto. We hadn't done anything like this since we held back the Persians.
>
> David: When did you hold back the Persians?
>
> Raffi (after a beat): 451.
>
> David: Fifteen hundred years before.
>
> Raffi (slight smile): Like I said. We go back.

Within Raffi's stories (of the cities of Ani and Van) are both the continuity of historical consciousness and the rupture caused by the historic Event popping up and disrupting the continuity of historical consciousness. On the one hand, the Event has ruptured Raffi's personal history (familial and national) and, on the other hand, a history is portrayed as continuous, going all the way back to the Battle of Avarayr, in A.D. 451.[19] Even though the Armenian army was defeated at the hands of the Persians, Raffi presents it as a (moral) victory. Similarly, the self-defense of Van is portrayed as a victory, and the Armenians as heroes, even though they had to retreat with the Russian army to the Caucasus and abandon their beloved city. With this particular story, Raffi tries to bridge two historical incidents within Armenian history, separated by fifteen hundred years: the Battle of Avarayr and the self-defense of Van. But this attempt of bridging is not enough to undo the real rupture caused by the Event.

At no point in the film does Egoyan present, or explicitly portray his self-reflexivity, his own personal experiences within the historical consciousness of diasporic Armenians. For him, the film itself is this project of presenting Armenian historical consciousness—memory and history—as a continuum for the Armenian community: history and memory without any breaks or gaps. But, of course, in this epic project there is the whole issue of denial and contestation that maintains the disruption of the historical consciousness of Armenian diasporan communities, and keeps the existence of the rupture alive.[20] It is this lively rupture that persistently prevents the historicization project from being realized. Egoyan tries to explain all the issues he wanted to address in the film. "[T]he screenplay had to tell the story of what happened, why it happened, why it's denied, why it continues to happen, and what happens when you continue to deny." The filmmaker feels the need to tell the story of the continuing effects of the Catastrophe, especially on the Armenians of the Diaspora. "The only concern was to find a way to give voice to a true history, to retrieve it from oblivion and make the viewers ask themselves why they have never heard of it."[21] He tries to use the authoritative role of his film in trying to tell us how history "really was." These multiple forms and narratives exist precisely because of this constant attempt at presenting "true" history as one continuous process where the rupture is suppressed. Who has the right and authority to tell stories? Who has access to history? There are all sorts of issues that constantly come up; issues of authority, authenticity, and truth. There are issues of rooting narratives, and rooting authors of the narratives, to their true places in history. There are issues of memory, and most important of all, there are issues of denial, both personal and of history itself. Egoyan continues his commentary:

> We have all these objects in the film. We have Ani's book, we have Edward's film, here we have a scene from it, we have Gorky's painting, we have Ruben's screen play, and we have Raffi's video diaries. [Of course, there is also the story of Ali, the Turkish-Canadian actor who plays the role of Jevdet Bey, the Turkish governor of Van, who carries out the massacres against the Armenians of Van and its surrounding

> villages]. All of these people are consumed into making something that is going to transmit their experience [their constructed stories]. Every story that we tell is given to interpretation. Nothing has the authority to represent absolute truth.

Even though the viewer is caught up in the crosscurrent of these multiple narratives where not a single one has the authority to represent "absolute truth," Egoyan creates a multilayered mosaic of histories and historicities as a mechanism of countering the denial that prevents the bridging of the gap. For him, the most important aspect of the film is to be able to embark on his historicization project in creating a continuity of "true" history. It is only then that he feels reconstruction and healing can take place. This becomes obvious at the end of his commentary and the film, with the scene where Gorky's mother sews the fallen button back onto his coat. Again, Egoyan's commentary:

> This is that moment, the mother sewing on this button. We are going right back to the root. And this scene isn't in Edward's film. It is a scene, the closest the film comes to sharing pure history. This is the most deeply felt image, the mother's hand reconstructing, this idea that you have to start reconstructing. You have to start putting things back together, and healing.

In the multiplicity of narratives, there are several counter-narratives that constantly disrupt the "official" narratives of the characters of the movie and prevent Egoyan from successfully fulfilling his project. David, the customs officer, disrupts Raffi's story on the true nature of his trip to Turkey. Celia, Ani's stepdaughter, disrupts Ani's story regarding her father's death and constantly confronts her in public. The story Edward, the director, and Ruben, the screenwriter, are trying to tell via their film *Ararat* is constantly disrupted by Ani's misgivings about the authenticity of the movie. As Arshile Gorky's painting, *The Artist and His Mother*, is literally slashed by Celia, thus destroying Gorky's representation of his story, Dr. Ussher's story is disrupted by Ani when she walks onto the set during filming. And, of course, Raffi's story is disrupted again, this time by the Turkish actor, who plays Jevdet Bey, when Raffi confronts him on the reality of the Armenian Catastrophe.[22] The film is unable to fully and conclusively "give voice to a true history," since "true" history is constantly disrupted by the official denial of the Turkish government that looms large over the narrative of the Armenian Catastrophe, above and beyond the film.[23] The historical consciousness of the Armenians, essentially that of diasporic Armenians who are the descendants of Ottoman-Armenians, is continuously contested, challenged, disrupted, and the historicization project becomes an unending endeavor, never complete.

Despite the array of stories, everything the viewer sees and hears in the film is concrete. All the stories are concrete. Memories and testimonies of the characters are concrete. Every aspect of any narrative in the film is concrete. Even postmemories are concrete. The massacre and deportation stories that the filmmaker Edward has heard from his survivor mother, upon which his movie is based, are concrete. There are no lapses in his memory. For Egoyan and the characters of the film, nothing is amorphous, fluid, tenuous, or beyond language and memories. In spite of the disruptions, gaps do not exist in the various stories, memories, and postmemories of the characters. It is this same concreteness that prevails in the literature of Armenian survivor memoirs and testimonies. In *Ararat*, Egoyan deals with the historical consciousness of diasporic Armenians as a communal group. He, as the director and screenwriter of the film, emerges as an author-historian where the collective memories of his subjects and communal group become his object of study and representation. But according to Pierre Nora, as the historian emerges as an author, a self-reflexivity should emerge in the voice of the historian. At the same time, Nora is skeptical of how the "new type of historian emerges, who, unlike his predecessor, is ready to confess the intimate relation that he maintains to his subject."[24]

Ararat does not give the viewer even a glimpse of the personal and lived experiences, the self-reflexivity of author-historian Egoyan, or the interpenetration of his personal experiences and autobiography with the collective memory of his communal group.[25] Personal gaps within his lived experiences and historical consciousness are absent, as are his personal postmemories. Some of his characters do impart their postmemories, but not Egoyan himself. Even though no single story comes across as "true" history, his larger narrative, the film, comes across as giving a concrete voice to the "true" story of the Armenian Catastrophe, with its concrete narrative and sense of continuity. But no matter how many stories and testimonies Egoyan includes in his film in an attempt to bridge the gap that is kept alive by denial, they are not enough. Historicization is never fully realized. And with the absence of any self-reflexivity, attempts of tackling the effects of the Catastrophe fall short. Egoyan deals with concrete aspects of memory. But what about the non-concrete aspects: the insubstantial, fluid, and tenuous parts, the ones that are unstable? How does one access them, frame them, and fix them in the historicization process?

It is through self-reflexivity that new narratives are engendered which ultimately create possibilities of realizing projects of historicization. Mythopoeia becomes this new form of narrative through which historicization is realized as exemplified in the works of Najarian, Bastajian, and Marcom Aharonian.

The Story of the Artist

> *"What do you remember, Ma?"*
> *"I remember many things but I can't remember my mother's face."*
> *"Tell me what you remember."*
> —Daughters of Memory, a story by Peter Najarian

With *Daughters of Memory,* Peter Najarian becomes one of the first author-artists born in the Diaspora, if not the first, to engage in self-reflexivity and tackle the issue of postmemories that keep escaping descendants of Armenian survivors.[26] Through self-reflexivity, Najarian positions himself within the narrative of his survivor mother and creates a whole new landscape for mapping the identity construction of a specific segment of diasporic Armenians: the generation of non-Armenian-speaking Armenian-Americans.

Daughters of Memory cover: Najarian's painting of his mother

The plot of *Daughters of Memory* is simple. Zeke, "a big-nosed, bald," Armenian artist, is reviewing his life's work. He ends up confronting the spirits of history and of his maternal grandmother, who perished in the desert wastelands of Mesopotamia. The story of the author and that of his protagonist are almost synonymous. It is his life story and the stories of his mother that he transposes to his character. As the narrator embarks on this journey of self-excavation and redemption, trying to give shape to the image of his grandmother, the reader encounters the many layers and crosscurrents of history through which his identity is formed and transformed. *Daughters of Memory* is a series of interwoven vignettes detailing Zeke's, and by extension Peter's attempt to grasp his unwritten and ruptured history. The narration is punctuated with a female chorus of survivors from his mother's generation.

In the first vignette, "The Old Grapevine," the searching and excavating tone is set:

> Lines upon lines, they flow like food for the tail-eating snake. They love the void and they grow in death . . . . Dear Death, dear dying friends, here are more of them, another mystery and a search.[27]

Here, already stories are mysteries, a concept that was missing in *Ararat*. The hunt begins with Zeke's mining the stories of his mother to salvage from oblivion whatever image he can of his maternal grandmother before he completely loses her with the death of his parent. "Who is she [my grandmother], what does she look like? He [the artist] wants to paint her as if she is the woman he's always wanted, and the quest for her figure leads him through the labyrinth of the mysterious female" forming within him.[28] He tries to draw his grandmother by drawing his models. As they are formed and shaped on his sketchpad, the models' gestures and images become his grandmother's. His quest not only leads him through the labyrinth of this mysterious female, but through a mysterious history as well. Since Zeke's mother is the sole remaining witness through whom he can develop an image of his grandmother, his mother's memories become the site of his archaeological excavation. But no matter how deeply he digs he cannot completely succeed, for his mother, also a survivor of the Armenian Genocide, is unable to remember her own mother's face. She recounts many of her childhood experiences, and throughout these stories the narrator's imageless grandmother is always present: "Once I heard her and my father make sounds in the night. My father was a gentle man but she was robust and strong. Her face however I can't remember at all."[29] And, in a story about her deportation route in the deserts of Syria: "I remember some women with rings in their nostrils and black lines on their cheeks. I can't remember my mother's face and yet I remember those women with rings in their nostrils and black lines on their cheeks when we stopped and tried to find some water."[30]

In spite of his mother's failure, Zeke keeps struggling to imagine the elusive face: "He tries to find her inside himself but his imagination fails, his memories interfere and they become like veils he can't clear away."[31]

It is through the narrator of *Daughters of Memory* that the author's experiences are manifested and transferred into an aesthetic realm with the attempt of historicization. In his dedication, Najarian writes: "For Grandma, who was born around the same time as Picasso and Joyce and who probably starved to death somewhere in the Syrian Desert when Degas died in Paris." But the narrator is not satisfied in placing and revealing his grandmother solely through great artists and authors who have been her contemporaries. He wants her to be more tangible, more accessible. Thus, he continues with the construction of her image:

> She washes her breasts and cups them with her palm as if to milk the eyes of her passionate grandson.
>
> He's obsessed with the crease of her buttocks and the swell of her nipples, the hair of her mound and the lips inside them.
>
> He has wanted to see her naked ever since he was not supposed to, the darkness under her dress and the contour of her bodice like mysteries he has wanted to solve . . .
>
> She was the secret underneath the clothes of the flesh, the darkness in the eye sockets of a cadaver on the sand, her stench drifting through the years.[32]

Zeke, in his frustration of not being able to completely penetrate the dark layers of memories, tries to penetrate the dark layers of her fleshy and sensual recesses. After he somewhat transfers his imageless grandmother into flesh and bones, he wonders what might have happened to her body:

> She lies buried in a valley, her bones the rocks now clean and smooth, her flesh the food for the meadows and the wood. Her eyes are the lupine and her voice purls in the breeze, her blood colors the petals of rose.[33]

Meanwhile, the artist still is trying to sketch his mother:

> "Ma, I can't draw you if you don't sit still."
>
> "Draw me from memory."[34]

With this command, his mother makes him confront the role of memories, of clinging to them in order to root oneself, one's family, and one's history. The artist must resort to memories to draw his invisible grandmother *and* his visible mother. His urge is so strong that while she is sleeping, he sneaks into her bedroom with pencil and paper. But even then he is confronted with the void, the faceless image of his grandmother. He sees his mother snoring, "dreaming of the dead, the face of her mother too deep to recall."

And then again, in the exchange between Zeke and his mother:

> "What do you remember, Ma?"
>
> "I remember many things but I can't remember my mother's face."
>
> "Tell me what you remember."
>
> "I remember in the winter we lived in town and she made bread in a small clay stove with wood fire. . . . On Sundays she always made *kuftah.* Most of thewomen made *kuftah* on Sundays . . . but her face however I can't remember at all."[35]

Najarian tackles issues of historicization by framing aspects of the non-concreteness of memories and in the process embarks on his project of integrating his own personal history with that of his family and the history of his nation. But what happens if certain aspects of experiences are beyond memories and beyond language? How does one access the aspects of memory and history that are outside any categories of conceptualization?

The Story of the Coffee Cup

> *Tell me what you cannot remember...*
> *Remember what you cannot tell me...*
> —Jagadakeer . . . between the near & east, a short film by Tina Bastajian

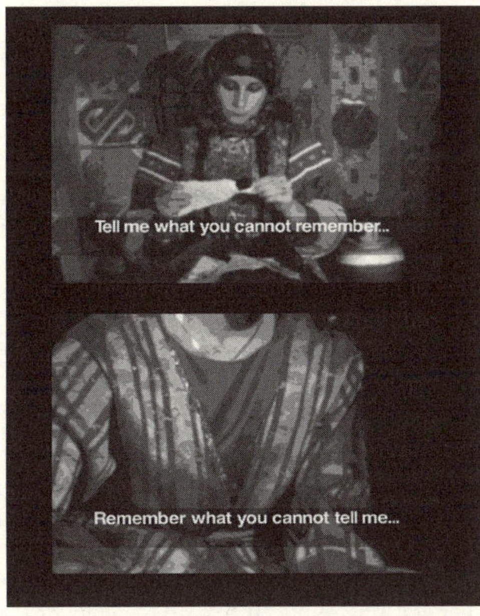

The sub-plot of *Jagadakeer . . . between the near & east* is similar in many ways to that of *Daughters of Memory*, even though the two are executed by artists from different generations and different historical backgrounds. Tina Bastajian, the creator of *Jagadakeer . . . between the near & east*, is two generations removed from the Armenian deportations and massacres. She is the granddaughter of child survivors who, like Peter Najarian's mother, were orphaned on the deportation routes. But with Bastajian, whose parents were born in the United States, there is a distancing from the massacres, the displacement, and their aftermath that is much more pronounced than Najarian's, who grew up among a generation of Armenians who were survivors and immigrants. As in *Daughters of Memory*, the searching and excavating tone of *Jagadakeer . . . between the near & east* is already evident in the first scene. Bastajian explains in "The Poetics and Tribulations of the Time-lag {in Making} *Jagadakeer . . . between the near & east*" that the film "explores personal and collective memory, nostalgia, displacement, absence, erasure and reconnection using the Armenian genocide as a point of reference, and as a visual/aural backdrop."[36]

The film opens with the projection of the first word of its title, *Jagadakeer*, followed by a tableau of a demitasse turned over on its saucer. The overturned demitasse sits on a table covered with an oriental rug. In the background hangs a reddish piece of cloth that is out of focus. A movie projector's flutter is heard; the flickering image of a tableau, with its sensual reddish hues. It is a film within a film. A voiceover of a woman speaking in Armenian is followed by her English translation:

When you read a coffee cup, you turn over the cup…

And then you open it and read the sediments, or whatever is left at the bottom.

Translate these sediments, read what is left behind.

Only after these utterances, does the rest of the movie title appear: . . . *between the near & east.* The film clip, squeezed between the two sections of the title, stands in for the ellipsis. In the ellipses of the title, a rupture is already sensed. Deciphering the sediments of the coffee cup becomes the key to sailing into the realm of "another mystery and a search."[37] Having to translate stories that are buried within the sediments of a coffee cup takes the viewer a step further away from the concreteness of events and into the realm of the ungraspable and the tenuous.

But in order to read sediments of an event, one has to have clairvoyance and the means of seeing beyond the range of ordinary perception. Like *Daughters of Memory, Jagadakeer* contains another mystery, another attempt at reconstructing the picture that existed before the traumatic events of the Catastrophe. But here, the image to be constructed is even further removed from the Event. Just as Bastajian is two generations removed from the events of the massacres and dispersion, so, too, is the first scene of the movie. The oriental setup of the coffee cup and its surrounding atmosphere, a film within a film, already takes us back in time. The shot is taken sometime in the past, and the off-screen utterances are translations of an almost forgotten language from a distant land and a remote past. Through the artist's search the viewer encounters the invisible and the absent, which reveal themselves only through reconstructed remnants—inherited postmemories. The filmmaker had heard very little about her maternal grandmother's childhood experiences of survival. As she recalls:

> From my mom, the one legacy, the one fragment that was repeated over and over again, because it was the only one that she knew, was that her mother, her grandmother and her great aunts crossed the Syrian desert naked and shaved all their hair on their heads and bodies to deter the Turks from raping them. It was a very odd thing to hear that as a little girl.[38]

She also learned from her mother that during the displacement, the women in her family concealed jewels and gold in their private places. This information echoes within the movie, the jewels that cover the navels of the belly dancers and the stories of Auntie Araxie, as Bastajian tries to tackle the fragmentary stories that she has inherited. The film is therefore incomplete and nonlinear, like its source material. Bastajian uncovers a new narrative that nevertheless crosses into the uncharted territory of unearthing and framing the invisible.

Negative of the original image and the composite family portrait from *Jagadakeer*.

In an effort to recreate a whole of his decimated family, Bastajian's great-uncle, Harutyun, took a family photograph shot in the early 1900s in Diarbekir and amended it by having the family members born after the photo added on to create a composite image of the whole family. This new image now included the family members who had died during the Genocide, the survivors, and those born afterwards. The family photograph becomes a compression both of time and space. By filling in the gaps, what Harutyun has done is create his family that would have existed if it weren't for the events of 1915. In the process of creating wholeness, a historicization has taken place. In creating *Jagadakeer*, Bastajian mirrors her great-uncle's impulse. She tries to recreate not only the moment the original photo was taken, but also the Event of the Catastrophe. This attempt unleashes an array of hidden subjects and problems. In the course of the artist's search, the viewer encounters remnants of whatever information she can gather, to complete her historicization project.

In conjunction with the reenactment of the original portrait session, Bastajian tries to construct a continuity from fragmentary pieces, where the process of historicization becomes revealing with the following clips. A man, in traditional Armenian dress, breaks open a pomegranate. The sound of the pomegranate cracking open is the same as the clicking sound of a camera. The two sounds are conflated. After cracking the pomegranate into two, he offers them to a woman. The framing of the shot only shows the arms of the two people. Voices from the game show *Jeopardy* are heard. The offering of the pomegranate is still on the screen. The voice of an Armenian photographer is heard, giving directions to family members as he poses them for a portrait and then tells them: "Be a bit happy . . .with happy faces. . . ." While the shutter clicks, the game show *Jeopardy* is heard. One of the contestants chooses "Near East" from the various categories of questions and the host asks, "Quoted in 1939, which infamous leader said: 'who still talks now of the extermination of the Armenians'. . . ." The negative image of Bastajian's paternal grandmother's family portrait, taken in the 1900s in Diarbekir, Turkey, now appears. As this image moves across the screen, an imaginary reenactment of the conversation taking place during the photo shoot between the photographer and Bastajian's great-grandmother is heard. Suddenly a female voice speaks in dialectical Turkish:

> *Yani, o yere ailenin ruhlar, a rılar vatanıdır, sürgünü kültürü da lısı*
> (where the ghosts of your family live, and the motherland of their pain, and the scars of a culture of exile).

No subtitle translates this utterance that at first seems out of context. It is followed by the continuation of the game show question: ". . . thus foreshadowing his rise to power?" which remains unanswered. It is a question whose answer most Armenians of the Diaspora know: Hitler. Next, a pastiche of scenes and dialogue unfolds:

> Armenian photographer: "Now pay attention . . ."

The next scene shows two torsos of belly dancers with a jewel in each of their navels, one green and one red. The green gem of the belly dancer on the left pops out as the photographer clicks his camera:

> Game show host: "Pat?"

> Armenian photographer: "It's done."

The viewer hears and sees the ruby pop out with the second click of the camera.

In the background, sounds of animal-drawn carts traversing rough roads are heard, simulating the caravans of deportees.

> A female voiceover commenting in Armenian:

> Auntie Araxie had known this silent wide expanse under her dress where she kept gold and secrets. . . .

The film takes the viewer back in time: the two belly dancers return, the jewels back in their navels. They are dancing behind a translucent veil. Their faces are still invisible, cut off by the frame. The color turns into a soft reddish hue, as the voice continues:

> . . . wrapped in an embroidered cloth
> that she would pass to my mother,
> who would then pass it on to me.
> She knew the silence of deserts,
> And the shriek of families floating down moaning rivers,
> And the smell of rotting children.

The translucent veil is lowered. The camera zooms in and back out. At last the faces of the belly dancers are revealed. These are all fragments of post-memories through which Bastajian is trying to reconstruct and create a linear historical narrative. The scene that opens with the cracking of a pomegranate signifies the breaking of silence and the telling of hidden and suppressed stories: the passing down of treasured memories from one generation to another. These scenes are rich with information. The precious stones in the navels of the belly dancers echo the jewelry that Bastajian's family members hid during the deportation. Also, perhaps, the treasure of the old culture that was lost. As the movie progresses, secrets are unraveled and silences broken. The gems pop out, the translucent veil drops and we now see the previously faceless dancers. Bastajian gradually excavates the missing parts of the story line, but the reconstruction is not linear; she creates her story from the gaps of history and memory, from what is between the near (the present) and the east (history). But within the process of historicization, the artist encounters gaps that she is not able to bridge: lapses of memories, forgetfulness, and incoherence. For example, in one scene a young woman in traditional dress is cutting onions, her eyes teary. We hear the voice of Bastajian's grandmother recounting her experiences of losing her family members one by one in the deserts of Mesopotamia; then suddenly her story breaks off. After a short pause, she says: "I cannot remember everything." Bastajian's grandmother is unable to remember her traumatic childhood experiences, either in a linear manner or in its entirety. Her narrative becomes disjointed and interspersed with pauses.

Several years before making this film, Bastajian had interviewed her paternal grandmother. Her initial interest in recording the old woman's stories was to have her "grandmother talk chronologically about [events] before, during, and after the genocide." She recorded the stories over a period of two years, but soon realized it was futile to try to arrange them in a coherent and linear way. Bastajian writes about the resulting frustration:

> Her stories were often very conflicting and incomplete, and usually not from her own experience but what were passed down to and through her. Though I didn't always understand which part came first, and who was who, she had her own special and endearing way of speaking and telling stories. I remember thinking then that I'd just let her talk and that I would figure it out later in the editing stage.[39]

At the time of the interview, Bastajian was not able to understand "that the overall incomplete, displaced, and often absent information was a byproduct of the [rupture created by the] genocide, and these remains would be the key to [her] film's content and structure."[40] Years later, she would employ the poignant off-screen voice to reflect these realizations.

In their efforts to excavate the invisible and the absent and thus engage in their historicization projects, both Najarian and Bastajian pose different versions of the same question. Zeke asks his mother directly: "Tell me what you remember"; whereas Bastajian's off-screen voice asks the grandmother: "Tell me what you don't remember. . . . Remember what you cannot tell me." As the authors get further away from the experience of the Event, the style of the excavation changes between first- and second-generation descendants of survivors, yet the desire and need for historicization is ever present. In both cases, within the process of historicization gaps created by the rupture cannot be bridged through concrete narratives. At this point, the narratives enter the realm of the mythical. Historicization becomes realizable only through mythopoeia: the creation of myths. The gaps are bridged through mythopoeia, thus creating continuity within the collective memory of the communal group, and the autobiography of the artist in its interpenetration with the collective memory. It is this mythopoeia that is encountered midway within both *Daughters of Memory* and *Jagadakeer*, but which is absent in the film *Ararat*.

The effort to reconstruct the whole from excavated fragments of memories eventually takes Zeke (and the author himself) to the lost homeland of historic Armenia that has become devoid of any Armenians, yet is inhabited by their ghosts and the descendants of the perpetrators of the Genocide. Using his family's survival stories and other accounts of the massacres, along with historical events, Najarian weaves a rich personal embroidery as he travels across the birthplace of his ancestors. Zeke's mind shuttles back and forth between the massacres and the encounters he has with the people who have now "settled in the homes of those who have died in the desert."[41] It becomes impossible for him to separate the current inhabitants of Turkey from their genocidal past. When he reaches the border, Turkish guards start searching the bus, but for him their act seems to say: "Come through the gate of flowers and bones."[42] Looking at the faces of the guards, he asks himself:

> Were these the faces that raped Aunty Zabel, were these the eyes that slaughtered Uncle Avedis? They stared back like innocent models. Nowhere else, not even in India, were they more friendly and hospitable. They had heard of the past but it was not theirs, it was erased from their history books.[43]

Here, the reader enters the fairyland of ghosts and their stories. The vignette titled "She Begins to Reveal Herself in Fairyland" is already telling of the nature of the narrative to come. The reader, in conjunction with the artist-narrator, is not able to separate the real and the present from the stories of the past. History slips into myth, and myth into history. It is not possible to differentiate the two anymore. It is within this fairyland that images start to form and stories reveal themselves. Najarian, through Zeke, is able to reconstruct history when he gets to his ancestors' birthplaces. After Zeke reaches Diarbekir, the birthplace of Najarian's father, his vision takes flight:

> These were the donkey lanes where his father played stickball with his gang. . . . These were the homes of Sunday feasts and evenings filled with music, Uncle Avedis playing the zither and Uncle Ashod singing like waves of wild wheat. These were the doorways of all those who did not escape, their bones the sand of Tigris below.[44]

As the narrator passes through cities once inhabited by substantial Armenian communities, the historical past mingles with the landscapes that unfold before him:

> From Diyarbekir the journey would continue through more hometowns and the never-ending saga of *mythical* kin. Through Severek where Harry Goshgarian's aunt was beheaded and through Urfa where Charlie Aramian's grandfather was tortured and hung by his feet . . . the terror of history impossible to draw, all drawing a transformation and every suffering doomed to become art.[45] [emphasis mine]

The reader enters an otherworldly realm with the narrator as "the journey takes us through hometowns and the never-ending saga of *mythical* kin." His process of historicization brings out the invisible, the mystery, and fills in the gaps created in his history. The rupture is bridged over through the construction of myths and stories, and the continuum that it establishes. While Zeke struggles with his task, the punctuating chorus of women survivors is not far away. These are the bits and pieces of stories that the author would hear while growing up in a community full of survivors. This one is about memories, trying to anchor oneself through them in the hope of not losing the self, and everything with it. But regardless, the ghosts of times past keep disturbing.

The Ghosts

- I wish I could write. I make marks on paper to help me remember and then I forget what they're for.
- That's okay, just keep trying. Don't lose your memory. If our memories go we're finished.
- We have to keep remembering or we'll be like Zarzavart in the nursing home. If you go there now she won't even know who you are.
- She lost touch with her family, that's how she got like that. There was no one to talk with but the walls.
- She talks with ghosts now. She looks out the window and talks with the ghosts in her head.[46]

When the artists and characters of both works enter legendary lands of bygone events, similar trajectories of historicization become integrated within the landscape of the mythical. Peter Najarian and his narrator ultimately tackle (their) history within the fairyland, now inhabited by ancestral spirits, by entering "the gate of flowers and bones." The author himself recounts how "he disappeared as if into *fairyland*," en route encountering the "never-ending saga of *mythical* kin" [emphases mine]. Similarly, Tina Bastajian and her invisible characters, always lurking in the background of the movie, confront the land in which the ghosts of their families now live: a landscape turned mythical. The characters in Bastajian's film are never fully present. All dialogues are done in voiceovers; the speakers are faceless, since they are spirits from bygone events.

It is in the next section of Batajian's film that the viewer is introduced to the concept of Armenia as a mythical place. We hear static sounds and changing of channels. The landscape of eastern Turkey is on a television screen. We hear the voices of the *Jeopardy* game show host and the contestants:

> "Pat, continue."
>
> "East for $900."
>
> "This small landlocked country, isolated by natural borders, seems a myth rather than a reality, often changing its borders, which at its widest extent stretched from 37-40 east longitude, and from 37.5-41.5 north latitude. Lee?"
>
> "What is Uzbekistan?"
>
> "No. Sorry. Pat?"
>
> "What is Georgia?"
>
> "Sorry. No one got that one. The correct answer was Armenia."

Not only does the host of the game show equate Armenia with a mythical place, but no one gets the answer right, since it is not a real or a concrete place. When I asked the filmmaker about her motivations for this portion of *Jagadakeer*, Bastajian replied: "This non-linear structure also provided a way to question mythical Armenian culture as it weaves the distinct tapestry that has become our lives, and voices—heard and unheard, seen and unseen."[47] The filmmaker tries to tackle the fragmentary stories that she has inherited. The film is therefore incomplete and nonlinear in the traditional sense, like its source material. Bastajian uncovers a new nonlinear style that nevertheless crosses into the uncharted territory of the mythical. As the movie progresses, secrets are revealed and silences broken. Bastajian gradually excavates the missing parts of the story line, but the reconstruction is not linear; she creates her story from the remnants of history and memory, from what is between the near (present) and the east (history).

Throughout the film, the viewer hears the off-screen voice prompting the grandmother to say what she does not remember, and to remember what she cannot tell, the grandmother reveals her stories in bits and pieces. In the next scene, a woman in folk costume and headscarf sits cross-legged on the floor and removes pieces of *lavash* bread from her mouth. She starts putting the torn pieces back together—morsels that she has already chewed and swallowed—and reconstituting the bread into its original whole. It is in this scene that we hear a voiceover in Armenian: "Tell me what you cannot remember," with the voice of a muezzin in the background, calling the faithful for prayer. Further through the film, we see a sitting woman's lower body, in traditional Armenian dress, scooping watermelon (symbolic of Diarbakir, the birthplace of Bastajian's grandmother) and the grandmother continuing with her deportation story. And then, the same Armenian voiceover is heard: "Remember what you cannot tell me." The scenes and voiceover are symbolic of the stories Bastajian is excavating. The woman in traditional costume (representing the link to a vanished past) is pulling forth Bastajian's heritage piece by piece, and the filmmaker is trying to put them together. Finally, the pieces in the film start falling in place and the viewer gets a discernible picture, though a montage.

In 1988, Bastajian traveled to Turkey with a friend of hers, a daughter of American missionaries who had lived in Adana during the 1970s. The experience later became key in framing the ungraspable in her work. Bastajian writes:

> As an Armenian traversing this complex landscape, a deep longing and curiosity was sparked. The idea of traveling to Turkey had always been a taboo subject to my family and to many Armenians, as it is the place where our ancestral ghosts live, cloaked in silence and denial. This trip allowed me to locate the displacement and absence I had always felt.[48]

With different historicities, different backgrounds, and diverse agendas, she and her travel partner have unforeseen encounters with respect to history and their relations to it. Bastajian had gone to Turkey with the stories of the deportations that she had heard from her grandmother and mother. For her, the journey takes on an extra dimension:

> While traveling in Turkey I experienced many unexpected and enlightening encounters with the Turks and my traveling companion Rebecca. This elicited many confused emotions that often fluctuated from my being ecstatic to the melancholic. I felt overwhelmed and sometimes conflicted over my internal emotions and the external stimulus of the complex landscape where I felt at once at home and estranged.[49]

But for her friend, the journey was a visit to the place of her childhood. The journey reaches a climax when her friend, Rebecca, is not capable of comprehending Bastajian's emotional state. Eight years later, only after being able to digest the complexities of their trip is Rebecca able to formulate her emotions. She writes the filmmaker a letter explaining her regrets and questioning her past attitudes in being insensitive regarding the Armenian Catastrophe and the nature of Turkish denials and in not being able to comprehend the state of an Armenian traveling through Turkey for the first time. As the film nears its conclusion, the voice of Bastajian's former travel partner, Rebecca, is heard reading her letter in Turkish, which she has translated from the original in English. The scene on the screen is a close-up of the negative of the family portrait:

> After our trip to Turkey, I began writing a project about memory, homeland, place, and the awaited return. . . . For that reason I owe you an apology. I was not truly sensitive to you . . . on our trip to Turkey . . . just to go there required courage. . . . Yes, danger was there, maybe not physical danger . . . but a danger to your soul and spirit . . . where the ghosts of your family live . . . and the motherland of their pain . . . and the scars of a culture of exile . . . I just didn't understand at the time . . . I am ashamed . . . and I am sorry.

Here, finally, the viewer understands the meaning of the disjointed, out of context, original Turkish utterance juxtaposed over the negative of the family picture at the beginning of the film, with no subtitles. For Bastajian, while traveling in Turkey, not only were the tragic stories and the ghosts of her ancestors weighing on her as she encountered the landscape "of flowers and bones" but the denial of the Turkish government in respect to the actions taken by the Ottoman regime in carrying out their genocidal policies. It wasn't enough for the filmmaker to hear an apology in English regarding the events of the Genocide and their effects on her identity. She wanted it said in Turkish. And in *Jagadakeer*, the apology is heard in Turkish, from her travel companion, which becomes a proxy for the one that the Turkish government has denied all along. The utterance in Turkish becomes a turning point in redeeming and revealing a history that has always been silenced and suppressed by the descendants of the perpetrators. Finally, the pieces in the film start falling in place and we get a more or less discernible picture. We have now been given the context of the Turkish utterance at the beginning of the film (juxtaposed over the negative of the family portrait) and its effect in framing the invisible. Finally, the process of historicization takes hold, mythopoeia being at the center of this process.

One of the last scenes of the film is home footage taken during one of Bastajian's birthday parties when she was still a child. She leans forward to blow out the candles on the cake while her mother and grandmother, one on each side, also lean forward with her in unison. For the filmmaker, this scene represents the passing down of stories and the postmemories that she has inherited from them: from the grandmother to the mother to the daughter.[50] A voiceover in Armenian is heard:

> Three skirts and gold dowry bangles . . .
> Float like dead women down the Euphrates . . .
> And sink like lentils, sifted by aunties.

As they sink, they become sediments waiting for their resurrection. Ultimately, they are brought back to life through the creation of mythical landscapes.

The Story of Rumor

> *She is writing a book of memory on her body and destroying it as she writes.*
> —Three Apples Fell from Heaven, a novel by Micheline Aharonian Marcom

With *Three Apples Fell from Heaven*, Micheline Aharonian Marcom dives straight into the vortex of the Event, the singularity where there is complete silence, and the absence of all memories.[51] She delves into the area that is beyond language. As she says in her interview:

> I was very interested in what goes unspoken . . . the shame of the body. For me, at the moment of the genocide, when all the rules and decorum of society have been stripped away, what is left, what is obvious is the body itself, and what happens to the body in those instances, and I was very struck by how in the memoirs of the surviving Armenians, almost all of them, skim over or alleviate the moments of suffering of the body. I felt it important that the body be present and what happens to the body.[52]

Aharonian Marcom embarks on the project of historicizing the most glaring void, which has been the absence of the body within the memoirs and stories of the survivors, especially the period covering the rupture. Her novel, set in 1915-17, takes places during the phase where the absence is the most glaring, where memory is nonexistent. It is not a matter of trying to salvage memories of survivors anymore, of grandmothers long dead.

In the chapter titled, "Inside 1917," Anaguil is modeled after the author's maternal grandmother. As an orphan, she is trying to remember her mother and her past by touching herself, digging her fingers into her skin. As the years go by, Anaguil struggles not to forget her Armenian past, her original identity:

> She touches her collarbone, then its hollow, her skin is dry and smooth; she runs her second and index fingers into the groove of the hollowed collarboned space. Anaguil thinks of her birth and its obligations. She thinks of death not as if she wants to die, but as if her death were a trapped moth pressing upon her lower back side with its wings, in the space of her back where her kidneys ache—the space inside where the moth flies and flutters ensnared by the skin. Constant. Constantly. She digs her fingers into her skin. . . .
>
> She touches herself to remember, Mama, Mama: I don't know if I can remember you in this skin and bone, collarbone, you gave me on the day of my birth. Enough.

She is writing a book of memory on her body and destroying it as she writes.[53] Anaguil's body has become a piece of vellum, a parchment for her text. These lines are phantasmagoric yet so accurately portray the absence of memory and of any text related to preserving memory. In this sense, Anaguil represents the multitude of survivors who have been unable to leave any records of their sufferings, either oral or textual. Whatever they have tried to remember has been lost. There is the constant struggle against forgetting one's self, one's parents, and one's history. Anaguil cannot prevent the slippage of her identity. And yet, it is through those destroyed parchments and the slippage of memory that the invisible is framed.

Micheline Aharonian Marcom is even more distanced from the events of the past than Najarian or Bastajian. She was eight years old when her maternal grandmother passed away and never had the chance to hear her stories directly. Nevertheless, her debut novel is drawn from her maternal grandmother, a child survivor of the Event. In 1997, Aharonian Marcom started writing the story of her grandmother because of a tremendous need to know the history of her family and to figure out her own place in this history. She wanted to fill in the invisible world behind the few scant phrases that she has inherited through her mother. During our interview, Aharonian Marcom said of her grandmother: "Even though I didn't know her very well, her absence was compelling." The author read as many memoirs of surviving Armenians as she could find. Slowly, the world of Anatolia with its silent history opened up in front of her, and she could place her grandmother within a tangible context.[54] Yet gaps remained, one of which was what happens to the body at the moment of transgression and rupture. She delineates the rupture through the transgression of the body. It becomes of utmost importance for the writer to understand the moments of suffering of the body. By historicization, the author's main objective ultimately became the positioning of herself within her own history and of human history at large. She is able to realize her project through the historicization of the ruptured body.

The book is comprised of a series of vignettes, connected to each other by descriptions of the body during extreme moments of suffering, death, and separation from family and community. Aharonian Marcom delves into the ontology of the physical body and its identity, and tries to understand the transformations when others appropriate it. There is always the story that history tells, a history written by official state narratives and governments in power. But how about the unwritten history experienced by both victims and perpetrators? How is the Event experienced and manifested by the parties involved? Aharonian Marcom details her interest in writing about this unwritten history:

> I am always interested in what has been left out, denied, desecrated, silenced, in the "howls restrained by decorum," as Whitman writes in *Song of Myself*. I became more interested in what wasn't said by Armenians and Turks. In the shame, the longing, the body.[55]

In an attempt to understand the human condition under such extreme circumstances, the author has no choice but to go into the realm of the bizarre and the fanciful. The *hamam*, or bathhouse, becomes the landscape in which the reader meets Anaguil and her four-year-old sister, Nevart, Armenian girls who are taken in by good-hearted Turkish neighbors after the death of their parents. But the price for survival is to be Turkified. The girls adopt new names: Anaguil becomes Fatma. She begins to hate going to the bathhouse with the Turkish Hanim, since it reminds her of going there with her Armenian mother. Her younger sister, however, has no recollection of her previous identity and is thus swiftly assimilated. Anaguil's inner torture and agony are revealed as she contemplates her history. One day, while walking through the *hamam,* she falls:

> There is a gaping hole, a hole from nowhere, she thinks, unexpected. Her toes slip out of the shoe and she falls down in the hallway. She hits her head upon the stone floor. There is also a falling down inside her, unexpected, that momentarily does not contain itself; it is louder than the music. She laughs. All of this is private, silent, until it breaks outside of her a little, and then a little bit more; bit by bit the laughs erupt like unstoppable stream from Anaguil's throat, her tongue, her teeth, her cracked lips. She laughs out loud. And then Anaguil notices the laughter as a foreign thing, as she herself has become to her self and to her town.[56]

Hitting her head functions as a trigger that leads to a hysterical instant of realization of what has happened to the physical body and the complex inner landscape and identity of an orphaned girl. Aharonian Marcom, in trying to unearth and frame the silenced, the left out, the denied, goes beyond the surface of the fate of the thousands of orphans who, like Anaguil, had to shed their identities, and articulates their inner voices. Yet Anaguil cannot prevent her fading past from coming through and disrupting her new life and identity. Her past is always there, disturbing the present.

The reader is plunged further into the abyss of madness with the poet Sargis disguised as a woman, hiding in an attic and slowly going insane. He watches from his hideout as the massacres and arrests are carried out in his town:

> . . . since I have lived here in this attic where the heat melts the hairs of my arms, and the constant perspiration on my skin has brought on a mutiny of red-pus sores. I am like a hairless dog, like bitches who live behind the *hamam* who burn to nothing and who die but still go again and again to the *hamam* in search of comfort . . . the same dogs reincarnated over and over again. [And] the people living there among the embers would kick the mongrels and cook them when all of their fur had been singed and removed, when their raised sanguine sores had made pattern on their skin—a facsimile of a new coat. It was an outdoor barbecue, reminiscent of summertime feast.
>
> Who shall cook me?
>
> You Turkish reed-sharpener, will you eat a dog although of another (and now repellent) race?
>
> My death will be like a dog's, like a *hamam*-dog's dying days in the heat of the ashes. I've removed my woman's vestments; I am the new Adam in the garden, the Garden of Heat-in-the-Attic: Sargis, the modern vitreous poet. I'll tell you of my dark days in this oven. I'm cooking. You'll eat me unseasoned in strips with bread (will you have bread then for your sandwich? Will the bakeries reopen?).[57]

Revealed through Sargis are the tumultuous interactions and relationships between Turks and Armenians during the critical years of the Event. During the massacres and deportations many Armenian men, like Sargis, disguised themselves as women to save their lives. Here, Sargis the poet has gone mad. Sitting in the attic, he writes his caca poems:

> I keep daily records of my excrements. Its changes. Its abeyances. Its texture: adamantine, fleshy, bushy, lithe, gelatinous, flaccid. What would its utterances be? I write my caca poems.
>
> For three days now there is nothing, only urine urine urine: yellow, gold, puce, quince, buff, sea-sand (O lovely!), desert-sand. I strain. I think: I am dying. My asshole hurts, the wrinkled squeeze-hole is like another burn. I sit on a cushion. My mama's needlework massages my bare ass—cream flowers and round edges caress me.[58]

Eventually, the rupture gets described through the transgression of the body, which plunges the characters into madness. Within this madness, the process of framing the invisible and the mute is conveyed in an odd, uncanny, and fantastic manner.

Aharonian Marcom tries to give voice to the voiceless, to the thousands of children who were abandoned on deportation routes, to the unnamed women who were thrown into wells or abducted. In chapter after chapter, the author puts a face to all these faceless people and delineates their inner landscapes via representational characters. We come to understand that the entire history of a nation has been horrendously silenced, and start to explore the contents of that silence through the violation of the body.

Whereas Najarian and Bastajian delve into the mythical realm midway through their creative works, at the moment when the concrete escapes them, Aharonian Marcom takes the reader right into the land of hyper-realistic fairy-tales and myth, since from the start she is exploring the absence of memories and history. Except for little morsels of reality, her novel is entirely mythopoeia. The title itself, *Three Apples Fell from Heaven*, refers to the traditional ending in Armenian fairytales, and the first chapter, "This Is the Story That Rumor Writes," uses a convention of Armenian fairytales that begin with—"There was and there was not":

> She writes it at night, while you are dozing.
>
> Rumor says things like, And so, and so
> There was and
> There was not
>
> Rumor tells stories, this is the story she writes.[59]

The more Aharonian Marcom delves into the mythical, the more lucid the void created by the rupture becomes.

As we come to the end of our readings of the last three artists, it becomes clear that gaps created by the Event in the collective memories of Armenians can be historicized through the process of mythopoeia, something that is missing in *Ararat*, where there are no gaps within the collective memories and post-memories of the characters. The further away the artist is from the rupture, and the more the discontinuity within the collectivity memory of their Armenian identity, the gaps become more pronounced and the idea of myth and the process of mythopoeia become more prominent within the works. Even though all three artists engage in self-reflexivity in creating their works, there are different levels of intimacy to the characters that have witnessed and lived the trauma of the Event. With Peter Najarian, the eldest of the three, it is almost impossible to separate the writer from his character, while with Tina Bastajian, the artist remains in the background, present yet invisible. And with Micheline Aharonian Marcom, the youngest of the three, even though the artist is not personally present, she is lurking in the context of the genesis and creation of the novel. The information that we gather about the novel being drawn from the life stories of her maternal grandmother is from the back jacket of the book, the articles that the author has written on the impetus of the novel, and her interviews. The scant pieces of postmemory that have been left behind by her grandmother become the foundation for the mythopoeia.

Conclusion

The rupture created by the Event of the Armenian Catastrophe has become crucial in the construction of identities of a new generation of Armenian-American novelists and artists. With the de-structuring of Armenian social and communal groups, first with their uprooting from the homeland and then with the eventual dispersion of various Armenian diasporan communities, there was also a de-structuring of collective memories that went hand in hand with the collectivity of the communities. Hence, a break was created within the continuity of Armenian historical consciousness—memory and history. As the descendants of the survivors moved further away from the continuity provided by their communities, coupled with the dispersion and assimilation, gaps developed within the collective memories of their Armenian identities. The more disconnected the artists have become from the continuity of the community and its collective memory, the wider the gaps have become.

The four artists discussed here embark on historicization projects trying to integrate the rupture created by the Catastrophe into the continuity of Armenian history and that of their personal histories. In comparing their works, Egoyan, with his feature film *Ararat*, stands out from the other three. Egoyan tries to implement his historicization project through a multiplicity of narratives and testimonies of various people. But no matter what, the forces of denial and counter-narratives keep disturbing his project. In *Ararat*, there is no interpenetration between his personal experiences and the collective memory of diasporic Armenians, no self-reflexivity. There are no gaps in the collective memories and histories of both the characters and Egoyan himself, even though their stories are constantly disrupted. No matter how many multilayered stories Egoyan incorporates within his epic narrative, his historicization project is never fully realized. It becomes a never-ending process of countering the denial of the Catastrophe. On the other hand, through mythopoeia, Najarian, Bastajian, and Aharonian Marcom are able to embark on their historicization projects much more successfully. Through the creation of myths, they are able to fill in the gaps created within the collective memory of their ethnic group and their own personal experiences as part of that same group. Through mythopoeia, they are able to bridge the disjuncture and gaps created between their own personal experiences, their autobiographies, and their re-structured communal group that is full of vestiges from the past. Myth has always been unstable, slippery, and full of contradictions. It is tenuous, amorphous, and fluid, difficult to frame and stabilize. There is slippage in its meaning. Thus, the historicization project for artists who are engaged in mythopoeia has been much more effective in circumventing the denial and contestation that maintains the disruption of the historical consciousness of Armenians in general, and for artists who have stuck with the concreteness of stories and in the representations of "true" histories. Through self-reflexivity, a new narrative emerges that realizes the process of historicization through mythopoeia.

The last scene of *Jagadakeer* shows an oriental room decorated with a red pillow and a red carpet. A woman's hand, with a gold bracelet, throws a pair of red dice on the red carpet, while a voiceover intones in Armenian:

> It is not on any map . . .
>
> True places never are . . .

Juxtaposed with the utterances, we see the dice going back into her hand, in reverse motion. And then the scene changes to the woman in traditional dress, who earlier was regurgitating and reconstituting the pieces of *lavash* bread. She is catching the composite family portrait that is being thrown back to her in slow motion. It is the first time that we see the photograph as a positive picture. The family picture and stories now completed, the gaps within the collective memory filled in, and historical consciousness made into a continuum, for the last three artists discussed here, the mythical homeland becomes a true place, even though it cannot be found on any map. Mythopoeia creates the possibility of historicizing the rupture created by the Catastrophe.[60]

Notes

1. Nearly all Armenians see the events of 1915 as an outright genocide committed against Armenians of the Ottoman Empire, whereas the Turkish state and official Turkish historiography deny the events as "genocide." I, personally, have chosen to use the terms "Event" and "Catastrophe," since the word genocide has become too politicized to be of much use for my analysis, and its definition has become too technical, devoid of human dimension or agency. In this context, the term "Event" refers to the specific events of 1915-1917 in relation to what transpired to the Ottoman-Armenians. It is a historical event, which since then has been referred to as *Mets Eghern* (approximately translated as "Great Crime"), *Taragrutiun* (Deportation), *Aksor* (Exile), *Jard* (Massacre), and most recently *Tseghaspanutiun* (Genocide). These are all terms that present the events that transpired in 1915 as historical ones. The historicity of this event gets interpreted and reinterpreted through time, thus the existence of different terminologies in describing it. I use the term "Event" only when referring to its historical connotation, which can encompass any or all of these terminologies. But the ontology of the "Catastrophe" is other than a historical event. Here, "Catastrophe" is used in its phenomenological sense. The term phenomenology has varied but related meanings in philosophy, psychology, and sociology. In cultural anthropology, it tends to take its sociological meaning: in this case, the study of the ways in which descendants of the survivors experience and understand the effects of the "Event." The term "Catastrophe" not only encompasses the "Event," but also the meaning that it acquires due to the extension of historical temporality. In this study, the ontology of the Catastrophe manifests itself in the construction of identities of present day non-Armenian-speaking Armenian-American artists.

2. In this study, "diasporic Armenians" refers in particular to Armenians who are the descendants of Ottoman-Armenian survivors.
3. In this chapter, I will only cover the rupture as it relates to Armenian historiography.
4. The break in this wall of silence occurs not only with the specified Armenians, but also within a segment of Turkish society. Starting in the early-1990s, we start hearing Turkish voices outside official Turkish historiography regarding the events of 1915. For an alternate periodization of Turkish historiography, see Fatma Müge Göçek, "Turkish Historiography and the Unbearable Weight of 1915," chapter 21 within this volume. In her attempt to reconstruct official Turkish historiography, Göçek embarks upon a process of periodization that consists of four stages, the fourth stage being the Post-Nationalist period, 1982 to the present. This period starts with the neo-liberalization of the Turkish economy, media, and communications under the Turkish president Türgut Özal. One of the most recent examples of this break in the wall of silence within official Turkish historiography has been the unprecedented conference on Ottoman-Armenians that took place on Turkish soil, where participants were able to present viewpoints outside official Turkish historiography. Worthy of mention is the series of workshops organized by Professors Ronald Suny and Fatma Müge Göçek, bringing Armenian, Turkish, and other scholars together to present papers and discuss the events of 1915.
5. For a background on this particular phenomenon—the separation of history and memory and the "culture of preservation," see Susan A. Crane, "Writing the Individual Back into Collective Memory," *The American Historical Review* 102, 5 (December 1997): 1372-1385.
6. In fact, the work of Maurice Halbwachs, *The Social Framework of Memory*, was an argument against Henri Bergson's concept of lived experience and Sigmund Freud's approach of leaving out the social group within the interpretation of individual psychology. For the concept of lived experience, see Henri Bergson, *Matter and Memory,* trans. Nancy Margaret Paul and W. Scott Palmer (London: S. Sonnenschein, and New York: Macmillan, 1911). In defining the interrelationship between individual memory and collective memory, Halbwachs gives preference to social procedures at the expense of the individual. He develops his ideas further in his collection of essays, *The Collective Memory*, English trans. (New York: Harper & Row, 1980).
7. The collective memories of Armenian-Americans discussed here refer only to the part that is connected to their Armenian identity.
8. Halbwachs, "Historical Memory and Collective Memory," in *The Collective Memory*, p. 55.
9. Lived experience is presented here in Henri Bergson's sense. For Bergson, memory occurs in the present, and is not archived somewhere in the brain. He emphasized the fact that recalling the past happens in the active present. Recalling and remembering become lived experiences.
10. Even though the concept of collective and historical memory was formulated in the early part of the twentieth century as a topic of scholarly research, the real boom in the scholarship on memory started in the 1980s with the publication of two works: Yosef Hayim Yerushalmi, *Zakhor: Jewish History and Jewish Memory* (Seattle: University of Washington Press, 1982); and Pierre Nora, "Entre mémoire et histoire," in *Les lieux de mémoire*, ed. Pierre Nora (Paris: Gallimard, 1984), pp. 23-43. The two authors, more or less, have the same stance on collective and historical memory; that historical memory has been replacing collective memory, and it is within historical memory that the past is preserved as fragments instead as continuity within collective memory.

11. See Roger Bastide, "Mémoire collective et sociologie du bricolage," *L'Année sociologique* (1970); and his *Les religions africaines au Brasil* (Paris: Presses universitaires de France, 1960).
12. By 1970, he had already brought in the role of the individual in the realm of memory studies, long before the scholarship on memory took off.
13. See the works of Marianne Hirsch, *Family Frames: Photography, Narrative, and Postmemory* (Cambridge, MA: Harvard University Press, 1997); Andrea Liss, *Trespassing through Shadows: Memory, Photography and the Holocaust* (Minneapolis: University of Minnesota Press, 1998); Ernt van Alphen, *Caught by History: Holocaust Effects in Contemporary Art, Literature, and Theory* (Stanford: Stanford University Press, 1997).
14. All are from the United States, except for Atom Egoyan, who resides in Canada.
15. Both Egoyan's film and the film within the film are called *Ararat.* Mt. Ararat occupies a prominent place in the ethos of the Armenian nation and its mythology.
16. In A.D. 961, Ani had become the capital of the Bagratuni Armenian kingdom.
17. In 1975, two groups were formed in Beirut, Lebanon, to combat Turkish denials of the Armenian Genocide and bring international attention to the forgotten Armenian Cause. They were involved in political violence and their main activities were the assassination of Turkish diplomats. One was the Armenian Secret Army for the Liberation of Armenia (ASALA), a Marxist-Leninist organization, and the other was Justice Commandos of the Armenian Genocide (JCAG), linked with the nationalist political organization, the Armenian Revolutionary Federation (ARF). In 1983, a new group was formed named Armenian Revolutionary Army (ARA) that replaced JCAG. The activities of all of these groups eventually petered out in 1985. In the film, which group Raffi's father belonged to is not specified.
18. Atom Egoyan, the grandson of Armenian survivors, was born in Egypt. At the age of four, his family immigrated to Vancouver, Canada, and he grew up in an environment where there was no significant Armenian community. He eventually became incorporated within the Armenian network at the age of eighteen, when he started attending the University of Toronto and became involved with Armenian causes. This was the time when Armenian organizations were engaged in political violence against the Turkish state.
19. Vardan Mamikonian, defending Armenia against the imposition of Zoroastrianism by the Persian shah in A.D. 451, went to battle against the superior Persian army and, though he was killed on the plain of Avarayr, helped to preserve Christianity in Armenia.
20. The film *Ararat* takes place in the Diaspora. It is where the new generation of Armenians and Turks encounter each other, and one of the main points of the film becomes the portrayal of this encounter.
21. Arsinee Khanjian relaying the words of her husband, Atom Egoyan, at the annual Bay Area Armenian National Committee's "Hai Tad" (Armenian Cause) event, March 6, 2004.
22. Egoyan, in his multiplicity of stories, also uses the published diary of Dr. Clarence Ussher, who was an American physician in Van during the events of 1915. His diary was published under the title: *An American Physician* in Turkey (1917). The screenwriter within the movie, Ruben, also uses the book to authenticate his story when confronted by Ani. There is also the story of Siamanto, who wrote a book of poems, *Bloody News from My Friend*, about the 1909 massacres of Adana. In it, Siamanto retells eyewitness accounts and testimonies, twice removed, of stories from the Adana massacres. Egoyan conflates the 1909 events of Adana unto the 1915 events of Van and instead of the stories being told as twice removed, he pres-

ents them as firsthand eyewitness accounts told by a German nurse to Dr. Ussher. Siamanto was one of the many Armenian intellectuals who were rounded up on April 24, 1915, and deported to central Anatolia, where they were massacred.

23. The Turkish government was on the offensive even before the film was premiered at the Cannes Film Festival, trying to force the distributor of the film, Miramax, into withdrawing it. Egoyan had to withdraw the film from the competition category at the Cannes Festival and have it screened separately. Immediately afterwards, the Turkish government published a book, *Art and Armenian Propaganda: Ararat as a Case Study* (2002), claiming that *Ararat* was a propaganda film in line with a whole history of Armenian propaganda films. The book was first published in Turkish in 2001, and later published in English.
24. Pierre Nora, "Between History and Memory: *Les lieux de mémoire*," *Representations* 26, 3 (1989): 18.
25. The lack of self-reflexivity is only true for *Ararat*. In those films where he is both director and screenwriter, there are indirect notions of self-reflexivity. Among these, the most personal and self-reflexive is *Calendar*, the only feature film where he appears on-screen.
26. Peter Najarian is the son of Zarouhi Najarian, an orphaned survivor of the massacres. He was born in New Jersey and then moved to California. *Daughters of Memory* was published in 1986, at about the same time that some elements in Turkey entered a post-nationalist period. It was also during this time that Armenian political violence ceased (1985). Thus, the second half of the 1980s becomes a pivotal period for both Armenian and Turkish historiography, with new voices being heard outside sanctioned nationalist narratives. On the Turkish side, in the early 1990s, the hegemony of the state over Turkish historiography was broken. On the Armenian side, with the cessation of the political violence carried out by various groups, the rhetoric of Armenian nationalism, induced and kept alive by Diaspora political organizations, gradually weakened. *Daughters of Memory* becomes the first innovative Armenian voice of this post-nationalist period dealing directly with the Catastrophe and its effects on the individual. Note: With the start of the conflict between Nagorno-Karabakh and Azerbaijan in the late 1980s, a new wave of nationalism took hold within the Armenian people. Unlike the previous nationalism, this one was a grassroots movement that began in Soviet Armenia. It was ironic that the Dashnaktsutiun, being the strongest and most nationalistic and anti-Soviet political party in the Diaspora, vehemently opposed the Armenian National Movement—the leadership behind the Karabakh movement—which was challenging the Soviet authorities.
27. Peter Najarian, *Daughters of Memory* (Berkeley, CA: City Miner Books, 1986), p. 3.
28. Ibid.
29. Ibid., p. 23.
30. Ibid., pp. 73-74.
31. Ibid., p.4.
32. Ibid., pp.47-48.
33. Ibid., p. 76.
34. Ibid., p.20.
35. Ibid., pp. 22-23.
36. Tina Bastajian, "The Poetics and Tribulations of the Time-lag {in Making} *Jagadakeer . . . between the near & east*" (unpublished manuscript).
37. Najarian, *Daughters of Memory*, p. 3.
38. Interview with the author.

39. Bastajian, "The Poetics and Tribulations of the Time-lag."
40. Ibid.
41. Najarian, *Daughters of Memory*, p. 134.
42. Ibid., p. 130.
43. Ibid.
44. Ibid., p. 139.
45. Ibid., p. 140.
46. Ibid., p. 134.
47. Interview with the author.
48. Bastajian," The Poetics and Tribulations of the Time-lag."
49. Ibid.
50. Interview with the filmmaker.
51. Micheline Aharonian Marcom is of Armenian heritage on her maternal grandparents' side, survivors of the Armenian Genocide. She was born in Dhahran, Saudi Arabia, and immigrated to the United States at a very young age, and grew up in a non-Armenian community.
52. Interview with the author.
53. Micheline Aharonian Marcom, *Three Apples Fell from Heaven* (New York: Riverside Books, 2001) pp. 53-54.
54. In ancient usage, Anatolia was synonymous with the peninsula of Asia Minor, the vast plateau between the Black Sea and the Mediterranean Sea. In modern usage, it is applied to the Asiatic portion of contemporary Turkey. *Anatolia* derives from the Greek term *anatole* "the east," originally "sunrise," literally "a rising above [the horizon]." See http://www.etymonline.com/index.php?term=Anatolia. In this context, I am using Anatolia as a reference to the whole landscape where the Event of the Catastrophe took place.
55. Micheline Aharonian Marcom. "In Her Own Words," *Ararat* 42, 164 (Autumn 2001): 50-52.
56. Marcom, *Three Apples Fell from Heaven*, pp. 21-22.
57. Ibid., pp. 136-137.
58. Ibid., p. 138.
59. Ibid. p. 1.
60. I would like to extend my gratitude to the four artists whose works I have utilized in this study. It is through their creative works that I have been able to expand my understanding of the legacy of the Armenian Catastrophe. I am indebted to them and to all the artists, writers, and friends who enriched the scope of my understanding."

10

The Diasporic Witness: Reconstruction of Testimony by Contemporary Los Angeles Artists

Ramela Grigorian Abbamontian

The Armenian Genocide of 1915 marked a traumatic turn in Armenian history: the first genocide of the twentieth century intensified the dispersal of Armenians to all parts of the world, especially the United States, heightening the sense of alienation resulting from a loss of a historic homeland. The aftershock of this moment in history unrelentingly impacted the lives, experiences, and identities of Armenians everywhere and bound them to one another by the thread of this historical memory, an ever-present burden on their diasporic identities. Collective memory, which transmits both the historical causes of the dispersion and a specific cultural heritage, is one of the attributes of a diasporan community.[1] It is this shared trauma that not only binds diasporan people together, but defines who they are, as David Waldstreicher poignantly suggests: "For Armenian Americans, the Genocide adds up to more than a historical tragedy; it remains the shaping event of their lives, and the reason they came to fashion a new life on a new continent. To ask that they forget is to ask them to forget who they are."[2]

How do artists visually articulate a calamity such as genocide endured by their own people? [3] Is it even possible to represent such a catastrophe and, more significantly, can it be represented by artists who have not experienced it firsthand? Could their non-experience be claimed as testimony?[4] What is the Genocide's impact on these artists and further how is their visual production an instrument to confront this historical memory, as they construct their diasporan identities? To address these questions, I consider the visual strategies employed by Los Angeles-based artists of Armenian descent in responding to the tragedy they inherited from a forcibly displaced people. The artists under consideration are Zareh Meguerditchian (popularly known as "Zareh"), Alina Mnatsakanian,

Sophia Gasparian, and Ara Oshagan, as well as photographers Oshagan and Levon Parian of The Genocide Project. Los Angeles serves as an ideal site of investigation because it is one of the largest centers of diasporan Armenians outside the Republic of Armenia, and burgeoning daily.

How are these artists, several generations removed from the event, nonetheless witnesses to it? Conventionally, a "witness" is one who has personal knowledge and firsthand experience of an incident.[5] In this chapter, I propose a modified designation wherein a witness is one who, though not having directly experienced a specific event, has nonetheless been privy to its aftershock and, hence, has the authority to recount it. These contemporary artists, then, are the witnesses to a post-genocide life and experienced its effect on their people, their families, and their own identities. Their story is also important; in fact, the story of the Armenian Genocide is incomplete without an account of its impact on subsequent generations.[6]

Interrogating these artists' stylistically varied works, I argue that their art attests to the Genocide's ongoing impact and reveals the inherent tensions of forging post-genocide diasporic identities. In other words, the artists attempt to comprehend the past in an effort to forge a contemporary identity. In this venture, the artists, by constructing the narrative of the Genocide and assuming the role of witnesses, inform others about the reality of mass murder and hence prevent the erasure of this historical memory. To that end, their works articulate the testimony of the Genocide and necessarily transform viewers into witnesses as well, confirming the reality of this event and preventing it from vanishing into oblivion.

An examination of selected works by these artists uncovers persistent threads in their artistic production. Foremost among these is that the artists' creativity has been triggered by Turkey's denial of the Genocide and by their consequent desire to raise awareness and bring about recognition, a process that must be fulfilled before healing can begin. Driven by a sense of responsibility as diasporan Armenians to do their parts for this cause, the artists also endeavor to perpetuate the historical memory of the Genocide. This prevention of erasure is prompted by the fact that as diasporan Armenians, living in a land outside of their "homeland,"[7] they are constantly reminded of the fact that their people were abruptly uprooted from their native hearths. In view of that, they also assert the survival of their community, despite the constant upheavals of history and immeasurable loss. In this process of reconstructing visual testimony of the Genocide and of survival, the artists and ultimately their viewers adopt the role of witnesses, becoming the historians, chroniclers, and storytellers who preserve the memory of this great crime.

Zareh

Angered by the general public's ignorance and the perpetrators' denial, Zareh (b. 1956) creates "a protest towards the silence" in *Turkish Soup Made with Armenian Bones* (1998) (Figs. 10.1-10.3).[8] Zareh was born in Syria and spent his early formative years in Syria and then Lebanon, where he moved at the age of seven. Spurred by the dangerous climate in Lebanon, he came to the United States in 1983, and after temporary stays in Dallas, Los Angeles, and back in Beirut, eventually made his permanent home in Los Angeles in 1986. The Genocide is a particularly sensitive issue for Zareh since his paternal grandfather Ohaness was shot in the head by Turkish soldiers and left to die, mercilessly dumped into a pit of other bodies. After about three days, Ohaness miraculously escaped, possibly with the help of neighborhood Arabs. Forty other members of Zareh's family, however, were not as fortunate; they all perished in the Genocide.

Not recoiling from referencing such brutality of the massacres, Zareh intrudes upon the viewer's space with *Turkish Soup Made with Armenian Bones.* A middle-aged man, clad in traditional Turkish costume and fez, operates a push-cart bearing the title words with "bones" mixed in "blood" visible through the transparent container atop the square base marked with the inscription, "Approved by U.N." The work has, similar to the Armenian experience, changed locations many times, standing often at busy street corners to shock and inform viewers. The installation/performance piece was exhibited during a nine-day period (April 16-24, 1998) at the following strategic locations: Third Street Promenade (Santa Monica, California); outside Borders Bookstore (Glen-

Figure 10.1
Zareh, Turkish Soup Made with Armenian Bones, **1998**

Figure 10.2

Figure 10.3

dale, California); Westwood Village (West Los Angeles, California); UCLA campus; Old Town (Pasadena, California); Downtown, Los Angeles; and at the Armenian Martyrs' Memorial Monument in Bicknell Park (Montebello, California). The installation was accompanied by a one-page flier providing brief information about the Armenian Genocide and identifying the various locations of the piece.

Zareh's intention is to draw attention to the inhumanity of the atrocious acts committed. He says, "When seeing this they may feel saddened. One of my goals in doing this is I wanted them to think about what has happened, what some humans have done to other people."[9] The various responses confirm that the installation has indeed stirred many emotions within its viewing public, albeit not always sadness. In fact, when the work appeared on the UCLA campus and in neighboring Westwood Village, many—including Armenians—were perplexed about the artist's ethnicity, wondering: would a Turk dare create such a display?[10] Some read the installation as making a mockery of the tragedy. Others felt its message was one of warning from Turkey to its protestors: "This is what we are capable of doing to you. We can do this again." Though certainly unanticipated by the artist, these initial responses raise a provocative point noted by Dora Apel in *Memory Effects: The Holocaust and the Art of Secondary Witnessing*. In terms of Holocaust imagery, she comments that postwar generation artists are "ultimately in the position of unwilling post facto bystanders," and theoretically could choose their specific position of identification: bystander, perpetrator, or victim.[11] She quotes Ernst van Alphen: "Soliciting partial and temporary identification with the perpetrators makes one aware of the ease with which one can slide into a measure of complicity."[12] While I am not suggesting that Zareh consciously chose thc gaze of the perpetrator, I am offering it as another way of considering the installation. Could Zareh's anger at the perpetrators' denial have triggered an unconscious attempt to understand what fuels this type of inhumanity?

As the work's life continued in the public sphere, a myriad of other responses were received.[13] Non-Armenians have walked by: disgusted, confused, and intrigued. Armenians, too, have had mixed responses. One woman, for example, said, "It is very sad, tragic, a great work . . . to inform the public about our history." Others have asserted, rather angrily, that Armenians have indeed survived; in the words of an elderly woman, with fists shaking in protest: "We did not become their soup. We lived. We are strong with our children and our future." The installation prompted another Armenian passer-by to share his family's story of struggle and survival, highlighting my assertion that by eliciting a witness response from its viewers, these works preserve the memory of the Genocide and celebrate survival.

Zareh, who works primarily on canvas, has employed an installation piece, pointing to the artist's desire to create a space of engagement with spectators and to elicit their responses. Installation pieces acquire life and meaning when in dialogue with the public. Nicolas de Oliveira comments that "the audience [is] the key site of the installation and the [piece] returns us to the body of the spectator, a space that is sentient and active: the empire of the senses."[14] *Turkish Soup* enters the public's space, making it difficult for people to avoid. The work confronts the viewers and seems to ask: Will you blindly walk by and pretend the blood does not exist? Will you cringe in disbelief and inquire about the impetus for such a work? Will you ask yourself why you weren't informed about the Armenian Genocide? Will you do something about it? The meaning of the piece is therefore activated in the people's sphere and in this process they are transformed from viewers into witnesses, a key intent of the artists in this study.

Are there any other witnesses to a genocide that is denied? Zareh posits an answer to this question with *The Red Trees of the Armenian Genocide* (April 2001) (Figs. 10.4-10.6). The performance is another instance in which the artist has invaded the spectator's space in order to inform and increase awareness about the Genocide among the uninformed public. In the performance, ten to twelve black-robed individuals walk, in various formations, gripping twisted and blood-red Manzanita tree branches. Once again, to reach the maximum number of people possible, the piece has been performed at five high-traffic locations, including the Third Street Promenade (Santa Monica, California), outside the Los Angeles County Museum of Art, in front of Borders Bookstore (Glendale, California), outside the Museum of Tolerance (Los Angeles, California),[15] and at the Armenian Martyrs' Memorial Monument in Bicknell Park (Montebello, California). Fliers were distributed at these performances as well.

Whereas in *Turkish Soup* Zareh alluded to the atrocious murders, here he points to the exhausting and demeaning deportation routes as another means to that same end. The walking performers evoke the repetition and orderly intervals of the long caravans of death marches where Armenians were forced to walk obediently, following their perpetrators' commands.[16] The methodical formation of the performers also points to the systematic and premeditated nature of the Genocide itself, refuting the murderers' claim that the deaths were an inevitable and unplanned aspect of war.

Zareh has taken this reference to the marches, the road to death, and subverted it. When the circle faces outward with the performers' arms extended upward, he deems them the protective internal posts of a structure.[17] When the performers form an inward-facing tight circle, Zareh identifies it as "a fire or unified protest," where the group's unity empowers its message.[18] Therefore, even though his intended audience is primarily the non-Armenian and uninformed public, I would also argue that he is attempting to appeal for unity within his fellow Armenians, a condition that would embolden their messages of protest.

Disrupting the silence and amplifying the call for recognition are the tree branches, once peaceful but now raising their blood-stained branches and "demanding justice."[19] For Zareh, the trees represented the ideal witnesses, natural

Figure 10.4
Zareh, The Red Trees of the Armenian Genocide, **2001.**

Figure 10.5

Figure 10.6

symbols of peace that have now come to bear the blood of the fallen victims. In a phone interview, Zareh animatedly shared: "I wanted to remove that peaceful situation. In an abnormal situation, the natural condition of the thing changed: it witnessed the Genocide, changed its look."[20] The blood of the brutally murdered victims saturated and tainted the very soil from which the trees absorbed their nutrients, eventually mirrored in the drastic color change of the now-sick trees. Ironically, the ill trees become the "living" proof, the natural witnesses,[21] confirming the reality of the Genocide. Their extended sharp, jagged, and "aggressive"[22] branches mimic, for Zareh, people's arms waving in the air, calling attention to danger of "fire or attack!"[23]

The bare tree branches could also imply the attempted obliteration of a rich cultural heritage. The Armenians, stripped of their land and history, were left to stand bare in a post-genocide world and resurrect any remains of a fragmented identity in order to construct a new one. Trees, here representatives of a destructed history as well as its silent witnesses, are evoked in the Armenians' contemporary lives with the Armenia Tree Project, an organization that launched a "memorial tree planting" in memory of the victims. The brochure reads:

> For every tear of sorrow, plant a seed of Life.
> For every fallen son and brother, grow a tree that stands for Truth.
> For every widow's wail of mourning, play the dawn's sweet symphony.
> For stolen daughters torched to dust, give us Beauty for their ashes.
> For every footprint swept beneath the desert sands, raise a tree of Hope.[24]

These new trees then, as "Seeds of remembrance. Roots of renewal,"[25] transform the former silent witnesses of genocide to contemporary witnesses of survival.

Alina Mnatsakanian

Alina Mnatsakanian (b. 1958), like Zareh, also evokes genocidal brutality in her performance piece titled, *Box/Cross/Dismemberment/Genocide* (1997), dedicated to abstract expressionist artist and Armenian Genocide survivor Arshile Gorky[26] (Figs. 10.7-10.10). Born and raised in Iran, Mnatsakanian left for Paris at the onset of the Iranian Revolution. She settled in Los Angeles in 1983 and, after twenty-two years and several sporadic trips to Armenia, recently relocated to Switzerland (September 2005). Mnatsakanian's uncle (by marriage) was a survivor who witnessed the murder of his entire family. Mnatsakanian's immediate family, however, wasn't directly impacted by the Genocide; she nonetheless claims: "I have something in me, a memory, a scar."[27] This memory then becomes the impetus for her works, including this specific performance piece.

In *Box/Cross/Dismemberment/Genocide*, a white box silently occupies the center of the gallery, generating questions about the contents within and perhaps indicating the initially untold stories guarded by genocide survivors. As the performance is about to begin, wearing black with a red shawl draped around her neck, Mnatsakanian, to the solemn tune of Edvard Mirzoyan's "Shoushanik Liric Ngar" (Shoushanik Lyric Image), opens each side of the box, revealing cast body fragments, old photographs, Armenian letters, and other markings on each board.

The opened box forms the shape of a cross, evoking images of the Crucifixion and the significance of Christianity as a key factor in the Genocide. Mnatsakanian then lights candles around the cross, as Lucine Zakarian's voice fittingly delivers a song of lamentation, "Lord, Open the Doors to Us." She pulls the red shawl over her face and sits at the foot of the cross, as a voice recording of Arshile Gorky's letter to his sister Vartoosh (February 25, 1941,

Figure 10.7
Alina Mnatsakanian, *Box/Cross/Dismemberment/Genocide*, **1997.**

Figure 10.8

Figure 10.9

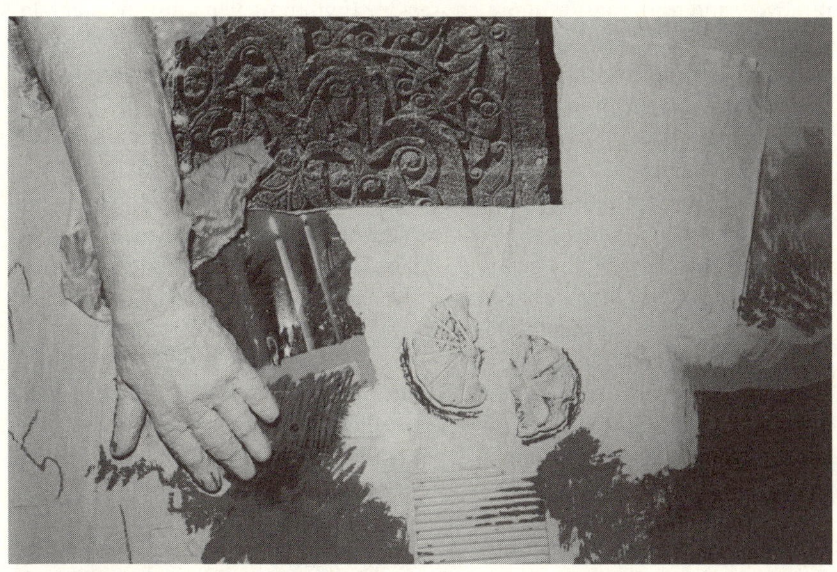

Figure 10.10

New York) reverberates through the gallery. The mourning ends, the shawl is removed, and to the faster, more aggressive rhythm of Vangelis' "Hispanola" (from the movie *1492*), Mnatsakanian takes apart each individual board, places it a distance from its original location, grabs seeds from the pouch around her waist, and plants them in the pot beside the board. This is repeated until each board is in a different location, except for the center board. She draws in the candles around this board, stands silently for a moment, and walks out, leaving the audience contemplating, in hushed silence, the fragmented body parts and what they have just witnessed. In some of the performances, audience members have subtly participated by echoing Mnatsakanian's lighting of the candles by lighting their own,[28] thereby becoming, like Zareh's viewers, critical components to the life of the performance.

The performance, however, is not intended merely as a commemorative piece. Mnatsakanian believes that the Genocide and the Armenian cause are political issues that need recognition, and this work is a means of telling that story.[29] Mnatsakanian recounts the genocidal events and their effect as she explains the performance:

> Six individual pieces symbolize the dismemberment Armenians experienced in 1915. Separating pieces reflects the desperate flight of Armenians from their homeland, while planting of the seeds illustrates the survival of the Armenian culture.[30]

As Mnatsakanian remarks, the dismembered body fragments recall genocidal dismemberment, and I would propose that since she uses the cast parts of her own body for the pieces, the dismemberment also signifies the fragmentation of a post-genocide diasporic identity. To defy the fragmentation, Mnatsakanian plants new seeds into the pots dispersed in different corners of the gallery—the world—and, like the trees of the Armenia Tree Project, indicates survival and regeneration. Interestingly, Mnatsakanian considers the central board with the head bust as Armenia and its surrounding pieces as the five continents which then became new homes for Armenians.[31]

Where Zareh draws attention to the murderous acts of the perpetrators, Alina Mnatsakanian marks the victims who were impacted by these acts in another piece titled *1 Person Died* (2003) (Fig. 10.11). The title phrase repeats 1.5 million times in three vertically displayed notebooks, "making a visual account for each person's death."[32] Through the years, the number 1.5 million has been repeated incessantly, possibly desensitizing the public's response to the calamity. But this work's extensive pages and the constant repetition of a *single* phrase endeavor to remember *each* life that was lost. Could these marked pages then also substitute for unmarked graves?

Though the persons who perished are not identified by name, the piece nonetheless evokes a memorial, similar to Maya Lin's *Vietnam Veterans Memorial* (1982) in Washington, D.C.[33] Maya Lin's reflective granite wall lists over

Figure 10.11
Alina Mnatsakanian, 1 Person Died, **2003.**

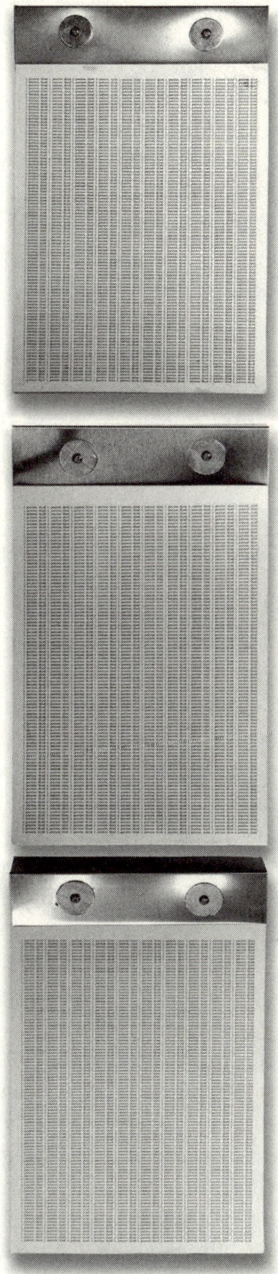

58,000 names of soldiers who died or were missing in action. She describes the impact and intent of this list: "These names, seemingly infinite in number, convey the sense of overwhelming numbers, while unifying those individuals into a whole. For this memorial is meant not as a monument to the individual but rather, as a memorial to the men and women who died during this war, as a whole."[34] It could be said that the listing of 1.5 million people, bound together in these notebooks, might also form some type of visual cemetery where the many names, and the bodies they symbolize, are brought together and honored. Since there is no gravesite where Armenians and others go to grieve, this work provides that private space of mourning. Maya Lin's words about her memorial are equally applicable to Mnatsakanian's: "Brought to a sharp awareness of such a loss, it is up to each individual to resolve or come to terms with this loss. For death is in the end a personal and private matter, and the area contained with this memorial is a quiet place, meant for personal reflection and private reckoning."[35]

What happens in that time of reflection? Referring to the *Vietnam Veterans Memorial*, Marita Sturken posits the following: "The most commonly noted response of visitors at the memorial has been to think of the widening circle of pain emanating from each name—to imagine for each name the grieving parents, sisters, brothers, girlfriends, wives, and children: to imagine, in effect, the multitude of people who were directly affected by the war."[36] Similarly, I would propose that the viewer, in the participatory act of turning each page of Mnatsakanian's piece, is also enveloped into a circle of pain, thereby becoming a witness to the impact of the Genocide on its ensuing generations.

Besides vicariously experiencing the pain linked to these losses, witnessing these names serves another purpose. "Through remembering, the past is retrieved and identity is recreated and affirmed," notes Lorne Shirinian when considering the use of photographs in survivor memoirs.[37] Likewise the remembrance of each life that was lost ensures the persistence of the memory of the Genocide and, moreover, ironically demonstrates the survival of those targeted for complete annihilation. In this way, Mnatsakanian takes on—and elicits from the viewers—the roles of historian, chronicler, and witness to the reality of the Genocide and its impact.

Sophia Gasparian

As Mnatsakanian memorializes the memory of those who have perished, Sophia Gasparian (b. 1972) visually employs surviving orphans to tell the story in the series *Dia De Los Muertos Armenianos* (Day of the Dead Armenians) (1999-2005) (Fig. 10.12). The topic of the Armenian Genocide is a relevant one for Soviet Armenia-born Gasparian. Gasparian's maternal great-grandmother Zaruhi Papazian was the only survivor in the family, with all others deported and massacred. Taken to Marseilles by French missionaries, Zaruhi married and began a new life, even attempting repatriation in 1948. Disappointed, she and her family left for Los Angeles in the 1970s; Gasparian and her family, similarly leaving corruption, oppression, and a dismal condition, joined them in 1988.

Painted individually, the images in *Dia De Los Muertos Armenianos* are hung together and comprise an installation.[38] Influenced by Japanese Manga (comic strips) and inspired by images from her childhood alphabet books in Soviet Armenia,[39] Gasparian's art utilizes cartoon images of orphaned children, because, "it is so much more effective to tell the story through an orphan's eyes—when people look at it, it's more powerful."[40] The choice of subject might be especially relevant to Gasparian since her great-grandmother was taken as an orphan to France after her entire family was massacred. Generally, however, orphans provided the critical link between the obliterated past and the uncertain future. As sole survivors of large families, they were the only witnesses left to tell of the atrocities they had encountered. They were also emblems of survival and the seeds of the next generation.

In *Turkey Says It's Sorry for the Armenian Genocide* (2000) (Fig. 10.13), the title's text evokes a newspaper headline. The use of the key phrase "it's sorry" instead of "it recognizes" denotes the step beyond acknowledgment, one equating to remorse and repentance. Is Gasparian, in marking her canvas

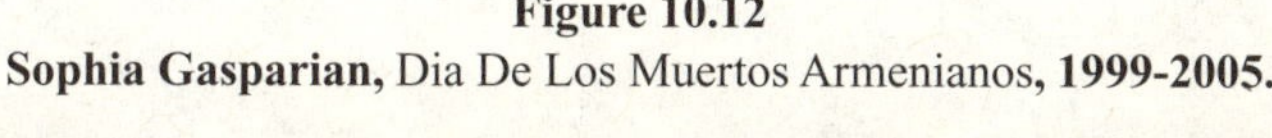

Figure 10.12
Sophia Gasparian, Dia De Los Muertos Armenianos, **1999-2005.**

Figure 10.13
Sophia Gasparian, Turkey Says It's Sorry for the Armenian Genocide**, 2000.**

with these words, proclaiming the purpose of her series: to bring recognition and reparation to the Armenian Genocide?

In this piece, the image of a train, according to Gasparian, "an innocent child's room drawing,"[41] dominates the picture space. Trains, appropriate for an orphan's tale, denote constant travel between two places. With this reference to movement and ungroundedness, Gasparian might be suggesting that the Genocide heightened the dispersal of Armenians and the fragmentation of their identities. Appropriately, beneath the train's wheels, the recycle logo from the grocery bag used as canvas bears fragmented words, which in full, probably read, "Assembling Required/15 items." These words might refer to the need to reconstruct or reassemble the fragmented identity. Additionally, they might point to the reparations owed to the Armenians, a notion supported by the train's smoke stack which contains newspaper text of the Senate Bill 1915 (approved in 2000) by California State Senator Charles Poochigian (Fresno) that allows victims of the genocide at the hands of Turks from 1915 to 1923 to file suits in California against life insurance policy companies to recover money allegedly owed from policies.[42]

In *What Have You Done to Assist the Armenians?* (2001) (Fig. 10.14), against the patchy red semblance of a blood-stained wall, a shoeless orphaned girl[43] locks eyes with the viewer and angrily demands to know, "What have you done to assist the Armenians?" To whom is her challenging question directed? On one level, Gasparian is addressing all of humanity, standing idly by as mass murder occurs everywhere, and is calling for an awakening of consciousness and a sense of responsibility. Gasparian could also be asking her own people, wondering if Armenians have done their part to remember the event, honor it, and bring recognition to it. In this way, the question is self-reflective, marking the artist's own thoughts about her sense of obligation to her own people. Many of these artists share the deep-rooted desire to contribute their part to the cause. In addition, considering the work is created and exhibited in the United States, it might also be directed at the host country of many Armenians, which has yet to acknowledge the "massacres" as premeditated genocide.[44]

Striking signifiers in the image are the shoeless feet as well as the life-size knife: the former possibly denoting the extreme distances walked by Armenians during the deportation routes and the latter perhaps recalling the instrument of murder for many, subtly recounted in the somewhat concealed newspaper print parallel to the knife (in the lower right), "Slash with a knife." The instrument of murder, the knife, points to the symbols of those guilty of the crime: the crescent moon and star.

In *Let's Not Chat About Despair* (1999)[45] (Fig. 10.15), Gasparian combines an old image from her alphabet book and considers the challenge of explaining such an atrocity to a little child. Gasparian's great-grandmother was from Turkey; at the age of six, she had endured the long marches through the deserts but was ultimately saved by French missionaries. "Yet nothing was ever talked

Figure 10.14
Sophia Gasparian, What Have You Done to Assist the Armenians?**, 2001.**

about," recalls Gasparian. The phrase, "Let's not chat about despair," is somewhat ambiguous. Are these the words of the indifferent little girl who would rather play with Grandma than hear yet another sad story? Or do they refer to the elderly woman who, with hunched shoulders, would rather not recall the slaughter? Even though the surviving generation was initially silent about the events it had endured, some voices gradually began to emerge—memoirs written, testimonies recorded—and they continued to rise. Therefore, I would suggest that the logo here "Recycle–Reuse" might reference the repetition of stories, or at the very least, the need to tell and retell stories in order to prevent the memory of the Genocide from expiring.

In *See That My Grave is Kept Clean* (2002) (Fig. 10.16), Gasparian once again engages text and, instead of asking a question or broadcasting headline news,

Figure 10.15
Sophia Gasparian, Let's Not Chat About Despair**, 1999.**

transmits the final request of the genocide victims to the surviving generations: "See that my grave is kept clean." Gasparian says, "I just feel that the least we can do is respect the dead people, if we can't do more, by keeping their graves clean."[46] Set against the yellow-gold background, the sad orphan girl, with her shoeless feet turned inward, drags a red wagon with a coffin in it. Little children normally carry toys in their red wagons, not coffins. This image becomes even more poignant considering the fact that the majority of genocide victims are without graves, as many died en route to the Syrian desert or were murdered and their bodies abandoned. This issue poses a difficult circumstance for the surviving generations: Where does one go to mourn? And how does one mourn? I would suggest that the little girl carrying the coffin of a victim in her wagon might further imply that the pain of the memory is a portable one, carried within every Armenian, from home to home, new life to new life.[47] And by extension, it could also mark the traveling identity of the Armenian: constantly moving but always seeking roots.

Like the works of Zareh and Mnatsakanian, Gasparian—with direct questions, requests, or news headlines—is also confronting the viewer and demanding participation in this dialogue about what happened to the Armenians. The spectator, once more, becomes an active agent, a witness, in the artwork. Moreover, he or she is called to transform prior inaction to urgent action.

Figure 10.16
Sophia Gasparian, See That My Grave is Kept Clean**, 2002.**

The Genocide Project

Gasparian's young orphans are transformed into the elderly survivors of The Genocide Project who preserve the story of what happened. Whereas Mnatsakanian had earlier documented that "1 person *died*," these photographs seem to affirm that "1 person *lived*." Launched in the mid-1990s, the mission of The Genocide Project is "to expose the Armenian Genocide to the world through the arts."[48] Photographers Ara Oshagan (b. 1964) and Levon Parian (b. 1955) take portraits of survivors in the Los Angeles area, while other members collect audio and video recordings of their eyewitness accounts. When exhibited, the photographs are identified by the name of the survivor, his/her year of birth, and birthplace. The complete work includes both the photograph as well as the text, which is a selection from the personal narrative of the subject.[49]

According to Parian, "It is harder to tell someone 'it never happened' when you are looking into those eyes and reading their story."[50] Lebanon-born Parian, who lived sporadically in the United States, Pakistan, and Afghanistan, before settling in the United States in 1973, also has a family story to tell. His paternal grandfather Levon Yotnaghparian, a soldier in the Ottoman army, transferred 4,000 Armenians to safety across the Syrian desert and then brought over orphans through the Armenian General Benevolent Union (A.G.B.U.). After completing such heroic deeds, he was informed by a Turkish neighbor that his father (Parian's great-grandfather) was hung in the town square. In addition to working on his grandfather's diary, Parian is also committed to photographing the many survivors.

When meeting the viewers' eyes, the survivors in these photographs seem to demand acknowledgment of the memory of the Genocide. The passing of time, manifested in the furrowed foreheads and wrinkled, vein-marked hands, has not erased the reality or the pain of the Genocide. Sometimes the survivors hold the sole objects that now offer them some sense of pride or peace and comfort, as in the Bible firmly grasped by Khatoun Pournazian (Fig. 10.17). The past and the present are merged in these photographs: the items detached from a past are held by the aged hands of the present life.

In the haunting black-and-white photographs, the subjects have been stripped of their surroundings, an artistic choice made after realizing that "their surroundings really had little to do with their past."[51] Their pasts, the life they had known, had been obliterated. Oshagan, in a *Los Angeles Times Magazine* article, explained the purposeful intent of the darkness: "We wanted the backgrounds of the photographs to be all black to represent the abyss. The light that surrounds them is the light that survived. And the focus is always on the eyes, which took in the horrors they witnessed."[52] It is also likely that the darkness behind these survivors represents the silence from which they have now emerged, articulating their experiences for the world to know.

The images are split, focusing only on the face and hands of the survivors, because these illustrate "the discontinuity of the killings, how their first life was stripped from them and a second forced upon them."[53] The rupture could also allude to the fact that the Genocide fragmented Armenian history and identity. In spite of that, the visual union of the two essential markers of one's physical identity, the face and the hands, also indicates the reconstruction of those fragments to offer a coherent narrative and a new identity, a symptom of the diasporic artist of Armenian descent. Further, the intense emphasis on the face and hands of the survivors ensures that each survivor is identified and accounted for. These are not headless torsos or indistinct faces. Each instance of survival has been remembered.

The work is deemed incomplete without the text. Oshagan and Parian have selected segments of the subjects' full narratives and juxtaposed their stories with their portraits. Even though the photographers initially resisted the oral history component of these portraits, their inclusion now points to the works' intended purpose and audience: to inform an uninformed public of the reality of the Armenian Genocide. The following is a segment from Haig Baronian's (Fig. 10.18) testimony:

> The caravan was getting smaller each day. At one place, my little grandmother, like Jeremiah incarnate, loudly cursed the Turkish government for their inhumanity,

Figure 10.17
The Genocide Project, Khatoun Pournazian

> pointing to us children she asked, "What is the fault of children to be subjected to such suffering." It was too much for a gendarme to bear, he pulled out his dagger and plunged it into my grandmother's back. The more he plunged his dagger, the more my beloved Nana asked for heaven's curses on him and his kind. Unable to silence her with repeated dagger thrusts, the gendarme mercifully pumped some bullets into her and ended her life. First my uncle, now my grandmother were left unmourned and unburied by the wayside. We moved on.

The juxtaposition of image and text undeniably indicates that these individuals have been transformed from being victims of the atrocities to survivors who now live to tell of their experiences. Their direct, confrontational gaze is no longer the terrified child of about eight or nine years of age fearfully looking into the perpetrator's eyes begging for his life, but rather it is the survivor, boldly looking out now and claiming a place, a voice in history. Robert Jay Lifton has explained that within the search for meaning among survivors, there is an "impulse to bear witness, beginning with a sense of responsibility to the dead, [which] can readily extend into a 'survivor mission'—a lasting commitment to the project that extracts significance from absurdity, vitality from massive death."[54] These portraits, like the survivors themselves, function as testimonies of the Genocide[55] and the subsequent lives in the Diaspora. They demonstrate, as Richard Brilliant proposes in *Portraiture,* "the individual's wish to endure."[56] In other words, these works are images of resistance, the visual equivalent of the "texts of resistance," suggested by Lorne Shirinian regarding survivor memoirs.[57] In addition to testifying to "life after the deportations, massacres, humiliation and indignation, and the indifference of the great powers,"[58] the survivor photographs, like the memoirs, also "testify to the spirit of the Armenians' ability—despite having fallen victim to the worst and barbarous of human behaviour—to survive; thus these memoirs are texts of life-affirmation."[59]

In these photographs, the eyes of the survivors meet those of their witnesses. In that momentary instance of the gaze, the survivor is bequeathing his/her story to the new generation of witnesses. The testimony of these survivors then becomes the testimony of the artists, who inherit the stories and the responsibility, and then in turn, transfer that to the viewers. By entrusting the story to the next generation, there is a transference of the witness role from the sitters to the viewers. Parian articulates it this way:

> They got on with their lives, raising children and making good in their new countries. But the guilt of it, the unfinished sorrows, are a huge wound opened in the Armenian psyche, and it's far from healed. We're the generation that has to, if not heal it, at least put a scab on the wound.[60]

These photographs then make the viewers noticeably aware of their new status as witnesses. In other words, by experiencing the events encountered by these eyes, the viewers also become witnesses to the same reality. The evolution of the exhibition title, from "Witness to Genocide" to "Eyewitness" to

Figure 10.18
The Genocide Project, Haig Baronian

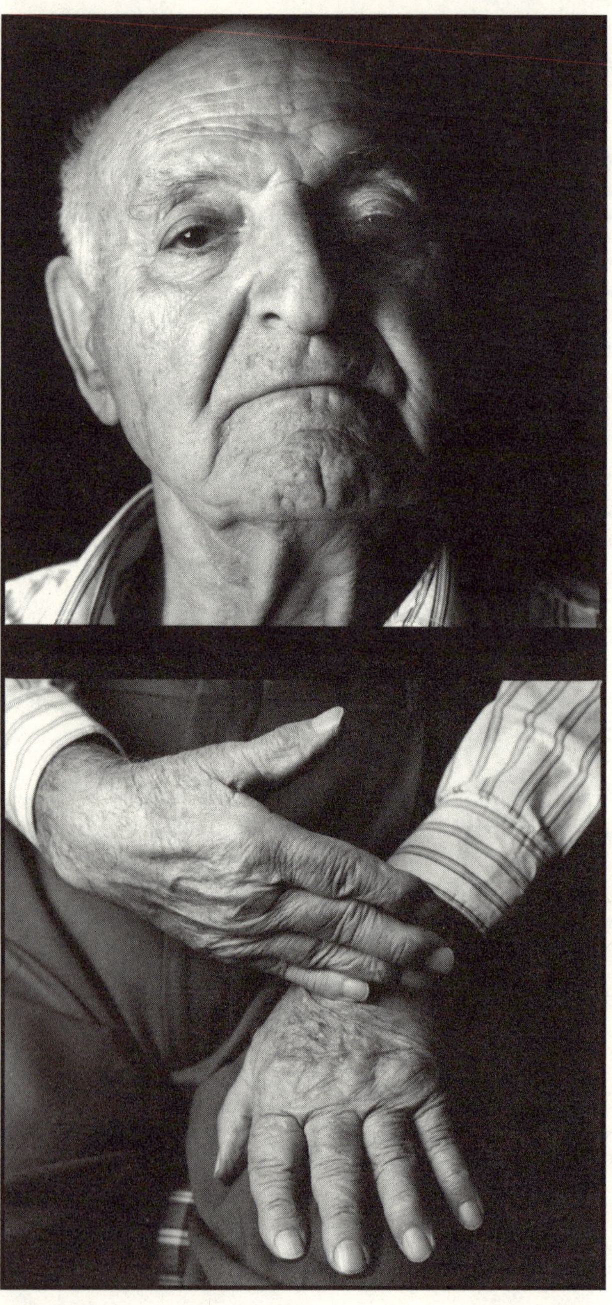

"*i*witness," illustrates this point. Sara Horowitz writes: "The act of testifying, then, constitutes the making of the witness. Much as the witness produces testimony, testimony produces the witness."[61] While her comment generally refers to survivors, I would argue that it is equally applicable to the "secondary witnesses," the artists, as well.

Ara Oshagan

In his extensive photographic series titled *Traces of Identity: An Insider's View of the L.A. Armenian Community, 2000-2004*, Ara Oshagan (b. 1964) explores Armenian life and culture, including the role of the Genocide in constructing a diasporic identity. Born in Lebanon, Oshagan moved to the United States in 1975 at the onset of the Lebanese Civil War. "We feel the effects of the survivors," muses Oshagan as he recalls the impact of the Genocide on his own family.[62] His paternal grandfather Hagop Oshagan, one of the preeminent intellectuals in Constantinople, escaped from capture seven times, living in gutters and attics to avoid authorities, until his final escape disguised as a German soldier. His maternal family was deported and forged a new life in the Middle East. These stories undoubtedly motivate Oshagan's photographic engagement with Armenian identity.

Oshagan's photographs of commemoration and protest, depicting the key features of Armenians' involvement in Los Angeles with the Genocide, construct multilayered sites of memory. [63] Any community that has experienced historical trauma honors and remembers the tragedy and its victims. This act of remembrance constructs sites of memory, asserted by James E. Young to be diverse and encompassing such things as archives, museums, parades, moments of silence, memorial gardens, resistance monuments, ruins, and commemorative fast days.[64]

Every year, Armenians gather at the Martyrs Monument in Montebello, California, the site of Oshagan's photograph, *Genocide Memorial, Montebello, April 24,2001* (2001) (Fig. 10.19). It depicts the hands of clergy members as they perform the religious ritual of placing incense (*khung*) on the plaque beneath the monument and praying in memory of the 1.5 million massacred. [65] Evoking Michelangelo's Sistine Chapel painting of God the Father's outstretched hand meeting the extended limp finger of Adam and igniting life within him, could the two hands in this image be attempting to give life to the victims and their memory? "I am here to keep our ancestors and the Armenian Genocide's story alive," one of the commemorators resolutely declared.[66] The diagonal pillars of the monument and the faces of the commemorators, like the incense smoke, are blurred in the background intimating yet again the distant memory of the Genocide and further reinforcing the intent of these commemorations to recall the tragedy and thereby prevent its disappearance from a collective historical memory.

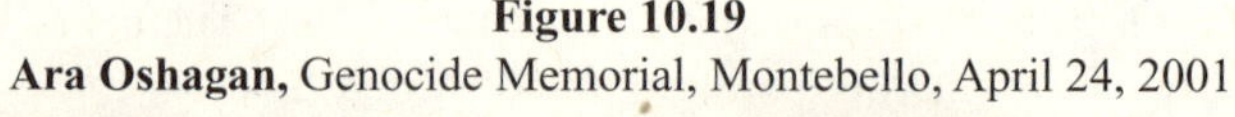

Figure 10.19
Ara Oshagan, Genocide Memorial, Montebello, April 24, 2001

Oshagan's photograph reveals different sites of memory, as previously suggested by James E. Young. Primarily, it marks the specific day of remembrance, April 24, which is also clearly designated by the artist in the title of the work.[67] As an extension of this memory marker, Young then asks: "How then is the remembrance day publicly performed? What do people remember in its ceremonies and moments of silence? To what extent do the forms of observance shape remembrance itself?"[68] This photograph responds to these inquiries with its reference to the commemorative event itself, a yearly gathering at the monument to participate in a program that includes the religious ceremony, laying of flowers at the plaque, and a number of speeches from political figures and community leaders. Yet as Young seems to suggest, the performance of remembrance is perceived differently among those present. Commemorators at the Montebello memorial have expressed the importance of the day, the event and their presence: "I am here to remember the victims, that it wasn't a waste. It is our responsibility and our desire to let the world know. We can't forget;"[69] and "I am here to commemorate, to remember, and to prevent it in the future."[70]

Another site of memory signified in this photograph is the monument, though not visible in its entirety but undoubtedly evoked by its heaven-bound pillars in the background. Necessitated by its abstract form and public presence, people have attached their personal interpretations to the monument.[71] They ascribe ideas of power, unity, peace, survival, and determination to it. Others suggest that it resembles a candle, a tower, or a statue. A few maintain that it is a symbol of protest and demands justice, similar to the angry branches of Zareh's *Red Trees*.

Finally, the photograph itself becomes another site of memory, through which Oshagan endeavors to understand the significance of the Genocide, its commemoration, and ultimately his own identity. In visually representing fragments—hands, heads, pillars—and assembling them into a single image, he attempts to comprehend and reconstruct the components of this historical memory: the memorial service, the gathering of people, the monument, and his role. The visual tension created between the distinctly outlined hands in the foreground and the hazy images in the background might allude to the internal conflict inherent in forging a post-genocide diasporic identity: the struggle between a self that is closely connected to a historic past and one that attempts to construct an identity in the present.

In tandem with commemorative memorial services, Armenians also gather yearly to raise their voices in protest to the fact that the Genocide has not been reaffirmed by the modern-day counterparts of the perpetrating nation as well the government of their own host country, the United States. Oshagan's *Genocide Commemoration Rally, Los Angeles, 2002* (2002) (Fig. 10.20) documents such a gathering. In the forceful engagement of the young man with the composition's foreground, the image illustrates once more the dynamic and undeniable presence of the Genocide in the lives of Armenians today. A crowd of many is present yet only one protestor's animated and angry face is clearly visible, bringing the large calamity to a human, personal level. The zealous young man is resolute in his, and the artist's, mission: "a political, social, emotional demand for recognition."[72] The two arms stretched upward, framing the young man, further reinforce the purpose of this gathering and photograph: protest. The indisputable meaning of this image is contrasted with the ambiguous nature of another photograph, taken the same day yet in a different location.

Genocide Commemoration Rally, E. Hollywood, April 24, 2002 (2002) (Fig. 10.21) is a depiction of another rally on commemoration day. In the far distance, a man—a witness—stands atop a UHAUL truck and records the scene, while children appear at play in the foreground and a man's face looks beyond the wall into our own space. The inclusion of youth, seen in the left margin, may highlight the fact that all members of the community are involved in the commemoration, that all know the story of the Genocide. However, the fact that the children are in play mode may indicate, like Gasparian's little girl in *Let's Not Chat about Despair*, that the severity of the Genocide is not fully comprehended by the young ones. To them, it may just be another part of their story of "being Armenian." I speculate that the gesture of the young girl reaching over across the brick wall points to the unattainable nature of this tragedy.

Rather appropriately but clearly unintentional, the presence of the UHAUL truck, like Gasparian's train in *Turkey Says It's Sorry for the Armenian Genocide*, could be read on multiple levels: the scattering of people triggered by the Genocide, the incessant movement of Armenians from one home to another and, in light of the man with the video camera, the notion that this message is portable and needs to travel to many areas, bearing the news of the atrocities.

Figure 10.20
Ara Oshagan, Genocide Commemoration Rally, Los Angeles, 2002

Figure 10.21
Ara Oshagan, Genocide Commemoration Rally, East Hollywood, April 24, 2002

Oshagan has employed fragments once more: the heads, hands, decapitated trees and light posts. Might this disarrayed arrangement refer to the fragmented identity of Armenians and their attempt to understand it? Could the concrete wall in the foreground mark the distant memory of the Genocide and the viewer's, specifically Oshagan's, attempt to gain entry into this historical memory, as indicated by the arm reaching over? These are questions Oshagan asks himself. In the following excerpt, he muses about the uncertain nature of the photograph and his involvement:

> There is an ambiguity of subject matter, you don't know what's going on. And then when you know what's going on, it's more ambiguous. So there's an ambiguity for the questioning of the political status of these commemorations. You can make an interpretation of that sort. Which I understand, because I question it myself . . . I am photographing these events and I am constantly thinking: why are we doing it this year, this way? Where is it getting us? We've been doing it for so many years. And why am I photographing now? . . . . Perhaps the ambiguity, the questioning of what's going on, that's how I feel myself. [73]

Might this very nature of the photograph provide the instrument through which the artist as well as the viewers gain access to their own roles in the preservation and maintenance of this historical memory? In response, James Ingo Freed's proposition is relevant: "Memory is important, letting that memory be sufficiently ambiguous and open-ended so that others can inhabit that space, can imbue the forms with their own memory."[74]

Conclusion

The visual engagement of contemporary artists with issues pertaining to the Genocide points to the integral impact of the event on the contemporary identities of Armenians. The artists in this study employ several stylistic strategies in their visual constructions of testimony, including the incorporation of text, references to the body, use of fragmented forms, a mixed-media technique, and viewer participation. These artistic devices are the tools through which the artists explore and reveal the effects of historical trauma on identity.

Predominant among these stylistic strategies is the use of text in most of the works, either in the form of fliers distributed with the installation or performance, a question or news headline directed at the viewer, the survivor's narrative alongside his/her portrait, or even recalling a modern grave with phrases such as "1 person died." Even the spoken word, in the form of songs or recited letters, is inserted into the works. What is the relationship of these words to the visual construction? What purpose do they serve? In his essay "Image and Word in Twentieth-Century Art," E. H. Gombrich proposed: "Unlike images, language can make that vital distinction which has concerned philosophers since the days of Plato, the distinction between universals and particulars."[75] Though the works of these Los Angeles artists are visually very effective, I would suggest that since the Genocide is not well known among the American public, the artists believe that some textual references would focus the viewer's experience of the work. That is, the words take the viewer from a universal notion of violent inhumanity to the particular case of the Armenian Genocide and its architects of mass murder, the Young Turks of the Ottoman government. For example, Zareh's push-cart bears the words, "Turkish Soup Made with Armenian Bones," lest a passerby assumes the unpleasant sight of blood refers to just any murder. Similarly the accompanying flier informs people that the installation is not a reference to arbitrary killing but rather to the premeditated slaughter of 1.5 million Armenians. Sophia Gasparian's orphans do not solely gaze at viewers, but they angrily challenge, "What have you done to assist the Armenians?" The Genocide Project's survivors do not only show signs of aging and a troubled life, but they tell viewers about the events that precipitated their deep wrinkles and defiant gaze. To that end, each photograph is titled very specifically with the name, birth year, and birthplace of its subject, all critical features to understanding when and where the premeditated plan of genocide was carried out and who were its targets. The incorporation of text is therefore critical to these works. As Gombrich summarized: "Where the artist cannot rely on cultural knowledge . . . he has to offer instructions for use in the form of titles, be they anecdotal, descriptive of motifs or individuals, or, for instance, referential."[76] Essentially, these visual testimonies merge image and text in order to create effective witnesses within their viewing audience, a goal intended by these artists in their attempt to ensure the enduring memory of the Genocide.

Another stylistic strategy employed by the artists is the skillful incorporation of the human body. Whether it is the artist or another person performing within the piece (Zareh and Mnatsakanian), or orphans and survivors telling their stories and making requests (Gasparian and The Genocide Project), or fragmented body parts referencing commemorative events (Oshagan), each artist's work in some way employs the human form. I would suggest that the motivation for incorporating the body is twofold. Primarily, as Mnatsakanian's *1 Person Died* reminds viewers, the Armenian Genocide claimed 1.5 million lives; these artists then, seek to evoke the devastating loss of life. Also, as I have proposed, they want to counter that loss by illustrating survival as well: the people who were intended targets for total extermination are indeed still very much present. These works, with their use of the body, consequently mark survival and celebrate life.

The works also utilize segmented forms, evidenced in the heads, hands, pillars, and words. These portioned representations might indicate the fragmented identities of the artists and of many others in the post-genocide generation. For instance, Oshagan's photographs are comprised of bodyless heads, extended arms, enlarged hands, pillar segments, and incomplete walls. Zareh uses tree branches, separated from their life source and made to wander as witnesses. Linda Nochlin explores the use of such forms in expressing the impact of modernity in *The Body in Pieces: The Fragment as a Metaphor of Modernity.* She considers the following question:

> But what of the larger implications of the topic, what of that sense of social, psychological, even metaphysical fragmentation that so seems to mark modern experience—a loss of wholeness, a shattering of connection, a destruction or disintegration of permanent value that is so universally felt in the nineteenth century as to be often identified with modernity itself?[77]

Artist and theorist R. B. Kitaj in *First Diasporist Manifesto* muses about an "unsettled mode of art-life,"[78] and notes that it constantly encounters issues of "history, kin, homelands, the scattering of his people (if he thinks he may have a people), and such stuff."[79] Both Nochlin and Kitaj point to identities that have witnessed historical upheaval and have resulted in a disintegration of wholeness, a symptom felt by the diasporic artists in this study.

As a further indication of the fragmentation of identity, these artists employ a mixed-media technique, where the final artistic product includes such things as objects, reused paper, painted surfaces, and sculptural forms. For example, Gasparian's works are often collage paintings reusing grocery bags and pasting forms onto the surfaces. In Mnatsakanian's *Box/Cross/Dismemberment/Genocide*, the boards include old photographs, dismembered casts of body parts, and half-marked surfaces. I argue that the artists' amalgamation of these various forms points to their preoccupation with their own identity, a desire to rearrange disparate fragments of their whole selves.

The viewer is an integral element to the works as well, as indicated by the intrusion of the installation pieces into the viewer's space as well as the various texts marking the works. Sophia Gasparian's work, for example, bestows a victim's final request to the viewers: "See that my grave is kept clean." In this way, these artists confront passivity and demand active participation with regard to genocide remembrance, acknowledgement, and further, prevention. Their works require the viewer to bear witness in order to further confirm the reality of the Genocide.

Through key stylistic features—text, body, fragments, mixed-media, and the viewer—the works of these contemporary Los Angeles-based artists not only authenticate the Genocide, but also explore its enduring impact on their post-genocide diasporic lives and identities. The artists' visual testimonies are the memorials for the Armenian Genocide, recalling what occurred and simultaneously working out their identities and finally their roles as witnesses. James E. Young explains: "While the survivors remember themselves and loved ones lost, their children build memorials to remember a world they never knew, an act of recovery whereby they locate themselves in a continuous past."[80] In this search, the artists identify key outcomes of the Armenian Genocide—namely, dispersion and fragmentation—and finally recognize the roots of their diasporic identities. Upon this realization, they assume the role of witnesses and attempt to prevent erasure of historical memory. By then educating the public about this catastrophic moment through their visual testimonies, they consequently create witnesses within their viewers. In this way, the memory of the Armenian Genocide is preserved.

Notes

1. William Safran, "Comparing Diasporas: A Review Essay," *Diaspora* 8, 3 (1999): 255.
2. David Waldstreicher, *The Armenian Americans* (New York: Chelsea, 1989), p. 105.
3. No comprehensive text has yet examined the impact of the Armenian Genocide on art. However, for the impact of the Holocaust on art, see the following: Ziva Amishai-Maisels, *Depiction and Interpretation: The Influence of the Holocaust on the Visual Arts* (Oxford and New York: Pergamon Press, 1993); Dora Apel, *Memory Effects: The Holocaust and the Art of Secondary Witnessing* (New Brunswick, NJ: Rutgers University Press, 2002); Monica Bohm-Duchen, *After Auschwitz: Responses to the Holocaust in Contemporary Art* (Great Britain: Northern Centre for Contemporary Art, Sunderland, in association with Lund Humphries, 1995); Ernst van Alphen, *Caught by History: Holocaust Effects in Contemporary Art, Literature, and Theory* (Stanford: Stanford University Press, 1997); James E. Young, *At Memory's Edge: After-Images of the Holocaust in Contemporary Art and Architecture* (New Haven, CT: Yale University Press, 2000); Barbie Zelizer, *Visual Culture and the Holocaust* (New Brunswick, NJ: Rutgers University Press, 2001).
4. This question is raised in response to Maurice Blanchot's *The Instant of My Death* (Stanford: Stanford University Press, 2000); "Description," *Stanford University Press* (2001-2005), www.sup.org/book.cgi?book_id=3325%203326 (July 21, 2005).
5. "Witness," *Merriam-Webster Online Dictionary* (2005), www.m-w.com/cgi-bin/dictionary?book=Dictionary&va=witness (August 1, 2005).
6. In *At Memory's Edge*, Young asserts that "without exploring why it's important, we leave out part of the story itself. Is it self-indulgent or self-aggrandizing to make the listener's story part of the teller's story?" (p. 4).
7. The term "homeland" here is understood as either historic Armenia or the present-day independent republic.
8. *Turkish Soup Made with Armenian Bones.* Produced and directed by Souren Karapetian, 33 minutes. Open Door Production, 2000, videocassette.
9. Rodney Tanaka, "A Macabre Reminder of the Genocide," *Glendale News-Press,* April 22, 1998.
10. Author's personal conversations with peers, April 1998.
11. Dora Apel, *Memory Effects,* p. 4.
12. Ernst van Alphen, "Playing the Holocaust," in *Mirroring Evil: Nazi Imagery/Recent Art*, ed. Norman L. Kleebatt (New York and New Brunswick, NJ: The Jewish Museum and Rutgers University Press, 2002), p. 77, as cited in Apel, *Memory Effects,* p. 5.
13. The following visitor responses have been observed in the documented film version of the installation.
14. Nicolas de Oliveira, Nicola Oxley, and Michael Petry, *Installation Art in the New Millennium: The Empire of the Senses* (New York: Thames & Hudson, 2003). Pages unnumbered.
15. Zareh had informed the museum (via a letter and phone call) that he would be exhibiting his work on the sidewalk outside their entrance, confirming that it would

be open on that specific day. However, much to his surprise, on the day of display, there was merely a sign posted on the door stating that the museum was closed; no other explanation was provided.

16. Interview with Zareh Meguerditchian, Glendale, California, April 15, 2005. Also, the trees could denote the fact that many Armenians were murdered by hanging.
17. Ibid.
18. Ibid.
19. Zareh's opening monologue in the film, *The Red Trees of the Armenian Genocide.* Produced and directed by Souren Karapetian, 20 minutes. Open Door Production, 2001, videocassette.
20. Interview with Zareh Meguerditchian, April 15, 2005.
21. Ibid.
22. Ibid.
23. Ibid.
24. *Armenia Tree Project*, brochure, 2005.
25. Ibid.
26. The piece was performed on several occasions between 1997 and 2002, most significantly at the commemorative events at California State University, Northridge, organized by the Armenian Students Association in April 1998.
27. Interview with Alina Mnatsakanian, Burbank, California, April 16, 2005.
28. Danielle C. Lee, "CSUN Honors Armenian Genocide Victims," *Daily Sundial*, April 28, 1998.
29. Interview with Alina Mnatsakanian, March 29, 2005.
30. Alina Mnatsakanian, *Box/Cross/Dismemberment/Genocide*, exhibition flier, 1997.
31. Interview with Alina Mnatsakanian, Switzerland (via email), February 22, 2006.
32. Alina Mnatsakanian, Artist's Portfolio, 2004.
33. For insightful essays about Maya Lin's memorial, see Marita Sturken, "The Wall, the Screen, and the Image: The Vietnam Veterans Memorial," *Representations* 35 (Summer 1991): 118-142, and Charles L. Griswold, "The Vietnam Veterans Memorial and the Washington Mall: Philosophical Thoughts on Political Iconography," in *Critical Issues in Public Art: Content, Context, and Controversy*, ed. Harriet F. Senie and Sally Webster (New York: Icon Editions, 1992), pp. 71-100.
34. Maya Ying Lin, "Design Submission to the Vietnam Veterans Memorial Competition, March 1981," *Vietnam Veterans Memorial Fund*, 2003, www.thevirtualwall.org/index.cfm (August 15, 2005).
35. Lin, "Design Submission."
36. Sturken, "The Wall," p. 126.
37. Lorne Shirinian, *Survivor Memoirs of the Armenian Genocide* (Reading: Taderon, 1999), p. 67.
38. The installation has changed form and number at different exhibitions.
39. Interview with Sophia Gasparian, Los Angeles, California, April 18, 2005. Gasparian explains that her alphabet books intrigue her because going to school in Soviet Armenia, the Communist government dictated the content of the books. "There was no talk about history. No mention of genocide or any kind of pain or suffering; it was this utopian society."
40. Interview with Sophia Gasparian, November 28, 2004.
41. Interview with Sophia Gasparian, March 26, 2005.
42. The bill was unanimously approved in the Legislature and signed by Governor Gray Davis.

43. Gasparian has used Japanese Manga artist Yoshitomo Nara's image, hence his small photo is included in the painting.
44. The United States government prefers to refer to the Armenian Genocide as "massacres." Despite this, successive governors of California (and many other states), including most-recently Arnold Schwarzenegger, have proclaimed April 24 as "A Day of the Remembrance of the Armenian Genocide."
45. According to Gasparian, the piece is based on a performance/song by Greek-American musician Diamanda Galas.
46. Interview with Sophia Gasparian, April 18, 2005.
47. Alina Mnatsakanian's installation *Journey* (1997) suggests a similar idea with the black-lined boxes carrying red crosses within them.
48. *The Genocide Awareness Project*, flier, 1996. Ara Oshagan and Garen Yegparian started the project. The organization's name eventually changed to *The Genocide Project.*
49. Artist Jeffrey Wolin, whose grandparents were survivors of the Holocaust, similarly photographs survivors; yet he writes their testimonies (either verbatim or in his own words) onto the photographs, "implicating himself in the construction of the narrative by implicitly making visible the presence of the listener, who inevitably affects how the stories are told" (Apel, *Memory Effects,* p. 93).
50. Interview with Levon Parian, Tujunga, California, March 27, 2005.
51. Interview with Levon Parian, March 27, 2005.
52. Janet Kinosian, "Witness to Fire," *Los Angeles Times Magazine,* May 23, 1999, p. 18.
53. Ibid.
54. Robert Jay Lifton, "Witnessing Survival," *Society* 15, 3 (March/April 1978): 43.
55. Claude Lanzmann refers to survivors as "living documents" in his film *Shoah* as cited in Sara Horowitz, "Rethinking Holocaust Testimony: The Making and Unmaking of the Witness," *Cardozo Studies in Law and Literature* 4, 1 (Spring/Summer 1992): 48.
56. Richard Brilliant, *Portraiture* (Cambridge: Harvard University Press, 1991), p. 14.
57. Shirinian, *Survivor Memoirs*, p. 69.
58. Ibid., p. 69.
59. Ibid., p. 70.
60. Kinosian, "Witness to Fire," p. 18.
61. Horowitz, "Rethinking Holocaust Testimony," p. 51.
62. Interview with Ara Oshagan, Glendale, California, February 22, 2006.
63. The photographs are from his series *Traces of Identity: An Insider's View of the L.A. Armenian Community, 2000-2004*.
64. James E. Young. *The Texture of Memory: Holocaust Memorials and Meaning* (New Haven, CT, and London: Yale University Press, 1993), p. viii.
65. The inscription on the plaque reads: "ARMENIAN MARTYRS MEMORIAL MONUMENT. THIS MONUMENT, ERECTED BY AMERICANS OF ARMENIAN DESCENT, IS DEDICATED TO THE 1,500,000 ARMENIAN VICTIMS OF THE GENOCIDE PERPETRATED BY THE TURKISH GOVERNMENT, 1915-1921, AND TO MEN OF ALL NATIONS WHO HAVE FALLEN VICTIM TO CRIMES AGAINST HUMANITY."
66. Interview with Koko Garabedian, Montebello, California, April 24, 2002.
67. For an extensive discussion of the relevance of a specific day of remembrance, see Young's chapter, "When a Day Remembers: A Performative History of Yom Hashoah," in *The Texture of Memory*, pp. 263-281.
68. Young, *Texture of Memory*, p. 272.

69. Interview with Mike (last name not given), Montebello, California, April 24, 2002.
70. Interview with Haik Antonyan, Montebello, California, April 24, 2002.
71. The following are based on random personal interviews conducted by the author and Jean Murachanian at the Armenian Martyrs Monument (Montebello, California), April 24, 2002.
72. Interview with Ara Oshagan, Santa Monica, California, July 15, 2005.
73. Ibid.
74. James Ingo Freed, "The United States Holocaust Memorial Museum," *Assemblage* 9 (1989): 61, as cited in Young, *Texture of Memory*, p. 283.
75. E. H. Gombrich, *Topics of Our Time: Twentieth-Century Issues in Learning and in Art* (Berkeley, Los Angeles, London: University of California Press, 1991), p. 167.
76. Ibid, p. 169.
77. Linda Nochlin, *The Body in Pieces: The Fragment as a Metaphor of Modernity* (New York: Thames and Hudson, 1995), pp. 23-24.
78. R. B. Kitaj, *First Diasporist Manifesto* (New York: Thames and Hudson, 1989), p. 21.
79. Ibid, p. 21.
80. Young, *Texture of Memory*, p. 285.

11

Musical Perspectives on the Armenian Genocide: From Aznavour to "System of a Down"

Jack Der-Sarkissian

"Ils Sont Tombés" (1975)[1]

They fell without knowing why.
Men, women, and children whose only wish was to live,
Fell heavily, like drunken people.
Who were mutilated, massacred, while their eyes were full of fear.

They fell while calling upon their God,
At the threshold of their church or doorstep.
Herded through the desert, staggering together,
Crushed by thirst, hunger, weapons, fire.

P.L.U.C.K.
(**P**olitically **L**ying, **U**nholy, **C**owardly **K**illers) (1998)[2]

Elimination, Elimination, Elimination.
Die, Why, Walk Down, Walk Down.
A whole race Genocide,
Taken away all of our pride,
A whole race Genocide,
Taken away, Watch Them all fall down.

"Ils Sont Tombés" and "P.L.U.C.K." are two songs that frame roughly a three-decade retrospective of the 1915 Armenian Genocide by American and Western European musical traditions. While both songs powerfully grieve the Catastrophe that occurred to the Armenian people, each utilizes the lament genre differently. These musical perspectives mirror the Armenian struggle spanning the last thirty years over the legacy of the Genocide. The perspective in the 1970s was one of cultural survival and revival, suggesting a population coming out of self-denial. The next thirty years would see no resolution, and in fact an exacerbation of the already-tense Armeno-Turkish relations. It comes as no surprise that the late 1990s differed from the earlier, more hopeful period by recognizing loss, displaying anger, and demanding action, even violence if needed, to right the wrongs visited upon the Armenian people.

In 1969, psychiatrist Elisabeth Kübler-Ross published *On Death and Dying,* which describes the steps experienced by those confronted with death.[3] Her theories subsequently have been expanded to explain reactions to disasters in general.[4] Kübler-Ross states that the initial reaction to a disaster is denial, by trying to avoid reconciling with the traumatic event. If the denial is overcome, it is replaced by anger as a frustrated outpouring of "bottled-up" emotion. Subsequent steps are bargaining, depression/grief and, finally, acceptance.

When a traumatic event occurs, a person's mind first responds by seeking rational ways of escaping the horrible experience. A range of defense mechanisms that ease anxiety may be triggered unconsciously yet distorts reality.[5] These defense mechanisms include denial, during which one refuses to acknowledge that an event has occurred. In its full form it is totally subconscious, though it may also have a significant conscious element. Closely related to denial is repression, which involves relegating uncomfortable thoughts to the subconscious in the hope that they will fade away. The degree of repression can vary, though repressed memories do not fully disappear. Other defense mechanisms include displacement, where emotions are redirected to a substitute target; intellectualization, whereupon one takes an objective viewpoint; projection, which involves attributing uncomfortable feelings onto others; rationalization, where one creates false but credible justifications; reaction formation, which is achieved by reacting to the trauma in the least likely manner; regression, or going back to acting as a child; and sublimation, in which one redirects "wrong" urges into socially acceptable actions.

The survivors of the Armenian Genocide undoubtedly utilized all these defense mechanisms when coming to terms with the horrors they experienced. As a whole these defense mechanisms emotionally tend to displace the individual mind (and, by inference, the collective unconscious) from the trauma, thus allowing a semblance of normalcy. Yet the traumatic event is not fully acknowledged in terms of achieving full closure. In this aspect, one can summarize this initial response as "self-denial" in the broad sense of the term. Given that the history of the Armenians has been mired in repeated tragedy, it is not surprising that the initial collective response to the Genocide was one of resignation and ultimately self-denial, utilizing all possible defense mechanisms to survive. A study of how Armenian musicians utilized Western music and developed their media from 1975 to 1998 demonstrates Kübler-Ross's theories about overcoming denial and progressing into anger, mirroring the collective Armenian struggle.

Starting in 1965, citizens in the Armenian Soviet Socialist Republic started the process of addressing and protesting the outcome of the 1915 Genocide.[6] Massive demonstrations marked the first collective step toward breaking down a partially self-imposed denial of the Genocide.[7] That episode, together with a thawing of the "Cold War" that separated the Diaspora from the Armenian homeland, was an important step in galvanizing Armenian self-consciousness, which ultimately was directed toward achieving international recognition of the Genocide.[8]

If this was the time for Armenian and Turkish communities to have an opportunity for reconciliation, it soon was marred. First, the Turkish government successfully maneuvered to delete references to the Armenian Genocide in a 1973 United Nations report that characterized the Armenian massacres in the Ottoman Empire as "the first genocide of the twentieth century." Similarly the United States Congress, under pressure from the State Department and Pentagon, failed to pass a resolution to designate April 24, 1975 as a "National Day of Remembrance of Man's Inhumanity to Man."[9]

Charles Aznavour and Alan Hovhaness

Since Western societies and institutions in the 1970s had distanced themselves politically from the Armenian Genocide, ethnic Armenians themselves decided to lobby their own cause. In addition to the regular methods of communication, advocates of the Armenian cause were also able to explore the Genocide using literature, fine art, dance, and music. The Armenian musical perspective in Western societies was born in this era and reached its first mass audience, both within and outside of Armenian societies, with a song titled "Ils Sont Tombés" or "They Fell," initially released in French but later also in English.

French-Armenian vocalist and lyricist Chahnour (Shahnur) Varenagh Aznavourian, popularly known as Charles Aznavour, released "Ils Sont Tombés" in 1975 on the sixtieth anniversary of the Genocide. "Ils Sont Tombés" is written and sung in the Western "pop" music style. At the time of its release, Aznavour was the foremost ethnically Armenian musician in the West. He released his song at a time when dormant issues regarding the Genocide were just beginning to resurface in every way within world politics. These trends mirrored Aznavour's willingness, and ultimate success, in using a traditionally "non-Armenian" musical style to further an Armenian political cause.

"Ils Sont Tombés" ultimately is an exploration of the legacy of the Armenian Genocide by an Armenian born and raised in France. While the work has the features of a lament, there are differences that mark it as a song of protest. Aznavour makes this quite apparent in the following stanzas:

No one objected in a euphoric world
While a people decomposed in their blood.
Europe was discovering jazz,
The noise of the trumpets was masking the cries of children.

They fell silently,
By thousands, and the millions, while the world remained silent.
In the desert, their bodies looked like minuscule red flowers,
Covered by a sandstorm, which also concealed their existence.

The protest movements then becoming evident in Western music are evident in these stanzas. Aznavour, possibly reacting to overtures by world leaders to Turkish deniers, lashes out to the uncaring world of 1915. He points to a global denial, and possibly an Armenian self-denial, with his allusion to an existence "covered by a sandstorm."

Aznavour is upset, upset at the apathetic world, yet makes no obvious demand of a just resolution beyond awareness. He treads his ground lightly within his native France by attributing his people's survival to their courage but also to the benevolence of others. He softens his general criticism by acknowledging the host countries that took in the survivors of the Armenian Genocide:

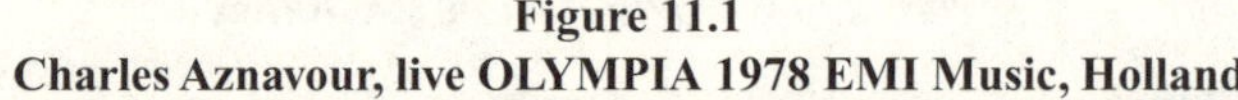

Figure 11.1
Charles Aznavour, live OLYMPIA 1978 EMI Music, Holland

They fell while naively believing,
That their children would hopefully live a normal childhood,
That they would one day march in a land of hope,
In open countries where people would welcome them.
I, myself, am of this race which now sleeps without a resting place,
Who chose to die rather than relinquish the faith,
Who never bowed their heads even in the face of insults,
Who survives despite everything without ever complaining.

SONG: "Ils Sont Tombés"
Album: *aznavour live, OLYMPIA 1978*, released 1978, Track # 4.

Aznavour proclaims his ethnic heritage with this song and conjures up heroic images of survival, with honor, despite an attempt at annihilation. He is ready to complain, for Aznavour is breaking the wall of self-denial surrounding this traumatic event. By embracing this song, the Armenians likewise affirmed that they had indeed been victimized and were ready to go forward.

In 1976, the Diocese of the Armenian Church of America commissioned classicalist Alan Chakmakjian, better known as Alan Hovhaness, of Armenian-Scottish heritage, to compose music in remembrance of the Holy Martyrs of A.D. 451. Hovhaness composed "Khorhoort Nahadagats—Mystery of the Holy Martyrs, Op. 251."[10]

In 1996 reviewer Kenneth LaFave, with George Mangigian, wrote:

> The "holy martyrs" of the title are the more than 1000 Armenian Christians slaughtered in A.D. 451. Armenia had been Christianized 150 years before and the nation's Persian conquerors saw the religion as an impediment to their absolute rule. Instead of subduing the Armenians, however, the mass-murder intensified Armenian Christianity and unified the nation against Persia. The third entry in Hovhaness' suite is a reference to this transcendence of genocide by spiritual and cultural solidarity: "Norahrash," meaning "new miracle."[11]

SONG: "Norahrash," third entry of the suite titled "Khorhoort Nahadagats."
Album: Alan Hovhaness, *Mystery of the Holy Martyrs Op. 251 & Symphony No. 3 Op. 148,* released 1996, Track #6.

The commissioning of "Khorhoort Nahadagats" by the Armenian Church was partly a reaction to the world's seeming indifference to those who had survived the Genocide. This was not lost upon Hovhaness, who used the themes of survival and resurgence in his work, again a basis for ending Kübler-Ross's self-denial of a traumatic event.

Hovhaness had explored the Armenian Genocide previously in his first symphony, Exile, Symphony No. 1, Op. 17, No. 2, in 1936, and, indirectly, again with St. Vartan in Symphony No. 9, Op. 180 in 1949.[12] Both symphonies celebrate the deliverance of and hope for the persecuted. While Hovhaness may have personally explored the impact of the Genocide some years before Aznavour's

Table 11.1

Charles Aznavour, "Il Sont Tombés (They Fell)," 1975

French Version (Aznavour/ Garvarentz)	**English Translation** (by Nanor Kabakian).	**English Version** (Aznavour/ Garvarentz/ Kretzmer)
Ils sont tombés sans trop savoir pourquoi Hommes, femmes et enfants qui ne voulaient que vivre Avec des gestes lourds comme des hommes ivres Mutilés, massacrés les yeux ouverts d'effroi	They fell without knowing why. Men, women, and children, whose only wish was to live, Fell heavily, like drunken people. They were mutilated, massacred, while their eyes were full of fear.	They fell that year, they vanished from the Earth, Never knowing the cause or what laws they'd offended. The women fell as well, and the babies they tendered, Left to die, left to cry, all condemned by their birth.
Ils sont tombés en invoquant leur Dieu Au seuil de leur église ou le pas de leur porte En troupeaux de désert titubant en cohorte Terrassés par la soif, la faim, le fer, le feu	They fell while calling upon their God, At the threshold of their church or doorstep. Herded through the desert, staggering together, Crushed by thirst, hunger, weapons, fire.	They fell like rain across the thirsty land. In their heart they were slain, in their God still believing. All their pity and pain in that season of grieving. All in vain, all in vain, just for one helping hand.
Nul n'éleva la voix dans un monde euphorique Tandis que croupissait un peuple dans son sang L' Europe découvrait le jazz et sa musique Les plaintes de trompettes couvraient les cris d'enfants	No one objected in a euphoric world While a people decomposed in their blood. Europe was discovering jazz, The noise of the trumpets was masking the cries of children.	For no one heard their prayers in a world bent on pleasure. From other people's cares, they simply closed their eyes. They created a lot of sound in jazz and ragtime measure. The trumpets screamed till dawn to drown the children's cries.
Ils sont tombés pudiquement sans bruit Par milliers, par millions, sans que le monde bouge Devenant un instant minuscules fleurs rouges Recouverts par un vent de sable et puis d'oubli	They fell silently, By thousands, and the millions, while the world remained silent, In the desert, their bodies looked like minuscule red flowers, Covered by a sandstorm, which also concealed their existence.	They fell like leaves, its people in its prime, Simple man, kindly man, and not one knew his crime. They became in that hour like the small desert flower, Soon covered by the silent wind in sands of time.
Ils sont tombés les yeux pleins de soleil Comme un oiseau qu'en vol une balle fracasse Pour mourir n'importe où et sans laisser de traces Ignorés, oubliés dans leur dernier sommeil	They fell, blinded by the sun, Just like a bird, in flight, which suddenly gets crushed by a bullet. Only to die anywhere, without leaving any trace, Ignored, forgotten as they were going into eternal sleep.	They fell that year before a cruel foe. They had little to give but their lives and their passion, And their longing to live, in their way, in their fashion, So their harvest could thrive and their children could grow.
Ils sont tombés en croyant ingénus Que leurs enfants pourraient continuer leur enfance Qu'un jour ils fouleraient des terres d'espérance Dans des pays ouverts d'hommes aux mains tendues	They fell while naively believing, That their children would hopefully live a normal childhood, That they would one day march in a land of hope, In open countries where people would welcome them.	They fell like flies, their eyes still full of sun, Like a dove, its flight, in the path of rifle, That falls down where it might, as if death were a trifle, And to bring to an end a life barely begun.
Moi je suis de ce peuple qui dort sans sépulture Qu'a choisi de mourir sans abdiquer sa foi Qui n'a jamais baissé la tête sous l'injure Qui survit malgré tout et qui ne se plaint pas	I, myself, am of this race which now sleeps without a resting place, Who chose to die rather than relinquish the faith, Who never bowed their heads even in the face of insults, Who survives despite everything without ever complaining.	And I am of that race who died in unknown places Who perished in their pride, whose blood in rivers ran. In agony and fright, with courage on their faces, They went into the night that waits for every man.
Ils sont tombés pour entrer dans la nuit Éternelle des temps au bout de leur courage La mort les a frappés sans demander leur âge Puisqu'ils étaient fautifs d'être enfants d'Arménie	They fell to enter the night. Having exhausted all their courage, Death struck them, regardless of their age, Their only crime being children of Armenia.	They fell like tears and never knew what for, In that summer of strife, of massacre and war. Their only crime was life; there only guilt was fear, The children of Armenia, nothing less, nothing more.

Figure 11.2
Alan Hovhaness, Mystery of the Holy Martyrs, OP 251, 1996, Soundset

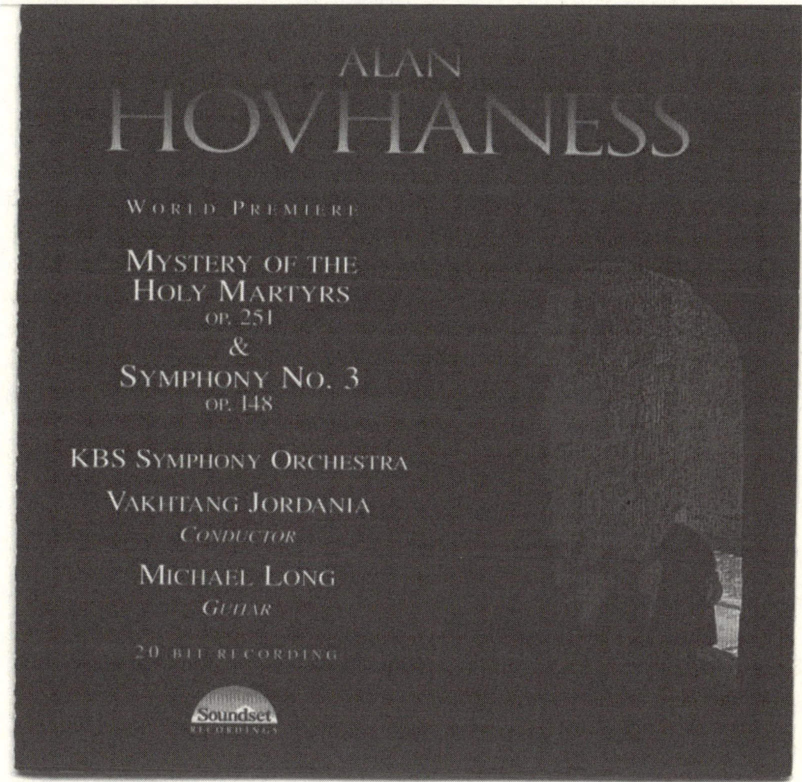

song, it was his commissioned and therefore communal work "Norahrash" in 1976 that stands with "Ils Sont Tombés" as providing an uplifting tribute to a people's survival, a celebration of revival, and an end to self-denial of the Genocide.

The Angry Generation

Both Aznavour and Hovhaness acknowledged that a catastrophe happened to the Armenian people, yet they ultimately praised their people's rebirth without making a clear statement regarding a "just" outcome for the Armenian Genocide. Some twenty years later, a new generation of Armenian-American artists took a different, somewhat darker and angrier approach to the issue.

In the intervening twenty years the fate of the world, and the Armenian people, changed radically. Most significantly the empire that provided relative "peace" for the Armenian nation collapsed in 1991. As the Union of Soviet

Socialist Republics was disintegrating in the late 1980s, the Armenians found themselves in an ethnic war with neighboring Azerbaijani Turks, reliving the victimization by the Ottoman Turks in 1915.[13] The Turkish republic's blockade of Armenia in solidarity with Azerbaijan reinforced the mood among the new generation of Armenians that the 1915 Genocide had never ended.[14] This anger and disillusionment was evident in the music of this new generation, which marked departure from the earlier patterns.

In 1996, jazz composer Gregg Bendian released "After Chomaklou Was a Desert (Threnody to the Victims of the Armenian Genocide)" in a free-form style of jazz.[15] Chomaklou (Chomakhlu) was a rural Armenian community near Caesarea/Kaiseri and Develi (Evereg-Fenesse). Chomaklou, plundered and razed, did not survive the Genocide.[16] Bendian chose to write a lament for the loss of his ancestral village. What temporarily survived was the Chomaklou Compatriotic Society, a benevolent and educational foundation, yet even this organization eventually dissolved, sealing the ultimate fate of this single community.

Figure 11.3
Gregg Bendian Project, *Counterparts*, 1996 CIMP

Bendian's profound sadness and anger become evident in his composition. Robert Iannapollo, in a review published in the jazz magazine *Cadence* in September 1996, observes:

> Its initial theme consists of a baleful melody. . . . While a funeral mood permeates much of the piece, midway through a series of crescendoing ascending/descending phrases and a speeding up of the tempo give the piece a powerful mood of defiance and affirmation. The final section returns to an uneasy quiet as the piece draws to its conclusion with Bendian dragging chains over his drums and bowing the cymbals.[17]

SONG: excerpt from "After Chomaklou Was a Desert (Threnody to the Victims of the Armenian Genocide)"
Album: Gregg Bendian Project, *Counterparts*, released 1996, Track # 3.

Bendian presents a world that was traumatized and never resurrected. He is angry. There is no resurgence, no survival to remember. The "dragging chains" that end his piece are symbolic of the decimation of the village and of its heritage. Bendian identifies the last section as a "Death March, Drone/Threnody":

> Here, the bass soloist represents the mournful voice of the people of Chomaklou (and the Armenian people as a whole) sobbing in the desert as they contemplate the aftermath of this largely unrecognized human tragedy.[18]

In 1998, the alternative hard-rock music group *System of a Down*, whose band members are all Armenian-Americans, released "P.L.U.C.K" or "**P**olitically **L**ying, **U**nholy, **C**owardly **K**illers." The song, written by Serj Tankian with music by Daron Malakian, has a heading on the lyrics page that reads:

> *System of a Down* would like to dedicate this song to the memory of the 1.5 million victims of the Armenian Genocide, perpetrated by the Turkish Government in 1915.

The first stanza of the song is similar in aspects to all the other works mentioned in that it acknowledges the Genocide and ends any remaining shred of self-denial. This is also explored later in the song:

> The plan was mastered and called Genocide,
> (Never want to see you around)
> Took all the children and then we died,
> (Never want to see you around)
> The few that remained were never found,
> (Never want to see you around)
> All in a system, Down ~

The line "The few that remained were never found" is reminiscent of Bendian's bleak outlook both on "Chomaklou" and on the current state of Armenian

Figure 11.4
System of a Down, 1998, American Recording

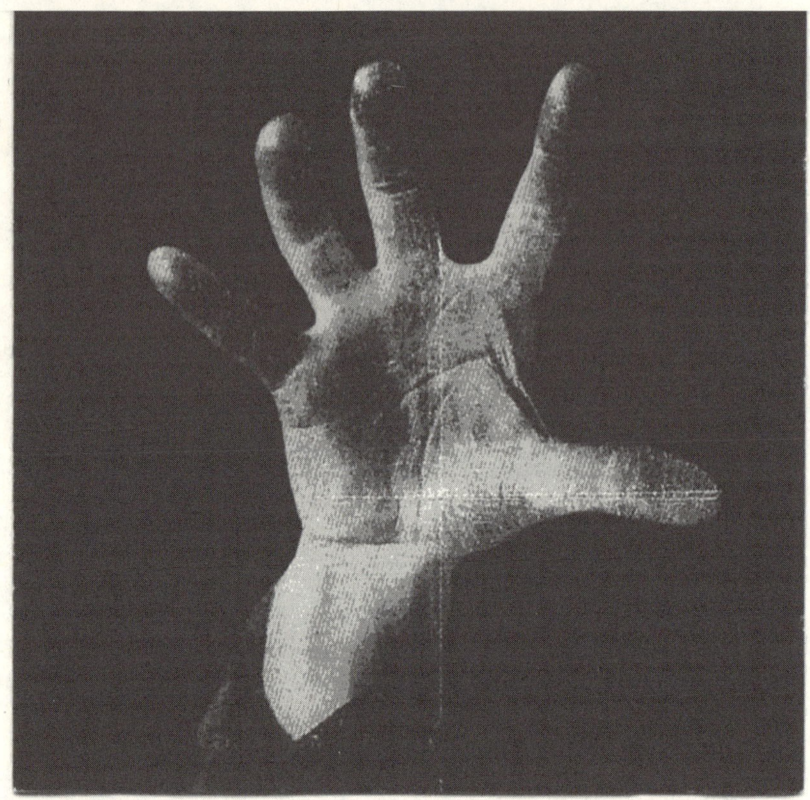

affairs. The implication is that the loss is unrecoverable. There is no mention of the heroic survival and cultural resurgence as reflected in Aznavour and Hovhaness. Moreover, *System of a Down,* unlike Aznavour, Hovhaness, and Bendian, goes a step further by demanding a "just" outcome for the Armenian Genocide. The following stanza is a departure from the earlier works because it signals a new direction in Genocide resolution vis-à-vis Armeno-Turkish relations:

> Revolution, the only solution,
> The armed response of an entire nation,
> Revolution, the only solution,
> We've taken all your shit, now it's time for restitution.
>
> Recognition, Restoration, Reparation,
> Recognition, Restoration, Reparation,
> Watch them all fall down.

Table 11.2

P.L.U.C.K. **(Politically Lying, Unholy, Cowardly Killers.)** **Album**: *System Of A Down* **Lyrics:** Serj Tankian **Music:** Daron Malakian **Musicians:** Serj Tankian, Daron Malakian, Shavo Odadjian, John Dolmayan **Date:** 1998	**"After Chomaklou Was a Desert"** **(Threnody to the Victims of the Armenian Genocide)** **Album:** Gregg Bendian Project *Counterparts* **Composer:** Gregg Bendian **Musicians:** Gregg Bendian, Mark Dresser, Paul Smoker, Vinny Golia **Date:** 1996
Elimination, Elimination, Elimination. Die, Why, Walk Down, Walk Down. A whole race Genocide, Taken away all of our pride, A whole race Genocide, Taken away, Watch Them all fall down. Revolution, the only solution, The armed response of an entire nation, Revolution, the only solution, We've taken all your shit, now it's time for restitution. Recognition, Restoration, Reparation, Recognition, Restoration, Reparation, Watch them all fall down. Revolution, the only solution, The armed response of an entire nation, Revolution, the only solution, We've taken all your shit, now it's time for restitution. The plan was mastered and called Genocide, (Never want to see you around) Took all the children and then we died, (Never want to see you around) The few that remained were never found, (Never want to see you around) All in a system, Down...... Down.....Down.......Down........ Walk Down...........Walk Down Watch them all fall down, Revolution, the only solution, The armed response of an entire nation, Revolution, the only solution, We've taken all your shit, now it's time for restitution. The plan was mastered and called Genocide (Never want to see you around) Took all the children and then we died, (Never want to see you around) The few that remained were never found, (Never want to see you around) All in a system, Down~	**COMPOSER'S NOTES:** Chomaklou was the Armenian village in Turkey where my grandfather grew up. He fled the village with his parents during the Turkish aggression of 1915. The Bendian family and the other villagers were marched out into the desert without food and water, to die. My grandfather Krikor's parents were murdered in the desert and he fled to the US with the help of his brother. With the music for "After Chomkalou" I wished to put forth, albeit in a visceral and abstract way, something of the impact of this nightmarish story. Although the music for "After Chomaklou" is not intended to be strictly programmatic in nature, there are definite sections which are intended to evoke a kind of unresolved five-part musical form. I. Opening: Solo percussion sounds represents the life, laughter and daily activity of a peaceful and happy village. II. First melodies: The strains of these suspended, abstract, but decidedly Armenian-inflected lines are meant to portray a sense of contentedness, while gradually moving toward a feeling of subtle foreboding. III. Tensions mount: There is now an inevitability to what will soon befall the people of Chomaklou. The ensemble's soloists speak out in turn, as the melodies become more pensive and desperate. IV. Conflict/Flight: The explosion of violence, screams of terror, and the cacophony of slaughter. V. Death March, Drone/Threnody: Here, the bass soloist represents the mournful voice of the people of Chomaklou (and the Armenian people as a whole) sobbing in the desert as they contemplate the aftermath of this largely unrecognized human tragedy.

SONG "P.L.U.C.K." (Politically Lying, Unholy, Cowardly Killers)
Album: *SYSTEM OF A DOWN*, released 1998, Track #13.

"P.L.U.C.K." epitomizes Kübler-Ross's transition from a state of denial to a state of anger. *System of a Down* chooses in "P.L.U.C.K." to advocate a "revolution" through an "armed response" in order to resolve the unresolved legacy of the Genocide. In addition, "recognition, restoration, reparation" outlines the necessity not only for acknowledgement but also for recovery and recompense. With respect to Kübler-Ross, this denotes potential progress toward the bargaining state yet the song as a whole remains imbued in violence. While the musical genre of alternative hard rock has the reputation of espousing violence,[19] *System of a Down* has been a relative exception by advocating for the disenfranchised in other works, such as "BOOM," which is an example of an anti-war song.[20] Yet violence is integral to "P.L.U.C.K." and exemplifies a state of anger.

Differing from Aznavour, Hovhaness, and Bendian, who never address righting the wrong, *System of a Down* grapples with this issue and offers a violent solution. That the musical group had the willingness, and ultimate success, in using a forceful, traditionally "non-Armenian" hard rock style to further an Armenian political cause clearly has its roots in the current irreconcilable state of Armeno-Turkish relations.

Musical perspectives from 1975 to 1998 mirror the Armenian struggle spanning the last thirty years over the legacy of the Genocide. The perspective in the 1970s was one of cultural survival and revival. It signified a time when the collective Armenian consciousness was able to admit that it was victimized, ending self-denial. Songs like "Ils Sont Tombés" and "Norahrash" served to acknowledge the traumas of the Armenian people yet also sought to celebrate their survival and cultural resurgence.

The next thirty years, in fact, would see no resolution but rather an exacerbation of the Armeno-Turkish conflict. Recurrent Turkish denials of the Armenian Genocide and Turkey's military support of Azerbaijan against the Republic of Armenia have created a new generation of diasporan Armenian musicians whose songs display a certain anxiety that the Armenian legacy will not survive. The "just" resolution of the Genocide appears equally bleak.[21] It then comes as no surprise that the late 1990s differed from the earlier, more hopeful period by recognizing loss and demanding action.

The trauma of the Genocide will resolve itself along the pathway delineated by Kübler-Ross. This applies both to the victim and the perpetrator. By embracing the various Armenian works in the Western musical styles over a thirty-year period, the Armenian people demonstrate how they have progressed beyond a form of self-denial into anger followed by bargaining through a call for action. This development has been fueled by the Turkish government itself, which has regressed further into self-denial and complicity by refusing to acknowledge and accept responsibility for the Genocide and by imposing economic hardships on the landlocked, small, existing Armenian republic in the South Caucasus.[22] The unfortunate divergence of these two nations will likely mean that the musicians of the next generation will have a ready audience for their songs.

Notes

1. Charles Aznavour, "Ils Sont Tombés," *aznavour live, OLYMPIA 1978,* Ý 978 EMI Music Holland BV, Ý 1998 EMI Music Fance.
2. System of a Down, "P.L.U.C.K.," *SYSTEM OF A DOWN,* Ý 998 The American Recording Company, LLC/ ÝThe American Recording Company, LLC.
3. See Harold I. Kaplan, Benjamin J. Sadock, and Jack A. Grebb, *Synopsis of Psychiatry: Behavioral Sciences, Clinical Psychiatry*, 7th ed. (Baltimore: Williams and Wilkins, 1994), pp. 76-77.

4. www.changingminds.org/disciplines/change_management/kubler_ross/kubler_ross.htm.
5. www.changingminds.org/explanations/behaviors/coping/defense_mechanisms.htm.
6. Richard G. Hovannisian, ed. *The Armenian People from Ancient to Modern Times*, vol. 2 (New York: St. Martin's Press, 1997), pp. 376-377.
7. www.chgs.umn.edu/Histories__Narratives__Document/The_Armenians/Denial/denial.html.
8. Hovannisian, *The Armenian People*, vol. 2, pp. 419-420.
9. www.armenocide.am.
10. Alan Hovhaness, "Norahrash," *Mystery of the Holy Martyrs Op. 251 & Symphony No. 3 Op 148*, Ý Ý 1996 Soundset Recordings.
11. Insert in *Mystery of the Holy Martyrs.*
12. www.hovhaness.com/hovhaness.html.
13. Hovannisian, *The Armenian People*, vol. 2, pp. 383-387.
14. Ibid., pp. 440-441.
15. Gregg Bendian Project, "After Chomaklu Was a Desert (Threnody to the Victims of the Armenian Genocide)," *Counterparts,* Ý Ý996 Creative Improvised Music Productions.
16. Aris Kalfaian, *Chomaklou: The Story of an Armenian Village*, trans. Krikor Asadourian, ed. and rev. with a preface and afterword by Michael Ekizian (New York: Chomaklou Compatriotic Society, 1982).
17. www.cadencebuilding.com/cadence/cadencemagazine.html.
18. Gregg Bendian, Personal communication, March 7, 2005.
19. www.newsmax.com/articles/?a=2000/9/13/181640.
20. www.systemofadownonline.com/vid/boom.htm.
21. www.armenocide.am.
22. www.chgs.umn.edu/Histories__Narratives__Document/The_Armenians/Denial/denial.html.

Part 3

Education

12

"No Mandate Left Behind"? Genocide Education in the Era of High-Stakes Testing

Nicole E. Vartanian

Ninety years after the perpetration of the Armenian Genocide and thirty years after the emergence of the field of genocide education in the United States, many questions remain regarding the most successful strategies for attaining an effective policy for teaching the topic of genocide. Can policymakers mandate what matters in public school classrooms? And even if so, to rephrase the landmark education legislation signed into law in 2001, will "every mandate be left behind" in the era of high-stakes testing?

To consider possible responses to this question, this discussion offers a brief review of Armenian Genocide education mandates in select states; provides a skeletal explanation of the legislation and testing guidelines under which schools are operating; considers the impact of this legislation on social studies curriculum; and explores the potential implications of pending legislation on the future of genocide education. Indeed, in light of the ubiquitous influence of high-stakes testing, as well as recent national policies that tie student achievement on standardized tests to federal funding for public schools, these issues require attention so that the topic of genocide is not fated to exist extraneous from and unincorporated into its intended educational frameworks.

Making of a Mandate

In the context of this complicated and politicized education landscape, the concept of genocide has had difficulty finding a secure place in public school curricula. One avenue that has been regularly pursued in an attempt to solidify this issue into curriculum guidelines has been through legislative mandates. In many states, these initiatives have been enacted via grassroots or political movements to adopt measures that would instruct school districts to teach the Holocaust and other genocides. These efforts are not always regulated, nor are they necessarily even implemented as prescribed, but they represent an important political and pedagogical victory for prioritizing this course of study.

Since the 1970s, an increasing number of states and school districts has tried to level the proverbial playing field for this subject and has turned to enacting mandates for teaching some form of history relating to human rights, genocide, and/or the Holocaust. Individuals involved in every state that has sought a mandate for teaching genocide have learned firsthand that politics is an inextricable part of sponsoring instruction on this topic. In this vein, states have achieved different levels of success with regard to mandating or supporting teaching about genocide in public schools. While dozens of states require teaching some version of the history of the Holocaust—and employ textbooks that include the subject—very few actually follow up on the mandate with evaluations of the instruction. To further complicate matters, instruction on other instances of twentieth-century genocide are mandated even more rarely, let alone included in approved texts, leaving students with the potential perception that the Holocaust was a uniquely horrific event, stripping the catastrophe of its precedent and antecedent context and obscuring the historical relevance of other genocidal acts.

In the case of the Armenian Genocide, it is no surprise that efforts to legislate teaching have consistently met with counter-pressures. As a result, the mandate processes have attained limited success, but to the present time seven states have adopted some form of educational mandate or guidance relating to the Armenian Genocide.

It is important to note that many teachers prioritized the teaching of this topic long before the mandates took effect and continue to do so with great attention and concern, whether or not they are held accountable for covering the material. Their work is to be modeled, particularly considering that they usually have had to teach these topics while independently ferreting out and utilizing supplemental teaching materials—such as state-recommended teaching guides, publications from educational organizations like Facing History and Ourselves, and materials developed by interested cultural groups.

National Legislative Context

While stakeholders can feel proud of the hard-fought legislative victories that these mandates represent, another potential challenge seems to be forming that threatens the implementation of these guidelines, namely the climate of high-stakes testing brought on by the landmark federal education legislation passed in 2001 known as No Child Left Behind (NCLB).

The four pillars of the legislation are as follows:

1. *Stronger accountability for results*: NCLB aims to close the achievement gap and make sure all students achieve academic proficiency. Annual state

and school district report cards inform parents and communities about state and school progress. Schools that do not make progress must provide supplemental services; take corrective actions; and, if still not making adequate yearly progress after five years, make dramatic changes to the way the school is managed.

2. *More freedom for states and communities*: NCLB aims to give schools, districts, and states more flexibility with the way that they use their federal funds. This allows districts to use funds for their particular needs, such as hiring new teachers, increasing teacher pay, and improving teacher training and professional development.
3. *Proven education methods*: NCLB puts emphasis on determining which educational programs and practices have been proven effective through rigorous scientific research. Federal funding is targeted to support these programs and teaching methods that work to improve student learning and achievement.
4. *More choices for parents*: In schools that do not meet state standards for at least two consecutive years, parents may transfer their children to a better-performing public school, including a public charter school, within their district. Students from low-income families in schools that fail to meet state standards for at least three years are eligible to receive supplemental educational services. Also, students who attend a persistently dangerous school or are the victims of a violent crime while in their school have the option to attend a safe school within their district.[1]

Of these four goals, the one that is most applicable to genocide education—and which has been the most contentious in states across the nation—relates to the first issue of accountability.

No one would argue against attempts to close the achievement gap for all students or to holding schools, districts, and states more accountable for student learning and achievement. This aspect of the legislation, however, has come under the most debate, largely as a result of the effects of its implementation. NCLB requires each state to design accountability systems for monitoring schools' annual yearly progress, which "must be based on challenging State standards in reading and mathematics, annual testing for all students in grades 3-8, and annual statewide progress objectives ensuring that all groups of students reach proficiency within 12 years."[2] The results of those annual examinations influence the level of federal funding states receive, so, given the high-stakes nature of these assessments for already cash-strapped states, it is no surprise that schools are making every effort to prepare their students to excel on these examinations.

Some educators, however, contend that one of the many unintended side effects of this increased focus on reading and mathematics assessment is that other core curricula are being pushed to the margins of an already over-extended school day. In fact, Theodore K. Rabb, Professor of History at Princeton University and a founder and board member of the National Council for History

Education, maintains: "It is clear that, with some notable exceptions nationwide, the amount of class time given to history, especially in the first eight grades, has been shrinking almost by the month."[3]

This growing concern has begun to fuel efforts on the part of the social studies community to call attention to the bleak outlook for this curriculum area and to galvanize support from policymakers and stakeholders for a renewed commitment to this subject. The National Council for the Social Studies (NCSS) has convened a group of representatives to explore issues surrounding instructional time in classrooms; the National Council for History Education has circulated a statement on what it sees as a "Crisis in History" forming; and the state of Maryland has commissioned a national and statewide study on "the state of social studies," to name but a few efforts underway to address the increasing tide of concern. It should be noted that this sense of alarm is not unique to the field of social studies—teachers in the arts and foreign languages in particular are signaling similar calls for action.

According to some experts, state policies that attach high stakes to student achievement in some subjects and not others have exacerbated this discrepancy. Further, there is research evidence illustrating that teachers are inclined to spend more time on subjects that are tested "and for which scores are used to rate schools' and students' progress" than on those that are not included in state testing programs. To this point, officials in the state of Maryland say that since the state eliminated its social studies tests in 2003, primarily because the assessment program did not fulfill federal requirements, a noticeable decrease in the attention given to the subjects has occurred.[4]

Supporters of NCLB point out that the legislation does nothing explicitly to encourage schools to cut back on core academic subjects like history or enrichment courses such as art or foreign language. However, educators argue, as school districts—particularly those that are classified as low-performing—struggle to demonstrate achievement under the auspices of the law's assessment requirements, this poses another layer of difficult decisions regarding how to parcel out the already burgeoning school day to meet all curricular demands.

In fact, so as to make certain that this obvious point was not lost, Florida's K-12 schools chancellor, Jim Warford, issued a memorandum to school districts in the fall of 2004, in response to complaints from teachers, reminding them that state law requires the teaching of social studies at all school levels. Time spent on social studies instruction in Illinois had already been diminishing in order to accommodate as much as 160 minutes daily of reading, when the legislature disposed of the state test in social studies, setting off a wave of criticism arguing that it would lead to further dissolution of instructional time for the subject area.[5]

The experience of Dana Lenzen, curriculum coordinator for elementary social studies at Lindbergh School District in St. Louis, Missouri, demonstrates how this translates directly to an elementary school classroom, when she asserts: "NCLB as well as all the state mandates have restricted social studies teaching enormously. I feel that we as social studies teachers have absolutely no latitude in what we teach. We are driven by NCLB and state testing mandates. Content in social studies is not looked upon favorably. I sneak in genocide teaching using Dr. Martin Luther King's birthday."[6]

In California, social studies instruction had already been facing an uphill battle for the past several years, according to Nancy McTygue, the interim executive director of the California Social Studies Project, a state-financed agency that provides professional development and curriculum support for the state's low-performing districts and schools. McTygue affirms that the field has suffered due to the lack of state accountability measures requiring schools to report achievement in social studies for the elementary and middle grades, a trend she contends has been exacerbated since the passage of the federal education law. "Low-performing schools have dropped history," she said, "choosing instead to have a three-hour block to teach a scripted reading program, in addition to two hours of mathematics and required [physical education] classes. If a student goes to a low-performing elementary school and then a low-performing middle school, they won't have history until they're 15 or 16, and all they'll have is 20th-century history," she cautioned.[7]

What does all this mean to those with an interest in the legacy of the Armenian Genocide? Depending on each state, it could mean different things regarding the teaching of this topic of study, but across the board at the very least it sounds an alarm to work even harder at helping ensure that the mandates that already have been enacted are in fact being implemented. This will become even more of a priority if Congress approves the administration's education budget for FY 2007 in its current state, which proposes that NCLB expands its reach into high schools, and at the time of this writing President Bush had submitted a request for $1.475 billion to fund these efforts. The new initiative would require two additional years of reading and mathematics testing; the original law requires states to test students at least once in grades 10-12.

If these changes are put into place, there is a growing concern over how social studies will fare at the high school level, too. Jesus Garcia, president of the National Council for the Social Studies and Professor of Social Studies Education at the University of Nevada, Las Vegas, points out: "If students do not get the basic skills in social studies in grades K-6, the result will be students entering high school with very little background information in any of the social studies subjects. That makes the job of the middle school teacher and high school teacher extremely difficult, because they will have to start from scratch."[8] The ripple effects of such a transformation of the social studies curriculum could be far-reaching, and certainly could threaten the teaching of topics such as genocide, which are already vulnerable subjects of study—even under the theoretically protective cloak of legislative mandates.

Actions for the Future

In light of the ever-changing landscape of educational reform, educators must adapt their strategies for supporting these efforts so as to maximize results. What follow are a few multilayered approaches for future actions, many of which are ongoing and others of which may seem obvious, but, hopefully, collectively will help inform the field's next steps in this process.

1. *Penetrate texts and tests*. At least twenty-one states, including influential California, Texas, and Florida, have committees that decide which books are to be utilized in public schools. As *Washington Post* education writer Jay Matthews notes: "The scrubbing and sanitizing that is imposed to satisfy the big states has affected all commercially produced textbooks. That means that even states without adoption laws end up using the same books as the ones written to please California and Texas."[9] For Stan Bartosiak, a high school world history teacher in the Glendale Unified School district, this translates into his using an assigned Prentice Hall textbook that was adapted by California and Texas, and includes *one paragraph* on the Armenian Genocide.[10] While the mere mention of the Genocide in a major, mainstream textbook represents a milestone of sorts, one paragraph quite obviously does not do justice to the legacy of this catastrophe. Hence, efforts must be focused on addressing this gross discrepancy, while recognizing that the textbook industry is just that—a very lucrative industry. In this vein, it is important to conduct an updated textbook analysis of major texts being adopted in Texas and California so there is clarity on the content that is driving the industry nationwide, and assess which publishers might afford an opening for the meaningful inclusion of genocide history.

2. *Inclusion of the topic of genocide on standardized tests*. This is an area that may be open to successful proactive efforts. Again, even with widespread criticisms surrounding the use of these examinations as high-stakes arbiters of student achievement—and certainly with the caveat that the vast majority of public school teachers work hard to dismantle the notion of "teaching to the test"—high-stakes assessments do offer both symbolic and substantive direction for teachers. Especially in states that boast genocide education mandates, social studies specialists who craft the examinations need to be encouraged to include this content in order to streamline the message of its importance. On this front, California and New York have seen progress but these efforts must be reinforced and expanded.

3. *Tailor efforts to each state*. The communications director of the Armenian National Committee in Washington, D.C. emphasizes that it is crucial to have an understanding of each state's approach to curriculum standards.[11] In the states where education mandates are pursued for teaching particular topics, it is important to learn the legislative climate of that state and work within it, in the context of community resources and strengths therein. On the other hand,

if a state generally does not pursue legislation, it is important to learn the mechanisms by which education standards are formed and work within those frameworks, vis-à-vis political coalitions and teachers' networks.

3. *Build coalitions at every turn.* Time and time again, the Armenian-American community turns to other groups to support Armenian Genocide legislation—both in and out of the arena of education—often without proactively offering its own backing to efforts in other ethnic and cultural minority communities. This can take place in many forums—for example, special interest group subcommittees of education associations are always seeking new members, and are the gathering grounds of many academics who go on to participate in the writing of textbooks on a myriad of subjects.

4. *Develop networks of teachers.* Countless passionate educators are committed to this genre of teaching, with or without mandates, and would embrace the collegiality and support that would come from coordinated efforts to interact with other like-minded professionals. On this point, The Genocide Education Project has taken the initiative to attend NCSS conferences and interact with teachers who prioritize the teaching of the Armenian Genocide in their classrooms. Many of those same teachers work with their respective states on setting curriculum standards or goals, or with state and district curriculum committees on the issue of textbook purchasing. These teachers can be the most effective grassroots foot soldiers in the effort to incorporate the Armenian Genocide in state- and district-level curriculum guidelines and texts.

5. *Produce and implement high-quality resources.* It is also crucial to develop cutting-edge materials and put them in the hands of teachers (not just delivered to school district curriculum directors) along with the tools to teach them. The number and nature of quality resources available to teachers is increasing all the time, but are only effective if they make their way directly to the teachers who are ready and waiting to implement them.

6. *Incorporate genocide into the NCSS National Standards for Social Studies Teachers.* As the organization that represents 26,000 socials studies educators, NCSS has compiled ten thematic strands of curriculum standards that make no mention of genocide. While the theme of human rights is evoked in the section "Global Connections," the topic of genocide could have fertile ground for application therein and/or within the rubric of "Power, Authority, and Governance." Such a high-level reference would send a powerful message to the social studies community regarding the importance and relevance of this topic of study.

It is clear that education reforms come and go, and mandates are enacted at political profit, but what endures in the classrooms of the nation's public schools are the lessons learned and the voices heard from the pages of collective human history. Ensuring that the legacy of the Armenian Genocide does in fact endure, and is never ever left behind, should be a shared responsibility for all those who feel invested with realizing this humble communal goal.

Appendix*

Excerpted text of Armenian Genocide education mandates in the following states:

CALIFORNIA

California History-Social Science Content Standard 10.5.5 requires that students in the public schools:

Discuss human rights violations and genocide, including the Ottoman government's actions against Armenian citizens.

History-Social Science Framework for California Public Schools:

Within the context of human rights and genocide, students should learn of the Ottoman government's planned mass deportation and systematic annihilation of the Armenian population in 1915. Students should also examine the reactions of other governments, including that of the United States, and world opinion during and after the Armenian genocide. They should examine the effects of the genocide on the remaining Armenian people, who were deprived of their historic homeland, and the ways in which it became a prototype of subsequent genocides.(Framework, p.127)

ILLINOIS

Illinois' Public Act PA 094-0478 mandates the teaching of the Armenian Genocide in public schools, although the framework has not been updated yet to reflect this change:

One of the universal lessons of the Holocaust is that national, ethnic, racial, or religious hatred can overtake any nation or society, leading to calamitous consequences. To reinforce that lesson, such curriculum shall include an additional unit of instruction studying other acts of genocide across the globe. This unit shall include, but not be limited to, the Armenian Genocide, the Famine-Genocide in Ukraine, and more recent atrocities in Cambodia, Bosnia, Rwanda, and Sudan.

MASSACHUSETTS

Massachusetts History and Social Science Curriculum Framework WHII.18 requires that students in the public schools:

Summarize the major events and consequences of WWI.
A. Physical and economic destruction
B. The League of Nations and attempts at disarmament
C. The collapse of the Romanov dynasty and the subsequent Bolshevik Revolution and Civil War in Russia
D. Post-war economic and political instability in Germany
E. The Armenian genocide in Turkey
F. The unprecedented loss of life from prolonged trench warfare

NEW JERSEY

New Jersey Social Studies Curriculum Framework, Chapter 2: Understanding History, Standard 6.4: Social History, Learning Activities for Grades 9-12 - World History period, requires that students in the public schools:

Locate and read other eyewitness accounts of the Holocaust and of other tragic examples of human destruction in history, such as the genocide of the Armenians; the horrors of Stalin's planned famine in the Ukraine, the genocide in Cambodia or Rwanda, the Trail of Tears in American history, the treatment of the Aborigines in Australia, the forced immigration and enslavement of Africans, and countless other examples of inhumanity. Compare and contrast the authors' views, thoughts, emotions, and experiences with those recorded by Anne Frank.

NEW YORK

New York State Social Studies Core Curriculum Unit Six: A Half Century of Crisis and Achievement (1900-1945), requires that students in the public schools learn about:

World War I
1. Europe: the physical setting
2. Causes
3. Impacts
4. Effects of science/technological advances on warfare
5. Armenian Massacre
6. Collapse of the Ottoman Empire
7. The war as reflected in literature, art, and propaganda

RHODE ISLAND

Rhode Island General Laws (R.I.G.L.), Title 16 on Education, Curriculum Chapter 16-22, Section 16-22-22 on Genocide and Human Rights Education, requires that the department of elementary and secondary education shall:

Pursuant to rules promulgated by the commissioner of elementary and secondary education, develop curricular material on genocide and human rights issues and guidelines for the teaching of that material. The material and guidelines shall include, but not be limited to: (1) the period of the transatlantic slave trades and the middle passage; (2) the great hunger period in Ireland; (3) the Armenian genocide; (4) the Holocaust; and (5) the Mussolini fascist regime and other recognized human rights violations. In formulating this program the department shall consult with practicing teachers, principals, superintendents and experts knowledgeable in genocide and human rights issues. Local school committees may incorporate the material into their elementary and secondary school curriculum.

VIRGINIA

Virginia World History and Geography: 1500 a.d. to the Present Curriculum Framework, Standard WHII.11b, requires that:

The student will demonstrate knowledge of the worldwide impact of World War II by examining the Holocaust and other examples of genocide in the twentieth century.

Examples of other genocides:

Armenians by leaders of the Ottoman Empire

Peasants, government and military leaders, and members of the elite in the Soviet Union by Joseph Stalin

The educated, artists, technicians, former government officials, monks, and minorities by Pol Pot in Cambodia

Tutsi minority by Hutu in Rwanda Muslims and Croats by Bosnian Serbs in former Yugoslavia

*Source: The Genocide Education Project's website for secondary school teachers, www.teachgenocide.org.

Notes

1. U.S. Department of Education website. www.ed.gov.
2. Ibid.
3. *Education Week* online, March 16, 2005.
4. Ibid.
5. Ibid.
6. Personal correspondence, March 24, 2005.
7. *Education Week* online, March 16, 2005.
8. Ibid.
9. *Education Week* online, March 16, 2005.
10. Telephone interview with Stan Bartosiak, March 23, 2005.
11. Telephone interview with Elizabeth Chouldjian, March 27, 2005.

13

Teaching about the Armenian Genocide

Adam Strom

In an era of increasing emphasis on standardized testing, schools are spending decreasing time on the study of history. History teachers report little professional development support for their work. Students report feeling unengaged and ask, "Why does history matter?"

Despite this environment, teachers are eager to find a place for content and methodology that inspires their students to care. These teachers fill Facing History and Ourselves workshops, institutes, community events, online forums, and join the online campus, hungry for the best practices in teaching history well. (These events can be found at www.facinghistory.org.) They want their students to sharpen their critical thinking skills; to learn to probe a particular history for its universal themes; and to discover that their choices matter now, in school, in their families, in their neighborhood, and later in their nation and world. They want tools that will help their students navigate the present and prepare for the future. This journey guides teachers as they face history and themselves.

Facing History and Ourselves has recently published its newest resource book, *Crimes Against Humanity and Civilization: The Genocide of the Armenians*. The book is anchored in the same intellectual and pedagogic perspective that has guided Facing History's thirty years of research and professional development about the collapse of democracy in Weimar Germany and the steps leading to the Holocaust, as well as other examples of mass violence and genocide in the twentieth century. Studying these histories provides students with the knowledge and skills for a deeper understanding of democratic citizenship.

The Armenian Genocide began what Pulitzer-prize-winner Samantha Power calls, "the age of genocide."[1] Less than a generation later, the Nazi Holocaust of the Jews, Gypsies, and others took place. Now at the opening of the twenty-first century students are witnesses to genocide as they turn on their televisions and click past high quality video images of mass violence from around the globe.

How could students, many soon to be of voting age, not recognize the inability of policymakers to stop the genocide today in Sudan? Teachers want to promote inquiry, interpretation, and discussion about difficult realities in our world. To avoid these realities is to risk apathetic, skeptical non-participants in our society and future. Too much is at stake if we fail to create a rationale for teaching about genocide and an interest in learning how to strengthen the political skill needed to make a difference in this world. Students will ask about "real politics." What's the difference between a massacre, genocide, and war? Is there a "just" war? What are the limits of national sovereignty? When should "we" intervene in another country's affairs? These are just some of the important questions that arise with a critical study of the Armenian Genocide.

Many teachers choose to teach the Armenian Genocide because it provides a "safe" distance from those questions, which reverberate so powerfully in our world today. This distance can help illuminate some of the questions that connect the present and the past. In the examination of these issues, complicated by rigorous historical inquiry, arguments about contemporary politics can become informed dialogue. With practice, the arrogance and dogma argued by those who wield the biggest stick or use the loudest voice to intimidate others into silence will be made impotent. Polarized views held so strongly by people so divided that there is no room for doubt or questioning yields paralysis. By facing history and ourselves at the same time, students learn to negotiate, offering opinions and practicing civil behavior. Good history teaching demands these practices. But teaching students to inquire about the past as a lens on the present is delicate, hard work. To do so, teachers need engaging content, powerful resources, and quality professional development, all of which are integral components of the Facing History and Ourselves rationale for teaching and learning about the Armenian Genocide.

Robert Melson, past president of the International Association of Genocide Scholars, describes the Armenian Genocide as the first "modern genocide" in which a nation—in this case an empire—turns on its own.[2] A student will eventually ask the teacher, "How did that happen?" In the introduction to his collection, *The Armenian Genocide: News Accounts from the American Press, 1915-1922,* Richard Kloian describes how the almost daily press coverage—more during its time than the Holocaust just one generation later—brought evidence of the extermination to politicians and ordinary people alike.[3] After students have read those headlines from the American newspapers they often are filled with outrage. As they get to know this history, students discover how Henry Morgenthau, the U.S. Ambassador to the Ottoman Empire, exclaimed internationally, "Do Something!" A student might ask: "Why didn't this make a difference?" Did awareness of these horrible atrocities influence the way people saw their relationship to the larger world? And if conscience inspired actions, why did efforts to stop genocide fail? Exploring such student questions, so timely, ought to be an important part of a rationale to teach about the Armenian Genocide.

After studying the particular historical moment, these students will be better equipped to make what former U.S. National Security advisor Anthony Lake calls "noise."[4] In *A Problem from Hell*, Samantha Power profiles "upstanders," whose activities on behalf of others provide models for individuals who have tried to move leaders to respond to the use of influence to make a difference. She begins her book with the story of Morgenthau in Constantinople.[5]

Studying the Armenian Genocide and the public campaign to protect Armenians in the face of escalating threats, massacres, and ultimately genocide provides an opportunity to reflect on the range of choices available to burgeoning human rights activists, ordinary citizens, and national leaders just before and after the turn of the twentieth century. Students who study the responses to the massacres of Armenians in the late nineteenth century and the activities of the Near East Relief, Inc. in the twentieth century come away with a more complete understanding of the period in which ideas about universal human rights first began to take shape. Indeed, Morgenthau's dilemma as a diplomat between vigorous international intervention during the genocide and settling for humanitarian relief has been echoed throughout the twentieth and the early years of the twenty-first century. A student studying the Armenian political movements of the late nineteenth century might ask: "How can groups advocate for equality in an unequal society?" and "What is my responsibility when I am aware of injustice?"

As headlines today record the efforts of the International Criminal Court to bring those responsible for genocide in Sudan to justice, there is an increasingly public debate over whether or not the United States should be a signatory to this International Criminal Court. For students of the Armenian Genocide who learn about the post-World War I international tribunals for the Young Turk leaders, the question of whether world recognition of the perpetrators' responsibility for "crimes against humanity" might have played a significant role in preventing the Holocaust and helping to deter subsequent genocides is most relevant. Too many people continue to believe that international legal responses to the mass murder of civilians began with the Nuremberg trials. Advocates for strong enforcement of international law argue that the prevention of genocide begins when there is no longer impunity for the perpetrators. Classroom discussions about America's role and responsibility for intervening in international cases of genocide are powerful and important, and Facing History and Ourselves resource book, *Crimes Against Humanity and Civilization: The Genocide of the Armenians,* provides the context for discussing perspectives, encourages questions, and challenges opinions.

Thirty years of teaching Facing History and Ourselves has taught us to trust our students. They can unquestionably become compassionate, ethical, and wise students of history. Such students make the search for a rationale for teaching history elegantly simple. Raquel Fernandez, a Facing History and Ourselves student at the International High School in Queens, New York, wrote about the power of history education:

> Sometimes school in Brazil was like sitting in a classroom with steamed up windows. Light came in, but you cannot see out. History, when taught well, can make that glass transparent. You can see and make clear the relationship between what we learn in school and our own lives.
>
> I know that we don't learn history to place blame. The members of my stepmother's family are all German. Am I to blame her for what happened during the Holocaust? How many generations of people can we hold responsible for the past? I'm responsible for what I do, not for what my ancestors have done.
>
> Now let's think about what history we learn. It is important that we learn the comfortable and the uncomfortable parts. It is from the uncomfortable parts that we really learn. It's there that we can find the conflicts that help us to understand ourselves. My mother's ancestors were both slave owners and slaves. Am I supposed to learn the history of slaves or the history of slave owners?
>
> Lastly, what do we do once we've begun to face the complexities of history? Our thoughts must affect our everyday actions. My father has been in Rwanda several times since the genocide helping people to rebuild. I'm not sure that I am ready to take those risks and sometimes I wonder how and where I can help. I try to keep in mind what journalist Bill Moyers said: "You can't do everything at one time, but you can do something at once."

Raquel's words offer powerful evidence of serious reflection from a budding moral philosopher. Good teachers know that adolescents often locate historical issues in their own lives. *That is simply how they make sense of the past.* Through the process of connecting past to present, Facing History and Ourselves students build an intellectual and emotional vocabulary to study history. That vocabulary will help them think about their own decision-making and the decision-making of others. In an increasingly globalized world, multiple perspective-taking matters, for it is through different perspectives that we learn to see ourselves in others.

In Facing History and Ourselves classes about the Armenian Genocide, as students navigate between past and present, they can learn to make a distinction between blame and responsibility. They might ask, as Raquel does: "Are the descendants of perpetrators to blame for the actions of their ancestors? How can people today accept responsibility for the past?" Attention to issues of judgment in the cases of the Armenian Genocide reveals how the failure of international justice and the continuing denial of the genocide leave a complicated legacy for the survivors and their families. That legacy continues to fuel anger, shame, sadness, and humiliation from generation to generation. The effort to understand the aftermath of genocide illuminates many of the issues that individuals, groups, and nations must confront if they are to transition from a culture of collective violence to a more peaceful society. This learning provides yet another reason to teach about the Armenian Genocide. It is instructive for those involved in conflict resolution and for those creating peace for today and tomorrow. These are the challenges for authentic civic education.

The stories of the survivors of the Armenian Genocide are powerful. They make a learner a contemporary "witness" of a sort of brutality and atrocity, and sometimes to stories of unimaginable courage—acts of kindness by a rescuer. Embedded in the records of survivors testimony are stories of people who risked their lives for their neighbors they knew and for the vulnerable victims they did not know.[6] From the particular details of each survivor's story, students raise the questions about altruism and about conscience.[7] Teachers do not need hypothetical moral dilemmas to promote moral discussions; the history and scholarly literature of the Armenian Genocide reveal the myriad choices made during this history, which provide extraordinary "teachable moments." Students ask questions: "What could have happened?" "What should have happened?" "What would I have done?" "What could I have done?" "Was the history inevitable?" Students ask those questions as the first step in making sense of the past. It is the role of the teacher to help students understand that we can never truly "know" definite answers to those moral and ethical dilemmas, yet it would be wrong to stop the students from asking.

In a Facing History and Ourselves classroom, there is a dialogue between the past and the present. In response to their questions, students encounter real stories from the past to ground them historically. There are also times to step back from the particular and ask our students, where can choices be made that protect the vulnerable before it is too late? When is prevention possible? Through careful study of this history students can learn to recognize the danger in creating an "other," in responding blindly to prejudice and propaganda, to question leaders who use fear to create obedience, and to recognize the use and abuse of the law in the name of cruelty.

Teaching about the history of the Armenian Genocide can and should reveal precious lessons about the kind of society that is built on the rule of law and human dignity, one that preserves rights and demands responsibility for the safety of our neighbor and encourages us to choose to learn how to participate. Ambassador Morgenthau, in the midst of the violence and brutality against the Armenian people, was asked by Talaat, the Young Turk Minister of the Interior: "Why are you so interested in the Armenians, anyway? . . . You are a Jew; these people are Christians."[8] Morgenthau replied: "I am not here as a Jew but as American Ambassador . . . I do not appeal to you in the name of any race or religion, but merely as a human being." Learning about the Armenian Genocide as Facing History and Ourselves has articulated in its rationale for teaching about the Holocaust, can be education for democracy. Ultimately, this is the essential question and the rationale for teaching the Armenian Genocide. How do we see ourselves in someone else's history? The global component challenges us to educate for interpersonal understanding. We expect the next "upstander" is sitting in our classroom or visiting our website, waiting to be inspired to make a difference in the world. We depend on it.

Notes

1. Samantha Power, *"A Problem from Hell": America and the Age of Genocide* (New York: Harper Collins, 2002), p. 1.
2. Robert Melson, *Revolution and Genocide: On the Origins of the Armenian Genocide and the Holocaust* (Chicago: University of Chicago Press, 1992).
3. Richard Kloian, "Reports from the Killing Fields: What Do They Tell Us?" in *The Armenian Genocide and the American Press* (Richmond, CA: Armenian Genocide Resource Center, 2005), p. 1.
4. Anthony Lake from an interview for the documentary, *The Ghosts of Rwanda*, www.pbs.org/wgbh/pages/frontline/shows/ghosts/interviews/lake.html.
5. Power, *A Problem from Hell,* p. xviii.
6. Richard G. Hovannisian, "Intervention and Shades of Altruism during the Armenian Genocide,"in *The Armenian Genocide: History, Politics, Ethics*, ed. R. G. Hovannisian (New York: St. Martin's Press, 1992), pp. 177-198.
7. Ibid.
8. Henry Morgenthau, *Ambassador Morgenthau's Story* (repr., Plandome, NY: New Age Publisher, 1975), pp. 333-334.

14

Exposure of the Armenian Genocide in Cyberspace: A Comparative Analysis

Hagop Gulludjian

The main reason for undertaking the topic of Armenian Genocide exposure on the Internet is the same as for most other research projects: the simple desire to discern between our perception of reality and what this reality actually is. In this case, it is an attempt to quantify and, to a lesser extent, to qualify the scope and magnitude of Armenian Genocide-related information present in the virtual space, mainly in comparison to other genocides.

Even though Armenian issues, including the Armenian Genocide, stepped late into the Internet, the trend has been increasing steadily during the past few years. Unlike bibliographies and resource lists that refer to traditional media, there are no comprehensive studies about genocide-related publications on the Internet. This is due to the virtual impossibility to catalog material that is very scattered and, besides, greatly volatile. That is the reason why a study must cover only a specific time frame and take into consideration as well that, unlike most published titles, websites might disappear without leaving traces.

Why study the Internet? Because it is the fastest and relatively easiest way to measure, on a broad basis, the reach of our subject matter. However, the drawback to this kind of study is that its usefulness happens to be not very long lasting because of the significant pace of change in this field, occasionally involving even the disappearance of an area of study. The speed of change is mind-boggling.

Virtual vs. Printed Media

A word about the difference between this kind of study and one involving traditional printed media. What we basically undertake here is a job of data-mining, trying to explore the information riches of cyberspace with technological tools that are, although far from perfect, not available yet to the printed, physical media. There is a huge difference in the indexing capabilities of electronic and printed worlds.[1] No library will ever index the complete texts of its entire holdings,[2] whereas this is a job usually done by most search engines on online literature, with certain limitations.

One of the main advantages of electronic literature vis-à-vis printed media is its widespread and immediate accessibility, while the main shortcoming is its lack of stability. However, this, too, is relative, because many categories of texts, like forum postings and newspaper reviews, may occasionally survive much longer on the Internet than in printed daily or weekly media.

Then there is a geographical advantage. Studying electronic texts on the Internet makes it possible to quickly and deeply cover occurrences of the researched subject all over the world, including even the remotest places. In the printed world, in contrast, it would be certainly unrealistic to expect somebody to cover absolutely all published media, including, for example, those in distant cities of a Chinese province or in Eastern Europe.

As for the value of these texts, we must admit that it is probably uneven in the field of scholarly content, which is best located in lengthy books not yet available in cyberspace, although not for long. However, this is compensated for by a strong presence in the field of political propaganda, educational resources, testimony, or current news and opinion. This information is placed within easy reach of almost everybody, and is organized in a highly ordered and easy-to-access data structure, be it in a hierarchical, tree-shaped, or a hypertextual or network structure. Online, we can find many aspects that would have been otherwise overlooked in printed media studies. These include multiple discussion forums, bookselling sites with a large number of reviews about genocide-related publications, short-lived news, opinions, blog sites, newsgroups, and so forth.

Another distinction between both worlds is the published matter's audience. It is relatively easy to establish the audience of printed information by means of considering its subject matter, the publishing house, or where it is distributed and accessed. We are certainly able to characterize the audience of articles in scholarly journals. However, that is not the case in cyberspace, because of the indiscriminate access to any commercially unprotected virtual text. The same information may be retrieved at the same time by elementary school students or scholars or by Turks and Armenians. Note that in contrast, most of printed data about the Genocide have been rather unreachable, banned, and illegal in Turkey.

One of the most significant topics worth mentioning is the opposing nature of investigative work in both worlds. While in printed media the key task is to dig up scarce information in hidden or hard to reach places, here it is quite the opposite: you have to uncover what is relevant in a superabundant, almost infinite flow of data. This is mostly a job of discarding instead of an activity of accumulation. Ultimately, it is the problem of abundance, or, better said, of redundancy, as opposed to the problem of scarcity.

I want to raise briefly here also the necessity to frame the study of the distinction between virtual and printed texts from a philosophical perspective. There are a number of issues. Of those, I will mention the peculiarity of hypertexts as virtualities, that is, potentialities presented to the reader in order for him to actualize a particular meaning of the text by way of building it through a number of linking decisions made by himself.[3] As a consequence, virtual texts produce a much broader array of possible outcomes, which have not been necessarily envisioned by the author. In addition, there is a change of attitude toward text by readers. The concept of textual authority carried by the printed text is being modified in a context of morphing online writings that refuse to be part of a permanent, rigid corpus. Therefore, a new kind of "fluid" text flourishes, constructed by readers and authors concurrently. Traditional text stability and authority are replaced by this fluidity, which leads to a sort of "secondary orality," featuring a distinctive dynamism and vitality.[4]

The Data Problem. What and Where?

When trying to get an objective idea on the Armenian Genocide's real presence on the Internet, we have to remember that online data are raw and perplexingly muddled. Among other troubles, there is much clutter coming from *spamdexing* (index spamming), which affects search results with false descriptions about unrelated links. The spam problem disrupts also the ease of use of search engines, currently the most suitable gateways to the Internet's riches. In addition to spammers, portals and directories, too, look constantly for ways to outmaneuver search engine algorithms, trying to appear in the first places of result lists. The consequence of these maneuvers is a sub-optimization of the search engines' usefulness, because they ultimately become a listing of portals and directories instead of offering direct results in their first pages. And we know that few will venture beyond those first pages.[5]

Nevertheless, unless the intention is the practically impossible task of cataloguing and individually describing our subject matter's presence, we have to stick to the only plausible way that can encompass a large portion of these massive and variable data. That is to say, search engines. However, there are a number of decisions concerning which engine and what kind of data to take into consideration.

Firstly, what are the search engines and how do they work? Basically, they are big servers with a software, called *spider*, which goes looking for new pages all over the Internet.[6] Once new pages are found, they are indexed in a database. When we order a search, what we access is this database. Spiders will not find a new page without relying on a reference that sends them to that page. Namely, they find it only if a link to that page exists in another page they already have in their database, or if it has been sent to them specifically by somebody. This is why the whole Web is not really covered by the search engines. What remains unseen is the *invisible Web,* which is estimated to be twice or three times larger than the *visible Web*, that is, the collection of indexed pages.[7]

Directories, which are guides or listings compiled by a human, are excluded from this study. Examples of directories are the original Yahoo, the Open Directory Project, Lycos, the formerly concept-oriented Excite, and other smaller ones. The reason for not considering them is that although they offer information of much better quality, they never cover the whole specter of our study's subject that is accessed by spiders. Their information is limited also because of their selective criteria for listing certain sites and not others. The selection they present is necessarily subjective. As a final point, the use of directories is gradually decreasing. This is verified by the fact that Yahoo, the pioneering directory, replaced its human-compiled listings first with the Inktomi engine some time ago and, from 2005, with a search engine of its own.

Once we delimit the field to search engines, we have to decide which engines to consider. Here we stumble with the problem that they keep shifting while data is collected. They change their search algorithms and the way they filter and render information. Overall, we do not even know what the bases for such changes are because they are generally kept as business secrets by the respective companies.

Four major search engines were considered initially: Google, Yahoo, MSN, and AskJeeves. The generalized belief that Google is omnipresent and is the most influential of the search engines had to be checked with a more factual and up-to-date analysis. MSN had been running with a newly developed engine and increasingly better results. On the other hand, while this study was developing, Yahoo modified radically its product as it replaced its engine on February 3, 2005. Although conveying much better results, they ceased to be statistically comparable to previous data. Moreover, the old market leader AltaVista and the search engine AlltheWeb were purchased by Yahoo. These important engines kept their own indexes; however, we do not know whether they were integrated to Yahoo's principal engine, or if they began nourishing it somehow. Another question is that search engines look for and classify information in different ways. Google favors a page's inbound and outbound links to determine its worth, while Yahoo used to prefer contents relative to the page itself, as keyword density, title tags, and description tags.[8] An added problem was that Google's results displayed generalized variations in March 2005 over their previous and subsequent trend. Lacking an explanation by Google, this may be due to corrections made by the company in its algorithms and filters. This is why, despite having established schemes to sort out genocide-related results' net evolution beyond the Internet's normal growth, the continuing instability in search engines' processes forced this study to abandon the analysis of absolute figures over a time frame and to focus the inquiry on the relation between numbers at a given date. That is to say, how the Armenian Genocide's occurrence ratio varies with respect to mentions of the other genocides. Only after this analysis does it become possible to study an evolution over time; that is, a survey of the dynamics of their comparative significance.

Comparative importance of search engines is a critical point. The important issue is not only the existence of occurrences on the Web, but how they are retrieved and visualized by surfers, because the engines are, basically, people's gateways to those occurrences. This issue may be examined, for example, in the total number of indexed pages by each engine. However, this is slippery ground. First, because numbers boasted by different companies are not synchronized. Then, they might not necessarily be true because companies, as a rule, are waging a commercial war. Finally, not all of the engines offer data about their progress in indexing. Sometimes these are estimates made by external analysts. Google informed about 8.1 billion indexed pages; estimation about Yahoo was that, excluding image files, they had indexed 4.2 billion pages until November 2004—that number most probably must be higher now; talk about MSN's index was around 5 billion, while AskJeeves announced 2.5 billion.[9] Claiming a large index does not necessarily mean that the search result will be better, because other factors intervene in the final picture. It could be likely that some of the engines modify the number of results offered during a search as a function of the probability of occurrence of a searched string in the texts that are not fully indexed.

The first topic to look for in determining the relative significance of search engines is their *market share* concerning the visits they receive. Available statistics were produced by different companies at different times. In April 2004, for example, on a sample of 25 million people all over the world, Google, Yahoo, and MSN led by 15.3, 10, and 7.2 percent, respectively, in what is called *share of visits*, with AskJeeves at 1.1 percent, and the other engines at negligible percentages.[10] These are visits—not visitors—to search-oriented sites during one month.

Audience reach is another classification, describing the percentage of Internet users estimated to have searched on each site at least once during the month. Here, too, we get a general picture of the relevant names to consider in a study: as of December 2004, Google had a 44.9 percent participation, while Yahoo, MSN, and AOL followed with 32, 25.2, and 17 percent.[11]

A relatively consistent finding was obtained as well employing the concept of *Share of searches* that focuses on the total number of searches performed by users in a particular sample group. In this case, 1.5 million English-speakers, two-thirds of them in the United States, performed 35 percent of their searches during December 2004 via Google, 32 percent through Yahoo, and 16 and 9, through MSN and AOL, respectively.[12] When search engines were replaced by the concept of Search Providers, which include channels and subsidiaries that use the same engine under different brands, the numbers varied somehow, without affecting the first three names (Google, 48 percent, Yahoo, 32, and

MSN, 16).[13] These figures might have been considerably altered in the following months because of the subsequent full-scale production of the new Yahoo and MSN engines.

At this point, there are a number of warnings and caveats regarding the use of information from search engines. First, consideration of data involved should be placed exactly within the corresponding time frame; this is because besides the continued modification of data, changes take place also in the way they are conveyed and the technologies utilized to compile and to index them. This means that an eventual long-term study would present lots of difficulties, nearly impossible to overcome.

In this respect, it is interesting to observe the evolution of the Internet and its contents. The size of the Web, as of June 1997, was estimated at 125 million static, distinct pages; in November 1997, at 200 million; and in March 1998, at 275 million.[14] Estimation about the *real* Web is that it is twice or three times as big as the *visible* Web. If, as we have seen, Google's indexed pages amount to 8 billion, we could risk the approximate number of 20 billion as the tentative size of the Internet. We would therefore imply that compared to March 1998, the Web has increased almost 75-fold. Certainly we have to view these figures with some caution, as remarks about this subject rarely go beyond guesswork embellished sometimes by allegedly scientific methods, that is, calculation based on overlapping and exclusion of samples from different search engines.

In June 1999, the then leading search engine AltaVista reported the word "Armenia" or "Armenian" in a quarter million pages.[15] In March 2005, the same engine showed "Armenia" in 20,600,000 pages, that is, almost 82 times the previous figure. Consequently, allowing for the difference in fifteen months, we may reasonably believe that the recurrence of the expression Armenia has kept an almost similar, maybe a slightly higher pace as the rest of the Web.

As the result of the general swelling of the Web and greater indexing, numbers seem to grow constantly on everything related to the Internet. However, the challenge is to detect differences in the growth of concepts that are the subject of this study, trying to establish if they are related to greater activity because of political momentum, increased propaganda, more education, or other issues. Nevertheless, to stay on pace with these dynamics is extremely complex, because of the existence of numerous variables we do not know or control. Numbers might be inflated as well because of duplicate content. Removal of such errors is a hopeless job. One kind of duplicate content is when search engines include pages about which the only information they possess are unchecked links that point toward those pages.[16] This is impractical to debug with accessible data, except by building and projecting from a complicated model. Within the limited precautions taken in this study in order to filter this kind of error was the use of search strings with and without quotes, with the purpose of comparing them later. Another way to clear up the findings was to perform searches within the *url* addresses of webpages. Nonetheless, the latter had to be abandoned because it quickly exposed what I suppose were errors of the search engines themselves, probably in some algorithm used to recover information from their databases: with certain strings, the number of occurrences within the url addresses exceeded the findings of keyword or phrase searches, which appears to be incongruous, as simple strings as "Armenian Genocide" are expected to happen in a page at least once, or more, if they are part of the url address of that page.

Another way to control results was to perform searches within the title of webpages, understanding as such not the actual title we see on the page, but the field whose content will appear on the browser's header. This result was much more reliable, provided there were enough data correlations to carry out an analysis of meanings on findings. Page title is generally assigned by the web designer, possibly resorting sometimes to automatic generation based on the page's real title or the prevailing subject in the virtual text. There were errors here, too. However, they were isolated, and it was possible to pull them out in order not to confuse general findings. These were validated also by carrying out comparative searches with diverse strings for each issue, as in "Armenian Genocide" and "Armenian massacres," or "Rwandan Genocide" and "Rwanda Genocide." Same for "Cambodia/Cambodian Genocide" and "Bosnia/Bosnian Genocide." The Holocaust presented a separate problem: it was difficult to clear up the results using "Jewish Holocaust" or "Jewish Genocide," because they are usually denoted just by the word "Holocaust." In this case, there was only left the possibility to make an assumption based on limited samples about the incidence ratio of the term "holocaust" in its generic, religious or literary sense. In any case, the extent of the occurrences of this word was so significantly higher from that of the word "Genocide," that it is evident that even if we found a way to discern the incidence of other uses of "holocaust," it would have resulted just in a slight variation of the relative standing of "Holocaust."

Surprisingly, the number of "Greek Calamity" occurrences was negligible. It was not so, however, in the case of the expression "Greek Genocide." There is an important caveat here: a basic survey of these pages shows that a significant number of them are about an alleged genocide committed by Greeks against Turks or Macedonians. It was reasonable to think that the same "false-positive" might take place in the Armenian case, too; however, it showed up after surfing a long time before finding one between positive references. Obviously, it is possible to observe a much higher incidence of this kind of reverse content in Turkish pages. Something similar happens, although to a much lesser extent, with the mentions of "Kurdish Genocide," when Assyrians are those who refer to the persecution and harassment they suffer from Kurds in the last decade, in the autonomous Kurdistan in Iraq.

Underexposure of occurrences in search results is another problem. Search engines do not necessarily consider the whole text of files they encounter. Some of them analyze only the content of the first 101 kilobytes, while others do it on 500 kilobytes or more.[17] The rest of the text remains unchecked. In the case of Google, for instance, it has been estimated that about 25 percent of pages included are not fully indexed, that is, it is not possible to search their full text.[18]

There are other errors hard to explain without having access to corporate information. In March 2005, for example, Yahoo and MSN outdid Google in the number of occurrences of Armenia, at the same time as Google showed a generalized decline in the majority of its figures. Greater indexing of one and a correction of an algorithm by the other? Maybe.

A problem affecting the truthfulness of search results is when analysis is focused on the language of considered webpages. Numerous non-English pages contain within their keywords or titles expressions in English, which may end in a misleading deviation.

Even if one planned to, there is no way to control the number of results search engines claim, because an attempt to do so would show that no search engine will expose more than 1,000 results, even if they claim to have found millions under certain search strings.

Finally, the last issue questioning the soundness of search results in general is about the controversy surrounding the authors of virtual texts. The Internet has generalized the possibility of publishing ideas and opinions under the cover of anonymity. It is not uncommon to come across websites that lack any information about the authors featured there or the institution backing them. No names, no addresses. Nevertheless, the major question is not anonymity, but pseudo-anonymity, which now seems to be more the rule than the exception. This is not the place to examine in detail the psychosocial implications of the virtual persona and the evolution of ethics in computer-mediated communication.[19] However, the issue is critical because, in this case, many people will resort to it in order to manipulate the perception of information users. That is how Amazon.com may display book reviews on the Genocide signed by non-Turkish, Anglo-Saxon surnames that claim to have had no previous information about the subject.[20] However, after the first couple of phrases pretending ignorance, neutrality, and a desire to learn more, you will get phrases that literally match the negationist lines heard from Turkish officials for many years. On the other hand, technological simplicity and the low cost needed to establish a website, when compared to costs associated with the publishing of a printed edition, encourage the creation of misleading websites. An example was aliyev.com, now disappeared, purportedly built by Armenians against the president of Azerbaijan during the 1990s.

The Survey

This study is based on more than 1,200 queries performed monthly, from December 2004 to March 2005, over diverse search engines, including Google, Yahoo, MSN, AskJeeves, AltaVista, and Excite. Major focus has been devoted to the first three. Because of unexpected changes in Yahoo's and MSN's engines,

Google is the only one with comparable findings along the researched time frame. This is the reason why, in order to circumscribe the survey to the most important data, we will concentrate especially on Google results, comparing them on occasion with Yahoo and MSN. AskJeeves will be left out of the analysis because it does not show the total number of results.

Queries were executed in English, Spanish, German, Portuguese, Italian, French, and Turkish language sites. Armenian was not methodically considered because of technical complications due to the lack of a unified standard for the Armenian characters, and the consequent difficulty to normalize results.[21]

Based on this survey, different typologies could be established for webpages dealing with the Armenian Genocide.

1. The first category concerns the authors of the sites. Among them are the *media,* with news and opinion pages; *scholars and academic institutions*, with articles, books, or reviews of related works; *governments*, with official websites or others sponsored by them; *nongovernmental organizations*, including what is usually understand as such, together with political parties and other associations; and finally, *student* and *individual* websites. Probably the latter are the most strident category. There is no restraint here in the way they speak out, and, aside from how questionable their contents might be, sometimes they can give an idea about the pulse of certain subcultures that would otherwise never appear in printed communication.[22]

2. Another classification involves the contents of dedicated or partial websites. Among these are *information resources,* such as bibliographies and reference sites, *memorial and testimonial* websites, including those about museums, monuments, survivor tales, pages about heroes and rescuers, expositions about the Genocide, and pages by survivors' descendants about their own plight and family memories. *Art and education* websites include pages about fiction works, film, and other media, such as plays, music, art expositions. *Discussion Forum* sites constitute an added kind of content in this classification, with a great and dynamic attendance. *Merchant* websites, too, are part of this group when they offer material related to the Genocide, and correlated reviews about them, which represent a whole new subset of on-the-fly opinions not found in traditional media. Interestingly, I have not found the Armenian equivalents of Holocaust sites about forgotten victims of the Genocide, in this case, Assyrians or Greeks, as there are Holocaust sites about Polish or Gypsy victims. There are neither anti-hatred sites, which would try to educate people from a more general, human perspective, nor webpages on concentration sites on the journey to Deir el-Zor. In this age of technological marvels and clickable maps, the only map about the routes and concentration and slaughter camps I have found is one you can barely read, with no zooming options and without taking advantage of the Internet's hypertextual capabilities to present further detail. While a distinct group of sites deals with Holocaust victims' dormant bank account issues, in the Armenian case, there are only a couple of links about New York Life Insurance

policyholder lists and information about the litigation involving that company and survivors of the Armenian Genocide.[23]

3. A third way to classify these websites is to consider the viewpoint expressed there. This important categorization is worth being studied in detail to get an idea about the relative number of sites dedicated to distort or misrepresent historical truths. There are many subtypes of this category. There are, of course, those websites *sustaining* the truth. Then there are *revisionist* and *negationist* pages, much similar to those found in printed literature. A third group comprises the sites that appear to be neutral. However, *true neutral* websites should be distinguished from *false neutral* sites. The first ones are those that either lack adequate information and are trying to position themselves at equal distance from both sides, or they do have the information, but because of political or other considerations, restrain themselves from being outspoken about it, staying in generalities. Examples of the latter are the official websites of the United States government. By *false neutral*, we understand those sites that adopt this stance as a way to influence more effectively the opinion of their readers.

The following are some of the conclusions obtained after numerical and graphical analysis of surveyed data. A certain disparity was observed between results of the three leading search engines for the words "Armenia" and "Armenian" (see Table 14.1). This might be due to the way each engine limits considering derivatives of a word. The value of these numbers alone, at this instance, is almost anecdotal. However, despite differences observed when comparing Genocide and Armenian Genocide, findings essentially illustrated a relative consistency between the three sources. "Genocide" had much less occurrences than "Holocaust"; almost one-third. Observation of small samples with the word "holocaust" demonstrated that even clearing up those occurrences with meanings different from "Jewish genocide," the statistical change was minor and did not significantly affect the proportion of Holocaust to Genocide. We can clearly see also an important presence of the expression "Armenian massacres," although just a fifth of the occurrences of "Armenian Genocide." The exact expression "Armenian Genocide" happened approximately half of the times compared to both words "Armenian" and "Genocide." This relation, alone, would not have a very useful meaning. However, if the same comparison is made between the string "Armenian massacres" and the words "Armenian" and "massacres," the ratio goes to one-fifth. This may mean several things, most importantly, that the expression "Armenian Genocide" emerges as *the* term that brands these events, just like Holocaust is the "brand name" of the Jewish genocide. This hypothesis is consistently confirmed in a series of different statistics.

Data were collected about the mentions of eleven genocidal events. Even though absolute numbers differed, the relationship between measured genocides was consistently analogous. Consistency was observed in the numerical relationship between the three engines, as well as in the evolution over the monthly measurements, with negligible deviations. Holocaust was measured also under the expression "Jewish holocaust" and "Jewish genocide." It has to be stressed that we are not talking about genocides per se, but about mentions of genocide. In some cases, as mentioned before, the same expression may mean different and quite opposite things for their authors, as in the case of "Greek Genocide," and in a few cases, about a supposed "Armenian Genocide against Turks" during World War I and later during the Karabagh war of independence. In order to get a comparable understanding of the different combinations of figures obtained in the survey, Armenian Genocide is made equal to 100, and the other figures have been adjusted accordingly (see Table 4.2).

In simple keyword searches, talk about the Assyrian Genocide was only 7 percent of the Armenian Genocide figure, which, in this case, in December 2004, was 231,000. On the opposite side, the Sudan Genocide, as understood for the Darfur events, as well as mentions of the Rwandan Genocide more than doubled the Armenian figures.

Similar numbers were obtained in March 2005, when the words "Armenian" and "Genocide" were found in the same files for 290,000 times. Additional talk was observed here about the Kurdish issue, probably because of the elections in Iraq. Cambodian figures also increased as a consequence to news about the financing of future tribunals to hear cases against implicated persons of the Khmer Rouge regime. The words "Jewish" and "Genocide" happened to be at the same time in 65 percent more pages than "Armenian" and "Genocide." Simultaneously, "Jewish" plus "Holocaust" had a ratio of six to one regarding "Armenian" and "Genocide." These are modest differences when "Holocaust" is considered alone against "Armenian" and "Genocide." The relation went to almost 23 to 1. However, we must remember that a simple keyword search does not say much about reality except some general and sometimes dubious trends. That is why searches were refined by resorting to *phrase search*, which is when the search string is placed within double quotes, meaning that we only

Table 14.1
Search engine results comparison, March 2005 (keyword search)

	MSN	Yahoo	Google
Armenia	13,420,000	19,800,000	12,600,000
Armenian	8,820,000	3,200,000	3,340,000
Armenian massacres	37,677	62,300	49,700
"Armenian Genocide"	84,000	195,000	162,000
Armenian Genocide	455,000	309,000	290,000
Genocide	1,960,000	5,710,000	3,020,000
Holocaust	5,700,000	8,540,000	6,580,000

Table 14.2
Genocide mentions comparison. Google, December 2004 and March 2005. Armenian Genocide is made equal to 100. Armenian Genocide value in December 2004=231,000; March 2005 (keyword search)=290,000; March 2005 (phrase search)=162,000; March 2005 (title search)=7,620

	Simple keyword search December 2004	Simple keyword search March 2005	Phrase search March 2005	Title search March 2005
Holocaust	2,632	2,269	4,062	2,808
Jewish Holocaust	844	597	42	12
Rwanda/n Genocide	265	194	73	60
Sudan Genocide	224	241	85	11
Jewish Genocide	180	165	4	4
Armenian Genocide	**100**	**100**	**100**	**100**
Greek Genocide	80	118	<1	1
Cambodia/n Genocide	78	89	10	8
Bosnia/n Genocide	48	127	1	7
Kurdish Genocide	39	47	<1	2
Ukrainian Genocide	26	18	5	3
Biafra Genocide	13	13	<1	<1
Assyrian Genocide	7	8	<1	2

get the occurrences of that exact same expression, in a unique order. Remarkably for this case, when we excluded the stand-alone expression "Holocaust," none of the other elements considered surpassed the mentions of the Armenian Genocide. Even Sudan and Rwanda, which previously doubled the mentions of the latter, stood now at 85 and 73 percent. The same happened, more so, to the expression "Jewish Holocaust," which stayed at a mere 7 percent of the previous comparison with keyword search, while "Armenian Genocide," with 162,000 mentions, was at a healthy 56 percent of the previous search. This may confirm the idea about "brand names" discussed before. The observed disparity might indicate either an error of the search engines while providing figures based on probability of association, or, more plausibly, it would point to a more developed and established online literature about the Armenian Genocide. Significant was the limited use of the expression "Jewish Genocide." Anyway, once "Holocaust" was included in the comparison, it outstripped the Armenian Genocide with yet a larger margin, by 40 to 1, tempting to apply now the same reasoning as above to this case.

Title search brings us closer to the "real thing." It delivers the occurrences of a given expression in the title of a webpage. Therefore, we may assume that the primary subject of that page is retrieved here. When contrasted with previous comparisons, the ratio divergence became much sharper. Within obtained results, most of other elements collapsed to less than 10 percent of the "Armenian Genocide" expression, except for Sudan (the latter, mainly in phrase search), which was quite explicable because of its political momentum at the time, and the Holocaust, which was about 28 times the Armenian Genocide. Rwanda, at a far 60 percent, demonstrates the idea of a settled literature, created during the Internet's expansion. Again, when these numbers are weighed against further relative decline of the expression "Jewish Holocaust" (only 4 percent of "Armenian Genocide"), we acquire additional evidence about the use of *Armenian Genocide* and stand-alone *Holocaust* as "brand names." Furthermore, this might possibly imply that expressions that increase their proportional presence when we restrict the search criterion, point to a corpus of texts with a major ingredient of what I would call *permanent literature*, as opposed to the mainly ephemeral character of the remaining texts. This might especially be true for the Holocaust, and also for the Armenian Genocide.

Figure 14.1
Frequency variation for the expression "Armenian Genocide" in webpage titles. Google, March 1 - March 31, 2005

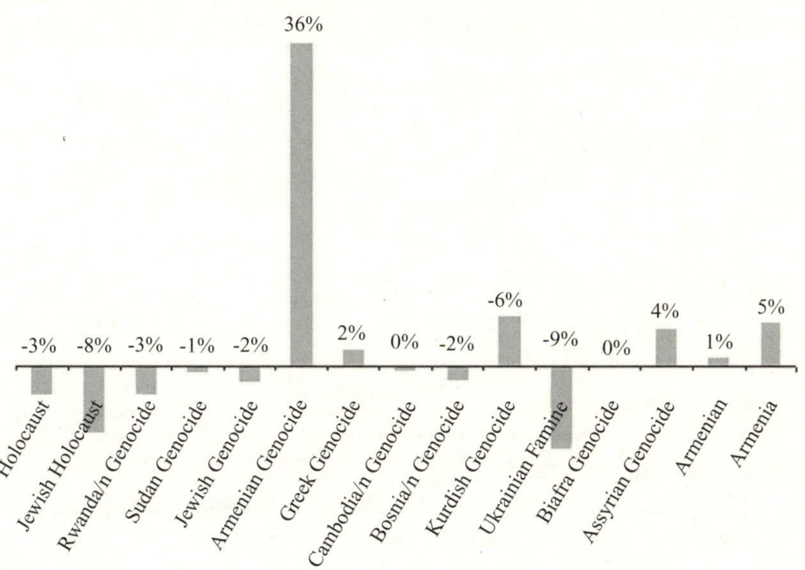

In simple keyword searches, talk about the Assyrian genocide was only 7 percent of the Armenian Genocide figure, which in this case, in December 2004, was 231,000. On the opposite side, the Sudan genocide, as understood for the Darfur events, as well as mentions of the Rwandan genocide, more than doubled the Armenian figures.

A "seasonal" effect is clearly seen in the number of mentions of the Armenian Genocide around the anniversary month of April (see Fig. 14.1). When data from March 1 is compared with results obtained on March 31, change is in the order of -9 to +6 percent for all genocide mentions except for the Armenian Genocide, which jumps a dramatic 36 percent. This is yet more impressive because "Armenian" or "Armenia" remain within the normal range of variation of the other elements considered during this period.

Figures 14.2, 14.3, and 14.4, which display dynamic data along the time frame of December 2004 to March 2005, demonstrate roughly the same associations we have observed so far, respectively on keyword search, phrase search, and title search. The stand-alone expression "Holocaust" is excluded in the charts to make the other elements' relative standing more visible.

A significant portion of the queries performed was about the degree in which the Armenian Genocide is exposed in a number of Western languages (English, French, Spanish, German, Italian, Portuguese),[24] plus Turkish. Here again, there was considerable consistency among data obtained along the considered time frame, with slight monthly increases (see Table 14.3 for results corresponding

Figure 14.2
Mentions of genocides - Comparative evolution. Google, December 2004 - March 2005 (simple keyword search). Armenian Genocide = 100

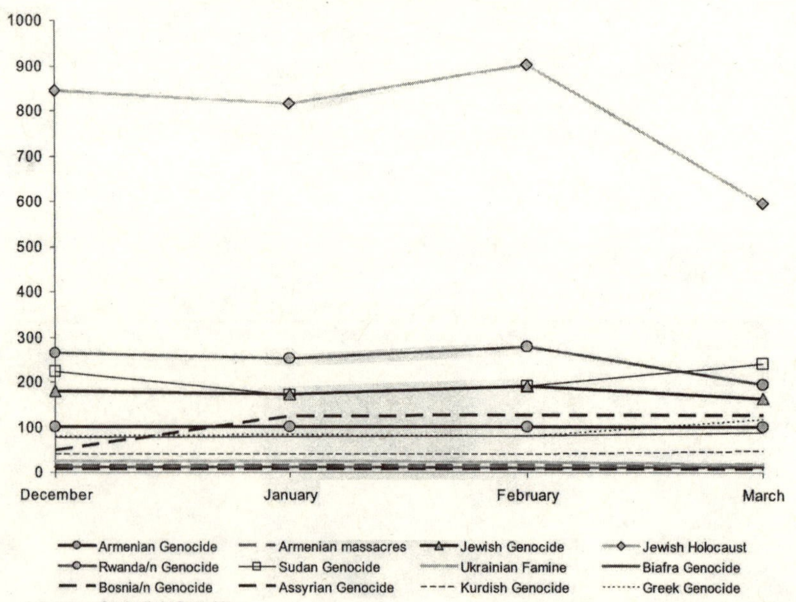

Figure 14.3
Mentions of genocides - Comparative evolution. Google, December 2004 - March 2005 (phrase search). Armenian Genocide = 100

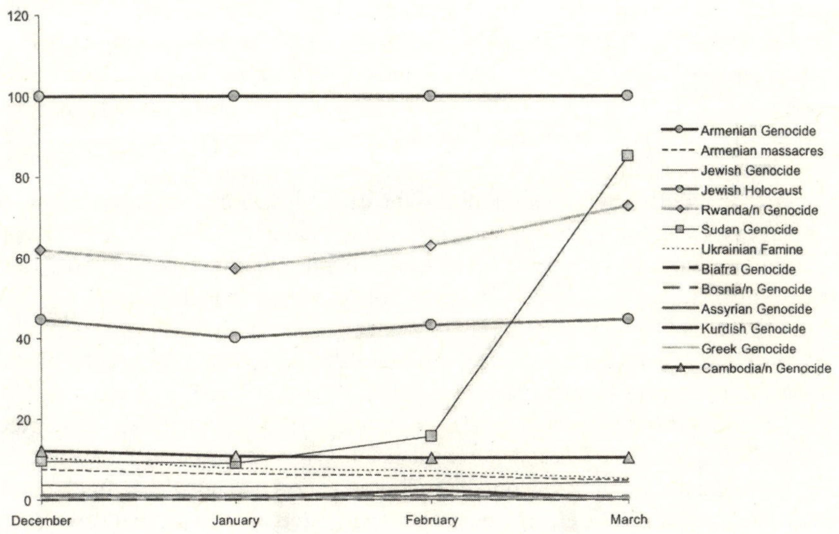

Figure 14.4
Mentions of genocides - Comparative evolution. Google, December 2004 - March 2005 (title search). Armenian Genocide = 100

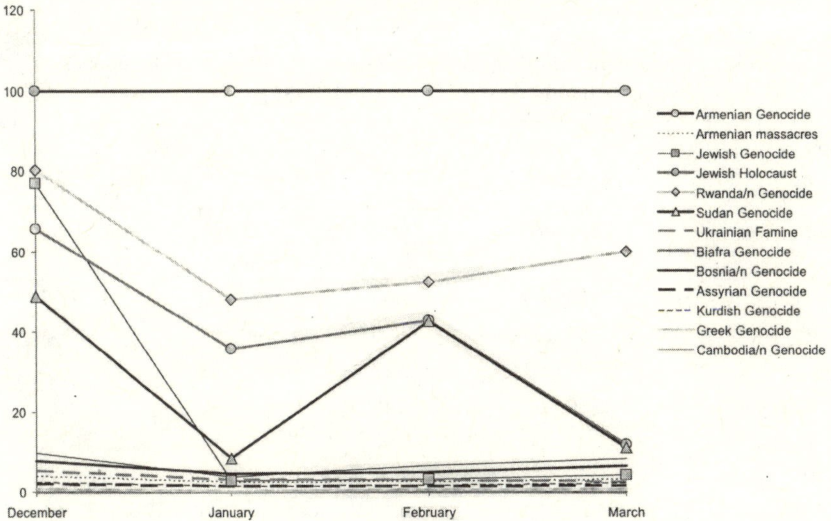

to March 2005). Once English is excluded, French stands out as the language in which the word "Genocide" is used most, perhaps because of the generally perceived French predilection for social sciences. Then come Spanish and German, with almost two-thirds of the French value and one-tenth of the occurrences observed in English. The relative lead of French numbers became greater when the keywords were Armenian+Genocide, suggesting that it is the language where the Armenian Genocide gets most of the attention in the subgroup, relative to overall "Genocide." However, the most remarkable figure was in the Turkish language, where the number of pages where both words were mentioned climbed to almost 80 percent of the number of pages with the word "Genocide." In the remainder of the group it was only as much as about 3 percent, except in French, where it reached 9 percent.

Phrase and title searches lead us to analogous conclusions (see Figs. 14.5 and 14.6). Turkish is the second language of the subgroup in title searches, while French is a far first. However, Turkish websites have the highest ratio in "Armenian Genocide"/ "Genocide," which demonstrates that their interest in genocide-related issues concentrates almost exclusively on the Armenian case.

Overall, the numbers suggest that compared to their relative mentions of the word Genocide, Spanish and Portuguese language websites refer too little to the Armenian Genocide, in contrast to Italian, German, and especially, French. On the other hand, it is clear that this is a highly dynamic issue, and very much responsive to developments in the international political field. As a sample of the wild changes in the number of mentions, see Table 14.4, which is an update of Table 14.3 data for August 2005. Notably, "Genocide" remains almost in the same numbers in Spanish, Italian, and Portuguese websites, whereas the expression "Armenian Genocide" more than doubles (it increases 3- to 5-fold

Table 14.3
Genocide mentions in sample group of languages. Google, March 2005. Queries performed only on websites with each language's header

	Genocide (Simple keyword search)	Armenian Genocide (Simple keyword search)	"Armenian Genocide" (Phrase search)	"Armenian Genocide" (Title search)
English	3,334,000	302,000	162,000	7,620
French	458,000	39,600	30,400	333
Spanish	358,000	3,530	688	47
German	330,800	6,146	132	21
Italian	138,000	4,190	586	42
Portuguese	56,200	491	271	5
Turkish	7,860	6,070	189	81

Table 14.4
Genocide mentions in sample group of languages. Google, August 2005. Queries performed only on websites with each language's header

	Genocide (Simple keyword search)	Armenian Genocide (Simple keyword search)	"Armenian Genocide" (Phrase search)	"Armenian Genocide" (Title search)
English	6,830,000	477,000	217,000	18,000
French	918,000	55,500	43,500	737
Spanish	354,000	9,250	6,370	225
German	257,000	8,910	136	8
Italian	141,000	9,100	5,140	70
Portuguese	60,200	886	562	6
Turkish	51,000	39,000	32,700	437

Figure 14.5
Distribution of mentions of the expression "Armenian Genocide" in sample group of languages. Phrase search, Google, March 2005

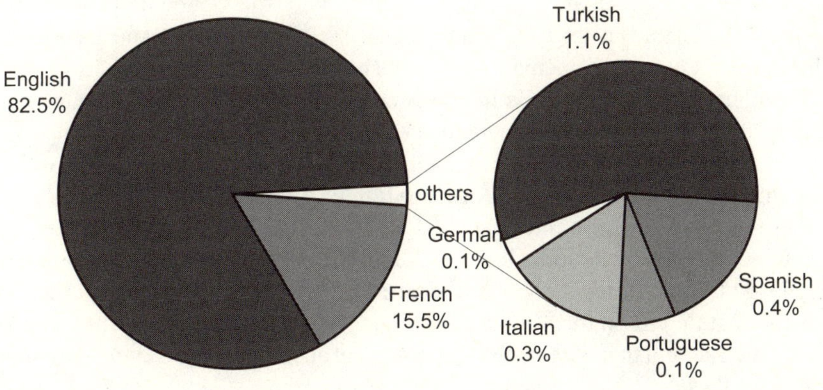

Figure 14.5
Distribution of mentions of the expression "Armenian Genocide" in sample group of languages. Title search, Google, March 2005

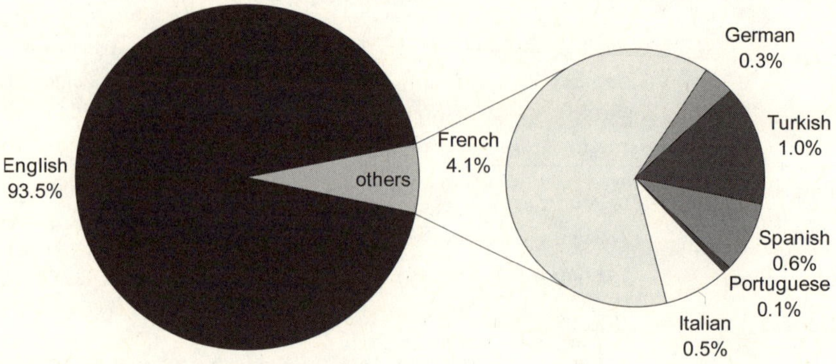

in Spanish). There is an even more explosive expansion in Turkish websites, in the order of 600 percent or more.

Conclusion

This has been a first attempt to describe the presence of the the Armenian Genocide on the Internet. It constitutes just one element of a larger issue concerning the online problematic of Armenian Studies. We have looked into some of the major meanings of the numerical analysis of this presence. Obviously there are many questions and different kinds of data in order to formulate further interpretations. One striking issue comes to mind when observing the example of Prevent Genocide International website, where the Genocide Convention is made available in thirty-five languages, including Turkish and Georgian; however, there is no Armenian version.[25] The depth and relevance of exposure is another area of study. So is the preparation of an evolving online catalog,[26] comprising the most important dedicated sites in thematic categories.

However, beyond and above a quantitative inquiry, it is vital to contemplate a number of deeper questions in order to frame adequately our further analysis. These include the study and awareness of the nature of virtual information, the ephemeral character of most Internet literature and the instability of sources as opposed to printed texts, the significance of the newer concept of multilogue in contrast to written monologues and dialogues, and so forth. We should also take into account that continuous technological advances may eventually render some of these questions obsolete.

As a conclusion, I would highlight the hypertextual attribute of Internet publications, which, by themselves, generate almost endless connections to other texts. This makes relevant their predominant function as part of a larger and customized text "manufactured" by the reader through linking decisions along his journey. Consequently, it broadens the interaction of Armenian Genocide studies with other issues, amplifying its audience in this way and contributing to its analysis from more diverse perspectives. That is, when people make a search about Darfur or the Holocaust, there is a high probability they will catch some links to Armenian Genocide-related information, and vice versa. Additionally, universal accessibility to information may result in an unexpected increase in the number of people concerned about the problem.

Finally, it is crucial to think about virtual information from the standpoint of a clearly defined philosophical and political framework. This is a time when availability of information has radically changed. From a scarce commodity, requiring painstaking search, it has become enormously redundant. Consequently, those who historically have tried to discourage access to insufficient information in order to exercise control may focus on this possibility to achieve the same misinformation, resorting instead to *hyper-redundancy*, making it difficult to find the truth. This is why the job of categorizing information and guiding research becomes so relevant, almost a whole specialty. Where do we stand in this respect a propos the Armenian Genocide? What kind of specialized web guides channel the inquiries and direct the search to specific sites? And what is ultimately the character and quality of the final information we receive?

All of this is a new area to explore, at least for Armenian Studies, where we must outline novel and adapting methodologies, delimit the confusing and over-extended field of study, and look toward other tasks we have yet to discover.

Notes

1. On the questions around print vs. electronic publishing, see John Lawrence, "Intellectual Property Futures: The Paper Club and the Digital Commons," in *Philosophical Perspectives on Computer-Mediated Communication*, ed. Charles Ess (Albany: State University of New York Press, 1996), pp. 95-114.
2. That is what we believe now. However, Google has an ongoing project to scan and make available for full text searches millions of volumes at American university libraries. See www.print.google.com/ googleprint/ about.html.
3. On this issue, see Hagop Gulludjian, "Network Communication, Culture and Diaspora," *Haigazian Armenological Review* 19 (1999): 367-392.
4. See Phil Mullins, "Sacred Text in the Sea of Texts: The Bible in North American Electronic Culture," in Ess, *Philosophical Perspectives,* pp. 271-302.
5. See Venivide (screen name), *Yahoo Search Forum,* Webmaster World, www.webmasterworld.com/ forum35/2777-3-10.htm (n.d.).
6. On this subject, see Linda Barrow, *The Spider's Apprentice*, Monash Information Services, May 11, 2004, www.monash.com/spidap.html.
7. Joe Barker, *The Best Search Engines*, University of California at Berkeley, January 3, 2005, www.lib.berkeley.edu/ TeachingLib/ Guides/Internet/SearchEngines.html (March 22, 2005).
8. Chris Richardson, "Google Results vs Yahoo Results," *Forum Home, P2L Articles,* November 8, 2004, www.pixel2life.com/forums/index.php?s=c9c8af9727a1f36fb 78d04cfd9279 (March 22, 2005).

9. Danny Sullivan, "Search Engine Size Wars V Erupts," *Search Engine Watch,* November 11, 2004, www.blog.searchenginewatch.com/blog/041111-084221 (March 2005).
10. Danny Sullivan, "Hitwise Search Engine Ratings," *Search Engine Watch,* May 17, 2004, www.searchenginewatch.com/reports/article.php/3099931 (March 2005).
11. Sample of 42,000 U.S. users, search-specific visits; includes image searches. Measured by Nielsen NetRatings December 2004. Danny Sullivan, "Nielsen NetRatings Search Engine Ratings," *Search Engine Watch*, February 11, 2004, www.searchenginewatch.com/reports/article.php/2156451 (March 2005).
12. Danny Sullivan, "comScore Media Metrix Search Engine Ratings," *Search Engine Watch*, February 11, 2005, www.searchenginewatch.com/reports/article.php/2156431 (March 2005).
13. Ibid.
14. Krishna Bharat and Andrei Broder, "Estimating the Relative Size and Overlap of Public Web Search Engines," paper presented at the 7th International World Wide Web Conference (WWW7), April 1998, www.research.compaq.com/SRC/whatsnew/sem.html.
15. Gulludjian, "Network Communication," p. 392.
16. About the high incidence of nonexistent pages retrieved by search engines, see Greg R. Notess, "Search Engine Statistics: Database Overlap," *Search Engine Showdown*, March 6, 2002, www.searchengineshowdown.com/stats/overlap.shtml (March 2005).
17. Chris Sherman, "Yahoo! Birth of a New Machine," *Search Engine Watch*, February 18, 2004, www.searchenginewatch.com/searchday/article.php/3314171 (February 2005).
18. Barker, *The Best Search Engines*.
19. About the ethical issue of anonymity and pseudo-anonymity in cyberspace, see Peter Danielson, "Pseudonyms, MailBots, and Virtual Letterheads: The Evolution of Computer-Mediated Ethics," in Ess, *Philosophical Perspectives,* pp. 67-93.
20. For a taste, see customer reviews of Donald E. Miller and Lorna Touryan Miller, *Survivors: An Oral History of the Armenian Genocide*, on Amazon.com, www.amazon.com/exec/obidos/tg/detail/ 0520219562/ qid=1124094863/sr=8-1/ref=sr_8_xs_ap_i1_xgl14/002-8416477-9715262?v=glance&s=books&n=507846.
21. The problem is about the ongoing use of the not fully standard Armscii-8 character set, and partial implementation of UNICODE in Armenian websites. In Armscii-8 websites, the truncated form "ó»Õ³ëå³ÝáõÃ," employed this way to avoid false results because of the dual orthography of the last letters, had approximately 2,500 occurrences (Google, March 2005).
22. Individual websites and discussion forums display, among other manifestations of little known subcultures, conversation threads, and self-presentation of Armenian youth groups acting "black," in a way idealizing rap and "gangsta" ways of life and communication (e.g., *Da genocide*). A few examples can be found at www.armenianplanet.com/post-2283.html and www.truehomiez.50megs.com/index.html.
23. See www.armenianinsurancesettlement.com and www.newyorklife.com/cda/0,3254,13529,00.html.
24. The following terms were used in the respective language searches: French, *Génocide arménien*; Spanish, *Genocidio armenio*; German, *Armenische Völkermord*, as well as *Genozid*; Italian, *Genocidio armeno*; Portuguese, *Genocidio armenio*; Turkish, *Ermeni soykirim/soykirimi* and also *Ermeni jenosidi*. Consistency of results was validated by observing the relative presence of the equivalent to the expression "Armenian massacres" and occasionally other related terms.
25. See Prevent Genocide International, www.preventgenocide.org/law/convention/index.htm#translations (April 2005).
26. There are resource lists on a number of university websites. However, most of them are partial lists and lack regular updating.

Part 4

Comparative Dimensions

15

The Assyrian Genocide in the Ottoman Empire and Adjacent Territories

Anahit Khosroeva

During World War I, the Armenian people fell victim to a policy of genocide perpetrated by the Young Turk government ruling Ottoman Turkey. The Armenian Genocide is presently understood by much of the world to have been the climax of a long history of oppression and violence for a group that had suffered for centuries as a Christian minority at the hands of greater powers, most notably the Turks. Less recognized is the fact that the Assyrians, whose ancestors stood at the cradle of civilization, have shared a similar history: that of a dispersed, Christian ethnic group with a prolonged experience of marginalization by foreign rule, particularly in the Ottoman Empire. This marginalization culminated in the same genocide that befell the Armenians in World War I.

Gaining recognition of the Armenian Genocide in the world community remains a crucial issue, but it has also overshadowed the plight of other ethnic groups who suffered similarly under Turkish rule. The Young Turk government implemented a like policy of extermination toward Assyrians, but scholarship on this group's experiences lags far behind that regarding the Armenians. A more complete picture of the Turkish massacres of other ethno-religious groups will further augment the powerful evidence contradicting Turkish denial of the genocide, which has been espoused since the outset and has misinformed many of its citizens and others around the world.

After the fall of the Assyrian Kingdom (605 B.C.), the descendants of the Assyrians continued to live on their historic land in ancient Betnahrain, which occupies the territory between the Persian Gulf, the Mediterranean Sea, Lake Urmia, and the Mesopotamian deserts. At the end of the nineteenth and the beginning of the twentieth century, they inhabited the eastern regions of Ottoman Turkey: in Hakkari *sanjak* of the *vilayet* (province) of Van in Western

Armenia and the vilayets of Erzerum, Diarbekir, Bitlis, Kharpert ((Kharberd), Sivas (Sebastia), as well as in the territories of Urmia in Iran, Mosul in Iraq, and the northwestern regions of Syria. Armenian and other sources show the number of Assyrians living in Turkish-controlled and adjacent territories during Ottoman times to be about one million.[1] This figure includes those peoples who possessed a common language, culture, national customs, and leadership under the cleric Mar-Shimoun Benjamin.

As part of the general Christian populace of the Ottoman Empire, the Assyrians were subjected to the same oppressive policies meted out by Turkish authorities to the Armenians and their religious kin. Many Assyrians studied in Turkish educational institutions, but they were denied public positions and opportunities to develop their regions economically. In the decades prior to World War I, the government's discriminatory practices against Christian minorities like the Assyrians and Armenians took a more violent turn, starting with the massacres of 1895-96 under Sultan Abdul Hamid II. A pivotal theme of Abdul Hamid's external and internal policies was Pan-Islam, which sought a religiously homogenous empire joining with Turkey all the neighboring territories populated with Muslims. To this end, the nationalist aspirations of non-Muslim elements in these regions were suppressed.

The massacres of Assyrians began in October 1895 in Diarbekir (Amid/ Amida) and spread to many other locations. On October 20, Turkish and Kurdish gangs began the slaughter of Christians in Diarbekir. The Assyrian Church of the Holy Mother of God gave refuge to many Assyrians, Armenians, and Greeks. In stark contrast to the fate of Assyrian villages, most of which were ruined and plundered by Kurds, the church was spared the anti-Christian aggressions. Here a revealing exchange occurred when several Assyrians suggested to their priest that the Armenian refugees be expelled from the building so as not to aggravate Turkish sentiment. The Assyrian cleric replied: "The people who cross themselves will stay in church to the end. Should we be killed, we will be killed together."[2] In the end, 119 villages in Diarbekir were scorched and ruined; 6,000 Christian families—about 30,000 people[3]—were killed. In October 1895, the Turkish army and *Hamidiye* regiments entered Urfa and killed 13,000 Assyrians.[4]

A well-known member of the Armenian national liberation movement and the Armenakan Party, Armenak Ekarian, recounted the slaughters that took place in southern Hakkari in early September 1896, where many Assyrians lived: "Taking the opportunity, the government wanted to get rid of that undesirable element and therefore sent there a large number of soldiers and hoodlums who killed hundreds of Assyrians."[5]

Sultan Abdul Hamid's anti-Christian pogroms had disastrous consequences for his Christians as up to 300,000 Armenians and 55,000 Assyrians died.[6] Many Christians were forcibly converted to Islam or murdered. About 100,000 people from 245 villages were Islamicized and countless Assyrian women were forced into Turkish harems.[7] While these numbers set a precedent in the extent of Turkish brutality toward its minority groups, World War I would provide the Young Turks with the opportunity to carry out its devastating Pan-Turkic dreams on a much grander scale.

The Young Turks' decision to enter World War I hinged on their belief that "participation in the war will considerably raise Turkey's authority, satisfy their vanity and dignity."[8] Moreover, the war allowed the Young Turks to test the viability of their Pan-Turkic vision, which found support among the military, bourgeois, and Ittihadist elite. During a talk with Dr. Mordtmann, an employee of the German embassy, Minister of Interior Talaat Pasha said that, exploiting the opportunity of martial law, the Turkish government would eventually get rid of its internal enemies—the Christians—without fear of foreign diplomatic intervention.[9] The ensuing events would bear out this sentiment, as thousands of Armenians, Assyrians, and others fell victim to the Turkish genocide while the world's great powers stood by. According to Dr. Johannes Lepsius, the Young Turk party's program stated: "Sooner or later all the nations under Turkish control will be turned into Turks. It is clear that they will not convert voluntarily and we will have to use force."[10] During one of the secret meetings the Young Turkish ideologist Dr. Nazim said: "The massacre is necessary. All the non-Turkish elements, whatever nation they belong to, should be exterminated."[11]

Ronald Stafford, an Englishman who was the former administrative inspector of Iraq's Ministry of Foreign Affairs, observed: "It would be a great progress for Turks if they could show that regardless of what happened to the Armenians, another Christian community in Turkey is quite satisfied with its fortune."[12]

The manner in which the massacres were organized and implemented serves as irrefutable evidence of the Turkish government's decision to eliminate a people whose nationalism and Christian identity ran contrary to the Young Turks' own ethnic and religious chauvinism.[13] The *vali* (governor) of Diarbekir, Reshid Bey, directed some of the earliest of these exterminations in his vilayet. The Assyrians of the Mardin, Midiat, and Jezire regions were especially victimized. The priest of the local Chaldean Assyrians, Joseph Naayem, reported that massacres had taken place since April 8, 1915. The culprits gathered men over sixteen years of age, beat, tortured, killed them, and afterwards put turbans on their heads and photographed them in order to prove to the world that Christians oppressed Muslims.

Turkish armed forces and Hamidiye units also slaughtered Assyrians in the region of Tur-Abdin beginning on June 5, 1915. Ten thousand Assyrians were killed.[14] One document reads: "The skulls of small children were smashed with rocks; the bodies of girls and women, who resisted rape or conversion into Moslems, were chopped into pieces live; men were mostly beheaded, or thrown into the nearby river; the clergy, monks and nuns were skinned or burnt live."[15]

In September 1916, the American publication *Martyred Armenia* translated an article by an Arab eyewitness of the massacres in Diarbekir. Alluding to the slaughters, the author Fa'iz el-Ghusein wrote that after many Assyrians had been killed in and around Diarbekir, belated orders were given "that only Armenians were to be killed, and that those belonging to other communities should not be touched." But when the Assyrians of the Midiat district learned what had happened to their brethren at Diarbekir, they fortified themselves in three villages "and put up a heroic resistance, showing courage beyond description." When the government was unable to subdue them, it offered amnesty on condition that the villagers lay down their arms, but the defenders "placed no reliance on it and did not surrender, for past experience had shown them that this is the most false Government on the face of the earth, taking back to-day what it gave yesterday, and punishing to-day with most cruel penalties him whom it had previously pardoned."[16]

Assyrians also suffered in the region of Van, where the vali Jevdet Bey had a "butcher'" regiment of 8,000 men that carried out unprecedented massacres. One striking example was the terrible slaughter in the Hakkari region in spring 1915, where Turks murdered about 60,000 Assyrians.[17] In the following years about 70,000 Assyrians were annihilated: some of them were murdered, others starved to death or were killed in battles against Muslims.[18]

In early June 1915, mass slaughters of Assyrians took place in northern Van, Timar, and Tuhum. The village of Kochanis, which was the residence of the Assyrian clerical leader, Mar-Shimoun, was completely destroyed. At the same time, Turks and Kurds plundered the Assyrian village of Mar-Zaya in Jelu and murdered its population. They entered and looted the church as well. About 7,000 Assyrians were slaughtered there during this period.[19]

On June 30, 1915, the American consul in Harput (Kharpert) Leslie Davis wrote to Henry Morgenthau, the American ambassador in Constantinople, that the Turks had found another way of exterminating the Christians—forced emigration. "On Saturday, June 28, it was publicly announced that all Armenians and Syrians were to leave after five days."[20] This was the way in which the deportations and massacres began in most regions.[21] The Assyrian slaughters continued in Bitlis and Sivas as well, emigration being the only form of escape.

Not all Assyrian communities suffered equally from the Turkish genocidal policy. The Assyrians of the mountainous regions of Hakkari near the boundary with Iran generally managed to elude the massacres. At the turn of the century, some 300,000 people lived there, of whom 100,000 were Assyrians.[22] Their militancy and the formidability of the area's topography spared these inhabitants from the extremes of Turkish aggressions, albeit with some loss of life.

Assyrians endured massacres not only inside the Ottoman realm but on its periphery as well. The destruction of Assyrian villages accompanied German and Turkish military operations in Iran, which the two allies intended to use as a corridor to the oil regions of Baku and thereafter to invade Central Asia. Iran thus became a battleground on which acts of mass violence were perpetrated against undesirable elements. The Assyrians of the Urmia region were among the most unfortunate elements. In September 1914, more than thirty Armenian and Assyrian villages were burned.[23] In October of that same year, the Russian vice consul in Urmia and the local governor visited Angar, Alvach, and other Assyrian villages ruined by Kurds, Turks, and Persian mobs. Commenting on the anti-Christian nature of the destruction, he wrote: "The consequences of jihad are everywhere."[24]

The unexpected retreat of the Russian army from Urmia in January 1915 had further tragic consequences for Assyrians living in Iran. Turkish troops along with Kurdish detachments organized mass slaughters of the Assyrian population. Only 25,000 people managed to escape death and take refuge in Transcaucasia.[25]

In January 1915, a platoon headed by Kachali Khan encircled and destroyed the largest and richest Assyrian village in Urmia—Gulpashan—where 300 Assyrian families (totaling about 2,500 people) lived. All but a couple of hundred were killed.[26] In addition to Gulpashan, massacres took place in Gyogtape, Ada, Khosrova, Haftvan, and other Assyrian villages, where local schools and churches were also ruined. In Khosrova, for example, the Assyrian population, which included refugees from neighboring villages (about 7,000 people), was gathered together and slaughtered.[27] In the Assyrian village of Haftvan 750 people were beheaded, and afterwards 5,000 Assyrian women were taken to Kurdish harems.[28] In the village of Kanachar 200 people were burnt alive.[29]

Turks, furious about the occupation of Dilman by the Russian army in April 1915, murdered the populations of the twenty neighboring Assyrian villages. The painful exodus from Urmia to Mesopotamia began and was accompanied by severe human losses. An English eyewitness noted: "I saw the picture of the tragic flight of an outcast nation. I speak about the Assyrians."[30] One of the refugees, American-educated Isaac Yonan, who had been miraculously saved, said that the situation was so unbearable it seemed that those alive envied the dead.[31] Ronald Stafford wrote that "the Assyrians' exodus is one of the most tragic pages of the military history. More than 17,000 Assyrians died on that way."[32]

In November 1916, the *New York Times* published an article by Dr. William W. Rockwell titled "The Total Number of Armenian and Syrian Dead," in which the author noted: "The Armenians are not the only unfortunates; the Syrians [Assyrians] also have been decimated. Great numbers have perished but no one knows how many."[33] Another American periodical, the *Atlantic Monthly*, wrote: "Within six months they [Young Turks] succeeded in doing what the Old Turks were unable to accomplish in six centuries . . . . Thousands of Nestorians and Syrians have vanished from the face of the earth."[34]

Various estimates have been given regarding the total number of Assyrian victims of Turkish genocide. In November 1919, the periodical *French Asia* wrote, "The Assyrian massacres resembled the Armenian slaughters. And as about this nation, which had 250,000 victims, has been spoken much less, it is necessary to inform the world about it."[35] Another source, Assyrian National Council Secretary C. Korek d'Kerporani, determined in 1922 that the losses of his people were more than 270,000.[36] Investigations into the massacres in later years pushed the figure still higher, as some scholars have placed the number of Assyrian victims at 500,000 and even 750,000.[37] Assyrians themselves have estimated that they lost two-thirds of their people during this period.

The systematic manner in which the massacres of Assyrians was conducted, along with the documented intentions of Turkish leaders and sheer number of individuals murdered, demonstrate that the Turkish government planned and, to a great extent, succeeded in fulfilling a policy of genocide toward the Assyrian people as well as the Armenians. World War I was an ideal context in which Turkey could accomplish this goal: the war not only absorbed the resources and focus of the world's major powers, but it also created a morally ambiguous atmosphere where brutality and death on a massive scale could be justified or trivialized. Thus, the Armenians and Assyrians—whose Christian identity and cultural durability were perceived by Turkish nationalists to be undesirable obstacles to the realization of a Pan-Turkic nation—found themselves bearers of a misfortune with reverberations lasting to this very day.

Indeed, the victims of the 1915-16 genocide and their ethnic progeny continue to struggle with its reality, a reality still denied by the Turkish government and other parties around the world. The Armenians, with the support of a legitimate government to their name, have had relative success in gaining recognition of the Armenian Genocide (albeit not from Turkey). However, while scholarship on the genocide of the Assyrians exists and is sometimes interlaced with that of their fellow Christians, the former group lacks both the greater numbers possessed by the Armenians and also its own country to promote the issue of the Assyrian Genocide. Such efforts as this essay aim to aid this promotion by shedding greater light on the injustices endured by an ethnic group—the Assyrians—whose experiences during World War I have been, to an extent, overshadowed by a better represented victim group—the Armenians. Perhaps more important, however, by supplying further evidence on the existence of genocidal practices and their devastating effects, such efforts will expand our current understanding of the scope of genocide, bolster the case against it, and thus hopefully prevent its occurrence in the future.

Notes

1. Sahak Mesrop, *Hayun taretsoyts* [Armenian Almanac] (Constantinople, 1913), pp. 67-68.
2. Tigran Mkund, *Amitai ardzaganknere* [Amida's Echos] (New York: Hye-Gule Press, 1950), p. 234.
3. Mkrtich Nersisian, *Genocid Armian v Osmanskoi Imperii* [The Armenian Genocide in the Ottoman Empire] (Erevan: Armenian Academy of Sciences, 1966), p. 120.
4. *Asuri-Süryani-Keldani halkının 1915 soykırım (SEYFO) dosyası: Bethnahrin yurtsever devrimci örgütü Asuri-Suryani halkına yönelik 1915, Soykırımı ve*

katliamlari ara tırma komisyonu [The Genocide File (SEYFO) of the Assyrian-Nestorian-Chaldean People: Bethnahrin, the Patriotic Revolutionary Organization, the Investigation Commission for the Genocide and the Massacres of 1915 against the Assyrian-Nestorian People] (Frankfurt, 1998), p. 55.

5. Armenak Ekarian, *Husher* [Memoirs] (Cairo: Nor Astgh, 1947), p. 111.
6. Joseph Naayem, *Shall This Nation Die*? (New York: Chaldean Rescue, 1921), p. 274.
7. Lev Sargizov, *Assiriytsi v Armenii* [Assyrians in Armenia], "Atra" no. 4 (St. Petersburg: Astranews, 1992), p. 71.
8. Akabi Nassibian, *Britain and the Armenian Question, 1915-1923* (London: Croom Helm, and New York: St. Martin's Press, 1984), p. 32.
9. Johannes Lepsius, *Deutschland und Armenian 1914-1918: Sammlung diplomatischer Aktenstücke* (Potsdam: Tempelverlag, 1919), p. 26.
10. Johannes Lepsius, *Bericht über die Lage des Armenischer Volkes in Türkei* (Potsdam: Tempelverlag, 1916), p. 220.
11. Mevlan Zade Rifat, *Osmanyan heghapoghutyan mut tsalkere ev Ittihati hayajinj tsragrere* [The Obscure Folds of the Ottoman Revolution and the Ittihad's Plans for Extermination of the Armenians] (Erevan: "KPH," 1990), pp. 98-99.
12. Ronald S. Stafford, *The Tragedy of the Assyrians* (London: G. Allen & Unwin, 1935), p. 27.
13. Joseph Alichoran, *Du génocide à la Diaspora: Les Assyro-Chaldéens au XX*[e] *siècle* (Paris: Revue Istina, 1994), p. 370.
14. Nikolay Hovhannisyan, *The Armenian Genocide* (Erevan: Zangak 97, 2005), p. 51.
15. *Documentation on the Genocide against the Assyrian-Suryoye-Chaldean-Aramaic People (SEYFO)* (Frankfurt, 1999), p. 9.
16. Richard D. Kloian, *The Armenian Genocide: News Accounts from the American Press (1915-1922)* (Richmond, CA: ACC Books, 1985), p. 161. For details on the tribulations of the Assyrian population in the Diarbekir region, see David Gaunt, "Death's End, 1915: The General Massacres of Christians in Diarbekir," in *Armenian Tigranakert/Diarbekir and Edessa/Urfa*, ed. Richard G. Hovannisian (Costa Mesa, CA: Mazda Publishers, 2006), pp. 309-359.
17. Makich Arzumanyan, *Hayastan 1914-1917* [Armenia, 1914-1917] (Erevan: Hayastan, 1969), p. 488.
18. Naayem, *Shall This Nation Die?* p. 275.
19. Thea Halo, *Not Even My Name* (New York: Picadore USA, 2000), p. 284.
20. Leslie A. Davis, *The Slaughterhouse Province. An American Diplomat's Report on the Armenian Genocide, 1915-1917* (New Rochelle, NY: Aristide D. Caratzas, 1989), pp. 143-144.
21. Wartkes Mikaeljan, *Die armenische Frage und der Genozid an den Armeniern in der Türkei (1913-1919): Dokumente aus dem Politischen Archiv des deutschen Auswärtigen Amts* (Erevan, Academy of Sciences, 2004).
22. Alichoran, *Du génocide à la Diaspora*, p. 370.
23. Gilbert E. Hubbard, *From the Gulf to Ararat: An Expedition through Mesopotamia and Kurdistan* (Edinburgh and London: W. Blackwood and Sons, 1916), pp. 257-258.
24. Lev Sargizov, *Assiriytsy stran Blizhnego i Srednego Vostoka* [Assyrians in the Countries of the Near and Middle East] (Erevan: Hayastan, 1979), pp. 25-26.
25. Abraham Yohannan, *The Death of a Nation* (New York and London: G. P. Putnam's Sons, 1916), p. 120.
26. *Mshak* (Tiflis), no. 55, March 14, 1915.

27. Naayem, *Shall This Nation Die*? p. 271.
28. Yohannan, *Death of a Nation*, pp. 127-128, 134.
29. Sargizov, *Assiriytsy stran Blizhnego i Srednego Vostoka*, p. 26.
30. Konstantin Matveev [Bar-Mattay], *Assiriyskii vopros vo vremia i posle Pervoi Mirovoi Voiny (1914-1923 gg.)* [The Assyrian Question during and after the First World War (1914-1923)] (Moscow, 1968), p. 49.
31. Kloian, *Armenian Genocide*, p. 9.
32. Stafford, *Tragedy of the Assyrians*, pp. 33-34.
33. Kloian, *Armenian Genocide*, pp. 188-189.
34. Ibid., p. 193.
35. Alichoran, *Du génocide à la Diaspora*, p. 370.
36. Levon Vardan, *Zhamanakagrutiun haykakan tasnhingi, 1915-1923* [Chronology of the Armenian (19)15, 1915-1923] (Beirut: Levon Bedirian, 1975), p. 90.
37. Halo, *Not Even My Name*, p. 8.

16

Greek Labor Battalions Asia Minor

Speros Vryonis, Jr.

The final collapse of the Greek armies in western Asia Minor at the battle of Afion Karahisar, August 13-15, 1922, constitutes the last and decisive phase of the reentry of the Kemalist armies into western and coastal Asia Minor. By early morning of Sunday, August 27, the Turkish irregulars entered Smyrna and by that evening the first detachments of Turkish regulars began their entry into the city. Killings, looting, and the final burning of the city (beginning August 31) were accompanied by comparable events and disasters/victories in the rest of western Asia Minor. The conditions of the defeated armies and the local Christian populations were swiftly and radically transformed by the measures that the Kemalists imposed. These conditions, for some fourteen months after the withdrawal of the Greek administration and armies from western Asia Minor, were followed by a harsh regime that envisaged the final destruction of any Christian (in western Asia Minor primarily Greek) populations. This policy had already been implemented in large parts of this region through the joint efforts of the German general Liman von Sanders and the Young Turk regime. The Kemalist government was to complete this erasure that had already begun during the years of World War I.[1]

In this short presentation an effort will be made first to examine one aspect only of this second phase, and this has to do with the conscription of so-called labor battalions of Greeks who were removed from the easily accessible maritime shores of the Aegean, marched off to various inland regions of Asia Minor and there subjected to lethal labors. The utilization of enforced conscriptions of labor battalions was a favorite device of the Young Turks, and one that was revived in 1941 when thousands of Greek, Armenian, and Jewish minorities were marched off into central Asia Minor.[2] The principal source under discussion here will be the literary-historical work of the Greek prose writer Elias Venezis, who was conscripted at age eighteen in 1922 and who served well into

1924. A native of Aivali, he was conscripted in a body of some 3,000 Greek Aivali males.

The author who will concern us is Elias Venezis, a man of considerable literary stature in the field of Modern Greek literature and generally associated with the so-called Generation of the Thirties. He is not completely unknown outside of Greece, as a number of his works have been translated into at least twelve European languages. As is the case with a number of twentieth-century Greek authors, Venezis was shaped by the wars and ethnic politics that absorbed the Balkans and Turkey and by the dire ethnic consequences that these wars had for the local and regional inhabitants. This is one of the factors and ingredients common to the modern literature of Turks, Greeks, Bulgars, Serbs, Bosnians, Armenians, and others.

Venezis and his family were caught up in the aftermaths of the Balkan wars, World War I, and the Greco-Turkish war of 1919-22. Specifically, he and his family lived in Aivali when the city was an important center of Greek culture, second only to Smyrna/Izmir in what the Greeks referred to as Aeolia and lonia.

After the collapse and final defeat of the Greek armies in western Asia Minor in the fall of 1922, the return of Turkish military administration brought in its wake a complete reversal of the fate of the Greeks in this region. Those who did not manage to escape were subjected to the rage and violent measures of their conquerors. What occurred in Smyrna was in part repeated in Aivali (that is, massacres and burning of Greek, Armenian, and foreign dwellings and businesses.[3]

Venezis, conscripted into these slave labor battalions at the age of eighteen, remained a slave without any rights and even without any official recognition of his existence for fourteen months. He entered as a youth who had enjoyed the ease, comfort, and education of a middle-class family. When he was finally exchanged fourteen months later, he was almost twenty and no longer a youth, but a man grown old as the result of all the difficulties and cruelties he had suffered at the hands of his military guards and often of local Turks. Later, when he compiled his individual essays on his captivity into a book of twenty chapters, each chapter was given a title, all of which were direct quotes from the lamentations in the Book of Psalms.

Soon after his liberation in the massive Greco-Turkish exchange of populations in 1924, Venezis wrote down his impressions and memories from the period of his "maturation" in the slave labor camps where he had been subjected to these harsh conditions. His work was thus written in its first form at the young age of twenty to twenty-one years and appeared as a serial in a local Greek newspaper on one of the isles from which he could see the Asiatic shores of his beloved fatherland. He later relates that he could not really face the text again until later when he polished it and turned it into the first of many editions in 1931. It may be that upon later reflection he introduced the stanzas from David's Psalms as titles for the various chapters.

The very title of the book, *To noumero 31.328: To vivlio tes skiavias*, is highly significant. By and large those thousands of Greeks in the slave labor camps had received no official identity as such. Therefore, they had no legal or official existence, and without this formally acknowledged identity their fate was of no consequence. They could (be made to) disappear quietly and without any fanfare.

Very soon the anxiety over this condition spread throughout the labor camps, and the fear that they might be killed permeated the immediate atmosphere. Thus the acquisition of an official number of each conscript became a general subject and accompanied all the expressions and discussions as their ultimate fates were foremost in both the minds and the conversations. Venezis was young, highly intelligent and sensitive to the almost innate differences of Greeks and Turks. With these qualities he managed to squeeze through the various tortures, beatings, killings, and illnesses that beset him. The title he has given to this book is thus doubly meaningful and is a direct reflection of the fact that the work is autobiographical. The first part of the book includes the official number that the Turkish authorities finally gave Venezis toward the end of his term as a slave laborer: No. 31.328. And the subtitle, *Vivlio tes skiavias*, translates as "The Book of Slavery."

How then does Venezis see his book? One literary critic wrote, "it is a work notable for its warlike style and tone." To this Venezis replied:

> But I do not speak of style and tone. I speak of burned "matter" (*hyle*), of the flesh which drips blood and thus floods the pages of the book; of the human heart which is being torn apart and not of the soul. Herein there is no soul whatsoever, for there is no space for a trip into the regions of the metaphysical. Then flesh when it is scorched as it is here with the red-hot iron, the flesh rises to the heights as an all-powerful deity, and all else becomes mute in its presence. It is often said that there is no pain which is the equal of a moral pain. Such things are uttered by wise men and by books. If, however, you go out on the streets and you inquire of the martyrs, that is to say those whose bodies were tortured while death commands them from above (and it is an easy thing to find such humans as our era has provided an abundance) and should you ask them, you will learn that there is nothing—indeed nothing—in existence which is more profound and more holy than a body which is suffering torture.

And, he concludes: "This book is a dedication or offering to this suffering that comes from pain." Indeed, as noted above, the twenty short chapters of the book carry titles that contain the moaning and weeping of the stanzas of the Psalms. The first chapter is headed by the Davidic phrase: "The travails of death consumed me and the horrors of death encircled me." And the second chapter: "They placed me in a deep grave in the darkness and shade of death." The descriptive narrative has a triple basis of mortal fear, cruel physical pain, and grim death (a death stripped of all alleviating niceties and honor).

Forced conscription of the eighteen-year-old Venezis into the slave labor battalions held but one promise: an anonymous but harsh death. He writes of his reaction and the reactions of the Greek male conscript upon learning of the conscription order:

"This news brought disaster on our people. For the labor battalions had a long past from the Great War. They had become legend. Thousands of Christians had left their bones in the labor camps. And the tears of their mothers had not yet dried."

Thus it was that Venezis' parents, four smaller sisters, and one young brother were able to take the last boat out of Asia Minor, whereas Venezis was prevented from disembarking with them and was taken instead to the dark, crowded basement of the Aivali jail. He had already been beaten savagely prior to the departure of the boat. This proved to be a ceremony that would constitute his daily diet for the better part of the year that was to follow. On three successive nights, the chief selected eight, then five, and finally two conscripted Greek laborers and had them marched outside the town to be bayoneted to death.

Eventually, the remaining forty-three Greek males were awakened during the night and ordered outside the camp there to begin their long trek (for the few who were to survive) to the various labor camps in the Turkish towns and villages of western Asia Minor. His was the fourth such recruited group that had been sent out from Aivali by the Turkish authorities. His group learned from a wounded recruit that all three of the previous groups, numbering in the hundreds, were bayoneted to death by order of the Turkish authorities. The night was cold, and after a period of some two hours of marching they were ordered to halt. The laborers feared that they were now going to be killed:

> They ordered us to sit down, and then they surrounded us at a certain distance. One says that they are going to shoot us. Another says that this cannot be the case for they would in such a circle be shooting at one another. Another replies, no. They will kill us with their bayonets. . . . The guards take two conscripts at a time down the hill and soon they were out of sight.

Since the remainder of the conscripts heard nothing, it was obvious that they were not going to kill the first two conscripts taken down the hill. Then the guards took Venezis and one other Greek down the hill in the same direction. The guards told them to take off their coats and then their jackets, then their pants, socks and shoes, "and we remained only with our undershirts and undershorts."

It was the end of October 1922 and though the sun during the day remained hot, the nights were very cold and accompanied by frost. The first torture had been physical and psychological: the murder by bayoneting of hundreds of Greek male conscripts from Aivali. This second exercise was not only psychological (denuding the conscripts) but also physical, as they were left unprotected from the extremes of the weather. Henceforth, the long and painful marches were carried out without the proper shoes and clothing necessary for sustaining such marches.

At their first nighttime stop, Ayasmat, other tribulations awaited them again. Venezis gives a graphic and dramatic description of the first night outside Aivali. They were quartered in a Greek church now converted into a stable and storehouse. In the meantime, they had taken on a Greek family of three: father, mother, and a young child:

> So soon as we had entered it we were assailed by the strong stink of animal dung, sulfur, and "holiness." Deathly silence prevailed. But soon we unleashed our noises from our bitter tasting mouths. We eventually stretched out on the floor tiles wherever we chanced to find ourselves. . . . In the depth of the church there "bedded down" near the altar the family. I understood that it was they from the crying of the little child. It must have been frightened by the darkness. . . . At about eleven, nighttime, the door of the building began to creak. Two or three soldiers began whispering quietly. I edged closer to Argyris, who came close to me as we began to observe. A light was lighted, a candle. And the soldiers began to search. They bent over the sleeping faces as they examined them. They were searching. Soon they reached us, the two male youths, and paused:
>
> "Do you want him?" the one said to the other as he pointed to Argyris.
>
> "Not for the moment."
>
> "Do you want the woman (the mother of the crying child)?"
>
> "Yes."
>
> "Yes."
>
> "Then you must await your turn."
>
> "I shall await my turn."
>
> They move away from us. Argyris understood all the conversation since he knew Turkish . . . as he lies very close to me I hear his heart beating rapidly, indeed, very rapidly. . . .
>
> "Elia," he murmurs, terrified: "Not that! Not that!" And I also was bathed with sweat from fear.
>
> The candle of the soldiers finally reached its destination, at the church's altar. We suddenly hear a female scream, which comes from that direction, as the screech slaps the bitter air. Then a second outcry, but it is abruptly halted as a hand stifles her mouth, for the soldiers do not want an uproar over the approaching issue. My comrades and I quietly and carefully moved toward the altar so that we can see. . . .
>
> The wife was holding on to her husband with both hands, not wanting to unglue herself from him. The small child lay between the father and the mother as it had not yet awakened . . . it was so calm and was probably immersed in its dreams. . . . In the beginning the soldier pulled the woman gently, but he began to pull more violently. His eyes were swollen with lust and as the resistance of the woman continued and as she continued to resist he pulled all the more violently.
>
> "Save me! Save me!" she cried out. The husband heard her, but he remained speechless and was unable to utter a word, though he tried. The wife cried out to him, "Why do you not kill me? Why do you not kill me?" Moved by her words he manages, desperately to beseech the soldiers: "Have mercy upon us! Have mercy upon us!"
>
> The soldiers gave him a kick in the ribs, and his great mass of a body suddenly reeled back. His wife lost physical contact with him. In an effort to grab at some firm object on which to base her desperate resistance, she accidentally grabbed the leg of the small child alongside her. And now, suddenly awakened, the child began to cry out, "Little mother! Little mother!" For a short while she dragged the child with her. Later she finally released it from her grasp.

> They exited from the altar and the soldiers and the woman came to a halt behind a column near the door. One of them took a nearby wooden plank . . . and rested it alongside the column to guard against the sight of the prisoners, but the plank was small and could not hide very much from our view. . . .
>
> And as we watched silently . . . one soldier was struggling to throw the woman down on her back. But she refused to fall. Then two of them grabbed her by her hands and the third soldier grabbed her legs. By now they had abandoned any gentleness as their own hands and bodies labored with rapid spasmodic movements, for they could no longer control themselves. They stretched her out on her back. The middle soldier was trying rapidly to remove her clothes as the others restrained her with their hands pressing down on her breast. In one last desperate effort she struggled to gather her last ounce of strength to resist. She would continue to slip out of their grasp and in doing so would bend and move like a serpent, all the while wailing, "Kill me! Kill me!"
>
> Finally she became calm. There could only be heard a weeping murmur, a complaint. And sporadically she continued to strike her head on the tile floor . . . and we could hear those who were "expressing themselves" on top of her.

To the violence of bayoneting, to the extremities of cold and heat, and to the unhealthy conditions of night stops and exposure to illnesses, now was added the violence of brutal rapes and the violation of the sanctity of the family. Rape was to become a daily exercise to the point that female prisoners were turned to prostitution to sate the appetites of the Turkish soldiers as well as local Turkish villagers. Many of them died from sexual abuse, while others became ill and shamed. Venezis had experienced all this in the first two days of his labor battalion's march from Aivali. All the above scenes were to be repeated ad nauseum for more than a year along with the appearance of ever-newer forms of dehumanization.

Unfortunately for the Greek male conscripts, their human environment underwent constant change because their fellow laborers were being murdered or were dying from the atrocious conditions placed upon them; all the while newer slave laborers supplanted those who fell by the wayside. In addition, guards were periodically changed most likely to prevent the development of close ties between them and their captives.

The unending itinerary brought Venezis to at least seven towns and villages in western Asia Minor. In many of these marches, Turkish cavalry units replaced the foot soldiers as guards. This signaled the beginning of other travails: during these journeys many laborers began to die off almost as if from preplanning:

> The new guards that took over were cavalry. They had the bright idea of abandoning the level road and of proceeding through the fields. This was a merciless trial for our naked bodies and swollen legs (and shoeless feet). The earth mounds were dry and hard from the sun as it had not yet rained. We tried to avoid them (the hard mounds) as they throw you off balance . . . but in avoiding them we fell in the thorny bushes which drove us mad:

> "I can no longer continue! I can no longer continue!"
>
> We were all screaming, and yet we all ran that we might not be left behind and thus killed by the guards. So one was trying to run past another—an insane competition that was drowning our complaints. We would remove the thorns from our feet while trying still to continue running. The cavalrymen ran behind us and were striking us with their rifle butts so that we could not stop. We were like a disheveled herd of animals that run about on the plain in search of some shelter as they smell the oncoming storm.

Earlier, both Venezis and Argyris had been forced to surrender their shoes and had managed to get the soldier's ill-fitting pair of army shoes—they were far too large, so the two laborers had split the pair so that one wore the right shoe and the other the left shoe. But, because of its ill-shaped form and poor manufacture, the single shoe proved to be an instrument of torture in their long and difficult journeys.

"I could not raise the weight of the comrade's large shoe. The sweating, stinking foot would slip and dance within this ill-fitting shoe. I took it off and held it in my hands. But then my instep, so used to its protection, began to tremble from the [hard] field. It became hot and threw off sparks. I tore a piece of my underwear that had been left me, and I bound the foot."

The forced removal of their shoes and clothes began to join in the assault on the health of the conscripts. To these were added severe thirst and hunger:

> The sun was ascending the skies, burning, hostile and merciless. And so, thirst began to burn us. The dust became glued to our tongues which came in and out of the mouth as though they had been wound up. We were spitting in order to get rid of the bitter taste . . . but our mouths were completely dry . . .
>
> We cried out, "Water, water!"
>
> "What?" replied the officer of the guard.
>
> "Su, su [water]," we would shout out in Turkish.
>
> "Water?" the guard responded. "Well [we shall see]."
>
> We arrived near a spring. But they kept us some 20 meters distant from the spring. The soldiers went in order, drank, watered their horses, and filled their canteens. They were drinking water by the handful, and much was falling and dripping about. The prisoners cried out, "Mercy," but to no avail. They kept us far from the water. They allowed only the females and the little child to go and drink. Then they marched the prisoners off for about half an hour until they came to a swamp, and there was deep green grass growing nearby. There were many mosquitoes. And the trees close by provided shade, and there were also small birds mating in the leaves.
>
> "Here, drink!" the commander ordered. We fell on the swamp water and were drinking it by the handfuls . . . this polluted water. We poured it on our burned faces and chests so that all our blood and life might be flooded with water . . . water. One of our comrades shouted, "Don't. Do not drink it, comrades. It is the white death."
>
> We responded: "White, black, green, let it come, comrade!" Our comrade made one last effort: "Dysentery will assail us." But, in the face of all this water in our mouths, and the latter were dripping water, and in the face of this challenge, our

> comrade was seized and so finally he buried his face in the swamp water where he drank and drank.
>
> Thus our thirst was assuaged. I stretched out on the grass. . . . Someone near me was chewing quietly. I gazed at his mouth and saw that he was eating grass and when he would spit it out he would proceed to chew fresh grass. I bent over the earth and I began to chew myself. For some time I chewed the bitter substance of the grass. I did this from a hidden joy of remembering how it is and what it was that a human eats.
>
> It was not long before dysentery appeared in the labor battalion, which was so weakened by the lack of clothing, healthy water, and food, and by the beatings and exhausting labors. The office of the guards knew full well that the swamp waters, grasses, and encampments filled with urine and excrement would eventually lead to death. Often there was no roof to shield the workers from the cold and rain, and so the human population of the work battalion was constantly changing, decimated by deaths and replenished by other equally suffering laborers. The drinking of swamp water became a regular part of the diet and those who survived, survived. The others met sorrowful and painful demises.

At one point, Venezis met up with a group of thirty Greek Orthodox priests from Aivali who had also been deprived of their clothing, save for their underclothing. On observing the beating of one of the priests, Venezis remarked that this particular man had given him Holy Communion in Aivali when he was still a child. On marching out of Fergamon, the priests had joined Venezis' labor caravan. The old priest gave out and could no longer walk:

> The column halted. Trouble. The soldiers were cursing. The old priest did not wish to continue. He fell. The commander ordered: "Grab him by the hands." Two of us grabbed him by his armpits and we continued the march. But his legs could not walk and so he was dragged. We halted once more. By now furious, the commander came from behind and struck him thrice in the small of the back . . . in order to "enliven" him. He slipped out of our hands . . . and fell. The soldiers dragged him to the side of the road and they released him face down and then began to beat him with their rifle butts. He did not even groan, only his tongue began to lick the earth to see if it were dry or bitter.
>
> From the heights of Attalus, a few meters from where we were, the Turkish children were playing, and they ran downhill to the scene. The soldiers withdrew in order to continue our march and the children began at once to stone the body which was in its death throes. For some time we could hear the dull thud of the stones as they began to accumulate atop the priest.

As they continued their march the same incidents marked their journey, a mere repetition of the hateful events and experiences that had marred their progress from the night that they left Aivali. Venezis now repeats them with almost monotonous regularity: "We began again to thirst mightily . . . . However they would not stop so that we could drink."

The soldiers had taken two young Greek girls for their sexual satisfaction. Finally, the commander of the guards realized that the young fifteen-year-old girl had been so brutally and frequently raped that she could no longer walk. As she lay down on the ground from exhaustion, dying, the officer kicked her with his booted foot and she fell from a height of some 10 meters and rolled into the rapidly flowing river below. So he ordered the death caravan to march on until midnight. The young girl could no longer service his needs.

By this time their thirst was now joined by hunger, both of which would experience constant interruptions:

> It was noon on the next day. We were marching on the plain. Suddenly in the middle of this desolation, a group of cavalry blocked our way. They were guerrillas, and they were armed to the teeth.
>
> "Halt!"
>
> What did they want? They took the soldiers aside and spoke with them, in the beginning with low voices which then gave way to shouts and quarrels. They did not agree. Suddenly and by signal these horsemen drew their pistols and aimed at us and at the soldiers. Pandaemonium broke loose . . . each one of us ran for cover behind the trees. When we recovered we saw that the horsemen had quickly disappeared. There were some rifle shots on either side. Later, silence. On gathering we observed that one of the girls was no longer with us. The last female that was now with us was the girl from Ayasmat, and she was weeping over the fate of her solitary female companion. . . . A few hours later hopelessness overcame us once more and we began once more to summon death.

After several days of forced marching they arrived at Kirkagach, where they were quartered in the basement of a church:

> In the morning they put us to clean the roads. Those who were ill remained behind where they were beaten for being sick. On the road the villagers gathered and, on spotting us, began to spit on us. Afterwards they took us back to the basement where, in a little while, the small children came to play. They had pieces of bread, cigarette butts, and melon rinds. The children would drop the melon rinds so that they would fall exactly on the beards and stomachs of the priests . . . .

The basement was narrow and small and so it was literally impossible for all the prisoners to lie down to sleep. Further, the guards, as usual, would refuse to allow them to leave their prison in order to relieve themselves at night, and so Venezis and the other captives were forced to relieve themselves where they were. But the most frightening event was that the guards removed half of the laborers, tied them together with a rope, and then took them away and murdered them.

In addition to such terrible developments, the weather was also changing:

> As the days passed the weather turned very cold and we struggled to cover our nakedness. I had found a sack thrown aside. I made a hole in the middle through which I passed my head and I tied it with string around my waist. It was good. I also managed to gather discarded paper and I fitted it in on my skin. And other comrades did whatever they could. Two had managed to beg for some women's [old and colored] clothing. Thus, when we gathered, these two stood out, like birds of paradise. We still suffered from our feet as we were barefooted. We also suffered from the lack of covers at night. We simply had none. It was thus that we were forced to go to bed one leaning against the other.

Venezis' labor battalion changed with the death of the majority of his original fourth group and by the infusion of remnˇants from other battalions, which had suffered similar decimations. Eventually, he was taken by train to Magnisa on the Aegean coast, where he received his long-desired official number 31,328 and so felt secure as the exchange of populations was now a diplomatic reality. He was one of the twenty-three survivors of the roughly 3,000 recruited male laborers from Aivali. Less than 1 percent had survived the brutal impositions of the Turkish regime. But even after he arrived in Magnisa in the large concentration camp, safety still was not certain. The weak surviving laborers often fell victim to epidemics of typhoid fever. The presiding officer would come into the camp in the morning and ask:

> "Are there any corpses?'
>
> "There are."
>
> And they gathered the corpses in tens or twenties, as many as there were and they would throw them into a ditch.

Indeed, the epidemic of typhoid fever had already destroyed the camp prior to the arrival of Venezis. As precautionary measures he and others were required to take baths and to have their heads shaved by slave barbers in order to do away with the lice:

> I had not been able to wash myself since that moment when I was apprehended, many months ago. I now scraped off the filth from my body—filth that was my own possession, and so I was somewhat saddened. My large fingernails were now packed with dirt, which eventually began to run down.

Though Venezis had survived untold hardships and had defied death in many forms, shapes, and circumstances, he still feared that now he might perish from the epidemic. Further, his diet did not improve much, and his difficult labors continued. The first sign of alleviation came with the announcement that Dallara, a Spanish official, was appointed to examine the conditions of the prisoners and the "care" that the Turkish government was providing them:

> Thus it was that one morning they took about sixty of us slave laborers for a small-scale forced-labor. The job was a little outside the town of Manisa. Near the railroad tracks there reaches a huge ravine within Mount Sipylo. It is called [in Turkish] Kirtikdere. It is reckoned that some 40,000 Christian men and women from Smyrna and Manisa were slaughtered during the first days of the catastrophe [the arrival of the Kemalist armies in Smyrna]. The corpses began to disintegrate and the water of the ravine, which descended from mountain, began to drive the corpses to the edge of the ravine where they reached the road and railroad tracks. Since the Spaniard Dallara, seated in his wagon-lit train, smoking a cigar, would have been looking out of his window and marveling at the beauty of the landscape, he would suddenly see the corpses. It would have been like the burst of some bomb-shell. Accordingly, our labor battalion was obliged, all day long, to shove the corpses back into the ravine

so that they could not be seen. In the beginning this labor consisted of grasping and holding in our arms these corpses and thus to carry them away. It was a repugnant labor. But after a few hours these emotional reactions passed and the slave laborers began to make a macabre joke of their task.

"What are you holding?'" one would ask.

The other looks down at what he is holding in his embrace, and as he continues walking, he replies: "Two skulls, five shin bones, six teeth."

"Are they male or female?"

"They seem to be male."

"You have not looked carefully, comrade."

On a number of shin and hand bones we found pieces of wire. The Christians must have been tied to one another . . . but with the downward journey [carried by the current of the water] the accompanying skeleton must have torn loose from its partner.

"Look here," he said. It was a little child. On seeing this, the disturbed Muslim guard murmured, "Allah! Allah!"

"How old was it?"

"Well it must have been two years old."

Early in the evening we had finished our job. The sergeant goes to the railroad tracks to see if anything is visible from the tracks. Nothing was to be seen, and he reported:

"Everything is in order."

On our return we stopped at a spring and washed our hands and faces, in order to have some relief. One of our comrades asked, "What will become of the bones?" Miltos looked at him calmly:

"Don't you know what happens to the bones?"

"No."

"They become fertilizer, comrade."

"What?"

"Fertilizer. You will see, for one day it will sell at a good price. You will see."

Miltos was a man who had traveled about, and he knew many things:

"Certainly, it will happen exactly like this: One day there will arrive from Southampton a certain person. He will straighten his eyeglasses, and he will examine the goods [the bones]. . . . He will grade the quality extra-fine for chemical fertilizer. 'How much a ton?' he will ask.

'So much'

And the purchaser will say: "But elsewhere we purchased Turkish goods, Bulgarian goods, Russian goods for less."

But the local commercial agent will respond, "But this is real Hellenic material."

"Really, it is genuine?"

"Yes."

"Well, in that case I shall pay the price."

And so the purchaser will agree to a price one *kurush* higher inasmuch as Pericles and Ictinos have entered the equation.

With this macabre reference to the slaying of thousands of Greek Christians, we abandon Venezis and his account of the life and fate of the conscripted labor battalions in western Asia Minor.

Venezis' account has informed us of the conscripted labor battalions recruited from Greek males in western Asia Minor. A second compact mass of

Greek Christians lived on the Black Sea coast and in the rugged mountain terrain immediately to the south of the coastline in the regions between Inebol and Sinope in the west and Trebizond and Batum in the east. The Greek Christians constituted important commercial and religious entities in the towns of Sinope, Oinoi, Ordu, Kerasus, Trebizond, Surmena, Rize, and Batum, as also in the agricultural zone and area of intensive animal husbandry in the many hundreds of Greek villages in the immediate plains and mountain slopes in the adjacent regions to the south of the coastal towns. The Balkan wars, which constituted an unmitigated disaster for the Ottoman Empire, resulted in the flight of thousands of Balkan Muslims (of various ethnic backgrounds) to what was left of the Ottoman Empire, eastern Thrace, and different parts of Asia Minor. Thus, it came about that many were sent to the Pontus region where the demands of the Ottoman government that they be given shelter and food by Greek villagers and city dwellers caused immediate friction between the newly arrived *muhajirs* (refugees) and the local Greeks. The embittered newcomers thus became the enemies of the local Greek population, an enmity that was to be reinforced by the needs of the Ottoman state, first, and then by those of the Kemalist state.[4]

The Young Turk regime implemented its nationalistic policies at the beginning of World War I, when it violently removed the Greek populations of Thrace and northwest Anatolia and granted their houses, shops, and fields to the muhajirs who came to replace them. Many Greeks were murdered.

When the war broke out and Turkey entered on the side of the Germans and Austrians, the successes of the Russian armies after the battle of Sarikamish transformed existing tensions in Pontus into the outright persecution of its Greek minority. The Turkish regime under Mustafa Kemal would finally remove all Greeks from the region. This was accomplished through a series of local and state actions that included massacres, the uprooting of most Greeks from their urban and rural habitats, the destruction of hundreds of villages, widespread looting and arson, the confiscation and destruction of property, the institution of massive slave labor battalions and death marches, and the reduction of women to what was often unremunerated prostitution.[5]

Between the persecutions of the Pontian Greeks, there transpired the meeting of the Ottoman Parliament in Istanbul on November 4, 1918, at which time the Greek member of Parliament from Pontus, Emmanuel Emmanouelides, set before the members of that body eight matters, of which the seventh had to do with the labor battalions:

> On the occasion of the conscription there were created the labor battalions. They [state authorities] destroyed through starvation and through general deprivations 250,000 from the men thus. . . . We ask: "What does the new government know of the perpetrators? What does it think on this matter? And, when will it initiate the measures that it is able to undertake?"[6]

Here we shall pursue the original sources on the specific matter of the conscripted labor battalions of Greek males subject to military conscription. Thanks to the recent publication of the huge fourteen-volume work *The Genocide of the Pontian Greeks* by Konstantinos Photiades we are faced for the first time with a systematic effort to martial thousands of documents and to write an orderly history of the event. The first three volumes of the work give Photiades' view of its history based on the following eleven volumes of documents. His documentation is, as a whole, consistent as to the rough numbers of conscripted, but it is not always clear whether the total numbers refer to conscriptions in Pontus or to more general figures of Greeks conscripted everywhere.

Photiades reproduces part of a German diplomatic report sent to Berlin on May 12, 1918, and which informs its superiors that "by the end of 1917 more than 200,000 Greeks were conscripted between the ages of fifteen and forty-eight. Many of them died from abuses, illnesses, starvation, and the cold weather."[7]

On October 12, 1918, the metropolitan of Trebizond informed the Greek Patriarch of Constantinople of the trials and tribulations of his flocks, singling out the creation of the conscripted labor battalions as the most fatal of the many measures that the Turks inflicted on the Greeks of Pontus. Though this document was composed in October of 1918, it is implied that these conscripted labor battalions had begun much earlier. Indeed they were already in the documentary evidence at least from 1916, when the metropolitan sent the patriarch an evaluation of the terrible conditions under which his people struggled to survive:

> The indigenous Greeks who have been conscripted, as they are not able to pay the fee for exemption, are forced to transport military supplies, or to work to build military bases, bath houses, and roads while they and their families are deprived of the provision of food. At times they [the Turkish authorities] threaten to deport them to Sivas or elsewhere [i.e., where cold climates increase the likelihood of death], and they are forced to pay money to avoid such movements. This tragedy continues today.[8]

As seen in the memoirs of Venezis, a very large percentage of those condemned to the labor battalions died before their labors could be finished. The contemporary memoirs of Antonios Gavrielides (1924) give a frightful description of the conditions under which the Pontian conscripts lived, worked, and died. Those who could afford to pay the 5 Turkish gold liras for the *bedel* (military exemption tax) had to pay annually and eventually had to sell their property to get the cash. At the same time, the wives, elders, and children of the conscripted laborers who were left behind endured the oppression of those who ruled them: sexual demands, the burning of houses, extortion, and so forth. The laborers, continues Gavrielides, were subjected to frequent and brutal beatings, starvation, illness, and frequent death.[9]

On March 10, 1916, the lower cleric of Argyropolis (Gumuskhane) reported to his metropolitan in Trebizond the conscription of all males between the ages of fifteen and fifty-one from Argyropolis and its environs into the labor battalions. On March 17, others were marched from Erzerum to Kelkit and Herriana to clean the roads.

On December 13, 1919, the total effect of the labor battalions on the local population was summarized by a document of the Greek Ministry of Foreign Affairs as based on the individual reports of the metropolitans of Trebizond, Chaldia, Colonia, Amisos, and Neocaesarea. The metropolitan of Trebizond reported, in addition, that the total number of his flock had been reduced from 52,000 in 1914 to 23,000 by 1919. He also made specific reference to the devastation wrought by the labor battalions:

> The relatively more prosperous were first robbed of their wealth and then sent off to the interior where they died from evil treatment and deprivations, the remainder were first conscripted and were put in the accursed labor battalions where a wretched death awaited them.[10]

As late as May 1919, the appearance of the Turkish army in the district of Kars (in Cilicia) brought into action the conscripted labor battalions in the region's twenty-seven villages.[11] The physical condition of the conscripted Greek labor battalions was of such poor quality that the death rate was very high. One Greek physician observed the following:

> During my stay in Islahiye, I saw labor battalions conscripted exclusively of 5,000 Greeks from Denizli. They were decimated in a very few months. Starvation, forced labor of a daily work schedule of twelve uninterrupted hours of hard labor, sunstroke, illness, and deprivation of all necessities brought conditions in which barely 1,000 managed to survive. There would enter the hospital daily 100 sick persons, the majority of whom would die the following day.[12]

The Kemalist regime continued the brutal conscription into slave labor battalions in both western and northeastern Anatolia after the fall of the imperial Ottoman regime. It was doubly "profitable" to Kemal and his new government since it destroyed the military and economic force of the Greek male population, all while utilizing the very last strengths and abilities of the Greek conscripts to build much of the material base and infrastructure of Turkey. As one Greek physician in the Turkish military service observed:

> I shall only describe here what I observed during my four-year military service [in the Ottoman armies]. I covered Anatolia from Erzerum to Kaiseri and from Kaiseri to Baku! I am bound to note here that the great highway from Erzerum to Ulukishla, with all its crossroads, were built during this war and they were built exclusively by Greek hands, that is by the (Greek) conscripts of the *amele taburu* [labor battalions] who labored and who died under the well-known circumstances.[13]

The testimony of Eleni Karipoglu concerning the final phase of the destruction of much of Bafra's Greek community by the Kemalist forces also contains a description of her sixty-day flight, along with women and children, in the snow-laden mountains toward Tokat. It is similar to the account of Venezis on Mt. Sipylon: "During this march we encountered thousands of corpses, some were frozen, and others had been killed, all surrounded by wild dogs which were eating the corpses."[14]

The pairing of the lethal but constructive labor of the Greek male conscripts with their death out of which the material foundations of the modern Turkish republic were often created calls to mind a medieval anecdote from the life of the famous Persian mystic Jalal al-Din Rumi, who lived in thirteenth-century Konia among Turks, Persians, Greeks, Armenians, and Jews with whom he had close relations. The anecdote is related by the fourteenth-century Mevlevi dervish biographer of Rumi and his successors as heads of the dervish order. On seeing that his friend Salah al-Din Zarqubi had hired Turkish workers to build and create a garden, Rumi chided Zarqubi, stating that for works of construction he should hire Greek workers; for work of demolition he should hire Turkish workers, as Allah had endowed the former with strength and stamina to build and had created the latter with the power to destroy. Though this is a myth of sorts, in the case of the situation in Anatolia during World War I and in the Greco-Turkish war, the Turks certainly destroyed the homes of their Greek neighbors, while the conscripted Greek labor battalions proved essential for the building of public works for the Turkish government.[15]

Notes

1. Taner Akçam, *From Empire to Republic: Turkish Nationalism & the Armenian Genocide* (London and New York: Zed Books, 2004), pp. 143-149, and more generally the entirety of chapter 4, "The Homogenizing and Ethnic Cleansing of Anatolia," pp. 115-156. For the collapse of the Greek front in western Asia Minor, see *Istoria tou ellenikou ethncus*, vol. 15, *Neoteros Ellenismos apo to 1913 os to 1941* (Athens: Ekdotike Athenon, 1998), pp. 98-247.
2. Speros Vryonis, Jr., *The Mechanism of Catastrophe: The Turkish Pogrom of September 6-7, 1955, and the Destruction of the Greek Community of Istanbul* (New York: Greekworks.com, 2005), p. 33. Alexis Alexandris, *The Greek Minority of Istanbul and Greek-Turkish Relations* 1918-1974 (Athens: Centre of Asia Minor Studies, 2003), pp. 213-214.
3. All that follows in the first part of this study has to do with labor battalions in western Asia Minor as they appear in the book of Elias Venezis, *To noumero 31.328: To vivlio tes skiavias,* 41st ed. (Athens: Vivliopleion tes Etias, 2000). The translations are my own.
4. Konstantinos Photiades, *E genoktonia ton Ellenon tou Pontou,* 14 vols. (Thessaloniki: Herodotus, 2002-2005).
5. For the detailed history of the region during this period, see Photiades, *E genoktonia ton Ellenon tou Pontou*, vols. 1-2. Volumes 4-14 contain a massive and rich collection of important archival documents.
6. Ibid., vol. 1, pp. 548-549 and note 415.
7. Ibid., p. 569.
8. Ibid., vol. 4, p. 169.

9. Antonios I. Gavrielides, *Seledes ek mauri ethniki symphora tou Pontou* (Athens: Eleuthere Skepsis, 2002), pp. 9ff.
10. Photiades, *E genoktonia ton Ellenon tou*, vol. 4, p. 237.
11. Ibid., p. 345.
12. Ibid., vol. 4, p. 564.
13. Ibid, vol. 1, pp. 565-566.
14. Ibid, vol. 6, p. 638.
15. This narrative is preserved in the fourteenth-century author Shams al-Din Ahmad al-Aflaki, *Manaqib al-Arif in*, ed. Tahsin Yazıcı (Ankara: Türk Tarih Kurumu Basimevi, 1980), vol. 2, p. 721. For translations:, see John O'Kane, *The Feats of the Knowers of God* (Leiden and Boston: Brill, 2002), pp. 502-503; Tahsin Yazıcı, ed., *Ahmet Eflaki, Ariflerin Menkıbeleri* (Istanbul: Hürriyet Yayınları, 1973), vol. 2, p. 153; Claude Hurat, *Les saints des derviches tourneur* (Paris: Editions Ernest Leroux, 1922), vol. 11, pp. 208-209.

17

Comparative Aspects of the Armenian and Jewish Cases of Genocide

Tigran Matosyan

Destruction of the Armenians in World War I became an ominous harbinger of other cases of mass killings in the twentieth century. The Jewish Holocaust less than three decades after the Armenian Genocide made it obvious that the crime has been perpetuated with impunity. The wholesale elimination of the Armenians, Jews, and other victim peoples also became a call for scholars in different scientific disciplines to undertake comparative research, with the primary objective to understand the motivations and preconditions of genocide. In particular, comparative studies of the Armenian and Jewish tragedies by a number of scholars such as Vahakn Dadrian[1] and Robert Melson[2] have proved to be important contributions in this endeavor. It goes without saying that both the Armenian Genocide and the Holocaust are unique, since each of these events was shaped by specific socio-political, cultural, geographical, international, and time factors. Taking into account these differences, it is also essential to bear in mind that comparative research is nonetheless useful and productive. Discovering similarities is especially important when one comes to recognize their analogous social determinants. In other words, by showing the similar features and by underscoring their universal roots, a basis is laid for a better understanding of the phenomenon of genocide. Better understanding, in turn, is a crucial precondition for predicting and eliminating this scourge of human society.

It has been stated frequently that one of the important common characteristics of the Armenian Genocide and the Holocaust is a long prehistory of victimization. The Armenians and Jews were ethnic and religious minorities, respectively, in the Ottoman Empire and in Europe. Their long-standing inferior status directly contributed to a range of negative consequences, including social oppression, pogroms, and massacres. It was natural that during both World War I and World War II, the perpetrators made use of the ominous legacy of anti-Armenian and anti-Jewish attitudes. Besides this fact, both the Armenians and Jews, in the long course of adaptation to the challenges of the dominant societies, had to construct special patterns of social behavior in order to avert or minimize the dangers threatening their societies. It is interesting—and also natural—that during the Armenian and Jewish calamities those patterns were to resurface by the force of historical necessity.

Prominent Holocaust scholar Raoul Hilberg in his *The Destruction of the European Jews* discusses the main collective behavior patterns of European Jewry before the Holocaust, in the meantime observing how these patterns were repeated during the war.[3] Hilberg's model of comparison can be applied effectively to the Armenian case. Moreover, the nexus between the social behavior patterns showed by the Armenians before and during their genocide becomes more understandable in the light of the Jewish experience.

The protection payments, bribes, and gifts given by Armenian and Jewish community leaders to their rulers through the centuries is a prime and recurring example. In order to stop the bloodshed of the Jews in Franconia in 1384, the Jewish community collected and paid 80,000 guilders to the representatives of the German king Wenzel; only then did the massacre cease.[4] As another example, in 1705, the judge of Bakhesh decreed that the children of the Christians converted to Islam must also become Muslims. However, the Armenian community's bribe of 700 *khurush* brought a swift rescinding of the decision.[5] It is not surprising that this kind of behavior surfaced during both genocides. Two examples personify these historical parallels. First, in order to delay the deportation of the Jews from Slovakia in 1942, the Jewish Relief Committee of Bratislava collected and paid $50,000 to SS official Dieter Wisliceny.[6] Similarly, receiving the order of deportation in 1915, the Armenians of Tokat paid a bribe of 1,600 Ottoman golden coins to the district governor (*mutasarrif*) in order to delay their deportation.[7]

In the past, Armenian and Jewish communities also resorted to the practice of applications and petitions to domestic and international powers. This more passive form of problem resolution was not as effective as ransom payments or bribery and often triggered negative reactions from dominant societies. However, this behavior also recurred during the Armenian and Jewish catastrophes. The examples are telling: in September 1942, some 350 Jews in Sofia, Bulgaria, rallied before the ministry of foreign affairs to petition for a postponement of their deportation.[8] When the deportation of the Armenians from areas near Aleppo started at the beginning of 1916, the Deportations Committee of the province had already received some 10,000 petitions from prospective Armenian deportees not to be displaced.[9]

Needless to say, the behavior of protection payments and petitions during the Armenian and Jewish genocides contributed negligibly at best to the salvation of the victimized communities. The victims were essentially left with few options: to resist, to flee, or to conform. Except for several cases of desperate self-defense (as at Musa Dagh or in the Warsaw ghetto) and individual examples of flight, the Armenian and Jewish communities chose to conform. As in the past, such behavior was a means of escaping physical destruction. The genocidal drive of the Turkish and German authorities during the two world wars, however, rendered even this mechanism ineffective and led to fatal consequences.

The probability of an armed resistance and self-defense in the face of total extermination is contingent not only upon a victim's previous experiences but also on the attendant domestic and international conditions. Central to the understanding of the main factors of the Armenian Genocide and the Holocaust is the notion that these two crimes were committed under the cover of world conflicts. The calculations of the perpetrators regrettably proved to be accurate: in each case, the international situation caused by a global war was to minimize any real possibility of foreign intervention. It is not surprising that the Ittihadists and the Nazis instantly grasped this rare "opportunity." Turkish and German leaders are reported to have spoken of the necessity to exploit the state of war. A collection of documents published in 1919 by Dr. Johannes Lepsius contains German Ambassador Hans von Wangenheim's report (Constantinople, June 17, 1915) to Chancellor Theobold von Bethmann-Hollweg on this subject: "Recently, Minister of Interior Talaat Bey has unequivocally stated to Dr. Mordtmann—who currently works at the Imperial Embassy—that the Turkish government wishes to take advantage of the war and completely settle the scores with its domestic enemies (local Christians), without having any disturbing diplomatic intervention on the part of foreign states."[10]

Rudolf Höss, the first commandant of the Auschwitz concentration camp, told the Nuremberg tribunal that in the summer of 1941 he was summoned to Berlin to be given the verbal orders of Adolf Hitler: "Himmler told me something to the effect—I do not remember the exact words—that the Führer had given the order for a final solution of the Jewish question. We, the SS, must carry out that order. If it is not carried out now, at this given time, then the Jews will later on destroy the German people."[11] That the expression "at this given time" should be more precisely understood as "under the cover of war" is quite logical; and that the war was closely interrelated in Adolf Hitler's worldview with clandestine criminal activity is corroborated by another fact. Already in 1935, six years before embarking on the extermination phase of the Final Solution, Hitler, analogous to Talaat's thinking, told a top Nazi medical officer that in case of war he would realize the plans of "euthanasia" since then such a program could be carried out more easily, and the general upheaval would not allow for public opposition take place.[12]

As a matter of fact, the impossibility of intervening was also felt by the active participants in the two wars who at given moments might have been considered potential saviors of the victimized groups. The Entente governments

(Great Britain, France, Russia) on May 24, 1915, took the unprecedented step of condemning the Turkish crimes against humanity and civilization. The authors of the statement made it clear that they were cognizant of the ongoing persecutions against the Armenian population, and gave notice that the members of the Turkish government and their agents involved in the massacres would be held responsible.[13] On October 30, 1943, the anti-Fascist coalition, headed by the Soviet Union, the United States, and Great Britain, made a similar statement based on information of the continuing mass destruction in Eastern Europe. Very much like the warning in 1915, the Moscow Declaration stated that the officials responsible for the barbarities would be personally tried and punished.[14] It is interesting to note that, besides these manifest messages, the two statements contained one latent meaning, that is, their authors could take no real measures at the time to relieve the victimized peoples.

The impossibility of intervening on behalf of the victims should be more precisely called relative impossibility. Historical data relating both to the Armenian Genocide and to the Holocaust show that there were moments when the Entente powers in World War I or the states of the anti-Fascist coalition in World War II were in position to extend a saving hand to the targeted peoples. Military objectives, however, took precedence over the cause of salvation. Contrary to the expectations of the Armenian leaders, the sudden and unexpected withdrawal of Russian troops from the city of Van in July 1915 (which they had liberated two months earlier) claimed additional tens of thousands of Armenian lives. The disinclination and refusal of the British and American military commanders to bomb the railway routes to Auschwitz and to stop further transportation of the Hungarian Jews to the death camp in the spring of 1944 can also be considered an example of prioritizing of military interests over humanitarian considerations.[15]

The conditions emerging from war influenced the genocidal process in other ways as well. In particular, the war economy dictated that the perpetrators satisfy the general needs and atmosphere of warfare, in other words, to make the genocide as effective as possible. First and foremost, this effectiveness was reflected in the killing methods applied by the Ittihadists and Nazis. Different as they were (because of an enormous economic and technological gap between Turkey and Germany in the respective periods), these methods shared one common and decisive feature—aspiration to maximum efficiency.

The fact that the use of bullets in the course of the Armenian Genocide was thrifty and that the perpetrators resorted to other killing methods—such as clubs, knives, daggers, and swords and by drowning, forced marches, starvation, exposure, and diseases—is the best example of this aspiration. The memoirs of U.S. Ambassador Henry Morgenthau attest to these objectives:

> At Angora all Armenian men from fifteen to seventy were arrested, bound together in groups of four, and sent on the road in the direction of Caesarea. When they

> had traveled five or six hours and had reached a secluded valley, a mob of Turkish peasants fell upon them with clubs, hammers, axes, scythes, spades, and saws. Such instruments not only caused more agonizing deaths than guns and pistols, but, as the Turks themselves boasted, they were more economical, since they didn't involve the waste of powder and shell.[16]

The introduction of gas chambers at the beginning of 1942 to replace the mass shootings demonstrates the importance of the efficiency principle for the Nazis.

The inclination of the Ittihadists and Nazis to kill a maximum number of people with the expenditure of minimum resources sometimes resulted in similar and even identical ways of action. For instance, the local organizers of the annihilation in Turkey frequently made crude use of the practice of suffocation, adopted later in the Nazi gas chambers. Arab lawyer Faiz el-Ghusein, a witness to the scenes of massacres in Turkey, was told a typical murder story by a Turkish officer: "In the province of Bitlis the authorities collected the Armenians in the barns full of straw (or chaff), piling up straw in front of the door and setting it on fire so that the Armenians inside perished in the smoke." According to the same source, sometimes hundreds were put together in one barn.[17] Another conspicuous example occurred in the vicinity of Deir el-Zor. Another witness, Aram Andonian (Antonyan), wrote that during the massacres in 1916 some 1,500 Armenian orphans were handed over to a local official named Ahmad Bey. He placed a part of these children in a cave, at the entrance of which he put wet hay, and set it on fire. The children died from suffocation.[18]

The Nazis, parallel to their modernized killing techniques, periodically resorted to some "antiquated" forms of murder. One such method, mass drowning, was repeatedly carried out against the Armenians throughout Turkey in 1915-16. Materials from the Nuremberg trials show that during the occupation of the Crimea the Nazis placed more than 100,000 people on rafts, took them out on the Black Sea, and dumped them to drown.[19] The Nazis also applied this "effective" method at the end of the war when an urgent necessity arose to conceal the evidence of committed crimes. In the first months of 1945, the inmates of the Neuengamme concentration camp were loaded onto two ships, taken out on the North Sea, and drowned.[20]

Unlike the Ittihadist *modus operandi,* application of antiquated forms of murder in the Nazi case was an exception to the general rules; as a matter of fact, it was quite spontaneous and contingent upon circumstances. The best way to exemplify this spontaneity is perhaps to consider the following example. During one of the killing operations in the city of Kursk, SS soldiers ran out of bullets; thereafter they were ordered to kill the remaining twenty-five victims "with gun-butts, spades, and other objects."[21]

The magnitude of dependence upon relatively simple killing means was high especially at times when the murder of the Jews was left to collaborators. Romanian forces, for example, did not possess the same technological advances of

Nazi Germany. Hence, like the Young Turks, they had to devise an extermination program in terms of the possibilities and "tools" at hand. It is not surprising that one can find a number of specific similarities in the killing techniques applied against the Armenians in 1915 and against the Jews in the Romanian realm during World War II. One of the common methods implemented by Turkish and Romanian forces was murder by starvation and dehydration, which in the following illustrations took on a form of outright rather than prolonged killing. The Arab lawyer el-Ghusein was told by a witness that "the Diarbekir authorities had killed the Armenians either by shooting, by butchery, or at times by putting numbers of them in wells or caves which were then blocked up so that they perished."[22] At the end of June 1941, thousands of Jews living in the Moldavian town of Jassy were sealed into a "death train," with no definite destination, "on the assumption that its already beaten-up occupants, crammed by the hundreds into closed cattle wagons, would without water and in high summer temperatures, asphyxiate to death."[23] In another case, 4,000 Jews in the camp at Acmecetca (Golta prefecture in Transnistria) were cordoned off from their surroundings and exterminated by hunger.[24]

The aspiration to efficiency played an active role not only in the killing process but also in the total plunder and appropriation of the victims' property. Having been deprived of all valuable belongings, the Armenians and Jews were often stripped of their clothes, and their gold teeth were pulled out before or after their murder. The following analogous examples show clearly the level of meticulousness of the perpetrators bent on making murder as profitable as possible. During his inspection trips around Lake Goljuk, Leslie Davis, the American consul at Kharpert (Harput), frequently saw burned bodies of Armenian victims. At first, he thought that this had been done as a sanitary measure, but subsequently he learned that the Kurds had burned these bodies in order to find any gold that the people may have swallowed.[25]

To draw a parallel, one need only to refer to the special procedure at Auschwitz. According to witness testimony, responsible persons appointed from the ranks of the inmates had to examine the ashes of the gassed victims outside the crematoria to find valuables.[26] This practice was common also at the sites of mass shootings such as Babi Yar in the vicinity of Kiev. Here the bodies were burned, and the ashes put through metallic sieves "in which the Germans were collecting the remains of golden teeth and other things like rings, etc."[27]

It is typical that in both cases a world war conditioned, among other things, the essence of anti-Armenian and anti-Jewish propaganda aimed at presenting the victim peoples as internal enemies and justifying their destruction. Besides this general line of accusation, the anti-Armenian and anti-Jewish propaganda was intended for consumption by the immediate participants in the mass killings. The authors of the genocides were keen on inspiring the killers and persuading them of the justness and necessity of their cause. Especially interesting are the similar methods of motivating the murder of the Armenian and Jewish children.

In both cases, the emphasis was placed on the idea of the thirst for revenge that the children of those being killed would have in the future. This provided a kind of psychological rationalization for the murderers, at the same time making them inordinately merciless. Examples are again telling. The chief organizer of the mass murder of the deported Armenians in Deir el-Zor, Zeki Bey, would often kill the Armenian children with his own hands, telling the underlings that even the newborn Armenians were guilty: "Don't think that I have killed an innocent being. Even the newborn babes of this people are criminals, for they will carry the seeds of vengeance in themselves. If you wish to ensure tomorrow, kill even their children."[28]

One of the former commanders of *Einsatzgruppe C*, Ervin Schulz, whose soldiers were carrying out mass shootings in the territory of the Ukraine, told the International Tribunal in Nuremberg that the *Einsatzgruppen* commanders had been given orders by Heinrich Himmler and Reinhard Heydrich, organizers of the extermination measures, to the effect that all Jews, including women and children, should be destroyed, lest they become avengers.[29] This way of motivation goes beyond the frames of the Armenian Genocide and the Holocaust. Its universality can be seen in some other cases of mass murder. For instance, the Rwandan Genocide of 1994 was also characterized by strong propaganda against the victims. The "Radio Television des Milles Collines," a Hutu station owned by relatives of President Juvenal Habyarinama, played a considerable role in preparing the massacres of the Tutsi population. The station used a propaganda mechanism that underscored the necessity to prevent today's children from becoming potential adult avengers. Consequently, one of the appeals of the station, urging the elimination of Tutsi children, went as follows: "We will not repeat the mistake of 1959. The children must be killed too."[30]

As noted, the Armenians and Jews had to resort to historically developed forms of social behavior in an attempt to avoid extermination. It was not only the victims, however, who were looking to the past experiences; the perpetrators themselves were making use of the rich heritage of previous anti-Armenian and anti-Jewish persecutions. In particular, this became clear in the Nazi and Ittihadist genocide propaganda that was characterized (especially in the Ittihadist case) by exploitation of the religious factor. Although the Young Turks and the Nazis, as pointed out by Christopher Walker, "despised conventional religion,"[31] they did not refrain from reviving old Muslim and Christian stereotypes and hatred against the prospective victims. In so doing, the authorities attempted to convert neighbors of the Armenians and Jews either into direct participants in murder or into passive or sympathetic bystanders.

In the case of the Armenian Genocide, the Young Turks harkened back to the concept of Holy War. By declaring *jihad* in November 1914, the Turkish government intended to channel Muslim religious sentiments not only against the Christian powers but also against the "disloyal infidels" within the Ottoman state. To understand how successful this propaganda technique was in

1915-16, one should turn to survivor accounts and memoirs that describe the Turkish and Kurdish mobs attacking Armenian caravans with shouts and cries of "Allah" and "jihad."[32]

The authors of the Jewish destruction were seeking support from the Christian populations of Eastern Europe in a similar mode—by reviving old anti-Jewish stereotypes or accusations of religious coloring. "Blood-libel," for instance, had been one of the most popular pretexts for persecutions and violence against the Jews. The top Nazi officials also calculated the possible benefits of rekindling this myth in the process of the Final Solution, as demonstrated in a letter of Heinrich Himmler to Ernst Kaltenbrunner, head of the security police:

> I have ordered a large number of the book, *The Jewish Ritual Murders*. . . . I am sending you 100 copies to distribute them among your *Einsatzgruppen* and, first of all, among people dealing with the Jewish question. . . . In general, the problem of the ritual murders should be investigated by experts in Romania, Hungary, and Bulgaria. I think then it can go to press, thereby making the expulsion of the Jews from these countries easier.[33]

Along with these similarities, the propaganda of both Ittihadists and Nazis was closely intertwined with the political ideologies of the Turkish and German ruling elites—Turkism and Pan-Turkism in the case of the Young Turks, and National Socialism in the case of the Nazis. These were skillfully employed not only to support the war effort but also to "substantiate" the extermination of the targeted peoples.

A cursory comparison of Pan-Turkism with National Socialism reveals that the ideas of Turkish nationalism had common features with Nazi nationalism, and that the Ittihadist ideas of territorial expansion or "Turanism" were parallel with the views of Nazi Pan-Germanism or *Lebensraum*. Looking closer, it becomes evident that there were even similarities in the respective racism of the Nazis and the Ittihadists (the early Pan-Turkist intellectuals considered Arthur de Gobineau to be one of their spiritual fathers[34]). Pan-Turkism contained some rudimentary forms of racist ideas that later became the main ideological weapon of the Nazis. To be more precise, the Young Turks and the Nazis shared a fascination with Social Darwinism, first applied to the Armenians and then to the Jews. Adherence of the Nazi leaders to the distorted theories of "natural selection" and "survival of the fittest" is apparent from their writings and speeches designed for propaganda. A case in point is a speech of Heinrich Himmler in Minsk. Immediately after a mass execution of Jews, the Reichsführer SS told the soldiers of *Einsatzgruppe B* to look at nature. In his opinion, combat was taking place everywhere, not only among human beings but also in the world of animals and plants; and whoever was too exhausted to battle had to disappear.[35]

In the written materials relating to the Armenian Genocide, there is scarce but convincing information on the Ittihadist inclination toward the ideas of

Social Darwinism. The spiritual leader of the Trebizond diocese, Archbishop Hovhannes (Jean) Naslian, noted in his memoirs that the official daily newspaper of the Ittihadist party, *Hilalı Ahmet*, was propagating ideas in a false scientific guise. For instance, one could read, "according to the laws of nature, inferior races should become food for superior ones."[36] If one gives credence to Mevlan Zade Rifat, his account also contains passages in which Ittihadist leaders reiterate these ideas. During a special meeting of the party's central committee before the Armenian Genocide, for example, Dr. Nazim, one of the masterminds of the annihilation, allegedly made analogous statements: "All animals and plants eat each other and prolong their lives by reciprocal destruction."[37]

Along with drawing historical parallels between the Armenian Genocide and the Jewish Holocaust, this comparative analysis perhaps supports the notion that social determinants of "universal" character (such as long-lasting minority-majority conflicts, total war, ideology) have a force in directing similar human action in various socio-historical contexts and situations. The realization of this interconnection becomes more important when the process of comparison is used for practical ends. Theoretical generalizations derived in the course of juxtaposition—in which are included other cases of genocide and mass destruction—may help to establish a unique methodological prism through which modern intergroup conflicts can be examined. Coupled with the good will and efforts of appropriate international organizations, the scholarly results can play an important role in predicting and preventing a conflict from escalating into wholesale extermination.

Notes

1. See the following representative interpretations by V. N. Dadrian: "The Historical and Legal Interconnections between the Armenian Genocide and the Jewish Holocaust: From Impunity to Retributive Justice," *Yale Journal of International Law* 23, 2 (1998): 503-559; "The Comparative Aspects of the Armenian and Jewish Cases of Genocide: A Sociohistorical Perspective," in *Is the Holocaust Unique? Perspectives on Comparative Genocide*, ed. Alan S. Rosenbaum (Boulder, CO: Westview Press, 1996), pp. 101-135; "The Convergent Aspects of the Armenian and Jewish Cases of Genocide. A Reinterpretation of the Concept of Holocaust," *Holocaust and Genocide Studies* 3, 2 (1988): 151-169.
2. See the following interpretative works by Robert Melson: *Revolution and Genocide: On the Origins of the Armenian Genocide and the Holocaust* (Chicago: University of Chicago Press, 1992); *On the Uniqueness and Comparability of the Holocaust: A Comparison with the Armenian Genocide* (Macquarie University, Sydney, Australia: Center for Comparative Genocide Studies, 1996).
3. Raoul Hilberg, *The Destruction of the European Jews* (Chicago: Quadrangle Books, 1967), pp. 14-17.
4. Ibid., p.15.
5. Manvel Zulalyan, *Arevmtian Hayastane XVI-XVIII dd.* [Western Armenia in the 16th -18th Centuries] (Erevan: Armenian Academy of Sciences, 1980), p. 75.
6. Hannah Arendt, *Eichmann in Jerusalem. A Report on the Banality of Evil* (New York: Viking Press, 1963), p. 144.

7. *Haikakan Jardere: Tokt. Iohannes Lepsiusi teghekagire* [Armenian Massacres: Dr. Johannes Lepsius' Report] (Beirut: Aztag, 1965), p. 68.
8. Hilberg, *Destruction of the European Jews,* p. 481.
9. *The Memoirs of Naim Bey: Turkish Official Documents Relating to the Deportations and Massacre of Armenians*, comp. Aram Andonian (London: Hodder and Stoughton, 1920), p. 40.
10. Johannes Lepsius, *Deutschland und Armenien 1914-1918: Sammlung Diplomatischer Aktenstücke* (1919; repr., Bremen: Donat und Temmen Verlag, 1986), p. 84.
11. *Niurnbergskii protsess nad glavnymi nemetskimi voiennymi prestupnikami: Sbornik materialov v semi tomakh* [The Nuremberg Trial of the Main German War Criminals. Collection of Materials in 7 Volumes], R. A. Rudenko, ed., vol. 4 (Moscow: Gosizdat Jurid., 1959), p. 418.
12. Lucy Dawidowicz, *The War against the Jews, 1933-1945* (New York: Bantam Books, 1986), p. 92.
13. *The Armenian Genocide. Documentation*, vol. 1 (Munich: Institut für Armenische Fragen, 1987), p. 306.
14. *Vneshniaia politika Sovetskogo Soiuza v period Otechestvennoi voiny: Sb. materialov i dokumentov* [Foreign Policy of the Soviet Union during the Patriotic War: Collection of Materials and Documents] (Moscow: Gosizdat Polit. Liter., 1946), pp. 418-419.
15. See David S. Wyman, "Why Auschwitz Wasn't Bombed," in *Anatomy of the Auschwitz Death Camp*, ed. Yisrael Gutman and Michael Berenbaum (Bloomington and Indianapolis: Indiana University Press, 1994), pp. 569-577.
16. Henry Morgenthau, *Ambassador Morgenthau's Story* (New York: Doubleday, Page, 1918), p. 312.
17. Faiz el-Ghusein, *Martyred Armenia* (repr., New York: Tankian Publishing Corp., 1975), p. 41.
18. Aram Antonyan, *Mets vochire. Haykakan verjin kotoratsnere ev Taleat Pasha* [The Great Crime. The Recent Armenian Massacres and Talaat Pasha] (Erevan: Arevik, 1990), p. 199.
19. See *Niurnbergskii protsess: Sbornik materialov v 8-mi tomakh* [The Nuremberg Trial: Collection of Materials in 8 Volumes], A. M. Rekunkov, ed., vol. 1 (Moscow: Jurid. Lit., 1987), p. 299.
20. In this and aforementioned cases of mass drowning, the nationality of victims was not mentioned. See *SS v deistvii: Dokumenty o prestupleniiakh SS* [SS in Action: Documents on the Crimes Committed by the SS], M. Iu. Raginskiy, ed. (Moscow: Progress, 1969), p. 317.
21. *Sudebnyi protsess o zverstvakh nemetsko-fashistskikh zakhvatchikov na territorii goroda Khar'kova i Khar'kovskoi oblasti v period ikh vremennoi okkupatsii* [Trial Relating to the Barbarities of the German-Fascist Occupants in the City of Kharkov and in the Kharkov Region during the Period of Its Temporary Occupation] (Moscow: Gospolitizdat, 1943), p. 68.
22. el-Ghusein, *Martyred Armenia*, p. 42.
23. Mark Levene, "The Experience of Genocide: Armenia 1915-16 and Romania 1941-42," in *The Amenian Genocide and the Shoah*, ed. Hans-Lukas Kieser and Dominic J. Schaller (Zurich: Chronos Verlag, 2002), p. 442.
24. Ibid., p. 454.
25. Leslie A. Davis, *The Slaughterhouse Province: An American Diplomat's Report on the Armenian Genocide, 1915-1917* (New Rochelle, NY: Aristide D. Caratzas, 1989), p. 80.

26. William Shirer, *The Rise and Fall of the Third Reich* (New York: Crest Books, 1960), p. 1267.
27. *Babyi Yar . . . chelovek, vlast', istoriia: Dokumenty i materialy v 5 knigakh* [Babi Yar . . . Man, Power, History: Documents and Materials in 5 Books], T. Evstafeyeva and V. Nakhmanovich, eds., Book 1 (Kiev: Vneshtorgizdat Ukraini, 2004), p. 225. A new dimension is added to this "meticulousness" by the following illustrations. Leslie Davis, *Slaughterhouse Province*, p. 83, noted in his account that nearly all bodies of the women he saw "lay flat on their backs and showed signs of barbarous mutilation by the bayonets of the gendarmes." The editor of the volume, Susan K. Blair, adds (p. 138, note 64) that "the Armenian women either hid, or were believed to hide, money in their vaginal orifice, according to an Armenian woman from Ordu . . . who related this detail to Dr. Ruth Parmalee of the Harput mission." Examples of the checking of dead women's bodies can also be found in accounts of other Armenian survivors. See, for example, Karapet Gabikian [Garabed Kapikian], *Eghernapatum Pokun Hayots ev norin metsi mayrakakhaki Sebastioy* [History of the Calamity of Armenia Minor and Its Great Capital Sebastia] (Boston: Hairenik, 1924), p. 145. The following quotation relating to the Belzec camp, from Richard Grunberger's *Hitler's SS* (London: Ebenezer Beyl & Son, 1970), p. 84, will suffice to recognize this universal feature of mass destruction: "At the end of another 32 minutes all were dead. . . . Some Jewish workers on the far side opened the wooden doors. . . . A couple of dozen workers checked the mouths of the dead, which they tore open with iron hooks. Other workers inspected anus and genital organs in search of money, diamonds, gold; dentists moved around hammering out gold teeth, bridges and crowns."
28. Andonian, *Memoirs of Naim Bey,* p. 46.
29. Yuri Schulmeister, *Gitlerizm v istorii evreev* [Hitlerism in the History of the Jews] (Kiev: Politizdat, 1990), p. 73. Alfred Streim, one of Germany's leading prosecutors of Nazi crimes, writes that "working through hundreds of interrogations produced in the proceedings against former members of the *Einsatzgruppen*," he could classify their answers and testimonies into several categories. One of them included assertions that sounded as follows: "Only several weeks after the invasion of the Soviet Union was the order issued to shoot all Jews, even Jewish women and children, 'so that no avengers can grow up'; this was the justification sometimes offered for this order." See Alfred Streim, "The Tasks of the SS Einsatzgruppen," trans. Henry Friedlander and Martha Humphreys, www.motlc.wiesenthal.com/resources/books/annual4/chap09.html.
30. Jonathan Glover, *Humanity: A Moral History of the Twentieth Century* (New Haven, CT: Yale University Press, 2000), p. 122. Another relevant example is what happened in Vietnam. On March 16, 1968, 120 American infantrymen, under the command of Captain Ernest Medina, organized the massacre of Vietnamese civilians in the village of My Lai while they were searching for a Vietcong battalion. Nearly 500 villagers were killed in four hours, including old men, women, and children. Before the attack, the soldiers were given instructions by Lieutenant William Calley, who described the villagers as enemy supporters, adding that "men had weapons, women carried packs, and the children were future Vietcong." Ibid., p. 58.
31. Christopher J. Walker, *Armenia: The Survival of a Nation* (London: Croom Helm, 1980), p. 191.
32. Grigoris Palakian (Krikoris Balakian), a witness to and survivor of the Armenian Genocide, writes in his memoirs that on the road of deportation he had a conversation with Captain Shukri, one of the organizers of the massacres at Yozgat. In response to Palakian's question of whether he felt remorse for his deeds, the

captain replied that he was participating in the Holy War, and it was not a crime to kill people during such a war. See Grigoris Palakian [Krikoris Balakian], *Hay Goghgotan: Drvagner hay martirosagrutenen* [The Armenian Calvary: Episodes from the Armenian Martyrdom] (repr., Erevan: Hayastan, 1991), p. 217.

33. *SS v deistvii,* pp. 227-228.
34. Taner Akçam, *Turetskoie natsional'noie "ia" i armianskii vopros* [The Turkish National "I" and the Armenian Question] (Moscow: Ario-Niks, 1995), p. 26. Ittihadist racism should not be equated with or understood in terms of the Nazi racism. By comparison, Ittihadist racial concepts were far less developed and did not view the Armenians as enemies based on race in the way that Nazism held the Jews and other peoples. See Melson, *Revolution and Genocide*, pp. 250-251.
35. Hilberg, *Destruction of the European Jews*, p. 219.
36. *Trapizoni temin vichakavor Hovhannes Ark. Nazliani hushere Merdzavor Arevelki 1914-1918 shrjani kakhakakan-kronakan depkerun masin* [Memoirs of the Prelate of the Diocese of Trebizond, Archbishop Hovhannes Nazlian, about the Political-Religious Events in the Middle East in the Period of 1914-1918], trans. H. Stepanian, vol. 1 (Beirut: Armenian Catholic Publishers, 1960), p. 11.
37. Mevlan Zade Rifat, *Osmanyan heghapokhutyan mut tsalkere ev Ittihati hayajinj dzragrere* [The Obscure Folds of the Ottoman Revolution and the Ittihad's Plans for Extermination of the Armenians] (Erevan: "KPH," 1990), p. 98.

18

The Armenian Genocide in the Syrian Press

Nora Arissian

The Syrian press is an extremely valuable unexplored source for study of the Armenian Genocide. There are hundreds of descriptions of the deportations and massacres, statistical data, testimonies, and analyses. As this is a new field, it is appropriate here to cast some light on these publications. This brief discussion is based on a much larger study that examines thirty Arabic newspapers and political journals. These point to an assignation of blame and try to give explanations.

While news of the Armenian deportations and persecutions appeared in the newspapers and periodicals of many countries, the Syrian press benefited uniquely from the region's location within the Ottoman Empire. Thus, Syrian dailies, periodicals, and other publications had greater access to relevant sources and bore actual witness to developments affecting the Armenians of the empire. When considering that Syria was under Turkish rule and subject to press censorship during the period of the Armenian Genocide, it is all the more remarkable that the Syrian news media described the Turkish massacres and deportations of Armenians so poignantly and in such an uncompromising fashion.

The Syrian press laid responsibility for the genocide on the commitment of the Young Turks to the ideology of Pan-Turkism and the preexisting general disdain for Armenians in Turkish society. It is significant that the articles used strong terms such as "extermination," "annihilation," and "uprooting of the race" and even the equivalent of the word "genocide." Various accounts and testimonies relating to the nature of the deportations and massacres were given. In these, German officials and soldiers were identified as playing a complicit role. The press also considered the impact of the Armenian Genocide on the Ottoman Arab population as it reported on the massacres, expulsions, and ultimate resettlement of the Armenian deportees and survivors in the Arab provinces.

It is remarkable that the Syrian press perceptively assessed the difference between the persecutions of the consecutive Hamidian and Young Turks regimes. In its opinion, the motivating factor in Sultan Abdul Hamid's policies of massacre, exile, and suppression of human rights was not primarily hatred toward the non-Turkish races but rather an attempt to retain firm Ottoman authority in a crumbling empire. The genocidal policies of the Young Turk or Ittihad party, on the other hand, were premeditated. The newspapers expressed anxiety that these policies would transform into Turkish intolerance and fanaticism toward all other peoples of the empire regardless of religion. Even before the outbreak of World War I, the Damascus daily *Al-Kabas* (The Torch) reported on January 13, 1914 that rumors of impending massacres were terrorizing the Armenian population, some of whom consequently were abandoning their homes and properties.

The independent weekly *Al-Kalam al-Hadidi* (The Iron Pen), published since 1913 in Sao Paulo, Brazil, by George Haddad, attributed the Ittihadist government's unwillingness to espouse egalitarianism to its Pan-Turkic ideology and policy of Turkification, which envisioned an ethno-religiously homogenous nation to be achieved through forced conversion, expulsion, and extermination of non-Turkic entities. In the issue of August 3, 1915, Haddad described the horrible scenes of massacres and lamented that once again ignorance and foolishness were the causes of another calamity in history. On March 1, 1916, the paper reported that the purpose of establishing the Turk Ojakh (Hearth) Union was to advance the Turkish language by eliminating all other languages in the Ottoman Empire and to engineer the "extermination" of the non-Turkish speaking nations under Ottoman dominion. On June 1 of that year, the newspaper wrote that starvation was a method utilized to kill the Armenian deportees gradually and was responsible for thousands of Armenian deaths in Lebanon and Syria. It further asserted that such a technique was implemented in accordance with the Turkish government's policy of ethno-religious extermination. A few months later, on January 26, 1917, it warned that the policy of the Young Turks was to subject the Arab nation (*al-umma*) to the same extreme measures already perpetrated against the Armenians.

The independent Paris weekly *Al-Mustakbal* (The Future), in its May 26, 1916 issue, attributed direct responsibility for the Armenian Genocide to orders given by Minister of War Enver Pasha and generally by Ittihad party leaders. The same publication commented on the failure of various Ottoman reforms to forestall the deportations and massacres of the Turkish Armenians. An article published on August 17 of that year addressed the inability of the European countries to compel Turkey to enforce various Armenian reform programs, a theme taken up by other journals in Syria itself, such as *Homs* on November 14, 1920. Much earlier, on September 18, 1913, the Damascus daily *Al-Muktabas* (The Firebrand) wrote that this policy had particularly disastrous implications for the Ottoman Armenians, whose economic success in certain professional crafts aroused the suspicions and disdain of many Turks. In the issue of May 10, 1918, well-known intellectual and former Syrian Prime Minister Haki al-Azem declared that the Ittihad party had intended "to inflict annihilation on the Armenian population, since the Turkish government had fears that they would continue to demand reforms." He attributed the decision for genocide to the Ittihadist leadership and pointed to its use of Turkish soldiers, sometimes assisted by Kurdish tribes, in carrying out its dirty work.

Syrian news articles in this period included numerous accounts concerning the nature of the deportations, abuses, and killings inflicted on the Armenians, which included the creation of conditions conducive to massive loss of life. On May 22, 1916, *Al-Mustakbal* reported that on June 28, 1915, the government ordered the deportation of Armenians from Erzerum within five days and arrested hundreds of intellectuals. A few days later, a correspondent wrote that the death caravans proceeded to unknown places. He described scenes of torture in which pregnant women and old men were marched under the lashes of whips. Some women who had managed to survive witnessed the killing of their children, beaten by the butts of guns or thrown in the river, and then were taken by Turkish officers and sold in the bazaars at very low prices. The victimization of the Armenians was termed as an offense against humanity, which "is living in pain and deprived of peace" and a crime that "humanity condemns" (*Al-Kalam al-Hadidi*, August 5, 1915, and June 1, 1916).

Articles in the Sao Paulo *Al-Afkar* (The Ideas) on January 2, 1918, and the Damascus official newspaper *Al-Asima* (The Capital) on February 27, 1919, stressed that the Turkish government's goal had been to drive the Armenian populations into the Syrian desert and that the authorities in Aleppo had ordered to deport into the interior even those Armenians who had settled in the city before the war. Eyewitness testimony was published in *Al-Afkar* on April 6, 1918, under the title "The Atrocities of the Turks in Armenia," in which the author described how Armenian women and children were thrown from boats and drowned in the Euphrates River and how horrible was the fate of the Armenians dying from thirst in the desert. When these wretched people approached a train, the Turkish guards beat the exhausted youngsters, women, and men, and kept them away from the train while they opened the faucets before the eyes of the deportees and "let the precious water spill on the sand." On July 6, 1918, the newspaper declared that there were no people on earth who had suffered and sacrificed so much as the Armenians to preserve their identity, serving as a source of inspiration to other peoples who continued to live under tyrannical rule. On September 14, it characterized the Young Turk policies as "political madness" and deplored the ignorance and fanaticism of the Turks, who were, the paper asserted, the direct descendants of the bloodthirsty Mongol hordes.

Multiple Syrian publications in this period also commented on the conscription of Armenian males into the army and the adoption of Armenian children by Turkish families as instruments employed by the Turkish government aimed toward the extinction of the entire Ottoman Armenian community. *Al-Afkar* reported on June 15, 1918, that the Young Turk government segregated Armenian men who had been conscripted into the army and then forced them into labor battalions. Turkish commanders made these battalions march virtually barefooted as far as the Sinai desert under the pretense of working on military routes, but the harsh conditions created for the conscripts resulted in starvation and massive loss of life, the Turkish government's intended outcome. In addition, *Al-Kalam al-Hadidi* on March 1, 1916, *Al-Mustakbal* on May 22, 1916, and *Al-Afkar* on March 20, 1918, reported that the Turkish authorities seized many Armenian children from the deported families and handed them over for adoption to Turkish families who raised them in the Turkish language and Islamic religion.

In its issue of March 17, 1916, *Al-Mustakbal* carried a report that included the testimony of Turkish soldiers regarding the mistreatment and torture of Armenians. Based on these interviews, the correspondent described scenes in which Armenian women had thrown their children into the river to prevent their being abused and killed by the Turkish soldiers. The soldiers would also gather children from the caravans, slaughter them in front of their parents, and then cast their bodies aside. On May 20, the paper reported that 492,000 Armenians had arrived in Aleppo, Damascus, Mosul, and Deir el-Zor by the beginning of the year. The majority of the deportees were women, children, and the elderly, who had been deprived of food and clothes and were decimated by disease. The article also cited a figure ascribed to Minister of Interior Talaat Pasha that 800,000 Armenians had been deported, of whom 300,000 had unfortunately died. The author corrected those figures, stating that in fact the number of those deported was 1,200,000 and those killed was 500,000.

The Syrian press also addressed the issue of German complicity in the Armenian Genocide. Germany, which was allied with the Ottoman Empire during World War I and whose political, military, and economic involvement in Turkish affairs expanded during this period, was in a unique position to observe and influence the developments in Turkey relating to the Armenian deportations and massacres. Syrian news sources marked Germany as the only European state to facilitate—directly or indirectly—the deportations and massacres of Ottoman Armenians. *Al-Mustakbal* on August 17, 1916, accused Germany of compliance and non-intervention. *Al-Afkar* on April 6, 1918, described German officers who were passive as they witnessed the Armenian caravans on the road to Aleppo and Ras-ul-Ain because they found it "improper to interfere." Syrian periodicals such as *Al-Afkar* in its issue of April 27, 1918, attributed Germany's role as an accomplice in the Armenian persecutions to its wish to maintain Turkish support in the war effort and to ensure domestic order in the Ottoman Empire.

Syrian publications during World War I also reveal the fear among Arab inhabitants of facing the same Turkification policies as those that destroyed the Armenian community. For example, *Al-Afkar* on June 5, 1918, in describing a speech given in Beirut by Jemal Pasha, showed that the Arabs were well aware of the intentions of the Ittihadists to "Turkify" the Arab population by subjecting it to measures similar to those applied against the Armenians. Under the title "The Arabs Tomorrow," Haki al-Azem writing *in Al-Mustakbal* on May 10, 1918, used the example of the Armenian massacres to urge the Arab public to protect the Arabic language and culture against the onslaught of the government's attempts at ethnic cleansing. He warned: "Next is our turn; if Syria remains under Turkish tyranny, then the Syrians will have their share of murder and torture at a huge level. The massacres in our country will be even more horrible than the Armenian massacres."

When studying the position of the Syrian press concerning the Turkification policy directed against the Armenian homelands and the Armenian people, it is obvious that many newspapers saw this policy as an explanation for the treatment not only of the Armenians but also increasingly of the Arabs. The Syrian periodicals realized that the Young Turks policies were based on eliminating all the non-Turkish groups regardless of their religion. Actions against the Armenians were aimed at uprooting and exterminating them whereas by and large the policy applied to the Syrians relied on the gallows, starvation, and measures for forced assimilation.

The calamity and the genocide of the Armenians left a deep impression on Arab memories and became a warning signal regarding the preservation of Arab identity. In these publications, one can observe not only the affirmation of the Turkish government's anti-Armenian measures but also the effect that these had in stoking fears that the Arabs, too, would be subjected to the ruinous Pan-Turkic policies of the empire's dictators.

As a consequence of the deportations and massacres, Armenian refugees and survivors established large communities in Syria, underscoring the significance of the geographical proximity of the Ottoman-Armenian regions to Syrian territory. This made Syria one of the havens in which Turkish Armenians could settle in relative peace. It also gave Syrian publications and their ethnic counterparts abroad a unique and credible vantage point from which to observe and report on the Armenian Genocide that unfolded under the cover of the Great War of 1914-18 and its aftermath.

19

A Legacy of Paradox: U.S. Foreign Policy and the Armenian Genocide

Suzanne E. Moranian

On the eve of the Armenian Genocide, the United States was a young nation with little experience in Middle Eastern affairs. The Genocide provided an opportunity for America to experiment with intervention. America's specific actions toward the Armenians from 1915 to 1927 established a general model that was to become a blueprint for its foreign policy worldwide ever since. In dealing with the Armenian Genocide, the United States established a legacy of paradox. The paradox is this: the self-interest that impelled the United States to engage on behalf of the Armenians is the same self-interest that impelled the United States to abandon the Armenians.[1]

From its beginnings, the United States traditionally shied away from foreign entanglements, as George Washington cautioned in his legendary *Farewell Address* when the first president was about to leave office in 1796. In his famous speech to "Friends and Fellow Citizens," he warned the young nation against risking its "peace and prosperity" by getting involved in European power struggles. "It is our one true policy," Washington declared, "to steer clear of permanent alliances with any portion of the foreign world."[2] This expedient advice has been cited in discourse on the foreign policy of America ever since.

However, throughout the nineteenth century, America's self-image and sense of its role in the world slowly edged away from isolationism and moved, at first warily, toward internationalism. Though they appeared to be opposite on the surface, these movements were ironically driven by the same impulse—to protect and strengthen the self-interest of the United States. Each was a search for power based on expediency. In the end, each would lead to the abandonment of moral principle in the case of the Armenians.

Americans, from the earliest Puritan settlers, regarded themselves as a unique, chosen people who were called upon to share their message. They envisioned themselves a glittering beacon of freedom—as a city on a hill—to inspire by example from afar. By the end of the 1800s, however, the United States had become convinced of its urgent obligation to export American principles of freedom and self-determination to what it viewed as a ruined, oppressed world. Instead of avoiding global involvement, America began to hunger to propagate its power and influence abroad.

With the rise of progressivism and its religious expression, the Social Gospel, in the increasingly urban and industrialized United States, Washington's isolationist *Farewell Address* developed competition as an engine for American foreign policy. The Social Gospel was a dynamic, new reform movement. It emerged as the nineteenth century gave way to the twentieth, with profound foreign policy implications. It blended private salvation with social justice and stressed that each person has a duty to himself and to society. It taught that the individual could seek his or her own salvation by helping others, especially those who were needy and powerless. This spirit infused the growing popularity of internationalism in America's foreign policy. Thus, the United States could seek its own national salvation by saving others. Soon, many Americans believed that the mission to save others—and this would come to include the Armenians–was enmeshed in the United States' own mission to pursue its chosen role in the world. Rescuing the "Starving Armenians" echoed as a slogan in America for many generations. It was true, as President Woodrow Wilson noted, that "the fate of Armenia has always been of special interest to the American people."[3] While seemingly altruistic on the surface, this impulse was driven by self-interest. One strengthens himself or herself by saving others. This outlook influences American internationalism even today.

The first wave of American imperialism in the Middle East began with American missionaries who established in the 1830s what was to become a thriving field of operation in Turkey. These Yankee evangelists paved the way for the American political involvement that eventually followed. The missionaries were torchbearers for what they saw as America's destiny to recreate itself, searching the globe for new and fertile fields. This ethos of social participation centered on the obligation to assume responsibility for the welfare of the world. These nineteenth-century American Protestant evangelists embodied a paradox, the legacy of which we may currently observe in President George Bush's mission in Iraq: they were confident that it was their special duty to impose their will on the lives of others, and they believed this while upholding the notion of the self-determination of all peoples.

It is astonishing to many to discover that until the 1930s, the United States did not have a coherent set of policy objectives in the Middle East. Besides safeguarding the American missionaries and their property there, there was no official U.S. policy in the Middle East. According to Oscar S. Straus, who served three times as American minister to the Ottoman Empire, President Grover Cleveland instructed him that "our chief concern in Turkey was the protection of the American missionary interests."[4] When Straus left his post, Lloyd C. Griscom became chargé d'affaires of the American Legation at Constantinople at the turn of the century. He noted that because "trade between the United States and Turkey was negligible," the Legation's real purpose was to advance the interests of the American missionaries scattered across Anatolia. On the eve of the twentieth century, "An American in Turkey was practically synonymous with missionary," Griscom explained.[5]

In fact, there was no official American ambassador to the Ottoman Empire until 1906. The U.S. State Department did not even have a Near Eastern Affairs Division until 1909—only six years before the Armenian Genocide. In attempts to overcome languid American diplomacy, the missionaries often pressed their own cases with Turkish officials. Indeed, historian John DeNovo aptly characterized the missionaries as "do-it-yourself diplomats."[6] In the late nineteenth and early twentieth centuries, the unchallenged missionary policy was the American policy in Turkey.

The American missionary movement flourished in this atmosphere. It stood in the vanguard of U.S. internationalism, and on the eve of the Armenian Genocide, the missionaries operated as America's foreign policymakers in the Middle East. The missionary leadership, acting in concert with President Wilson, as well as the U.S. Congress, launched an unprecedented humanitarian relief drive on behalf of the Armenian people.

Only a few weeks after the Genocide began, on April 24, 1915, America's ambassador to Turkey, Henry Morgenthau, urgently cabled Wilson's Secretary of State, William Jennings Bryan, requesting relief funds for the Armenians: "Some say starvation threatens. Please help quickly."[7] Bryan immediately forwarded this request to America's premier missionary statesman, James L. Barton, the prominent Foreign Secretary of the American Board of Commissioners for Foreign Missions (ABCFM). Headquartered in Boston, the ABCFM was the largest American missionary organization operating in Turkey, with 145 missionaries, 800 native workers, 114 churches, 13,000 converts, 60,000 students, and 132 higher grade schools and 1,100 lower grade schools in 1900.[8] When Bryan contacted the ABCFM upon receiving Morgenthau's distressing cable to address relief for the Armenians, he wedded the U.S. government and missionaries in Middle Eastern pursuits.

The missionaries in the Turkish field worked jointly with the U.S. consuls there to help over 150,000 survivors who fled to Syria and over 200,000 Armenians who fled to the Russian Caucasus. Thinking in 1915 that $100,000 would be enough, American relief organizers gleefully raised almost double that goal. Quickly realizing the overwhelming need for more money, fundraising efforts took on the practices of a multinational business. In 1916, almost $2.5 million was donated, and that doubled to $5 million the following year.

The receipts for 1918 jumped to just over $7 million. Following the armistice, the relief field opened up. In 1919, the U.S. Congress granted a charter to the Near East Relief (NER) organization. The NER raised a staggering $19.5 million that year. The U.S. government would eventually donate $25 million in supplies, service, and cash.[9]

Over a fifteen-year period, NER spent $116 million in assistance, helped between 1 million and 2 million refugees (two-thirds of whom were women and children), and educated 132,000 orphans in the NER schools.[10] Because of the American missionaries, supported by the U.S. government, America assumed the moral mandate of the Middle East. New ground was broken by expanding the foundation of support of American philanthropy in the region. The United States led the world in feeding, housing, clothing, and educating the Armenian refugee population. As an American peace negotiator was to declare in 1920, it was "no exaggeration to say that the Armenians would have disappeared as a nation" had it not been for America's missionary-led relief efforts.[11]

This unprecedented outpouring of American philanthropy, which transcended any known national charity at that time, was a clear expression of the Social Gospel. Americans gave to save the Armenians, not only out of sympathy, but because the country as a whole looked actively to transplant a blend of Christianity and American democracy overseas in an act of self-propagation. The mission to save Armenians became enmeshed in America's mission to pursue its chosen role in the world. Americans embraced international activism and disregarded the cautionary *Farewell Address*. In a repudiation of Washington's warning against overseas entanglements, Americans believed that it was their duty to save Armenians.

The American media, in response to the humanitarian drive to rescue the Armenian people, sounded the cry over and over that it was America's unique task to help the Armenians. A 1919 editorial in the *New Republic* was typical of published commentary at the time. It exhorted Americans to remember their unique obligation to the Armenians: "Let us not imagine that we can wash our hands of the responsibility for Armenia's fate. If we fail at this juncture to vindicate Armenia's right to freedom we shall never again persuade the world that our moral sentiments are anything but empty rhetoric playing over a gulf of selfishness and sloth."[12] This was an outright moral and political test of the special mission of the United States. In step with the Social Gospel, Americans believed that their own strength as a nation came from their deliverance of the Armenians. The motive was dualistic: it was charitable and self-serving at the same time. Its morality purified its expediency.

The record-breaking humanitarian relief drive also benefited the Protestant progressives. In the rapidly changing United States, the Social Gospel leadership sought to establish Protestantism as a powerful voice via their foreign programs. The Protestant progressives used outreach ministries, such as Near East Relief, to recreate Christianity globally, and, at the same time, to enhance their role in a newly secularized America. The swift rise of cities, ethnic populations, and industrialization transformed the nation and replaced the prevailing rural, Protestant culture that had defined America. However, Protestants saw that through the Social Gospel—which included their popular overseas missionary enterprises—they could reshape the lives of others in sweeping ways, boost their membership at home, and raise unprecedented sums of money from the general public. Early on, the followers of the Social Gospel discerned that due to the rise of industrialization and urbanization, power was organized differently than before. Protestantism in America had to reinvent itself, as the diversity of the twentieth century replaced the homogeneity that had defined America from its birth.

The Protestant churches faced a difficult question. What role were they to play? The Social Gospel was the first Protestant movement to address the vast changes sweeping the United States. Ironically, the Protestant quest for power at home depended in part on their humanitarian programs abroad. Using radical approaches abroad to achieve traditional, if not conservative, goals at home has endured as a model throughout interventionist American foreign policy. After World War I, however, the American missionaries saw their assets and power threatened with the rise of Mustafa Kemal, later called Ataturk. In 1920, Undersecretary of State Frank Polk was set to retire. He complained that the Allies after the war were "doing all in their power to perpetuate war and disturbances in the Near East." It would be "the same old game. The Turks will come back and each country will be vying for its favor."[13] In only a few years, Polk had been proved to be right.

Starting with the Mudros Armistice with Turkey at the end of World War I, the course of postwar settlements only worsened conditions for the Armenians. The Allies were actually reviving Turkish power and sovereignty. Americans could scarcely believe it, but gripped by isolationism, they were unwilling to do anything about it. The role of the Allies in putting the Turks back in the saddle, unintentional at first, began to dawn on Americans in 1920. The Allied policies, secret agreements and internal squabbling fed into the hands of the Turks, helped to rebuild their army, unified the fragmented Turkish citizenry, and repaired their broken spirit. The Allies forced the unwilling Turks to sign the Treaty of Sèvres on August 10, 1920, threatening them with the loss of Constantinople. However, the ascendancy of Kemal rendered the treaty a dead letter, unacceptable to the Nationalists. Before long, the Turks were restored to power, flushed with success. Despondent, the old Scotsman and staunch Armenian advocate, Viscount James Bryce, remarked to Barton in 1921: "Armenia seems entirely abandoned here."[14]

This held poor consequences for the American missionaries in Turkey. The xenophobic Nationalists clamped down on foreign missionaries as unwanted intruders. The secular Kemalist regime expelled numerous missionaries, levied oppressive taxes, seized their valuable property, shut down thriving missionary medical facilities, and allowed only for secular schools promoting Turkish studies. With nearly $100 million and a hundred years of work invested in the Turkish field, the American missionaries were dangling in a precarious situation. They also knew that neither the United States nor the Allies were about to come to their rescue. They were on their own and at the mercy of Mustafa Kemal.

The missionaries chose, therefore, to accommodate themselves to the Kemalists in order to continue their egoistic religious imperialism. However, the Turks would not tolerate the Americans unless they severed their ties with the Armenians. Faced with this dilemma, the missionaries deliberately opted to cut themselves loose from the Armenian community to work among the Muslims of Turkey. The ethical cost of this appeasement included missionary censorship of internal dissent regarding this decision, official revisionism with regard to Turkish crimes against the Armenian people, and, of course, their abandonment of the Armenians. Thus, as a requisite to preserving their Anatolian operation, the American missionaries elected to sever their bonds with the very Armenian Protestant community they created.

The American Board's missionaries stationed across Turkey gathered together in Constantinople in January 1923 to discuss their policy of rapprochement with the Turkish Nationalists. It was not a coincidence that at the very same time, the Allies were negotiating in Lausanne, Switzerland, with the Turks for a postwar peace settlement that recognized the political triumph of the Kemalists over the Western powers. Barton was in Lausanne to advance missionary interests with the Turks. He then journeyed on to Turkey to attend the American Board's decisive January assembly, which was also driven by the restoration of Turkish sovereignty. Missionary Luther Fowle announced at this meeting that the purging of Armenians and Greeks from Turkey served, in fact, to the ABCFM's advantage in their future proselytizing of the Turks. The "great exodus of Christians," he declared, created "an unparalleled opportunity for establishing relationships with a large group of Mohammedans."[15] Only a few missionaries opposed what they considered the Board's hypocritical and un-Christian policy of appeasement with the Turks and subsequently resigned. Thus, the search for power that had driven the missionary involvement with the Armenians would now come to drive missionary abandonment of the Armenians. This is the paradox that was to replay itself over and over in American policy not only toward the Armenians but toward the world in general.

The self-interested nature of American internationalism was revealed upon America's entry into World War I. The liberalism of President Wilson's foreign policy featured his promises of self-determination. His power as a world leader involved the tenet of self-government for oppressed peoples. Thus, Wilson stood as a beacon of hope to the Armenians. They believed that he represented moral principle outweighing expediency. However, Wilson, heavily influenced by missionary leaders whose enterprises he endorsed, pursued a policy of American neutrality toward Turkey. Many Americans urged the United States to declare war on Turkey as a way to rescue the Armenians, following America's entry into the war against Germany in April 1917. Also, as a belligerent, they believed that the United States would be in a better position to dismantle the Ottoman Empire and therefore have a stronger hand in delivering justice to the Armenians.

Wilson, safely guarding the missionaries, believed that such a move was impractical. He argued that war with Turkey would threaten relief efforts to help the Armenians, as the Turks would shut down the missionary programs and expel the Americans. He was determined to preserve the vast American philanthropic enterprises in Turkey. Wilson's Secretary of State, Robert Lansing, also defended neutrality, citing the protection of ongoing relief measures as well as the missionary properties and investments in Turkey. Such longtime Wilson foes as the pro-war Theodore Roosevelt and Henry Cabot Lodge, however, openly denounced the Turks and their atrocities against the Armenians. They ardently accused Wilson of ignoring Armenian interests, noting that only war with Turkey would stop the massacres of the Armenians. "Frankly," insisted the formidable Roosevelt, "I do not think that the question admits of any debate whatsoever. . . . We are guilty of the greatest dereliction of duty in not going to war with Turkey."[16] In response to his critics, Wilson promised the Armenians that he would seek justice on their behalf "in the general reckoning after the war."[17]

Yet, when the peace finally came in 1919, the Armenians were no better off for it. Wilson purposely forestalled action in Washington on behalf of the Armenians at its most critical juncture. He was driven to protect his personal goal of promoting America's membership in the League of Nations. He issued generalized, if not confusing, promises of "autonomous development" to the Armenians throughout the Paris Peace Conference. These were publicly highlighted with his famous Fourteen Points framework for peace, as well as privately in quiet, back-channel remarks to world leaders. Wilson, France's Georges Clemenceau, and England's David Lloyd George agreed to a resolution regarding American mandates over Armenia as well as Constantinople and the Straits. Wilson emphasized, on behalf of the United States, that his agreement was subject to the consent of the Senate in Washington. On the surface, his proposals invested great hope in the Armenian cause. Before leaving Paris, Wilson affirmed to General James G. Harbord on the train station's platform that he would take up the Armenian matter.[18]

Back home, however, the isolationists were already circling like buzzards around the mandate issue. The prominent Republican Charles Evans Hughes, for example, fought against the mandate citing Washington's *Farewell Address*. Hughes admired George Washington's "live and let live" concept, with no imperialistic designs, as the key to modern national security. Hughes reflected the times, as a demoralized, postwar America swiftly retreated from internationalism. World War I became a repudiation of idealism as well as America's faith in its mission on secular and religious levels. Historian Richard Hofstadter has noted keenly: "War has always been the Nemesis of the liberal tradition in America."[19]

In such a national mood, Wilson was thus confronted with the nearly impossible task of convincing the American people to endorse entry in the newly formed League of Nations. At the same time, the plight of the Armenians was worsening rapidly, especially with the imminent withdrawal of the British forces that had temporarily occupied the railway from Baku to Batum and other parts of the Caucasus. As Wilson confided dramatically to Senator John Sharp Williams: "I wish with all my heart that Congress and the country could assent to our assuming the trusteeship for Armenia and going to the help of those suffering people in an effective way."[20]

Delay in assuming their mandate meant certain disaster. Undersecretary of State Polk urged Wilson to stir up the passion of the Congress, since the entire resolution of the Armenian mandate rested on Senate approval. The chances in the increasingly isolationist Senate would dim with every passing day, so Wilson's timing was key to the mandate's success. Literally, the world was waiting. What Wilson then did was nothing short of astonishing. He sent a simple note to Secretary of State Lansing. It was short and blunt. He clearly understood its immediate consequences. Although it was not Wilson's long-term intention, that note killed any chance that the United States might have intervened on behalf of the Armenians. What did Wilson say? "I fear," he wrote, "that it would be most unwise to put before Congress just at this stage of its discussion of the Covenant [of the League of the Nations] either a proposal to promise to assume the Mandate for the Armenia or a proposal to send American troops there to replace the British and assume the temporary protection of the population; and yet will our own public opinion tolerate our doing, at least attempting, nothing?"[21] So there it was. This was the same reformist Wilson who envisioned a moral America healing a wounded postwar world by transplanting a protective liberalism. The missionaries had been doing this for years using the Gospel. Wilson believed that the United States could deliver peace and justice by recreating itself globally and prevailing over tyranny. Armenia was a good place to start.

Yet, by August 1919, Wilson confronted a forbidding challenge in winning the fight to persuade America to join the League of Nations, which he viewed as crucial to the strength and power of America. He did not want the Armenian mandate issue to jeopardize the success of his overriding priority—ratification of the German peace treaty of Versailles and entry into the League of Nations. He gambled that once the United States joined the League, the push for the Armenian mandate would then follow. He realized that the Armenians would have to pay an inhumane price for the strategic postponement. As is well known, by the time the mandate issue reached the Senate floor for a vote, the moment had passed, and the mandate died. Wilson, thus, purposely forestalled action in Washington on behalf of the Armenians at its most pivotal juncture to promote instead America's membership in the League of Nations. In the end, both initiatives were to fail. Wilsonian liberalism was repudiated, and the desperate Armenians were cut loose. Paradoxically, in Wilson's search for American power, which compelled him to rescue the Armenians from brutality, he thereby severed himself from them.

After Wilson's presidency ended, President Warren G. Harding and his fellow Republicans fervently clamored for a return to American isolationism, while at the same time actively pursuing expanded foreign business investments in the Middle East. Harding offered no assurances to the Armenians who were suffering atrocities at the hands of the Kemalists. Unsophisticated in worldly affairs, Harding never rose above his beginnings as a party functionary from Ohio. In striking contrast to Wilson's example, Harding feared the United States becoming "unduly involved" on behalf of the Armenians, as he believed it would undermine American power. Unlike the progressive Social Gospelers, Harding's coterie believed that saving other peoples served to weaken, not strengthen, the United States. Opposing interventionism in Turkey, the resolute conservative contended that it was wrong for people to think "America can dictate the settlement of the tremendously tangled situation there."[22]

This conviction foreshadowed dim prospects for the Armenians at the Lausanne conference—the final chapter in the Armenian Question. Lausanne would be the last chance for Armenians to establish any rights, security, and even a homeland, in Turkey. Caleb F. Gates, president of Robert College in Turkey, an American institution closely aligned with the Protestant missionaries, remarked on the anticipated Lausanne conference. No decent settlement would be secured on behalf of the Armenians or Greeks in Turkey. He predicted eerily that the Kemalists would confront the Lausanne peace negotiators "with a *fait accompli* and be able to say to them—'there are no Christian Minorities, they have all left the country.'"[23] It was a prophetic remark.

The Turkish Nationalists wanted formally to end hostilities with the Allies but refused to recognize the Treaty of Sèvres that the Allies had imposed on the sultan's government in August 1920. Kemal therefore left unanswered the Allied proposals made during the London conference of premiers in 1921. Now, a major obstacle remained the issue of the minority populations in Turkey. Before the Turks arrived at the conferece in Lausanne in December 1922, they opted to settle this problem once and for all. They decided to rid their land of the remnant Christians so as to end the matter in advance of new negotiations with the Allies. The Nationalists forced nearly all non-Muslims to leave Turkish territory in 1922.

Fearing for their lives, most of the Armenians and Greeks choked all passageways trying to flee Turkey amid misery and destruction. The desperate mass exodus from their ancestral homes was confirmed in Associated Press dispatches from Anatolia: "Every road converging upon the Black Sea and Mediterranean ports is crowded beyond capacity with emigrants, all suffering from extreme cold, and many freezing to death." Worse, complained *The Literary Digest*, the statesmen of the civilized nations "meekly accepted the Turkish dictum."[24] In

1924, Archibald Cary Coolidge's political commentary captured the gloomy mood of the West. "There have been times in the last ten years when, in the old world at least, men have been tempted to despair of humanity. The aftermath of the war," he sadly observed, "has seemed to some more cruel than the war itself and they see no end to it."[25]

Lausanne was wintry in late November 1922. Brilliant sunshine glittered from the snow-capped Alps to Lake Leman. There were so many hotels that James Barton said that Lausanne looked like Atlantic City perched on a hill. It was there that representatives from the Allied nations and Turkey congregated to negotiate their formal peace ending World War I. One of the most important postwar conferences, it sanctified the Kemalists as rightful participants on the world stage.

All parties had high stakes riding on such issues as freedom of the Straits, protection of the remaining minorities, and the capitulations or economic privileges for foreign countries. These complex issues went to the heart of the political, economic, social, and judicial structure of Turkey, as well as the vital strategic and financial interests of the West. Even American missionary and philanthropic enterprises would be inordinately affected. The future would be written at Lausanne. The daunting agenda was, as historian Harry N. Howard noted, "a veritable Gordian knot."[26]

The American Board was determined that the United States must send representatives to Lausanne, since their entire Turkish operation was at stake. American public opinion reinforced this demand, upset that the Turks were back and menacing the Christians. However, the aloof Harding administration was loathe to become embroiled in these difficult territorial settlements, which, mindful of Washington's warning against entangling alliances, it thus far had successfully avoided. Further, Harding emphasized that the United States had never been at war with Turkey. Yet, his administration was aware that Lausanne would decide several matters important to America. Many Americans also pressed the point that the world was changing fast, and George Washington's cautionary advice was no longer applicable. Allen W. Dulles of the State Department's Near East Division (subsequently director of the Central Intelligence Agency) studied the question of whether or not the United States should be represented in Lausanne. He identified essential priorities including American rights in Turkey under the capitulations, the protection of American missionary and philanthropic organizations, the protection of American commerce and the creation of an Open Door trade policy, indemnity for American losses since 1914, the independence of the Straits, and, only because American opinion demanded it, the protection of the Christian minorities. This report mapped out what was to become America's policy with Turkey for the next several years.[27] Favoring the resumption of diplomatic relations with Turkey, which required a treaty of its own to be negotiated soon, Harding finally agreed to send two representatives to uphold the American position at Lausanne.

The head of the American delegation was Richard Washburn Child, the American ambassador to Italy, and second was Joseph C. Grew, minister to Switzerland. The State Department asked Barton to serve there as an official advisor to the American representatives. Child and Grew were weak, unknowledgeable about Middle Eastern affairs, and were so disorganized at the start of the conference, complained a shocked Barton, that "Grew does not know whether he or Child is chief."[28] Barton was worried that the "clean-shaven and youthful-looking" Child, as the *New York Times* described him, as well as Grew, Child's Harvard classmate, would be no match for Turkey's "belligerent" negotiator and Kemal's foreign minister, General Ismet Pasha.[29]

As the conference progressed, Barton became anxious that no one was making the case for the security of the Armenians. The American missionary leaders had not yet decided on their future course within Turkey, including their relationship with the Armenians. As it turned out, the missionaries were on the very brink of severing their commitment to the Armenians. However, during the Lausanne proceedings, the missionaries continued their advocacy of Armenian interests, as they had done from the start of the Genocide. When it came to encouraging the American delegation to advance the Armenian cause, Barton noted with disappointment that Child "is not very clear on that subject it seems to me."[30] Indeed, in a meeting to discuss the future of the Armenians, Child took Barton by surprise. The ambassador inquired by what possible authority the United States had the right to dictate to Turkey how to treat its subject populations. "How would we take it if Turkey and perhaps France and Italy should presume to dictate to us how we should deal with our Negroes?" Child inquired. He announced to the other delegations that it was not the purpose of the United States "to force any of our opinions upon" Turkey and that other nations must allow Turkey the right "to work out her own destiny."[31] Later, Child told Barton that the Turks had promised to protect the Armenians and would offer them a "square deal." He naively asked Barton: "Why should we assume that they will not do it?"[32]

Barton was further alarmed on behalf of the Armenians because of the apparent lack of remorse on the part of the Turks. Throughout the conference, the Kemalists continued to deny their behavior and responsibilities toward the Armenians. Ismet insisted that the Armenian exodus in November was purely voluntary. The Turks also refused to attend the session when the Armenians formally presented their case to the conference. Even Benito Mussolini could not persuade the Turks to overcome their opposition to the Armenians. Barton thought that a strong word from the U.S. government would "rally the Allies and bring the Turks to terms in twenty-four hours," especially regarding the proposal for a national home for the Armenians. However, Barton protested, the Harding administration "was ready to receive or grab everything but not ready to give anything." The veteran internationalist bemoaned that the United States "was the weakest of all of them in our inability to influence or shape or carry out conclusions of a vital character." [33]

At the start of the conference, there were high hopes for the establishment of an Armenian National Home. The Allies initially coalesced on that point and appeared ready to coerce Turkey into providing land for the Armenians, most likely in eastern Cilicia. However, the Kemalists insisted that they would sign no document in which the words "Armenian National Home" appeared. Lord Curzon, Britain's Secretary of State for Foreign Affairs, then informed Ismet that the question would not come up again. "It seems tacitly agreed that the Armenian National Home will not be pressed," Barton complained. The Allies removed the Armenian Question from the docket, with no American protest. "Under the name of 'Exchange of Populations,' Turkey was given the tacit authority to drive all the Greeks and Armenians out of Turkey except from Constantinople," Barton bitterly declared, "and to leave Turkey absolutely and alone to the Turks." Child conceded to Barton, "the Turk is winning" in Lausanne. One by one, the Allies expressed sympathy for the Armenians but declined to threaten use of force against the unrepentant Turks. Curzon commented to Barton that Great Britain, the other Allies and the United States were simply not going to wage war with Turkey to secure a national home for the Armenians. "America weeps," Barton uttered, "and refuses to lift a finger to prevent the crucifixion of a race."[34] Even Grew noted in his diary, referring to the idea of an Armenian territory in Anatolia, "There is no subject upon which the Turks are more fixed in their obstinacy."[35]

Press reports from Lausanne signaled the dismay of Armenian supporters. "As regards the Armenians, they were virtually thrown overboard by the conference," and were "relegated to obscurity," concluded the *New York Times*.[36] The writer William T. Ellis agreed. He observed that the case for the Armenians was now hopeless, sanctioned by the Lausanne conference, "for there is no square mile of Turkish territory wherein a majority population of Armenians can claim, as a right, the privilege of self-government." Ellis concluded: "The Turks have got rid of the problem of Christian minorities by getting rid of the Christians."[37]

There, once and for all, Armenian hope for justice was denied by a reinvigorated Turkey, which enjoyed the cooperation of the Allied Powers and the United States government. At Lausanne, thought Armenian defenders, wrongs were to be righted. Yet, the Turks refused steadfastly to discuss the rights of their remnant Armenian population, with no objection from the American negotiators. Harding and his isolationist cohorts thought the best way to keep America strong and preserve its self-interest was to accommodate the demands of the Turks and cut the American government off from the Armenian Question. Long sympathetic to the Armenian cause, the American public was outraged at what they saw to be a dishonorable peace.

Unlike the Armenians, the American missionary and philanthropic concerns in Turkey fared much better at Lausanne. General Ismet was eager to maintain these educational and charitable enterprises, as long as the Americans refrained from proselytizing the Turkish people and adhered to various regulations. It bettered Turkey's chances of being accepted as a civilized nation to treat the American missionaries with kindness and respect. He promised to investigate the acts of intimidation and violence that the Kemalists had allegedly committed against the American Protestants; he vowed that the missionaries would be safe in the future. The American missionaries thereby preserved their lucrative holdings in Turkey. Thus, after the Lausanne conference ended, the missionaries embarked upon a campaign in the United States to rehabilitate the image of the Turks. Driven by their self-interests, the missionary leaders—who once depended on the Armenians for past achievements in Turkey—now broke their bonds with the Armenians to attempt continued evangelical success there. Again, the American people, loyal to the Armenians, could forgive neither the Turks nor the missionaries, since the price for appeasement was desertion of the Armenians.

Falling apart at the seams with contentious personalities and age-old rivalries, the Lausanne conference recessed until April 1923. When negotiations resumed, Grew headed America's Special Mission at Lausanne. Ismet was anxious to work out a treaty of amity and commerce with the United States. Waiting until after the Turks and the Allies concluded their peace settlement, Grew did not commence negotiations with the Turks until June. The treaty was signed on August 6. It was a diplomatic rendering of the political reality that the Turks were in control. The purpose of the treaty was not to revisit the conditions of the war, but instead to establish new ties with the Turkish Nationalists. American opinion was hostile to the negotiations, as it emerged that the Turks forbade any discussion of the Christian minorities. Grew feared that the glaring absence of the Armenian issue from the treaty would make it a public relations disaster to sell at home. Grew's assistant G. Howland Shaw correctly predicted that many Americans would find the treaty unsatisfactory and "nothing less than an unaccountable surrender." The essential fact that most Americans missed, he asserted, was that "unless we were willing to fight, we all had to accept pretty much what the Turks were willing to give us."[38] Overall, the negotiators were pleased that the United States gained most-favored-nation status in their efforts to establish a commercial relationship, as well as recognition for nearly all American missionary and philanthropic institutions operating in Turkey.

The ensuing reaction in America, however, exceeded the most dismal expectations. The omission of the emotionally-charged Armenian issue crippled the requisite support of the treaty by the American people. They were too entrenched in their compassion for the "martyred" Armenians. At the time, Grew rationalized this failure, revealing to a journalist, "I do not personally consider that this was a matter of great importance."[39] Thirty years later, Grew felt compelled to justify the situation remarking, "I had not been able to pull impossible rabbits out of impossible hats."[40]

American opposition to reconciliation with Turkey was rampant and would not quiet across the country. This vehement outcry prevented the treaty agreement of amity and commerce, which was signed in 1923, from coming up for a Senate vote until 1927. On January 27 of that year, the Lausanne treaty failed to earn the requisite two-third Senate vote after years of delay. By then it hardly mattered.

In mid-February, the State Department exchanged notes with Turkey. This was an executive agreement that did not need Senate consent, and therefore it sidestepped public hostility. It restored formal diplomatic relations. Both nations agreed to maintain the status quo and behave generally as if the president had ratified the treaty. In May, with input from such missionary statesmen as Barton, the State Department named Grew as the new ambassador to Turkey. He arrived in Turkey in September 1927, although Senate approval lagged until the following April.

Turkey appointed Ahmed Mouhtar (Moukhtar) as its ambassador to Washington. His arrival unleashed a renewed wave of protest from those opposed to rapprochement. In December 1927, President Calvin Coolidge officially received Mouhtar. After ten years of a turbulent relationship, Turkey and the United States had come full circle. The indignant adversaries of accommodation complained, however, that the price of this diplomatic reunion was the abandonment of the Armenian Question. Americans were appalled that Turkish rehabilitation came at the expense of the expulsion and annihilation of the Armenians from their ancient homeland.

Kemal himself bragged about this very circumstance. His remarks were recorded in a confidential diary entry by Admiral Mark Bristol, the United States High Commissioner in Turkey after the war. Several weeks after the Lausanne treaty was defeated in the Senate, a ball was held at the Anatolian Club in Constantinople for the foreign diplomatic corps, including the Americans. Bristol complained that it was "not a great social success" until Kemal arrived. He assured Bristol that the recent Senate vote did not diminish Turkey's friendship with America. Kemal said, however, that he did not understand how a "fanatical minority could impose its will on an enlightened majority." Kemal declared that he was "not bloodthirsty," but he bragged that in the past he had "caused blood to flow," and would, if needed for the accomplishment of his high purpose, "cause it to flow again." Kemal complained that he "had experienced the power of the minorities," whom he referred to as "noxious." Their power, he pledged, was something to be obliterated, along with the minorities themselves."[41] Thus, he boasted of the cruel truth that his modern Turkish republic was born of the persecution of its own Christian peoples.

As a final insult to the Armenians, the American missionaries acted jointly with the American government as architects of the postwar reconciliation with the Turks. It better served the self-interests of both the Washington policymakers and the missionary leadership to disengage from the Armenians in the 1920s and instead align themselves with Kemal's Turkey. Thus, the self-interest that initially underwrote American commitment to the Armenians drove its very demise.

Self-contradiction is the enduring legacy that marks American foreign policy even today. On the one hand, there seems to be an opposition to nation-building and foreign entanglements, making Washington's *Farewell Address* still relevant. On the other hand, however, American leaders have espoused a missionary-like dedication in exporting American democracy and in advocating American intervention around the world–both impulses driven by a desire to empower America without relying on any other country.

Notes

1. This chapter is drawn from Suzanne E. Moranian, "The American Missionaries and the Armenian Question: 1915-1927," Ph.D. diss., University of Wisconsin–Madison, 1994.
2. George Washington, "Farewell Address: To the People of the United States," September 17, 1796, www.usgovinfo.about.com.
3. Archives of the American Board of Commissioners for Foreign Missions (cited hereafter as ABCFM archives), ABC 16.9.1, vol. 2, no. 174, Woodrow Wilson to M. Paul Hymans, November 30, 1920. All ABCFM material quoted in this chapter is published by permission of the Houghton Library, Harvard University, as well as Wider Church Ministries, United Church of Christ.
4. Oscar S. Straus, *Under Four Administrations* (Cambridge, MA: Riverside Press, 1922), pp. 44-45.
5. Lloyd C. Griscom, *Diplomatically Speaking* (Boston: Little, Brown and Company, 1940), p. 134.
6. John A. DeNovo, *American Interests and Policies in the Middle East: 1900-1939* (Minneapolis: University of Minnesota Press, 1963), p. 20.
7. ABCFM archives, ABC 16.9.3, vol. 40, no. 26, William Jennings Bryan to James L. Barton, May 17, 1915.
8. Edwin Munsell Bliss, Henry Otis Dwight, H. Allen Tupper, eds., *The Encyclopedia of Missions*, 2d ed. (1904; repr., Detroit: Gale Research Co., 1975), pp. 29-31.
9. James L. Barton, *The Story of Near East Relief, 1915-1930: An Interpretation* (New York: Macmillan Co., 1930), pp. 409-411.
10. ABCFM archives, ABC Personal: James L. Barton papers, 8:6, James L. Barton, "American Philanthropy in the Near East."
11. Benjamin Burges Moore, "Some Facts about Armenia," *New York Times, Current History Magazine* 12 (June 1920): 508.
12. "Our Duty to Armenia," *New Republic* 20 (September 10, 1919): 163-164.
13. The Papers of Mark L. Bristol (Library of Congress, Washington, D.C.), box 32, Frank L. Polk to Mark L. Bristol, June 3, 1920.
14. ABCFM archives, ABC 16.9.1, vol. 2, no. 243, James Bryce to James L. Barton, June 21, 1921.
15. ABCFM archives, ABC 16.9.2, vol. 5, no. 57-58, Report of Addresses at Conference of Turkey Missionaries, January 9, 1923.
16. ABCFM archives, ABC 14.2, vol. 7, no.122, Theodore Roosevelt to James L. Barton, May13, 1918.
17. The Papers of T. Woodrow Wilson (Library of Congress, Washington, D.C.), series 4, reel 337, no. 204106, Woodrow Wilson to Joseph P. Tumulty, July 1918.
18. The Papers of Henry Morgenthau (Library of Congress, Washington, D.C.), Henry Morgenthau, "Diaries," June 30, 1919. Harbord was preparing to lead a mission of investigation to Anatolia and Armenia.

19. Richard Hofstadter, *The Age of Reform* (New York: Vintage Books, 1955), p. 272.
20. The Papers of John Sharp Williams (Library of Congress, Washington, D.C.), box 2, Woodrow Wilson to John Sharp Williams, August 12, 1919.
21. U.S. National Archives, Record Group 59, General Records of the Department of State, 860J.01/26½,Woodrow Wilson to Robert Lansing, August 4, 1919.
22. ABCFM archives, ABC Personal: Barton papers, 4:9, Warren G. Harding to James L. Barton, September and October 5, 1922.
23. Morgenthau papers, box 6, C.F. Gates to A. W. Staub, November 3, 1922.
24. "Christians Ordered Out of Turkey," *Literary Digest* 75 (December 16, 1922): 13.
25. Archibald Cary Coolidge, "Ten Years of War and Peace," *Foreign Affairs* 3, 1 (September 15, 1924): 21.
26. Harry N. Howard, *The Partition of Turkey: A Diplomatic History, 1913-1923* (1931; repr., New York: Howard Fertig, 1966), p. 278.
27. Laurence Evans, *United States Policy and the Partition of Turkey, 1914-1924* (Baltimore: Johns Hopkins Press, 1965), pp. 393-397.
28. ABCFM archives, ABC 16.5, no. 202, James L. Barton to All at the Rooms, November 19, 1922.
29. ABCFM archives, ABC 16.5, no. 203, James L. Barton to Patient and Gentle Readers, November 20-26, 1922; *New York Times, Current History Magazine* 17 (January 1923): 531-535.
30. ABCFM archives, ABC 16.5, no. 205, James L. Barton to Patient Readers, December 3-7, 1922.
31. ABCFM archives, ABC 16.5, Report of Barton to Constituency, February 3, 1923; Bristol papers, box 78, Am[erican] Mission to Constantinople, January 31, 1923.
32. ABCFM archives, ABC 16.5, no. 207, James L. Barton to ABCFM, December 12-14, 1922, and James L. Barton to Patient Friends, December 15-19, 1922, ABC 16.5, no. 208.
33. ABCFM archives, ABC 16.5, no. 209, James L. Barton to Folks, December 20-27, 1922.
34. ABCFM archives, ABC Personal: Barton papers, box 2, Barton to Constituency, February 3, 1923; Barton to Boarders January 1923; Barton, "Program for the Near East."
35. Papers of Joseph C. Grew, Houghton Library, Harvard University, "Diary,1923," vol. 22, MS Am 1687.
36. "The Lausanne Conference," *New York Times, Current History* 17 (February 1923): 747.
37. William T. Ellis, "Lausanne: A Close-Up," *American Review of Reviews* 67 (March 1923): 269-274.
38. U.S. Archives, RG 59, 711.672/173, G. Howland Shaw, Memorandum, August 1923.
39. Grew Papers, vol. 23, MS Am 1687, Joseph C. Grew to Elbert F. Baldwin, August 7, 1923.
40. Joseph C. Grew, "The Peace Conference of Lausanne, 1922-23," *Proceedings of the American Philosophical Society* 98 (February 1954): 2.
41. Bristol papers, box 7, "Confidential Diary," January 31, 1927.

20

French Society and the Armenian Genocide

Philippe Videlier

I do not know if the fame of Jean Jaurès has reached the shores of America. He was the key figure of socialism in France and was killed in 1914 in Paris in the "Café du Croissant"—which had nothing to do with the Turkish flag and its crescent but with French pastry. This murder was, for France, the first blast of World War I. Jean Jaurès was a member of French Parliament.

On November 3, 1896, after the great massacres of Armenians in Anatolia and Constantinople, Jaurès addressed the French Parliament about the extermination campaign that had begun in Turkey against the Armenian populations, and he denounced the political abstention of the government and the silence of the press which, he asserted, had been paid off by the sultan. Addressing the French government, he declared that, seeing all this blood, watching all these abominations, all this savagery, all these violations of human rights, it had not uttered a word and was thereby an accomplice in the crime.[1] In response, the chairman of the Chamber warned Jaurès that he was insulting the government and Minister of Foreign Affairs Gabriel Hanotaux protested that Jaurès was insulting all the previous governments as well because the policies toward the Ottoman Empire had long been based on the principle of *realpolitik.*

Hanotaux, a very important person, was also a good friend of Turkey and did not want to aggravate Sultan Abdul Hamid, because it could be bad for commerce and strategic plans. Turkey, yesterday like today, was in a key position between Europe and Asia, between the Middle East and Russia, and it was a lucrative area for investment and profits for the big companies, arms dealers, railways, and banks.

Everyone in Europe knew about the great massacres of 1894-1896. Eyewitnesses and diplomats sent reports, letters, and telegrams to their governments. A *Blue Book* of official documents was printed in London and a *Yellow Book* in Paris. In Berlin, Pastor Johannes Lepsius published *Armenien und Europa*; in

France, Victor Bérard wrote *La politique du Sultan* (1897) and Pierre Quillard and Lucien Margery published *La Question d'Orient et la politique personnelle de M. Hanotaux*. The politician Georges Clemenceau, who was to be the prime minister of France prior to and during World War I, declared: "What we call politics is only a crime and even a stupidity."[2]

At that time, Turkey was an exotic country for the French people, the terminus of the Orient-Express, the rolling deluxe hotel fast traveling from Paris Gare de l'Est to Constantinople via Vienna and Budapest in 67 hours and 35 minutes. At the very dawn of cinematography, invented by the Lumière Brothers in Lyon, the first films about Turkey were shot by Eugène Promio: "Constantinople—Panorama de la Corne d'Or"; "Constantinople—Panorama du Bosphore"; "Constantinople—Artillerie turque"; "Constantinople—Défilé de l'infanterie turque"—the last of these being shown in Lyon on April 25, 1897.

But France, too, was exotic to the educated Ottomans and much safer than Constantinople for the sultan's political opponents. This is why the Young Turks found haven in Paris where in the Latin Quarter their paper *Meshveret* was published by Ahmed Riza. This paper was called "la presse des opprimés" (the press of the oppressed), along with the Armenian *Hairenik* (Fatherland) in Boston, *Kurdistan* in Folkestone, England, and *l'Arménie* in Paris. In 1902 and 1907, the Ottoman political refugees and oppositional elements in Europe held conferences in Paris. The second of these brought together the Turkish Committee of Union and Progress (CUP), the party Dashnaktsutiun (Armenian Revolutionary Federation), the Jewish Committee of Egypt, and the Ottoman League of Private Initiative for Decentralization and Constitution, among others. They declared that they fought together for the "Holy Light of Liberty and Justice." At the turn of the twentieth century, prominent intellectuals, among them the novelist Anatole France and Jean Longuet (grandson of Karl Marx), launched the journal *Pro-Armenia*, with the goal to make known "the deplorable condition of the Armenians in Turkey."[3]

One idea spread among French society, in these years, from high classes and bourgeois intellectuals down to the most common people: in an Oriental country ruled by a bloody tyrant, the Red Sultan, an oppressed people suffered, the Armenian people, victim of periodic massacres. Some people thought that religion was the cause of that sad situation: Islam against Christians, while other thought that it was mainly a question of politics: regressive barbarity against modern democracy.

In January 1908, Jean Jaurès' daily newspaper *L'Humanité* published on the front page an interview with a leader of the Armenian Revolutionary Federation. "We are going to take the Ottoman Bastille," he declared.[4] So when in the summer of 1908 revolution broke out in Turkey, it was welcomed and applauded by the French people. Jaurès, as the representative of progressive opinion, gave assurances in *L'Humanité* that all the good-hearted people, all freedom-loving democrats would be grateful to the Turkish people for the work of regeneration that they surely would accomplish. Public opinion in Europe was highly optimistic in this respect.

When, in April 1909, Abdul Hamid tried to reverse his fate by promoting a coup d'état and lost the game, Jaurès wrote: "The bloody ghost vanished forever."[5] But, as was soon seen, he was wrong. At almost the same time, in April 1909, the "Adana event" occurred. During these massacres in Adana and the surrounding areas in Cilicia, between 20,000 and 30,000 Armenians died under the blows of both Islamists gangs and Young Turk constitutional troops. "One more time," wrote *Le Petit Journal* on May 2, "Armenian Christians had been massively murdered. . . . In Adana, their bazaars have been looted and burned. . . . An eyewitness of these horrors wrote that the town seems like 'a slaughterhouse.'" Two weeks later on May 15, *L'Illustration*, the largest popular weekly in France, wrote: "It is still impossible to have an exact idea of what were these actions of savagery, even to estimate the number of the dead."

At that time, there were few Armenians in France, a number of merchants and intellectuals. But the situation changed after World War I and the accompanying Armenian Genocide. Nearly 1.5 million Armenians perished by deadly deportations and massacres. The "New Turkey" was a Turkey without Armenians. As Talaat Pasha said to his friends "I have accomplished more toward solving the Armenian problem in three months than Abdul-Hamid accomplished in thirty years!"[6]

In France, as in the United States, Great Britain, and even Germany, there were many publications dealing with the annihilation (the term "genocide" did not exist then). Among these were the following: *L'Arménie sous le joug turc*, 1915, with a speech by Paul Doumer—a prominent politician who later became president of the Republic; *L'Arménie, les massacres et la question d'Orient*, 1916, by Gaston Doumergue, another eminent politician who also became president of the Republic; *La supression des Arméniens*, by René Pinon, 1916; *Une victime du pangermanisme: l'Arménie martyre*, 1916, by the priest Abbé Eugène Griselle; *Au pays de l'épouvante*, by Henry Barby, with a preface by Paul Deschanel, another future president of the Republic. In addition, books by the American Herbert A. Gibbons, Englishman Arnold Toynbee, and German Johannes Lepsius were translated into French. And there were already pamphlets by deniers such as the novelist Pierre Loti of l'Académie Française, who, in *Les massacres d'Arménie*, explained that all this clamor was exaggeration and fabrication by the enemies of "our good friend Turkey."[7] French society was aware and informed of what happened in the Ottoman Empire during the war. At the end of the conflict, survivors found refuge in orphanages and camps in Syria, Lebanon, Cyprus, Greece, and other countries of the eastern Mediterranean region.

A report of the Republic of Armenia's delegation in Paris, "*L'Arménie et la question arménienne, avant, pendant et depuis la guerre*" (Paris, 1922), listed the postwar distribution of Armenian refugees as follows: Syria, 75,000; Palestine,

3,000; Mesopotamia, 6,000; Macedonia, 30,000; Salonika, 5,000; Athens and Piraeus, 15,000; Bulgaria, 10,000; Black Sea/Crimea, etc., 20,000, as well as a half million in the Caucasus region.

After the war, the Middle East was divided into zones of influence by France and Great Britain. More than 60,000 Armenian refugees were living near Aleppo and more than 20,000 in and around Beirut. At the end of 1922, the French Army in Lebanon and Syria organized large camps, with tents and shacks that became shantytowns. Living conditions were so bad that in 1926 the camps were struck by plague.

In the early 1920s, some of these refugees came to France, because France was looking for cheap labor for its plants and factories. At the end of 1922, the S.S. *Tourville* transported several hundreds of refugees from Smyrna to Marseilles. The great French journalist Albert Londres called Marseilles the gate of the south: "That's a harbor, one of the most beautiful of all the shores. It is famous under all the latitudes."[8] Perhaps. But the first settlements of these new immigrants in Marseilles were camps, too: Camp Mirbeau and Camp Oddo on Boulevard Oddo, a piece of land given to the army by the Railway Company Paris-Lyon-Méditerranée. By 1923, there were more than 3,000 people living in this camp.

But the refugees, who were considered "stateless persons," were also immigrant workers. Looking for jobs and housing they moved northward, along the Valley of the Rhône, stopping group by group along this route. Some settled in Valence, which, of course, has nothing to do with romantic Valencia in Spain; some settled in Vienne, which, of course, has nothing to do with stately Vienna, the capital of Austria, but rather these are two small towns lying between Marseilles and Lyon on the Rhône River.

There are a number of accounts of the newcomers' first contact with French life, this one from a man born probably in 1908, coming to Valence via Marseilles:

> When I arrived, my weight was 35 kilos. I was only skin and bones, God in Heaven and nobody on Earth. . . . [We stayed] at Hôtel Louvois, Place d'Aix; it was a slum; we were seven in a room. We had no mattress, we lay flat on bricks. I paid three francs a day for rent, and I earned 5 a day working to trim pieces of metal in M. Fouques' foundry.[9]

This was the fate of almost all immigrants.

In Vienne, some Armenians lived in a former factory they called "le Kemp," using an American pronunciation they had learned in Syria and Lebanon from the missionaries and employees of the Near East Relief. It was a factory near the railway Paris-Lyon-Méditerranée, with its chimney "like a cathedral."[10] During the war, the plant manufactured guns and after the war, sewing machines. And then the owner made up his mind to enter into politics, so he sold the building to a rich widow who sold it again to a textile company, Pascal-Valluit

& cie., for the manufacture of calico, its specialty being soft flannel. The company sent someone to Marseilles to recruit Armenian workers, as did the shoe manufacturer Pellet, for its *cousues main* (sewn by hand). This is the reason that many Armenians lived in Vienne, Isère, 30 kilometers (18 miles) south of Lyon along rue Peyssonneau (*le Kemp*), for those working in "Chez Pascal," or rue Lafayette, 150, for those working in "Chez Pellet." Other companies along the way followed suit.

From one industrial town to another, Armenians made their way north again, into the heart of France and its capital—Paris. The trail was not a straight one, however, for along the way, settlements were born to the left and right of the river, according to the possibilities for work. Some refugees, for example, settled in the little villages lost in Ardèche, a pretty mountainous district on the right bank of the Rhône, where there was work in the silk mills for women and girls and in metalwork foundries for men. At Le Pouzin, there were 400 Armenians; others settled in Joyeuse, Largentière, and Aubenas.

In a flea-market I found a directory of the Armenian community of France, *Annuaire des adresses arméniennes*, published in 1932 by the Librairie Arpi in Paris, with advertisements for shopkeepers and artisans, a mixture of Occidental and Oriental references and values: "Café Sultan"—rue d'Angoulême, Paris; "Imprimerie Euphrate"—Tateossian, rue Villeroy, Lyon, Rhône, depuis 1927; "Raki Sainte Sophie" Distillerie de Pantin; "Yoghourt Select" Colombes (Seine); Henry Minelian, Tailleur, "elegance et qualité," rue de Crimée, Paris; "Danel Chausseur Paris—Marque déposée": manufacture of shoes for women (Danielian changed his name to the more French-sounding Danel).[11]

The directory gives a list of Armenian people town by town. The names are printed in Armenian and the addresses in French. The towns did not reproduce a map of France; rather, they drew the map of the Armenian settlements in France: Marseilles, Nice, Valence (Drôme), Vienne, Pont de Chéruy, Charvieu, Décines (Isère), Saint-Chamond (Loire), and then the areas surrounding Paris: Alfortville, Colombes, Asnières. The directory acts as a mirror where the Diaspora can see its physiognomy. It builds a new geography whose scales are upset and where big capitals have less importance than unknown suburbs. These unknown suburbs are famous within the Diaspora everywhere. Even the frontiers do not exist anymore, as this French directory of Armenians annexes the small communities of Belgium, England, Germany, Switzerland, Italy, Bohemia—Brussels, Antwerp, London, Manchester, Berlin, Geneva, Venice, Torino, Prague.

A woman living in Décines, an industrial suburb of Lyon, since 1927 told the story that a boat brought her and her parents to Marseilles: "I was twelve," she said. "Then, we went to La Ciotat"—a harbor not far from Marseilles where the Lumière brothers had an estate and in 1895 made one of the first movies in the world: "*L'arrivée du train en gare de La Ciotat*" (The Coming of the Train into La Ciotat Station). So, she and her family went to Marseilles, to La Ciotat, "and then we went to Saint-Chamond" (near the industrial town of Saint-Etienne, Loire), where there was a silk factory—Fabrique Pascal. She added:

> It is closed now. [It was artificial silk.] Natural silk, it was in Ardèche. We worked there too. Not far from Privas. . . . Aubenas. With my brother. And then we asked for the ID card for my brother. We wanted to go to Saint-Chamond; we stayed one year or two. I could not work because I was not fifteen. But the prefect was very kind. He gave me my work record. He wrote I was 15. We cheated. I was born in 1912, but on my ID card, it's 1910. We do not have exact age. Some were noted 10, others 15. Nobody knows. And then the bosses of Décines came to take workers and then went to Décines, in 1927, all the family. My father, my mother, my little brother, and me. In Décines, they made propaganda, you know, in Décines they have built a house with a lot of Armenians in it. And all the group came, several families.[12]

Décines was a village in the early 1920s, with only 1,500 people, mainly farmers and peasants. But in 1923, a large industry with a new technology moved there: rayon—artificial silk. And the firm needed many workers—2,500. In an advertising booklet in the 1930s, the firm justified its choice of location: "Should we recruit the labor force we needed in the suburbs of Lyon and bring it by special trains, tramways, or buses? After study, it appeared that it would be too great a cost, every year, with the inconvenience of running the factory with people more or less contaminated by life in working class boroughs of the town."[13] That was clear. They wanted immigrants to run the factory because it was cheaper and safer socially. By chance, the big boss knew an Armenian little boss in Ardèche; together they choose an Armenian labor force and built houses for them. For this reason, in 1924-25, Décines became the main Armenian town in that region.[14]

In France, Armenian intellectuals published a daily paper in Paris. Most intellectuals were in Paris, while the Armenian majority, the workers, were in towns throughout the country. The daily *Haratch* (Forward) was established in 1925 by Schavarch Missakian (Shavarsh Misakian). What is very instructive is that the paper created a link connecting the Diaspora. From time to time, there were articles on the lives of Armenians in the various towns or villages where Armenians had settled. Most of these articles were written by Armenian workers. The first article from the different towns was always moving, because it seemed to be taken from the Bible, telling of the arrival of a wandering and tired people in the Promised Land. It was like poetry. It described pleasant scenery. Anyone who knows these industrial towns would not describe them as the "promised land." But these writers were refugees coming from the deserts of Syria and Mesopotamia, from camps in Athens, from orphanages in Syria and Lebanon, and for them, the area had, as they said, "a taste of paradise." Of course, it was a very special paradise, with big machines, requiring nine or ten hours a day, six days a week, to produce textile or metal.

"At half an hour from Lyon, Décines is a little town built on a large plain, with Good Air and Good Water," wrote *Haratch* on June 23, 1926. Good

Air—Good Water? You wouldn't say this if you knew Décines. Good Air and Good Water—in Armenian: *Otn u Choure*. This description was poetic and, as noted, very similar to a biblical expression. But, nonetheless, in all the places where Armenians settled in France, either lost in the countryside or near the big towns, it was always "*Otn u Choure*":

> At 44 kilometers from Lyon, Tarare is an attractive village of 10,000 people, in the middle of woods. Water and air are good there. It has twenty-five factories, silk for the most part. The number of Armenians is six, coming with contracts from Beirut three months ago. Next, two families and ten orphan girls will come too. (*Haratch,* October 3, 1926)

> One can imagine how good the air and the water were with twenty-five textile factories! Pont de Chéruy is an attractive village in the Département de l'Isère. It is nearly 40 minutes from Lyon and possesses a big factory of electric threads. . . . Life of the community goes on normally. In this smiling natural site 500 Armenians are living, linked to the enormous Grammont factory. (*Haratch*, June 9, 1926)

Years ago, I saw the destruction of the old workers' flats of Pont-de-Chéruy, just near the Grammont factory, which still exists with its big chimney.

Migration and Diaspora have their own patterns, which do not seem always rational but are in fact. The map of the Diaspora is designed by History, that is to say, by hazard and necessity. Accounts, living memory, when still possible, and documents in the archives tell us the complexity of this map.

The academic works about migration in the 1930s offer special versions of the story, as if they see their subject from a great distance, biased by prejudice. This is the case of the main dissertation on the subject: Georges Mauco's *Les étrangers en France,* published in 1932. About Armenians, he wrote:

> Greeks, Turks, and Armenians, because of their preference for trade and of their little capacity for hard manual work are grouped in big towns where they are artisans or middlemen. From Marseilles, where a large colony resides, they are going up the Rhône Valley, concentrating in big numbers in Lyon, and then Paris.[15]

What is said about their occupation was, of course, untrue—an image of prejudice. A census of foreigners in 1939 for the Département of Rhône, shows that of a total of 3,000 Armenians (children included), 1,700 were employed, and of this number more than 83 percent were manual laborers (compared, for example, with 70 percent for Italians) and less than 12 percent were shopkeepers.[16]

When the Armenians arrived as fugitives, the nationality of the refugees was recorded in many different ways: Armenian, even though there was no Armenian nation state, and also as Turk, Lebanese, Syrians (or just Arabian), Russian, Bulgarian, Persian, Greek. In 1925, the Armenian population in France was estimated at 30,000. Since 1924, they were covered by the Nansen status for stateless people under the auspices of the League of Nations. In the Diaspora, the Armenians of France made up the most important community in Europe: outnumbering those in Bulgaria, Rumania, Greece, Great Britain, and Italy. It is said that presently there are 120,000 people of Armenian origin living in France.[17] For many years, the first generation of Armenians in France remained silent about the Genocide. They survived, they worked, and they died.

However, I found something strange in the archives. In April 1935, just twenty years after the Genocide, six different Armenian associations asked the French authorities to ban a film: "*Le Martyre d'un peuple*"—about the martyrdom of the Armenian people. The argument they used was as follows:

> This film reminds us of the slaughters of Armenian population by the Turkish government of that time. We, who are speaking in the name of thousands of Armenian immigrants, in the name of those whose parents were murdered during those years, point out that we do not want to reawaken this atrocious memory in ourselves.[18]

Thus, the film was banned. It is well known, however, in the United States as *Ravished Armenia*, starring Aurora Mardiganian, a survivor who died in Los Angeles in 1994.

But this attitude changed after two decades and a new generation. The memory of the Genocide was always present within families but remained hidden in their private lives. Public recognition of the Genocide was the task, the duty, and the struggle of the third generation. It began in the 1970s and continues up to the present.

The first monument in memory of the Armenian Genocide in France, I believe, was dedicated in 1972 in Décines. Subsequently, monuments were erected in Marseilles, Issy-les-Moulineaux, Vienne, Alfortville, and Valence. An opinion poll of April 1996 showed that 69 percent of the French population was aware of the Armenian Genocide and 75 percent of that group thought that the French government should recognize it officially.[19] This was done in 2001 by a law that states simply: "The French Republic publicly recognizes the Armenian Genocide of 1915."[20]

Since that time, the public debate has turned to the issue of the integration of Turkey into the European Union, with many holding that this should be made conditional on the ability of Turkey to face its past, to break with denial, and to conform to democratic standards of life and thinking, because the Armenian Genocide belongs to the collective memory of all civilized persons.

Notes

1. Jean Jaurès, *Oeuvres: Pour la Paix*, vol. 1: *Les alliances européennes: 1887-1903* (Paris: Editions Rieder, 1931), p. 132.
2. Georges Clemenceau, April 7, 1897, in Gustave Meyrier, *Les massacres de Diarbekir* (Paris: L'inventaire, 2000), p. 235.
3. Pierre Quillard, *Pour l'Arménie: mémoire et dossier* (Paris: Cahiers de la Quinzaine, 1902), p. 153.

4. Jean-Marie Carzou, *Un Génocide exemplaire: Arménie 1915* (Verviers: Marabout, 1977), p. 87.
5. Jean Jaurès, *Oeuvres: Pour la Paix,* vol. 4: *Europe incertaine: 1908-1911* (Paris: Editions Rieder, 1934), p. 101.
6. Henry Morgenthau, *Secrets of the Bosphorus* (London: Hutchinson, 1918), p. 225.
7. Pierre Loti, *Les massacres d'Arménie* (Paris: Calmann-Lévy, 1918).
8. Albert Londres, *Marseille, Porte du Sud* (Paris: Le Serpent à Plumes, 1995) p. 9.
9. Frédéric Bourgade, *Les Arméniens de Valence: Une intégration réussie* (Valence: Les Bonnes Feuilles, 1991), p. 16.
10. Jean Ayanian, *Le Kemp: Une enfance intra-muros* (Marseille: Editions Parenthèses, 1996), p. 68.
11. *Annuaire des adresses arméniennes* (Paris: Librairie Arpi, 1932).
12. Philippe Videlier, Interview with an Armenian woman (Décines, Rhône, 1991).
13. Pamphlet of the Société Lyonnaise de Soie Artificielle (Lyon, 1933).
14. Philippe Videlier, *Décines: Une ville, des vies* (Vénissieux: Paroles d'Aube, 1996).
15. Georges Mauco, *Les étrangers en France* (Paris: A. Colin, 1932), p. 172.
16. Préfecture du Rhône, *Etat de la population étrangère par nationalités et par type de professions: 1939*, Archives Départementales du Rhône, 4M422.
17. Aïda Boudjikanian-Keuroghlian, *Les Arméniens de la région Rhône-Alpes: Essai géographique sur les rapports d'une minorité ethnique avec son milieu d'accueil* (Lyon: Association des Amis de la Revue de Géographie de Lyon, 1978), p. 7. "Ancestry Group" statistics do not exist in France. Some Armenian associations claim that the number of persons of Armenian origin is as high as 400,000 to 450,000.
18. Letter to Préfet du Rhône: April 15, 1935, Archives Départementales du Rhône, 4M484.
19. *Le Monde*, April 7-8, 1996.
20. *Journal Officiel de la République Française*, January 30, 2001.

Part 5

Historiography and Reconciliation

21

Turkish Historiography and the Unbearable Weight of 1915

Fatma Müge Göçek

Even though ninety years have passed since the traumatic events of 1915, there are still questions that haunt Turkish society; specifically, how does one narrate what happened to the Anatolian Armenians? How can one talk about 1915? How and why did 1915 happen? What can one term 1915 and who can write about it?

For instance, the traumatic events of 1915 have been referred to by various terms in Turkish society throughout the ninety years' of its history. The initial Ottoman legal term employed to refer to the action taken against the Armenians in 1915 was *tehcir* (*tehjir*), loosely translated as "forced migration," which etymologically derives from the Arabic root *h-j-r*, meaning to migrate from one place to another. This was distinct from the Ottoman term *sürgün*, translated as "the transfer of populations"—the latter was an ancient practice ordered by the Ottoman state more to repopulate regions of the empire in an attempt to increase its revenue base. Applied mostly to Muslims, it was often accompanied by tax breaks and land allocations in the settled regions. Tehcir did not contain any of the advantages of sürgün and was much more punitive in nature. The term Ottomans employed after World War I to refer to the atrocities committed against the Armenians during the forced deportations was *kıtal*, translated as "massacre," or "mass killing." It is this term that I employ in relation to 1915.

I am aware, however, that the common practice among Armenians and most English-language speaking scholars is to refer to 1915 as "genocide." I do agree that if one were to define genocide "as sustained purposeful action by a perpetrator to destroy physically a collectivity directly or indirectly through interdiction of the biological and social reproduction of group members sustained regardless of the surrender or lack of threat offered by the victim,"[1] what happened in 1915 was genocide. I prefer to employ the term massacres because my aim is to develop a historical sociological analysis from the standpoint of Ottoman history as it is negotiated in Turkish society today. Ottomans themselves did not have access to the term genocide because it was not yet formulated—the term was first coined by Raphael Lemkin in his 1944 book entitled *Axis Rule in Occupied Europe*; the Turkish state in turn has politicized the term to such a degree that its employment automatically shuts off any possible venues of communication with Turkish society at large.

Since my aim is to communicate my ideas to Turkish society and hopefully start a dialogue, I choose to employ the traditional Ottoman term. Also, the term genocide contains a very strong moral responsibility—it would not be fair to expect Turkish society that is barely aware of what happened in 1915 to be ready to assume this responsibility. After all, ignorance is "one condition that is generally recognized as a morally valid excuse" provided, of course, that this does not translate into "self-deception and culpable ignorance."[2] The term "massacre" also captures, and hopefully problematizes the current contention in Turkish society against the term genocide. Turkish society first has to be communicated the historical events that transpired in 1915. I am sure that once it has processed and interpreted this knowledge it will correctly decide what to call the events.

The Turkish translation of the term genocide is *soykırımı*, which could be translated back into English as the "slaughter, carnage of a race." Turkish scholars who are attempting to start a dialogue in Turkish society often prefer instead to employ the Turkish term *kırım*, thus removing the racial component, to thereby refer to 1915 as "slaughter, carnage," or *katliam,* roughly equivalent in meaning to massacres.

In this discussion, I address the first two of my earlier questions, namely the narration of what happened to Anatolian Armenians and how one can talk about 1915 within this narration. I must note at this juncture that I employ the term "Anatolian Armenians" to refer to those affected and destroyed by the traumatic events of 1915 as this term captures not only their place of origin, their centuries-old homeland, but also refers to how they socially and culturally identified themselves as a community. I have to emphasize, however, that the term as such does not capture the horrid deaths of hundreds of Armenian intellectuals arrested on April 24, 1915 and deported from Istanbul/Constantinople by train to be massacred and the tens of thousands likewise deported from Adrianople, Rodosto, and other Ottoman territories in Europe (Rumelia) only to perish en route. Most of the other Armenians in Istanbul escaped the same tragic fate as did those of Izmir/Smyrna, at least until 1922.

Part I commences with the acknowledgement that the current narrative structure available in Turkish to communicate the massacres of 1915 contains a very strong naturalized nationalist subtext that subtly marginalizes, normalizes, and legitimates this tragedy. I, therefore, propose a new framework for

Turkish historiography that gives agency to the experience of minority groups and suggest that the current hegemonic nationalist historiography be replaced by it. In Part II, I move to the next question of how to locate 1915 within this new post-nationalist historiography. Though 1915 is powerful when unmediated, unframed, and unassimilated, once it is located within historiography, its trauma becomes normalized. This has also been evinced in the only other context like 1915, both in terms of the scope of the tragedy as well as its disastrous aftermath, namely the Holocaust.[3] Hence, I analyze the problem of the contextualization of 1915 in relation to the Holocaust.

Part I: A New Post-Nationalist Turkish Historiography

Even though the work of historiography is centrally bound to concerns in the nature of knowledge production, it is also always engaged as an ethical exercise in a promise of justice to the other, to the excluded.[4] This is especially the case in my attempt to reconstruct a post-nationalist historiography, because the current one, I contend, excludes the experience of the minorities. I should note, at this juncture, that neither is Turkey alone in constructing such a nationalist narrative nor I in challenging it. Nationalist historiographies are recently being challenged in other parts of the world as well. Two cases in point are the current debates in Israel[5] and Indonesia.[6]

When the current Turkish historiography pertaining to the Anatolian Armenians is analyzed in detail, the elements of Turkish nationalism and the violence of the events of 1915 emerge as the two elements that need to be examined critically and deconstructed. The domination of the ideology (read Turkish nationalism) and the historical event (read 1915) that have diffused into much of the existing scholarship on Turkey remain unexamined as scholars approach historical sources uncritically and often accept the textual rhetoric as historical reality. Yet such histories epistemologically manipulate the role and significance of certain social groups (read Sunni Turks) at the expense of all others through their selective employment and deployment of history. In so doing, they eliminate outright certain possible choices and trajectories (read non-nationalist solutions) not only from history but, by implication, from scholars' analyses as well. They thus introduce a certain historical determinacy whereby the nationally triumphant groups (read the now secularized Turkish elites) always persevere by soaring to historical success against all odds, and the vanquished (read the rest of Turkish society, including all minorities) seem destined to failure. A case illustrating this depiction is the construction of the point of origin of the official historiography of the Turkish republic.

I conjecture that it was the famous *Speech* (*Nutuk*) that Mustafa Kemal delivered in 1927 at the Second Congress of the Republican People's Party—which he had founded and now led—that laid the foundation stone for the official historiography of the Turkish republic. In that speech, Mustafa Kemal narrated his own historiography of the War of Independence and that particular historiography eventually became that of the Turkish nation. I should note, however, that Mustafa Kemal was not alone in his attempt to create a nationalist history for the new Turkish republic. Public narratives were often employed to create nationalist narratives for history that often made a nation; a case in point is the creation of the story of American nation-building.[7]

The first sentence of Mustafa Kemal's speech actually declared the point of origin of his own historiography—and therefore, by implication, of all the official Turkish historiographies thereafter—as follows: "I alighted in Samsun on the 19th day of May of 1919." The ensuing text not only covered the events from the year 1919 onward, but did so from the vantage point of 1927, namely four years after the establishment of the Turkish republic and the suppression of various revolts throughout Anatolia. It is noteworthy that at the particular historical juncture when Mustafa Kemal took to narrating his version of this new nation's past, all the minority groups in Turkey, including the Armenians, had already been very effectively marginalized. Given these epistemological parameters, it was virtually impossible within the confines of Turkish nationalist historiography predicated on such a historical framework to ever recover and fully recognize the agency of such ethnic and religious groups in Turkey.

And the ensuing Turkish nationalist discourse neatly categorized these ethnic and religious groups along strictly maintained boundaries of inclusion and exclusion. It defined the included Turkish secular elites as historically triumphant and then proceeded to naturalize their norms and values into society as "historical reality." The nationalist ideology also idealized the emerging Turkish secular elites as it simultaneously allocated them exclusive determining power over the course of Turkish history and also purified them of all the vice they had once engaged in by censoring history; it thus presented the Turkish elites morally and metaphorically as "white." By the same token, Turkish nationalist ideology articulated and narrated the excluded minorities as the vanquished and then proceeded to attribute to them the exact opposite characteristics: the excluded were stripped of most of their agency, and the very little they were permitted to exercise was of course depicted within parameters defined by the triumphant group, thereby appearing totally subversive and immoral. Turkish nationalist ideology thus embellished history by selectively employing only those historical events that portrayed the excluded minorities in a negative light, thereby saturating them with vice. It therefore ended up conveying Turkish minorities morally and metaphorically as "black." And when scholars, they themselves socialized within the Turkish nation-state where such an ideology was predominant, approached this highly selective representation of Turkish history within this framework, they, too, directly or indirectly reproduced historical actors as either black or white, with no consideration at all of either the possible shades in-between or other colors.

The official Turkish nationalist historiography also selectively retold the historical events before 1915 in a way that both legitimated what happened to the Anatolian Armenians and took pains to demonstrate that the same, if not more, happened to the Turks as well. This epistemological restructuring of the past, undertaken to emphasize the unavoidability of 1915, enabled Turkish nationalist historiography to deny both its extent and intentionality. Hence, 1915 was employed to structure all existing Turkish historical accounts onto itself with insurmountable force and, in so doing, obliterated all critical historical analysis and eliminated all events, institutions, social groups that might not have foreshadowed this ultimate outcome in the following manner: Anatolian Armenians were portrayed in history initially as a wealthy and content "loyal" social group who turned ungrateful and treacherous mostly at the instigation of the Great Powers; the same powers were also narrated, in the same stroke of the pen, as aggressing upon the Turks in their attempt to wrest the empire away from the "rightful owners." As a consequence, both the Turks and the Armenians were depicted as suffering "equally" during World War I, which was brought upon them by the Great Powers.

In official Turkish historiography, both the hegemony of Turkish nationalism and the hegemony of 1915 ended up dramatically limiting the historical repertoire of the scholars engaged in the research of Turkey's past. The official employment of history thus portrayed very selectively the social conditions of the Ottoman Empire, the agency of various social groups within, the repertoire of choices these groups had, and the range of historical events they encountered. Given this state of affairs, I argue here that it would not be possible for official Turkish historiography to make any significant empirical and methodological advances without reconstructing its framework through engaging in critical analysis. I propose to reconstruct such a historiography by reconsidering in particular its periodization so that it is not solely based on the naturalized nationalist history of the Turks that eventually emerges hegemonic, but rather on the intersections of the experiences of *both* the Turks and the minority groups, in this case the Anatolian Armenians, of the empire.

Alternate Periodization of a Post-Nationalist Turkish Historiography

The alternate periodization of such a post-nationalist Turkish historiography needs to comprise, in relation to the Ottoman *millet* and imperial structures, five stages: (1) Formative Period, 1453-1639; (2) Institutionalization Period, 1639-1839; (3) Reform Period, 1839-1902; (4) Nationalist Period, 1902-1982; and (5) Toward a Post-Nationalist Period, 1982-2004.

In determining the temporal boundaries of the *Formative Period of 1453-1639*, even though the origins of what became the Ottoman Empire could be traced to the establishment of the Ottoman principality in the Iznik (Nicea) region around 1299 and the interaction of the semi-nomadic Ottoman Turks with the non-Muslims residing in Anatolia even a century earlier, I conjecture that it was probably with the conquest of Constantinople from the Byzantine Empire in

1453 that the Ottoman Turks started to develop not only the ideal but also the realization of an imperial structure populated by social groups from multiple ethnicities and religions. It is then that the first outline of a policy regarding the conditions under which non-Muslims was to exist within the confines of Ottoman lands starts to form.[8]

According to this policy, the non-Muslim minorities were organized into religious communities termed millets, where the Greek, Armenian, and Jewish communities comprised the main categories. Each millet community was organized around its religious institution and headed by its particular elected religious leader who oversaw the internal administration of the community and was legally responsible for it, especially in terms of the payment of communal taxes to the Ottoman sultan. Under this arrangement, even though the non-Muslim minorities possessed economic rights, they lacked significant social and political rights in that they could not bear arms, travel on horseback within cities, or hold administrative office except when appointed by the sultan. Since their civic rights were based on their religion, they also could not marry Muslims without religious conversion and, if they chose to do so, lost their legal rights within their own communities. As a consequence, during this formative period, given the conditions under which they functioned, the Ottoman minorities ended up becoming active and prominent in one sphere—the economic one—where they faced the minimum restrictions. They thus specialized in particular professions and utilized their multilingual skills especially in inter-imperial trade.

The fact that the position of the Ottoman minorities was restricted in relation to their social interaction with the rest of the population, however, produced significant repercussions throughout society. The Ottoman social system, established as such, ended up naturalizing the superiority of the Muslims in that there were no such political, social, and economic restrictions placed upon them; they could bear arms, hold office, and also live in a society that operated within the Islamic legal framework. In short, one could claim that during the formative period, the social system allowed the Ottoman minorities to coexist peacefully with their non co-religionists—a state of affairs quite advanced given the persecutions of religious minorities throughout Europe but favored, in the last instance, the Muslims. I set 1639 as the endpoint of this formative period because of a change that then occurred in the particular position of the Armenians within the empire: it was with the treaty of 1639 between the Ottoman and Safavid empires that the social location of the Armenians in the Ottoman social system became finalized.[9]

The periodization I propose differs from that currently provided by the Turkish nationalist historiography in the following dimensions: The latter's portrayal of this period is one of continuous peace where "Turkish magnanimity and Muslim benevolence" grants rights to the religious minorities living in their midst; the narrative then *imputes* how religious minorities received this noble act (without historically researching to find out what they actually thought in relation to their existence in the Ottoman Empire) by stating that they in turn became and remained peaceful "out of gratitude." Hence, the moral tone of benevolence on the side of the Turks and gratitude on the receiving side of the minorities is already established by the Turks for the minorities, without the latter's participation in the process. The Turkish nationalist historiography then proceeds to select carefully and mention frequently other contemporaneous historical events with the intent to demonstrate the superiority of the Ottoman treatment of minorities over others; one such frequently mentioned historical event involves the violence inflicted by the Spanish Inquisition upon religious minorities resulting in their death and deportation. That the Ottoman sultan welcomed such minorities into his empire further strengthens the nationalist narrative. Hence the initial positive moral tone set by the domestic treatment of the religious minorities in the Ottoman Empire is extended here to establish moral superiority over contemporaneous European empires.

In developing the above-mentioned narrative, Turkish nationalist historiography thus selectively highlights the favorable dimensions of the minority existence in the empire. Yet, in so doing, it also, again selectively, fails to mention other aspects of Ottoman minority existence. Specifically, Turkish nationalist historiography underplays or silences the obligations the Ottoman minorities had to fulfill in return for what they received, namely the additional taxes they were obligated to pay, and also the legal, social, political, and administrative restrictions they faced within Ottoman society because of their religion. In addition, Turkish nationalist historiography assumes the naturalized dominance of the Ottoman administrative perspective as it treats the Ottoman minorities as one undifferentiated, rather stereotyped, social group; it thus fails to take into account, for instance, the internal dynamics and divisions of the religious minorities such as the ones that existed between those residing in the capital as opposed to those living in the provinces, or the inter-communal strife among them that was also present from the onset. Also overlooked in this particular historical juncture is the tension that existed between the Ottoman Muslims and minorities as their interests often came into conflict. The absence of these factors in the Turkish nationalist historiography idealizes and thereby dehistoricizes the relationship between the Muslim and minority communities; in so doing, it indirectly sets the stage for the later mythification of Muslim and minority relations. It is therefore no accident that with the advent of domestic strife in nineteenth-century Ottoman society, this selective representation "naturally" leads to the placement of the blame for the social strife unto the treachery of the ungrateful Ottoman minorities.

I chose 1639 as the starting point of the *Institutionalization Period of 1639-1839* for it is during the period of Sultan Suleiman II that the Ottoman social structure takes shape as the now established relations between the Muslims and minorities start to reproduce themselves.[10] During the ensuing two hundred years, even though the Ottoman Muslim and minority communities do indeed coexist relatively peacefully, they continue their transformation not as one social unit, but as two separate communities, one Muslim and the other non-Muslim, that evolve internally within themselves and in quite limited interaction with one another. Hence the initial legal separation based on religion becomes institutionalized into the Ottoman social structure creating a very strong defined and maintained bifurcation. As the Ottoman subjects practice their religions within their own communal spaces, their social and communication networks develop most strongly within themselves rather than across the divide; as the same subjects cannot marry or inherit across the religious divide, their transfer of knowledge, wealth, and resources also occurs within their own communities separately from one another. In particular, the restriction placed upon minorities of not being allowed to bear arms as non-Muslims excludes them from the Ottoman military profession, which becomes the exclusive domain of the Muslims. Even though this restriction proves to be quite advantageous to the Ottoman Muslims during the expansion of the empire in that it brings them not only material wealth but higher social standing, it nevertheless starts to work to their disadvantage in the late eighteenth and nineteenth centuries when the Ottoman Empire stops expanding. Thus, the Ottoman army starts to face increasing defeats, and the Ottoman Muslims manning the military not only fail to acquire wealth and status through warfare but begin to lose their lives at alarmingly high rates.

What limits Ottoman imperial expansion during the same historical period is the rising West. It is the emergence of European powers now equipped not only with the products of the Industrial Revolution but with new military warfare techniques that establishes a strong stand at the borders of the Ottoman Empire. This Western transformation, which places the Ottoman Muslim subjects at a disadvantage, provides new opportunities for the Ottoman non-Muslims. Because of the European economic expansion that ensues as a consequence of the Industrial Revolution, European trade with the Ottoman Empire escalates and the Ottoman minorities who have for ages been domestically directed to specializing in trade and the economy acquire, unlike their Muslim counterparts, increased advantages because of their linguistic, cultural, and religious affinity with Europe. The Ottoman sultans make use of the skills of some Ottoman minorities by appointing them to significant administrative posts, often relying on either their domestically developed economic skills or their linguistic skills; hence, many end up heading Ottoman economic institutions or engaging in diplomacy with European powers on behalf of the Ottoman sultan. Yet, the minorities manning these high-level administrative posts differ from their Muslim counterparts in one significant dimension: the Ottoman sultan often establishes control over the Muslim post-holders by marrying them to women from his own household to guarantee their loyalty, or the Muslim post-holders are able to resist the sultan's control by networking with their powerful relatives or by passing their advantages on to their children. Since the Ottoman minority post-holders are socially located outside of such family and marriage networks, their hold on the power they acquire places them in a much more precarious position and often does not extend beyond their own lifetime.

The political developments in Europe in the form of the Enlightenment and the ensuing French Revolution also impact the Ottoman social structure and with it the Ottoman Muslims and minorities in quite different ways. The most significant outcome of this Western political development is undoubtedly a discussion of rights of individuals as citizens rather than as imperial subjects. A preordained world is gradually replaced by one where individuals operate in a society within which they acquire contractual rights and responsibilities to become citizens of equal standing. As such, these citizens want to make the societies they live in their own and, when prevented from doing so, undertake revolutions to actualize their visions, visions that are often termed "visions of modernity."

It is no accident that the penetration of these European visions into the Ottoman Empire occurs indirectly through education and directly through the Ottoman minorities who have both the closest economic contact with Europe through trade and also often send their sons to Europe for education to sustain the economic advantage they have been able to build in the empire. It is also not surprising that it is the Ottoman minorities who become conscious and increasingly dissatisfied with their position within the Ottoman social system. After all, the Ottoman minorities and Muslims do coexist within an overarching imperial culture and their language, music, architecture, and arts have been affected by one another through the centuries. For instance, Armenian architects build mosques, Greek musicians compose musical pieces, and Jewish artisans create clothing. Yet when all the material culture by Muslims and minorities creates the Ottoman public space, the cultural ownership often ends up getting attributed to the socially, politically and legally dominant Muslim community. What the Ottoman minorities produce is only theirs privately; they do not have, because of the societal restrictions placed upon them, as much claim on public ownership, no particular space of their own within the Ottoman public sphere other than their carefully bounded communal space. Even though the Ottoman minorities increasingly participate in the creation of the Ottoman public space, they are not publicly recognized as a part of it; they are instead obligated to retire to the privacy of their own communal space.

As a consequence of these political and economic developments in Europe and the concurrent Ottoman internal transformation, the positions of Ottoman Muslims and minorities become affected in disparate ways, however. The interaction between the external and internal dynamics impacts the Ottoman minorities more favorably than the Muslims. While the Ottoman minorities are advantaged by the economic developments, the new political ideas increasingly highlight their disadvantaged location within Ottoman society. The Muslims increasingly lose the advantages of their normalized dominance in society as the

Ottoman imperial expansion tapers off and they, too, become dissatisfied with their location within society. It is in the next historical period that both social groups, especially the younger cohorts educated in Western-style institutions, turn to reforms in an attempt to redefine their locations; both groups note that the problems are embedded in the existing Ottoman social system, both identify the preordained nature of Ottoman imperial rule as the possible origin of such problems, and both start work for the introduction of an Ottoman constitutional government that would, in theory, ensure them larger public space for increased political participation. I chose 1839 as the end point of this period because it is then that both groups start to work toward reforming the empire.

Once again, the periodization I propose diverges from the narrative provided by Turkish nationalist historiography in the following ways: in the nationalist narrative, there is no differentiation of the formative and institutionalization periods of Ottoman social structure in relation to the lives of its Muslims and minorities. Ottoman history is instead bifurcated into the "classical period" that covers all the centuries preceding the nineteenth-century European impact, that is, roughly five hundred years (1299-1839, and then the ensuing "reform period" that articulates the Ottoman transformation occurring as a consequence of the impact of about eighty years (1840-1922) until the foundation of the Republic of Turkey. The lack of differentiation of the Ottoman classical period produces two consequences: it further dehistoricizes the societal locations of the Muslims and minorities by overlooking the transformations they underwent through the four centuries. Particularly, how the disparate locations of the Muslims and minorities gradually become embedded in the Ottoman social structure and how a deep structural divide was established between them are overlooked. The nationalist historiography also mythifies both the characteristics of Ottoman minorities and the Muslim benevolence toward them as unchanging over the course of the centuries.

The only source of change the nationalist historiography then ends up highlighting is not internally generated, but externally enforced by the expanding West. The increasing involvement of European powers in the Ottoman Empire therefore becomes interpreted negatively as the intervention of these powers in Ottoman internal affairs in general and their pressuring for reforms for the Ottoman minorities in particular. The interaction also assumes a moral character as it is clearly defined, in line with nationalist rhetoric that categorizes all actions as either "good" or "bad" for the nation and all actors as "black" or "white," that the latent intention of Western powers is, from the start, to weaken and destroy the Ottoman Empire. The economic and political impact of Europe is also selectively highlighted in relation to the unrest it produces among the Ottoman minorities alone; the negative impact of the European transformation on the location of the Ottoman Muslims in relation to the minorities is overlooked. The Muslims enter the nationalist rhetoric only in terms of the increasing tension between the Ottoman sultan who holds on to his power and the newly emerging Western-style educated Muslims who want to share that power.

It is within this epistemological context that the historical analysis of the reform period, the period of visible Western European impact on the Ottoman social structure, commences. From the start, however, the Turkish nationalist historiography treats the Western impact on Ottoman Muslims and minorities as two independent—rather than *interdependent*—phenomena, thereby ideologically reading into the text their subsequent failure to transform peacefully along the same lines.

I start the *Reform Period of 1839-1902* with the year 1839 because it is then that both the Ottoman minorities and the Western-style educated Muslims start to process and interpret the political, social, and legal ideas generated in Europe within the dynamics of Ottoman society. Especially the younger generations of both the Ottoman minorities and the Muslims observe the West, increasingly receive their education there and, most importantly, in order to reproduce the military and economic success of the West, start establishing educational institutions in the Ottoman Empire along similar lines. In the educational and social reforms they undertake, the Ottoman minorities are primarily supported by the emerging class of merchants and tradesmen who benefit from the increasing economic and trade relations with Europe, while the Ottoman Muslims must rely on the Ottoman state.

The disparate nature of this support impacts the Ottoman social structure differently: the reforms pertaining to the Ottoman minorities are successful mostly when undertaken by minorities themselves and, as such, remain constricted to the minority communities. The reforms by the Ottoman state targeting in theory both the minorities and the Muslims are mostly triumphant in the case of the Muslims and fail to overcome in praxis the institutionalized structural divide in society between the Muslims and the minorities. Still, the reform period is marked by intense efforts on all sides, namely the Ottoman state administration and the existing Muslim elites, the minorities and their local governance structures, and the Western-style educated Muslims with their new political visions to reform the empire into a form that would fit all their needs.

The Ottoman imperial administration spearheaded the reform efforts by undertaking three administrative legal reforms approximately every two decades (1839, 1856, and 1876) to ascertain equal rights to the Ottoman Muslims and minorities.[11] The persistence of these three efforts reveals, I think, how deeply ingrained the Muslim-minority inequality was in the Ottoman social system that it took three unsuccessful tries to overcome. Muslim dominance was so deeply naturalized in the system that efforts had to be introduced each time as alleviating problems with the social locations of *both* the Muslims and the minorities, whereas they in essence attempted to bring the status of the minorities up to the level of the Muslims.

The first proclamation in the *Tanzimat* reform period was promulgated on November 3, 1839, whereby the individual rights of both the Muslims and minorities of the empire were recognized together equally for the first time. What is noteworthy here is the novel legal treatment of both social groups under a single decree, which was bound to highlight the legal inequalities that existed between the Ottoman Muslims and minorities especially when they were placed side by side rather than treated as two entirely structurally separate categories. The following proclamation called the *Islahat,* promulgated on February 28, 1856, further attempted to negotiate and bring about equality between the Muslims and minorities of the empire. As noted above, the necessity to proclaim a second reform approximately two decades after the first suggests the depth of the necessary structural adjustment to the Ottoman social system to alleviate the sources of inequality: these extended from equal opportunity in recruitment into educational and administrative institutions to equal representation in courts to equal opportunity for membership in provincial assemblies.

These reform proclamations had to be followed by a third almost two decades later when, on December 23, 1876, a more drastic legal reform termed the *Meşrutiyet* was undertaken with the declaration of the Ottoman constitutional system and the formation of an Ottoman national assembly. Even though European powers interpreted this Ottoman move as a pre-emptive move to relieve the European pressure placed upon the empire for reforms, it nevertheless did enable all subjects some degree of representation in an assembly and led to the first elections of the empire. I think that the Ottoman state did indeed try to reform the empire along Western lines in an attempt to capture European patterns of imperial success, but failed when it was unable to overcome the deep structural divide that had developed in Ottoman society between the Muslims and the minorities.

The difference in societal reactions to these state-initiated reforms is noteworthy in that there were strong generational differences in reception both among the Ottoman minorities as well as Muslims. Most of the younger generations of Ottoman minorities favorably received the potential improvement to their legal status and their closer integration into the larger Ottoman society that these reforms, but they were frustrated with the slow pace with which the reforms were executed and the resistance they faced both within their own communities and also from Ottoman Muslims. Older generations of Ottoman minorities predicted that these legal reforms would increase the sense of loss of communal identity as their communities became more and more integrated into Ottoman society at large; they therefore wanted to retain their special language, legal system, local practices, and special privileges even when these sometimes brought with them exclusionary practices from the larger society.

The reactions of the Muslims were also complex; those younger generations of Ottoman Muslims educated in Western-style institutions embraced, in theory and in principle, the Western European ideology of the brotherhood of all men under equal rights and therefore realized and supported these reforms as a necessary component of modernity. As they had naturalized their dominance in the existing system, they were not yet aware how this equality would directly affect their lives in practice. The older generations of Ottoman Muslims protested vociferously, stating that they did not want to destroy a system that had worked so well for so many years, and some even voiced the opinion that they did not want the Ottoman minorities who had been beneath them for so many centuries to be elevated to the same legal status as them.

The Ottoman minorities participated in the Ottoman state-initiated reforms as individuals and in the reforms of their own local administrations as groups.[12] Probably the state-initiated reform that had the most influence on Ottoman minorities was the first 1839 Ottoman reform proclamation in that it enabled the establishment in millets of mixed tribunals. Previously, the local administrative bodies of the Ottoman minorities were dominated by the power of religious leaders, yet this reform created space for lay members in these tribunals who in turn introduced new ideas and reforms into their particular millets. The participation of laity in religious affairs brought dynamism to all three minority communities of the empire, namely the Jews, Greeks, and Armenians. The concurrent changes in the Ottoman taxation system also contained in the reform edict enabled Ottoman minority merchants and artisans to participate more fully in the local millet administration thereby providing increasing support to the reformist elements and their new ideas. It was also during this period that the first stirrings of nationalism set in as Greece was established as an independent state in 1830, and all communities struggled with the issue of defining their identities within an imperial framework in a world still structurally dominated by empires. The ensuing rebellions in Wallachia, Moldavia, Montenegro, and Serbia in the 1850's, and the increasing influence of the Russian Empire in the Balkans and the north and the northeast in the 1890's brought the Ottoman Empire more and more under pressure for reforms to improve the rights of its Christian subjects.

The interpretation by Turkish nationalist historiography of this period of Ottoman reform is marked by a deep ambivalence in that, while it has to recognize and legitimate the Western ideas and institutions of reform that later provide the founding stones of the Turkish republic, it also has to criticize the Western powers instigating those ideas and institutions. The nationalist historiography therefore treats the recipient Ottoman societal elements selectively: it does not recognize the differentiation within the Ottoman minorities because it treats them as one stereotyped unit that has no agency of its own so the minority reaction to the reforms is interpreted solely in terms of how they fall under the influence of Western powers to "turn against" the Ottoman Empire. The contributions of those minorities in Westernizing Ottoman society are therefore overlooked.

In relation to the Ottoman Muslims, those older generations that react adversely to the reforms are likewise dismissed as "the traditional religious" elements that do not have the interests of the empire at hand. In so doing, the nationalist historiography obfuscates and dismisses the most significant criticisms of the reforms undertaken by this group, that these reforms eliminated the natural dominance of Muslims in Ottoman society. The only Ottoman group that emerges triumphant with its agency unscathed is the young Ottoman Muslim reformists as these were the intellectual forefathers of Turkish nationalists. In this case, too, however, the nationalist historiography treats historical facts selectively by employing the most significant methodological fallacy of nationalism: the rhetoric of the reformists is treated as historical reality. Even though the Ottoman reformists do pay a lot of lip service to legal equality in theory, their record becomes much more checkered when one analyzes the degree to which such reforms were actualized in Ottoman society. As noted previously, there was significant structural resistance to the application of the reforms, which often goes unmentioned.

By overlooking the discrepancy between the rhetoric and reality of the reforms and by treating the rhetoric as reality, Turkish nationalist historiography manages to portray the impact and reception of reforms much more favorably than they actually were. In the narrative of nationalist historiography, if problems with reforms do exist, the culprits are either the Western powers who pressure too hard or the Ottoman minorities who want too much too soon; the reactions of the Ottoman Muslims are overlooked. Hence, it is only the agency of reform-minded Ottoman Muslims that is recognized within Ottoman society.

I think a new era commences in Ottoman history with the introduction of the idea of nationalism into the empire. Hence, I start the *Nationalist Period of 1902-1982* with the historical event of the 1902 Congress of Ottoman Opposition Parties in Paris, even though the seeds of nationalism were sown earlier throughout the empire at disparate locations during the latter half of the nineteenth century, as indicated by the many rebellions from the Balkans to Syria, Lebanon to Jeddah. I argue that it is at this 1902 congress that political parties belonging to the Muslims and minorities of the Ottoman Empire met in Paris to discuss their common future, if there was to be one. As such, they all had a fair chance as participants in the congress to become significant players in determining the future of the empire, and history had not yet eliminated some at the expense of others.

If my starting point of the 1902 congress is compared with that of nationalist historiography, which commences with the Turkish War of Independence in 1919, it becomes evident that two social factors eventually become silent in the nationalist historiography. The first factor to disappear is the ideology of nationalism that had started to take shape among some of the Young Turks—it seems as if it has disappeared in the ensuing Turkish historical narrative because it becomes such a natural part of it that one can no longer recognize it as a distinct factor. The second factor that is literally lost is the multicultural, multiethnic structure of the Ottoman Empire initially reflected in the various groups of Kurds, Armenians, Assyrians participating in the congress—this multiethnic, multicultural factor is gradually marginalized in Turkish historical narrative as these groups lose their agency to survive only as the "other."

I should note here that these two factors are intimately connected to each other as well: the gradual marginalization of the ethnic and cultural groups is justified and legitimated by the escalating nationalist rhetoric embedded in the same narrative. The physical removal of these groups, often by force and violence, accompanies this symbolic disappearance. When one then approaches the events of 1919 from such a standpoint, it becomes evident that at that particular time period those who had committed to fight a War of Independence, including Mustafa Kemal, were already ambivalent about where ethnic and religious minorities of the empire fit in the ensuing state they aimed to establish on *their* homeland. In addition, two such minorities, namely the Anatolian Armenians and the Greeks, had already been uprooted once from their ancestral lands for the good of the "homeland" upon the orders of the Committee of Union and Progress.

The events of 1902 that I propose to focus on present a different framework, however, one where nationalism and its destructive treatment of minorities have not yet left their marks on the historical narrative. In 1902, the historical repertoire at the congress still included all the ethnic and religious groups of the Ottoman Empire, and the ideology of nationalism was one among the many that were feverishly discussed. Such a point of origin thus enables me to map out the many paths of social transformation possible for the Ottoman Empire that Turkish nationalism then eradicated by either suppressing, deporting or eliminating the various ethnic and cultural groups; I am also able to capture in its own terms the agency of such victimized groups as they attempted to resist this escalating nationalism. In 1902, the Ottoman social groups still came to the Paris congress as groups of an empire, but it soon became clear both there and soon thereafter that a peaceful coexistence was to prove impossible because the Muslim-Turkish element was not willing to forego its naturalized dominance in the Ottoman social structure, and the millet system had generated a Muslim-Christian divide that was beyond repair. The environment was thus too polarized for the various social groups to come together to act in unison for they had led separate communal lives for such long centuries. I should note that I would argue it was at this congress that the Young Turk movement started its transformation from an intellectual endeavor into a political entity, a process that eventually produced the 1908 revolution when the Committee of Union and Progress formed by a segment of the Young Turks seized power from the Ottoman sultan.

The period as a whole was thus marked by the nationalisms not only of the Ottoman minorities themselves, but also by the nationalism of the dominant Muslim group against them, which was to eventually wreak havoc on them through forced deportation in the case of the Armenians, forced population exchange in the case of the Greeks, and gradual attrition in the case of the Jews. I think that from the viewpoint of the history of Muslims and minorities, the founding of the Turkish republic in 1923 was not a very significant turning point in that the minorities retained their rights by the Lausanne treaty and their acquisition of the rights and responsibilities of Turkish citizenship remained mostly limited to responsibilities rather than rights. Even though they did *rhetorically* acquire full rights, they did not do so *in practice* as demonstrated by the following incidents all instigated by the Turkish state almost once every decade: before and during World War II: the Turkish Jews were forcibly deported from Thrace to prevent possible collaboration with the enemy; all three minorities—Greeks, Armenians, Jews—were forcibly conscripted into the military to work as laborers; all three were targeted to pay a "Wealth Tax" (*Varlık Vergisi)* that literally wiped out their resources; a decade later, on September 6-7, 1955, the state set street mobs upon the minorities in Istanbul to destroy their shops, houses, and places of worship; and still another decade later during the Cyprus events of 1963-64 many Greeks were compelled to emigrate with savings not to exceed the equivalent of $100. It is at the termination of this nationalist period that the minorities are virtually destroyed and the path of elimination followed by Turkish nationalism is almost complete.

I think that mapping out the nationalist movement from its Ottoman inception to its Republican phase not only brings narrative coherence to the historical events that transpire, but also connects the trauma of 1915 with its nationalist aftershocks into the 1960s. My periodization of course differs dramatically from the nationalist historiography which refuses to recognize the significant historical continuities between the Ottoman Empire and the Turkish republic. But I would contend that that very refusal fragments the narrative history of state-sponsored prejudice and violence against the minorities and thereby enables the Turkish state to disclaim any historical continuity in its attitude toward the minorities. Specifically, the exclusion of the period from 1902 to 1922 from nationalist historiography obfuscates the most virulent formative stages of Turkish nationalism that flourished under the Young Turks.

With the foundation of the Turkish republic in 1923 and the ensuing radical Westernization, Turkish nationalism became neatly folded—and hidden—in the Western "civilizational" project. Turkish nationalists gained much more international recognition and respect as ardent Westernizers and pursued their national projects under this guise; their sustained prejudice and violence against the religious minorities in Turkey were also justified in the name of this civilizational project: all social groups who criticized state projects were immediately accused of obstructing Turkey's path through Western civilization toward progress.

I mark the advent of a new era hopefully termed the *post-nationalist period from 1982 to the present* with the year 1982, for it is then that the neo-liberalization of the Turkish economy, media, and communications occurred under the Turkish president Turgut Özal. This liberalization process created pockets of public space not controlled by the Turkish state and it was within those spaces that social groups finally started to discuss what their own society meant in their own terms. The political oppression wrought upon society by the military at exactly the same time might even have helped along this societal implosion by getting people focused on "non-political" topics such as identity formation. It was also during this period that a substantial amount of Armenian/Greek/Jewish minority literature was translated into Turkish and the memoirs of minorities appeared for the first time. Even though the Turkish state was literally forced into this neo-liberalization due to its changing location in the world conjuncture at the end of the Cold War, it nevertheless did end up creating new pockets of public space in Turkey that still are not directly controlled by the state. Whether these pockets have the potential to transform into political space capable of empowering minorities in Turkey remains to be seen.

The official Turkish minorities of Jews, Greeks, and Armenians are currently so decimated in number that they no longer possess their former social, political, and economic significance. The Turkish state recognition of and apology for its policies of prejudice and violence against these communities would therefore have symbolic significance at best. The other most significant unofficial minority, the Kurds, is still not fully recognized by the Turkish state in terms of their rights. Yet the rights of all social groups in Turkey vis-à-vis the state—as opposed to their responsibilities which they have always been forced to fulfill—have recently become significant on the national agenda in relation to Turkey's impending European Union membership. The recent public discussions around these and other social issues and the often violent reactions of nationalist elements, however, have demonstrated how deeply ingrained and naturalized nationalism still is in contemporary Turkish society. The next decade in Turkey shall witness the challenge of the liberal elements in Turkish society against the nationalist hegemony to bring in what I, hopefully, intend to term the "post-nationalist European Union period."

One problem that I still have not resolved with this new historiography is the location of 1915 as this is a highly traumatic event that ultimately resulted in the terminal removal of Anatolian Armenians from their ancestral homeland. Even though I have criticized the employment of 1915 by Turkish nationalist historiography and attempted to correct the historical subversions implicit in its narrative through my proposed historiography, locating 1915 within the Nationalist Period of 1902 to1982 contextualizes and thereby implicitly normalizes the trauma and tragedy of 1915. And it is to this problematic issue that I next turn.

Part II: The Location of 1915 within the Post-Nationalist Turkish Historiography

In studying traumatic events that are almost beyond human comprehension, scholars find guidance in the literature on the Holocaust, for the Holocaust, like 1915, is not a historical event but rather "signals human motives and actions that put human nature at risk and subject civilization to judgment," leaving "an indelible mark on our consciousness about the nature of evil, of extreme victimization, of the limits of suffering and despair."[13] There have been a number of scholars who have compared 1915 with the Holocaust, starting with Vahakn Dadrian who drew upon social-psychology for formulating hypotheses about the profiles of the perpetrators and the victims.[14] Richard Rubenstein was the first Holocaust scholar who first acknowledged that the Armenian massacres constituted the first full-fledged attempt by a modern state to practice disciplined organized genocide, and that therefore the Holocaust had to be placed within the context of mass death in relation to it.[15] Irving Louis Horowitz made a similar argument.[16]

Helen Fein elaborated upon the comparison by stating that in both cases the political formula legitimating the raison d'étre of the state as a vehicle of destiny for the dominant group was adapted by a new elite in a state in decline to exclude the victims.[17] The next scholar to undertake an extensive comparison was Robert Melson who argued that it was the relative success of both victim groups in modernization that set the preconditions for their persecution.[18] Benjamin Valentino follows Fein's conceptualization as he groups Turkish Armenia, Nazi Germany, and Rwanda under "ethnic mass killings" to argue then that all three resulted from the efforts of the political leaders to transform radically the ethnic, religious, or national composition of society at the expense of certain groups.[19] Patricia Marchak employs the same argument as she finds in both cases, among many others, the commonality of terror sponsored by the states committing human rights crimes against their citizens.[20]

Yehuda Bauer compares the two events in relation to their characteristics and, while agreeing that the Armenian Genocide is arguably the closest parallel to the Holocaust, contends that the motivation of the former was political, chauvinistic, pragmatic, and ethnic while the latter was ideological, universal, total, and racial.[21] Martin Shaw proposes an intrinsic connection between war and genocide in that genocide is a particular form of modern warfare, which the Armenian Genocide was the first of the modern ideologically motivated genocides, and, as such, set the precedent for the Holocaust.[22] Ward Churchill makes a similar claim; he argues that 1915 served as an example to the Holocaust.[23] Maud Mandel undertakes an interesting comparative study of what she identifies as "the victims of the two twentieth century genocides" as she analyzes their reestablishment patterns in France.[24]

Still, these comparisons only provide guidance to the essential problem that exists in both cases, which is the problem of how to approach the study of such human tragedy, by itself or in relation to other events and, if the latter, how. Saul Friedlander addresses this problem in philosophical terms as a decision a scholar has to make either by studying the event in and of itself to the exclusion of everything else, or contextualizing it within everything else.[25] The exclusive focus on the event alone highlights it, but ends up removing the event from the people; its contextualization instead within the rest of history normalizes the event, but in so doing makes the event more accessible to people. The issue and the implied decision was widely discussed in the course of 1986 to become referred to as the "Historians' Debate."[26]

The parameters of this decision are particularly significant in my case because I am also ethnically a Turk, therefore by implication a member of the social group that perpetrated the unspeakable crimes of 1915. If I contextualize the massacres of 1915 in my historiography as I have within a long Turkish nationalist period that ends up normalizing 1915 and thereby, by implication, mitigating and obliterating the trauma associated with 1915, then I need to discuss critically the location of 1915 in and of itself to address this possibility. It is therefore particularly imperative for me to acknowledge that I as a Turkish scholar convey the critical stand I take in relation to 1915 in the historical narrative I construct.

In referring to this debate, scholars tend to argue that it is not the contextualization—and the ensuing normalization—that is problematic, but rather its uncritical, non-self-reflexive manner. What is at issue then is the ethics one employs in undertaking the contextualization. In attempting to find a constructive solution to this problem, Saul Friedlander argues that what is missing is "a narrative that includes both the voice of the scholar as well as the memory of the survivors, commentary and overt interpretation of events that deepen the historical record and resist hasty ideological closure."[27] The scholar thus has to work out a subject position and come to terms with his implication in the grid of tragic participant positions—it can be argued that in relation to the trauma, this stance locates the scholars closest to that of an innocent bystander. This also is the position Michael Mann seems to assume in his extremely significant work.[28]

Yet, the position of the scholar has to be a more complex one, Dominick LaCapra argues; it has to acknowledge the resister, listen attentively and respect the position of the victim, and also appreciate the complexities introduced by the oppressors to make accomplices out of victims.[29] In other words, the "network of interrelated subject positions" has to be "investigated empirically, analyzed carefully and critically, and attempted not to be replicated in one's voice." What is significant here is the strategic negotiation LaCapra asks the scholar to engage in with the trauma and its historical actors. The conventional distance that scholars place between themselves and their texts is no longer there; the strategic negotiation enables scholars to do a couple of things simultaneously: they capture the complexity of the trauma, contextualize it without normalizing it, and, by reflecting on their own subject position during this process, are able to clarify their ethical stand in relation to the trauma.

Yet I think this strategic intervention needs to be taken a step further in the direction suggested by feminist theory, which calls for the presence of the first-person narrative of the scholar within the text.[30] Feminist theory contends that the existing power relations in society that naturalize the dominance of males also affect the creation of knowledge about society at large to imbue them with the interest of the males at the expense of females. The social science texts written by male scholars therefore often end up hiding their power and authority through particular strategies such the use of the pronoun "we" or the passive sentence structure; these strategies not only obfuscate the agency of the male scholars but also indirectly end up legitimating their authority. Hence, as Michel Foucault comments in relation to scientific disciplines, the males exercise power "by tying themselves to scientific or moral definitions of who they are."[31] Just as the hidden intentions of scholars contextualizing trauma can end up normalizing it, so do the intention of male social scientists contextualizing women's experiences end up marginalizing them in society. Feminist scholars have argued that these "power relations" implicit in texts can be made transparent by introducing the standpoint of women to the texts. One strategy employed by feminist scholars like Dorothy Smith is, in opposition to what is practiced by their male counterparts, the interjection of their own voices into the texts to make their particular vantage points, their relation to the text, transparent.

It is for these reasons that I, in a strategic move, have employed and continue to employ the first person narrative in this text. One should, however, note the one major criticism that could be made against such a move, that it may distort existing power relations in society at large by privileging the voice of the scholar. Such relativism also "lacks a commitment to truth and morality."[32] Both of these criticisms center on the issue of the ethical accountability and moral responsibility of the scholar. Both as a scholar and as someone who also happens to be a Turk, that is, a member of the social group that perpetrated the massacres, what is my moral responsibility in studying 1915?

Good moral character comprises, according to David Jones, "having certain traits, or moral virtues, among which are benevolence, conscientiousness, courage, autonomy and self-control, self-knowledge, self-respect and practical wisdom."[33] The most significant manner in which societies have held individuals accountable for their actions is through the imposition of legal punishment. Holding scholars accountable for their writings and interpretations is what the academic community endeavors to do, yet if one takes a step back and focuses on the act of knowledge production itself, what are the guidelines a scholar has to follow to ensure that she is morally responsible toward her subject matter while producing the text?

The Frankfurt School and critical theory have revealed that there are human interests hidden behind knowledge that is purportedly scientific and therefore objective, and they have proposed "aggressive critique" as a way to uncover the ideologies hidden in the text. Yet if the scholar does not reveal her vantage point, this aggressive critique might privilege the standpoint of the scholar engaging in the criticism. It is for this reason that I propose that one has to, following the lead of feminist theory, interject the voice of the scholar into the text for the purpose of *transparency*. For in the world of the academe, the scholar can only establish her morally accountability in relation to her text by revealing her own voice—in so doing, she enables her audience to assume the position of enforcing moral responsibility that the legal system assumes in society.

When 1915 is thus approached within the epistemological framework of the Holocaust and with the inclusion of the voice of the scholar, two possible interpretations of 1915 emerge. The first is that 1915 was, like the Holocaust was initially framed, "an aberration in history," a viewpoint still held by the Turkish nationalist historiography. The second is that 1915 was, like the Holocaust has been defined by most scholars, a product of modernity. In relation to the latter, what has not yet been adequately studied is the impact of Ottoman modernity on society at large. Even though there have been many detailed descriptive accounts of the Ottoman reforms and established institutions, how these actually affected the lives of the subjects of the empire need to be further analyzed.

1915 as an "Aberration in Ottoman History"

It is interesting to note that the Turkish state historiography refers to the traumatic events of 1915 as "a deviance that occurred during a state of war" and often blames the conditions of World War I for the unfortunate turn of events. This mode of explanation is similar to the argument made about the initial portrayal of the Holocaust by scholars as an aberration, a catastrophe, an "ethnic cleansing that ran out of control," "a case of neglect producing a kind of guiltless guilt," a deviation from the Enlightenment.[34] This was one of the ways in which scholars managed to avoid approaching the analysis of the subject, which would have led them to questioning the fundamental premises of Western civilization. Also such portrayal created a space for the suffering of the Germans under the same conditions as well. In his analysis of the construction of Holocaust historiography, Dan Stone therefore states[35] that what marked the aftermath of World War II as well as the Nuremberg trials was "a desire, which still holds, to isolate Nazism, to ensure its place firmly outside of the Western tradition." This "aggressive silence" that continued while the Allies set upon to reconstruct a Germany fit to fight the Cold War and while parliamentary democracy was becoming triumphant was only broken in 1961 with the publication of Raoul Hilberg's *The Destruction of the European Jews*. It was only then that the Holocaust became an acceptable area for institutionally-based scholarly inquiry.[36] In terms of silences, the postwar German historiography was initially terrifyingly similar to the prewar one in that German postwar selective memory was ready and willing to talk about the suffering of the Germans, but not the Jews.[37] So the issue was not that they did not or could not remember but that they did so selectively even though, as Yehuda Bauer has noted, "the horror of the Holocaust was not that in it humans deviated from human behavior; the horror is that they didn't."[38]

The Turkish case demonstrates interesting similarities and differences from the German one. World War I, in which the Ottoman Empire was defeated, led to the partial occupation of Istanbul by the Allied Powers, which motivated the

Ottoman government to bring those who perpetrated the atrocities against the Armenians to trial. Yet the British, who took the lead in these affairs, committed a major error by arresting and imprisoning such perpetrators with persons who had resisted the Allied occupation with arms or had written critically about the Allies. What was thus an imprisonment of those who had committed the crimes against the Armenians in particular and a crime against humanity in general became intermixed with the imprisonment of those nationalist patriots who had attempted to defend their Turkish homeland from the Allied occupiers.

Of the large number tried for the Armenian massacres, only a few ended up being hanged for their crimes. Yet even more significant was the fate of those perpetrators of the atrocities who, in their attempts to elude the Allied Powers and escape trail, disappeared into the Anatolian countryside. Upon the consolidation of the Turkish War of Independence around the former Ottoman general Mustafa Kemal, which started after the Greek occupation (with Allied approval) of Izmir in 1919, these perpetrators joined the Turkish resistance movement and also fought alongside Mustafa Kemal in Anatolia, thereby throwing in their lot with the nationalists against the Allies. The eventual success of the War of Independence not only enabled them never to account for the crimes they had committed against the Armenians, but many of them became prominent statesmen in the Turkish National Assembly. In addition, their initial lack of accountability for the violence they had committed led them to sanction violence against minority groups in future Turkish events as well.

How this trajectory of lack of accountability for initial violence leads to violence sanctioning action later on is best demonstrated in the case of the prominent Turkish statesman Celal Bayar. Neither his official biography nor his autobiography mentions certain significant events in his life, thereby preventing the access of Turkish society to this significant knowledge demonstrating the close connection between lack of accountability and violence. Bayar entered political life by first becoming a member of the Committee of Union and Progress and later of its secret organization, the *Teşkilat-ı Mahsusa.* He was especially committed to creating a Turkish Muslim bourgeoisie to replace the existing cosmopolitan Ottoman Christian one and this led him to assume a hostile stand against the Christian minorities of the empire. Bayar's first significant undercover operation in 1911 was the threatening and scaring of the Ottoman Greeks living in western Anatolia, thus employing informal force to get them to immigrate to Crete and other parts of Greece, away from Asia Minor which the Union and Progress leadership had started to consider in the aftermath of the Balkan wars as "the Turkish homeland." His success in this endeavor enabled him to rise quickly within party ranks and also led to his imprisonment by the British after World War I.

Upon his release from this imprisonment, Bayar joined the Turkish National Assembly to become one of its longest serving members. He attended the Lausanne treaty negotiations as a financial expert and later became the Minister of Finance. He was serving as the president of the Turkish republic when the September 6-7, 1955, the state instigated and orchestrated attacks on the properties and, in some instances, on the lives of members of the Greek, Armenian, and Jewish minorities of Istanbul. Even though he was later tried in relation to his role in this and related events, he was acquitted by the military due to old age. I think this case and total lack of knowledge about it in Turkish society demonstrate that what is remembered and forgotten in a society is ultimately decided by those who control collective memory.[39] While following Santayana's famous dictum that those who do not remember the past are condemned to repeat it, Turkish society has had to face time and time again state violence against its minorities, as the state elites, following Claus Offe's counter-dictum that "those who remember history are condemned to repeat it," have kept employing the same extreme measures against the minorities.

In the remembrance of suffering, there is a difference between the German and Turkish cases because of the historical sequencing of events. Since the initial Ottoman defeat in World War I was followed soon thereafter by the Turkish War of Independence and the successful establishment of the Turkish republic in 1923, the Turks, unlike the Germans, initially did not have a long aftermath of defeat during which to privilege their suffering over that of the other. Once they established the republic, not only did they not mourn the loss of their empire, but instead celebrated with nationalistic fervor the victory they had won against what they perceived to be the Allied Powers in particular and the West in general. As a consequence, they instead talked about the new modern nation they were going to build and "put all the suffering behind them." Peter Burke states that the victors can afford to forget and also have the tools to enforce their forgetting; they also take what they have for granted.[40]

Hence the Turks, being the victors, could afford to forget and systematically erased the connection between memory and place so that there were almost no references left physically, historically, and culturally to the existence of an Armenian past in Anatolia which, in turn, made it easier to deny the Armenian suffering. A case in point is the erasure of topographical names in Anatolia that are of Armenian origin.[41] All was replaced by a nationalist rhetoric of a nation reborn from the ashes of an old, now destroyed empire; the nationalist victory and the Republic it produced were their compensation for all the suffering. I should note, however, that Turkey is not alone in choosing to forget the suffering in its past. In Spain, for instance, in the years following the dictator Franco's death, there was an unwritten agreement that the years of repression and human rights violations should be forgotten, at least in public.[42]

Since the Turkish republic was formulated in opposition to the Ottoman Empire, it had to define and defend its legitimacy against it which meant that the sole foundation of the Republic was predicated on repudiating any continuity with the Ottoman past in any shape or form. The Turkish state and nation was thus not only to forget the sufferings it had caused the Anatolian Armenians and other groups in its past, or the sufferings it had experienced itself, but that it actually had a past. Every endeavor was instead oriented to the bright future that was to come. So the issue was not the selective remembrance of the Germans, but the total lack of remembrance. When the Turkish republic created a national past for itself, it was no accident that its vision first went past the Anatolian homeland to locate and create a mythical past in Central Asia that defined the Turkish nation as the source of all humanity and civilization, and by implication as the original people of Anatolia.

The nationalist rhetoric reproduced in the textbooks also hindered, until very recently, the critical examination of this imagined nationalist past that placed the Turks at the center of the world. And it is the persistence of the vestiges of this naturalized nationalism that enables the Turkish state to sustain its denial within Turkish society today. It is no accident, however, when 1915 has been recently discussed that the Turkish sufferings which had been initially repressed immediately surface as a defensive measure to delegitimate the Armenian claims. I should note in the context of denial that the Turkish state is not alone in denying the nature of the events in its past; Japan, for instance, likewise still denies the violence it engaged in on the Asian continent during World War II.[43]

Given the enormity of the tragedy, there exists in the German case "a guilt on the collective consciousness of a proportion that goes beyond the individual guilt of a relatively few perpetrators."[44] In addition, "because the victims were slain solely because they belonged to a particular community and not because of any individual transgression, the amount of guilt rebounds onto the entire collective" inviting, in turn, collective guilt which cannot be collectively resolved. The same dynamics also work for the Turks in that the entire Turkish nation stands accused because of the crimes perpetrated certainly by a smaller number. Those who did not participate in the atrocities are also overlooked; differences across time and space in the perpetration of the crimes are also rarely taken into account. In addition, the denial of the Turkish state of the intentional nature of 1915 compounds the problem. When the guilt spread over the entire nation is also denied, Anthony Kauders notes in the case of the Holocaust, it becomes "much easier for the population to deny its responsibility for the events of the past: being guilty amongst the guilty could not lead to the isolation or ostracization encountered by someone who is guilty and surrounded by the innocent."[45] Hence, in the case of the Turkish society as well, individual Turks draw comfort from the state denial because no one in civil society, which is still under the influence of the nationalist state rhetoric, admits to guilt either. This produces the rather farcical situation whereby denial of suffering and guilt, sustained by legal sanctions against declaring 1915 a genocide, thrives within the boundaries of the Turkish republic while the rest of the scholarly world outside declares the same event a genocide.

The Turkish collective guilt has the potential to turn into shame when Turkish state and society are eventually confronted with the interpretation of 1915 by the rest of the scholarly world. And such an opportunity has presented itself when

Turkey started talks to join the European Union. It was therefore no accident that the discussion of 1915 has become a significant topic of public discussion since the December 17, 2004 decision by the European Union that formally started Turkey's membership process. After all, according to Aristotle, shame emerges if "those who admire us, those whom we admire, those by whom we wish to be admired, those with whom we are competing, and those whose opinion of us we respect" think poorly of us. Hence, shame requires the presence of others to be actualized.[46]

And that is what the Turkish state has recently experienced when the European Union as well as the American government mentioned the necessity for Turkey's coming to terms with 1915. As these political bodies comprised the "civilized" moral communities the Turkish state and society had aspired and still aspires to join, a quandary ensued. The fallback position in Turkey was the nationalist rhetoric of denial while there are attempts within civil society for an alternate post-national recognition of the past. Ultimately, however, the current stand would only collapse "when the people lose confidence in the moral validity of their social and political systems."[47] Whether this would actualize depends on the strength of Turkish civil society in overcoming the nationalist rhetoric.

1915 as a "Consequence of Ottoman Modernity and the Ensuing Turkish Nationalism"

Recent scholarship has emphasized that the Holocaust, rather than an aberration in history, was located within and triggered by modernity. After all, as Cristina Rojas contends[48] "the process that made 'civilization' an element of the national consciousness of the West was the same process that authorized violence in the name of civilization. The self-consciousness of civilization authorized bringing civilization to others by violent means." Likewise, Zygmunt Bauman claims that modernity was a necessary but not sufficient condition for the Holocaust and as such "the Holocaust represents the greatest achievement of the principles of modernity, not a departure from them, where the principles are rationalization, bureaucratization, legislation, surveillance and social engineering."

Four dimensions of modernity become evident in the unfolding of German history that triggered the Holocaust; these four measures to create a more "modern and efficient" German society comprised of (1) bureaucratic rational planning, (2) resettlement, (3) scientific reasoning and (4) the exclusion of irrationality. First, Gotz Aly and Susanne Heim's historical research on the entire bureaucracy of the Third Reich demonstrated that the Holocaust owed little to racial hatred and much more to bureaucratic rational planning to create a more productive and efficient society under German domination.[49] Second, the Holocaust could only be understood in relation to a wider resettlement policy whereby ethnic Germans were forcibly settled from where the Jews were removed; hence a positive and negative population policy was practiced.[50]

Even though this social engineering was partially responsible for the Holocaust, however, it nevertheless did not explain the origin of the task.

Third, these tasks originated in scientific reasoning that, unchecked by moral imperatives and legitimated in the name of objectivity, started to develop totalizing patterns of thought.[51] As scientists aimed for progress, they set targets, as they reached them they set higher ones and, in the absence of moral parameters, kept sacrificing more to reach them. It was the outcome of concerns with racial hygiene and a better civilization that led them to remove the Jews to accomplish it.[52] This factor still does not explain the targeting of the Jews in the first place and the rage and fury behind it, however. Fourth, modernity suppressed irrational thinking. The violent impulses occurred because of modernity's exclusion of the irrational, of the forces that already existed in society which were repressed in a rational system. These were unleashed in Germany at the age-old hatreds that had sustained themselves, but had initially found outlets in religion and such beliefs. In all, as one scholar noted "the Holocaust was not a 'reversion to barbarism,' nor a 'break with civilization,' still less an '*Asiatic deed*.' But it was also far from being a 'historic black hole,' somehow beyond language, poetry and historical understanding, but rather a possibility inherent in European civilization itself."[53] I would further contend that outlets in religion and such beliefs were replaced in modernity with the ideology of nationalism; it was nationalism's exclusionary urge and ability to sacrifice all, especially human life, for the greater cause, especially for the sake of the homeland, that legitimated violence throughout the twentieth century causing it to be the bloodiest century in human history.

The similarities of the Holocaust to 1915 are striking in that all four factors of modernity could already be identified in the Ottoman case. Rational planning was the one significant dimension about which the Committee of Union and Progress had continually criticized the autocratic rule of the Ottoman sultan, arguing that the entire Ottoman administrative cadre should be made up of recent graduates of Western-style schools modeled after the "modern" European schools. This tension was referred to in the case of the military as between those officers who had risen through the ranks (*alaylı*) against those who had been "schooled" (*mektepli*) after Western models. A similar reorganization of Ottoman state and society ensued after the Young Turk revolution took place in 1908: it was actually the reorganization of the military and the retirement of elderly officers without Western-style military training acquired in the new Ottoman military academies modeled after their counterparts in the West that in an unprecedented swift Balkan defeat in 1912-13 created a flood of Muslim immigrants into Anatolia and also polarized and escalated Turkish nationalism and hatred against Christians.

Likewise, the existence of the principles of self-determination had alerted the Young Turk leadership to population proportions especially in the six provinces commonly referred to *Vilayet-i Selase*. In an attempt to reduce the proportion of Christians in the population, the leadership re-districted these six provinces along with other provinces where the Christians were a majority in the cities. Following the Balkan wars, the Muslim immigrants were resettled consciously with these Anatolian Christian populations in mind. Even during the subsequent Armenian deportations, when the center received queries as to what to do with Armenian remnants, mainly women, children, and the elderly, the reply always was "disperse them in a manner so that they will not constitute more than 5 percent of the population." It is difficult to assess the radicalization thesis, although one scholar has successfully argued that this did indeed occur in the case of the measures taken by the Committee of Union and Progress.[54]

Yet probably the most significant and dramatic similarity comprises the last factor, namely the suppression of irrationality, which was unleashed against the Anatolian Armenians in 1915 under the guise of nationalism. The traumatic events of 1915 were committed by what were presumably the most civilized and educated elites of the empire who were educated in Germany and France. These were the leaders who had initially arrived in Constantinople in 1908 to proclaim, in the name of modernity, a constitution that was to complement and eventually replace the perceived arbitrary violence of the Ottoman sultan. They undertook social engineering to "remove the cancerous elements from the sick man" in an attempt to nurse him back to health. That the most radical instigators of the Armenian massacres, such as Dr. Nazım and Dr. Behaeddin Şakir (Shakir), were actually physicians ought to be noted in this context. The Union and Progress Committee attempted to save the empire and create a fatherland for the Turks. The target was the minorities in general and the Armenians in particular because the millet system had already defined their position in society as precarious; when one as an Ottoman considered the possibility of building a new Ottoman society, the bifurcated millet system already placed the minorities outside the imagined boundaries of the Turkish nation.

The Armenians, like all ethno-religious groups of the empire, attempted to become legal equals in Ottoman society since this was what modernity had promised everyone—just like the European Jews later attempted to so become in Europe after them with the same tragic results. The Armenians were also wealthy and, finally, could be replaced by the Turkish Muslim Balkan immigrants flooding the capital in the thousands to create a more ethnically homogenous population, one that would stop the European intervention in Ottoman administration. Hence, it is ironic that the European criteria imposed on the Ottoman Empire (of reform and equality), combined with the Enlightenment ideals of progress that the Ottoman educated groups had acquired, ignited under the pressure of war and nationalism to wreak vengeance on the most structurally precarious social group, the Ottoman Armenians. That the Europeans could not see the parallels between this act of extermination and the European Enlightenment has of course been one of the biggest surprises when I study the sources of the time. And yet, given what is noted in the literature on the Holocaust, that it took so many decades after the Holocaust for the Europeans to recognize the calamity as a consequence of modernity rather than as a historical aberration, this may not be so surprising.

In relation to 1915, there was the additional filter of Orientalism that enabled the Europeans to dismiss what happened to the Armenians as an "Asiatic deed" executed by people of a "different faith" thereby emphasizing the difference of culture and religion to overlook totally the very strong discourse of nationalism and modernity under which these massacres were ordered, and then to refuse to come to the aid of the Armenians when the latter attempted to establish their own homeland after the war. Why was it that the Europeans were not able to draw upon the similarities, fathom the patterns of nationalism that had emerged in the Ottoman Empire at the time, formulated after German Romanticism, to "wipe out unwanted elements?" This was undoubtedly a result of the Orientalist posture, of seeing the Ottoman Empire dominated by the Turks who were Muslims as the "Other."

The modernist notion of progress combined experience and expectation and anticipated it in the spheres outside of Europe and, in so doing, precipitated events there in ways that led to 1915. The hegemonic paradigm of the Enlightenment story views modernity of non-Western societies such as the Ottoman Empire as a consequence of Western impact and influence. Yet when one expands, as Stuart Hall suggests,[55] the boundaries of the West "to the Rest," it becomes evident that the West would not have been able to represent itself as the summit of history without comparing itself to the Rest. This expanded scope highlights the significance of experiences outside of the West in the formation of modernity, actually providing early sightings of what was to come. Indeed, one might argue that 1915 became the laboratory of the dark side of modernity, foreshadowing what was to emerge a few decades later in Europe.

Yet if the research on the Holocaust is any measure, the scholarly attempt at an explanation that I have presented above will still not be satisfactory to the victims, in this case the descendants of the Anatolian Armenians who suffered so much from what transpired in 1915. In the case of the Holocaust, the memory of those who have been directly affected by the crime differs significantly from the memory of others who study the crime. While "the victim's perspective is guided by the question of the perpetrators' motives . . . researchers who lack any direct or indirect affiliation to the collectives involved with the crime tend to universalize its meaning."[56] In identifying the elements of European modernity as interpreted by the Ottomans as the main cause leading to 1915, I too have attempted to seek broader universal dynamics instead of the particularities in the characteristics of the perpetrators. In their own accounts, scholars of Armenian origin instead emphasize the religious, ethnic, cultural characteristics of the perpetrators—the Turks. Ultimately, however, it would be the ability of all scholars to be able to recognize each other's standpoints and to jointly respect and mourn the suffering caused by the trauma of 1915 that is going to make research on this extremely significant tragedy of Armenian, Anatolian, Turkish, and human history possible. For it is only through "a democratic practice of history in which an ever growing chorus of voices is heard"[57] that one can make sense of the world.

Notes

1. Helen Fein, *Accounting for Genocide: National Responses and Jewish Victimization during the Holocaust* (New York: Free Press, 1993), p. 24.
2. David H. Jones, *Moral Responsibility in the Holocaust: A Study in the Ethics of Character* (London: Rowman and Littlefield, 1999), pp. 7, 17.
3. James E. Young, *Writing and Rewriting the Holocaust: Narrative and the Consequences of Interpretation* (Bloomington: Indiana University Press, 1988), p. 15.
4. See Mark Jackson, "The Ethical Space of Historiography," *Journal of Historical Sociology* 14:4 (2001): 80, for a detailed discussion of this ethical dimension.
5. See, for instance, Anita Shapira and Derek Penslar, eds., *Israeli Historical Revisionism: From Left to Right* (London: Frank Cass, 2003).
6. See, for instance, Gerry Van Klinken, "The Battle for History after Suharto—Beyond Sacred Dates, Great Men and Legal Milestones," *Critical Asian Studies* 33, 3 (2001): 323-350.
7. See, for instance, Joyce Appleby, Lynn Hunt, and Margaret Jacob, eds., *Telling the Truth about History* (New York: W. W. Norton, 1994), p. 102.
8. See, for a more extensive discussion of this point, Benjamin Braude and Bernard Lewis, eds., *Christians and Jews in the Ottoman Empire,* 2 vols. (New York: Holmes and Meier, 1982).
9. See Gerard J. Libaridian, *Modern Armenia: People, Nation, State* (New Brunswick, NJ: Transaction Publishers, 2004), p. 13, for a discussion of the ending point of the formative period.
10. See Fatma Müge Göçek, *Rise of the Bourgeoisie, Demise of Empire: Ottoman Westernization and Social Change* (New York: Oxford University Press, 1996), for a discussion of the parameters of this period.
11. For a more detailed discussion, see Fahir ArmaoÝlu*Şiyasi Tarih 1789-1960* [Political History 1789-1960] (Ankara: Sevinç, 1964).
12. See Vartan Artinian, "The Armenian Constitutional System in the Ottoman Empire 1839-1963," Ph.D. diss., Brandeis University, 1970, for a fuller discussion of this distinction.
13. Gulie Ne'eman Arad, "Nazi Germany and the Jews: Reflections on a Beginning, a Middle and an Open End," *History and Memory* 9, 1 (1997): 422.
14. See, for instance, Vahakn Dadrian, "The Structural Functional Components of Genocide: A Victimological Approach to the Armenian Case," in *Victimology*, ed. I. Drapkin and E. Viano (Lexington, MA: Heath, 1974), pp. 123-135; idem., "A Typology of Genocide," *International Review of Modern Sociology* 5 (1975): 201-212.
15. Richard Rubenstein, *The Cunning of History: The Holocaust and the American Future* (New York: Harper, 1978).
16. Irving Louis Horowitz, *Genocide and State Power* (New Brunswick, NJ: Transaction Publishers, 1976).
17. Ibid., p. 26.
18. Robert Melson, *Revolution and Genocide* (Chicago: University of Chicago Press, 1992).
19. Benjamin A. Valentino, *Final Solutions: Mass Killings and Genocide in the 20th Century* (Ithaca, NY: Cornell University Press, 2004).

20. Patricia Marchak, *Reigns of Terror* (Montreal: McGill Queens University Press, 2003).
21. Yehuda Bauer, *Rethinking the Holocaust* (New Haven, CT: Yale University Press, 2001).
22. Martin Shaw, *War and Genocide: Organized Killing in Modern Society* (Cambridge: Polity Press, 2003).
23. Ward Churchill, *A Little Matter of Genocide: Holocaust and Denial in the Americas, 1492 to the Present* (San Francisco: City Lights, 1997).
24. Maud Mandel, *In the Aftermath of Genocide: Armenians and Jews in Twentieth Century France* (Durham, NC: Duke University Press, 2003).
25. Saul Friedlander, *Memory, History, and the Extermination of the Jews of Europe* (Bloomington: Indiana University Press, 1993), p. 95.
26. See Dominick LaCapra, *History and Memory after Auschwitz* (Ithaca: Cornell University Press, 1998), pp. 43-72, for a discussion of this debate.
27. Quoted in James E. Young, "Between History and Memory: The Uncanny Voices of Historian and Survivor," *History and Memory* 19, 1(1997): 48.
28. Michael Mann, *The Holocaust in History* (New York: Meridian, 1987).
29. Ibid., pp. 41-42.
30. See the works of Dorothy Smith, esp. *The Conceptual Practices of Power: A Feminist Sociology of Knowledge* (Boston: Northeastern University Press, 1990).
31. Cited in Jon Simons, *Foucault and the Political* (London: Routledge, 1995), p. 2.
32. See Omar Bartov, "Intellectuals on Auschwitz: Memory, History, Truth," in *A Holocaust Reader: Responses to the Nazi Extermination*, ed. Michael Morgan (New York: Oxford University Press, 2001), p. 309, for a discussion of this point.
33. Ibid., esp. pp. 7, 45-58.
34. See, for instance, Dan Diner, "On Guilt Discourse and Other Narratives: Epistemological Observations Regarding the Holocaust," *History and Memory* 9, 1 (1997): 302, 307.
35. Dan Stone, *Constructing the Holocaust: A Study in Historiography* (London: Vallentine Mitchell, 2003), p. 84.
36. Ibid., pp. 87-88.
37. Stone, *Constructing the Holocaust*, p. 97; Diner "On Guilt Discourse and Other Narratives," pp. 301-302.
38. Yehuda Bauer, "Holocaust and Genocide: Some Comparisons," in *Lessons and Legacies*, ed. Peter Hayes (Evanston, IL: Northwestern University Press, 1991), p. 38.
39. See Gil Eyal, "Identity and Trauma," *History and Memory* 16, 1(2004): 5-6, for a discussion of this remembering and forgetting.
40. Peter Burke, "History as Social Memory," in *Varieties of Cultural History* (Cambridge: Polity, 1997), p. 54.
41. For a general discussion of this practice, see Meron Benvenisti, *Sacred Landscape: The Buried History of the Holy Land since 1948* (Berkeley, Los Angeles, London: University of California Press, 2000).
42. Andrew Rigby, "Amnesty and Amnesia in Spain," *Peace Review* 12, 1 (2000): 73-79.
43. Jordan Sand, "History and Public Memory in Japan: The 'Comfort' Women Controversy," *History and Memory* 11, 2 (1999): 115-122.
44. Diner, "On Guilt Discourse and Other Narratives," p. 303.
45. Anthony Kauders, "History as Censure: 'Repression' and 'Philo-Semitism' in Post-War Germany," *History and Memory* 15, 1(2003): 100.

46. See, for the articulation of this point, Jon Elster, *Alchemies of the Mind: Rationality and the Emotions* (Cambridge: Cambridge University Press, 1999), pp. 63, 152-153; Bernard Williams, *Shame and Necessity* (Berkeley, Los Angeles, London: University of California Press, 1993), pp. 78-82.
47. Daniel Chirot, "What Happened in Eastern Europe in 1989?" in *Popular Protest and Public Culture in Modern China: Learning from 1989,* ed. Jeffrey N. Wasserstrom and Elizabeth J. Perry (Boulder, CO: Westview, 1991), p. 221.
48. Cristina Rojas, *Civilization and Violence: Regimes of Representation in Nineteenth-Century Columbia* (Minneapolis: University of Minnesota Press, 2002), p. xiii.
49. Stone, *Constructing the Holocaust,* p. 242.
50. Ibid., p. 243.
51. Ibid., pp. 244-245.
52. Ibid., pp. 246-247.
53. Gotz Aly, "The Planning Intelligentsia and the "Final Solution,'" in *Confronting the Nazi Past*, ed. Michael Burleigh (London: Collins and Brown, 1996), p.153.
54. Donald Bloxham, *Genocide on Trial: The War Crimes Trials and the Formation of Holocaust History and Memory* (New York: Oxford University Press, 2001).
55. Stuart Hall, "The West and the Rest: Discourse and Power," in *Modernity: An Introduction to Modern Societies*, ed. S. Hall et al. (Cambridge, MA: Blackwell, 1996), p. 221.
56. Diner, "On Guilt Discourse and Other Narratives," p. 308.
57. Appleby, Hunt, and Jacob, *Telling the Truth about History,* p. 11.

22

Venturing into the Minefield: Turkish Liberal Historiography and the Armenian Genocide

Bedross Der Matossian

Historiography normally refers to the act of writing history, the collective writings of history and the history of such activities over time.[1] This chapter addresses the collective writings of history by a group of scholars of "Turkish origin," mainly deriving from a tradition of leftist sentiments. What is particular about this group of Turkish liberal historians is that they provide an alternative historical interpretation[2] of a specific historical event that is otherwise accepted by the official Turkish history (*resmi tarih*) as an historical travesty.[3]

Historical events, which are conventionally regarded as the "building bricks of history," are composed into a certain form that acts as a vehicle for the creation and representation of historical knowledge and historical explanation.[4] In other words, in the writing of history, events are placed into narrative form. Historians argue that narrative is important because it is through it that we understand the relationship between form and content, the word and the world.[5] Furthermore, in this process of the creation and the representation of historical knowledge and historical explanation it is narrative that transcends the geographic, religious, national, ethnic, and cultural boundaries in conveying its messages. Hayden White argues on this point saying: "Far from being a problem, then, narrative might well be considered a solution to a problem of general human concern, namely, the problem of how to translate knowing into telling, the problem of fashioning human experience into a form assailable to structures of meaning that are generally human rather than culture-specific.... This suggests that far from being one code among many that a culture may utilize for endowing experience with meaning, narrative is a meta-code, a human universal on the basis of which trans-cultural messages about the nature of a shared reality can be transmitted."[6] The shared reality that is being transmitted in this case through the medium of narrative is the historical event of 1915: the Armenian Genocide. Though the historical event of 1915 is considered to be a "shared reality" for both the "perpetrator group"[7] and the "victimized group," it does not mean that both groups have a common consensus or single definition and interpretation of this shared reality. Whereas the "victimized group" for decades has been fighting for international recognition of the historical event itself through using the medium of narrative in its historical explanation, the "perpetrator group" has been trying for decades to hinder the reality of the historical event through creating a narrative of its own by using the methodology of negation, rationalization, relativization, and trivialization of the Armenian Genocide.[8] Hence, the emergence of a new trend in Turkish historiography that provides an alternative interpretation of the historical event of 1915 ought to be considered as an important step toward a critical assessment of the state's narrative on the historical event of 1915.

Though an alternative interpretation of the historical event of 1915 or a critical assessment of Turkish state narrative on the event is considered to be a sound approach, still one needs not forget that histories are always shaped by both the perception of the historian and the way the historian would like the events to be understood by others through the form of narrative. White argues on this point saying "history can never provide the story, rather it is a narrative designed by the historian as he/she organizes the contents in the form of a narrative of what he/she believes the past was about."[9] Furthermore, it is the conglomerations of narratives of the historians that constitute an essential component in the act of collective writing of history that eventually become historiography. Thus, without narrative there can be no reconstruction of the past and without historical imagination there can be no history and without collective writing of histories there can be no historiography. For White "it is the success of narrative in revealing the meaning, coherence, or significance of events that attests to the legitimacy of its practice in historiography. And it is the success of historiography in narrativizing sets of historical events that attests to the 'realism' of narrative itself."[10]

This analysis assesses the contents of the narrative of Turkish liberal historiography on the event of 1915, otherwise known by Turkish liberal scholars as *soykırım*[11] (genocide), *kıyım*[12] (massacre), *katliam*[13] (massacre), *etnik temizlik*[14] (ethnic cleansing) and the widely used term by Turkish liberal scholars, *kırım*[15] (mass murder). One needs to take into consideration that each of these terminologies that define the historical event have different meanings ranging from the magnitude to the premeditated nature of the event. This suggests that the employment of different concepts by Turkish liberal historiography in defining the historical event of 1915 demonstrates the variety of their treatment of the historical event and thus shows their non-monolithic approach, contrary to what appears in Turkish official history.

However, in order for an account of past events to count as a proper history, it is not enough that it display all the features of narrativity. White argues that "in addition the account must manifest a proper concern for the judicious handling of evidence, and it must honor the chronological order of the original occurrence of the events of which it treats as a baseline not to be transgressed in the classification of any given event as either a cause or an effect. . . . The events must be not only registered within the chronological framework of their original occurrence but narrated as well, that is to say, revealed as possessing a structure, an order of meaning, that they do not possess as mere sequence."[16]

Reform, economic advancement, revolt, immigration, nationalism, and oppression constitute an essential chronological elements in the narrative of Turkish liberal historiography on the event of 1915. Moreover, this series of interconnected events constitutes the historical background and the historical explanation in the interpretation of the Turkish liberal narrative of the deterioration of the Armeno-Turkish relationship and its culmination in the Armenian Genocide. Hence, after discussing these interconnected events in the narrative of Turkish liberal historiography on the deterioration of the Armeno-Turkish relationship, I will dwell on the concept of causation and contextualization in the historical explanation of the Armeno-Turkish relationship and then will move to discuss the narrative of the event itself through the medium of premeditation-implementation and aftermath.

Reform

In his recent book, Taner Akçam indicates that the real effects of important social events can be felt only one hundred years after their occurrence. Based on the theory of the German sociologist Norbert Elias,[17] Akçam indicates that in order "to understand the Armenian Genocide it is essential to take perspective of at least a hundred years, back to the beginning of the dissolution of the Ottoman Empire."[18] The continuous European pressure on the Ottoman Empire in the nineteenth century played a decisive role in the internal administrative and legal reforms of the *Tanzimat* period. This was evident in particular with the position of the Christians and especially the Armenians in the Ottoman Empire. Though the primary goal of these reforms was purely political, that is, to satisfy the European powers, this does not mean that there was not an internal will to improve the administration and the status of the non-Muslim elements living in the Ottoman Empire. In addition, these reforms in particular in the provincial system aimed at strengthening the control of the center over the periphery and consequently a process of centralization began as an ultimate reaction to the "dissolution" of the Ottoman Empire. For example, in 1864, a complete overhaul of regulations on the organization of provincial government was initiated, a move that aimed at bringing the periphery closer to the grip of the center.

However, the nineteenth-century reforms in the Ottoman Empire did not have the same impact on the Muslims as they did on the non-Muslims. Fatma

Müge Göçek argues that the effects of the reforms on the Ottoman Muslims were largely negative. The Muslims interpreted the rights promised to the minorities as a loss of their privileged position in the empire.[19] It is this feeling of the loss of a privileged position and the "elevation" of the status of the non-Muslims that led to the deterioration of interethnic relationships. Furthermore, these reforms also had an impact on changing the dynamics of power inside the Armenian *millet* in the Ottoman Empire and culminated in the creation of the Armenian National Constitution and the crystallization of the Armenian identity. However, for Turkish liberal historiography reform also meant international pressure as reform became a strong catalyst that "opened the way for the imperialist powers to interfere in the Ottoman Empire's internal affairs, and almost every national or religious group would ultimately receive patronage and support from one of the Great Powers." [20] Subsequently, after the Congress of Berlin in 1878 when the Armenian Question became internationalized, the issue of reform became a stronger catalyst for European pressure. However, the deplorable condition of the periphery led the Armenians constantly to demand reforms and appeal to the European powers for intervention. Thus, the issue of reform and international intervention were important factors that were to haunt the Armenian-Turkish relationship until the collapse of the Ottoman Empire.

Economic Advancement and Nationalism

The Anglo-Ottoman Convention of 1838 and various trade agreements with European powers in the nineteenth century led to a dramatic increase of European trade in the Ottoman Empire. Foreign trade in the Ottoman provinces fell slowly under the monopoly of non-Muslim Ottoman merchants, chiefly of Greek and Armenian origin. For Turkish liberal historians economic advancement had direct connection with the emergence of nationalism. After demonstrating the economic advancement and integration of the Armenians in the Ottoman society, Fikret Adanır poses the question, "Why did the Armeno-Turkish relationship become catastrophic?"[21] One decisive factor that he demonstrates is nationalism.[22] For Halil Berktay, Göçek, and Adanır commerce had a direct impact on the emergence of Armenian nationalism. Berktay indicates that "trade, the money economy, and capitalism first developed among the non-Turkish and non-Muslim population groups of the empire. In this way these groups became more open to nationalist movements and engaged in struggles against the empire in order to establish their own nation states" [*ulus devletlerini kurmak için*].[23] However, Göçek indicates that "Turks and Muslim Arabs did not benefit from the changing patterns of commerce as much as the Greeks and Armenians; in the case of the Ottoman Turks, the commercial success of the Ottoman minorities generated enmity and fostered Turkish nationalism."[24] Her observation is important because it indicates that the economic advancement of the Armenians had a double impact. It not only fostered Armenian nationalism, but Turkish reactionary nationalism as well. The various boycotts against the Austrians, Greeks, and Armenians in the last decade of the Ottoman Empire enhanced the radicalization of the Turkish nationalism, and, as Göçek indicates, "these boycotts led the Unionists to conclude that only a national economy and a Turkish bourgeoisie could withstand foreign intervention and domination."[25] In addition, Göçek considers some other factors that played an important role as determinants of the structure of nationalisms that emerged in the nineteenth-century Ottoman Empire.[26] These include war and reform movements, the new visions of history that emerged in the intelligentsia of the ethnic groups living in the Ottoman Empire and, finally, their literature and education which gave meaning to them. She continues on this point arguing: "The combination of war, commerce, and reforms that transformed existing social relations thus interacted with new visions painted by history, literature, and education and, under the parameters set by the existing organizations of philanthropic and secret societies and political parties, determined the patterns the nationalisms within the Ottoman empire took." [27]

Revolts and Immigration

Demographic changes in Anatolia as a result of immigration of Muslims from the Balkans and the Caucasus and events taking place in the Balkans had an important impact on the deterioration of the Armeno-Turkish relationship. It is impossible to examine the historical background of the Armeno-Turkish conflict without taking into consideration two important factors: revolts and immigration. It is worthy to mention that in a span of twenty years, from 1862 to1882, the immigration of the Muslim population from the Balkans and Russia increased the Ottoman population by at least 40 percent.[28] A good number of these immigrants populated areas where Armenians were living thus creating population imbalance and consequentially creating friction among the local populations and the immigrants.[29] The special status that the Armenian merchants enjoyed under the protection of the European powers led these new immigrants, persecuted by the tsarist regime in Russia, to be more antagonistic toward the Armenians. It is worth mentioning that the situation in some parts of the Anatolian provinces was already deteriorating. Frequent attacks by the Kurdish tribes on the Armenians, heavy taxation, friction with the newly immigrated Muslims from the Caucasus and the Balkans, corruption in the administration, and failure of Armenian efforts to solve these problems in a diplomatic way led to the emergence of Armenian revolutionary groups. The Treaty of San Stefano in March 1878 was followed in July by the Treaty of Berlin, considered by the Armenians a disastrous diplomatic failure.

It seems that between 1878 and 1880 there was a major ideological shift within the Armenian communities of Anatolia. It is only after 1880 that the revolutionary movement emerged in the provinces. The Balkan insurrections on the other hand had an impact on the emergence of the Armenian revolutionary groups.[30] The nationalist uprising of the Balkan groups, beginning with the Serbian revolt of 1804 and culminating belatedly in the Bulgarian revolt of 1875, had an impact on the Armenians living in Anatolia and shattered all kinds of possible unity under the banner of Ottomanism.[31] Adanır indicates that the beginning of these revolutionary activities in the eastern provinces was aimed at resisting the encroachment of the Kurdish tribes. However, he indicates that with the arrival of the Hnchak and the Dashnaktsutiun (Armenian Revolutionary Federation) underground groups the policy changed.[32] These organizations, he asserts, aimed for the independence of Armenia and acted to gain European involvement through the tactic of provocation-massacres-intervention.[33] Turkish liberal historiography downplays the approach of Armenian historiography to these revolutionary groups as pure self-defense units intended to protect the Armenian-inhabited areas from the Kurdish encroachments. For example, Selim Deringil argues on this issue, stating that the well-armed Armenian partisan groups that were active in Anatolia were more than "self-defense units."[34] In order to understand better the nature of these groups and their relations with the Turkish and the Kurdish population, Deringil suggests concentrating more on the interethnic periphery relationships. "What were the relations between the sedentary Armenian population and the nomadic Kurds, say between 1880 and 1915?" asks Deringil. "How did the state policy articulate with local balances? What were the dimensions of collaboration with Russia?"[35] Deringil suggests that in order to understand better the breaking points between the Armenians and the Turks a considerable initial corpus of micro-level monographic studies needs to be conducted.[36] Deringil raises an important point here and that is the lack of micro-level monographic studies that deal with the Armeno-Turkish conflict in particular on the periphery level as most of the studies tend to deal more with the diplomatic and political history of the period. [37]

As mentioned, the activities of the guerrillas in the Balkans and the events that accompanied the Ottoman defeat by Russia in 1877-78, were hard blows to the Ottomanist vision for a fraternal union of the people of the empire.[38] Consequently, this led to the immigration of hundreds of thousands of Muslims who were escaping the Russian army or expelled by the Christian state and looked for refuge in Asia Minor. Berktay argues that in this period the Ottomans tried to repress nationalist uprisings in the Balkans and perpetrated massacres. Then Turkish Muslims in the region were massacred and they fled as a result to Istanbul and Anatolia.[39] Adanır and Berktay highlight the issue of the immigration as an important factor in the deterioration of the Armeno-Turkish relationship. According to Berktay, this is an important point because the bitterness of the uprisings in the Balkans caused great hatred (*büyük bir hınç biriktirdi*) and desire for revenge among Turkish Muslims. He continues: "The Armenian affair cannot be understood without paying attention to this hatred" [*Ermeni olayı bu hınç birikimi dikkate alınmadan anlaşılamaz*].[40]

Oppression

According to Deringil a "legitimacy crisis" took place in the Ottoman Empire in the second half of the nineteenth century. This legitimacy crisis, which had internal and external dimensions, resulted from the challenges of the time. Deringil indicates that "by the reign of Abdulhamid, the desire of the state to administer and control with hitherto unprecedented intensity led to a situation where the role of the center had to be constantly re-defined."[41] One of the challenges of the time was the rising Armenian nationalism that was reflected in the Armenian revolutionary movements. Deringil indicates that as the tension between Muslims and Armenians mounted in the 1890s, the Ottoman center became more attentive to the smallest detail that could influence inter-community relations.[42] Furthermore, the center began monitoring every single movement regardless if it was by a revolutionary group or a philanthropic one that could endanger its entity and hence by taking the necessary measures it tried to diminish that threat. For this, Deringil illustrates an interesting example of Ottoman counter-espionage against the Hnchak revolutionaries in 1894. The counter-espionage took place in the United States in order to monitor the activities of the Hnchak party in Boston. The Ottoman government through the Turkish consul in Boston tried to enlist an Armenian informant to gather information about the activities of the local party organization. In the end, the attempt failed as the Armenian informant began to demand higher compensation.[43] The case indicates that the Ottoman government was active internationally in monitoring the activities of the other branches of the revolutionary groups that were present in the Ottoman Empire.

Meanwhile, Islam was used by the state as a mobilizing force of solidarity and hence for demographic reasons the Muslim immigrants from the Balkans and the Caucasus were resettled in Asia Minor, particularly in Armenian-populated areas. The resettlement of refugees in these areas played an important role in the escalating Armeno-Turkish tensions. Furthermore, in order to combat the Russians, in 1891, Sultan Abdul Hamid II created the irregular *Hamidiye* regiments, primarily from among the Kurds, but as Adanır indicates, "in reality these were against the local population, and contributed in deteriorating the Armenian situation."[44] Deringil, Berktay, and Engin Akarlı argue the same. According to Deringil: "There was certainly a policy during the Hamidian era to use Kurdish tribes as Cossack-inspired irregulars [Hamidiye units] against the Armenians, as there was a search for a new base of solidarity on a recharged Islamic basis."[45] Berktay, on the other hand, highlights the issue of irregular troops in his comment on the massacres during the Hamidian period: "In any case, during the 'century of dissolution [*çözülüş yüzyılı*]' the Ottoman administration repeatedly chose to use not the standing army [*düzenli ordudan*], but irregulars and undisciplined [*düzensiz güçleri*] in these affairs, relying on their primitiveness and violence."[46] This point of irregular troops is an important one that Berktay raises again when discussing the Armenian Genocide of 1915.

In addition, most of these scholars do not see a continuity between the Hamidian massacres and the Young Turks policies as it is attested in some trends of the Armenian historiography on the Armenian Genocide.[47] Deringil on this point indicates that the "Hamidian policies of ad hoc, semiofficial and official massacres were qualitatively different from the systematic persecution carried out in the Young Turk era."[48] Similarly, Akarlı indicates the need to distinguish between Abdul Hamid's relatively measured repression of the Armenians and the annihilative policies of the Committee of Union and Progress (Young Turks). He continues on this point saying: "For all his faults, Abdulhamid felt more bound by certain traditions of statecraft, which should help explain why the Ottoman state lasted so long on such wide-flung territories."[49]

Causation and Contextualization

In discussing premeditation, implementation, and aftermath in the narrative of Turkish liberal historiography, it is necessary to consider the issue of causation and contextualization in Armeno-Turkish relations. Generally speaking, causal relations exist between events, that is, if event A occurs, then event B follows, and "it can be reasonably demonstrated that event A explains the subsequent (temporal sequential) occurrence of event B."[50] Some historians tend to place an emphasis on causation. Noted British historian E. H. Carr, for example, maintained that the study of history is the study of causes.[51] Carr elaborates further on this point: "The relation of the historian to his causes has the same dual and reciprocal character as the relation of the historian to his facts. The causes determine his interpretation of the historical process, and his interpretation determines his selection and marshalling of the causes. The hierarchy of causes, the relative significance of one cause or set of causes or of another, is the essence of his interpretation."[52] Thus, the hierarchy of causes is the essence of interpretation.

Hayden White has a different perception. For him, focusing on the causes of an event "fails to recognize the variety of narratives that can be told and that themselves prefigure the type of causal connections to be made."[53] Because, as Alan Munslow states, "White sees history as a literary artifact, he believes that historians make causal links as part of their overall constitution and prefiguration of the historical field through the exercise of their historical imagination and the employment of trope, emplotment, argument, ideological preference and philosophical orientation."[54]

As stated, Turkish liberal historiography tends to represent the historical background of the Armeno-Turkish conflict by using causal relations. Thus, for example, if there had been no Armenian economic advancement there would not have been the growth of nationalism, and if there had been no resettlement policy in the Armenian provinces there would not have been ethnic friction, and if there had been no revolt there would not have been oppression, and so forth. The use of causal relations by Turkish liberal historiography in explaining the historical events of 1915 limits the variety of other narratives explaining those events.

The employment of causal relationships in Turkish liberal historiography raises the concept of contextualization. Although, in such horrendous events such as genocide, contextualization may help to explain the crime, it might also demonstrate its inevitability and minimize the level of the catastrophe. Thus, a scholar is faced with the dilemma of reconstructing the past through the integral use of causal relations and through contextualization and normalization of the event to give it proper historical meaning but without losing the ethical component. Göçek captures this dilemma with the following words:

> If I contextualize the massacres of 1915 in my historiography, as I have, within a long Turkish nationalist period that ends up normalizing 1915 and thereby, by implication, mitigating and obliterating the trauma associated with 1915, then I need to critically discuss the location of 1915 in and itself to address this possibility. For I am doubly implicated, not only as a scholar but also as a Turk. It is therefore particularly imperative for me to acknowledge that I as a Turkish scholar convey the critical stand I take in relation to 1915 in the historical narrative I construct.

What Göçek argues is that it is not contextualization and the ensuing normalization of the event that is problematic rather its uncritical manner. She continues on this point: "What is at issue then is the ethics one employs in undertaking the contextualization." [55] So how should scholars approach a subject such as genocide? Based on Dominick LaCapra,[56] Göçek suggests that the scholar should engage in a strategic negotiation with the trauma and its historical actors: "The conventional distance scholars place between themselves and their texts is no longer there; the strategic negotiation enables the scholar to do a couple of things simultaneously: he captures the complexity of the trauma, contextualize it without normalizing it, and by reflecting on his own subject position during this process, is able to clarify his ethical stand in relation to the trauma."

Premeditation-Implementation-Aftermath

Turkish liberal historiography examines the concepts of premeditation, implementation, and aftermath through the lens of the second constitutional period (1908-18).[57] In other words, the second constitutional period becomes the ultimate tool for the contextualization of the historical event of 1915. Although the contribution of Turkish liberal historiography on the historical event of 1915 is still in its infancy,[58] the phase leading to the second constitutional period has been examined thoroughly by shedding new light in particular on the Armeno-Turkish relationship in the pre-revolution era and the level of their cooperation.

In a painstaking study, Sükrü Hanioğlu has demonstrated the relationship of the Young Turks with the Armenians, in particular with the Armenian

Revolutionary Federation, which was more inclined to Prince Sabaheddin's decentralization ideology.[59] Furthermore, Hanioğlu has demonstrated that the relationship between the Young Turks and the Dashnaktsutiun was not great because they disagreed on a number of points, especially the issues of foreign intervention and decentralization.[60] Though in the first congress of the Ottoman oppositional groups in 1902 the relationship of the Armenians with the Young Turks was tense,[61] between 1905 and 1907, the relationship between the Young Turks and the Dashnaktsutiun improved, and as a result of Sabaheddin Bey's efforts, the two sides reached a serious agreement for the first time in the history of the Young Turk movement.[62] Consequently, the Dashnaktsutiun began to take part in the revolutionary propaganda that was not only confined to the Armenian circles; rather it appealed also to the Turkish circles inviting them to common action.[63] Furthermore, bogus organizations were formed in order to maximize the spectrum of the revolution. The most important of these bogus organizations established by the Dashnaktsutiun was the so-called Turkish Allied Party. Hanioğlu indicates that the real object of the Dashnaktsutiun, a rapprochement between Turks and Armenians, became the most common theme in the Turkish Allied Party's propaganda.[64]

Regardless of the level of cooperation, the selective Armeno-Turkish cooperation against the regime of Abdul Hamid II is an important point that contradicts the official Turkish history (*resmi tarih*), which contends that the Armenian revolutionary activities, in particular those of the Dashnaktsutiun against Abdul Hamid, were rebellious acts aimed at the establishment of an independent Armenia and disregards Armenian cooperation with the Young Turks whose goals were the overthrow of the oppressive sultan's regime and reinstatement of the Ottoman constitution.[65] Despite this fact, two main issues remained as serious obstacles in the Armeno-Turkish relationships: decentralization and international intervention. It is no surprise that the Armenians like the Arabs and the Albanians were more inclined to Prince Sabaheddin because of his decentralized approach influenced by the theories of Demolins.[66] This is also evident in the Armenian press in the post-revolution period by the entrance of Sabaheddin to Istanbul. Hanioğlu indicates that following his failure to interest the Armenian committees, some of which were bargaining with Sabaheddin at the same time, Behaeddin Shakir [67] decided to abandon his grandiose scheme of uniting all the Young Turks, Ahmed Jelaleddin Pasha, and the Armenian committees in an organization that would in reality be under his control.[68] The result was that the organization adopted the name the CUP (Committee of Union and Progress),[69] Behaeddin Shakir became responsible for the creation of four independent divisions of the central committee, a fact that according to Hanioğlu helped Behaeddin Shakir to gain the upper hand in the organization and made him the hidden leader of the new organization.[70] What is the significance of Behaeddin Shakir in the central committee after the revolution? To what extent did Behaeddin Shakir manipulate this role in the liquidation process of the Armenians in 1915?

As mentioned, between 1905 and 1907, relations between the Young Turks and the Dashnaktsutiun improved. This led the Armenian party to take a more active role in a second congress of Ottoman oppositional parties in 1907. The CUP, Prince Sabaheddin's League of Private Initiative and Decentralization, and the Dashnaktsutiun, jointly organized that congress in which general agreement was reached among the three committees.[71] According to Hanioğlu, "the Year 1908 thus opened with a tactical alliance in place among three opposition committees. For those who had witnessed the endless debates between the leaders of the Dashnaktsutiun and the CUP. . ., this seemed a considerable success."[72]

To what extent was this cooperation between the Dashnaktsutiun and the CUP productive or vital for the realization of the Young Turk revolution? To what extent was this cooperation sincere? To what extent did the Young Turks trust the Armenians? Hanioğlu comments on this point, saying: "The CPU [CUP] papers and available Ottoman documents reveal that the joint CPU-Dashnaktsutiun revolutionary activities were very insignificant and that the CPU never trusted the Dashnaktsutiun. . . . The CPU alliance with the Dashnaktsutiun played no role whatsoever in that revolution and was for practical purposes almost worthless."[73] This indicates the level of the distrust that existed between the Committee of Union and Progress and the Dashnaktsutiun, the only Armenian party cooperating with the CUP. Why did the Young Turks not have sincere confidence in the non-Muslim elements, in particular the Armenians? According to Akçam, the Young Turks looked no more favorably on other non-Muslim elements living in the Ottoman Empire. In the Young Turks' view the non-Muslims represented a potential threat that would or could split the empire.[74]

The Young Turk revolution of 1908 brought with it hopes of freedom and equality. It was with the reinstatement of the Ottoman Constitution of 1876 that a new phase began in the Ottoman Empire and which ended in the collapse of the empire after World War I. This phase was characterized by overlapping "*isms*," identities, and loyalties, ranging from Ottomanism to Islamism, Turkism, and Arabism. This phase was also characterized by immense international pressure on the Ottoman Empire, loss of territories, and mounting politicization of the ethnic boundaries.

The hopes for the ideal Ottoman society based on equality and justice after the post-revolutionary period under the banner of Ottomanism began to fade as a result of political ruptures in this process. One of the most important ruptures was the counterrevolution of 1909, which was initiated by the reactionary forces in the Ottoman Empire. The counterrevolution, widely known as the *31 Mart olayları* (the March 31 incidents), and the accompanying massacres in Adana and throughout Cilicia had a tremendous impact on disrupting the equilibrium of this transitional period. Most Turkish liberal historians fail to address this important point.[75] Although the Cilician massacres were not the ultimate manifestation of the radicalization of Turkish nationalism,[76] they opened a serious gap between the Armenians and the Turks. For most of the Turkish liberal historians it was the

Balkan wars that led to the radicalization of Turkish nationalism and a drastic change in the government's policy toward the Christian elements living in the empire, in particular the Armenians. Adanır comments on this issue:

> The Balkan wars (1912 and 1913) constituted a turning point in the evolution of the relationship between the Young Turks and the Armenians. Two changes of political direction seem to be significant in this regard: the first turning point is seen in the new conception of the CUP about the national question. Confronted with a new wave of Muslim refugees coming from the Balkan, the majority of the Young Turks abandoned their egalitarian Ottomanist attitude and began to utilize the demands of the Muslims in a campaign of defamation of the non-Muslim populations. . . .
>
> The second turning point took place within the Armenian camp. After the disastrous Ottoman defeat in the Balkan wars and the fact that certain promises of the Young Turks—such as those concerning the issue of the Armenian territories—did not materialize, the Armenian Revolutionary Federation decided to place again the solution of the Armenian Question in the hands of the Great Powers.[77]

According to Adanır, this consequentially led to a grave crisis in the Young Turk-Armenian relationship in 1913-14.[78]

Rejecting the view that it was during the Balkan wars that Turkish nationalism began to be radicalized, Hanioğlu, utilizing the private papers of several secretaries of the CUP's secret central committee, maintains that the CUP was a more intensely Turkish nationalist organization from an earlier date than many historians have thought.[79] Commenting on this point, he writes: "It is obvious that the Young Turks had strong nationalistic feelings even before the Young Turk revolution of 1908. Contrary to commonly held views, this policy did not begin after the Balkan wars of 1912-1913."[80] So, if Turkish nationalism was evident even before the 1908 revolution, does this mean that there was a long-term plan by Turkish nationalists to establish a Turanic empire in which the Armenians were considered to be a huge impediment for the realization of this ideology and does this mean that Pan-Turkism was the ultimate motive behind the Armenian Genocide? Most Turkish liberal historians refute Pan-Turkism as the ultimate ideology or the motive behind the annihilation of the Armenians.[81] Akarlı comments on this point saying: "Since they are called 'Young Turks' by common convention, and because some of them sometimes sang songs of a mythical 'Turan' or Pan-Turkish state, we cannot jump at the conclusion that they thus wanted to get rid of all the Armenians once and for all to clear the way to the Turan. If the UPP [Union and Progress Party] leadership agreed on anything, it was the preservation of Ottoman state as a centralized structure, however much of it could be preserved, and at whatever cost."[82]

The issue of Turkification or centralization still remains a lively debate among Turkish liberal scholars. So what was the motive behind the Armenian Genocide? Akçam argues that the feeling of vengeance, formed among Ottoman Turkish officials as a result of continual territorial losses, was largely directed at the non-Muslim minorities, "the "servants of yesterday," who lived on these lands. And during World War I this revenge, which could not have been taken against the Bulgarians or the Greeks, was instead taken out against the "ungrateful" Armenians, who, by "collaborating with the imperialists, struck us from behind."[83] Akçam continues on this issue stating: "In short, the ruling members of an Empire that was continually losing territories, that stood on the verge of collapse, perceived the national and democratic demands of their Christian subjects through the psychoses of isolation, fear and annihilation, and adopted an approach to them that was in line with these feelings."[84]

According to Berktay and Akçam, it is this feeling of "total annihilation" that led the military dictatorship of the CUP to take such a drastic step especially after the Armenian demands for reform.[85] Akçam continues on this issue stating that the ruling members of the empire approached these national demands with the understanding that they would have to conduct a "war for survival." And the only way to win this "war of survival" was through the homogenization of troubled, heterogeneous areas.[86] I think that the concept of "total annihilation" or "war for survival" should be understood more as wartime rhetoric manipulated by the CUP for the justification of the annihilation of the Armenians rather than reflecting the "true" feelings of the CUP leadership. Regarding the premeditation issue, Akçam demonstrates that the decision for the annihilation of the Armenians was taken in March 1915, when a clandestine decision was made against the Armenians and Behaeddin Shakir was tasked with its implementation.[87] Akçam, Berktay, and Deringil believe that the decision for the annihilation of the Armenians was given orally to the regions.[88] Berktay argues that in the orders for deportation there was no mention of massacre (*katlıam*) and mass murder (*kırım*). However, at the same time, separate unwritten special orders were given (*ayrı ve yazlı olmayan özel emirler verilmiştir*) to the most rapacious members of the Special Organization (*Teşkilat-i Mahsusa*) who "worshiped violence and were not bound to any moral codes" [*hiçbir toplumsal ahlak kayıdıyla bağlı olmayan*]. [89] In the arguments of Akçam, Berktay, and Deringil, one notices a special emphasis on the Special Organization and the total exclusion of the Ottoman army from the responsibility of the Genocide. Isn't the army at the end of the day the symbol of the state? Wasn't this army the one who waged the War of Independence that led to the establishment of the Turkish republic? Akçam sees a strong relationship between the Armenian Genocide and the foundation of the Turkish republic: "I think the main reason the Turks avoid any discussion on history and make it a taboo lies in the reality of this connection between the Armenian Genocide and the foundation of the Turkish Republic."[90]

Ayhan Aktar has demonstrated that this taboo was discussed in the Ottoman Parliament long before the foundation of the Turkish republic.[91] In dealing with the Ottoman parliamentary debates of 1918, Aktar emphasizes that no one from the Ottoman deputies at that time has shed any doubt about the actuality of the mass murder. By using the terminology *imha edilmek* (to be annihilated), *cinayeti azime* (macabre murder), *Ermeni kıtalı* (Armenian massacre), and

Ermeni faciası (Armenian catastrophe), the Ottoman Parliament confirmed that "crimes against humanity" had been committed against the Armenians during the world war. Aktar draws the following conclusions:

1. The deputies in the Ottoman Parliament, Muslim and non-Muslim, did not enter a mode of saying: "this matter [massacres] did not take place and all the sayings are false" (*bu iş olmamıştır, söylenenlerin hepsi yalandır*). However, the proposals brought by Ottoman deputies of Armenian and Greek origins to punish those responsible met with obstacles, as the deputies of the Committee of Union and Progress were a majority in the Parliament.[92]

2. The CUP deputies, on the one hand, were saying, that "Turks also died" and the minority deputies, on the other hand, were saying that the bandit organizations (*çete yönetimi*) were responsible for the massacre and asked for their punishment;

3. The current debates surrounding the Armenian deportation revolve around two poles: on the one hand, there are those who adhere to the premeditated character of an organized "genocide" and, on the other hand, there are those who justify expulsions of hundreds of thousands of people as a simple administrative measure necessitated by the wartime conditions (*şavas şartlarının gereği olan basit bir idari tedbir*).

Aktar summarizes: "And within this polarized context of 'blacks and whites,' it becomes almost impossible to maintain an academic discussion. In this climate the voices of social scientists who are seeking truth in 'gray zones' [*gri alanlarda*] are intimidated into silence and are asked to be condemned by the law of 'national treachery' [*hıyaneti vataniye*]."[93]

The most recent incident of this sort is that of the conference organized by Bosporus (Boğaziçi), Bilgi, and Sabancı universities and entitled "Ottoman Armenians during the Era of Imperial Decline: Academic Responsibility and Issues of Democracy" which had been scheduled to take place at Bosporus University during May 25-27, 2005. The conference was deferred because of the strong reactions of the government and both the ruling and the opposition parties. Following Minister of Justice Cemil Çiçek's characterization of the conference "as a treason against Turkey" [*Türkiye'ye hıyanet olarak*], Bosporus University announced the postponement of the conference.[94] However, after weeks of deliberations and numerous attempts by the Turkish government to block the conference, it was held on September 24-25 at Bilgi University.[95] The conference is considered an important step for Turkish liberal historiography, because for the first time since the founding of the Turkish republic in 1923, a meeting within a Turkish university questioned the state narrative on one of the most sensitive issues—the Armenian Genocide, whether or not it was given that name.

Conclusion

In historical narrative it is "narrativity" that, as Paul Ricoeur puts it, "brings us back from within-time-ness to historicality, from 'reckoning with' time to 'recollecting' it."[96] This chapter has attempted to assess the "recollecting" of Turkish liberal historiography of an important event in the history of the Ottoman Empire and modern Turkey. In doing so, it has shown that the narrative of Turkish liberal historiography is not as monolithic as the narrative of the *resmi tarih* (official history). Despite having some commonalities with the Armenian historiography, Turkish liberal historiography still provides different perspectives to understanding the Armenian Genocide. Moreover, Turkish liberal historiography in its historical explanation of the event tends to deal more with causal relations by using contextualization as a tool. In studying horrendous events such as genocides, contextualization may yield a better understanding of the event, but it might also tend to demonstrate its inevitability and thereby minimize the level of the catastrophe. In addition, most Turkish liberal historians refrain from dealing directly with the mechanism of the event itself, as they tend to describe the macro-history of the event rather than dealing with it on the micro-level. Turkish liberal historiography on the Armenian Genocide is still in its infancy, because a Turkish critical approach to the history of Turkey and the Ottoman Empire in general is still on the threshold of achieving what Göçek calls "post-nationalist critical narrative." One also need not forget that the task of Turkish liberal historians, in particular those who "venture into the minefield" or roam in the "gray zones," is an intricate one. Through workshops, dialogues, and conferences Turkish liberal historiography can be fostered. Moreover, such events must focus first and foremost on Turkish society through publishing their proceedings in Turkish translation in order to promote the "narratives of society" that challenge the "state narrative."[97]

Turkey today is standing on the threshold of entering the European Union. Some will argue that this move will yield positive outcomes for Turkish liberal historiography. However, the ongoing massive campaign by the Turkish government, the Justice and Development Party (Adalet ve Kalkınma Partisi or AKP), and the Republican People's Party (Cumhuriyet Halk Partisi or CHP), both against the Armenian "claims" and the Turkish "collaborators," conveys another message.

Notes

1. The phrase "Venturing into the Minefield" was used by Selim Deringil in an article titled "The Study of the Armenian Crisis of the Late Ottoman Empire, or, Seizing the Document by the Throat," in *New Perspectives on Turkey* 27 (Fall 2002): 35. On historiography, see Alan Munslow, *The Routledge Companion to Historical Studies* (London, New York: Routledge, 2000), p. 133.
2. In the past two decades a new trend emerged in Turkey that began a critical assessment of Turkish history and historiography. It is important to mention the following

among many others: Nergis Canefe, "Turkish Nationalism and Ethno-Symbolic Analysis: The Rules of Exception," *Nations and Nationalism* 8, 2 (2002): 133-55; Ayla Göl, "Imagining the Turkish Nation through 'Othering' the Armenians," *Nations and Nationalism* 11, 1 (2005): 121-139; Ayşe Kadioğlu, "The Paradox of Turkish Nationalism and Construction of Official Identity," *Middle Eastern Studies* 32, 4 (1996): 177-193; Fatma Müge Göçek, "The Decline of the Ottoman Empire and the Emergence of Greek Armenian, Turkish, and Arab Nationalisms," in *Social Constructions of Nationalism: In the Middle East*, ed. Fatma Müge Göçek (Albany: State University of New York Press, 2002), pp. 15-83; idem, "Silences in the Turkish Republican Past: An Analysis of Contemporary Turkish-Armenian Literature," presented at a workshop at the Hagop Kevorkian Center for Near Eastern Studies, New York University, October 27, 2003; idem, "Reconstructing the Turkish Historiography on the Armenian Deaths and Massacres of 1915," in *Looking Backward, Moving Forward: Confronting the Armenian Genocide* , ed. Richard G. Hovannisian (New Brunswick: Transaction Publishers, 2003), pp. 209-230; Taner Akçam, *Insan hakları ve Ermeni sorunu* [Human Rights and the Armenian Question] (Istanbul: Image Press, 1999); idem, *Turk ulusal kimliği ve Ermeni Sorunu* [Turkish National Identity and the Armenian Question] (İstanbul: İletişim Publications, 1994); idem, *Ermeni tabusu aralanırken: Diyalogdan başka bir çözüm var* mı? [As the Armenian Taboo Is Being Unsilenced: Is There A Solution Other than a Dialogue?] (İstanbul: Su Publications, 2000); idem, *From Empire to Republic: Turkish Nationalism and the Armenian Genocide* (New York: Zed Books, 2004); Taner Timur, *Türkler ve Ermeniler: 1915 ve sonrası* [Turks and Armenians: 1915 and Its Aftermath] (Ankara: Image Press, 2001); Fuat Dündar, *Ittihat ve Terakki'nin Müslümanları iskan politikası (1913-1918)* [Union and Progress Party's Muslim Resettlement Policy (1913-1918)] (İstanbul: Iletişim Press, 2001); Osman Selim Kocahanoğlu, *İttihat-Terakki'nin sorgulanması ve yargılanması: meclis-i mebusan zabıtları* [The Interrogation and Trial of the Union and Progress: Proceedings of the Ottoman Assembly] (Istanbul: Temel Press, 1998); Şükrü Hanioğlu, *Preparation for a Revolution: The Young Turks, 1902-1908* (New York: Oxford University Press, 2001); idem, *The Young Turks in Opposition* (New York: Oxford University Press, 1995); Aykut Kansu, *1908 Devrimi: The Revolution of 1908 in Turkey*, trans. Ayda Erbal (İstanbul : Iletişim, 1995, 2006); idem, *Revolution of 1908 in Turkey* (Leiden and New York: E. J. Brill, 1997); idem, *Politics in Post-Revolutionary Turkey, 1913-1918* (Leiden and Boston: E .J. Brill, 2000).

3. The Turkish official history (*resmi tarih*) on the Armenian Question is embodied in the work of Esat Uras, *Tarihte Ermeniler ve Ermeni Meselesi* [Armenians in History and the Armenian Question] (Ankara: Yeni Press, 1950). The book was translated and appeared in English with a number of additions in 1988 (Istanbul: Documentary Publications). See also Y. G. Çark, *Türk devletinin hizmetinde* Ermeniler (1453-*1953)* [Armenians in the Service of the Turkish State] (Istanbul: Yeni Press, 1953). For a criticism of the Turkish official history, see Etienne Copeaux, *Espaces et temps de la nation turque: Analyse d'une historiographie nationaliste 1931-1993* (Paris: CNRS editions, 1997), esp. pp. 322-338. See also Göçek "Reconstructing the Turkish Historiography on the Armenian Deaths."
4. Munslow, *Routledge Companion to Historical Studies,* p. 169.
5. Ibid., p. 170.
6. Hayden White, *The Content of the Form: Narrative Discourse and Historical Representation* (Baltimore and London: John Hopkins University Press, 1990), p. 1.
7. In this sense, the concept perpetrator is used to represent the side that belongs to the perpetrator.

8. For more information on this issue of denial, see Richard G. Hovannisian, "Denial of the Armenian Genocide in Comparison with the Holocaust Denial," in *Remembrance and Denial: The Case of the Armenian Genocide*, ed. Richard G. Hovannisian (Detroit: Wayne State University Press, 1998). See by the same author, "The Armenian Genocide and Patterns of Denial," in *The Armenian Genocide in Perspective*, ed. Richard G. Hovannisian (New Brunswick, NJ: Transaction Publishers, 1986), pp. 111-133.
9. Hayden White, *Tropics of Discourse: Essays in Cultural Criticism* (Baltimore: John Hopkins University Press, 1978), p. 85.
10. White, *Content of the Form*, p. 55.
11. The concept *soykırım* has been used mainly by Taner Akçam. See his *Ermeni tabusu aralanırken*.
12. The concept used by Taner Akçam in the past decade. See his *Insan haklari ve Ermeni sorunu,* and *Turk ulusal kimli i ve Ermeni Sorunu*.
13. The concept of *katliam* has been used even before the foundation of the Turkish republic in 1923, during the Ottoman parliamentary debates of 1918. See Ayhan Aktar, "Son Osmanlı Meclisi ve Ermeni Meselesi: Kasım-Aralık 1918" [The Last Ottoman Parliament and the Armenian Question: November-December 1918], *Toplum ve Bilim* [Society and Science] 91 (Fall 2002): 142-165.
14. This is the term used by Halil Berktay in an interview with Derya Sazak: "Tehcir kanunu etnik temizlik" [The Deportation Law (is) Ethnic Cleansing] in the Istanbul newspaper *Milliyet*, March 7, 2005.
15. This is the term used by such leftist historians as Mete Tunçay. See, for example, in Ferhat Kentel, "Nefret" [Hatred], in *Gazetem*, February 10, 2005.
16. White, *Content of the Form*, p. 5.
17. Norbert Elias, *Was ist Soziologie* (Munich: Juventa Press, 1981).
18. Akçam, *From Empire to Republic*, p. 46.
19. Göçek, "Decline of the Ottoman Empire," p. 28.
20. Akçam, *From Empire to Republic*, p. 79.
21. Fikret Adanır, "Le génocide Arménien? Une Réévaluation, " in *L'actualité du génocide des Arméniens: Actes du colloque, organisé par le Comité de Défense de la Cause Arménienne à Paris-Sorbonne, les 16, 17 et 18 avril 1998* (Paris: Edipol, 1999), p. 408.
22. Ibid., p. 407.
23. "Ermenileri özel örgüt öldürdü" [A Special Organization Killed the Armenians]: Interview with Halil Berktay in the Istanbul newspaper *Radikal*, October 9, 2000.
24. Göçek, "Decline of the Ottoman Empire," p. 22.
25. Ibid., p. 28. For more information regarding these boycotts and in particular regarding the nationalization of economy, see Ayhan Aktar, "Economic Nationalism in Turkey: The Formative Years, 1912 -1925," *Boğaziçi Journal, Review of Social and Administrative Studies* 10, 1-2 (1996): 263-290.
26. This is in the case of the Greek, Armenian, Turkish, and Arab nationalisms.
27. Ibid., p. 55.
28. Kemal Karpat, *The Politicization of Islam: Reconstructing Identity, State, Faith, and Community in the late Ottoman State* (New York: Oxford University Press, 2001), p. 97; Idem, *Ottoman Population, 1830-1914: Demographic and Social Characteristics* (Madison: University of Wisconsin Press, 1985).
29. The final phase of the settlement policy of the immigrants in the Ottoman Empire was initiated during the second constitutional period by the Committee of Union and Progress. For more information on this issue, see Dündar, *Ittihat ve Terakki'nin Müslümanları iskan politikası*.

30. On the social groups and nationalism in the Balkans, see Dimitrije Djordjevic, Revolutions nationales de peuples balkaniques, 1804-1914 (Belgrade: Istorijski Institut, 1965).
31. On the emergence of the Armenian revolutionary groups, see Louis Nalbandian, The Armenian Revolutionary Movement: The Development of Armenian Political Parties through the Nineteenth Century (Berkeley and Los Angeles: University of California Press, 1963); Anahide Ter Minassian, Nationalism and Socialism in the Armenian Revolutionary Movement (1887-1912), trans. A. M. Berrett (Cambridge, MA: Zoryan Institute, 1984).
32. Adanır, "Le génocide Arménien?" pp. 408-409.
33. Ibid., p. 408. The Armenian revolutionary groups did not have a monolithic approach in their aims and demands. For example, while the Dashnaktsutiun sought an autonomous status for the six Armenian provinces within the framework of the Ottoman Empire, the Hnchaks called for independence from the Ottoman Empire.
34. Selim Deringil, "In Search of a Way Forward: A Response to Ronald Grigor Suny," Armenian Forum 1, 2 (1998): 66.
35. Ibid., p. 71.
36. Ibid., p. 69.
37. See, for example, a recent M.A thesis that deals with the issue on the level of the periphery: Uğur Ü. Üngör, "A Reign of Terror: CUP Rule in Diyarbekir Province, 1913-1918," M.A Thesis, University of Amsterdam, 2005.
38. Adanır, "Le génocide Arménien?" p. 408.
39. Berktay, "Ermenileri özel örgüt öldürdü."
40. Ibid.
41. Selim Deringil, *The Well-Protected Domains: Ideology and the Legitimation of Power in the Ottoman Empire, 1876-1909* (London: I. B. Tauris, 1998), p. 166.
42. Ibid., p. 14.
43. Deringil, "Study of the Armenian Crisis," pp. 46-47.
44. Adanır, "Le génocide Arménien?" p. 408.
45. Deringil, "In Search of a Way Forward," p. 67.
46. Berktay, "Ermenileri özel örgüt öldürdü."
47. Vahakn N. Dadrian, *The History of the Armenian Genocide. Ethnic Conflict from the Balkans to Anatolia to the Caucasus* (Providence, RI: Berghahn Books,1995); idem, *Warrant for Genocide: Key Elements of Turko-Armenian Conflict* (New Brunswick, NJ: Transaction Publishers, 1999).
48. Deringil, "In Search of a Way Forward," p. 67.
49. Engin Akarlı, "Particularities of History: A Response to Ronald Grigor Suny," *Armenian Forum* 1, 2 (198): 59.
50. Munslow, *Routledge Companion to Historical Studies*, p. 38.
51. E. H. Carr, *What is History? The George Macaulay Trevelyan Lectures Delivered in the University of Cambridge January-March 1961* (Houndmills, Basingstoke: Macmillan, 1986), pp. 81-82.
52. Ibid., p. 97.
53. White, *Content of the Form*, p. 41.
54. Munslow, *Routledge Companion to Historical Studies*, p. 41.
55. See Göçek's chapter, "Turkish Historiography and the Unbearable Weight of 1915," in this volume.
56. Dominick LaCapra, *History and Memory after Auschwitz* (Ithaca, NY: Cornell University Press, 1988), pp. 41-42. In approaching events such as the Holocaust or what LaCapra calls other limit-events he argues the following: "The conventional

stance for the historian is often closest to that of the innocent bystander-onlooker. But this safe position is particularly in the case of the Holocaust and other extreme or limit-events. The most tempting position is probably that of the resister with marked sympathy for the victim and antipathy for the perpetrator or collaborator. . . . I think the historian should attempt to work out a complex position that does not simply identify with one or another participant-position. While acknowledging in particular the need to honor the resister and to listen attentively to and respect the position of the victim (or the multiple and variable positions of the victims), as well as to appreciate the complexities introduced by what Primo Levi called the gray zone of relations induced by the Nazi policy of trying to make accomplices of victims, the historian should attempt to prepare the way for overcoming the entire complex of relations defined by the grid: perpetrator-collaborator-victim-bystander-resister.

57. The brief first constitutional period refers to the short span from December 1876 to early 1878 when Sultan Abdul Hamid II allowed for constitutional rule and a parliamentary system. In February 1878, during the Russo-Turkish war, he prorogued the Parliament and suspended the constitution. Afterwards, an absolute monarchical rule was established for three decades. The Hamidian absolutist regime ended with the Young Turk revolution of 1908 and the reinstatement of the Ottoman constitution of 1876. Thus, the second constitutional period lasted until 1918. During this period, the sultan had little authority and the Committee of Union and Progress ruled the empire.
58. The only complete studies remain those of Taner Akçam. See note 1 above.
59. Hanioğlu, *Preparation for a Revolution,* pp. 82-129.
60. Hanioğlu, *The Young Turks in Opposition*, pp. 194-195.
61. Ibid., pp. 173-199.
62. Hanioğlu, *Preparation for a Revolution*, p. 95.
63. Ibid., pp. 99-100.
64. Ibid., p. 101.
65. I use "selective Armeno-Turkish cooperation," since only one party (Dashnaktsutiun) actively collaborated with the Young Turks.
66. Edmond Demolins (1852-1907) was the leading representative of the Le Play School and the editor of the journal *Science Sociale*. He frequently argued that decentralization was one of the primary reasons for what was perceived as Anglo-Saxon superiority. Sabaheddin believed that the Ottomans should follow the theories of Demolins in order to solve the problems of the empire. For more information on Demolins' theories, see Edmond Demolins, *A quoi tient la supériorité des Anglo-Saxons* (Paris: Firmin-Didot, 1899)
67. Behaeddin Shakir, who played an important role in the liquidation process, led the special organization called *Teshkilat-i Mahsusa*. In 1920, he was tried in Constantinople in absentia and was sentenced to death.
68. Hanioğlu, *Preparation for a Revolution*, p. 136.
69. The organization was also known as the Committee of Progress and Union (CPU).
70. Hanioğlu, *Preparation for a Revolution*, p. 139.
71. Ibid., p. 191.
72. Ibid., p. 206.
73. Ibid., p. 207.
74. Akçam, *From Empire to Republic,* p. 84.
75. See Aykut Kansu, *Politics in Post-Revolutionary Turkey,* pp. 122-125.
76. According to the Armenian, Turkish, and Arabic newspapers of the time the Adana massacres were perpetrated by the reactionary forces in the Ottoman Empire. Later

CUP organs blamed Abdul Hamid as the sole instigator of the counterrevolution, which resulted also in the massacres of Adana.

77. Adanır, "Le génocide Arménien? " pp. 410-411.
78. Ibid., p. 411.
79. Rashid Khalidi, ed., *Origins of Arab Nationalism* (New York: Columbia University Press, 1991), p.x.
80. Şükrü Hanioğlu, "The Young Turks and the Arabs Before the Revolution in 1908," in Khalidi, *Origins of Arab Nationalism*, p. 43.
81. See, for example, Adanır, "Le génocide Arménien?" p. 413.
82. Akarlı, "Particularities of History," p. 60.
83. Akçam, *From Empire to Republic,* p. 97.
84. Ibid., p. 105.
85. Ibid.
86. Ibid., p. 150.
87. Ibid., p. 166.
88. Akçam, *From Empire to Republic*, p. 172. Berktay, "Ermenileri özel örgüt öldürdü." Deringil, "The Study of the Armenian Crisis," p. 56, indicates that there were two levels of decision making: one, the official level, which issued orders not necessarily in bad faith; the other, a secret organization whose express purpose was to carry out forbidden activities.
89. Berktay, "Ermenileri özel örgüt öldürdü."
90. Akçam, *From Empire to Republic,* p. 240.
91. Aktar, "Son Osmanlı Meclisi ve Ermeni Meselesi," pp. 142-165.
92. Ibid., p. 163.
93. Ibid. , p. 164.
94. "Konferans Ertelendi" [The Conference Has Been Postponed], *Radikal*, May 25, 2005, p. 7.
95. Some argue that because of pressure from the European Union, Prime Minister Recep Tayyip Erdoğan quietly encouraged the organizers of the conference to reschedule the conference for September, days before the planned start of negotiations for Turkey entering the EU.
96. Paul Ricoeur, "Narrative Time," *Critical Inquiry* 7, 1 (1980): 178.
97. Most of the scholarship written by Turkish liberal historians on the Armenian Genocide is in English.

23

Can Memory of Genocide Lead to Reconciliation?

Elazar Barkan

Conflicts that deteriorate into wars, interethnic violence, including ethnic cleansing and genocide, are often the result of historical memory of earlier animosity. In the postmodern and postcolonial world, history has become a formative experience that shapes the national identity and is recognized to be malleable and subject to ideological construction. As such, history is no longer an academic exercise, rather a political battlefield. Memory and the narrating of memory shape the politics of countries, the ability to reconcile with enemies or deteriorate into war. Few nations have had their past history dominating their contemporary history as Armenians: both in Armenia and in the Diaspora. The memory of the Genocide has been the most formative experience in the identity of the Armenian Diaspora and is at the core of the conflict with Turkey. Oftentimes the attitude of reconciliation methods is to propose ignoring the past and exploring shared interests as a basis for future cooperation. But as is well known, the past refuses to give way. Therefore, I propose that it is by engaging memory and history that conflict resolution, and even reconciliation, may take place. It is the active memory of genocide that may provide a new space for reconciliation, a space constructed through acknowledgement of responsibility. I explore this through comparative examination of how other nations deal with their own historical crimes and injustices, as a way to rethink the Armenian-Turkish conflict. The discussion of the current state of the concept of genocide aims to show that politically it is both central and crucial for the identity of the victims and cannot be wished away just because of a lack of precision or because the legal definition diverges from the daily usage. I conclude by discussing the memory of the Armenian Genocide and support a constructive engagement between Armenian and Turkish historians, preferably the formation of a formal historical commission by the two countries. Such collaboration ought to construct a memory that respects the victims, shows empathy for the suffering, rejects denial, points to the responsible individuals and government crimes but does not indict the Turkish nation—and certainly not today's Turkish people—for the Genocide. A historical commission has to engage in redress not retribution and that can best be achieved through collaboration between scholars and intellectuals on both sides of the dispute.

Historical Memory and National Conflicts

The recounting of history has been exploited to provoke conflict, incite war, and inflame genocides. The genocide in Rwanda and the war in the former Yugoslavia are perhaps the best-known recent examples of ethnic conflict where leaders incited the crimes and violence by inflaming animosity through reference to the historical rivalry. Whether it was Milosevic and the continuous references to the historical suffering of Serbia at the hands of the Muslims or the Hutu propaganda that framed the domination of the Tutsis as a result of historical oppression, the place of history was central in igniting the conflicts. When a team of researchers attempted to tell the story of the dissolution of Yugoslavia, they concluded that a core cause was "the persistence of irreconcilable national historical narratives that helped to sustain separate identities," which led to the ethnic animosity. History was not merely the past, but rather remained a question of current Yugoslav identity.[1] But these genocides were not exceptions. One can safely generalize to say that national and ethnic conflicts are rooted in historical narratives and in constructing the enemy as the Other, often inhuman and dangerous.

As the memory of national suffering and historical traumas comes to constitute an increasing share of the national identity, the challenge today is to integrate these memories into a productive national agenda. The Turkish-Armenian conflict of memory tends to be on the extreme, but it is clearly far from being unique or even an exceptional phenomenon. Indeed, the resistance of the Japanese to acknowledge and confront the imperial legacy of Japanese colonialism is a major stumbling block in East Asia politics. That China refuses to engage in any soul searching about its own atrocities and historical crimes does not lend it credibility, but neither does it diminish the Japanese culpability. While there are less adamant cases of repressed memory, for the present purposes it might be more productive to recognize those cases in which repressed memory of historical crimes have been addressed.

Shifts in National Memory—The Rediscovery of Guilt

I have traced elsewhere a whole list of cases in which countries following a period of prolonged denial have come to recognize that past policies have led to war crimes, atrocities, and even genocide.[2] The most prominent category is that of the attitude of former British colonies toward their indigenous populations.

It is a long story, but suffice it here to say that New Zealand, Canada, Australia, and the United States in different ways have begun—and on occasions have gone to great length—to acknowledge their culpability toward the indigenous peoples. Pope John Paul II apologized on numerous occasions for the mistakes of the Church, though his apologies were not directed to the victims but to God. Great Britain apologized to Ireland for the Great Famine, and the list goes on. Indeed, the acknowledgement today of historical crimes and injustices has become common.

Voluntary redressing guilt is not only growing, but it is taking multiple forms. Among others, these include reparation, restitution of real property, restoration of cultural property, historical commissions, and apologies as a form of atonement. Over the last three decades, these forms of redress have been increasingly integrated with new democracies. And while transitional justice has become a growth industry, perhaps one significant aspect of redress that is rarely integrated in discussions of transition to democracy or human rights is the role of historical commissions. Let me highlight three cases that I think would be pertinent in different ways to the memory of the destruction of the Armenian people in 1915.

The United States faces the dilemma of how to address the legacy of slavery. There was never an apology, reparation, or recognition of the wrong. Whatever the American Civil War was about, it stopped the crime of slavery, but it did not amend or address its legacy. The moral case for an apology is made by Roy Brooks:

> No government can commit an atrocity as large as American slavery and simply walk away from it without so much as offering an apology and expect to have credibility in the community of moral nations. Apologizing for slavery is something our government, with the support of the American people, should choose to do because it is the morally correct (rather than the politically expedient) thing to do. Moral apology, in the end, gives shape and substance to flag waving. It says to the world that America has not only grown stronger over the years, it has grown up, too.[3]

Recognition is larger than the material reparation and presumably would have a higher register than symbolic reparation. There is much moral conviction in this statement, though the observation that people pay more attention when money is involved may not be unwarranted. Even if compared with the crime the payments are symbolic, these could still be substantial for the victims.

Over the past fifteen years, a trickle of previous activism has increased dramatically, and the question of responsibility is popping up in numerous sites. In addition to lawsuits that capture headlines, even if the long-term result is less than desired and the focus of politics continues at the national level, much of the activities take place on the local level. For example, cities such as Chicago and New York demand accountability from companies doing business with the city by requiring them to disclose profits derived from slavery.[4] Brown

University, as another example, reexamines its own complicity in the slave trade, illuminating New England's role in the slave economy and the legacy of slavers in the most revered contemporary institutions. In the South, sites are recognized for representing oppression, not heroism, and a trickle of renaming, reevaluating, establishing commissions, building museums, and moving to recognize the complicity and responsibility of the society in slavery is gathering momentum. The evil of slavery was never a secret, but the social amnesia and lack of responsibility certainly was and largely still is. The process of recognition transforms and taints many heroes of American history. If New England is not only about abolition but also about slavers, the legacy and the identity have to be viewed differently.

The Tulsa Race Riot Commission of the late 1990s investigated the turmoil in Greenwood in 1921. Its task was to salvage the history of the riots and place it at the center of the city's historical identity as well as to bring justice to the victims. Some of the survivors were hoping for justice in the form of reparation, but the commission was more successful in illuminating a long-forgotten tragedy and bringing a measure of recognition to the memory of the victims and the destroyed community. Indeed the commission's work, which was as comprehensive as could have been expected, underscored not only the importance of such enterprise but also its limitations: our power to remake the world is limited. By expanding historical knowledge—that is, both through research constructing new narratives and by dissemination of wider academic knowledge—these new recognitions began to remake Tulsa.[5] Such local efforts are taking place in numerous places in the United States. It is often a result of local initiatives and local pains that particular local memory is reconstructed, as is the case on university campuses where building names and statues commemorating racists such as Ku Klux Klan leaders are being challenged and occasionally renamed. [6]

The destruction of Native Americans has elicited mostly indirect responses. On the one hand, there is more of an institutional and legal framework to acknowledge the special responsibility that the United States has toward its indigenous peoples, whereas, on the other hand, it is almost exclusively indirect. Much is in the language and policies of welfare or dependent nations and very little through explicit acknowledgment of responsibility for suffering. It is against this background that at the height of the movement for political apologies at the end of the Clinton presidency that the apology from Assistant Secretary for Indian Affairs Kevin Gover was both unique and controversial.[7] The apology was not for the controversial designation of genocide of indigenous peoples but rather a more limited one for past actions of the Bureau of Indian Affairs (BIA).

The rewriting of history shapes the national agenda and the self-perception of the people. Some, no doubt, view these revisions as an attack on the very being of the country, as sacrilege, and advocate extremely nationalist positions. Others see this as an opportunity to understand the national history as more complex and to allow room in it to those people who had suffered in the past and may or may not be part of the contemporary nation. Poland is a good example.

In 1939, Poland was divided between Nazi Germany and the Soviet Union. In June 1941, Germany attacked the Soviet Union ("Operation Barbarossa") and conquered the western parts of the Soviet Union within a few months, including eastern Poland. In the immediate aftermath of the Nazi occupation, there was extensive violence against Jews in Poland, which has become a central part of the story of the Holocaust. Although the role of non-German populations as collaborators and perpetrators of the Holocaust has always been part of the Jewish narrative, it was and to a degree continues to be denied in Eastern Europe. In Poland a major shift took place as a result of the publication of the book *Neighbors* by Jan Gross (2000), which dealt with the massacre of the Jews in Jedwabne. It was in Jedwabne that, following the German occupation and in the midst of the confusion, a pogrom carried out by the Polish population killed hundreds of Jews, most of the local population. After the war, several trials took place and individuals were punished, but the event disappeared from national memory. Following the publication of *Neighbors*, the case captured Polish public opinion and subsequently received international attention. The investigation and the memory of the pogrom has helped to transform Polish attitudes toward their own history. It has led to extensive public discussion, formal investigations and commissions, presidential apologies, further ongoing investigations of the extent of similar events, the complicity of the Poles in the Holocaust, and anti-Semitism in general. Some right-wing nationalists and anti-Semites remain vocal in denying responsibility, but generally speaking Poland acknowledges its historical responsibility and is eager to examine its own history. Anti-Semitism was not a secret in Poland, and many Jews have always viewed Poland as responsible for much Jewish suffering before and during the Holocaust. But it was only the Polish self-examination as a result of Jedwabne that allowed for a greater reconciliation between the two peoples. While the horrific crime could have aggravated the relationship between them, because of the engagement by Poland, both its government and civil society, the memory of the event became a catalyst for greater discussion, and, one dare say, closer relations between Jews and Poles.

Fortuitously, Poland had established a couple of years earlier the Institute of National Remembrance (IPN) for the purpose of investigating Nazi and Communist crimes. A potentially rather boring task of caring for historical documentation and archives was transformed into a major role in coming to terms with the past. One could not overestimate the role of the IPN in transforming the engagement with the past from an accusatory to a professional and eventually a moral process.

The lesson one may draw from this is that the recognition of the crime by the perpetrators, acknowledging both guilt and responsibility, is not news to the victims. Thus, it does not ipso facto worsen the interactions. However recognition enables more empathy for the suffering of the victims. It also alerts at least some of the victims (and this is a process) that a part of the perpetrator side has discovered remorse. It is a long process and when the diachronic perspective is incorporated in cases of multigenerational victimization, the shifts are slower still. It is after all a matter of collective corporate responsibility—the actual perpetrators being long gone. The suffering is being retold either by very young witnesses and survivors who in their advanced years may relate fragmented memories or by the historical records. There is growing literature on the phenomenon of second- and third-generation survivors in particular regarding the Holocaust, but there is little doubt that the phenomena are widespread. It is also true that the suffering of later generations from the atrocities cannot approximate the physical suffering during the atrocities. The suffering is transformed from the individual physical body to the memory of the group, to the identity and psychology of the descendant. The confrontation or discussion between the descendants of the victims and the descendants of the perpetrators is moved away from a question of criminal responsibility and guilt toward moral responsibility and politics. The question of bringing individuals to justice—of retribution—is no longer pertinent. Thus, responsibility and guilt become more voluntary and political. It cannot be forced by a court or a victorious army but rather is more of a moral statement, which occasionally is backed by some form of reparations, and oftentimes by hard negotiations and political pressure. As such, the acknowledgement not only declares ownership of the crimes, but it does a double duty: accepting the genealogy of the crime and simultaneously declaring that the current generation is different. Not only do those who take responsibility assume a duty that both morally and legally is indirect—we do not believe in punishing children for the crimes of their parents—but with the public recognition they become virtuous, not merely tainted by their history, but even more important transforming the guilt into a morally uplifting act.

Guilt has many meanings. Karl Jaspers spoke of four circles of guilt: criminal, political, moral, and metaphysical. Only the first carries a penalty. Yet, if we recognize that guilt is not collective—it is not all Germans who were criminally guilty for the Holocaust, only those who perpetrated it—so the punishment can only be directed at those guilty. Thus, in the case of the Armenian Genocide, the guilt is not Turkish (or Ottoman) but rather that of those individuals responsible for the atrocities. The healing, the recognition, has to be among descendants, and as such it is about the identity of the groups. Shifting the blame from the group to the individuals may distance the descendants from the identification with the perpetrators and find alternative forms to represent the national narratives.

Reconstructing Narratives

In Israel, the traditional story of the war of independence viewed the Palestinians not only as the aggressors but also held the Palestinian refugees wholly responsible for their own fate. The traditional narrative is that the Palestinian leadership encouraged the civilian population to flee in order to allow the invading Arab armies a clear battlefield, with the expectation of a quick Arab victory over Israel to be followed by the return of the refugees to their homes. The small size of Israel, its overall demography relative to the Arab nations that fought against it, and the commitment to nation-building, all lent credibility to the story. But in the 1980s, Israeli historians began, using Israeli and British archives, to uncover the role of Israel in expelling many Palestinians. The Palestinian exodus—the story of the refugees has become much more complex. Some fled, others were expelled, and the vast majority was never allowed to return. This history is far from complete. It is told largely by one side, the Israeli one, even if that "side" has multiple narratives. The Palestinians have begun to tell part of their own narrative, and increasingly oral histories are being collected. But as a national comprehensive narrative, the Palestinians are yet to write their own story. For both sides to reach a "shared history," these multiple perspectives have to be developed. It may be less difficult than one might imagine. The national positions are not polarized, and there is a process of bringing these histories together. From the Israeli perspective, the new narrative that underscores the Israeli culpability in the Palestinian *Al Nakba*—the catastrophe—has transformed the national perspective of the war of independence, which turns out to play a primarily role in reshaping the understanding of the current political situation. This history contributed to the Israeli willingness to view the conflict as a national conflict and the Palestinians as victims as well, not merely as aggressors. That many Palestinians see themselves as merely victims suggests the gap that is yet to be breached. Yet Israeli responsibility for the refugee problem was never publicly acknowledged in Israel. The historical research provided new knowledge that has had a direct impact on the Israeli approach to possible solutions to the conflict. For various reasons, the Palestinian position is different. There is little doubt that the rewriting of the history has led to a rethinking of national identity in Israel and to different political perceptions.[8]

When Hitler reputedly referred to the collective amnesia about the annihilation of the Armenians, he was obviously making a reference to an event that largely disappeared from public conversation but was hardly forgotten, certainly not only by the survivors but also by many others. Hitler's declaration was an act of remembering in itself. In contrast, he did not mention technically the first genocide of the twentieth century, which went unnoticed by the world, was quickly forgotten, and was continuously ignored until recently. The genocide perpetrated by German colonialists against the Herero of South-West Africa, today's Namibia, is receiving growing academic and political attention. It is subject to legal proceeding in the United States, and the process shows that forgetting is potentially never complete. There does not have to be a physical continuity of commemoration for the memory to survive.

The Herero genocide was the result of an effort by German settlers to seize land. The German army tried to annihilate the Hereros between 1904 and 1907 by killing or expelling tens of thousands to die in the desert. Since then, Germany's recognition of its guilt for the Holocaust has transformed its own self-perception. An analogous recognition by Germany of the Herero genocide will never have a comparable impact on the German identity, nor will it have economic effects of any significance. Although the stakes are relatively low for Germany, it has been very hesitant and reluctant to acknowledge the destruction of the Herero as genocide. Although Germany recognizes its own responsibility for the suffering of the Hereros, it has not recognized it as genocide or provided reparations. It does give disproportionate material aid to Namibia, which obviously is directly related to the colonial legacy and the genocide. Namibia itself is not advocating recognition of the genocide, and the Hereros are now a discriminated minority in the country. All of this makes the unpacking of guilt and contemporary policies more complex.[9]

Rediscovery of national guilt increases around the world. The rationale and support for denial is diminishing, and it seems to be a losing political proposition. Yet the appeal of historical acknowledgements is in part because it is very difficult, for despite the claim by some that it is only political expediency or even blatant cynicism, such action is significant for both victims and perpetrators. Some acknowledgements are more difficult than others. The German reluctance to acknowledge the killing of the Hereros as genocide is an example that the admission to the ultimate crime remains particularly problematic, even for a country with its own self-identity steeped in guilt.

The memories of the Arab-Israeli war of 1948 have direct impact on the current violent conflict. The question to be raised is whether the distance from the violence changes profoundly the intensity of the memories or the impact on the contemporary politics. A tentative answer may suggest that the distance is not really a factor when the identity of the victims is fixed, frozen in a way by the crime. Even in cases when interaction of memory and politics is supposedly more distanced, such as the Polish-Jewish historical memories or the Hereros in Namibia, where the violence ceased decades earlier, the identities and interrelations of the groups are closely intertwined with memory.

The Current State of the Concept of Genocide

The worst national catastrophes and sufferings are named holocaust and genocide, followed by ethnic cleansing and other war crimes. In the context of contemporary politics that ascribe moral capital to those most greatly victimized, victims and their descendants campaign to name their catastrophe as a genocide or holocaust. Others object to such cheapening of the sacred term Holocaust. This discussion intensified during the 1990s, as the claim of genocide became frequent currency in disputes over widespread violence. Both in the former Yugoslavia and Rwanda the massive violence was judged to be ethnic cleansing and genocide. The international community refuses to rank legally the various crimes, and the International Criminal Court treats all crimes as of equal gravity. Yet there is little doubt that politically and publicly the naming of the crimes ranks the severity of the victimization. Ethnic cleansing generally is not viewed as being comparable in severity with genocide. War crimes cover a whole array of violations and oftentimes are horrific, but these are different qualitatively in the public perception than genocide. This is presumably true, even if historically many of the worst crimes have not been named genocide.

Political violence in the twentieth century was so widespread that to draw attention to the suffering of one's own group has become a Sisyphean task. Because of the expansion of the concepts of holocaust and genocide, together with ethnic cleansing, to characterize all such violence, it is hard to draw attention to historical suffering that is designated merely as war crimes and crimes against humanity or as human rights violations. The claims to label a particular victimization as genocide can be seen at times as political grandstanding but at other times a request, a plea, from victims to win attention. The significant point of the proliferation of the terms holocaust and genocide is the attempt of victims and their supporters to engage the Holocaust and derive from it a space for sympathy. If social and historical justice is sought by victims through recognition, memory, commemoration, and reparations, the comparison to the Holocaust has to be viewed for what it seeks—its own legitimization.

As a result of this proliferation of genocide discourse, the United Nations Genocide Convention is under increasing stress of becoming irrelevant, since it designates the most horrendous of crimes and since an increasing number of groups see their own suffering as the ultimate victimization and as such deserving of the designation of genocide. The imprecision of the Genocide Convention means that there is no minimal threshold for determining what constitutes genocide. As a result of the open-ended definition of genocide and the intense political stakes involved, there is a disjunction between the popular and the legal definition of genocide. The Genocide Convention states explicitly that it is not dealing with a new phenomenon, rather "that at all periods of history genocide has inflicted great losses on humanity." This clearly contextualized genocides as having a long history even if the term and the convention were new. The attribution of the term "genocide" was to be applied widely from the very beginning.

In practice, however, it was not. During the first decades after World War II, the Cold War dominated the Genocide Convention, which was never evoked to stop or intervene in any of the worst violence and conflicts of the era: not in Biafra, Bangladesh, or Cambodia. It should be remembered that although the Convention acknowledges ethnic, racial, and religious motivations for genocide, it does not recognize political or economic destruction or repression. Indeed most killings have been perpetrated in cases that do not technically qualify as genocide: foremost in China and the Soviet Union, where tens of millions have died.

Indeed, even in most horrendous crimes, the concept of genocide is applied in a constraining way. A recent dilemma presented for the understanding of genocide in historical perspective is displayed in Brussels, where the show, "Memory of Congo: The Colonial Era," in the Royal Museum of Central Africa is one of the most explicit attempts to confront the question of genocide under colonial rule. Although the exhibit investigated the extent and displayed the crimes under colonial rule, the committee of experts could not validate the accepted estimate of 10 million killed. That figure was first advanced by Edmund Morel, who formed the Congo Reform Association and was the most prominent critic at the time.[10] Demographic studies persuaded the committee that the Congo's population fell by at least 20 percent during the half-century after 1875, which included disease and violence. A contemporary commission appointed by King Leopold concluded in its report (1905) "that the state administration and the contracting companies were implicated in atrocities, as were numerous militias who terrorized the region."[11] Although the commission was planned as a sham, it turned out to be a real investigatory commission, and the testimonies and evidence it collected were horrific. Yet King Leopold managed to control its dissemination, and the firsthand testimonies did not become public for decades. [12]

The terminology of genocide is avoided but the exhibit highlights the extensive list of horrendous crimes. While Congo is embroiled in its current phase of violent war, with possibly 2 million fatalities, the historical memory of the atrocities inflicted by Belgium as a colonial power is mostly a Belgian domestic affair. Its apology and historical studies of the horror have not become a subject of international controversy. This is in contrast with the case of the Hereros, whose destruction is increasingly recognized as genocide. Ironically, one case involving tens of thousands of victims is designated genocide, while the other involving millions of victims is not.

The most formal and comprehensive investigation of the status of genocide as the ultimate crime was recently conducted by the UN study of Darfur, published in January 2005. The commission explicated the meaning of the 1948 Genocide Convention. In addition to articulating the various stipulations regarding genocide, with particular emphasis on the intent of the perpetrators to destroy, "in whole or in part, the group as such." The report clarifies the international case law regarding the question of the intent to destroy a group "in part." It shows that this requires "the intention to destroy 'a considerable number of individuals' or 'a substantial part,' but not necessarily a 'very important part'." The analysis is based on judgments by the Rwanda and the Yugoslavia tribunals.[13] The examples given are of more than passing interest. First the report points to the recent example "of the attempt to kill all Muslims of Bosnia-Herzegovina, or all Muslims living in a region of that country"; then it points to a historical example of the attempt "to destroy all the Jews living in Italy"; and finally to "the Armenians living in France." The committee interprets the "in part" in the definition of genocide to counter an anticipation of the criminal defense, arguing that "they did not intend the destruction of the group as a whole," because like the Turkish government, which targeted in 1915 the Armenians "within its borders, not those of the Diaspora," or the Nazis, who intended to destroy all the Jews living in Europe, the Rwandan extremists did not intend to eliminate the "Tutsi population beyond the country's borders."[14]

This example of the Armenians in France while not explained must strike the reader as being peculiar. It involves two parts. Among the cases mentioned to explain "in part" the destruction of the Armenian population in Turkey in 1915 is referenced indirectly through the footnote to William Schabas. It is he, not the report, that refers to 1915 and the Armenians. It is prefaced by the heading: "Instances mentioned in either case law or the legal literature." This may have been intentional in that it is harder to object to the citation of literature. The report itself refers to the "Armenians living in France." It is curious because this is the only reference to an imaginary situation and not an actual attempt of destruction. Together it allows the report to refer to the Armenians and to introduce Schabas' perspective without taking a stand on the question in a way that would pressure Turkey to object. The reference, while politically careful, raises awareness of the Armenian Genocide of 1915 and creates symmetry between Jewish and Armenian diasporic communities. It serves the purpose not only of showing that even a small minority in a country can be subject to genocide, even if not the whole group. After all, the reference to a small minority was also accomplished by evoking the Jewish example in Italy. The not so subtle purpose in using the Armenian example in France is to remind the reader of the permanent dispute over the question of the Armenian Genocide without forcing Turkey to object to the report.

In exploring the definition of the groups potentially subject to genocide, the report declares that based on the Rwanda tribunal, the definition of the group is not limited to the categories in the UN Convention but includes groupings based on "the self-perception of the members of each group." The Tutsi may not be national, religious, ethnic, or racial group, but it was victimized as a group and saw itself as such. This somewhat pragmatic definition clarifies the otherwise rather imprecise categories: "the approach taken to determine whether a group is a [fully] protected one has evolved from an objective to a subjective standard to take into account that 'collective identities, and in particular ethnicity, are by their very nature social constructs, 'imagined' identities entirely dependent on variable and contingent perceptions, and not social facts, which are verifiable in the same manner as natural phenomena or physical facts."[15]

Genocide has been called the "crime of crimes" and as such designating an event as genocide carries a special weight. This designation is justified, especially given the Genocide Convention and the special obligation it bestows on signatories. However, despite the special stigma assigned to genocide, it is of interest to note that this implied ranking of crimes is beginning to be viewed as having a negative impact. The UN report indeed makes an effort to counter the hierarchy of crimes when it states "that some categories of crimes against humanity may be similarly heinous [to genocide] and carry a similarly grave stigma," underscoring the Rwanda tribunal's rejection of the notion of crime of crimes "because there is no such hierarchical gradation of crimes."

It is useful to examine the general use of the term genocide in the Darfur case, since it is indicative of changing standards. In June 2004, the definition of the humanitarian crisis in Darfur began to be viewed as genocide. There were declarations by the U.S. Congress (June 24, 2004), various media outlets, followed by Secretary of State Colin Powell's testimony in the Senate (September 9, 2004) declaring that "genocide has been committed in Darfur and that the Government of Sudan and the Jingaweit bear responsibility." The accompanying documents that the State Department published did not, however, explicate the accusation but just provided evidence of the atrocities. The European Union did not join the United States in declaring the catastrophe a genocide, nor did Human Rights Watch or the International Crisis Group. The one major humanitarian organization that declared it genocide was Physicians for Human Rights (PHR), which in an extensive published report wrote:

> PHR has concluded that the forcible removal of Darfurians from their land, the total destruction of their villages and livelihood, the deliberate obstruction of aid, and the resulting mortality that humanitarian agencies and human rights organizations now are managing to discern and predict describe a criminal intent and criminal accomplishment completely commensurate with instances of past mass killing the world has only belatedly called genocide.

The U.S. isolation internationally, its effort to take the moral high ground in Darfur, while being criticized for its Iraq policies and the abuse in Abu Ghraib prison, was viewed as manipulative, and there was never a follow up after Powell's testimony. Indeed, in 2005, the government of Sudan denied there was a genocide and called the claim of genocide "exaggerated," asserting that it was a tribal warfare, which is very "common in Africa."[16] Inexplicably, the position was backed by the United States when on November 9, 2005, U.S. Deputy Secretary of State Robert Zoellick stated: "It's a tribal war . . . and frankly, I don't think foreign forces ought to get themselves in the middle of a tribal war of Sudanese." In March 2006, the United States continued its flip-flopping when President George W. Bush declared: "When we say genocide, that means genocide has to be stopped,"[17] a position that has been enunciated numerous times by John Bolton, U.S. ambassador to the United Nations.

The United Nations in the meantime came as close as possible to labeling it a genocide without actually doing so. The Internet and various media publications since 2004 have used the designation of genocide. If, in 2004, on the occasion of commemorating the tenth anniversary of the Rwandan genocide, calling the crimes in Darfur a genocide was newsworthy, within two years it had become the norm but had little if any impact. Bush's comments were hardly reported, much less announced as a policy initiative. Indeed, rhetoric became the policy, if it could be categorized as such. For anyone who believes in the power of words and the role that moral castigation ought to have in public and international politics, the government of Sudan is a somber check of reality in the mockery it makes of any such obligations. In the first three months of 2006, Sudan hosted both the African Union summit and the Arab Summit, a clear testimony that there was no effective international condemnation. The category of genocide remains the crime of crimes, but the public is made numb to it. The Darfur crisis and genocide conveys a pessimistic approach either to prevention or containment of genocide. There is dissonance between the significance attributed to the use of the concept of genocide when it is avoided or rejected and the relative little impact it has once it is employed. One would have expected that the use of the term in Darfur would have made a change in policy and attitude; instead, only normalization followed. This leaves open the question of what is the impact of the absence of the concept of genocide on politics—the unavailability of the designation of genocide and the struggle over its employment—especially in cases that refer to historical events that remain contentious at present, as the dispute over the Armenian Genocide exemplifies. Could the absence enhance its significance, while its abundance normalize and minimize it?

The normalization of the concept of genocide results from its wide-ranged deployment. Not only is it evoked for extreme cases, but because of the tension between legal ambiguity and public political use and the clear payoff in public attention when an event is called genocide, many forms of gross violation of human rights are being termed genocide, even in cases where the designation conflicts with the public perception of the concept. This includes cases of extreme violence—for example race riots as was the issue with the worst racial mass violence in the United States—the Tulsa riots. The concept of genocide was employed when the headline, "Compensation sought over 'black holocaust,'" descried the lawsuit brought by about 100 descendants of individuals who were victims of the race riots. Or the designation of genocide against the Aborigines in Australia that was formulated by the "Bringing Them Home" commission to describe the violence against the aborigine children, primarily the removal of lighter-skinned children with the goal of placing them with white families or in institutional settings, although no killing took place. The designation of genocide in this case was based on the Genocide Convention, Article 2(e) "Forcibly transferring children of the group to another group." So while genocide has a legal definition, and its application is subject to political controversies, it is the very contention and constrained usage by the international community that enhances its value and importance for victims.

The appropriation of the concepts of genocide and holocaust often stems from desire for equality as a form of social justice. It comes from those who are most frustrated that their suffering has been least attended to and their claim for equality as a demand for recognition. As the case of Darfur suggests, naming may come to stand for policy and action, political rhetoric in place of prevention. Despite the depressing thought that the Genocide Convention lacks implementation globally and does not facilitate prevention, paradoxically it may be more useful in reconciliation and resolving historical conflict. This conclusion may be merited by the recognition that the crime of crimes is more powerful as a form of acknowledgement than of prevention.

Historic Response as a Form of Reconciliation Why Do We Need an International Criminal Court? . . . To Achieve Justice for All

> *For nearly half a century—almost as long as the United Nations has been in existence—the General Assembly has recognized the need to establish such a court to prosecute and punish persons responsible for crimes such as genocide. Many thought . . . that the horrors of the Second World War—the camps, the cruelty, the exterminations, the Holocaust—could never happen again. And yet they have. In Cambodia, in Bosnia and Herzegovina, in Rwanda. Our time—this decade even—has shown us that man's capacity for evil knows no limits. Genocide . . . is now a word of our time, too, a heinous reality that calls for a historic response.*
> —Kofi Annan, United Nations Secretary-General

What does a historic response mean? Annan calls for a retributive justice as a historic response. If it is to be historic, new standards will need to be set. Annan is correct in emphasizing that the response to exceptional horrors has to be historic. But what would make it "historic"? Bringing criminals and perpetrators to justice would be a good beginning. But this, after all, ought to be the norm, even in less heinous crimes. The exceptional response, however, may be the attempt to set a new standard and procedure to bring to justice perpetrators for crimes against humanity, war crime, and foremost genocide. Many hope the International Criminal Court (ICC) will provide deterrence, though this has always been a highly optimistic notion. Indeed, the article in the *New York Times* about Luis Moreno-Ocampo, chief prosecutor of the ICC action in Darfur, conveyed exactly the reverse of what it claimed: that there may be justice even in the absence of peace.[18] The grim conclusion instead ought to have been that even if there may be indictments, and in the unlikely event that these would translate into arrests, trials, and punishments, the notion that this would be justice may be more offensive and distressing than uplifting. So, is it the prevailing view that the ICC has already failed? It certainly ought to be given a chance to fulfill its goal, which may in the long run have the unintended consequences of being instructive to conflict resolution and to peace, even if less to justice. The judicial process may prove productive in creating a narrative that may contribute to conflict resolution. Such a historical response would be to engage history as a form that transcends legal standards and trial procedures and addresses the identity issues, the cultural and the political, the material and the national issues stemming from the gross violations in history.

The Armenian-Turkish Case

Today international recognition of the Armenian Genocide and the Turkish denial of historical facts is widespread. Turkey's efforts in rejecting the designation of "genocide" for the atrocities and crimes committed against the Armenians have failed to persuade the international public. Two main causes for this increasing trend to recognize the genocide of the Armenians are foremost the activism by the Armenian Diaspora and the international shift in attending to crimes and injustices and in applying more widely the term genocide. This increased attention is anchored in broader attention to human rights in general. Since the 1970s and most noticeably following the end of the Cold War, the centrality of the Holocaust to twentieth-century history and with it heightened attention to analogous and comparable events has been growing. Evidence of this can be seen in the frequency with which the term genocide appears in historical abstracts (see Table 23.1).

There is a substantial increase in the number of references, and although there was a dip in citations per year referring to the Armenian Genocide in the 1990s the trend has been reversed since 2000. At the very least, this indicates an increased academic interest in the subject. But this is only one approximation. Another more widespread indication is a Google search, which showed more than 47 million links for "genocide" and over 2 million links for "Armenia"

Table 23.1
International Writings about the Armenian Genocide (Historical Abstracts)

Entries for Genocide	3489	Per year	Armenian Genocide Total:161	Per year	Massacres (but not genocide)
1951-1979	258	32.2	19 (since 1968)		
1980-1989	843	84.3	55	5.5	
1990-1999	1395	139.5	49	4.9	7
Since 2000	992	165	38	6.3	8

and "Armenian genocide" (April 2006)—four times as many links as "Rwanda genocide." By comparison, Holocaust has 70 million links and Holocaust and Jews has 17 million. "Chinese," "Russian," and "German" are linked with genocide more often than "Armenia," but there are very few links to "Bosnian' and "Bosnian genocide." Turkey and genocide are linked to 3.5 million. There is much to be investigated regarding these data, but here the simple observation may be made that interest in and the discussion of the question of Turkey and the Armenian Genocide is widespread, perhaps exceeding all others except the Holocaust and the largest Communist countries, where the magnitude of the killing involved tens of millions of people.

It is clear that the Internet has changed the way knowledge is produced and consumed. *Wikipedia* is perhaps the single most successful alternative to traditional sources of reliable knowledge. Its comparison with the *Encyclopaedia Britannica* for accuracy, despite a slight disagreement in the interpretation of the results, is the best testimony that not only is Wikipedia larger and more detailed than any printed source today, but its accuracy insures that it is fast becoming the first choice for searches. It is therefore particularly interesting to see the changes in Wikipedia as a reflection of the community view. The article on "Armenian genocide" has all the markings of a dispute—it has been vandalized, editing is restricted, and the neutrality of the article declared "disputed." The data reflect public discussion. If this estimate is approximately correct, the article is a testimony of the Turkish denial as a lost cause. The preponderance of evidence, even more than an academic perusal of various databases and abstracts, suggests that the shift—unless there are structural changes—is irreversible. The Armenian Genocide is acknowledged as a fact. Intense interest in the subject by Armenians and the international community and the place the debate occupies as a proxy regarding the issue of democratization in Turkey suggest that the genie can no longer be put back into the bottle. Thus, the production of knowledge through the Internet means that more documents and resources will find their way into the public domain.

These data give a representative impression of the views of the international community and academic experts in regard to the growing engagement with the question of Armenian Genocide. Other indications support this conclusion, from several attempts to establish joint Turkish Armenian committees (including the Turkish-Armenian Reconciliation Commission to solicit legal opinion on the matter in New York) to the more political votes in Europe and the United States that acknowledge the Genocide. Perhaps another indication—but which is too soon to be conclusive—is the growing attention to the topic in Turkey since the summer of 2005 and the large number of conferences and publications organized on the subject. Turkey and the Armenian Genocide is the topic of articles in several daily papers and magazines, and attempts in Turkey to prosecute intellectuals who write on the subject only adds to its wider publicity. In addition, hundreds of articles are published yearly in dailies and magazines that discuss the Genocide in multiple ways.

One would expect that this international near consensus would more or less bring the dispute to a close. If a majority of persons, beyond Turkey and its supporters, accepts that genocide took place, why has it remained such a controversial topic? The reason is that denial hurts victims and festers conflict. Robbing victims of their memories of suffering seems to reenact the offense. When central aspects of the Holocaust, which is not only widely acknowledged but which has become the paradigm of ultimate suffering and victimization, are denied, a general outcry occurs. Those who deny the Holocaust are a particular breed of anti-Semite and their claims are vehemently denounced, legislated against, and generally frowned upon. Yet, although their position is weak, Holocaust deniers do wield inordinate power by their very existence, which is offensive to the victims. In an analogous way, if somewhat different, Polish right-wing nationalists deny Polish responsibility for the killing of Jews, and some Germans attempt to save their national honor by denying the atrocities against the Hereros. In this context, Turkey's adamant rejection and denial of the Armenian Genocide, or even its extensive war crimes or atrocities, and its presentation of Turkish losses as being on a par with the Armenian losses, have been particularly offensive to the victims and their descendants. Denial of the Genocide has failed in the past to persuade outside "impartial" observers; however, political fallout is bound to place Turkey under increasing international pressure, as well as to stir up domestic controversy. This environment is characteristic of current politics in Turkey as it pursues both an accession status to the European Union and domestic democratic reforms. The tension can only result in more public controversy. Yet, notwithstanding the global community's acceptance of the Armenian position, it is only Turkey, and the official Turkey, not merely the academic or private citizens in Turkey, that can lift the denial. As long as the perpetrators do not acknowledge the crime, victims see their identity and suffering as being denied.

Turkey has provided no viable alternative to those who recognize the catastrophe yet refrain from using the term genocide. It has not explained the killings in any way that makes sense to the outside world, and its ongoing attempts to deny Armenian claims leave outsiders with no recourse but to choose sides. In this event, Turkey repeatedly loses in public opinion. It appears that pressure on Turkey will increase further in the future. In part this has to do with the increased ease of communication in general and the growing role of human rights in international conversation, in which attention to gross violations occupies increasing space. Another reason is the activism of the Armenian Diaspora (including such initiatives as a proposed Armenian Genocide museum in Washington, D.C.) and human rights activists in Turkey, as well as Turkey's bid for accession to the European Union.

It has been claimed that Turkey fears that if it accepts its guilt, the resulting moral and material burdens may be too much to bear.[20] Not only will Armenia demand territory and reparation, but the dissonance will be too much. These suppositions sound like domestic propaganda and are not persuasive to the external observer. Armenia's explicit statements regarding denial of territorial claims ought to be addressed by a formal Turkish response. Moreover, dissonance in Turkish self-perception in accepting responsibility for the Armenian Genocide does not have to be destabilizing; indeed, it is more likely to be empowering once it takes place, for it is the ability to deal with the past that liberates public discourse and allows for reconciliation.

A nation being dragged and forced to admit responsibility may have ambivalent feelings. Consider the Swiss resolution of the bank accounts of Holocaust victims. The initial high moral aspirations were hijacked by right-wing Swiss nationalists, causing an increase in anti-Semitism and xenophobia toward immigrants and refugees as well. On the other hand, liberal Swiss began to emphasize a greater willingness to be involved in international politics and to question the morality of Switzerland's benefiting from its bystander status in world conflict. (As a result one of the impacts was the relaxation of banking secrecy laws, which had previously provided a safe haven for wealth siphoned off by the world's worst dictators and an increase in the possibility of restitution.) Historical memory needs to be managed to become productive. At present, Turkey would have to be transformed to accept its responsibility and to reformulate its nationalism. Although the current growth of nationalism in Turkey may be a passing phenomenon it could turn out to be a major obstacle to any reconciliation. Much of what happens depends on the international community; however, in the final analysis it will be Turkey that will determine how it will handle its own memory and responsibilities.

A frequent Turkish response, which is not a new claim but one that has resurfaced recently more explicitly, has been to argue that it is up to the historians to resolve the dispute. Turkey's Prime Minister Recep Tayyip Erdogan has on several occasions, including a discussion with the speaker of the French Parliament Jean Louise Debre, suggested that this dispute over history be left to historians. This, however, is not a neutral statement because of the long-standing, intense Turkish effort to construct a historical narrative that denies the Genocide and attempts to answer point by point the Armenian narrative. Erdoğan's suggestion ought to be viewed as coming on the heels of extensive historical research sponsored by the state and carried out by "patriotic" historians.

Despite this context, the Turkish declaration may well be a very good suggestion that ought to be pursued. The claim has the potential of moving the dispute into a relatively professional arena. However, historians can be as partisan as any nationalist and over the generations have contributed much to national conflicts. Thus, much propaganda and disinformation has been batted about in the dispute. Both sides ought to engage the historical inquiry and find external professional bodies to sponsor a professional investigation without preconditions. Contemporary politics would only benefit from such an investigation, and perhaps contemporary reconciliation, not as a precondition, would be the outcome of such an investigation.

In the last generation a new form of reconciliation emerged as part of the transition of societies to democracies. The growing stature of truth and reconciliation commissions, as well as historical commissions that are informed by current human rights standards and are staffed by professional historians, provides for new mechanism of reconciliation. The members of these commissions are not only representatives of both sides in a conflict but also include outsiders, and by assuming a semi-judicial stance, they offer a new opening for reconciliation.

In a structured situation, a professional historical discussion can demarcate that part of the narrative that can be agreed upon. Secondly, a historical description can be created to indicate how the debate has evolved and show that despite current disagreements, many areas of agreement exist, that is, from a political perspective, even a historiographic examination would show the changes in the narratives. Once historians are engaged to provide a narrative that delineates agreements and disagreements about particular and specific aspects of the events, the areas of disagreement could be clarified and the evidentiary disputes adjudicated by an international panel. In theory, agreement could be reached. But the first step must be taken.

Turkey and Armenia are both in transitional phases of their history. Historical legacy casts its shadow on the relations between the two countries and serves to destabilize the Caucasus region, while also affecting the domestic democratization processes by providing fodder for nationalists and xenophobia, casting every dispute as a potential national cataclysm. It is in this context that the memory of the Armenian Genocide, and not its repression, can lead to reconciliation. To reach this point of acknowledgement both sides must participate in the journey willingly and hopefully benefit from it. Historical examples suggest that this is possible, but it is also full of risks. Relying on international good will, it is up to both sides, Turkey and Armenia, to bring about a reconciliation.

Notes

1. "The Scholars' Initiative," Research Team 2: The Dissolution of Yugoslavia.
2. Elazar Barkan, *The Guilt of Nations: Restitution and Negotiating Historical Injustices* (New York: W. W. Norton, 2000). See also Elazar Barkan and Alexander Karn, eds., *Taking Wrongs Seriously: Apologies and Reconciliation* (Stanford: Stanford University Press, 2006).
3. Roy L. Brooks, "The New Patriotism and Apology for Slavery," in Barkan and Karn, *Taking Wrongs Seriously*, pp. 230-231.
4. The Chicago City Council in 2000 passed a resolution urging Congress to discuss compensation for the descendants of slaves. This included a series of hearings. In 2002, the council passed "a first-of-its-kind ordinance requiring companies that seek city business to disclose any profits that they, or their predecessor companies, made from slavery." In 2005, the New York City Council held a hearing on "Slave Era Disclosure Bill and Reparations Resolution."

5. Alfred L. Brophy, "The Tulsa Race Riot Commission, Apology, and Reparation: Understanding the Functions and Limitations of a Historical Truth Commission," in Barkan and Karn, *Taking Wrongs Seriously*, pp. 234-258.
6. Alfred L. Brophy, "Considering Universities' Moral Culpability in Slavery," conference paper, Brown University, March 2005. The conference was organized by Brown's Steering Committee, which itself is a leader in campus responses to "Historical Injustices: Restitution and Reconciliation in International Perspective," the title of the conference.
7. Rebecca Tsosie, "The BIA's Apology to Native Americans: An Essay on Collective Memory and Collective Conscience," in Barkan and Karn, *Taking Wrongs Seriously*, pp. 185-212.
8. Benny Morris, *The Birth of the Palestinian Refugee Problem Revisited* (Cambridge and New York: Cambridge University Press, 2004); Sari Hanafi, "Right of Return and Its Application: Opening the Debate about Sociology of the Return," in *Exile and Return: Predicaments of Palestinians and Jews*, ed. Ann Mosely Lesch and Ian S. Lustick (Philadelphia: University of Pennsylvania Press, 2005), pp. 55-82; Gershon Shafir, "Palestinian and Jewish Memories and Return," in manuscript form. A useful source for current Palestinian research is Shaml, Palestinian Diaspora and Refugee Center, www.shaml.org/.
9. Jan-Bart Gewald, *Herero Heroes: Socio-Political History of the Herero of Namibia, 1890-1923* (Oxford: James Currey, and Athens: Ohio State University Press, 1999); Isabel V. Hull, *Absolute Destruction: Military Culture and the Practices of War in Imperial Germany* (Ithaca, NY: Cornell University Press, 2005); Mark Cocker, *Rivers of Gold, Rivers of Blood: Europe's Conflict with Tribal Peoples* (London, Jonathan, Cape, 2000) pp. 269-370.
10. Adam Hochschild, *King Leopold's Ghost: A Story of Greed, Terror, and Heroism in Colonial Africa* (London: Macmillan, 1998). On Edmund Morel and racism, see Elazar Barkan, *The Retreat of Scientific Racism: Changing Concepts of Race in Britain and the United States between the World Wars* (Cambridge and New York: Cambridge University Press, 1991), pp. 24-25.
11. Alan Riding, "Art Show Forces Belgium to Ask Hard Questions about Its Colonial Past," *New York Times*, February 9, 2005.
12. Hochschild, *King Leopold's Ghost*, pp. 250-255.
13. "Report of the International Commission of Inquiry on Darfur to the United Nations Secretary-General, Pursuant to Security Council Resolution 1564 of 18 September 2004" (Geneva, January 25, 2005), p. 124.
14. William Schabas, *Genocide in International Law* (Cambridge, Cambridge University Press, 2000), p. 235.
15. Ibid., p. 127.
16. Vice President Ali Osman Taha, quoted in *Agence France-Presse*, November 13, 2005.
17. *Deutsche Presse-Agentur*, March 29, 2006.
18. Elizabeth Rubin, "If Not Peace, Then Justice," *New York Times*, April 2, 2006.
19. The first citation is Richard G. Hovannisian, "The Allies and Armenia, 1915-18," *Journal of Contemporary History* [Great Britain] 1968 3, 1: 145-168.
20. Taner Akçam, "Fear of Facing History: Essential Steps toward Turkish-Armenian Reconciliation," in manuscript form.

24

Anatomy of Post-Genocide Reconciliation

Simon Payaslian

"Dwell on the past and you will lose an eye.
Forget the past and you will lose both eyes."
—Russian proverb

In recent years there has been a growing interest in efforts toward Armenian-Turkish reconciliation, an issue of fundamental significance for the Armenian people, who ninety years ago fell victim to the Young Turk policy of genocide.[1] Reconciliation between Turks and Armenians became the subject of much heated debate after the establishment of the Turkish-Armenian Reconciliation Commission (TARC) in 2001 in the form of "unofficial" Track Two Diplomacy.[2] As of this writing, however, reconciliation appears to be far removed from the realities on the ground as dictated by domestic and regional political and ideological constraints and geopolitical considerations. The paucity of scholarly treatment of Armenian-Turkish reconciliation, nine decades after the Genocide, is perhaps indicative of the remoteness of such an eventuality. Although during the past three decades there has emerged a vast literature on reconciliation in general, references to the Armenian Genocide or to Armenian-Turkish reconciliation across the full spectrum of that literature have been too few in number to bear any significance on the development of the theory and practice of reconciliation.[3]

A cursory examination of the literature on reconciliation suggests several perspectives ranging from constitutionalism, international law and organizations, human rights, peace studies, conflict resolution, and criminal justice to the psychology and theology of forgiveness and healing, moral reconstruction, and transitional and restorative justice.[4] Each approach requires some form of juridical and administrative reforms to institute confidence-building mechanisms between groups in conflict and to facilitate intergroup, intercommunal dialogue. These perspectives rely on normative, moral, and spiritual propositions, aspirational humanitarian values, and legal principles for successful mediation. Given the nature of the Armenian-Turkish conflict, however—which involves the annihilation of 1.5 million Armenians, the dispersion of the Armenian people, and geopolitical and territorial issues—most of the existing approaches and perspectives cannot be meaningfully applied to this case. What is instead proposed here is a two-phase reconciliation process, whereby the first step would institute an ad hoc multilateral reconciliation tribunal vested with advisory and adjudicatory authority, which upon fulfillment of its task would subsequently guide bilateral arrangements for reconciliation.

The principal responsibilities for the conduct of bilateral and multilateral diplomacy toward reconciliation rest with the governments of Armenia and Turkey. Yet, the Turkish-Armenian case is further complicated by the presence of diasporan communities, a significant factor in any negotiations regarding the Genocide (a topic requiring separate treatment). The central problem to be addressed here is the identification of the guiding principles undergirding Armenian-Turkish reconciliation. Two fundamental principles are essential for the removal of barriers to post-genocide reconciliation: truth and justice.[5] The first requires a recognition by the perpetrator (the Turkish government) of the factuality of the crime (genocide) committed against the victim (the Armenian people); the second, specification of matters pertaining to restitutive and compensatory justice. It is commonly believed that Turkish recognition of the Armenian Genocide would serve such purposes as, for example, the restoration of the historic Armenian homeland to its rightful owners, healing the emotional wounds of the survivors and their descendants, and securing pecuniary compensation. Turkish recognition is also said to create an opportunity for reconciliation and normalization, leading to the establishment of formal diplomatic relations between Armenia and Turkey and the attendant privileges of and obligations in the exchange of good offices. It is worth stressing here, however, that the most essential ingredient with respect to compensatory justice—namely, the restitution of the Armenian homeland to the Armenian people—cannot be accomplished through recognition or reconciliation.[6] Further, contrary to the conventional view, nor would the exchange of diplomatic offices necessarily enhance the national security of either party, for it is the preponderance of military power that ultimately determines the nature of relations between states.

Matters of Truth and Justice

Reconciliation is predicated upon the axiom that "the truth shall set us free" and assumes that perpetrator and victim can be brought face to face to reconcile their differences regarding the past. The principal point thus emphasized is that both parties—perpetrator and victim—arrive at a common understanding of what constitutes the truth concerning their past behavior and its consequences, that is, the truth about history. Clearly, there can be no just reconciliation without a consensus on the truth.[7] Premised upon this fundamental principle, analysts often refer to several truth commissions as exemplifying workable models for reconciliation (for example, the South African Truth and Reconciliation Commission, Ghana's National Reconciliation Commission, Chile's National Commission on Truth and Reconciliation, and Peru's Truth and Reconciliation Commission).[8] Such commissions commonly require confessions on the part of the perpetrator and forgiveness on the part of the victim for the physical and mental damages caused to the victims of violence. The perpetrator is expected to confess the crimes committed against the victim, leading to a "self-purging," often cathartic in nature, and to the potential for a redemptive transformation in the perpetrator's perception of the crime as a historical fact. Public apology by the perpetrator and forgiveness by the victim begin the process of reconciliation, and only after the perpetrator no longer denies the past can perpetrator and victim transcend anger and hostilities, thus leading to closure. In the case of South Africa, for instance, individual testimonials by victims and perpetrators exposed the offenses and in so doing offered an opportunity to punish the perpetrators by "shaming" and by "social censure and ostracism." Ruti Teitel has emphasized the consequences of the end of the perpetrator's denial of the truth: "When the 'truth' becomes known, when certain critical knowledge is publicly recognized, the shared knowledge often sets in motion other legal responses, such as sanctions against perpetrators, reparations for victims, and institutional changes."[9]

Martha Minow has identified "a spectrum of goals" for truth commissions. Most of the points she enumerates, however, are applicable to experiences of national crises but cannot realistically be expected of Armenian-Turkish negotiations. According to Minow, a truth commission can, for example, enable a society to "overcome communal and official denial of the atrocity and gain public acknowledgment" (point 1) and doing so would "restore dignity to victims" (point 8).[10] The Turkish government, however, has been denying the Armenian Genocide for nine decades, and its policies to that effect are too familiar to comment on here. Suffice it to note that any "public acknowledgment" of the Genocide on the part of the government in Ankara to "restore" the "dignity" of its Armenian victims seems impossible in the foreseeable future. As a result, a truth commission modeled after the African or Latin American experiences may be useful regarding the Turkish government's human rights violations and perhaps may even promote political liberalization within Turkey, but the political reality remains that no such commission would bring about official Turkish recognition of the Armenian Genocide.

Critics of truth commissions have noted that such panels and processes as witnessed in Africa and Latin America quickly become politicized by the state and competing interests. One of the principal objectives of truth commissions and the reconciliation processes has been to enhance the political legitimacy of the post-crisis government, which in most cases employed in its bureaucracies the very same people who had participated in the crimes.[11] The truth and reconciliation commissions, "designed more for perpetrators than victims,"[12] are therefore established to delineate a point of demarcation between the "old" and the "new," a point of departure (even if only symbolic) from deplorable human rights practices to the promotion of national reconciliation, from a morally and legally unsustainable authoritarian rule to a sustainable legitimate commonweal.[13]

The practices of transitional justice as experienced in the former Soviet bloc may be of certain utility in delineating, as a point of departure, the general contours of a legal framework for the debate on matters of compensation within the context of international human rights. Yet, the difficulties involved in applying the model of post-Communist transitional justice are in a sense similar to those discussed above concerning the truth and reconciliation commissions. The functionality of the post-Communist successor state has required adjustments in, and rectifications through, municipal law formulated and administered within the context of dismantling the single-party political system and its centralized economy for the purpose of developing market economy. Transitional justice in the post-Communist state, therefore, is a matter of domestic or internal reconciliation through political and economic liberalization and re-privatization. "The guiding principle [in the former Soviet bloc] is harmony, so that the reparations for past wrongs are justified in juridical terms, as legal entitlements and 'rights' to the extent and insofar as they are compatible with the goals of the economic transition."[14]

Moreover, truth commissions also have a tendency to develop a degree of moral equivalencies, whereby the perpetrator's crime is couched in justifications for the atrocities. For example, the second volume of the South African Report of the Truth and Reconciliation Commission first describes the role of and egregious human rights violations by the apartheid regime against which appears an analysis of the anti-apartheid "liberation movements" and the violence committed by the latter. The victims are thus presented as being equally criminal as the perpetrators.[15] Further, in emphasizing such concepts as "healing" and "forgiveness" as essential ingredients for reconciliation, the literature on this subject tends to be unduly optimistic with respect to expected results, as works in this area envision processes insulated from power and disparities in influence.[16]

Another problem in these models is that the activities and jurisdictions of the truth commissions are limited essentially to the national level. The Chilean National Commission on Truth and Reconciliation is illustrative. The law instituting the Commission states that "the truth had to be brought to light, for only on such a foundation . . . would it be possible to . . . create the necessary conditions for achieving true *national* reconciliation."[17] In a similar vein, what Teitel has aptly noted regarding transitional justice in the German case applies to some extent to the Turkish experience: "War-related guilt borne by the country as a whole was deemed to prevent a transition to lasting democracy. The view of national justice as hopelessly political represents prior postwar policy, with apparent repercussions for the century."[18]

Post-genocide reconciliation in the Armenian case, however, is fundamentally different from these forms of reconciliation. Post-genocide reconciliation and the attendant matters pertaining to indemnification involve more than mere domestic political and economic liberalization in Turkey. While truth and reconciliation commissions deal with issues pertaining to violence committed by authoritarian regimes, such commissions cannot address the problems associated with the Armenian Genocide, as the intent of the Young Turk genocidal policies was the total removal and annihilation of the Armenian people. For example, the truth commission on Rwanda is not applicable to the Armenian-Turkish case because, unlike the Tutsi and the Hutu who continue to live together in Rwanda, the entire Armenian population—with the exception of the community in Istanbul—has been removed from their ancestral homeland. Also, the subject of Armenian-Turkish reconciliation cannot be considered a matter of transitional or restorative justice, for that concept implies, as witnessed in the former Soviet bloc, that damages can, even if to a limited extent, be rectified by restoring the status quo ante (for example, pre-Stalinization). Nor are conflict resolution methods applicable, as the hour to resolve the Armenian-Turkish crisis—which can be said to have escalated at least as early as the 1870s but certainly in the 1890s—has long passed. By the time the crisis reached its conclusion in 1923, the Armenian population in the Ottoman Empire had been virtually eliminated and the remnants of the survivors dispersed throughout the world. Regarding historical justice, Teitel writes:

> "History will be the judge"—the truth will withstand the passage of time. Common sayings reflect popular intuitions regarding the relation of historical interpretation of time, suggesting that somehow historical judgment evolves with its passage. Certainly at the descriptive level, this appears true. Often many generations pass, whether after war or repressive rule, before societies are able to confront their history. . . . With the passage of time, interceding political events and historiographical developments all bear on historical interpretation, which means that such interpretations undergo change.[19]

The conference held in Turkey on the Ottoman Armenians in September 2005 reportedly inaugurated a genuine *Historikerstreit* (Historians' Debate) on matters pertaining to the Armenians in pre-1923 Turkey. The views expressed certainly seemed to have challenged the prevailing Young Turk-Ataturkist paradigm of Turkish historiography that has for years denied the history of the Armenian people and therefore, and more emphatically, denied the Armenian Genocide.[20] A discussion of the political objectives pursued (for example, joining the European Union) by permitting such a conference to take place in the first place is beyond the scope of this discussion. Suffice it to note that, like the case of the de-Communization processes in the former Soviet bloc, the Turkish political system and culture must certainly experience a de-Ataturkification process before democratization can be consolidated. It is worth noting, however, that such *Historikerstreit*, while perhaps promotive of liberalization in Turkey, is not necessarily promotive of Armenian-Turkish reconciliation. The concept of "transitional justice," therefore, while providing a certain theoretical framework to formulate a conceptualization of reconciliation, is better suited for processes of political liberalization along the lines of Ataturkist-liberal reconciliation within Turkey rather than Armenian-Turkish reconciliation.[21] Whether the current debates in Turkey will lead to political liberalization remains to be seen, but reliance on the Armenian Question as a vehicle to that end should not be construed, or presented, as automatically leading to Turkish recognition of the Armenian Genocide. Domestic political liberalization may be a necessary though certainly not a sufficient condition toward that end.

In a word, most of the studies on reconciliation encompass terminologies and methodologies that have limited applicability to the Armenian-Turkish case, as they do not address the problems of post-genocide reconciliation. As the TARC experience has demonstrated, post-genocide reconciliation is not likely to be accomplished through commissions lacking international competence and legitimacy with respect to the Armenian Genocide. The legal and moral matrix of a just reconciliation requires in this case a conceptualization or re-conceptualization of just reconciliation in terms of international human rights, that is, the international human right to recognition and reconciliation. Such a conceptualization would enable the victim, whose military capabilities are no match to those of the perpetrator's, to gain access to the instrumentalities of international legal mechanisms for various forms of sanctions in order to buttress its claims through bilateral channels in the process of reconciliation. Reliance on international human rights enhances the legitimacy of that process. At the international level, the United Nations, as the global institution with universal legal and moral legitimacy, would function as the third-party facilitator of reconciliation negotiations between perpetrator and victim.

Political and Moral Legitimacy

In addition to matters pertaining truth and justice, it is essential that the parties and mediating agencies involved in post-genocide reconciliation possess universally acceptable legal and moral legitimacy. The formation of a truth and reconciliation commission in the Armenian-Turkish case must have greater transparency and must be representative of the Armenian people. The TARC experience demonstrated that that process lacked a sufficient degree of public legitimacy, and as a result it could not function as a mediator. Moreover, while the independent study conducted by the International Center for Transitional Justice (ICTJ), as commissioned by TARC, correctly concluded that "the Events, viewed collectively, can thus be said to include all of the elements of the crime of genocide as defined in the Convention,"[22] the ICTJ too lacked political legitimacy. Neither TARC nor ICTJ was representative of the Armenian people. Inclusivity does not necessarily facilitate diplomatic deft and dexterity, but it does enable the negotiators to hear "the voices of the aggrieved"—for "memory and repair depend on 'our willingness and our capacity to act on behalf of the victims.'"[23]

Further, legitimization of reconciliation procedures requires integration of truth values and adherence to the principle of procedural representation.[24] The UN Charter, the Universal Declaration of Human Rights, the UN Convention on the Prevention and Punishment of the Crime of Genocide, the International Covenant on Civil and Political Rights, and the International Covenant on Economic, Social and Cultural Rights, to name a few, require legitimate representation of victims. Truth values have a crucial role in the process of reconciliation if the parties to the process share the expected "goal events" and to a significant extent shape public policies that are in turn accommodative of reconciliatory tendencies as "international political goods."[25] International reconciliatory agencies facilitate—albeit incrementally[26]—the realization of morally and legally legitimate values and contribute to the "reserves" of public support that such agencies "accumulate or accrue to the 'legitimacy account.'"[27] Reconciliation construed as international human rights with bilaterally shared "goal events" confers legitimacy upon the agencies established for that purpose.

Legitimacy thus requires attention to rights and values in international law. This point is worth emphasizing in the Armenian case particularly because the post-World War I courts-martial failed to bring to justice the architects and executors of the genocidal policies. The failure by the Turkish government to do so then has, as demonstrated for the past ninety years, led to failure in accountability. The international community has been equally derelict in its responsibility, as it vacillated in the enforcement of the Mudros Armistice (1918) between the victorious Allied Powers and the Ottoman Empire, ignored the Treaty of Sèvres of 1920, and thereafter altogether neglected all matters pertaining to justice for the Armenians, when in fact international law provided for state culpability and obligated the Allies to punish the perpetrators. On May 24, 1915, the Allied Powers (England, France, and Russia) issued a joint declaration proclaiming to "hold personally responsible" for crimes "all members of the Ottoman Government and those of their agents." Crimes against humanity, though not codified at the time, were nevertheless derived from the principle of *jus in bello* in customary law and the Law of the Hague as formulated in international conferences of 1899 and 1907 and considered the crimes of forced deportations, tortures, and massacres committed by states as "offenses that transcended the confines of national law" and violated "the laws of all nations."[28] The Hague Convention of 1907 also contained provisions for the protection of all property in time of armed conflict, and subsequent instruments in later years (for instance, the Additional Protocols to the Geneva Conventions of 1977) expanded protections to that effect. The failure on the part of the international community to obtain accountability by holding the Ottoman state as a perpetrator of "crimes against humanity" has meant the absence of punishment and therefore of closure.

International Human Rights and Reconciliation

Two general views dominate the debate regarding the viability of international human rights law. Proponents of the view that international human rights law is "soft law" contend that the relevant documents such as the UN Charter, the Universal Declaration of Human Rights, the International Covenants on Civil and Political Rights, and Social, Economic, and Cultural Rights, are "mere guidelines" and as such they impose no legal obligations on states to observe international standards set therein. Accordingly, this view holds that state parties to the UN Charter and other international instruments are under no legal obligation to respect international human rights law. The second view, on the other hand, maintains that the above-mentioned documents as well as numerous other resolutions and conventions by international bodies represent "hard law" and constitute "a part of international customary law and, as such, are binding on all states."[29] This "hard law" view considers governments—signatories and non-signatories alike—as sovereign states obligated to respect international human rights law regardless of their domestic constitutional, political, and economic conditions. It is this second view that must be considered as the foundation for Armenian-Turkish reconciliation. Accordingly, this case would require that parties involved be held accountable as international law imposes certain non-derogable legal responsibilities, including adherence to international human rights standards. The key advantage in an Armenian-Turkish reconciliation commission predicated upon international human rights law and values would be the strengthening of the legitimacy of the multilateral and bilateral processes.

International human rights law as developed under the UN Charter and the International Bill of Rights has acquired the same status and "binding character as other international law and agreements."[30] The "general principles" of international law and both conventional and customary law lend strong legitimacy not only to human rights agreements but also to declarations and resolutions adopted by the United Nations, regional international organizations, and state parties. Five decades ago, Lauterpacht argued that "as a result of the Charter of the UN—as well as of other changes in international law—the individual has acquired a status and a stature which has transformed him from an object of international compassion into a subject of international rights."[31] The UN Charter, as the supreme legal document in international law and the "highest instrument in the international hierarchy of international and domestic documents," affirms the fundamental human rights of the individual, whose legal rights it recognizes as part of international law independently of the state and "as part of the constitutional law both of states and of the society of states at large."[32] Although such an approach may "generate tensions" between non-state entities and state parties to international human rights instruments, nevertheless the universality of the UN Charter, the Universal Declaration of Human Rights, and the International Covenants have made these instruments an inextricable part of international human rights values and standards.[33] This is particularly so since, as Lauterpacht has argued, "in modern international society the interests to be protected and regulated can no longer be entrusted exclusively to States. These interests call for the recognition of new subjects of rights and duties conceived as the rational means of international social welfare."[34]

Given that under current international law only the state possesses legal standing in matters of administrative justice, the governments of Turkey and Armenia (despite their long repressive legacies), as sovereign entities operating in the international community, cannot abrogate their obligations to observe international human rights standards.[35] International law thus imposes on both governments the legal responsibility to observe principles of human rights as they enter into bilateral or multilateral negotiations toward a just reconciliation. Such a responsibility for the government of Armenia ultimately entails legal representation of the Armenian nation in matters pertaining to the Genocide; for the government of Turkey, it entails the duties of recognition of and reparation for the crime of genocide committed against the Armenian nation. The reconciliation process could also obligate the Turkish government to issue public acknowledgments of the crimes committed by its predecessors and directly engage with the descendants of victims through, for example, agencies to institutionalize group level reconciliation. To be sure, punishment of the crime of genocide may be but one, though in no way guaranteed, of the outcomes of the multilateral and bilateral reconciliation procedures. A clear identification of the criminal and the victim is the first step toward any attempts at reconciliation. Confusion and distortions in the political discourse as to the criminal and the crime, as practiced by the Turkish government and its sympathizers, lead to false premises and therefore to unworkable measures toward reconciliation.

Multilateral Arrangements for Reconciliation: The First Phase

The Genocide Convention (Article VI) expects national judiciary, as the court of first instance, to enforce punishment for the crime of genocide committed within the perpetrator's territorial jurisdiction. The Convention neither grants nor recognizes territorial, jurisdictional exclusivity, however, and legal precedence (as established by the *Eichmann* case)[36] has reaffirmed the applicability of international legal standards and universal jurisdiction to genocide.[37] The same holds true for crimes against humanity and war crimes, as well as related areas of international criminal law, where the jurisdiction of international tribunals is recognized based on the principle of universality, as affirmed under customary and conventional international laws, including, for example, the Geneva Conventions (1949), the Hague Convention for the Protection of Cultural Property in the Event of Armed Conflict (1954), the Slavery Convention (1956), and the Torture Convention (1984), to name but a few. Such cases include the International Military Tribunals at Nuremberg and for the Far East (Tokyo) after World War II, the International Criminal Tribunal for the Former Yugoslavia, and the International Criminal Tribunal for Rwanda (1990s). The latter two, the Statutes of the International Criminal Court, as well as municipal laws in certain countries (such as France, Canada, Belgium, and Australia) have also established linkages in the accountability of culpability of not only state but also of non-state actors.[38] As Teitel has noted, established principles of universal jurisdiction transcend both temporal and spatial constraints:

> The crime against humanity is conceived as an offense to all humanity, and hence prosecutable by all nations, giving rise to the related jurisdictional principle of "universality." . . . [T]he crime against humanity is considered an offense "among civilized nations" and therefore punishable with, or without, prior legislation. . . . If, under the traditional jurisdictional principle of territoriality, the wronged community is considered contiguous to the site of the crime, it is in the nature of the crime against humanity that the relevant wronged community is all nations, and the relevant offense perpetrated against humanity.[39]

National administrative and juridical forums in Turkey are ill-prepared and not likely to serve as mechanisms for purposes of assigning culpability and accountability. The abortive courts-martial under the post-World War I dysfunctional system and the persistent denial by the Turkish government of the Genocide (in addition to the absence of respect for human rights in general) since then have amply demonstrated the failure of the Turkish government to administer internal justice, rendering any Turkish claims to the principle of territoriality in legal jurisdiction nugatory. Ratner and Abrams write:

> States parties to treaties obligating them to penalize certain offenses under domestic law must have domestic criminal law statutes implementing this obligation, or a domestic law system that permits prosecution directly under international law; if they do not, they are violating their international legal commitments. . . . The scope of any obligation or right under international law and the extent to which the state implements any obligation through domestic law—incompletely, fully, or by going further than the obligation—will permit those concerned with accountability to choose a proper forum for prosecution.[40]

It must be stressed that Armenian-Turkish reconciliation is ultimately a bilateral reconciliation, where the governments of Armenia and Turkey agree on a set of values and procedures to formulate and implement relevant policies, but the pursuit of accountability, arrived at multilaterally and bilaterally and premised upon the principle of universality, is necessary as a first step toward just reconciliation. A multilateral venue would include, for example (unlike TARC and unrelated to it) the formation of an ad hoc international tribunal with the legally legitimate authority as sponsored and publicly sanctioned by an international organization, such as the UN Security Council or the General Assembly; UN's judicial agency, the International Court of Justice; or the International Criminal Court. The International Criminal Tribunal for the Former Yugoslavia and the International Criminal Tribunal for Rwanda, for example, were established by the UN Security Council.

International sponsorship, especially by the United Nations, and the rules and procedures derived from the legal and moral legitimacy of the sponsor strengthen the legitimacy of the reconciliation tribunal,[41] enhance the credibility of the process, as well as grant the benefits of neutrality, financial support, and international awareness.[42] Unlike TARC, the said international tribunal would be composed of representatives of Armenian, Turkish, UN agencies, Western and non-Western governments, as well as representatives of diasporan communities. When confronted with the challenge of national sovereignty in the case of East Timor, for instance, the UN Human Rights Commission requested that the UN Secretary-General include "Asian experts" as commissioners for "adequate representation." As Ratner and Abrams have noted, "a commission's success will depend heavily on the independence, stature, and moral authority of its members. The nature and history of the abuses that the commission will be examining may also make diversity in its composition—whether as to ethnicity, politics, profession, or other attributes—critical to establishing credibility."[43] Unlike TARC, members of the commission must include high-ranking officials from both the governments of Armenia and Turkey so as to enhance the feasibility of reconciliation in subsequent bilateral negotiations between the two parties. Such a reconciliation process should not be entrusted to the auspices of a single mediating government. Neither the United States nor any other government commands sufficient credibility to function as the sole mediator between Armenia and Turkey. Moreover, the international tribunal must operate within a clearly specified set of methodologically sound procedural standards, with a healthy degree of transparency that can uphold and sustain its credibility for the duration of the multilateral and subsequent bilateral negotiations.

The multilateral model relies on the ability of the sponsoring international organizations to "galvanize the necessary political will"[44] and the financial resources for the effective mediation by the international tribunal. Joe Verhoeven has correctly pointed out: "It should be the elementary right of the victims to have access to an independent (international) body simply for the truth to be established officially. And it should be the obligation of the state concerned to cooperate with such a body. No such right or obligation presently exists or is clearly admitted."[45] The pursuit of the Armenian case through such international means can also contribute to the development of international law in general and of international human rights law in particular.

Such an international tribunal may facilitate reconciliation through both dialogue and adjudication, and therefore matters pertaining to evidentiary principles and admissibility of related records are essential for its effective functioning. Adjudicatory procedures would require the granting of certain prosecutorial authority to the international tribunal, for the Armenian case requires holding the Turkish state accountable for the Genocide, necessitating thereby a legal formulation and enumeration of the punitive damages and a determination as to the nature and extent of punitive measures to be implemented.

The difficulty in this case is that only after the dialogue is set in motion can the international organization sponsoring the tribunal assume the responsibility of facilitating adjudicatory obligations. Further complicating matters is that in order for the ICJ or any other international judicial body to hear the case of *Armenia v. Turkey*, both parties must accept the jurisdiction of the adjudicating agency. As Verhoeven has noted, it would be very surprising "if Turkey ever agreed to submit to the ICJ or any other international tribunal a dispute that could call into question its denial of the Armenian Genocide."[46] If, as a first step, negotiations at the multilateral level prove successful in formulating a framework for reconciliation, the second step would involve negotiations at the bilateral level for the effective implementation (with the direct support of the sponsoring international organization) of the processes agreed upon by the international tribunal.

Bilateral Arrangements for Reconciliation: The Second Phase

Successful negotiations toward reconciliation at the international level are essential to facilitate further bilateral negotiations and, with public confidence, to encourage compliance at the domestic level, particularly if both parties are to overcome domestic opposition. Integration of the institutions of the perpetrator and victim governments and of international organizations into the reconciliation process is essential. Post-genocide reconciliation requires acceptance and acknowledgment on the part of the perpetrator government that it has committed genocide. Moreover, in order to be successful, the governmental bureaucracies—both from the Turkish and Armenian sides—must participate in the process. In the case of the government of Turkey, the military establishment, which for eighty years has viewed itself as the bastion of Ataturkism, is likely to feel threatened by such proceedings. In the case of the government of Armenia, suspicions (in Armenia and the diasporan communities) of political compromises regarding issues related to the Genocide may undermine the process.

In bilateral negotiations, the processes of foreign policy decision making by both governments would involve a number of ingredients facilitative of reconciliation. These would include the institutionalization of principles, rules, and procedures for the articulation of specific interests and values and, in the long term, the routinization of decisions supportive of patterns of reconciliatory behavior, itself the "accretional character" of piecemeal (even if at first incoherent) set of decisions.[47] Bilateral decisions are the products of the integration of a set of "cognitive beliefs" as shaped by each nation's worldview, which, in turn, as individuals or collectivities, shape the operative values in the formulation and implementation of policy objectives.[48] This is not to say, however, that internal struggles below the leadership level do not exist or suddenly terminate once the reconciliation process is set in motion, for inter- and intra-bureaucratic struggles to define and redefine the preconditions for the process, to formulate and reformulate its objectives, and to delineate the legal and moral contours of policy implementation remain as much an integral part of the bilateral process as in a single country's policy formulation and implementation processes.

Bilateral negotiations toward reconciliation would also contain certain identifiable characteristics, including a consistent and mutual complementariness and synchronization of both governments' leadership and bureaucratic activities with respect to reconciliation, and a significant degree of regularity in bilaterally established patterns of behavior and "established norms of diplomatic practices" distributed among legal and administrative facilities.[49] The latter would consist of the core decision makers in foreign policy (such as the head of state and personal envoys, key advisors, cabinet members, the legislative branch, and political parties) who, in turn, mobilize the general public[50] for the legitimization of reconciliation processes. Failure to institutionalize routinization in Armenian-Turkish bilateral foreign policy behavior would indicate failure in the reconciliation dialogue. As Ratner and Abrams have pointed out with respect to international tribunals possessing prosecutorial jurisdiction, failure to institute and effectuate reconciliation would render the entire process "at best an academic exercise and at worst a cynical set-back for international law and justice."[51]

The Future of Armenian-Turkish Reconciliation

The process of just reconciliation, guided by normative principles consisting of universalist and egalitarian values,[52] is expected to determine reparatory compensations for damages incurred by the Armenian people as a result of the genocidal policies of the Young Turk regime. As the entire Armenian population suffered, so steps toward reconciliation and measures for compensation must be premised upon universalist obligations toward the Armenian nation.[53] Such a task cannot be accomplished without a legitimate and fair representation of the Armenian people. And the only viable entity with a sufficient degree of legal legitimacy is the government of the Republic of Armenia. It will remain the responsibility of that government, as obligated under international human rights law and in collaboration with the diasporan communities, to develop the means to formulate the specific processes toward the just representation of the Diaspora in legal and political matters pertaining to reconciliation with the Republic of Turkey.

A perpetrator government accused of genocide and crimes against humanity is held accountable for various reasons. The most significant reasons appear to be that accountability permits the victims and their relatives and friends "a sense of justice," healing from the traumatic experiences, and eventually a sense of closure, although closure can never be guaranteed. A workable process of reconciliation would seek to develop and embrace public dialogues regarding the historical record of both the perpetrator and the victim. Accountability may also encourage the offending government to reform its legal structure and bureaucracies so as to institute a more just political system in an environment conducive to democratization.

Furthermore, "a retributive theory of justice would regard accountability as just punishment for those who do wrong."[54] Primarily moral in proscription, "satisfactory reparation" entails first and foremost "a formal apology" by the perpetrator or condemnation of an act by an international tribunal. It is the former, the perpetrator's apology, however, that essentially serves as a necessary though not necessarily a sufficient condition toward reconciliation. The key question concerning the Armenian-Turkish reconciliation process is whether acceptance of responsibility by the Turkish government can lead to a just restitution and compensation, which necessarily leads to issues of territory—that is, territory as the Armenian historic homeland—and confiscated movable and immovable properties. As noted above, however, given the current regional and global configurations of power, neither recognition nor reconciliation can facilitate such a just restitution. Whether pecuniary compensation can function as "a substitute for restoration of the *status quo ante*"[55] will be left to the descendants of the victims and survivors to decide—a mathematically daunting undertaking and morally an impossible task. Nevertheless, pecuniary compensation would be necessary in the Armenian case, since restorative justice is impossible; this is certainly true as of this writing and is likely to so remain for the foreseeable future. Martha Minow has most aptly presented the moral dilemma:

> The symbolic gesture and the struggle for it give victims a chance to reclaim their dignity and their history. But at the heart of reparations is the paradoxical search to repair the irreparable. Once paid, compensation may wrongly imply that the harms are over and need not be discussed again. Money can never remedy non-monetary loss, however, and the fight over money carries the risk of trivializing the harms.[56]

A fundamental philosophical question in the case of Armenian-Turkish reconciliation is whether a later generation—a generation removed from the actual, physical experience of the Genocide—has the moral right to forgive the perpetrator. This issue of trans-generational moral obligations frequently appears in the literature on reconciliation, and it is particularly relevant to the Armenian-Turkish case. However, most of the published material on truth and reconciliation commissions (in the South African case, for example) assume that the perpetrator and the victim can meet face to face, recount their experiences of torture and bloodshed, and having arrived at some common understanding or agreement on the crimes committed, also agree to move on with their lives and return to some form of normalcy. Such a scenario is not applicable in the Armenian case, especially by now, after ninety years. The survivors of the death marches—those who lost members of their families, those who lost their homes and land—are no longer with us. However, there is a Turkish government that has inherited the moral burdens of the perpetrator, and there is an Armenian government that has inherited the physical and emotional scars of the crime of genocide. As observed in a number of truth and reconciliation commissions, one of the principal functions of their hearings has been to provide a forum for the perpetrator to ask the victim—"Can you forgive us?"[57] Can representatives of the Turkish government meet face to face with representatives of the Armenian government and ask: "Can you forgive us?" At first blush, insistence on such a gesture for forgiveness may seem backward-looking; however, a statement to that effect may in fact be forward-looking, facilitating, in piecemeal processes, the removal of emotional, psychological obstacles toward workable reconciliation schemes. In the end, "Apologies are most meaningful when accompanied by material reparations; and reparations are most meaningful when accompanied by acknowledgment of their inadequacy in the effort to apologize and make amends . . . taken together, apologies and reparations offer responses to mass atrocity that demand recognition of wrongs done without obliging survivors to forgive."[58]

Summary

Post-genocide Armenian-Turkish reconciliation is certainly more than a policy issue. Unlike "normal" public policy dealing with issues such as inflation,[59] unemployment, health care, and the like, reconciliation in the Armenian-Turkish case requires accountability and acknowledgment of responsibility after ninety years of denial of the crime. And given the magnitude of the crime and the political and economic conditions and legal standards evolved since then, reconciliation schemes "transcend conventional understandings of corrective and distributive justice."[60] Teitel notes that "Compensation is often justified on the basis of rights created under natural law or international law, as sources of continuous norms that take no notice of political change. Under international law, the greatest support is for the most grave abuses, the 'jus cogens' norms."[61] Such a principle, however, while applicable to the former Soviet bloc, is not commensurable with the situation concerning Armenian-Turkish reconciliation, not to mention reparations. In the case of the former, the post-Communist state possesses the "mandate to equal protection,"[62] a mandate which the Turkish government a fortiori lacks given the absence of the Armenian inhabitants of the Armenian provinces and across the former Ottoman Empire. While it may be argued that attention to and preoccupation with issues pertaining to compensation can hinder negotiations toward reconciliation, given the considerable differences in the political and economic environments before and after the Genocide, such negotiations cannot ignore international law, particularly international human rights law, in constructing the rights of the victim (the Armenians) in reconciliation processes.

A host of questions must be answered before any Armenian-Turkish reconciliation process can be effective. It needs to be determined whether the Armenian-Turkish reconciliation process should be confined to secret or closed door negotiations as it was with TARC, or become more transparent, based on or operating in an environment of openness and wider participation. Moreover, it also needs to be decided whether the reconciliation process should be confined to bilateral diplomacy or become integrated into a multilateral process where credible and legitimate institutions and parties—such as the United Nations—directly participate in the process. A two-step process is a necessary, if not a sufficient, condition for a successful Armenian-Turkish reconciliation: an international tribunal, having rectified the difficulties encountered with TARC, would first strengthen the moral and legal legitimacy of the reconciliation process and subsequently guide the Armenian-Turkish bilateral negotiations. The analysis presented here thus insists on the direct and open participation of at least three parties: the government of Armenia and the government of Turkey, and the United Nations or a UN agency with full legal competence in matters of genocide. Contrary to the more optimistic prognoses and expectations of the truth commissions at the national level, the Armenian Genocide falls within the domain of international politics, so that an Armenian-Turkish tribunal is not likely to produce positive results without the direct participation of internationally legitimate institutions. Complicating matters further is the fact that, unlike other truth and reconciliation commissions, the survivors of the Armenian Genocide and their descendants are dispersed throughout the world, necessitating therefore representation of the Armenian diasporan communities in the reconciliation process. Further, the realities of international politics in general and regional geopolitics in particular, at least in the foreseeable future, cannot provide the observer cause for optimism in movements toward reconciliation. As of this writing, neither the government of Turkey appears ready to accept responsibility as the perpetrator of the Genocide, nor does the government of Armenia seem prepared to place these issues on the international agenda.

Notes

1. The literature on the Armenian Genocide is enormous. For useful background information and analyses, see, for example, Vahakn N. Dadrian, *The History of the Armenian Genocide: Ethnic Conflict from the Balkans to Anatolia to the Caucasus* (Providence, RI: Berghahn Books, 1995); Richard G. Hovannisian, ed., *The Armenian Genocide: History, Politics, Ethics* (New York: St. Martin's Press, 1992); Richard G. Hovannisian, ed., *The Armenian Genocide in Perspective* (New Brunswick, NJ: Transaction Books, 1986).
2. David L. Phillips, *Unsilencing the Past: Track Two Diplomacy and Turkish-Armenian Reconciliation* (New York and Oxford: Berghahn Books, 2005).

3. See, for example, Martha Minow, *Between Vengeance and Forgiveness: Facing History after Genocide and Mass Violence* (Boston: Beacon Press, 1998), p. 1.
4. See, for example, Vincent Taylor, *Forgiveness and Reconciliation: A Study in New Testament Theology* (London: Macmillan, 1960); Alex Moraine, Janet Levy, and Ronel Scheffer, eds., *Dealing with the Past: Truth and Reconciliation in South Africa* (Capetown: IDASA, 1994); Ruti G. Teitel, *Transitional Justice* (Oxford: Oxford University Press, 2000); Michael L. Hadley, ed., *The Spiritual Roots of Restorative Justice* (Albany: State University of New York Press, 2001); Gerry Johnstone, *Restorative Justice: Ideas, Values, Debates* (Devon, UK, and Portland, OR: Willan, 2002).
5. Minow, *Between Vengeance and Forgiveness*, p. 9.
6. Simon Payaslian, "After Recognition," *Armenian Forum* 2,3 (Winter 2001): 33-56, 75-76.
7. Ervin Staub, "Healing and Reconciliation," in *Looking Backward, Moving Forward: Confronting the Armenian Genocide*, ed. Richard G. Hovannisian (New Brunswick, NJ: Transaction Publishers, 2003), p. 270.
8. See examples in Priscilla Hayner, "Fifteen Truth Commissions—1974 to 1994: A Comparative Study," *Human Rights Quarterly* 16 (1994): 597.
9. Martha Minow, "Breaking the Cycles of Hatred," and Nancy L. Rosenblum, "Justice and the Experience of Injustice," in *Breaking the Cycles of Hatred: Memory, Law, and Repair*, ed. Martha Minow (Princeton: Princeton University Press, 2002), pp. 17-18, 98-99; Teitel, *Transitional Justice*, pp. 88, 90. See also Russell Daye, *Political Forgiveness: Lessons from South Africa* (Maryknoll, NY: Orbis, 2004); Michael Humphrey, *The Politics of Atrocity and Reconciliation: From Terror to Trauma* (London: Routledge, 2002).
10. Minow, *Between Vengeance and Forgiveness*, pp. 87-88.
11. See, for example, Richard Wilson, *The Politics of Truth and Reconciliation in South Africa: Legitimizing the Post-Apartheid State* (Cambridge, UK: Cambridge University Press, 2001). Such problems are not limited to the Third World countries. The trial of Klaus Barbie is said to have accomplished a similar legitimization and unification in France. See, for example, Alain Finkielkraut, *Remembering in Vain: The Klause Barbie Trial and Crimes against Humanity*, trans. Roxanne Lapidus with Sima Godfrey (New York: Columbia University Press, 1992).
12. Ellis Cose, *Bone to Pick: Of Forgiveness, Reconciliation, Reparation, and Revenge* (New York: Atria Books, 2004), p. 15.
13. Steven R. Ratner and Jason S. Abrams, *Accountability for Human Rights Atrocities in International Law*, 2d ed. (Oxford: Oxford University Press, 2001), p. 229; Hayner, "Fifteen Truth Commissions," pp. 597, 599, 604.
14. Teitel, *Transitional Justice*, p. 131.
15. Ibid., p. 86.
16. Mark R. Amstutz, *The Healing of Nations: The Promise and Limits of Political Forgiveness* (Lanham, MD: Rowman and Littlefield, 2005).
17. Quoted in Teitel, *Transitional Justice*, p. 110, emphasis added.
18. Ibid., p. 31.
19. Ibid., p. 89.
20. See, for example, Clive Foss, "The Turkish View of Armenian History: A Vanishing Nation," in *The Armenian Genocide: History, Politics, Ethics*, ed. Richard G. Hovannisian (New York: St. Martin's Press, 1992), pp. 250-279; Fatma Müge Göçek, "Reconstructing the Turkish Historiography on the Armenian Massacres and Deaths of 1915," in Hovannisian, *Looking Backward, Moving Forward*, pp. 209-230.

21. Belinda Cooper and Taner Akçam, "Turks, Armenians, and the 'G-Word,'" *World Policy Journal* (Fall 2005): 81-93.
22. The International Center for Transitional Justice, "The Applicability of the United Nations Convention on the Prevention and Punishment of the Crime of Genocide to Events which Occurred during the Early Twentieth Century," Legal analysis prepared for the International Center for Transitional Justice, on the basis of the Memorandum of Understanding entered into by The Turkish Armenian Reconciliation Commission on July 12, 2002. Available at http://www.ictj.org/downloads/TARC.memo.eng.pdf.
23. Rosenblum, "Justice and the Experience of Injustice," pp. 80-81, quoting Judith Shklar, *The Faces of Injustice* (New Haven, CT: Yale University Press, 1990), p. 2. On restitution, see Elazar Barkan, *The Guilt of Nations: Restitution and Negotiating Historical Injustices* (Baltimore and London: Johns Hopkins University Press, 2000).
24. Although it is possible that such a process may lead to "delegitimating the predecessor regime." Teitel, *Transitional Justice*, p. 72.
25. Philip Jacob and James Toscano, eds., *The Integration of Political Communities* (New York: Lippincott, 1964), pp. 209-210; Harold Lasswell and Abraham Kaplan, *Power and Society* (New Haven, CT: Yale University Press, 1950), p. 16; Gabriel Almond and G. Bingham Powell, *Comparative Politics*, 2d ed. (Boston: Little, Brown, 1978), pp. 395-396, 415-416.
26. Richard Falk, *A Study of Future Worlds* (New York: Free Press, 1975), pp. 72-74.
27. Almond and Powell, *Comparative Politics*, p. 356.
28. Teitel, *Transitional Justice*, pp. 60, 61.
29. Luis Sohn, "The New International Law: Protection of the Rights of Individuals Rather than States," *American University Law Review* 32,1 (1982): 12. See also Luis Sohn, "John A. Sibley Lecture: The Shaping of International Law," *Georgia Journal of International and Comparative Law* 8,1 (1978): 18-22; B. G. Ramcharan, *Humanitarian Good Offices in International Law* (The Hague: Martinus Nijhoff Publishers, 1983); Paul Sieghart, *The International Law of Human Rights* (Oxford: Clarendon Press, 1983).
30. Louis Henkin et al., *International Law: Cases and Materials*, 3d ed. (St. Paul, MN: West, 1993), p. 1007.
31. Hersch Lauterpacht, *International Law and Human Rights* (New York: Praege. Sohn, "New International Law," p. 13; Burns Weston and Richard Claude, eds., *Human Rights in the World Community* (Philadelphia: University of Pennsylvania Press, 1989), pp. 184-190; Tom J. Farer, "The United Nations and Human Rights: More than a Whimper," *Human Rights Quarterly* 9 (1987): 550-586; Evan Luard, ed., *The International Protection of Human Rights* (New York: Praeger, 1967); Karel Vasak, ed., *The International Dimensions of Human Rights* (Westport, CT: Greenwood Press, 1982); Richard A. Falk, Samuel S. Kim, and Sam H. Mandlovitz, eds., *The United Nations and a Just World Order* (Boulder, CO: Westview Press, 1991); Egon Schwelb, "The International Court of Justice and the Human Rights Clauses of the Charter," *American Journal of International Law* 66 (1972): 337-351; Lauterpacht, *International Law and Human Rights*, pp. 34, 123-124.
33. Theodor Meron, *Human Rights and Humanitarian Norms as Customary Law* (Oxford: Oxford University Press, 1989), p. 81.
34. Lauterpacht, *International Law and Human Rights*, p. 18; Rosalyn Higgins, "Conceptual Thinking about the Individual in International Law," *New York Law School Law Review* 24 (1978).
35. Vojin Dimitrijević, *The Insecurity of Human Rights after Communism* (Oslo: Norwegian Institute of Human Rights, 1993).

36. Adolf Eichmann was a leading member of the Gestapo in Berlin whose primary responsibility consisted of the deportation and murder of Jews in Germany and in the occupied countries during World War II. He fled to Argentina after the war but was taken prisoner to Israel in 1960 and tried for crimes against the Jewish people and crimes against humanity. He was found guilty and sentenced to death.
37. Ratner and Abrams, *Accountability*, pp. 163-164.
38. Ibid., pp. 68-69, 107-108; Teitel, *Transitional Justice*, pp. 60, 61.
39. Teitel, *Transitional Justice*, pp. 60, 61.
40. Ratner and Abrams, *Accountability*, pp. 160-161, 167.
41. Minow, "Breaking the Cycles of Hatred," p. 21.
42. Ratner and Abrams, *Accountability*, p. 230.
43. Ibid., p. 231.
44. Ibid., p. 221.
45. Joe Verhoeven, "The Armenian Genocide and International Law," in Hovannisian, *Looking Backward, Moving Forward*, p. 148.
46. Ibid., p. 150.
47. Charles W. Kegley, Jr., "Decision Regimes and the Comparative Study of Foreign Policy," in *New Directions in the Study of Foreign Policy*, ed. Charles F. Hermann, Charles W. Kegley, Jr., and James N. Rosenau (Boston: Allen and Unwin, 1987), pp. 252-253. See also Stephen Krasner, "Structural Causes and Regime Consequences: Regimes as Intervening Variables," in *International Regimes*, ed. Stephen Krasner (Ithaca, NY: Cornell University Press, 1981); Miriam Steiner, "The Search for Order in a Disorderly World: Worldviews and Prescriptive Decision Paradigms," *International Organization* 37,3 (Summer 1983): 373-413; Mark W. Zacher, "Toward a Theory of International Regimes," *Journal of International Affairs* 44,1 (Spring/Summer 1990): 140.
48. Kegley, "Decision Regimes," pp. 252-253. See also Oran R. Young, "The Politics of Regime Formation: Managing Natural Resources and the Environment," *International Organization* 43,3 (Summer 1989): 360.
49. Kegley, "Decision Regimes," p. 258; Peter M. Haas, "Do Regimes Matter? Epistemic Communities and Mediterranean Pollution Control," *International Organization* 43,3 (Summer 1989): 381.
50. John Spanier and Eric Uslaner, *American Foreign Policy Making and the Democratic Dilemmas*, 5th ed. (Pacific Grove, CA: Brooks/Cole, 1990), pp. 18-25; John Burton, *Global Conflict* (Brighton, Sussex: Wheatsheaf Books, 1986), pp. 39-41, 131-136, 143-144; Graham T. Allison, *Essence of Decision* (Boston: Little, Brown and Company, 1971), p. 157.
51. Ratner and Abrams, *Accountability*, pp. 222-223.
52. Teitel, *Transitional Justice*, p. 132.
53. On various approaches to compensatory justice, see John W. Chapman, ed., *Compensatory Justice: Nomos XXXIII* (New York: New York University Press, 1991).
54. Ratner and Abrams, *Accountability*, p. 155.
55. Georg Schwarzenberger and E. D. Brown, *A Manual of International Law*, 6th ed. (Milton: Professional Books, 1976), p. 147, italics in the original.
56. Minow, "Breaking the Cycles of Hatred," p. 23.
57. See Cose, *Bone to Pick*, passim.
58. Minow, "Breaking the Cycles of Hatred," pp. 23-24.
59. See, for example, Taner Akçam, *Dialogue Across an International Divide: Essays towards a Turkish-Armenian Dialogue* (Toronto: Zoryan Institute, 2001), p. 25.
60. Teitel, *Transitional Justice*, p. 133.

61. For an example from the experiences of transition in the former Soviet bloc, see *Law on Extrajudicial Rehabilitation ("Large Restitution Law")*, repr. in *Central and Eastern European Legal Texts* (March 1991), as cited in Teitel, *Transitional Justice*, p. 134, notes 40 and 57.
62. Ibid., p. 134. Also, unlike the debates in the former Soviet bloc countries regarding the "baseline" to determine compensatory damages and the right to redress (most of which agreed on 1948 as "the cutoff date"), the "baseline" in the Armenian case appears, at least as of this writing, to be more clearly established at 1915.

About the Contributors

Ramela Grigorian Abbomontian is Assistant Professor of Art History at Los Angeles Pierce College, a Ph.D. candidate in Modern Art, with a minor in Armenian Studies, at the University of California, Los Angeles, and an educational consultant for the Ararat-Eskijian Museum in Mission Hills, California. Her dissertation examines the visual construction of diasporic identity by Armenian-American artists in Los Angeles. Additional research interests include Diaspora theory, museum studies, Armenian art, photography, public art, and genocide art. Among her honors is the UCLA Distinguished Teaching Assistant Award.

Nora Arissian is Lecturer of History at Damascus University, where she completed her undergraduate training. The recipient of a doctoral degree from the Institute of Oriental Studies of the National Academy of Sciences of Armenia, she is the author and translator of works in Arabic and Armenian based on research in the Syrian archives and on primary sources in several languages. She is a contributor to Armenian and Arabic newspapers and journals. Her published books (titles in translation) are *The Position of Syrian Intellectuals toward the Armenian Genocide*, and *Echoes of the Armenian Genocide in the Syrian Press (1877-1930)*.

Elazar Barkan is Professor of International Public Affairs and co-director of SIPA's Human Rights Concentration at Columbia University. He is also the director of the Institute for Historical Justice and Reconciliation at the Salzburg Seminar, which promotes dialogue in societies divided by conflicts and human rights abuses. His research interests focus on the role of history in contemporary society and politics, with particular emphasis on the response to gross historical crimes and injustices. His publications include *The Guilt of Nations: Restitution and Negotiating Historical Injustices*, and the co-edited volumes *Claiming the Stones/Naming the Bones: Cultural Property and the Negotiation of National and Ethnic Identity*, and *Taking Wrongs Seriously: Apologies and Reconciliation*.

Bedross Der Matossian is a PhD candidate in the Department of Middle East and Asian Languages and Cultures at Columbia University. He received his B.A. degree from the Hebrew University of Jerusalem where he also began his graduate work in Islamic and Middle Eastern Studies. His areas of concentration are the inter-ethnic relationships in the Ottoman Empire during the second constitutional period (1908-18), the socio-political and the economic history of the Armenians in the nineteenth-century Ottoman Empire, and the Armenian Genocide.

Barlow Der Mugrdechian is Lecturer in Armenian Studies at California State University, Fresno, where he teaches Armenian history, language, and culture. He has taken groups of students on study tours to Armenia and was the project director of a five-year grant, 1999-2004, for a Faculty and Development Program in Business and Economics at Erevan State University. In 2000, he was awarded an honorary doctorate from Erevan State University. He served as President of the Society for Armenian Studies for four years and has a variety of other executive positions within the SAS.

Jack Der Sarkissian is Doctor of Medicine with the Southern California Permanente Medical Group and the associate program director for the family medicine residency at the Group's UCLA-affiliated Los Angeles Medical Center. He was instrumental in establishing a Center of Excellence for Armenian Language Services in the Los Angeles Medical Center and has lectured to many groups regarding the needs of the Armenian patient placed in a historical context. He participated in the UCLA series on Historic Armenian Cities and Provinces with a paper titled "Case Studies in Survival: Two Armenian Physicians in 1922 Smyrna." He is an amateur musician, who records and performs in the greater Los Angeles area.

Fatma Müge Göçek is Associate Professor of Sociology and Women's Studies at the University of Michigan. Her studies focus on social change in the Middle East. Her publications include *Rise of the Bourgeoisie, Demise of Empire: Ottoman Westernization and Social Change,* and *East Encounters West: France and the Ottoman Empire in the Eighteenth Century.* She is an initiator of the Armenian-Turkish Workshop, which fosters dialogue relating to the events culminating in the elimination of most of the Armenian population of the Ottoman Empire.

Hagop Gulludjian is a Lecturer in Western Armenian at UCLA and previously was Associate Professor of Armenian Studies at the Universidad del Salvador, Buenos Aires. He has been the publisher and/or editor of numerous periodicals and has also assisted the Argentine government in technology policy issues. In addition to Armenian studies, his research and occasional publications involve the study of virtuality and the interrelation of technology and culture.

Richard G. Hovannisian is Holder of the Armenian Educational Foundation Chair in Modern Armenian History at the University of California, Los Angeles, and editor of this series. His publications include *Armenia on the Road to Independence*, the four-volume *The Republic of Armenia*, four volumes on the Armenian Genocide, and seventeen other volumes and sixty research articles relating to Armenian, Caucasian, Middle Eastern, and Islamic studies. A Guggenheim Fellow, he has received many honors, including encyclicals from the supreme patriarchs of the Armenian Church, two honorary doctoral degrees, and election to membership in the National Academy of Sciences of Armenia.

Anahit Khosroeva is Senior Researcher in the Institute of History, National Academy of Sciences of Armenia, and has been a scholar in residence at North Park University in Chicago, where she taught a course on twentieth-century genocides. Her dissertation is titled "The Assyrian Massacres in the Ottoman Turkey and the Adjacent Turkish Territories (End of the Nineteenth to the First Quarter of the Twentieth Century)." She is the author of the two books and numerous articles on the history of the Assyrian people.

Marc Aram Mamigonian is Director of Programs and Publications at the National Association for Armenian Studies and Research (NAASR) and editor of the *Journal of Armenian Studies*. He is the co-author of commentaries on James Joyce's *Ulysses* and *Stephen Hero* as well as numerous articles and reviews on Armenian, Joycean, and other subjects. His most recent article, "Solar Patriot: Oliver St. John Gogarty in *Ulysses*" (co-authored with John N. Turner) appeared in *James Joyce Quarterly*. He is the editor of *The Armenians of New England: Celebrating a Culture and Preserving a Heritage* and *Rethinking Armenian Studies: Past, Present, and Future* (special issue of the *Journal of Armenian Studies)*.

Tigran Matosyan is a Candidate in History at the National Academy of Sciences of Armenia. His research and publications focus on historical comparison of the Armenian Genocide and the Holocaust. As a member of the Critical Sociology Network/Caucasus Academic Project, he is currently involved with a research team studying perceptions about Europe as expressed in the public discourse in Armenia and Georgia from the twentieth-century to the present.

Suzanne E. Moranian is a graduate of Wellesley College and the University of Wisconsin-Madison, where she prepared a Ph.D. dissertation titled "The American Missionaries and the Armenian Question, 1915-1927." Her publications include "The Armenian Genocide and American Relief Efforts," in *America and the Armenian Genocide of 1915,* Jay Winter, ed., and "Bearing Witness: The Missionary Archives as Evidence of the Armenian Genocide," in

The Armenian Genocide: History, Politics, Ethics, R. G. Hovannisian, ed. She is the recipient of the William Hesseltine History Prize and the Martha Edwards American Association of University Women Fellowship Award and has been a Visiting Research Scholar at the Wellesley College Centers for Women. She is the president of the Armenian International Women's Association.

Jean Murachanian is a Ph.D. candidate in Art History at the University of California, Los Angeles, where she specializes in modern art with a minor in Armenian Studies. Her doctoral dissertation is titled "Léon Tutundjian: Trauma, Identity and Modern Art in the Aftermath of Genocide." She is the recipient of the UCLA Graduate Division Dissertation Year Fellowship and the Edward A. Dickson History of Art Fellowship. Her research interests include trauma theory, ethnic studies, Diaspora theory, identity politics, and museum studies.

Marc Nichanian is Visiting Professor of Armenian Language and Civilization at Columbia University. He has lectured widely on Armenian literature and on historical interpretations and literary responses to the Armenian Genocide or *Aghet* (Catastrophe). His publications include *Ages et usages de la langue arménienne*; *Writers of Disaster: Armenian Literature in the Twentieth Century*; *La Perversion historiographique;* and the first volume in a series titled *Entre l'art et le témoignage,* as well as many articles on Armenian literature. He has edited six volumes of *GAM*: *A Journal of Analysis*.

Michael Papazian is Associate Professor of Philosophy and chair of the Department of Religion and Philosophy at Berry College in Rome, Georgia. His publications include *Light from Light: An Introduction to the History and Theology of the Armenian Church*, a translation of Eghishe's *Commentary on Genesis,* and articles on ancient philosophy and on medieval Armenian philosophy and theology.

Simon Payaslian is Holder of the Kaloosdian/Mugar Chair in Armenian Genocide Studies and Modern Armenian History at Clark University. He is the author of *United States Policy toward the Armenian Question and the Armenian Genocide*; *The Armenian Genocide, 1915-1923: A Handbook for Students and Teachers*; *U.S. Foreign Economic and Military Aid*: *The Reagan and Bush Administrations*; and *International Political Economy: Conflict and Cooperation in the Global System* (co-author); as well as articles on the United Nations, international law and human rights, peace studies, the Kurdish Question, and U.S. foreign policy.

Rubina Peroomian is a Research Associate at the University of California, Los Angeles, where she earned her Ph.D. in Near Eastern Languages and Cultures. She has taught Armenian Studies courses and has lectured widely. Her publications include: *Literary Responses to Catastrophe: A Comparison of the Armenian and the Jewish Experience*, a series of secondary textbooks on the Armenian Question with an emphasis on the history of the Armenian Genocide, and several research articles on the Armenian Genocide and diasporan literature. Her most recent publication is a compilation of materials, lesson plans, and strategies to teach the Armenian Genocide the Armenian students from kindergarten to twelfth grade.

Adam Strom is the director of planning, research, and development of new projects at Facing History and Ourselves (FHAO), Inc. He was the principal writer and editor of FHAO's resource book titled *Crimes Against Humanity and Civilization: The Genocide of the Armenians* (April, 2004). He is also the primary author and editor of *Engaging the Future: Religion, Human Rights, and Conflict Resolution* (2003), an international on-line forum and a series of readings growing out of the forum, and *Identity, Religion, and Violence: Considering the Legacies of September 11th*, an on-line study guide for educators.

Henry Theriault is Associate Professor of Philosophy at Worcester State College and Coordinator of the College's Center for the Study of Human Rights. His research focuses on genocide and human rights. His publications include "An Analytical Typology of Arguments Denying Genocides and Related Mass Human Rights Violations" (*Comparative Genocide Studies*, vol. 1, 2004), "Free Speech and Denial: The Armenian Case," (*Looking Backward, Moving Forward: Confronting the Armenian Genocide*, ed. R. G. Hovannisian), and "Universal Social Theory and Genocide Denial" (*Journal of Genocide Research*, 2001, reprinted in *Defining the Horrific: Readings on Genocide and Holocaust in the Twentieth Century*, ed. William L. Hewitt.

Hrag Varjabedian is a Ph.D. candidate in Cultural Anthropology at the University of Wisconsin-Madison. The focus of his research has been the construction of national and ethnic identities of Armenian people of both the Diaspora and of Armenia. He has conducted his fieldwork research in Armenia on an International Research and Exchange (IREX) fellowship. His most recent publications are: "Shared Landscapes, Divergent Myths: The Mythical Landscape of Anatolia," and "The Archaeology of Memory: Framing the Invisible."

Nicole E. Vartanian is a university administrator and instructor who earned a doctorate in the sociology of education from Teachers College, Columbia University. She has served as a research scientist in the Institute for Education Sciences of the U.S. Department of Education and as a Fulbright Scholar in Armenia to teach and work on issues relating to civic education and educational policy. She has also been a consultant for a USAID-sponsored Discovery workshop for stakeholders across Armenia's educational sector and for Project Harmony's

Legal Socialization Project to present strategies for police officers and teachers to educate students about laws and their responsibilities for upholding them.

Philippe Videlier is a researcher at the Centre National de la Recherche Scientifique (CNRS), France, where he is the director of the "Sociétés en mouvement et representations" program in Lyon. His research focuses on nineteenth- and twentieth-century migrations, social movements, ideologies, and popular cultures. Among his nine published volumes are studies on the suburban industrial towns of Vénissieux, Saint-Priest, and Décines in the Lyon area. His most recent book (2005) is titled *Nuit Turque* and relates to the Armenian Genocide. He has also studied Armenian migrations in the 1920s and 1930s, when genocide survivors were brought from Greece and Syria to work in the artificial silk industry. He was active in the movement for recognition of Armenian Genocide by the French Parliament. His present work deals with the creation of a "Centre de la Mémoire des Villes ouvrières" in the Lyon suburb of Villeurbanne.

Speros Vryonis, Jr. is Professor Emeritus of the University of California, Los Angeles, where he served as the Director of the Near Eastern Center, and of New York University, where he headed the Alexander S. Onassis Center for Hellenic Studies. He also founded and directed the Speros Basil Vryonis Center for the Study of Hellenism in Los Angeles and Sacramento, California. A Guggenheim Fellow and Fulbright Scholar, he has been elected as a fellow of the American Academy of Arts and Sciences, the Medieval Academy of America, and the American Philosophical Society. His extensive bibliography includes *The Decline of Medieval Hellenism in Asia Minor and the Process of Islamization from the Eleventh Through the Fifteenth Century*; *Byzantium and Europe*; *Studies on Byzantium, Seljuks and Ottomans*; *Byzantium: Its Internal History and Relations with the Muslim World*; *Studies in Byzantine Institutions and Society*; and *The Mechanism of Catastrophe: The Turkish Pogrom of September 6-7, 1955, and the Destruction of the Greek Community of Istanbul.*

Index